THE LONG TWELFTH-CENTURY
VIEW OF THE ANGLO-SAXON PAST

Studies in Early Medieval Britain and Ireland

Series editors:

Joanna E. Story, University of Leicester, UK
Roy Flechner, University College Dublin, Ireland

Studies in Early Medieval Britain and Ireland illuminates the history of Britain and Ireland from the start of the fifth century to the establishment of French-speaking aristocracies in the eleventh and twelfth centuries, for historians, archaeologists, philologists and literary and cultural scholars. It explores the origins of British society, of communities, and political, administrative and ecclesiastical institutions. It was in the early middle ages that the English, Welsh, Scots and Irish defined and distinguished themselves in language, customs and territory and the successive conquests and settlements lent distinctive Anglo-Saxon, Scandinavian and Norman elements to the British ethnic mix. Royal dynasties were established and the landscape took a form that can still be recognised today; it was then too that Christian churches were established with lasting results for our cultural, moral, legal and intellectual horizons.

Studies in Early Medieval Britain and Ireland reveals these roots and makes them accessible to a wide readership of scholars, students and lay people.

Other titles in the series

Bede and the Future
Edited by Peter Darby and Faith Wallis

Heaven and Earth in Anglo-Saxon England
Theology and Society in an Age of Faith
Helen Foxhall Forbes

Bede and the End of Time
Peter Darby

Women's Names in Old English
Elisabeth Okasha

The Long Twelfth-Century View of the Anglo-Saxon Past

Edited by

MARTIN BRETT
Robinson College, Cambridge, UK

and

DAVID A. WOODMAN
Robinson College, Cambridge, UK

ASHGATE

© Martin Brett, David A. Woodman and the contributors 2015

All rights reserved. No part of this publication may be reproduced, stored in a retrieval system or transmitted in any form or by any means, electronic, mechanical, photocopying, recording or otherwise without the prior permission of the publisher.

Martin Brett and David A. Woodman have asserted their right under the Copyright, Designs and Patents Act, 1988, to be identified as the editors of this work.

Published by
Ashgate Publishing Limited
Wey Court East
Union Road
Farnham
Surrey, GU9 7PT
England

Ashgate Publishing Company
110 Cherry Street
Suite 3–1
Burlington, VT 05401–3818
USA

www.ashgate.com

British Library Cataloguing in Publication Data
A catalogue record for this book is available from the British Library

The Library of Congress has cataloged the printed edition as follows:
The long twelfth-century view of the Anglo-Saxon past / edited by Martin Brett and David A. Woodman.
       pages cm. – (Studies in early medieval Britain and Ireland)
   Includes bibliographical references and indexes.
   ISBN 978–1–4724–2817–2 (hardcover : alk. paper) – ISBN 978–1–4724–2818–9 (ebook) – ISBN 978–1–4724–2819–6 (epub)
   1. Anglo-Saxons – Historiography. 2. Great Britain – History – Anglo-Saxon period, 449–1066 – Historiography. 3. Civilization, Anglo-Saxon – Historiography. 4. Civilization, Medieval – Historiography. 5. Middle Ages – Historiography.
   I. Brett, M. II. Woodman, D. A. (David Anthony), 1981–
   DA152.L66 2015
   942.01072–dc23   2014027143

ISBN 9781472428172 (hbk)
ISBN 9781472428189 (ebk – PDF)
ISBN 9781472428196 (ebk – ePUB)

Printed in the United Kingdom by Henry Ling Limited,
at the Dorset Press, Dorchester, DT1 1HD

Contents

Acknowledgements — *vii*
List of Figures — *ix*
List of Tables — *xi*
Abbreviations — *xiii*

1   Introduction — 1
     Martin Brett

PART I: THE ANGLO-SAXON SAINTS

2   The Viking Hiatus in the Cult of Saints as Seen in the Twelfth Century — 13
     R. Bartlett

3   Folcard of Saint-Bertin and the Anglo-Saxon Saints at Thorney — 27
     Rosalind Love

4   Bede's *Historia Ecclesiastica* as a Source of Lections in Pre- and Post-Conquest England — 47
     Teresa Webber

PART II: ANGLO-SAXON ENGLAND IN THE NARRATIVE OF BRITAIN

5   Danish Ferocity and Abandoned Monasteries: The Twelfth-century View — 77
     Julia Barrow

6   Symeon of Durham's *Historia de Regibus Anglorum et Dacorum* as a Product of Twelfth-century Historical Workshops — 95
     David Rollason

7   William of Malmesbury's Diatribe against the Normans — 113
     R.M. Thomson

8	Normandy's View of the Anglo-Saxon Past in the Twelfth Century *Elisabeth van Houts*	123
9	Richard of Devizes and 'a rising tide of nonsense': How Cerdic Met King Arthur *John Gillingham*	141

PART III: ANGLO-SAXON LAW AND CHARTER

10	Historical Literacy in the Archive: Post-Conquest Imitative Copies of Pre-Conquest Charters and Some French Comparanda *J. Crick*	159
11	The Use and Abuse of Anglo-Saxon Charters by the Kings of England, 1100–1300 *Nicholas Vincent*	191
12	Pre-Conquest Laws and Legislators in the Twelfth Century *Bruce O'Brien*	229

PART IV: ART HISTORY AND THE FRENCH VERNACULAR

13	'History' in Anglo-Norman Romance: The Presentation of the Pre-Conquest Past *Judith Weiss*	275
14	The Scribe Looks Back: Anglo-Saxon England and the Eadwine Psalter *C. Karkov*	289
15	The Anglo-Saxon Tradition in Post-Conquest Architecture and Sculpture *Malcolm Thurlby*	307

Bibliography   359
General Index   409
Index of Manuscripts   421

Acknowledgements

This book is the result of a conference held at Robinson College, Cambridge, in March 2011. The conference would not have been possible without generous research grants from the British Academy, from the Department of Anglo-Saxon, Norse and Celtic at Cambridge University, and from Robinson College itself. The editors had long held the conviction that while much work had been done on the use (and abuse) of the Anglo-Saxon past in the early twelfth century, there was scope for more investigation of this phenomenon, stretching to the later end of the century. We were therefore all the more grateful that the contributors to this volume agreed to bring their significant, and complementary, areas of expertise to the venture. We are further indebted to them for their great patience while it was being brought to completion. We would like also to thank Professor Joanna Story and the Ashgate publishers for accepting the volume in the series, *Studies in early medieval Britain*. One of the original speakers at the conference, Professor Nicholas Brooks FBA, sadly passed away on 2 February 2014. We hope that the book's appearance may serve in a modest way to recall Nicholas's own interests in all aspects of the Anglo-Saxon past, and his distinguished contribution to its study, crowned by the publication of his long-awaited edition of the pre-Conquest charters of Canterbury cathedral in 2013.

Martin Brett and David Woodman
Robinson College, Cambridge

List of Figures

6.1 The development of the *Historia de regibus Anglorum et Danorum* (versions 0-0$_4$) and its relationship to other works.   107

10.1 S 602. King Eadwig's gift to his thegn, Æthelnoth, of land at Darlaston, Staffs. Purported original of AD 956, from the archive of Burton. Stafford, William Salt Library, MS. 84/1/41 (230 × 360 mm), reproduced at a scale of 45% of the original size. Reproduced by permission of the Trustees of the William Salt Library, Stafford.   173

10.2 S 646. King Eadwig's grant to Archbishop Oda of forty hides at Ely, Cambs. Original of AD 957, from the archive of Ely. Oxford, Bodleian Library, MS. Eng. Hist. a. 2, no. V (190 × 490 mm), reproduced at a scale of 35% of the original size. Reproduced by permission of the Bodleian Libraries, the University of Oxford.   175

12.1 Paris, Bibliothèque nationale de France, lat. 4771, p. 63 (The End of the *Genealogy*).   249

12.2 Paris, Bibliothèque nationale de France, lat. 4771, pp. 3, 14, 30, 34, 42, 46 and 58 (The Corrector's Hand).   250

12.3 Paris, Bibliothèque nationale de France, lat. 4771, p. 7 (The Corrector's Insular and Pregothic Scripts).   251

12.4 Bibliothèque nationale de France, lat. 4771, p. 12 (Insular and Pregothic treatments of pre-Conquest legal terms).   253

12.5 Paris, Bibliothèque nationale de France, lat. 4771, p. 1 (Colbertine *Cnut*'s Prologue).   263

14.1 Cambridge, Trinity College Library, MS R.17.1, fo. 5v. By permission of the Master and Fellows, Trinity College, Cambridge.   291

14.2: Cambridge, Trinity College Library, MS R.17.1, fo. 6r. By permission of the Master and Fellows, Trinity College, Cambridge.   294

14.3 Cambridge, Trinity College Library, MS R.17.1, fo. 5v (detail). By permission of the Master and Fellows, Trinity College, Cambridge.   298

| 14.4 | Cambridge Trinity College Library, MS R.17.1, fo. 283v. By permission of the Master and Fellows, Trinity College, Cambridge. | 300 |

15.1	Earls Barton, All Saints, W tower, exterior from SW.	312
15.2	Great Paxton, Holy Trinity, interior to W from chancel.	313
15.3	Worcester cathedral, chapterhouse, interior.	330
15.4	Water Stratford, St Giles, tympanum of S doorway.	341
15.5	Bradbourne, All Saints, W tower, detail of S doorway.	344

List of Tables

10.1	Preliminary list of single-sheet copies of pre-Conquest diplomas and charters copied in the long twelfth century.	165
10.2	Preliminary list of single-sheet copies of purportedly pre-Conquest writs copied in the long twelfth century.	168
10.3	Indicative list of published identifications of single-sheet imitative copies of Merovingian and Carolingian diplomas from the eleventh and twelfth centuries.	179
10.4	Indicative list of published identifications of single-sheet imitative copies of non-royal documents from the eleventh and twelfth centuries.	182
10.5	Documents in the names of English kings from the archives of Saint-Denis in script showing influence of English exemplars.	184
11.1	References to pre-Conquest kings in the charters of Henry II, 1154–1189.	207

Abbreviations

AB	*Analecta Bollandiana*
Ann. mon.	*Annales monastici*, ed. Luard
ANS	*Anglo-Norman Studies*
ASC	Anglo-Saxon Chronicle, cited by manuscript and *sub anno*
ASE	*Anglo-Saxon England*
ASS	*Acta Sanctorum...*, ed. J. Bollandus and others
BEC	*Bibliothèque de l'École des chartes*
BL	London, British Library
BnF	Paris, Bibliothèque nationale de France
Bodl. Lib.	Oxford, Bodleian Library
CCCC	Cambridge, Corpus Christi College
CCSL	Corpus Christianorum Series Latina (1953–)
Colgrave and Mynors	*Bede's ecclesiastical history of the English people*, ed. Colgrave and Mynors
DN	*The 'Draco Normannicus' of Étienne of Rouen* in *Chronicles of the reigns of Stephen* [etc.]
EHR	*English Historical Review*
Gaimar, *Estoire*	Geffrei Gaimar, *Estoire des Engleis*
G. Mon.	Geoffrey of Monmouth, *The history of the kings*
GND	William of Jumièges, *Gesta Normannorum ducum*
HBS	Henry Bradshaw Society
HE	Bede, *Historia ecclesiastica*
HH	Henry, archdeacon of Huntingdon, *Historia Anglorum*
HR	Symeon of Durham [attr.], *Historia regum*
HsC	*Historia de sancto Cuthberto*
JEH	*Journal of Ecclesiastical History*
JW *Chronicle*	*The chronicle of John of Worcester*
LE	*Liber Eliensis*, ed. Blake
Malmesbury, *GP*	William of Malmesbury, *Gesta pontificum*
Malmesbury, *GR*	William of Malmesbury, *Gesta regum*
MGH	Monumenta Germaniae Historica
MLGB	N.R. Ker, *Medieval libraries of Great Britain*
OCCC	Oxford, Corpus Christi College

ODNB	*Oxford Dictionary of National Biography*
OSF	*Facsimiles of Anglo-Saxon manuscripts*
OV	Orderic Vitalis, *Historia ecclesiastica*
PL	*Patrologia Latina*
PRO/TNA	Public Record Office / London, The National Archives
RCHME	Royal Commission on Historical Monuments (England)
RRAN	*Regesta regum Anglo-Normannorum*
RS	Rolls Series
S	P. Sawyer, *Anglo-Saxon charters*
SS	Surtees Society
Symeon, *LdE*	Symeon of Durham, *Libellus de exordio*
TRHS	*Transactions of the Royal Historical Society*
VCH	*Victoria history of the counties of England*
Wace, *Brut*	*Wace's Roman de Brut*
Wace, *Rou*	Wace, *The Roman de Rou*

Chapter 1
Introduction

Martin Brett

The chapters published below originated in a conference held at Robinson College, Cambridge on 29–30 March 2011. This was structured around three convictions of the organisers, each amply confirmed by the papers that were given, and the discussion that they provoked. The first was that the ways in which post-Conquest writers and artists positioned themselves in relation to the Anglo-Saxon past could tell one much about the world they thought they inhabited themselves. The second was that a great deal of valuable work was being done in all these fields, and that it would be useful to take stock of the present state of scholarship, at least under some of its aspects. The third was that the topic continues to reward study long after Anglo-Saxon England became Anglo-Norman England or even a Plantagenet empire. The constraints of time and space demanded that this could be explored only until the opening years of the thirteenth century, but much might be said of succeeding centuries too. The choice of contributors also reflected a desire to avoid any tendency for subject specialists to treat 1066 as a watershed in scholarship as well as in experience. The intention was to ensure that experts in the pre-Conquest period would be able to control exaggerated claims which might be made for innovation in the twelfth century, or indeed for the survival of earlier intellectual or practical patterns.

At one level the questions we ask are part of the most enduring issue in all English historiography. Why and how the Norman Conquest happened, and what consequences followed from it, are problems which were central to the first great flowering of historical activity in England among the chroniclers writing in the reigns of Henry I and Stephen,[1] were as critical to the ecclesiastical polemic

---

[1] For the general historiographical context, see, for example, R. Southern, 'Aspects of the European tradition of historical writing, 4: the sense of the past', *TRHS* xxiii (1973), 243–63; A. Gransden, *Historical writing in England, c.550–1307*, New York 1974; *The writing of history in the Middle Ages: essays presented to Richard William Southern*, ed. R.H.C. Davis and others, Oxford 1981; J. Campbell, 'Some twelfth-century views of the Anglo-Saxon past', in idem, *Essays in Anglo-Saxon history, 400–1200*, London 1986, 209–28; A.G. Rigg, *A history of Anglo-Latin literature, 1066–1422*, Cambridge 1992; A. Galloway, 'Writing history in England', in D. Wallace (ed.), *Cambridge History of medieval English literature*, Cambridge 1999, 255–83. For the so-called 'renaissance' in historical writing in England, see A. Williams, *The English and the Norman Conquest*, Woodbridge

of Matthew Parker in the sixteenth century, for whom the Conquest marked the moment in which the English Church turned from its apostolic origins to Romish error, and played a leading role in the great debates over law, kingship and the social order of the seventeenth century. Nineteenth-century historians, in Germany and France as well as England, sought to identify the contribution of notions of Germanic and Roman or at least Latin social order to the origins of representative government. If such great narratives began to fragment in the twentieth century, particularly with a growing recognition of the resemblances between English history and that of Europe rather than their differences, historiographic debate continued unabated. In recent years one could point, for instance, to the high claims advanced for the nature and powers of the late Saxon state,[2] or even for some kind of 'English conquest' over the Normans in the four or five generations before 1200.[3]

Such great questions commonly expect large answers, but large answers tend to become less convincing in detail the more they seek to explain. Our concern was to explore the diversity of answers which might be given, rather than to offer a single new synthesis.

While the contributors all addressed the general theme of twelfth-century understandings of the shaping power of the past, they approached it by exploring particular sources in which they were expert, not only chronicles and saints' lives, but law tracts and charters, manuscript painting, building and vernacular romance. Predictably, it soon became apparent that the answers offered in one field are often far from easy to align with those in another, and that these differences provoke new and sometimes unexpected questions.

The variety of sources one could examine for the purpose is wide, but some more or less demanded inclusion. The cult of the saints must figure very largely in any enquiry, for their shrines, and the habit of devotion to them, were a fixed point in the landscape whatever the turmoil around them, and their rights were central to the prosperity of the religious centres which gathered round them, whoever now ruled the community. The devotion to earlier saints always required

---

1995, 165–86. But see also T.N. Bisson, *The Crisis of the Twelfth Century: Power, Lordship, and the Origins of European Government*, Princeton and Oxford 2009, who suggests a rather more chaotic view of the twelfth century in general.

[2] For the probable existence of some kind of centralised agency in control of the production of charters, at least from the early tenth century onwards, see S. Keynes, *The diplomas of King Æthelred 'the Unready', 978–1016: a study in their use as historical evidence*, Cambridge 1980. For broader analysis, see, for example, J. Campbell, *The Anglo-Saxon state*, Hambledon and London 2000; J.R. Maddicott and D.M. Palliser (eds), *The medieval state: essays Presented to James Campbell*, Cambridge 2000; N. Brooks, *Anglo-Saxon myths: State and Church, 400–1066*, London 2000.

[3] H. Thomas, *The English and the Normans: ethnic hostility, assimilation, and identity, 1066–c.1220*, Oxford 2003.

a continuous tradition of reshaping according to changing views of their function and the challenge of new forms of devotion. The arrival with the Conquest of a new audience gave this general proposition a distinctive character in the English twelfth century. The chapters by Bartlett and Love explore this process, examining the influence of hagiographic models little exploited earlier, the ways in which the urgent concerns of ancient houses led to a vigorous literature in which Saxon texts were adapted to new debates, or demanded the composition of accounts of Saxon saints compiled often on the basis of minimal earlier information. The pervasive influence of Bede in twelfth-century writing is a commonplace of modern scholarship; within months of Archbishop Lanfranc's arrival at Canterbury he could rely on his potent authority as the *doctor Anglorum*, the more significantly since he was seeking to invoke it in the service of a doctrine of primacy that was as novel in England as it was anywhere in Europe. Webber's examination of the use of lections from Bede in the liturgy of the night office of matins is a significant demonstration of the ways in which his influence could be diffused much more widely than is obvious in the study of purely narrative texts. To start with hagiography is more than a matter of convenience, for the saints' lives were the first narrative responses to the Conquest to survive in England, and many of the chroniclers who addressed the relation of past and present from the reign of Henry I to the end of the twelfth century were hagiographers as well as, and sometimes before, becoming historians.[4]

These extended chronicles of the English in the twelfth century have been the subject of numerous modern studies, and particularly those of Sir Richard Southern in 1973 and James Campbell in 1984 were the starting point for several further chapters.[5] All appear in some sense to be shaped by a determination to reassert an underlying continuity across the Conquest, and a distinctively English one at that. One has to wait until the *Abbreviationes* by Ralph of Diss at the end of the century for a chronicler who looks at length beyond English sources to write something approximating to a chronicle of the Angevin lordship as a whole.[6]

There have been new editions and much detailed discussion of the set of chronicles in the names of Eadmer, William of Malmesbury, John of Worcester

---

[4] For a useful overview of the production of hagiography throughout this period, see M. Lapidge and R.C. Love, 'The Latin hagiography of England and Wales (600–1550)', in G. Philippart (ed.), *Hagiographies: international history of the Latin and vernacular hagiographical literature in the West from its origins to 1550*, iii, Turnhout 2001, 203–325.

[5] See above, n. 1.

[6] For the writings of Ralph of Diss, see R. Sharpe, *A handlist of the Latin writers of Great Britain and Ireland before 1540*, Turnhout 1997, 446. See also the entry for 'Diceto, Ralph de', in *ODNB*, by J.F.A. Mason and B. Smalley, *Historians in the Middle Ages*, London 1974, 114–19.

and Henry of Huntingdon,⁷ all of whom depended heavily on the Anglo-Saxon Chronicle, but the Durham *Historia regum* has been more neglected.⁸ Rollason shows in new detail how Durham's idiosyncratic pre-Conquest traditions were articulated around a larger narrative of England developed in other monastic centres further south as part of a widespread collaborative enterprise. The *Historia regum* is in part an exercise in connecting the years after the Conquest with the long history of St Cuthbert earlier, in part a fuller incorporation of the world of St Cuthbert in the story of the realm of England before as much as after the Conquest.⁹

Barrow surveys the struggle of twelfth-century writers to explain apparent discontinuities in the history of extant religious houses, and equally the extinction of religious life at sites known or said to have been communities earlier, and refounded (or said to be so) more recently. It is striking that post-Conquest authors found it necessary to invoke heathen destruction far more widely than had their tenth-century predecessors, reflecting apparently a need to supply earlier explanations which their sources embarrassingly lacked.

---

⁷ For Eadmer's work, see *Eadmeri Historia novorum in Anglia et opuscula duo de vita Sancti Anselmi et quibusdam miraculis ejus*, ed. M. Rule (RS [lxxxi], 1884). The first four books have been translated by G. Bosanquet, *Eadmer's history of recent events in England*, London 1964. For an edition and translation of William of Malmesbury's chronicles about kings and bishops of England, see William of Malmesbury, *Gesta regum Anglorum*, [i] ed. and tr. R.A.B. Mynors, R.M. Thomson and M. Winterbottom, Oxford 1998; ii, *General introduction and commentary*, R.M. Thomson, Oxford 1999 and William of Malmesbury, *Gesta pontificum Anglorum, i. Text and Translation*, ed. and tr. M. Winterbottom with R.M. Thomson, Oxford 2007; ii. *Introduction and commentary*, R.M. Thomson, Oxford 2007. For an edition and translation of the Worcester Latin chronicle attributed to John, see *The chronicle of John of Worcester:* ii, *The annals from 450 to 1066*, ed. R.R. Darlington and P. McGurk, tr. J. Bray and P. McGurk, Oxford 1995; iii, *The annals from 1067 to 1140*, ed. and tr. P. McGurk, Oxford 1998. For Henry of Huntingdon's work, see Henry, archdeacon of Huntingdon, *The history of the English people*, ed. and tr. D. Greenway, Oxford 1996.

⁸ The classic account of this difficult text (and manuscript) remains P.H. Blair, 'Some observations on the *Historia regum* attributed to Symeon of Durham', in N.K. Chadwick (ed.), *Celt and Saxon: studies in the early British border*, Cambridge 1963, 63–118, reprinted in P.H. Blair, *Anglo-Saxon Northumbria*, ed. M. Lapidge and Pauline Hunter Blair, London 1984, no. ix. For the remarkable breadth of historical writing emerging from Durham in the late eleventh and early twelfth centuries, see, especially, H.S. Offler, *Medieval historians of Durham*, Durham 1958, reprinted in idem, *North of the Tees: studies in medieval British history*, ed. A.J. Piper and A.I. Doyle, Collected Studies, Aldershot 1996, no. i.

⁹ W.M. Aird, *St Cuthbert and the Normans: the church of Durham, 1071–1153*, Woodbridge 1998, has much useful discussion of the desire of the Anglo-Norman members of the Cuthbertine community to fashion a history which emphasised their connections with their Anglo-Saxon past.

Thomson demonstrates the remarkable way in which William of Malmesbury in his later years came to express a startlingly hostile view of the Normans quite unlike the more measured judgements familiar in his earlier works.[10] The passage challenges almost all conventional accounts of the decline of 'ethnic' hostilities by the mid-century, and the more so since Malmesbury seems to assume that his audience might be at least receptive. William's mind and art were of exceptional subtlety, and no single explanation for his larger works will do much to explain them. Nevertheless they can be interpreted in some part as an effort to interpret the Anglo-Saxon past to a partially Norman audience. The passage Thomson discusses, appropriately enough from the commentary on the Lamentations of Jeremiah, suggests that William may have approached the task with less optimism or readiness than we have supposed.

The degree to which Norman writers after 1100 absorbed any part of the longer narrative of Britain has been little treated outside Chibnall's magisterial studies of Orderic Vitalis.[11] Liesbeth van Houts takes up the topic, in her account of the very modest place of Anglo-Saxon or even post-Conquest history of England in Norman chronicles, apart from Orderic, until Robert of Torigni's annals came to provide an account of the twelfth century which does treat the Norman lordship either side of the Channel as something more like the Norman empire of much recent scholarship.[12] Up to this point the contributors have been discussing the influence of a vision of the Anglo-Saxon past which can claim to rest on written record or living memory, however incomplete or tendentious. Robert of Torigni, however, introduces the ever more powerful influence of the fictive history of Britain of Geoffrey of Monmouth – which Robert first showed to an astonished Henry of Huntingdon.

The influence of Geoffrey is demonstrated by Gillingham in what might well seem the least expected of places, and certainly one of the least studied, in the largely unpublished work of Richard of Devizes. Richard has often been represented as the most sceptical, ironic and even secular-minded of observers of his own time. There is no doubt that he speaks in a distinctive voice, but Gillingham shows that he was prepared to give significant space to Geoffrey's imaginary world, and indeed to do more, for Richard seems to have worked over his source with some imagination and thought. James Campbell's 'tide of nonsense' is shown to have risen higher, and spread further, than we had supposed – so that the relative value attached to the fictional history of Britain

---

[10] See also R.M. Thomson, *William of Malmesbury*, 2 edn, Woodbridge 2003.
[11] M. Chibnall, *The world of Orderic Vitalis*, Oxford 1984 and eadem, *Anglo-Norman England, 1066–1166*, Oxford 1986.
[12] See, too, the valuable accounts Professor van Houts gave earlier of the Battle *Historia de conquestu Anglie*, or of the so-called 'Hyde chronicle', much briefer works that share some of this focus on the double lordship.

as against the (partially) sober history of Anglo-Saxon England becomes a yet more pressing object for reflection.

The next group of studies turn from hagiography and chronicle to issues of law and government. Vincent analyses the charters of the Norman and Angevin kings up to the reign of John, tracing the extent to which these draw explicitly on the acts of their Anglo-Saxon predecessors. His conclusion, based as it is on a comprehensive corpus for the period, is striking, for he finds that these are barely represented at all in genuine texts, with the qualified exception of those of Edward the Confessor. This is a challenging result, for it has to be set against the apparently widespread production of forged charters in the name of many more pre-Conquest kings, as well as bishops and occasional laymen, which are attributed more or less securely to the twelfth century. Vincent's conclusion is surely sound, and if so the origins and purpose of this large corpus of later forgery demands much further thought than it has yet received. It also fits uneasily with recent discussion of the Norman claim to a direct line of legal transition from the Saxon kings, suggesting that such arguments, though clearly discernible in some sources, were far from universal, or even perhaps prevalent.

Julia Crick's minute examination of a number of examples of the conscious imitation of earlier script in some post-Conquest examples of royal acts illustrates the same problem in a particular aspect, and with great clarity. It is particularly convenient that she provides a list of the single-sheet representations of pre-Conquest diplomas which are certainly or probably later – of these only some 20 per cent are attributed to the Confessor. The list, of course, would be enormously extended if it incorporated copies too. She is able to demonstrate two points of particular relevance – the extreme care with which many of them were executed, and the complexity of the motives for which the enterprise may have been conducted. In a broader perspective she compares her findings with those of French diplomatic, with the surprising observation that English forgers manufactured documents predominantly from the tenth and early eleventh century, while the French preferred to father their efforts on late Merovingian or early Carolingian authors.

Vincent's programme is also difficult to harmonise with the lessons taught by the numerous twelfth-century law-codes, mostly attributed to Cnut and the Confessor, examined by Bruce O'Brien, building on the work of Patrick Wormald.[13] His study underlines the remarkable energy and care with which these pseudonymous compilations were constructed, the elaboration of their claims to ancient authority and the apparent value attached to them into the thirteenth century, attested by the number and date of the copies in which they survive. The specific case of the 'Colbertine' Cnut is a powerful demonstration

---

[13] P. Wormald, *The making of English law: King Alfred to the twelfth century, i. Legislation and its limits*, Oxford 1999.

of the minute attention which could be devoted to these texts. It has long been remarked that this is a significant problem, for the gap between the late-twelfth-century editions of the old codes and the handbook of 'Glanvill' of the same date is as wide as the Atlantic, and there is very little reason to suppose that the law of these compilations continued to be practised on any scale. O'Brien observes that these apparently antiquarian collections can travel in the company of undoubtedly current texts, Roman law tracts on procedure or even early collections of the decretals of Alexander III. The difficulty of explaining this fact has long been familiar, and it is striking that placing it more fully in the context of charter and script only increases the difficulty.

The study of Judy Weiss on Anglo-Saxon England in vernacular romance reveals a complex set of references to the Anglo-Saxon past, which cannot be forced into any easy pattern of thought. She does however contribute a new piece of evidence to the problem of ideal and current law. The theme of the good law of King Edward reappears in her analysis of *Waldef*, where it is expounded at London against the tyrannical conduct of 'King Fergus' of London, by the authoritative voice of Edward the sheriff, 'very old and ... wise in the laws and royal customs'. *Waldef* is thought to have been written in East Anglia around 1200–1214, so this is a specially resonant observation. The law codes later attributed to King Edward show a clear concern for good law as ancient law, and particularly for consent. Much beloved by seventeenth-century lawyers, these passages were soon dismissed by Anglo-Saxonists as manifest alterations made in the twelfth century. O'Brien's study reminds us how carefully the passages were framed and revised, and Weiss shows the effect of that association of ideas among a lay audience. As is well known, they figured largely in the *Leges Londinienses* of *c.*1200, which in turn seems to have influenced the East Anglian and northern magnates whose rising led ultimately to the drafting of the Great Charter. If this very plausible suggestion is adopted, there is a certain irony in the fact that Edward is represented as frustrating the arbitrary punishment of a mercenary, for King John's mercenaries were singled out for proscription in the Charter.

The forms of memory examined in these studies, Crick's partially excepted, are conditioned in part by the choice of the narrator, in part by the processes by which narrative or legal tradition evolved over time. The two studies by Karkov and Thurlby take a different turn, by considering the response of later artists and craftsmen to monuments of an earlier time which they confronted directly. Karkov's minute analysis of the illumination of the Eadwine psalter is a precise demonstration of the reaction of later artists to their exemplar, in which she shows how they departed from it, often to accommodate changed patterns of liturgical or exegetical observance.

Thurlby's extended survey of the materials for attempting a history of architectural practice across the Conquest years reflects much recent work, particularly on the surviving archaeological record from greater Anglo-Saxon churches subsequently destroyed. The effect of this research has been to cast doubt on many claims for distinctively Norman decorative techniques, and so to emphasise the degree to which post-Conquest craftsmen continued to work with an established repertory of ornament or even structural practice. This makes it more difficult than was once supposed to identify a post-Conquest caesura in tradition, or a period of conscious recovery of earlier styles in the twelfth century. At first sight the contrasting ground plans of St Augustine at Canterbury in 1066 and after Abbot Scolland's rebuilding, for example, seem as dramatic an assertion of discontinuity as one could wish, but Thurlby's study shows how much more limited the gap may be when considered more closely.

The unity of all these studies lies in the material to which they are devoted, and not in the conclusions they suggest, and this is itself a matter of importance. Instructive though these explorations are, they all take place in the context of specific and local interests. They cannot be understood except against a background of pressing immediate concerns, whether the preservation of the rights and dignity of individual monastic houses or of the whole order in the face of criticism of new forms of religious life, the challenges of an ever more pervasive royal authority, the evolving needs of litigants in courts adopting new procedures, new forms of liturgical practice or changing methods of exposition of texts and doctrine. On the other hand, few of these local concerns derived from processes and debates which were specific to England. This constant reinterpretation of the past was also a response to broader changes across the whole Latin West.[14]

The detail of the Eadwine psalter shows the influence of biblical commentary as it was being developed in the contemporary French schools, where so many writers of the later twelfth century had themselves studied. The debates in England over the merits of the apostolic life of the regular canons or the claims of the reformed orders to preserve the monastic tradition in its primitive purity were only part of much larger controversies, with which local writers were entirely familiar. Correspondingly, this relatively limited line of enquiry illuminates virtually every aspect of the learned, and sometimes the secular, culture of the twelfth century. The variety of the results which are offered reflects the fact that all memories of the past might be refracted through different lenses, and selected for different purposes. There can be no question of a definitive answer to the question implied in our title, any more than one could suppose that Anglo-Norman or Plantagenet identity could ever be represented as a universal or even widespread set of values or, consequently, that it could follow some unitary process of evolution.

---

[14] For the general context, see T.F.X. Noble and J. van Engen, *European transformations: the long twelfth century*, Notre Dame 2012.

What these studies are intended to do is show how many strands there were to this identity, each appropriate to different contexts and how distinct these strands could be. The lack of a great answer is itself the best illustration of the richness and variety of the whole period.

PART I
The Anglo-Saxon Saints

Chapter 2
The Viking Hiatus in the Cult of Saints as Seen in the Twelfth Century

R. Bartlett

When Geoffrey of Courlon, monk of the abbey of St-Pierre-le-Vif at Sens, drew up a list of his abbey's relics in 1293, he was able to identify dozens of them, often giving their provenance and describing the reliquaries that enshrined them, but there remained a vestigial class. This consisted of:

> Many other holy martyrs, confessors and virgins, whose names and written texts (*nomina vel scripture*) cannot be discovered, on account of the age of the writing (*litterarum vetustas*), and on account of destruction by pagans, Vandals and Northmen, and by certain wicked local inhabitants, and because of the devastation of fires, which have burned the abbey three times.[1]

This is a fairly useful summary of some of the dangers which threaten historical – including hagiographical – record: sources that cannot be read, destruction by human violence and by fire. The monks and clergy of twelfth-century England would have recognised this list and the problem it generated: a gap in knowledge, a rupture in that continuous history which was both the desire and the assumption of the great churches of Christendom. Just as there were dangers if they could not demonstrate continuous tenure of their properties, so too they were unsettled by any fissure in the narrative connecting them with their saintly founders and patrons.

Geoffrey's phrase *litterarum vetustas* can be interpreted in more than one way: the physical deterioration of the documents themselves, or a change in script rendering earlier texts difficult to read, or perhaps simply antiquated style. Hermann the archdeacon, writing his *Miracles of St Edmund c.*1100, explained

---

[1] 'Et aliorum plurimorum sanctorum, martyrum, confessorum atque virginum, quorum nomina vel scripture, propter litterarum vestutatem et propter paganorum, Euvandalorum, Norhtmannorum et quorundam pessimorum inhabitantium destructionem, insuper et per vastationes ignium quibus per tres vices dictum cenobium fuit enormiter concrematum, possunt minime reperiri': *Libellus super reliquiis sanctorum et sanctarum que in monasterio sancti Petri Vivi Senon' continentur*, BnF, MS nouv. acq. lat. 311, pp. 6–7; printed, *Le Livre des reliques de l'abbaye de Saint-Pierre-le-Vif de Sens*, ed. G. Julliot and M. Prou, Sens 1887, 7.

that his information came partly from oral sources, and partly from an earlier unnamed or anonymous writer, who had evidently presented him with some problems, wielding 'a very difficult, or, I might say, adamantine, pen'.[2] In the case of post-Conquest England, there were also problems of language. When monks from La Charité-sur-Loire were brought to the Shropshire church of Much Wenlock, around 1080, they learned that the site was associated with the Anglo-Saxon saint Milburga, but had little information about her, and the location of her tomb was unknown. They then happened upon an ancient piece of writing. This was 'written in English letters, so that no one could read it or understand it unless he were knowledgeable in that language'. Someone was eventually found to translate it, and it turned out to describe where Milburga's body could be found.[3] At this period it might be easy to find a person who could read Old English and also speak French or Latin, but this clearly became more difficult as the generations passed.

Apart from the veil of difficulty created by changes in language, style and handwriting, there was also, as Geoffrey of Courlon points out, simple destruction. Geoffrey's choice of fire as a primary destructive force is understandable. Canterbury cathedral was devastated by fire in 1067 and in 1174, while in 1087 St Paul's London was burned by a fire 'so fierce that it seemed to unleash the fury of an angry God', although the cloth on the shrine of St Erkenwald inside was miraculously preserved.[4] William fitz Stephen, great champion of London though he was, observed that 'the only plagues in London are the immoderate drinking of fools and frequent fires'.[5] Both have threatened London subsequently. But, of course, some of the first culprits to blame for a

---

[2] 'calamo cujusdam difficillimo, et, ut ita dicam, adamantino': Hermann the archdeacon, *Liber de miraculis sancti Edmundi* in *Memorials of St Edmund's abbey*, ed. T. Arnold (RS [xcvi], 1890–96), i. 26–92, at 27. Antonia Gransden argued that the author of this work was not called Hermann but Bertrann: 'The composition and authorship of the *De miraculis Sancti Eadmundi* attributed to "Hermann the archdeacon"', *Journal of Medieval Latin* v (1995), 1–52, but a vigorous counter-case was deployed in T. Licence, 'History and hagiography in the late eleventh century: the life and work of Herman the archdeacon, monk of Bury St Edmunds', *EHR* cxxiv (2009), 516–44.

[3] 'carta tamen illa anglicis litteris scripta erat, ut nemo legere aut intelligere posset, nisi de illius lingue idiomate peritus esset': P.A. Hayward, 'The *Miracula inventionis beate Mylburge virginis* attributed to "the Lord Ato, cardinal bishop of Ostia"', *EHR* cxiv (1999), 543–73, at 565–6.

[4] 'ut ... furorem offensi dei ... videatur aperire': Arcoid, *Miracula sancti Erkenwaldi* c. 4, in *The saint of London: the life and miracles of St. Erkenwald*, ed. E.G. Whatley, Binghamton 1989, 100–164, at 120–28 (quotation p. 120).

[5] 'Solae pestes Londoniae sunt immodica stultorum potatio et frequens incendium': William fitz Stephen, *Vita sancti Thomae* prologue, in *Materials for the history of Thomas Becket*, ed. J.C. Robertson (RS [lxvii], 1875–85), iii. 1–154, at 8.

break in historical record would be the barbarians, not, in the case of Anglo-Norman writers, Geoffrey's Vandals (a curiously elastic and elusive group in medieval Frankish historiography),[6] but certainly the Vikings.

When Orderic Vitalis, monk of the Norman monastery of St-Évroult, was attempting to piece together the story of the life of its founding father, who had lived more than four centuries earlier, he had recourse not only to chronicles but also to what he learned 'not from written sources but from what I have been told by my elders'. Such oral tradition was especially important because of the destruction of many earlier written materials: 'In the great storms that raged so horribly in the time of the Danes, writings of our forebears perished in fire, along with churches and buildings ... When the books perish, the deeds of the men of old fall into oblivion ...'.[7] For Orderic, the doings of the saintly Évroult lay on the other side of the fiery chasm of Viking savagery, and had to be reconstructed carefully, drawing on whatever sources might be at hand. He was not alone among twelfth-century writers who looked at the past in this way.

The *Life and Miracles* of St Bega, which were written probably at St Bees in Cumbria late in the twelfth century or possibly early in the thirteenth, give an account of the saint, supposedly an early-medieval Irish princess, and of her burial. St Bega then lay hidden in her tomb for around 460 years: 'Danish devastation (*Danica depopulatio*) destroyed from human knowledge the miracles with which she had been resplendent while still in the flesh or also when freed from the bonds of the flesh.'[8] So record of both Bega's *in vita* and posthumous miracles had been obliterated. Even knowledge of her tomb was lost, before it was disclosed by divine revelation to be in the cemetery at Hackness, whence she was translated to Whitby, perhaps *c.*1140. Writing not long after this event, Ailred of Rievaulx recalls the desolation of Northumbria after the Danish raids, and especially the damage done to the church of Hexham: 'whatever was made

---

[6] According to Geoffrey, St Ebbo, who lived in the time of Dagobert III (d. 715/16) and yet died in 808, saved Sens from Vandals: *Libellus super reliquiis* (as in n. 1 above), 58, *Le Livre des reliques*, 63; Ademar of Chabannes had to refute the story that King Pippin of Aquitaine, who died in 838, had defeated a Vandal army: Ademar of Chabannes, *Chronicon*, III. c. 56, ed. P. Bourgain-Hemeryck, R. Landes and G. Pon (Corpus Christianorum, continuatio medievalis cxxix, 1999), 175–7; the thirteenth-century French prose *Life of St Nicholas* refers to 'les Wandes qui sont unes gens Sarrazinnes': BL, MS Add. 17275, fo. 230; cf. the reference in Jean Bodel, *Le Jeu de Saint Nicolas*, ed. F. J. Warne, Oxford 1968, p. xiv.

[7] 'quae non scripto sed seniorum relatione didici ... In nimiis enim procellis quae tempore Danorum enormiter furuerunt, antiquorum scripta cum basilicis et aedibus incendio deperierunt ... Codicibus autem perditis antiquorum res gestae oblivioni traditae sunt': OV iii. 282–4.

[8] 'miracula quibus fulserat in carne degens, sive eciam vinculis carnis absoluta, Danica depopulatio delevit ab hominum noticia': *Vita et miracula sancte Bege virginis*, in *The register of the priory of St Bees*, ed. J. Wilson (SS cxxvi, 1915), 497–520, at 508.

of wood, was burned, and the noble library ... completely disappeared. In this devastation the records of the life and miracles of the saints that the holy fathers had transmitted in writing to the knowledge of later generations were destroyed.'[9]

William of Malmesbury provides a classic statement of this theory of a caesura or gap in the hagiographic record. His comments were stimulated by his visit to the monastery of Tavistock. William liked Tavistock. It was a pleasant spot, with plenty of fish, and he admired the way that the river had been routed through the monks' toilets to carry away 'whatever was superfluous'. But he lamented the absence of sources about the local saint, Rumon: 'he is adorned with a beautiful shrine, but what is said about him is not buttressed by the solid authority of writers (*nulla fides scriptorum assistit opinioni*)'; 'you will find this the situation not only here but in many places in England', William adds, where 'only the bare names of the saints (*nuda tantum sanctorum nomina*)' are known. And he believes that knowledge of the exploits of the saints had been destroyed by the violence of enemies.[10]

Being trained in rhetorical effects, and grounded also in the dramatic stories of the Old Testament, the writers of the twelfth century were able to paint powerful verbal pictures of Viking devastation. They might go for the spectacular (and here, since it is hard to better, I use Dr Love's translation):

> the fearful and impious people of the northern regions, gnashing and raving to sate the hunger of its ferocity, and longing to quench the hunger of its spite with the outpouring of human blood, sprang up from the frozen places of its birth, and ploughing through the vast ocean with no small fleet of boats, reached the shores of Britain, and encircling the entire island now by sea now by land, began to lay waste to it by fire's blaze and iron's blade.[11]

---

[9] 'Quidquid de lignis fuerat, ignis absumpsit. Bibliotheca illa nobilissima ... tota deperiit. In qua denique devastatione monimenta, quae de vita et miraculis sanctorum sancti patres ad posteritatis notitiam stilo transmiserant, constat esse consumta': Ailred of Rievaulx, *De sanctis ecclesiae Haugustaldensis* c. 11 in *The priory of Hexham*, ed. J. Raine (SS xliv, xlvi, 1864–5), i. 172–203, at 190.

[10] '... pulchritudine decoratus scrinii, ubi nulla scriptorum fides assistit opinioni. Quod non solum ibi sed in multis locis Angliae invenies, violentia (credo) hostilitatis abolitam omnem gestorum notitiam, nuda tamen sanctorum nomina ... sciri': Malmesbury, *GP* i. 316 (bk ii. 95).

[11] 'Etenim aquilonalium plagarum gens atrox et impia sue ferocitatis exercende fame frendens ac seuiens, humanique sanguinis effusione sitim malignitatis potare cupiens, a gelidis natiuitatis sue sedibus prosiliuit, et cum non minima nauali classe uastum sulcans pelagus Brittannie litora tenuit, totamque ipsam insulam nunc mari nunc terra circuiens, flammis ac ferro cepit depopulari': *Miracula sancte Ætheldrethe virginis* c. 1 in Goscelin of Saint-Bertin, *The hagiography of the female saints of Ely*, ed. R.C. Love, Oxford 2004, 95–130, at 107.

Or they might ponder the destruction in a more elegiac mood. The ruins of Ebchester in county Durham, supposedly a nunnery founded in the seventh century,

> teach us today quite clearly what it was once like and how great it once was when it was standing. For times changed, as they do, and its inhabitants were killed ... Ebchester was destroyed and turned into forested wastelands and grazing places for animals, as it appears today.[12]

There is no doubt of the strong dramatic impact of the picture of nameless hordes of pagans coming across the North Sea and destroying everything in their path, while melancholy musings among the vestiges of the past can be evocative, but they lack individual villains. This could, however, be remedied. By the twelfth century standard characters in the cast of the Viking devastations were the brothers Ingvar and Ubba (sometimes aspirated as Hingvar and Hubba). Ingvar seems to represent the historically attested Ivarr, a Viking leader of the ninth century, and, although he has gone down in legend as Ivarr the Boneless, it does seem possible to construct at least a skeleton biography for him.[13] He was a leader of the Great Army, is mentioned in the Anglo-Saxon Chronicle *sub anno* 878, and is probably the same as the successful Viking chief Ímar who made his fortune in Ireland. Ingvar crops up again, as a leader of the Great Army, in Æthelweard's chronicle at the end of the tenth century.[14]

The chronicle references are simply that – references. The most important text to bring life to the two Viking brothers was Abbo of Fleury's account of Edmund king and martyr, composed *c*.986, which contains the first mention of Ingvar's brother Ubba, and attributes Edmund's martyrdom to Ingvar. The brothers are diabolic figures, coming from the frozen north, where Satan placed his seat, and aim at the complete extermination of Britain. Abbo gives his account of them an apocalyptic twist by associating them with the cannibal and Hyperborean nations who are to come at the time of Antichrist.[15] Abbo's *Life*

---

[12] 'Quod quale quantumque in se olim fuerit dum staret ex ruinis suis manifeste nunc docet, mutato namque ut solet statu temporum, interfectis habitatoribus suis ... Subversum est et in plurimam nemorum vastitatem et animalium pascua, sicut hodie videtur, commutatum': *Vita et miracula S. Æbbe virginis* c. 2, in *The miracles of St Æbbe of Coldingham and St Margaret of Scotland*, ed. R. Bartlett, Oxford 2003, 1–66, at 10.

[13] Usefully summarised in M. Costambeys, 'Ívarr (d. 873)', in *ODNB*, Oxford 2004, xxix. 443–5.

[14] *Chronicon Æthelweardi*, ed. A. Campbell, London and Edinburgh 1962, iv. 2 (pp. 35–6).

[15] Abbo of Fleury, *Passio sancti Eadmundi* c. 5, ed. M. Winterbottom, *Three Lives of English saints*, Toronto 1972, 67–87, at 71–2.

of Edmund was a popular text, and launched Ingvar and Ubba on an extensive literary career.

The F text of the Anglo-Saxon Chronicle gives their names as an interlinear addition to its account of the death of Edmund, and the early-twelfth-century *Life* of Sexburga, which describes a premonition that the saint has of the Viking invasions, specifically mentions the devastations of Ingvar and Ubba.[16] John of Worcester makes Ingvar and Ubba responsible for the flight of Cuthbert's community from Lindisfarne.[17] Henry of Huntingdon describes them as 'most brave but most cruel', and, perhaps with a novelistic urge to differentiate his characters, says that Ingvar was extremely intelligent while Ubba had amazing courage.[18] In contrast, Geoffrey of Wells credits Ubba, not with manly courage, but with a mastery of demonic arts and sorcery.[19] Ingvar, 'the pagan king', is responsible for the devastation of Ely according to the *Liber Eliensis*, which also tells how his *collega* Ubba was killed at the battle of Ashdown (871).[20] Fortunately we do not have to depend on such an unreliable source for the ultimate fate of Ingvar and Ubba, for this is recorded in the Book of Hyde, a fifteenth-century compilation from Hyde Abbey, Winchester: 'While crossing a ford in Berkshire, Ingvar drowned, and to this day the ford is called *Hyngurford* by the local people. But while Ubba was out riding, suddenly the earth opened up its mouth and swallowed him alive.'[21] Perhaps this story of Ubba's fate has some connection with Gaimar's assertion that, after Ubba was killed in battle, the Danes made a great mound over him at the site in Devon now called Ubbelaw.[22]

Not all writers of the long twelfth century placed the Viking caesura in the time of the Great Army, or relied on the Chronicle's unforgettable account of

---

[16] ASC MS F, fo. 54; *Vita beate Sexburge regine* cc. 14–15, in Goscelin of Saint-Bertin, *The hagiography of the female saints*, 133–88, at 162–4.

[17] JW *Chronicle* ii. 444–6, s.a. 995.

[18] '… viri strenuissimi sed crudelissimi. Hingvar erat ingentis ingenii, Vbba vero fortitudinis admirande': HH 280 (bk v. 5).

[19] Geoffrey of Wells, *De infantia sancti Edmundi*, c. 7, in *Memorials of St Edmund's*, i. 93–103, at 41–2.

[20] *LE* 53–4 (bk i. 39).

[21] 'Qui Hyngwar, dum quoddam vadum pertransiret, in comitatu Barokensi, dimersus est, quod vadum usque hodie, ab ejus nomine, a comprovincialibus *Hyngurford* appellatur. Hubba vero dum equitaret, subito terra aperiens os suum vivum absorbuit': *Liber monasterii de Hyda*, ed. E. Edwards (RS [xlv], 1866), 10.

[22] Geffrei Gaimar, *Estoire des Engleis (History of the English)*, ed. and tr. I. Short, Oxford 2009, lines 3144–56, at p. 172. Writing of the defeat of the Danes in 878 at Kinwith near Bideford in Devon (now identified as Countisbury), E. Conybeare, *Alfred in the chroniclers*, Cambridge 1900, 33, says 'The Hubba Stone, a huge barrow amongst the sandhills by the estuary (now swept away by the tide), enshrined for eight centuries the name and the bones of the pirate chief here slaughtered.' See also *Two of the Saxon chronicles parallel*, ed. C. Plummer and J. Earle, Oxford 1892–9, ii. 93.

ninth-century England with her back to the wall. Faricius' *Life* of Aldhelm, composed in the 1090s, places the crucial break not at that time, but at the period of the late tenth-century Danish raids. In fact, the first disruption that Faricius notes in the centuries following the death of Aldhelm in 709 occurs under King Eadwig (955–9), whose policy was the replacement of monks and nuns by worldly canons.[23] Faricius, followed by William of Malmesbury, states that a volume of Aldhelm's miracles had been lost 'at the time of the Danes, when they still persecuted Christ's Church', and that the saint's body had been translated from a precious shrine into a plain stone coffin in order to avoid desecration by the Vikings, well known for 'their foul greed for the gleam of precious metal'. This translation of the relics ('or rather concealment', writes Faricius) was effected by Archbishop Dunstan, and took place on 5 May, 'as many martyrologies testify'.[24] The complete absence of any such references in extant sources could lead us to doubt Faricius' accuracy, or it might remind us how fragmentary the surviving evidence is.

Faricius, then, when he writes 'the savagery of the Danes began to rage over the English', has in mind the raids that began in the 980s and 990s and culminated eventually in the Danish conquest of England.[25] Glastonbury's twelfth-century claim to possess the body of St Dunstan likewise rested on a story about this period, which described how the monks of Glastonbury had removed the relics from Canterbury in 1012 after that city had been devastated by the Danes.[26] Taking us yet further from the Danes of the Great Army is the description of the shrine of St Ecgwine at Evesham at the time of his translation in the later 1030s. The saint's relics were kept at that time in 'a shrine at one time beautifully adorned with precious gold-coloured metal' but this had been despoiled 'by the Danes thereabouts (*a Dacis circumcirca*)', and therefore presumably by a resident and settled Danish population.[27]

---

[23] Faricius, *Vita sancti Aldhelmi* c. 14, ed. M. Winterbottom, 'An edition of Faricius, *Vita S. Aldhelmi*', *Journal of Medieval Latin* xv (2005), 93–147, at 111.

[24] 'Danorum tempore, cum adhuc Christi ecclesiam persequerentur; in carioris metalli specie eorum spurcam aviditatem; Hanc autem translationis et, ut verius dicam, fidelem absconsionem; ut multa testantur martyrologia': ibid 98 (preface), 113 (c. 16); Malmesbury, *GP* i. 582 (bk v. 236), 632 (bk v. 267); William of Malmesbury, *Vita Dunstani* ii. 10. 4, in William of Malmesbury, *Saints' Lives*, ed. and tr. M. Winterbottom and R.M. Thomson, Oxford 2002, 165–302, at 258–60.

[25] 'Danorum super Anglos furere cepit sevitia': Faricius, *Vita sancti Aldhelmi* 112 (c. 15).

[26] R. Sharpe, 'Eadmer's letter to the monks of Glastonbury concerning St Dunstan's disputed remains', in L. Abrams and J.P. Carley (eds), *The archaeology and history of Glastonbury abbey*, Woodbridge 1991, 205–15, with bibliography and references.

[27] 'in quodam scrinio quondam precioso fulvoque metallo bene adornato, set iam pridem a Dacis circumcirca expoliato': Thomas of Marlborough, *History of the abbey of Evesham*, ed. J. Sayers and L. Watkiss, Oxford 2003, 72 (bk i. 63).

Danes of various sorts could thus be invoked to explain any disappointing deficiencies in the hagiographic record. But some writers looked for other explanations of the gap in their knowledge when gazing into the dark backward and abysm of time. For example, conventional statements, found in the historians and in charter preambles as well as in hagiographic writing, about the value of writing things down, and the evanescence of events that are not put into written record, could lead to the conclusion that it is the men of old who are at fault here. Reproach is then aimed not at Viking destruction but at English sloth. Arcoid, canon of St Paul's and author of the *Miracles* of St Erkenwald of *c*. 1140, notes the inadequacy of the record available to him, for, while 'the faithful people' of the past had appreciated the saint's miracles and remembered what they saw and heard, 'alas! they neglected to tie them down with letters, lest they escape'.[28] Ecgwine's miracles, too, 'had been consigned to oblivion by the negligence and carelessness of writers'.[29]

Likewise, the twelfth-century author of the *Life and miracles* of Oswin, king of Deira, criticises 'the negligence of the men of old (*antiquorum incuria*)' for failing to leave a proper record of the seventh-century saint. But he then goes on to advance another reason, of a quite different kind, why 'the memory of the holy martyr Oswin had faded away and been completely effaced'. This was the attitude of the Anglo-Saxons towards funeral monuments. In that distant period and place, writes our author, 'the rough nation (*rudis natio*)' did not attach much importance to 'the glory of sepulchres', and hence Oswin had been interred simply and anonymously. This is a judgement that goes beyond the commonplace point about the lack of written sources, and advances to a historical perception, a sense that customs change over time, with a hint of the primitiveness of earlier times.[30] It also, of course, rebuts the potential objection that Oswin could not have been a saint, for, if he had been, he would surely have had a glorious tomb-shrine.

Eadmer has a particularly thorough discussion of the issue of missing evidence. He explained the lack of miracles attributed to St Bregwin, the eighth-century archbishop of Canterbury, in the following way. One possibility, he says, is that Bregwin performed miracles in his lifetime, but they were not

---

[28] 'Fidelis ... populus ... litteris ligare ne aufugerent, proh dolor, neglexit': Arcoid, *Miracula sancti Erkenwaldi* 'proemium' in *The saint of London*, ed. Whatley, 100–102.

[29] 'negligentia et incuria scriptorum scimus oblivioni tradita esse': Thomas of Marlborough, *History of Evesham*, 76 (bk ii. 65).

[30] 'Et quia rudis natio illis temporibus et illis in locis non multum efficiebatur circa sepulchrarum gloriam, reverendum corpus sarcophago lapideo impositum in abdito sinu terrae reconditum est ... Tali occasione memoria sancti martyris Oswini obsoleta et penitus deleta ...': *Vita Oswini regis Deirorum* prologue and c. 4 in *Miscellanea biographica*, ed. J. Raine (SS viii, 1838), 1–59, at 1, 11; for discussion of the revival of Oswin's cult and the sources that describe it, see P.A. Hayward, 'Sanctity and lordship in twelfth-century England: Saint Albans, Durham, and the cult of Saint Oswine, king and martyr', *Viator* xxx (1999), 105–44.

recorded in writing. Alternatively, they might have been written down, but the written record had disappeared through the long passage of time or because of some incident (Viking destruction could fit in here, of course). It is in any case quite clear, he argues, that Bregwin *could have* performed miracles in his lifetime, because there is no doubt that he did so posthumously – we know that 'by indubitable report (*certa relatione*)'. Finally, there is the possibility that he did not perform any miracles in his lifetime because 'those times, in which the faith of Christ was well established, did not require miracles, which are aimed at unbelievers rather than believers'.[31]

* * *

So, the monks and clergy of the long twelfth century, looking back over earlier times, could explain a break in their traditions in various ways. They could even make a virtue of such a break, by turning it into a heroic tradition of its own kind. The wanderings of the community of St Cuthbert, in flight from the Vikings, between their abandonment of Lindisfarne in 875 and their eventual settlement at Durham in 995, in all likelihood still with the body of the saint they had started with, generated an epic of its own. Tradition was preserved into the twelfth century of the names of the companions who had accompanied the body of the saint during its wandering years, and remarkable stories were told about them. Similar knowledge was handed down about those who had kept the faith with the body of St Edmund before it reached its final destination.[32]

But one thing, that is perhaps surprising, is that not many martyr cults sprang from the blood of the Vikings' victims, either in historical reality or in the imagination of later generations. The Danes made few saints and, with the exception of Edmund king and martyr, and, in a slightly different mode, Alphege, these saints did not have notable cults. It is only the *Aberdeen Breviary*,

---

[31] 'illa tempora fide Christi quaque fundata non egebat signis miraculorum, que ... infidelium sunt potius quam fidelium': Eadmer, *Vita Bregwini* 5, ed. B.W. Scholz, 'Eadmer's Life of Bregwine, archbishop of Canterbury, 761–4', *Traditio* xxii (1966), 127–48, at 140–41. The idea goes back to I Corinthians 14: 22 ('linguae in signum sunt non fidelibus, sed infidelibus') and there was a lively tradition of debate on the subject: M. van Uytfanghe, 'La controverse biblique et patristique autour du miracle, et ses répercussions sur l'hagiographie dans l'Antiquité tardive et le haut Moyen Âge latin', in *Hagiographie, cultures et sociétés, IVe–XIIe siècles: actes du colloque organisé à Nanterre et à Paris 2–5 mai 1979*, Paris 1981, 205–33.

[32] Symeon of Durham, *Libellus de exordio atque procursu istius hoc est Dunhelmensis ecclesie*, ed. and tr. D.W. Rollason, Oxford 2000, bk ii. c. 6 (pp. 100–104), ii. 10–13 (pp. 110–26); iii. 1 (pp. 144–8); Reginald of Durham, *Libellus de admirandis beati Cuthberti virtutibus*, cc. 12–15, ed. J. Raine (SS i, 1835), 16–28; Hermann the archdeacon, *Liber de miraculis sancti Edmundi*, 30.

for example, printed in 1510, that informs us of St Adrian and his companions, who were killed on the Isle of May in the Firth of Forth, 'when the fearful madness of the Danes was raging, who had destroyed almost the whole of Britain, which is now called England'.[33] According to various twelfth-century versions of her Life, St Osyth was killed by the ubiquitous Ingvar and Ubba,[34] and Roger of Wendover, followed by Matthew Paris, writes that the same villains were also responsible for the death of Ebba of Coldingham – not the seventh-century abbess, but a later namesake who encouraged her nuns to cut off their noses and upper lips, in order to make them less attractive to marauding Danes. In this way they avoided rape – although not being burned alive.[35] But these are minor cults or no cults at all.

Despite all the traditions of destruction and the ebullient prose that the authors of the twelfth century devoted to Viking murder and arson, they also tell how cults and communities could be re-established. Indeed, this is usually the primary purpose of their narratives. Take the case of St Oswin. After his death in 651, no one knew where Oswin's body lay, as it was buried in the nondescript tomb already mentioned, until, in the year 1065, the saint himself appeared in a dream to the pious Edmund, sacristan of the church where his bones lay. Edmund went to the bishop of Durham, Aethelwine, and the bishop evidently contacted Countess Judith, Tostig's wife, who put in a request for a portion of the relics if the body could be found. Needless to say, the body was found. Countess Judith received some hairs, and, when she saw crowds assembling, she 'wished to strengthen their faith and devotion towards St Oswin'. She had the hairs of the saint placed on a fire and when they were unharmed, 'the venerable countess and the innumerable crowd of people standing around the fire were made more certain of the merit of the martyr'.[36] A minor cult came into existence.

---

[33] 'seuiente tremulenta Danorum rabie, qui totam fere Britanniam, que nunc Anglia dicitur, deuastauerant': *Breviarium Aberdonense* (Edinburgh, 1510; facsimile reprint, Bannatyne Club, London, 1854), Sanctorale, fos 62v–63; for excavations on the Isle of May, including evidence of pilgrimage, see *Excavations at St Ethernan's monastery, Isle of May, Fife, 1992–7* (Tayside and Fife Archaeological Commitee, Monograph 6, 2008).

[34] *La Vie seinte Osith, virge e martire*, line 771, ed. D.W. Russell, *Papers on Language and Literature* xli (2005), 339–445, at 384; D. Bethell, 'The Lives of St Osyth of Essex and St Osyth of Aylesbury', *AB* lxxxviii (1970), 75–127, esp. 88.

[35] Matthew Paris, *Chronica majora*, ed. H.R. Luard (RS [lvii] 1872–83) ii. 391–2, s.a. 870; there is a dramatic eighteenth-century engraving of this scene, reproduced in J.T. Schulenburg, *Forgetful of their sex: female sanctity and society, 500–1100*, Chicago 1998, pl. 10, after 132.

[36] 'Devota femina ... voluit eos solidare in fide et sancti Oswini devotione ... Quod videns veneranda comitissa et plebs igni circunstans innumera de martyris merito certior est effecta': *Vita Oswini* c. 4 (pp. 12–15).

The story invokes both visionary validation – the appearance of the saint in a dream – and the test of relics by fire – a not uncommon occurrence in the eleventh century, both intended to demonstrate that the body turned up in 1065 really was that of the king who had been killed more than four centuries earlier.[37] But it is worth pointing out that the name of this saint would have disappeared long before if it had not been preserved in the writings of Bede. For the churchmen of the twelfth century were not completely without landmarks or signposts when they contemplated past centuries. They had Bede. And Bede is so important a source for the seventh century that it is hardly an exaggeration to say that the men of the twelfth century knew just as much about that time as we do. In some cases, like that of Oswin and of Ebba (the seventh-century abbess, not the legendary nasolabial self-mutilator), it is probable that Bede and Bede alone explains the birth of cult in the long twelfth century.[38] And, in the absence of Bede, other texts might fill the lacuna. The sickly Modwenna of Burton upon Trent, a saint about whom very little could be said, received a strengthening blood transfusion from a borrowed Life of an Irish saint with a somewhat similar name, Monnina.[39] A Life of St Rumon of Tavistock, the lack of which was so lamented by William of Malmesbury, was subsequently concocted from the Life of Ronan of Brittany.[40] The rich hagiography of the Irish and Bretons could afford to be a generous lender.

For monastic and clerical writers of later centuries, the ravages of the Vikings became something of a topos, a recognizable stereotype to be invoked, often to explain a gap in the recorded hagiographic traditions. This is clearly relevant to the long and still-lively controversy about the destructiveness of the Vikings, associated particularly with the name of Peter Sawyer and his opponents and

---

[37] One way of testing the authenticity of a relic was to subject it to trial by fire. Thomas Head, who has worked on this subject for some time, gave a provisional list of such incidents, which includes three instances from England. All three date to the mid-eleventh century: a hair of Cuthbert, in the possession of the famous relic collector Alfred Westou, so in the period 1040–70, although this was not really a trial – Symeon, *LdE* 162 (bk iii. 7); Oswin in 1065; Wigstan and Credan at Evesham in the period 1077–89 (*Chronicon abbatiae Ramesiensis*, ed. W.D. Macray (RS [lxxxiii] 1886), 323); T. Head, 'Saints, heretics, and fire: finding meaning through the ordeal', in S. Farmer and B. Rosenwein (eds), *Monks and nuns, saints and outcasts*, Ithaca 2000, 220–38; idem, 'The genesis of the ordeal of relics by fire in Ottonian Germany: an alternative form of "canonization"', in G. Klaniczay (ed.), *Procès de canonisation au Moyen Âge: aspects juridiques et religieux / Medieval canonization processes: legal and religious aspects*, Rome 2004, 19–37.

[38] On Oswin, n. 30 above; on Ebba, *The Miracles of St Æbbe*, ed. Bartlett, pp. xiv–xvi.

[39] Geoffrey of Burton, *Life and miracles of St Modwenna*, ed. R. Bartlett, Oxford 2002, pp. xi–xx.

[40] P. Grosjean, 'Vie de S. Rumon; vie, invention et miracles de S. Nectan', *AB* lxxi (1953), 359–414, at 361–75.

defenders. Were the Norsemen horrifying marauders of unparalleled brutality, whose ravages left large parts of western Europe in smoking ruins, or, alternatively, in Wallace-Hadrill's immortal words, 'should we view the Vikings as little more than groups of long-haired tourists who occasionally roughed up the natives?'[41]

England experienced the double hiatus of the general disruptions of the ninth and tenth centuries, however much weight we give to the Vikings as the cause of that disruption, and then the very specific experience of the Norman Conquest, in the aftermath of which there was an influx of foreign bishops, abbots and monks, both into existing houses and into new religious houses founded by French monks, often as dependencies of French houses. The hagiography and the history of local cults needed to accommodate this situation.

In his book of 1994, *Phantoms of remembrance*, Patrick Geary wrote about processes of remembering and forgetting around the new millennium, with reference to 'the new past forged in the eleventh century', based on 'the image of destruction, disintegration, and confusion in the tenth century, followed by painful rebirth of a new society'; he stresses the 'perception of discontinuity and … the process of selection and creation of a past that embodies this perception.'[42] Many literate people in the eleventh and twelfth centuries did indeed see European society as emerging from a long period of darkness and disruption to a more promising future. We are familiar with Raoul Glaber's 'white mantle of churches'. 'It was', he writes, 'as if the world were shaking itself and throwing off the past.'[43]

Monks and canons of this period, looking at their inheritance, at the shrines, relics and records of their churches, often asked themselves about their past, and frequently found only hazy answers. They were a little like a drunk after a particularly spectacular night of indulgence, waking up to find a muddle of objects, some familiar, like the pile of clothes lying in the corner, some less explicable, like that parrot cage or the note in an unfamiliar hand. The historians and hagiographers of the eleventh and twelfth centuries had plenty of fragments

---

[41] J.M. Wallace-Hadrill, *Early medieval history*, Oxford 1975, 220; some representative publications in the debate are P. Sawyer, *The age of the Vikings*, 2 edn, London 1971; S. Coupland, 'The Vikings in Francia and Anglo-Saxon England to 911', in R. McKitterick (ed.), *The New Cambridge medieval history*, Cambridge 1995, 190–201; A. Smyth, 'The effect of Scandinavian raiders on the English and Irish churches: a preliminary reassessment', in B. Smith (ed.), *Britain and Ireland, 900–1300: insular responses to medieval European change*, Cambridge 1999, 1–38; J.L. Nelson, 'Presidential address: England and the Continent in the ninth century: II, the Vikings and others', *TRHS* 6 ser. xviii (2003), 1–28.

[42] P.J. Geary, *Phantoms of remembrance: memory and oblivion at the end of the first millennium*, Princeton 1994, 23, 26.

[43] 'Erat enim instar ac si mundus ipse excutiendo semet, reiecta vetustate, passim candidam ecclesiarum vestem indueret': Rodulfus Glaber, *Historiarum libri quinque*, ed. J. France, Oxford 1989, 116 (bk iii. 13).

of the past, but usually lacked a convincing explanation of how they had got to their present; or, the same thing in other words, a convincing narrative. But they were intelligent men, trained in Latin rhetoric, with its rules of history and criteria of plausibility. They were able to create their stories, from a blend of real historical information, misinterpretation of real historical information, and invention, cynical or not. This is an age of great creativity in hagiography, as well as in the 'invention' – that is, discovery – of saintly bodies. Both the saints' Lives and the holy bodies were, for the great churches, title deeds, and could be created if they were lacking.

Chapter 3
Folcard of Saint-Bertin and the Anglo-Saxon Saints at Thorney

Rosalind Love

Sixty-four churches are known to have been dedicated to St Botwulf (or Botolph, as he is usually known now) in England, and a further sixteen across Denmark, Norway and Sweden, witness to his significant popularity in the Middle Ages.[1] Scattered early evidence presents a picture of the saint as a leading light in the seventh-century monastic movement. The anonymous *Life* of Abbot Ceolfrith, written at Monkwearmouth-Jarrow in Bede's time, notes that in his twenties (in about 670) Ceolfrith had visited Botwulf in East Anglia to learn about monasticism:

> He came to the East Angles, so as to see the establishment of Abbot Botwulf, whom rumour had made famous everywhere as a man of unique life and teaching, filled with the Spirit's grace; and when he had been fully instructed, as far as was possible in a short time, he returned home.[2]

For the year 654, the Anglo-Saxon Chronicle (A, B, C and E for 653) records two events: 'In this year King Anna was slain. And Botwulf began to build the minster at *Icanho*'; *Icanho* is now agreed by most scholars to be Iken, on the Alde estuary in Suffolk.[3] There are also signs that in the later 670s Botwulf's

---

* This chapter is preliminary to an edition and translation of the works of Folcard which I have in hand for the Oxford Medieval Texts Series; all quotations from Folcard's hagiographies cited here derive from that edition, but references to existing editions in print will also be provided in the notes. All translations are my own unless otherwise stated.

[1] On the Scandinavian dedications, see the summary in J. Toy, 'St Botulph: an English saint in Scandinavia', in M. Carver (ed.), *The cross goes north: processes of conversion in northern Europe, AD 300–1300*, York 2003, 565–70.

[2] 'Peruenit et ad Anglos Orientales, ut uideret instituta Botuulfi abbatis, quem singularis uitae et doctrinae uirum, gratiaque Spiritus plenum, fama circumquaque uulgauerat; instructusque abundanter, quantum breui potuit, domum rediit': *Vita sanctissimi Ceolfridi abbatis* c. 4, in *Venerabilis Baedae opera historica*, ed. C. Plummer, Oxford 1896, i. 389.

[3] 'Onna cyning wearþ ofslægen. 7 Botulf ongon mynster timbran æt Icanho.' On the identification of *Icanho* as Iken, see N. Scarfe, *Suffolk in the Middle Ages*, Woodbridge 1986, 39–51.

foundation was able to establish some kind of daughter house in faraway Shropshire. The *Life* of St Mildburh of Much Wenlock, written towards the end of the eleventh century by Goscelin of Saint-Bertin, incorporates a document known as 'St Mildburg's Testament', describing the endowment of the saint's monastery at Much Wenlock (Shropshire) and quoting what are believed to be authentic charters of early date.[4] One of these states that Abbot Æthelheah of *Icheanog* and the *familia* of Botwulf gave land in Shropshire and Herefordshire to Mildburg, and in return received from her land at *Homtun* (perhaps Hampton in Shropshire).[5] This suggests that Iken's influence, possibly through connections established by the East Anglian royal dynasty, extended well beyond Suffolk. Yet, however famous he might have been in his day, if there was an early written account of Botwulf it does not survive, and we have only the *Vita* composed in the eleventh century by Folcard, former monk of Saint-Bertin, then abbot of Thorney, the monastery that claimed some of Botwulf's relics. It is fair to say, however, that his account has not been accorded much value: Dorothy Whitelock wrote 'it is doubtful whether one can accept anything on the authority of the Life of St Botulf written by Folcard.'[6] Still, it is all we have, and we must interrogate Folcard's text as best we can; the aim of this chapter, then, is to ask how Folcard constructed Botwulf's sanctity, and what there was in his own personal background and the circumstances at Thorney which may have led him to write as he did. We may thereby gain some sense of his perspective on the distant Anglo-Saxon past and of Thorney's desire to establish a link with that past.

Folcard's *Vita Botulfi* survives in five twelfth- or thirteenth-century manuscripts and several abridgements, and then his account makes its way into later compilations such as John of Tynemouth's *Sanctilogium* from the

---

[4] The *Vita s. Milburge* remains unpublished, although A.J.M. Edwards presented an edition in her unpublished Ph.D. dissertation 'Odo of Ostia's history of the Translation of St. Milburga and its connection with the early history of Wenlock Abbey', University of London 1960, 41–91, 176–9 and 262–71. I have an edition and translation in preparation, and have argued for Goscelin's authorship of the text on a number of occasions; see R.C. Love, '"Torture me, rend me, burn me, kill me!" Goscelin of Saint-Bertin and the depiction of female sanctity', in P. Szarmach (ed.), *Writing women saints in Anglo-Saxon England*, Toronto 2013, 274–306. The attribution to Goscelin is doubted by P.A. Hayward, 'The *Miracula inventionis beate Mylburge virginis* attributed to "the Lord Ato, cardinal bishop of Ostia"', *EHR* cxiv (1999), 543–73.

[5] See H.P.R. Finberg, *The early charters of the West Midlands*, 2 edn, Leicester 1961, 197–211, with Mildburg's Testament printed (from the *Vita Milburge* in BL, MS Add. 34633) at pp. 201–4; this evidence was also discussed by D. Whitelock, 'The pre-Viking age Church in East Anglia', *ASE* i (1972), 1–22, at 12.

[6] Whitelock, 'The pre-Viking age Church', 11.

fourteenth century.[7] Lessons for the Office on Botwulf's feast-day, 17 June, abridged from Folcard's text, can be found in twenty-five whole or fragmentary liturgical books from Scandinavia, from the twelfth century to the fifteenth, not to mention the printed breviaries, putting Botwulf among the most successful of all the Anglo-Saxon saints exported to the Scandinavian church.[8] And it is Folcard's depiction of Botwulf that became the standard narrative.

In the preface to his *Life* of Botwulf, Folcard offers his reasons for writing, in what seem to be striking personal terms; as we shall see, self-revelation, real or feigned, is a hallmark of his work.[9] Referring to himself as 'monachorum minimus' ('least of the monks'), he states that he finds himself, as penance for his sins, in charge of the monks at Thorney in the Fens, but the place itself is no penance, rather it has a profound appeal, for a variety of reasons which he then goes on to unfold. Thorney, he says, is a place where 'like the ass or the ox at the Lord's manger, become a beast of burden, I intend to cling always, until evil be overpassed (Ps. lvi. 2).'[10] As we shall have cause to note in due course, Folcard was well read in the classics, but surely also in the Scriptures, so it cannot have been far from his thoughts that a standard exegesis of the animals present at Christ's birth is that they represent the faithful of the new covenant – Jew and gentile, clean and unclean – approaching the holy altar – the manger – for spiritual nourishment. Augustine put it this way, quoting Isaiah i. 3: 'two animals approach the manger, two peoples, "the ox knows his owner and the ass his master's manger". So, approach the manger, do not be ashamed to be the Lord's beast of burden. You will bear Christ, you will not err as you walk on the way.'[11] In likening himself to these beasts of burden, Folcard thus portrays Thorney as his refuge, but as more: food for the soul. A dumb animal, not ashamed to be thus in humble subjection, he approaches adoringly.

Folcard refers in this preface to 'the saints who rest in this church' ('sanctos in eadem basilica pausantes'). Apart from Botwulf, those saints were Botwulf's

---

[7] The contents of the *Sanctilogium* were edited by C. Horstman, *Nova Legenda Anglie*, Oxford 1901, with Botwulf at i. 130–33.

[8] See J. Toy, *English saints in the medieval liturgies of the Scandinavian churches* (HBS, Subsidia vi, 2009), 65–86, and also Toy, 'St Botulph'.

[9] The preface to Folcard's *Life* of Botwulf was omitted in the Bollandists' text in *ASS*, Junii III, 402–3, but was printed by T.D. Hardy, *Descriptive catalogue of materials relating to the history of Great Britain and Ireland* (RS [xxvi], 1862–71), i. 373–4.

[10] 'ut asinus uel bos ad presepe Domini, apud quem, ut iumentum factus, semper adherere, "donec transeat iniquitas" ex eius gratia, proposui.'

[11] 'Accedant ad praesepe duo animalia, duo populi: agnouit enim bos possessorem suum, et asinus praesepe domini sui. Attende ad praesepium: noli erubescere esse iumentum Domini. Christum portabis, non errabis ambulans per uiam': Augustine, Sermon 189, ed. G. Morin in 'Sancti Augustini sermones post Maurinos reperti', *Miscellanea Agostiniana* i (1930), 211.

supposed brother *Adulfus* (Æthwulf, or perhaps Æthelwulf), and three anchorites, claimed as Thorney's own original saints, the siblings Thancred, Torhtred and Tova. After founding the Benedictine community at Thorney in 973, on its behalf Æthelwold had also apparently rounded up several other sets of relics, including those of the founder of Monkwearmouth-Jarrow, Benedict Biscop. For all of these saints, Folcard constructed a group of texts: the *Life* of Botwulf, a homily about Thancred, Torhtred and Tova, and an account of the translation of all the relics at Thorney. The preface to the Botwulf *Life* effectively serves as a prologue for the whole dossier.

Returning to that preface, we may also note that Folcard professes to like Thorney first because it is dedicated to Mary, who offers hope of forgiveness: 'because she is known as the Mother of Mercy, by the fallen who are wishing to rise up again, in the hope of gaining forgiveness she is held first and foremost in respect'.[12] Its setting appeals too, a bosky solitude conducive to holiness: at this period Thorney was still an island surrounded by fen, perhaps reminiscent of Folcard's former home at Saint-Omer, at the head of a marshy estuary. And thirdly, he says, the fact that it was Æthelwold's favourite commends it as well. Folcard addressed this preface to Walchelin, bishop of Winchester (1070–98), *Desiderantissimo patri et domino suo, et eque reuerentissimo presuli* ('To his dearest father and lord, and likewise a most reverend prelate'). While he may thus have been making some kind of personal appeal to Walchelin, we may also be justified in reading the dedication of Thorney's hagiographical dossier as a reflection of institutional concerns. In that case, it is important to ask why Walchelin was the dedicatee, and why Thorney's diocesan bishop, Remigius, was not. Remigius had been consecrated in 1067 as bishop of Dorchester, and in 1072 moved the see to Lincoln, but before that, in 1070, he was put under suspension because he had been consecrated by Stigand, and was obliged to go to Rome in 1071 to obtain papal pardon.[13] If we wanted to find a reason why Folcard dedicated the Thorney dossier to Walchelin rather than Remigius, this hiatus in 1070–71 would be one straightforward explanation, and would thus date its composition or completion to those years. Alternatively, and perhaps more convincingly, we could see this dedication as a deliberate attempt by Folcard to reinforce Thorney's old connection with Winchester through Æthelwold and Godeman, whom Æthelwold appointed as abbot. Such a pointed gesture may have been in part an attempt to deflect the desire of another institution, Peterborough, to claim control over Thorney by its own rewriting the Anglo-Saxon past, as we shall see later.

---

[12] 'quia mater misericordie dinoscitur lapsis resurgere uolentibus, sub optentu uenie prior et principalis respectus habetur.'

[13] See D. Bates, *Bishop Remigius of Lincoln, 1067–1092*, Lincoln 1992, 5.

To emphasise the Æthelwold connection, Folcard's preface to the *Life* of Botwulf goes so far as to assert that Æthelwold had hoped to retire to Thorney's solitude: 'where, so they say – and it is sufficiently credible – he would have chosen to end the course of his life communing with the divine.'[14] That claim is made in more detail elsewhere in the dossier, in Folcard's account of Botwulf's translation:[15]

> He [Æthelwold] even set up not far from that monastery, namely in the place where the blessed virgin of Christ Tova had been enclosed, a stone oratory in the form of a pyramid, divided up by very slender lattices and with two chambers, dedicated with three small altars, surrounded on all sides right up to the walls with trees of various types, in short a hermit's cell for himself, should the grace of the Ruler on high permit, who instead kept such a great light on the episcopal candlestand, for the illumination of the whole English world.[16]

Folcard thus implies that of all his foundations, Thorney's seclusion was especially dear to Æthelwold. Not surprisingly this detail is not to be found in any earlier source. Perhaps it was a fondly cherished house tradition at Thorney, but it may equally have been an elaboration which grew out of Folcard's own conception of sanctity and his view of the abbey's need to shape a particular account of its history. We shall have reason to note in due course that contemplative retreat from the world was a theme in Folcard's hagiography, but first a brief look at Folcard's personal story seems appropriate.

Apart from the throwaway comments in the Botwulf preface, little is known about the circumstances which brought him to Thorney. Orderic Vitalis reported that the Conqueror appointed Folcard, *sancti Bertini Sithiensis monachum multa*

---

[14] 'In qua, ut aiunt, et satis credi potest, cursum presentis uite finire delegerit in conuersatione theorica.'

[15] The translation-narrative was printed from the twelfth-century BL, Harley 3097 as an appendix to *Liber vitae: register and martyrology of New Minster and Hyde abbey, Winchester*, ed. W. de Gray Birch (Hampshire Record Society, 1892), 286–90; the quotation here derives from a more correct version of the same narrative preserved in Cambridge, St John's College, H. 6, fos 179r–82v, also twelfth-century. The translation is my own. For a brief discussion of both the Harley and St John's manuscripts, see C. Clark, 'Notes on a *Life* of three Thorney saints, Thancred, Torhtred and Tova', *Proceedings of the Cambridge Antiquarian Society* lxix (1979), 45–52.

[16] 'Construxit etiam non longe ab eodem monasterio in eo scilicet loco ubi beata uirgo Christi Toua inclusa fuerat lapideam ecclesiolam in modum pyramidis, delicatissimis cameratam cancellulis et duplici area, tribus dedicatam altaribus permodicis, undique usque ad ipsos eius muros uallatam arboribus diuersi generis, sedem scilicet heremiticam sibi si permisisset gratia supremi rectoris, qui magis tantam lucernam retinebat in candelabro pontificali, ad illuminationem totius orbis anglici.'

eruditione ualidum ('a very learned monk of Saint-Bertin'), as acting abbot there, and that Folcard served for sixteen years – unblessed (*absque benedictione*) – until 1085, when he 'withdrew' (*recessit*) because of disagreements with Bishop Remigius.[17] It is hard to escape the impression that those disagreements and the lack of an episcopal blessing for all those years may have been connected. Folcard's situation is reminiscent of that of Simeon, the prior of Winchester who was made abbot of Ely in 1082 but refused to accept the blessing which Remigius was trying to foist upon him as diocesan bishop, and asserted Ely's freedom of choice in the matter. Simeon thus went unblessed and the dispute dragged on until his brother, Bishop Walchelin of Winchester, persuaded the octogenarian abbot to submit to Remigius's blessing, and prevailed upon the Ely monks not to reject him for having capitulated.[18] This was over ten years after Folcard's appointment, which according to Orderic would have been in 1069, but there may nonetheless have been similar long-running problems at Thorney, another possible explanation for the decision to dedicate its hagiographical dossier to Walchelin, ignoring Remigius pointedly (thus we would not then be obliged to restrict the dossier's completion to 1070–71). It has been suggested that there was also a political motivation for Folcard's deposition, that he was regarded as too unwarlike to be at the fenland frontline of the Danish invasion which William feared in 1085.[19] If the self-portrait that we shall slowly reconstruct from Folcard's autobiographical hints is in any way a true likeness, then one begins to see why he might not have been entirely trusted to hold the line. We have no record of where Folcard went afterwards, nor yet of when he died. There seems no particular reason why he could not simply have retreated into the ranks at Thorney to live out his days in that adopted fen home.

Our knowledge of what Folcard did before Thorney is just as hazy, and emerges only from the frequent, if evasive, autobiographical notes in his surviving writings. Of those, the text that seems most likely to have been composed just before the move to Thorney is his *Life* of John of Beverley. Its preface, addressed to Ealdred, archbishop of York, who died in 1069, hints plangently at Folcard's personal difficulties and subsequent rescue by an unnamed queen and by Ealdred, who commissioned him to write about John.[20] In an extraordinary but frustratingly allusive passage, worth quoting in full, Folcard claims to have been the victim of some kind of attack:

---

[17] OV vi. 150–51.

[18] These events are described in the twelfth-century *Liber Eliensis*, LE 200–202 (bk ii. 118).

[19] J. Maddicott, 'Responses to the threat of invasion, 1085', *EHR* cxxii (2007), 986–97, discussing Folcard's case at 993.

[20] The *Life* was printed by J. Raine, *The historians of the church of York and its archbishops* (RS [lxxi], 1879–94), i. 239–60.

> For indeed when the sea of my struggling community was much tossed, and with almost all the very dear offspring of the monastery groaning deeply, because he who had occupied the place of pastor and physician, should, in me, his weakling little lamb, have pursued not so much retribution for a fault but the age-old damage of domestic hatred; and when <my brethren>, summoning up all their energies, tried to protect me, their fellow sheep against the onslaught of the – alas! – all too familiar wolf, he used wrongfully-acquired secular power to push me out of the monastic boat and plunge me into the ocean swell.[21]

Folcard presents himself as a sickly lamb attacked by an all too well-known wolf who was supposed to be his shepherd, presumably his abbot; the reasons for the attack hide behind the phrase 'domestic hatred', suggesting that this community in crisis was no setting to which Folcard was a newcomer. The sickly lamb cannot but recall that lost sheep in the parable, which exegetes tended to interpret as the straying sinner.[22] Here, then, we might dimly perceive some hint that Folcard knew that he was not entirely innocent, an impression that one gains also from the Botwulf preface, with its comments about Mary, to whom the fallen turn in hope of forgiveness. Whatever the rights and wrongs of his situation, however, in the preface addressed to Ealdred, Folcard then states that just when he seemed about to drown, someone rescued him, pitied his open wounds, and entrusted him to Ealdred's care. He cannot keep silent about her identity:

> And in order that all posterity may know of such kindness, I say that she is the queen, whose honest qualities the eloquent loquacity of no orator, however skilled, could ever expound. We therefore believe her to be joined by heaven to the king's side, that the great adroitness of her watchful industry might provide benefits for the present kingdom.[23]

---

[21] *Historians of the church of York*, i. 240: 'Turbato siquidem fluctuantis cenobii mei pelago gementibusque pene cunctis carissimis pignoribus monasterii, quod is qui pastoris et medici locum occupauerat in languente ouicula non culpe pressuram sed ueterem familiaris odii insectatus sit iacturam; et cum collatis totius animi sui uiribus consociam ouem in irruentem – proh dolor! – nimis familiarem lupum conarentur tueri, perperam comparato seculari potentatu exturbatum a carina monasteriali fluctibus immersit ponti'.

[22] See, for example, Jerome's Commentary on the Gospel of Matthew, book 3 on Matt. xviii. 10–14, in *S. Hieronymi presbyteri opera, pars I opera exegetica 7: commentariorum in Matheum libri IV*, ed. D. Hurst and M. Adriaen (CCSL lxxvii, 1969), 160: alii uero in nonaginta nouem ouibus iustorum putant numerum intellegi, et in una ouicula peccatorum ('some believe that in the ninety-nine sheep should be understood the number of the righteous, and in the one lamb, the number of sinners').

[23] *Historians of the church of York*, i. 240–41: 'Vtque tantam pietatem omnis noscat posteritas, reginam dico, cuius probitates nullius unquam quantumlibet diserti retoris

In the context of the quest for an author for the *Life* of Edward the Confessor and evaluating the case for Folcard, Frank Barlow debated to which queen Folcard could have been referring here, concluding that it was probably Edith, Edward's consort.[24]

As to the question of whence Folcard could have been ejected so wretchedly, Barlow considered the claims of Canterbury or Thorney, before advancing what seemed to him the more plausible theory that it must have been Saint-Bertin.[25] In this matter there is significant benefit to be had from reading this preface to the *Life* of John of Beverley alongside that of Folcard's earliest known work, his *Life* of Bertin, composed before he came to England.[26] Again we find cryptic autobiography. The preface addresses the abbot of Saint-Bertin, Bovo, and can thus be dated to his term of office, 1042–65. Bertin's relics had been translated in 1052 by Bovo, who wrote his own first-person narrative of those events.[27] It is plausible that Folcard's *Life* was intended to provide a fresh account of the patron saint to celebrate that occasion. There had been an early composite biography of Saints Omer, Bertin and Winnoc, which, in focusing primarily on Omer, would have come to seem inappropriate for the needs of Bovo's abbey.[28] Folcard refers in his preface to the 'old' *Life* of Bertin which he does not feel that his own ought to displace: 'Yet if you command me thus, in accordance with what they say about the wooden and earthenware vessels serving alongside the golden ones in the Lord's temple [1 Tim. ii. 20], so this effort of my insignificance may be kept alongside the old one.'[29]

A noteworthy feature of this Bertin preface is Folcard's strutting familiarity with works of Horace, the *Sermones* (*Satires*) and the *Ars poetica*, quoted or paraphrased no fewer than seven times. Highly allusive, it is also written in rather oblique style. After the inscription, Folcard opens immediately with a reference to Bovo's criticism of him, that he was a wastrel: 'rightly you very

---

facunda euoluet loquacitas; quam idcirco diuinitus adiunctam regio credimus lateri, ut tanta eius uigilantis industrie solertia emolumentum prouideatur presentis regni'.

[24] *The Life of King Edward who rests at Westminster*, ed. F. Barlow, 2 edn, Oxford 1992, liv–lvi.

[25] *Life of King Edward*, lvi.

[26] The text was printed by the Bollandists, as the *Vita tertia Bertini*, in *ASS* Septembris ii. 604–13.

[27] *Bovonis abbatis relatio de inventione et elevatione S. Bertini*, ed. O. Holder-Egger (MGH Scriptores xv.1, 1887), 524–34. The text is discussed by K. Ugé, *Creating the monastic past in medieval Flanders*, Woodbridge 2005, 72–87.

[28] The composite life was edited by W. Levison in *Vitae Audomari, Bertini, Winnoci* (MGH, Scriptores rerum Merovingicarum v, 1910), 753–75.

[29] *ASS* Sept. ii. 604: 'sed si ita iubes, secundum illud quod lignea et fictilia uasa cum aureis aiunt in templo Domini, sic hec mee paruitatis descriptio seruetur cum ueteri'.

often rant at your servant, that I only take up space, like that useless fig-tree'.[30] This refers to the fruitless fig-tree of the Gospels (for example, in Luke xiii. 7), cursed and doomed to be cut down, a type of the faithless and errant chosen race. There is a real sense that Folcard is aware he has strayed, yet he will lay the blame elsewhere. He goes on to observe that if he is useless, it is all Bovo's fault for pushing him too soon, expecting him to 'swim without a float' (*nimis impulisti ut narrem sine cortice*). Here he borrows an image which Horace had used to refer to his father's advice about waiting till he was a bit older to indulge in illicit affairs with married women (Horace, *Satires* i.4.119–20: *simul ac duraverit aetas / membra animumque tuum, nabis sine cortice*, 'as soon as time has toughened your body and your mind, you'll swim without a float').[31] Bovo gave Folcard too much freedom too early, so that sin's blight set in, he says, but the time has come to channel his hitherto misapplied intellectual energy in a more appropriate direction. A chance to do so presents itself, because the brothers at Saint-Bertin want something new on the patron saint, but Folcard thinks that the notion is just too ridiculous (*absurdum nimis esset*). And – oh! – he says, I could hardly be bothered to check over what I have done; you can do that! *Seruo tuo alter Aristarchus fias*, 'Be a second Aristarchus to your servant'. Folcard thus appropriates Horace's reference to Aristarchus of Samothrace, a byword for frank literary criticism (Horace, *Ars poetica* line 450).[32]

The overall tone of this preface seems somewhat cheeky, perhaps sarcastic, or it is a private joke between teacher and pupil now drawn close. Certainly only a well-trained eye will have appreciated the Horatian allusions (which passed by the Bollandist editor unnoticed). If the banter is affectionate, still the criticism Folcard directs at Bovo is inescapable: he pushed him too hard too soon, and has offered nothing but criticism since. One wonders what this personal anecdote has to do with the account of St Bertin which follows, except as a rather overblown attempt at expressing the conventional modesty required of an author. The *Life* which follows is fairly unadorned, offering for the most part a workmanlike presentation of Bertin as monastic founder. Perhaps the frustration that seems to seethe between the lines of the preface and the adverse reaction that they maybe elicited from Bovo were causes for the 'familiar hatred' to which Folcard ascribed his downfall in the preface addressed to Archbishop Ealdred. This archly languid tone can hardly have seemed appropriate for the new *Life* of a patron saint, but was it sufficient to get a monk kicked out of his community? Alas, we may never know.

---

[30] *ASS* Sept. ii. 604: 'merito frequentius stomacharis, quod solum terram occupem, ut ficus illa inutilis'.
[31] *Q. Horati Flacci opera*, ed. E.C. Wickham, rev. H.W. Garrod, Oxford 1901, 149.
[32] *Horati Flacci opera*, 267.

From the prefaces to the *Lives* of John of Beverley and Bertin the murky outlines of a personal story emerge, of a gifted and well-read mind combined with a rather supine nature, a weak will, perhaps, but one brought to its knees by the consequences of its own cleverness. All this is the baggage that Folcard brought to Thorney, beloved refuge. At this point we should return to the preface to the *Life* of Botwulf. Folcard states there that he was moved to write out of indignation, 'seeing that the saints who rest in this church have not been commemorated by any author'.[33] That is, he had found no hagiography at Thorney. He then goes on to describe the sources that he did have in rather hackneyed terms:

> I have found some material recorded rather poorly in old books and some briefly noted down by that same outstanding prelate in the charters of this abbey, and the rest from the recounting of our elders, who had it from their forbears.[34]

Here are three distinct elements: old books, charters and local anecdotes. To maintain that you are recording oral tradition handed down by elders is a trope of hagiography; similarly commonplace is the claim that there are poorly written old books. That leaves the things noted by Æthelwold in charters. In the case of Thorney's own saints, Thancred, Torhtred and Tova, there is indeed a brief account of them in S 792, the purported foundation charter of King Edgar from the 970s, for the place once called *Ancarig* now known as Thorney. There is no copy of the document older than the thirteenth century. Although believed to incorporate early materials, the charter is not regarded as genuine as it stands.[35] Comparison of its content with Folcard's sermon on Thancred, Torhtred and Tova highlights a small degree of verbal similarity, and a roughly similar narrative outline.[36] On two occasions in the sermon Folcard makes explicit reference to the fact that he is drawing on something that Æthelwold wrote concerning the saints, and each time this is immediately followed by the closest verbal parallels with the charter. This is part of Folcard's account of the hermit saints:

> Inter hec duorum sanctorum fratrum sancta preconia, nequit latere prelucidi splendoris Dei margarita, eorum scilicet soror et socia gloriosa Christi uirgo Toua. Que sicut beatus Christi presul et eiusdem loci primus constructor et abbas

---

[33] Hardy, *Descriptive catalogue*, i. 374. 'Videns autem sanctos in eadem basilica pausantes, nulla scriptorum memoria commendatos'.

[34] 'Reperta sunt tamen quedem in ueteribus libris uitiose descripta, quedem ab ipso precipuo presule in priuilegiis eiusdem cenobii sunt breuiter annotata, cetera ex relatione ueterum, ut ab antiquioribus sunt eis exhibita.'

[35] S 792, *Charters of Peterborough Abbey*, ed. S.E. Kelly, Oxford 2009, appendix 4, with accompanying discussion.

[36] The verbal parallels were noted in brief by Clark, 'Notes', 48.

> sanctissimus <u>Atheluuoldus in suis testatur scriptis</u> **non solum** erat tantorum sanctorum soror **carnali propinquitate sed etiam uirtutum** sedula **imitatione**. Hec itaque longius et quasi miliario uno remotius in silua uirili pectore sibi singulare delegerat tugurium, ut scilicet terrena consolatione et societate eminus deserta, diuinum familiarius optineret amminiculum. Triumphato mundi tyranno in tali **agone**, **menbrum** Christi facta **caput** meruit **Christum** habere, cui unita est in compage corporis ecclesie in illa uidelicet celesti sanctorum communione.³⁷

The Thorney 'foundation charter' speaks similarly of the third sibling of the group:

> Tova uero eorum soror, non **solum carnalis propinquitatis** federe compaginata **set etiam imitacione uirtutum** et caritatis repagulo connexa, in ultima huius insule parte anachoreticam uitam ducens, **agonem** sancte conuersationis decentissime complens ac putidam huius fragilitatis mortem deserens, **membrum** tripudians perrexit ad **caput** quod **Christus** est.³⁸

Folcard then goes on to write about the martyrdom of Thancred, before reporting thus:

> Frater uero eius sanctus Torhtredus aeque **antistes** Domini, ut predictus Dei pontifex Atheluuoldus eadem scriptis suis edocet, in **confessionis gloria** inimicum et mundum deuincens **ad Christum** in pace obdormiens **migrauit** ... .³⁹

---

³⁷ *Liber vitae*, 285: 'Among the holy praises of the two saintly brothers, God's pearl, of bright splendour, cannot lie hidden, namely their sister and companion, Christ's glorious virgin, Tova. As Christ's holy bishop and this place's first constructor and abbot, the most reverend Æthelwold, testifies in what he wrote, she was a sister to those great saints not only by fleshly affinity, but also in tireless imitation of their virtues. For with manly heart she had chosen for herself a separate hut in the woods further off, indeed almost a mile away, so that far removed from earthly comfort and company, she might more intimately receive divine support. Having triumphed over the tyrant of the world in such a struggle, and become Christ's limb, she deserved to have Christ as her head, to whom she is united by the joining of his body, the Church, to wit in that heavenly communion of saints'.

³⁸ *Charters of Peterborough*, 370: 'But Tova, their sister, joined not only by the bond of fleshly affinity but also connected in imitation of the virtues and by the link of affection, living an anchoritic life in the farthest part of this island, most fittingly fulfilling the struggle of the holy way of life and abandoning this frailty's foul death, went rejoicing, as a limb to join the head which is Christ...'.

³⁹ 'His brother, St Torhtred, also the Lord's priest, as God's bishop Æthelwold tells in his writings, vanquished his enemy and the world with a confessor's glory, passed over to Christ falling peacefully asleep.'

One can compare this with the immediately preceding sentence in the charter:

> Nam in ipso prefato loco, anachoreticae uite aptissimo, duo quondam precipue sanctitatis germani **antistites**, Thancredus uidelicet et Torthredus, celestis uite beatitudinem, alter martyrio, alter **confessionis gloria**, obtinentes, cum gloriosa aegregii triumphi palma **migrau**erunt **ad Christum**.[40]

On the face of it, considering the suspect nature of the charter, there is no reason why we could not try to argue, if we so wished, that the passage in the charter was written after Folcard's text, and was based on it, or even that it was written at about the same time, rather than that the relationship necessarily went the other way, and that Folcard was, as he claimed, drawing on a version of this charter. An alternative is that both drew upon a common source. Susan Kelly, in discussing the charter, does suggest that the fabrication as it stands incorporated early material relating to the endowment of Thorney by Æthelwold.[41] Whatever we think of the origins of S 792 it is perhaps worth noting that the document, purporting to record the privileges that King Edgar granted to Thorney in 973, and his confirmation of its lands, makes no mention whatsoever of Botwulf, referring only to the monastery's dedication to Mary and the connection of the site with the three hermits. One way to interpret that silence might be to see the early material on which the charter was based as deriving from a stage in Æthelwold's establishment of Thorney that preceded his quest to adorn the house with further sets of relics brought from elsewhere.

Both Folcard and the 'foundation' charter refer to the two brothers as *antistes*, report that one was a martyr, the other a confessor, and put their sister in an anchorage near by. What the charter does not do is locate the three saints explicitly in time; it merely observes that *Ancarig*, now known as Thorney, was subsequently devastated by heathens (*paganis*, for which read Vikings) and controlled thereafter by seculars.[42] Folcard, perhaps guessing or following house tradition, pinned Thancred's death to the time of Edmund's martyrdom, which effectively means the same as what the charter says, but highlights Thorney's saintly connections more firmly by making a link with one of England's most famous martyrs. Otherwise Folcard fills out his page with pious reflections, but

---

[40] *Charters of Peterborough*, 370: 'For in that same aforementioned place, very suitable for the anchoritic life, two brothers, formerly bishops of outstanding holiness, namely Tancred and Torhtred, attaining the blessedness of the heavenly life, one by means of martyrdom, the other by means of the glory of confession, passed over to Christ bearing the glorious palm of their excellent triumph'.

[41] Ibid. 374; such early material may have taken the form of detailed memoranda about individual estates, discussed by Kelly at 46–7.

[42] *Charters of Peterborough*, 370.

one intriguing feature of his sermon is the tone he takes concerning the nature of the calling of Torhtred, Thancred and Tova:

> Rightly we proclaim saints who are in the world yet lofty in their contempt for the world, but nothing prevents us proclaiming also those who, for love of God, spurn such things and seek solitude's peace, so as to pour all their attention into carrying out holy things alone.[43]

The implication seems to be that Folcard felt the need to justify veneration for hermits who chose contemplative retreat rather than the active life.

Apart from their inclusion among the saints of Thorney in the Old English *List of saints' resting-places* that has been dated to before 1031, there is no other evidence for the story of Thancred, Torhtred and Tova.[44] They may have been dredged up in the 970s to give Thorney some kind of monastic pedigree; even if the precise contours of their story were just local legend, there is no reason why that island in the Fens could not indeed have been used as a refuge from the world at some point in the past. There are signs from not long after Folcard's day that Peterborough Abbey was looking to establish an ancient origin for a right to control Thorney. A charter in the Peterborough archive, purporting to record King Wulfhere's grants to St Peter's, *Medeshamstede* (that is, Peterborough) in 664, but patently a much later fabrication, incorporates a claim that Peterborough's first abbot, Seaxwulf, asked Wulfhere for permission to establish a hermitage at a place called *Ancarig* ('Anchorite island'), later to become Thorney.[45] By contrast, Folcard's Thorney dossier at no point looks to provide any kind of foundation-legend for the house going back as early as the seventh century and certainly makes no mention of Seaxwulf. If the Peterborough version of events were known at Thorney in Folcard's day, it may not have suited the community to have the story called to mind. Peterborough's

---

[43] *Liber vitae*, 285: 'Predicamus digne sanctos in seculo contemptu tamen seculi sublimes, predicare quoque nichil prohibet eos qui talia pro Dei amore contempnentes solitudinis petiere quietem, ut in sola diuinorum exequutione omnem sui infunderent intentionem'.

[44] *Die Heiligen Englands: angelsächsisch und lateinisch*, ed. F. Liebermann, Hanover 1889, 15; and also D.W. Rollason, 'Lists of saints' resting-places in Anglo-Saxon England', *ASE* vii (1978), 61–93, at 65 and 91. The list is in two halves, one rather earlier in origin than the other, and Thancred and co. occur in the section whose completion Rollason dates to the year 1013 or before (ibid. 68).

[45] S 68; *Charters of Peterborough*, no. 1. For further discussion of this charter and the discovery in 2012 of the earliest surviving copy of it in the Northamptonshire Record Office, see R.C. Love, 'The Anglo-Saxon saints of Thorney Abbey and their hagiographer', in L. Lazzari and P. Lendinara (eds), *Hagiography in Anglo-Saxon England: adopting and adapting saints' Lives into Old English prose (c.950–1150)*, Porto, 2014, 488–534, at 511–12.

ambitions might, indeed, be another explanation for Folcard's direct appeal to Walchelin and Winchester, with the preface to the *Life* of Botwulf pointedly calling to mind a different, and later, foundation, namely that by Æthelwold. To create a sense of Thorney's connection to the first beginnings of monasticism in England, Folcard had recourse instead to rather artificial means, which brings us back to Botwulf.

No charter comparable to S 792 survives which records anything of Botwulf, and in his *Vita* Folcard makes no claim to have a source similar to Æthelwold's notes for Thancred, Torhtred and Tova. Given that Botwulf's relics (only half of the body, in fact: the head went to Ely, and part of the body was retained for the royal relic collection) had been translated from Iken, possibly via another resting-place, there is no particular reason for us to expect that Thorney should have had any earlier record of him.[46] One wonders, therefore, what Folcard and the Thorney monks did know about Botwulf. Like Guthlac of Crowland, the saint failed to make it into the pages of Bede's *Ecclesiastical history*, perhaps the more surprising because, as we have seen, Bede's abbot, Ceolfrith, had visited Botwulf's famed community. Folcard cannot have been aware of that anecdote, because he would surely have incorporated it into the *Vita* to enhance Botwulf's standing as a leading light in the spread of monasticism.

Of Folcard's three securely attributed *Lives*, that of Botwulf is by far the shortest, some 1,700 words; the whole Thorney dossier only 2,200. The *Life* of Bertin amounts to around 6,000 words; that of John to some 4,000. The style of the Botwulf *Life* is simple and the narrative mostly so bland that it could describe any founding abbot. It is as if Folcard kept things minimal for lack of secure information. Perhaps he did not have the instinct for verbose elaboration possessed by his confrère Goscelin of Saint-Bertin – here we may recall Folcard's own self-portrait, in the *Life* of Bertin, as clever but somewhat lazy – or at the least he saw only the need to provide a narrative of sufficient length to serve as lections for the purposes of the liturgy.[47] So he recounts in simple terms how Botwulf is born of noble parents, goes to study monasticism on the Continent, is an apt pupil, and then later an abbot who applies discipline with gentleness, is prophetic, humble, sage in discourse, troubled with illness in old age; overall, few specific details. In fact, there are just two key scenes in Folcard's narrative.

The first scene is as follows: while abroad Botwulf meets some young Anglo-Saxon noblewomen who have also been sent to study monasticism, and upon learning that he is intending to return home they arrange for him to be received

---

[46] It is Folcard who records the division of Botwulf's body, in his narrative on the translation of all the Thorney relics, *Liber vitae*, 288.

[47] In BnF, lat. 13092, dating from the twelfth century, the *Vita Botulfi* is transmitted together with antiphons and responsories for the saint's feast, which may also have been composed by Folcard.

there by their brother.⁴⁸ Folcard calls this brother Æthelmund, king of the South Angles, a minor whose mother Sæwara is ruling on his behalf. When Botwulf goes to Æthelmund, the latter's royal kinsmen, Æthelhere and Æthelwald, add their support to the saint's request for some land on which to construct a monastery, and express an eagerness to add lands of their own to endow the new establishment (*de suis prediis, si suscipere uellet, cupiebant illi largiri*). Now to those looking for data about the seventh century, this narrative has seemed fatally flawed. Folcard had already lost credibility sooner, though. Early in the *Life*, Folcard has Æthwulf, supposedly Botwulf's brother, cross the Channel with him and end up as bishop of *Traiectensis*, usually interpreted as referring to Utrecht. That would make him an unlikely predecessor to Willibrord, seventh-century apostle to the Frisians, usually reckoned as the first bishop of Utrecht; of a Bishop Æthwulf at Utrecht there is no record, perhaps not surprisingly.⁴⁹ Although the *Vita Botulfi* says nothing of Æthwulf's death or burial, it emerges from Folcard's account of the translation of the Thorney relics, in which he reports that Botwulf's body became too heavy to move, taken as a miraculous sign that the saint wished his brother's remains to be moved from Iken too, providing the monks in charge of the translation with a 'double joy', as Folcard put it.⁵⁰ We might well imagine that two sets of relics were found, those of Botwulf the founder, and those of an Æthwulf or Æthelwulf, about whom nothing was known apart, perhaps, from the fact that he had been a bishop. Folcard was thus obliged to incorporate this figure into his narrative, and did so rather maladroitly.

Just like Æthwulf, then, Æthelmund of the South Angles and his mother, Sæwara, seem to come out of nowhere: as Dorothy Whitelock observed, they are 'unknown to history'.⁵¹ Æthelwald and Æthelhere, their kinsmen, can be found in the pages of Bede's *Ecclesiastical history*,⁵² as brothers of Anna, king of the East Angles, who succeeded him one after the other in the late 650s and early 660s. This much Folcard could have pieced together, since the Anglo-Saxon Chronicle, as we have seen, reports Anna's death in the same year as Botwulf's founding of Iken, in 654. If he did his research with care he could also have learned from the pages of Bede's *Ecclesiastical history* that princesses from East Anglia, Anna's daughter, Æthelburh, and his stepdaughter, Saethryth,

---

⁴⁸   *ASS* Junii. iii. 402.
⁴⁹   As reported in *HE* v. 11. See W. Fritze, 'Zur Entstehungsgeschichte des Bistums Utrecht: Franken und Friesen, 690–734', *Rheinische Vierteljahrsblätter* xxxv (1971), 107–51. I have suggested elsewhere that Folcard may have meant by *Traiectensis* not Utrecht but the more ancient diocese of Tongeren-Maastricht, though there is no record of a Bishop Adulfus/Athwulf there either; see Love, 'The Anglo-Saxon saints of Thorney Abbey'.
⁵⁰   *Liber vitae*, 287–8.
⁵¹   'The pre-Viking age Church', 11 n. 1.
⁵²   *HE* iii. 22 and 24.

had been abbesses at Faremoutiers-en-Brie.[53] Is it right, then, to assume that Folcard invented Æthelmund and Sæwara, and, if so, on what basis other than his own imagination? Could he really have dreamed up such plausible names? He needed to pin Botwulf to real people and a known monastic movement. The well-attested trend for young women from aristocratic families to study abroad seems to have been his best shot, but that story and the persons of Æthelmund and Sæwara are assumed by modern scholarship to be absurdities. What seems slightly puzzling is the uneven mix of the specific and non-specific in Folcard's narrative: if you are going to invent a tall tale, why not also give names to the two sisters of Æthelmund whom Botwulf meets abroad, and, for example, call Sæwara's daughter Sæthryth? (After all Bede described Sæthryth as 'the daughter of King Anna's wife' without naming that wife.) I am inclined to feel that it is more likely that Folcard found some kind of document that named Æthelmund and Sæwara, perhaps even Æthelwald and Æthelhere too. On the whole, though, the narrative raises questions for which there seem at present to be no confident answers.

The other key scene follows immediately.[54] Folcard states that Botwulf, not wishing anyone to alienate good land for his new monastery, heads out into the wilds and fixes upon Iken, almost as isolated today as it was then, on the estuary of the Alde. Botwulf comes upon a demon-infested waste, and its devilish occupants harangue the saint as he approaches:

> Why, Botwulf, cruellest guest, do you drive us from these dwellings? We have not offended you, not infringed your rights. What do you seek from our expulsion, what do you want to prepare for yourself in this our region?[55]

Without much of a struggle, the sign of the cross ensures that the place is vacated so that Botwulf can establish his monastery. This was not the first time Folcard had had cause to describe such a founding moment. The major turning-point in his first hagiography, the *Life* of Bertin, comes when the saint casts himself adrift in a boat on the marshes near Saint-Omer, and chooses the spot where he lands to build a monastery.[56] The story is already present in the earlier narrative concerning Bertin which was Folcard's source, but he makes certain changes, the chief of which is to present Bertin as working alone in striking out from Omer's first foundation, whereas in the earlier composite life he sets out with

---

[53] *HE* iii. 8.
[54] *ASS* Junii iii. 403.
[55] 'Cur, Botulfe, seuissime hospes, nos his depellis sedibus? Nihil in te offendimus, nihil tui iuris inquietauimus. Quid petis in expulsione nostra, quid tibi parare vis in hac regione nostra?'
[56] *Vita tertia Bertini*, cc. 13–16, ed. *ASS* Sept. ii. 606.

St Mummolin.⁵⁷ He also injects some drama into the scene, including towering waves, a phenomenon that would have been somewhat unlikely, one might suppose, in the marshy terrain that surrounded Saint-Omer. Just as Bertin's boat stops, the saint has reached verse 14 of Psalm 131 ('This is my rest for ever and ever: here will I dwell, for I have chosen it'). The spot seems inauspicious: God's choice of site for a monastery would not necessarily have been man's; as Folcard puts it, 'Bertin recognised from these unmistakeable signs that the place had been chosen for him by God, even though the place's nature was ill-suited to weighty construction work.'⁵⁸ Bertin is presented as seeing before him difficult, inhospitable terrain, but Folcard was not moved to go further and present the place as a desert possessed by demons. It was not in his immediate source, the composite life, nor did he choose to add that hagiographical colouring to his own version of the story. He seems to have been more drawn by the theme of the *peregrinus*, trusting to the wind and waves.

In the case of Botwulf we shall never know what Folcard had as a source and so we cannot verify how Botwulf's choice of site was presented, if it had been at all, before Folcard picked up his pen. His account of Botwulf's arrival at the chosen spot owes something to the stories of demonic possession in the synoptic Gospels, in particular the occasion when Christ drives out unclean spirits into a herd of pigs. Before he does so, the demons scream, 'What have you to do with us? Why do you torment us?' (Matt. viii. 28). Botwulf is similarly accused, as we have seen, and Folcard thus shows him as Christ-like in his power over evil. Another obvious comparison would be with the story of Guthlac, whose fen hermitage at Crowland, not so very far from Thorney, was also the habitation of demons, whose persistent houndings were vividly described in the eighth-century Latin *Life of Guthlac* by Felix.⁵⁹ It is worth noting, however, that although Felix's Guthlac had a prolonged set-to with demonic foes, they are never made to address to him as Botwulf's do; that is a dramatic touch that is particular to the Old English poetic manifestation of the story, *Guthlac A*.⁶⁰ As well as aligning Botwulf with Guthlac, Folcard also tacitly places Botwulf in the ancient tradition of St Antony the hermit, whose famed battles with demons in the Egyptian deserts had inspired Felix's narrative. Yet what Botwulf is shown establishing at Iken turns out very clearly not to be a hermitage but a monastery, based on what he had experienced on the Continent, so the hagiographer claims. That continuity of practice is a point which Folcard repeatedly emphasises later

---

⁵⁷ See *Passiones vitaeque sanctorum*, iii. 760–61.
⁵⁸ *Vita tertia Bertini*, c. 16, ed. *ASS* Sept. ii. 606: 'Earum ergo rerum euidentibus signis beatus Bertinus locum illum a Deo sibi electum cognoscens, quamquam natura sua operose molis fuerit impatiens'.
⁵⁹ *Felix's Life of St Guthlac*, ed. and tr. B. Colgrave, Cambridge 1956.
⁶⁰ *The Anglo-Saxon poetic records: a collective edition*, ed. G.P. Krapp and E. van Kirk Dobbie, London 1931–42, iii. 49–72; see especially lines 208–17.

in the text. Botwulf, exhorting his flock from his deathbed, 'thought it sweet and pleasant to talk over and over about (*loqui et sepius repetere*) the rules observed at the monasteries he had visited as a pilgrim.'[61]

In his two longer *Lives* we have the advantage of being able to measure how Folcard shaped the sanctity of the subjects against the sources he used: for Bertin, as we have already noted, it is the composite Life of Omer, Bertin and Winnoc. That source shows Bertin appointing his successor as abbot, and one of Folcard's major departures from it in his own version is to suggest that Bertin's motive in doing so was a desire to devote himself wholly to prayer and fasting in an oratory he had built for the purpose: 'just as he now, as abbot, fulfilled Martha's role, Bertin foresaw that he should also labour in Mary's best part' (*uti qui iam uices peregit Marthe, laborandum sibi preuidit etiam in optima parte Marie*).[62] Folcard emphatically redirects Bertin's sanctity towards the contemplative.

Folcard's source for his *Life* of John of Beverley was Bede's *Ecclesiastical history*, which recorded that the elderly John retired from his role of bishop, having identified a successor. Folcard follows Bede very faithfully and records that retirement briskly enough. But it is noteworthy that one of the few episodes he adds to Bede's account, by far the longest, focuses on otherworldly contemplation. Folcard shows John praying in St Michael's church in York, as he says 'eyes raised heavenwards and hands uplifted, pouring out his soul like water in God's sight' (*intentis in celum luminibus erectisque manibus, in conspectu Dei effundentem sicut aquam animam suam*), that is, weeping tears of contrition.[63] The church was ablaze with light, the Holy Spirit in the form of a dove came to rest on John's head, signifying the great purity of his tearful prayer. The scene moves John onwards from the practical miracle-working of the healings which Bede described in his account of the saint – Martha's busyness – to pure God-wards contemplation, Mary's best part.[64]

Writing as he was in a hermit's paradise, Thorney, in dealing with Botwulf Folcard made no such narrative choice as he had in the cases of Bertin and John, though he presumably had relative freedom to do so. Instead, he uses Botwulf's relics to lend to Thorney a connection with a tradition whose moment of origin was assuredly in the eremitic spirit of Antony and Guthlac, but a tradition that is, in its source of inspiration and regulated shape, firmly and influentially coenobitic, exemplifying the community life by which Folcard maintains Botwulf had been so inspired on the Continent. This stands distinct from

---

[61] *ASS* Junii iii. 403.
[62] *ASS* Sept. ii. 610.
[63] *Historians of the church of York*, i. 258.
[64] On Folcard's impulse to present the saints about whom he wrote as having 'anchoretic inclinations', similar to that observable in the work of his former confrère, Goscelin, see now the perceptive analysis by T. Licence, *Hermits and recluses in English society, 950–1200*, Oxford 2011, esp. 62–3.

Thorney's own claim, through Thancred, Torhtred and Tova, to a tradition of *anachoresis*, which Folcard applies also to Æthelwold. Yet his Thorney dossier taken as whole carefully provided the community with a claim to be involved in every phase of the monastic history of Anglo-Saxon England.

Chapter 4
Bede's *Historia Ecclesiastica* as a Source of Lections in Pre- and Post-Conquest England

Teresa Webber

Just over a third of the seventy-odd surviving English manuscripts of Bede's *Historia ecclesiastica gentis Anglorum* date from the long twelfth century, material witnesses to engagement with the Anglo-Saxon past.[1] The appeal of the text in the later eleventh and twelfth centuries was investigated some thirty years ago by Antonia Gransden and R.H.C. Davis.[2] Both took as their starting-point the high percentage of copies surviving from this period but thereafter focused primarily upon narrative and documentary evidence. They used these sources to demonstrate the various ways in which Bede's history was deployed: to inspire and justify not only the restoration of monastic life in the north of England during the second half of the eleventh century but also the establishment there of Cistercian communities during the twelfth, and as an authority in various cases of dispute. The copies themselves provide evidence of a further application for selective reading of the text during the eleventh and twelfth centuries: as

---

[1] M.L.W. Laistner, with the collaboration of H.H. King, *A hand-list of Bede manuscripts*, Ithaca, NY 1943, 93–103, with additions and corrections noted by the following: N.R. Ker, review in *Medium Ævum* xiii (1944), 36–40; V. de Montmollin, review in *Revue du Moyen Âge Latin* iv (1948), 395–6; C.H. Beeson, 'The manuscripts of Bede', *Classical Philology* xlii (1947), 73–87; K.W. Humphreys and A.S.C. Ross, 'Further manuscripts of Bede's "Historia ecclesiastica", of the "Epistola Cuthberti de obitu Bedae", and further Anglo-Saxon texts of "Cædmon's hymn" and "Bede's death song"', *Notes and Queries* xxii (1975), 50–55; H. Silvestre, 'Le hand-list de Laistner-King et les mss bruxellois de Bède', *Scriptorium* vi (1952), 287–93. For a full revised list, see J.A. Westgard, 'Dissemination and reception of Bede's *Historia ecclesiastica gentis Anglorum* in Germany c.731–1500: the manuscript evidence', unpubl. Ph.D. diss., Chapel Hill 2005, 135–41.

[2] A. Gransden, 'Bede's reputation as an historian in medieval England', *JEH* xxxii (1981), 397–425, repr. in eadem, *Legends, traditions and history in medieval England*, London 1992, 1–29; R.H.C. Davis, 'Bede after Bede', in C. Harper-Bill, C.J. Holdsworth and J.L. Nelson (eds), *Studies in medieval history presented to R. Allen Brown*, Woodbridge 1989, 103–16.

hagiographical lections delivered in the night office of matins on major feast days. They thus contribute to our knowledge not only of the reception of the *Historia ecclesiastica* but also of the cult of early Anglo-Saxon saints in England before and after the Conquest, and the local and wider circumstances that shaped such practice.

Matins Lections and Hagiography in the Early Middle Ages

Eleven of the thirty-one known English copies of the *Historia ecclesiastica* that date from between the late tenth and the late twelfth centuries contain marginal additions in the form of one or more sequences of roman numerals corresponding to the lections of the night office of matins.[3] On Sundays and major feast days matins took an extended form of three nocturns, each of which included (in addition to psalmody, antiphons and, for the third nocturn in monastic practice, canticles) a set of readings and responsories: four readings and responsories per nocturn (twelve in all) according to the liturgical *cursus* set out in the Rule of St Benedict, three per nocturn (a total of nine) in the so-called 'Roman' *cursus* practised by both secular clergy and Augustinian canons.[4] On ferias (ordinary weekdays) and lesser feast days in both the Benedictine and 'Roman' *cursus*, there were only three readings (or just one on ferias during summer, according to the Rule). During the earlier Middle Ages there was some fluidity in the precise length of the passages read on a particular day each year, but manuscript evidence suggests that from the late tenth century onwards the length of the individual lections was becoming predetermined within each local usage (although still liable to periodic modification).[5] The selected passages were either compiled in liturgical order in office lectionaries (or smaller *libelli* containing the relevant texts and/or chants for individual feasts of special local importance), or demarcated by marginal annotations in copies of the full texts

---

[3] See below, Appendix. Fragments of two further copies survive as CCCC, MS 270, fos 1 and 197 and BL MS Egerton 3278, dating respectively from the late and the early eleventh century.

[4] The most accessible account of the two traditions is provided by J. Harper, *The forms and orders of Western liturgy from the tenth to the eighteenth century: a historical introduction and guide for students and musicians*, Oxford 1991, 86–97. For a more detailed treatment of the monastic *cursus*, see J.B.L. Tolhurst (ed.), *The monastic breviary of Hyde Abbey, Winchester, volume vi. Introduction to the English monastic breviaries* (HBS lxxx, 1942).

[5] F. Dolbeau, 'Notes sur l'organisation interne des légendiers latins', in P. Riché (ed.), *Hagiographie, cultures et sociétés, ive–xiie siècles: actes du colloque organisé à Nanterre et à Paris (2–5 Mai 1979)*, Paris 1981, 11–31, at 12; A. Davril, 'La longueur des leçons de l'office nocturne: étude comparative', in P. de Clerck and E. Palazzo (eds), *Rituels: mélanges offerts à Pierre-Marie Gy, O.P.*, Paris 1990, 183–97.

from which they were drawn.⁶ In the latter case, the start of each lection was typically indicated in the margin with a roman numeral (sometimes preceded with the abbreviation 'L' (*lectio*)); in those cases where the sequence of lections did not run continuously through the text, or for the final lection of a nocturn, the end might also be indicated by 'F' (*finis*), or, in the latter case, by 'T' or '*Tu autem*' (the beginning of the brief formula that usually concluded the readings of each nocturn: 'Tu autem Domine miserere nobis').

No single lectionary for the office liturgy emerged during the earlier Middle Ages, although a broadly similar framework for two of the principal components of the matins lections – an annual cycle of biblical reading and homilies on the gospel of the day – became widely disseminated between the late eighth and the eleventh centuries.⁷ There was inevitably much wider variation in the choice of hagiographical texts, given the extent of local variety in the observance of saints' feasts as well as some diversity of opinion regarding the extent to which hagiography was appropriate in this liturgical context.

Until the late eighth century the use of hagiography within the liturgy of western Christendom had been restricted, albeit to differing degrees according to the particular liturgical tradition.⁸ The Rule of St Benedict made no mention of hagiography in its prescriptions for readings at matins, specifying only scripture and patristic exegesis: 'Besides the inspired books of the Old and New Testaments, the works read at Vigils should include explanations of Scripture by reputable and orthodox catholic Fathers' (ch. ix).⁹ Its chapter on the practice of

---

⁶ For the evidence for office lectionaries in late Anglo-Saxon England, see H. Gneuss, 'Liturgical books in Anglo-Saxon England and their Old English terminology', in M. Lapidge and H. Gneuss (eds), *Learning and literature in Anglo-Saxon England: studies presented to Peter Clemoes on the occasion of his sixty-fifth birthday*, Cambridge 1985, 91–141, at 120–21.

⁷ In late Anglo-Saxon and early Norman England, to judge from what survives, the annual biblical cycle was based upon *Ordo Romanus* XIIIA (M. Andrieu, *Les Ordines Romani du haut Moyen Âge*, Louvain 1931–61, ii. 469–88), while the gospel homilies were taken primarily from variously expanded versions of the Homiliary of Paul the Deacon: M. McC. Gatch, 'The office in late Anglo-Saxon monasticism', in Lapidge and Gneuss, *Learning and literature*, 341–62, at 350–56; Gneuss, 'Liturgical books', 122–5. See also A.G. Martimort, 'La lecture patristique dans la liturgie des heures', in Giustino Farnedi (ed.), *Traditio et progressio: studi liturgici in onore del Prof. Adrien Nocent, OSB* (Analecta liturgica xii, 1988), 311–31, at 320–22, 325–7.

⁸ A.G. Martimort, *Les Lectures liturgiques et leurs livres* (Typologie des sources du Moyen Âge occidental lxiv, 1992), 97–100; E. Palazzo, *A history of liturgical books from the beginning to the thirteenth century*, tr. M. Beaumont, Collegeville, MN 1998, 156–7.

⁹ *The Rule of St Benedict in English*, ed. Timothy Fry, Collegeville, MN 1982, 39; 'Codices autem legantur in uigiliis diuinae auctoritatis tam ueteris testamenti quam noui; sed et expositiones earum, quae a nominatis et orthodoxis catholicis patribus factae sunt': *Benedicti regula, editio altera emendata*, ed. R. Hanslik (Corpus scriptorum ecclesiasticorum latinorum lxxv, 1977), 61.

the office on saints' feasts and solemnities (ch. xiv) ruled that at matins the psalms, antiphons and lections should be those 'belonging to the feast day', but did not explicitly supplement the prescriptions of ch. ix, by permitting or prohibiting the use of hagiography in general.[10] The pseudo-Gelasian *Decretum*, however, widely copied from the late eighth century onwards as the canonical statement of which scriptural, patristic and other texts were orthodox and which were not, declared that 'the deeds of the holy martyrs ... according to ancient custom ... are not read in the holy Roman Church'.[11] Nevertheless, hagiographical readings were accepted within the Gallican and other non-Roman liturgies, and by the late eighth century the prohibition recorded in the *Decretum Gelasianum* was becoming relaxed even in Rome.[12] From the Carolingian period onwards the use of hagiography in the night office continued to expand, as major saints' feasts, whether observed widely or only locally, came increasingly to be furnished with proper readings, chants and prayers. In some instances the readings of all three nocturns on feasts of twelve (or nine) lections were taken from hagiographical narrative; in others, the readings of the final nocturn were taken from a homily, either one proper to the saint or from one of those designated for the common of apostles, martyrs, confessors or virgins.[13]

The early stages of the development of the office liturgy for saints' feasts in England are largely obscure before the late tenth century, with the exception of a liturgy for St Cuthbert.[14] The texts of chants for a mass and office in his honour conclude the original contents of a copy of Bede's two *Lives* of St Cuthbert, probably produced in southern England between 934 and 939, and presented by King Aethelstan to the community of St Cuthbert at Chester-le-Street (CCCC, MS 183).[15] The scribe, however, did not provide nor specify the texts to be read as

---

[10] 'In sanctorum uero festitiuitatibus uel omnibus sollemnitatibus, sicut diximus dominico die agendum, ita agatur, excepto quod psalmi aut antiphonae uel lectiones ad ipsum diem pertinentes dicantur.' Ibid. 69.

[11] 'gesta sanctorum martyrum ... secundum antiquam consuetudinem singulari cautela in sancta Romana ecclesia non leguntur': *Das Decretum Gelasianum de libris recipiendis et non recipiendis*, ed. E. von Dobschütz (Texte und Untersuchungen zur Geschichte der altchristlichen Literatur xxxviii/4, 1912), 39–40.

[12] B. de Gaiffier, 'La lecture des actes des martyres dans la prière liturgique en Occident: à propos du passionaire hispanique', *AB* lxxii (1954), 134–66, and idem, 'La lecture des passions des martyrs à Rome avant le IXe siècle', *AB* lxxxvii (1969), 63–78.

[13] Martimort, 'La lecture patristique', 325–7.

[14] For the difficulties of establishing the practice of the divine office in Anglo-Saxon England, see the preliminary survey in Gatch, 'The office', 341–62. A detailed study of the office in Anglo-Saxon England, by Jesse D. Billett, is forthcoming in the Subsidia series of the Henry Bradshaw Society.

[15] S. Keynes, 'King Athelstan's books', in Lapidge and Gneuss, *Learning and literature*, 143–201, at 180–85; C. Hohler and A. Hughes, 'The Durham services in honour of St.

office lections (although he supplied rubrics and incipits for those for the mass), nor are any traces of lection marks visible in either of Bede's lives that precede the liturgical items. Sets of marginal lection numbers were, however, added to two tenth-century copies of Bede's prose *Life* of Cuthbert from Canterbury: Cotton Vitellius A. xix (mid-tenth-century, probably from St Augustine's) and BL MS Harley 1117 (late-tenth-century, probably from Christ Church).[16] Unfortunately the date of these annotations cannot be determined with any precision, since the component graphs (*i*, *v*, *x* and *L*[*ectio*]) are insufficient to permit close dating on palaeographical criteria.[17] Nevertheless, their presence in a number of late-tenth and early-eleventh-century English copies of accounts of saints' lives and miracles would seem to suggest that it was from around this date that the practice of annotating manuscripts with marginal lection marks was introduced. Among such manuscripts are four late Anglo-Saxon copies of Bede's *Historia ecclesiastica*: BL MS Royal 13. C. v, Bodleian Library, Oxford, MSS Bodley 163 and Hatton 43, and Winchester Cathedral, MS 1 + BL MS Cotton Tiberius D. iv, vol. 2, fos 158–66.

More closely datable evidence for the liturgical use of hagiography in Anglo-Saxon England is provided by Ælfric, in the customs he compiled for his community at Eynsham *c*.1005, which adapted the liturgical customs of the *Regularis concordia*, compiled in the early 970s by Æthelwold, bishop of Winchester.[18] The *Regularis concordia* did not elaborate upon the Rule's prescriptions for matins, but Ælfric concluded his text by responding to a request from his monks to set out the annual cycle of the biblical readings, in the course of which he remarked that 'on all the feasts of the saints, throughout the entire year, we read lives or passions of the saints themselves, or sermons appropriate to the given solemnity, and [we sing] proper responsories, if these are to be had; if not, we sing other appropriate ones, and adopt for the third position [readings] from a homily on the gospel, as we do always and everywhere'.[19] In other words, it was to be the custom at Eynsham on major saints' feasts for the eight readings of the first two nocturns to be hagiographical in content, with the four readings of the final nocturn to

---

Cuthbert', in C.F. Battiscombe (ed.), *The relics of St. Cuthbert*, Oxford 1956, 155–91; D. Hiley, 'The music of prose offices in honour of English saints', *Plainsong and Medieval Music* x (2001), 23–37, at 31–7; L.M. Sole, 'Some Anglo-Saxon Cuthbert *liturgica*: the manuscript evidence', *Revue bénédictine* cviii (1998), 104–44.

[16] H. Gneuss, *Handlist of Anglo-Saxon manuscripts: a list of manuscripts and manuscript fragments written or owned in England up to 1100*, Tempe, AZ 2001, nos 401 and 427.

[17] Changes in the proportions of nib-width to minim height introduced from the late eleventh century onwards, and the introduction of new features of style in more cursive handwriting of the later twelfth century, sometimes permit one to distinguish lection marks added in the twelfth century from those of an earlier date.

[18] *Ælfric's Letter to the monks of Eynsham*, ed. C.A. Jones, Cambridge 1998, 3–12.

[19] Ibid. 144–9, 217–28, esp. 146–7, 222 n. 344.

be from an appropriate gospel homily, as was the case whenever matins took the extended form of three nocturns. A sampling of late Anglo-Saxon manuscripts containing lection marks suggests that the custom of restricting hagiographical narrative to the first two nocturns was widely, although not invariably, practised elsewhere in eleventh-century England, to judge from the preponderance among the annotations of the numerical sequence i–viii (rather than i–xii).[20]

Bede's *Historia Ecclesiastica* as a Source for Lections at Matins

Ælfric's own hagiographical works provide only equivocal evidence for the liturgical use of passages from the *Historia ecclesiastica*. In the Latin and Old English prologues to his *Lives of the saints* Ælfric remarked that in his two series of *Catholic homilies* he had translated the passions and lives of the saints celebrated with feast days by the English nation, whereas in the *Lives of the saints* he presented the passions and lives of the saints whom monks honour in their offices.[21] Since a full set of propers for the mass and the office may not have yet existed for each of the saints included in these three works, one cannot assume a correspondence between the sources drawn upon by Ælfric and the contents of the office lections delivered on the major saints' feasts at one or more of the religious houses known to him.[22] It would therefore be unwise to infer from Ælfric's use of the *Historia ecclesiastica* as one of his sources for the lives of Gregory and Cuthbert in the second series of his *Catholic homilies* and for the lives of Alban, Oswald and Æthelthryth in his *Lives of the saints* that the relevant passages were already being read as office lections for each of these saints by the final decade of the tenth century, although this remains a possibility.[23]

---

[20] For evidence of the arrangement of eight hagiographical and four homiletic lections for the feast of Swithun at the Old Minster, Winchester, see M. Lapidge, *The cult of St Swithun*, Oxford 2003, 104–5, nn. 116–17, and 116–17. A mid-tenth-century copy of Bede's prose *Life of Cuthbert* from St Augustine's, Canterbury (BL MS Cotton Vitellius A. xix), however, contains both the sequence i–viii in the margins of chs i–iv, and i–xii in the margins of chs xxxvii–xxxix.

[21] 'coenobite officiis uenerantur ... mynster-menn mid heora þenungum betwux him wurðiað': *Ælfric's Lives of saints: being a set of sermons on saints' days formerly observed by the English Church*, ed. W.W. Skeat (Early English Text Society original ser. lxxvi, cxiv, 1881–1900), i, 2–5.

[22] M. Gretsch, *Ælfric and the cult of saints in late Anglo-Saxon England*, Cambridge 2005, 160.

[23] For the suggestion that a compilation of *vitae* of Anglo-Saxon saints, including extracts from the *Historia ecclesiastica* pertaining to Alban, Cuthbert, Oswald, Birinus and Aethelthryth (surviving in Paris, BnF MS lat. 5362, a late-eleventh- or early-twelfth-century manuscript later owned by the Norman abbey of Fécamp), may represent a compilation made

Unequivocal evidence for the use of the *Historia ecclesiastica* for liturgical lections in late Anglo-Saxon England is provided instead by liturgical *libelli* for the feasts of Alban and Birinus. An office for St Alban, including the text for the first eight lessons, taken verbatim from the *Historia ecclesiastica*, i. 6–7, is one of a number of liturgical elements in an eleventh-century composite manuscript from St Albans (Morgan Library and Museum [formerly Pierpont Morgan Library], New York, MS M 926); the office (fos 44r–51v) is written in a hand of the mid- or second half of the eleventh century.[24] According to the *Gesta abbatum sancti Albani*, the chants had been composed by Abbot Ælfric (an error for Leofric, abbot by 993), who 'being warned in a vision of St. Alban composed the History (*historia*) and provided musical notation for it'.[25] The term 'historia', in this context, refers to a set of newly composed office chants with a narrative basis, and could be extended to include newly composed readings as well. Here, however, it must refer just to the chants, but since the texts of some of these derive from Bede's narrative it is possible that proper readings were supplied from the *Historia ecclesiastica* at this date also.

By the second half of the eleventh century a proper office of chants and readings also existed for the West Saxon saint Birinus, whose cult had been given fresh stimulus by the translation of Birinus's remains c.980 within the newly rebuilt Old Minster at Winchester, and became widespread during the eleventh century.[26] A second booklet in Morgan, M 926, contains (on fos 74r–75v) several chants for the office written in hands of the second half of the century,[27] while a booklet from an eleventh-century composite manuscript from Abingdon (Oxford, Bodleian Library, MS Digby 39, booklet iv, fos 50–56) contains a copy of the *Historia ecclesiastica*, iii. 7, with crosses in the margin, presumably intended to indicate its

---

by Aelfric, see Wulfstan of Winchester, *The Life of St. Æthelwold*, ed. and tr. M. Lapidge and M. Winterbottom, Oxford 1991, cxlviii–ix.

[24] K.D. Hartzell, 'A St. Albans miscellany in New York', *Mittellateinisches Jahrbuch* x (1975), 20–61, at 26–37 and 52 7; R.M. Thomson, *Manuscripts from St Albans Abbey, 1066–1235*, Woodbridge 1982, i. 115–16. The copy specifies that the final four lections are to be supplied from the gospel homily for the common of martyrs: 'Require in natale unius martyris' (fo. 51).

[25] Hartzell, 'A St Albans miscellany', 26–7; 'Iste (Ælfric), visione praemonitus Sancti Albani, quae nunc cantatur, composuit Historiam, et eidem notam melicam adaptavit': *Gesta abbatum monasterii sancti Albani*, ed. H.T. Riley (RS [xxviii], 1867–69), i. 32. See also A. Hughes, 'British rhymed offices: a catalogue and commentary', in S. Rankin and D. Hiley (eds), *Music in the medieval English liturgy: Plainsong and Medieval Music Society centennial essays*, Oxford 1993, 239–84, at 252–3.

[26] R.C. Love (ed.), *Three eleventh-century Anglo-Latin saints' Lives: Vita S. Birini, Vita et miracula S. Kenelmi and Vita S. Rumwoldi*, Oxford 1996, lx–lxxi.

[27] Hartzell, 'A St Albans miscellany', 38–42, 58–9.

division into eight lessons.²⁸ It is likely that earlier exemplars from Winchester (or perhaps Dorchester-on-Thames, the original place of Birinus' burial) lie behind both the texts in Bodl. Lib. MS Digby 39 and the chants in Morgan M 926.²⁹

The account of St Alban (although not that of Birinus) is one of twelve such narratives that are marked up as one or more sets of lections in copies of the *Historia ecclesiastica* produced in England between the late tenth and late twelfth centuries.³⁰ As may be seen from the following list, in several cases (Alban, Gregory, Mellitus, Paulinus, Fursey and John of Beverley) the relevant passage is annotated in only a single extant copy, but passages narrating the lives and/or miracles of Oswald, Æthelthryth and Cuthbert are marked up in three copies, and Augustine, Æthelburh of Barking and Wilfrid in two. (Details concerning the dates, origin and ownership of these manuscripts are provided below in the Appendix.)

ALBAN

BL MS Royal 13. C. v, fo. 10v: *HE* i. 7 (traces of two sequences of 8 lections remain visible).

AUGUSTINE

BL MS Harley 3680, fos 20v–21v, 22r–23v: *HE* i. 23 (lections i–iii), i. 25–6 (lections iv–viii).
Bodl. Lib., MS Hatton 43, fos 20v–21r, 21v–22v: *HE* i. 23 (lections i–iii); *HE* i. 25–6 '..caelestis amplecteretur' (lections iv–viii, partially erased).

---

²⁸ Love, *Three saints' Lives*, lxvi–vii, lxxv–lxxvi; Gneuss, *Handlist*, no. 609. The handwriting is an English Caroline minuscule that lacks both the distinctive features of the variety that became widely diffused in England during the second half of the eleventh century and any evidence of continental influence, and can be dated no more closely than to the second half of the century or perhaps even earlier. The early-twelfth-century date assigned in R. Gameson, *The manuscripts of early Norman England (c.1066–1130)*, Oxford 1999, 135 must refer to fos 57–92 (containing a newly composed *Vita S. Birini* and a copy of Osbern's *Vita S. Ælfegi*), which are in a later hand, and commence on a new quire.

²⁹ Love, *Three saints' Lives*, lxi–lxxi; Hartzell, 'A Saint Albans miscellany', 38–42.

³⁰ The manuscripts may once have been more heavily annotated than is now apparent, earlier layers of annotation having been erased. In some instances such erasure is only apparent from the still-visible traces of the occasional numeral from a once full sequence. Two such partial sequences of eight lections, indicating successive revision of the readings for the feast of St Alban, are visible in BL MS Royal 13. C. v, (fo. 10v). It is possible that marks for lections may also have been supplied as dry-point annotation, now visible only when lit from a certain angle (for the use of dry-point annotation as readers' prompts in a tenth-century copy of the Rule of St Benedict and the Martyrology of Usuard, see T. Graham, 'Cambridge, Corpus Christi College 57 and its Anglo-Saxon users', in P. Pusiano and E. Treharne (eds), *Anglo-Saxon manuscripts and their heritage*, Aldershot 1998, 21–69, at 42, 45–7.

GREGORY
Winchester Cathedral, MS 1, fos 26v–27r: *HE* ii. 1 'Nam alii quidam pontifices.. (end)' (lections v–viii).

MELLITUS
BL MS Royal 13. C. v, fos 53v–55r: *HE* ii. 3–4 '..serui seruorum dei' (lections i–viii).

PAULINUS
BL MS Add. 14250, fo. 41r–v: *HE* ii. 9 'Ordinatus est autem..(end)' (lections i–iii).

OSWALD
Durham, Dean and Chapter Library, MS B. II. 35, fo. 127r–v: *HE* iii. 9– beginning of 10 (traces of lections i–viii, now partially trimmed).
Bodl. Lib., MS Bodley 163, fos 74v–75r: *HE* iii. 1 (lections i–iii); fo. 76r–v: *HE* iii. 2 'Quidam de fratribus..(end)' (lections i–iii); fo. 86r: *HE* iii. 11 'Est monasterium nobile'.. 'Unde factum est..(beginning of lectio iii)' (lections i–iii); fos 86v–87r: *HE* iii. 11 'Lota igitur ossa \sancti oswaldi regis/..(end)' (lections i–viii); fos 135v–137r: *HE* iv. 14 (lections i–viii); fo. 249v, three lections added in the mid-twelfth century, the first re-worked from *HE* iii. 1–2, lections ii–iii taken verbatim from *HE* iii. 2.
Bodl. Lib., MS Douce 368, fos 32v–33r, 34r–v: *HE* iii. 9 (lections i–iv); *HE* iii. 12–13 (lections v–viii).

FURSEY
Bodl. Lib., MS Hatton 43, fos 84v–88r: *HE* iii. 19 (as far as '..diem clausit ultimum') (lections i–viii).

ÆTHELBURH
BL MS Royal 13. C. v, fos 138v–139v: *HE* iv. 9 '\In tempore illo cum mater pia æþelburga/ esset rapienda..(end)' (lections i–viii).
Bodl. Lib., MS Bodley 163, fos 128r–130r: *HE* iv. 8–9 (lections i–iii).

ÆTHELTHRYTH
Cambridge, Trinity College, MS R. 5. 27, fos 90v–92r: *HE* iv.19 (17) (lections i–viii).
BL MS Royal 13. C. v, fos 151r–153v: *HE* iv.19 (17) (lections i–xii).
Bodl. Lib. MS Hatton 43, fos 121v–122r: *HE* iv.19 (17) (as far as '..esse coepit et monitis') (lections i–iii).

CUTHBERT
BL MS Harley 3680, fos 131r–v, 132r–133r: *HE* iv. 27 (25) (as far as '..propria actione premonstraret.') (lections i–iv); *HE* iv. 28 (26) (lections v–viii).

Bodl. Lib., MS Hatton 43, fos 136v–138r: *HE* iv. 29–30 (27–28) (lections i–ix).
Bodl. Lib., MS Douce 368, fos 58v–59v: *HE* iv. 27 (25) (beginning '\Vir domini cuthbertus/ Qui quidem a prima ętate') – iv. 28 (26) '..in quibus beatę memorię theodorus primatum tenebat.' (lections i–viii).

JOHN OF BEVERLEY
Durham, Dean and Chapter Library, MS B. II. 35, fos 183r–184r: *HE* v. 2– beginning of v. 4 (start of lectio viii) (traces of lections i–viii, partially trimmed).

WILFRID
BL MS Add. 38817, fos 82v–83r: *HE* v. 19 'At ille britanniam..ut supra docuimus' (lections i–vi).
Bodl. Lib., MS Hatton 43, fos 160r–162r: *HE* v. 19 'Cum esset \wilfridus/ puer.. (lection viii) Scriptum est hoc modo..(ending not indicated)' (lections i–viii).

The predominant liturgical tradition reflected in these manuscripts is Benedictine. Only three of the extant manuscripts contain lection marks that correspond with the secular 'Roman' cursus. Two of these are from houses of Augustinian canons: BL MS Add. 38817, from Kirkham priory, contains six lections for the first two nocturns of a secular office for Wilfrid, whilst BL MS Add. 14250, from Plympton priory, contains three lections for the commemoration of Paulinus as a lesser feast. The presence in Bodl. Lib., MS Hatton 43 of a sequence of nine lection marks indicating the commemoration of St Cuthbert according to the secular cursus is more difficult to account for, since this manuscript also contains lections according to the Benedictine cursus for Augustine, Æthelthryth and Wilfrid, and, by the earlier twelfth century at least, was at Christ Church, Canterbury.

Lection marks are wholly absent from the surviving Cistercian copies.[31] This may be coincidental or correspond with the generally lower incidence of such marks in copies dating from the mid- and later twelfth century, perhaps because by this date the passages were becoming more commonly included either in liturgical sequence in office lectionaries or in passionals. It may, however, reflect adherence to the restricted number of feasts in the official Cistercian kalendar as it evolved over the twelfth century (many saints were included only with commemorations), and the limited inclusion of hagiography within the

---

[31] BL MS Add. 25014 (from Newminster), Oxford, St John's College, MS 99 (from Jervaulx), and probably Oxford, New College, MS 308 (a thirteenth-century list of popes added on fos 2v–3v refers to Eugenius III as 'nostri ordinis'). The presence of both flex punctuation and single-colour initials in Oxford, Magdalen College, MS lat. 105 might suggest a Cistercian origin for this copy also.

standard lectionary as presented in the late twelfth-century *Ecclesiastica officia*.[32] The survival of only a single (late medieval) Cistercian breviary from England (BL MS Burney 335) makes it impossible to gauge how far English houses during the twelfth century were obedient in their practice of the office to the norms that had evolved by the 1180s. David Chadd, however, has drawn attention to the inclusion of 'irregular' saints in two late-twelfth-century English Cistercian missals (CUL Add. 4079; Harley 1229) as well as in Burney 335, and concluded that 'the allowance [by the General Chapters] of special pleading for the observance of local feasts ... was an inevitable erosion of liturgical universality.'[33] It would be unwise, therefore, to discount completely the possibility that the *Historia ecclesiastica* was used liturgically in Cistercian houses in England during the twelfth century.

The specific local contexts in which copies that do contain lections came to be thus marked and the lections introduced into the matins liturgy can be established only to a limited extent, given the incomplete nature of the evidence for the ownership history of the manuscripts involved, and the difficulty in closely dating the handwriting of the marks themselves. While the twelfth-century provenance of all but one of the late-eleventh- and twelfth-century copies with lection marks can be determined, albeit with varying levels of certainty (only Bodl. Lib., MS Laud Misc. 243 wholly resists localisation), the eleventh- and twelfth-century ownership-histories of those produced before the mid-eleventh century is much less clear. In a few instances, however, the liturgical evidence provided by the lection marks can itself provide some assistance.

The addition of lections for the observance of a full octave of proper office readings for the feast of St Oswald in Bodl. Lib., MS Bodley 163 reinforces other evidence that points to the presence of the manuscript at Peterborough abbey (where Oswald was specially culted) by the twelfth century.[34] Likewise, a twelfth-century Christ Church, Canterbury provenance for Bodl. Lib., MS Hatton 43, another early eleventh-century copy of unknown origin but corrected by a

---

[32] B. Backaert, 'L'évolution du calendrier cistercien', *Collectanea ordinis cisterciensium reformatorum* xii (1950), 81–94, 302–16; xiii (1951), 108–27; R. Grégoire, 'L'homéliaire cistercien du manuscrit 114(82) de Dijon', *Cîteaux: Commentarii Cistercienses* xxviii (1977), 133–207. For Cistercian legislation as it evolved during the twelfth century, see *Narrative and legislative texts from early Cîteaux*, ed. C. Waddell (Cîteaux: Commentarii cistercienses, Studia et documenta ix, 1999); *Twelfth-century statutes from the Cistercian General Chapter*, ed. C. Waddell (Cîteaux: Commentarii cistercienses, Studia et documenta xii, 2002).

[33] D. Chadd, 'Liturgy and liturgical music: the limits of uniformity', in C. Norton and D. Park (eds), *Cistercian art and architecture in the British Isles*, Cambridge 1986, 299–314, at 307–14. See also R.W. Pfaff, *The liturgy in medieval England: a history*, Cambridge 2009, 248–60.

[34] For the non-liturgical evidence of Peterborough provenance, see N.R. Ker, *Catalogue of manuscripts containing Anglo-Saxon*, Oxford 1957, no. 304, p. 358.

Christ Church scribe in the early twelfth century, is bolstered by the addition of lection markings for major feasts not only for Augustine of Canterbury but also Fursey and Wilfrid, whose relics were claimed by Eadmer to be housed there.[35] Conversely, an early Gloucester provenance for BL MS Royal 13. C. v (evidently there by the early thirteenth century, since it contains annotations in the same hand as those found in other manuscripts from Gloucester abbey) is cast into doubt by the marking up as eight lections (for major feasts) the accounts of Mellitus, bishop of London and archbishop of Canterbury, and Æthelburh of Barking,[36] saints whose feasts (respectively 24 April or 18 September and 7 July or 11 October) are not recorded in the twelfth-century Gloucester kalendar (Oxford, Jesus College, MS 10, fos 1–6v).[37] The place of origin of this copy is uncertain, although the hand of the main scribe has been identified in a manuscript with Worcester connections.[38] Nevertheless these saints are not recorded either in the kalendar from Worcester that accompanies the first volume of a mid-eleventh-century Worcester legendary (Cambridge, Corpus Christi College, MS 9, pp. 3–14).[39] Mellitus and Æthelburh were both culted as major feasts not only within London and its vicinity but also further afield, such as at St Augustine's, Canterbury,[40] so it is not possible to localise closely the earlier ownership history of the manuscript on these liturgical grounds alone.[41]

---

[35] Eadmer, *De reliquiis sancti Audoeni et quorundam aliorum sanctorum quae Cantuariae in aecclesia domini salvatoris habentur*, ed. A. Wilmart, in 'Eadmeri Cantuariensis cantoris nova opuscula de sanctorum veneratione et obsecratione', *Revue des sciences religieuses* xv (1935), 362–70, at 364–6. Eadmer's record of the head of Fursey among the relics at the east altar in the pre-Conquest church 'ut antiquitas fatebatur' (ibid. 365) is the earliest reference to its presence at Christ Church. N.P. Brooks, *The early history of the church of Canterbury: Christ Church from 597 to 1066*, Leicester 1984, 37–42, 53; H.M. Taylor, 'The Anglo-Saxon cathedral church at Canterbury', *Archaeological Journal* cxxvi (1969), 101–29.

[36] Lection numbers iv–viii for Mellitus have been partially erased, indicating a subsequent downgrading of the feast to one of three lessons.

[37] R.M. Thomson, 'Books and learning at Gloucester abbey in the twelfth and thirteenth centuries', in J.P. Carley and C.G.C. Tite (eds), *Books and collectors, 1200–1700: essays presented to Andrew Watson*, London 1997, 3–26, at 3, 11, 19; F. Wormald, *English Benedictine kalendars after A.D. 1100* (HBS lxxvii, lxxxi, 1939–46), ii. 39–55.

[38] CCCC, MS 448, ii: T.A.M. Bishop, *English Caroline minuscule*, Oxford 1971, 20, n. 1. For a revised date for the handwriting, see D.N. Dumville, *English Caroline script and monastic history: studies in Benedictinism, A.D. 950–1030*, Woodbridge 1993, 55–6, n. 245.

[39] F. Wormald, *English kalendars before A.D. 1100* (HBS lxxii, 1934), no. 18; Rebecca Rushforth, *Saints in English kalendars before A.D. 1100* (HBS cxvii, 2008), no. 20.

[40] Office chants for the feast of Mellitus were copied in the late eleventh century on the front endleaves of CCCC, MS 267 (*s.* xi ex, from St Augustine's): K.D. Hartzell, *Catalogue of manuscripts written or owned in England up to 1200 containing music*, Woodbridge 2006, no. 33.

[41] For calendrical evidence from Anglo-Saxon England, see the tables in Rushforth, *Saints*, under 24 April and 18 September (Mellitus); 7 July and 11 October (Æthelburh). For

In those instances where the passages marked as lections for a major feast concern saints of known special local significance, the annotations may be assessed alongside other evidence for the particular contexts in which those cults were revived or provided with additional liturgical embellishment.

St Oswald at Peterborough

The most precious of the relics that Peterborough abbey claimed to possess at the time of the Norman Conquest was the incorrupt right arm of St Oswald, king of Northumbria.[42] Even the new Norman abbot, Turold, condemned by Hugh Candidus as a despoiler of the abbey, took pains to recover the arm from Ramsey abbey, where it had been secreted for safe-keeping after its theft from Peterborough by Hereward and his Danish allies in 1070.[43] The relic was publicly displayed in its golden reliquary on at least three occasions during the first half of the twelfth century.[44] The sequence of numbers for eight lections that was supplied in the margins of book iii.11 (on the initial translation of the body of Oswald to Bardney) cannot be dated more closely than to the eleventh or early twelfth century. Further sets of lections, however, can be shown to have been supplied on at least two separate occasions between the late eleventh and the mid-twelfth centuries, reflecting repeated activity in enhancing the festal liturgy for the saint. The first set, a second sequence of eight lections (*HE* iv. 14), is datable to no earlier than the late eleventh century, since the annotations accompany a chapter (from the *m*-text of the *Historia*) that had been lacking from the original copy (a representative of the *c*-text), supplied over erasure (fo. 135v) and on an additional bifolium (fos 136–7) in a late-eleventh-century hand.[45] A later (twelfth-century) hand added marginal numbers for two sets of three lections against book iii. 2 and book iii. 11, and a different hand supplied lection numbers for a further set of three readings in the margins of book iii. 1. Another (mid-twelfth-century) scribe, who revised the text at the start of the

---

later evidence, see Wormald, *English Benedictine kalendars after A.D. 1100*; the completion of the edition of English kalendars after 1100 is currently in hand, under the editorship of Nigel Morgan.

[42] D.W. Rollason, 'St Oswald in post-Conquest England', in C. Stancliffe and E. Cambridge (eds), *Oswald: Northumbrian king to European saint*, Stamford 1995, 164–77, at 171–2; Islwyn Geoffrey Thomas, 'The cult of saints' relics in medieval England', unpubl. Ph.D. diss. London 1974, 198–203.

[43] *The chronicle of Hugh Candidus, a monk of Peterborough*, ed. W.T. Mellows, London 1949, 79–81, 83.

[44] Ibid. 52, 105–6.

[45] B. Colgrave and R.A.B. Mynors (eds), *Bede's Ecclesiastical history of the English people*, Oxford 1969, li.

copy by replacing the outer leaves of the first quire and rewriting the text on what are now numbered fos 1, 6 and 7, also supplied the text for a further three lections for Oswald on fo. 249v that comprises a reworking of part of book iii. 1 and (more or less verbatim) the first part of book iii. 2 (ending at 'mox sanitate restituuntur'). Taken together, this second set of eight lections and several sets of three lections bear witness to the celebration of the octave of Oswald's feast, and the provision (perhaps incrementally, or with subsequent revision) of proper readings for the ferias within the octave. Evidence that the cult of Oswald was enhanced after the Conquest by the introduction or revision of propers for a full octave of liturgical commemoration is also provided by office chants for the full octave in a thirteenth-century Peterborough antiphoner (Cambridge, Magdalene College, MS F. 4. 10), which combine chants from an office of Oswald also found in a mid-twelfth-century Durham manuscript (Cambridge, Trinity College, MS O. 3. 55), with additional chants from a north-eastern French or Flemish office.[46] The 'English' and the 'Flemish' office are hard to date on textual or musical grounds, but a date no earlier than the twelfth century has been proposed for both.[47] The somewhat awkward insertion of chants from the Flemish office into the sequence of English chants enabled the provision of proper responsories for the ferias within the octave, different from those sung on the feast itself and its octave. It is tempting to speculate that the chants reflect successive endeavours at Peterborough to embellish the liturgy for Oswald hinted at by the lection evidence in their copy of the *Historia ecclesiastica*.

Wilfrid and Fursey at Christ Church, Canterbury

The addition of annotations marking up narratives concerning both Wilfrid and Fursey as lections in Bodl. Lib. MS Hatton 43 is very likely to correspond with the liturgical promotion of their cults at Canterbury in the late eleventh or early twelfth centuries, almost certainly at the initiative of Eadmer. After a fire of 1067 and the rebuilding of the cathedral, the relics of Wilfrid (originally moved from Ripon to Canterbury, perhaps in the immediate aftermath of the burning of the

---

[46] D. Hiley, 'The office chants for St Oswald, king of Northumbria and martyr', in O. Kongsted, N. Krabbe, M. Kube and M. Michelsen (eds), *A Due: musical essays in honour of John D. Bergsagel & Heinrich W. Schwab: Musikalische Aufsätze zu Ehren von John D. Bergsagel & Heinrich W. Schabe*, Copenhagen 2008, 244–59; idem, 'The saints venerated in medieval Peterborough as reflected in the Antiphoner Cambridge, Magdalene College, F.4.10', in E. Hornby and D. Maw (eds), *Essays on the history of English music in honour of John Caldwell: sources, style, performance, historiography*, Woodbridge 2010, 22–46.

[47] Hiley, 'Office chants', 255.

monastery of Ripon by King Eadred in 948),[48] together with those of other saints, were moved to a comparatively inaccessible position above the north transept.[49] Eadmer's disapproval of what, for him, constituted a failure to venerate these saints and their relics appropriately is evident in several of his works, and his efforts to restore their cults at Christ Church included their commemoration in appropriate liturgical form as well as new hagiography.[50] Eadmer appears to have believed that he was restoring pre-Conquest liturgical practice, but calendrical evidence suggests that neither Wilfrid nor Fursey had been commemorated with major feasts at Christ Church in the decades before the Conquest, since neither is recorded in the original hand in the kalendar in an early-eleventh-century psalter from Christ Church, now BL MS Arundel 155.[51] Major feasts in their honour, however, had certainly been introduced by the second quarter of the twelfth century, since both are recorded as higher-grade feasts in the original hand in the kalendar in Bodl. Lib. MS Add. C. 260, but whether before or after Eadmer accompanied Anselm into exile (1097–1100, and again 1103–1106) cannot be determined.[52] None of the lection annotations in Hatton 43 is closely datable; those for Wilfrid and Fursey are in different hands, neither of which is the same as that of the early-twelfth-century Christ Church scribe who made numerous corrections to the text.

---

[48] D.W. Rollason, 'Relic-cults as an instrument of royal policy, c.900–c.1050', *ASE* xv (1986), 91–103, at 95–6; Brooks, *Early history of Canterbury*, 227–8.

[49] J. Rubenstein, 'Liturgy against history: the competing visions of Lanfranc and Eadmer of Canterbury', *Speculum* lxxiv (1999), 279–309, at 289–98.

[50] Ibid. 298–307. For a further perspective, see P.A. Hayward, 'St Wilfrid of Ripon and the northern Church in Anglo-Norman historiography', *Northern History* xlix (2012), 11–35, at 13–21.

[51] Wormald, *English kalendars before 1100*, no. 13: Rushforth, *Saints*, no. 11.

[52] T.A. Heslop, 'The Canterbury calendars and the Norman Conquest', in R. Eales and R. Sharpe (eds), *Canterbury and the Norman Conquest: churches, saints and scholars, 1066–1109*, London 1995, 53–85, at 54–5, 70–77 (Fursey: 16 January, written in capitals; Wilfrid: 12 October, written in coloured capitals). Lanfranc's *Monastic constitutions*, which describes in detail the three highest grades of feasts of twelve lessons, and mentions in passing a fourth grade (§73 'sicut priuatis duodecim lectionibus'), itemises only some of the saints observed with feasts of twelve lessons of the third grade, and none of those of the fourth, so is not helpful in establishing which saints were thus culted at Christ Church during Lanfranc's archiepiscopate (*The monastic constitutions of Lanfranc*, ed. and tr. D. Knowles and C.N.L. Brooke, Oxford 2002, §62–73). It cannot therefore be safely used as evidence for the absence of a liturgical cult of those, including Wilfrid and Fursey, whose names are not mentioned.

St Augustine at St Augustine's, Canterbury

Extracts from the *Historia ecclesiastica* were also deployed in the liturgical enhancement of the cult of St Augustine at St Augustine's, Canterbury at the end of the eleventh century. A copy of the full text is not known to survive from St Augustine's,[53] and it is impossible to know from what date it was first used there to supply proper lections for an office of Augustine. Nevertheless, liturgical items at the end of a copy of Goscelin's *Historia et miracula S. Augustini* (with the *sermo* but lacking the account of the *translatio*) and *Historia minor de aduentu beati Augustini* dating from the first half of the twelfth century (Cambridge, Corpus Christi College, MS 312, pp. 272–97) show that sometime during the earlier twelfth century the relevant passages from Bede's *Historia* had been combined with extracts from Goscelin's two works to provide a full octave of proper lections, as well as proper chants for vespers, for the feast of Augustine on 26 May and its octave.[54] The lections for the feast itself and the following two days comprise extracts from the *Historia ecclesiastica* i. 23 – ii. 2 (with minor modifications and reworking); those for the octave and Sunday within the octave are taken from the *Historia maior*, and the remainder of the ferial readings from the *Historia minor*.[55] From this evidence alone it is not possible to determine whether the lections from Goscelin's works represent additions to a pre-existing office liturgy that already drew its lections from Bede, in order to expand the proper liturgy of the feast to an entire octave. Nevertheless, the inclusion of extracts from the *Historia maior* and *Historia minor* demonstrates that the festal liturgy of St Augustine certainly was embellished sometime after the completion of these works (in the wake of the translation of his relics and those of the other early saints of Canterbury in 1091), while the account of Augustine's life in Bede's *Historia ecclesia* provided the lections on the feast day itself.[56]

---

[53] Fragments of a late-eleventh- or early-twelfth-century copy survive now as endleaves of CCCC, MS 270 (fos 1 and 197), a sacramentary produced at St Augustine's between 1091 and 1100: Gneuss, *Handlist*, no. 75.

[54] Hartzell, *Catalogue*, no. 36; D. Hiley, 'Chant composition at Canterbury after the Norman Conquest', in B. Hangartner and U. Fischer (eds), *Max Lutolf zum 60. Geburtstag. Festschrift*, Basel 1994, 31–46, at 43; Other proper chants for Augustine survive in the following manuscripts from St Augustine's: Cambridge, St John's College, MS 164 (F.27), BL MSS Cotton Vespasian D. vi and Egerton 874: Hartzell, *Catalogue*, nos 56, 145 and 150.

[55] The sources were identified by Eleanor Rutherford as part of a codicological essay submitted in partial fulfilment of the M.Phil. in Musicology, University of Cambridge, 2010. I am very grateful to her for giving me permission to report these findings.

[56] For the circumstances surrounding the translation and Goscelin's hagiographical activity at St Augustine's, see R. Sharpe, 'Goscelin's St Augustine and St Mildreth: hagiography and liturgy in context', *Journal of Theological Studies* xli (1990), 502–16; idem, 'The setting of St Augustine's translation, 1091', in Eales and Sharpe, *Canterbury and the Norman Conquest*,

However, a significant number of the narratives marked as lections, for both major and lesser feasts, do not relate to patronal saints or to those with major relic cults at the community concerned. For example, the widespread cult from at least the eleventh century onwards of Cuthbert, Oswald and Aethelthryth beyond their major cult centres is reflected by the marking of eight lections for a major feast for one or more of these saints in copies of Bede's *Historia* from respectively Christ Church, Canterbury, Winchcombe and Rochester (in the case of Cuthbert), from Winchcombe (in the case of Oswald), and from an unidentified Yorkshire house (perhaps St Mary's abbey, York) and an unidentified monastic community perhaps in the West Midlands (in the case of Aethelthryth).[57] The partial survival of two layers of annotation for lections for the first two nocturns of a major feast of twelve lessons for St Alban in BL MS Royal 13. C. v (a manuscript with no obvious connection with the abbey of St Albans) attests to the wider celebration of his feast with proper readings, and perhaps also chants, since according to Matthew Paris, Archbishop Ælfric had given authority for the newly composed *historia* for St Alban to be 'made public in many places in England, and had the day of the same martyr honoured'.[58]

Manuscript evidence for the use of Bede's *Historia ecclesiastica* in the liturgy thus contributes to the more complex picture of the history of the cult of early English saints in late Anglo-Saxon and early Norman England that has emerged in recent decades.[59] Some of the annotations reinforce the evidence

---

1–13. The *Historia maior* was completed sometime in or after 1099: Sharpe, 'Goscelin's St Augustine', 516.

[57] Cuthbert: Bodl. Lib. MSS Hatton 43 (Christ Church, Canterbury), and Douce 368 (Winchcombe), BL MS Harley 3680 (Rochester); Oswald: Bodl. Lib. MS Douce 368 (Winchcombe); Æthelthryth: Cambridge, Trinity College, MS R. 5. 27 (?St Mary's abbey, York), BL MS Royal 13. C. v (?West Midlands). For the liturgical observance of the feast of Cuthbert, see Gretsch, Ælfric, 96–101; for that of Oswald, A. Thacker, '*Membra disiecta*: the division of the body and the diffusion of the cult', in Stancliffe and Cambridge, *Oswald*, 97–127, at 119–27; Rollason, 'St Oswald', in ibid. 164–77; for that of Æthelthryth, Goscelin of Saint-Bertin, *The hagiography of the female saints of Ely*, ed. R.C. Love, Oxford 2004, xxiii–xxv, xxxii–xl; Gretsch, Ælfric, 162–71.

[58] 'et auctoritate fratris sui, Archiepiscopi, multis locis Angliae fecit publicari, diemque ejusdem Martyris honorari': *Gesta abbatum*, i. 32; Hartzell, 'A St. Albans miscellany', 27.

[59] For an initial re-evaluation of Norman scepticism towards Anglo-Saxon saints and their cults, as expressed in D. Knowles, *The monastic order in England*, 2 edn, Cambridge 1963, 118–19: R.W. Southern, *Saint Anselm and his biographer*, Cambridge 1963, 277–87 and idem, *Saint Anselm: a portrait in a landscape*, Cambridge 1990, 312–20, see S.J. Ridyard, '*Condigna veneratio*: post-Conquest attitudes to the saints of the Anglo-Saxons', *ANS* ix (1987), 179–206; R.W. Pfaff, 'Lanfranc's supposed purge of the Anglo-Saxon calendar', in T. Reuter (ed.), *Warriors and churchmen in the high Middle Ages: essays presented to Karl Leyser*, London 1992, 95–108. For subsequent modifications and additional perspectives, see T.A. Heslop, 'The Canterbury calendars and the Norman Conquest', in Eales and Sharpe,

for the impetus given to the liturgical enhancement of saints' cults provided by perceived threats to or local rivalries between monastic houses in the decades after the Conquest. Eleventh-century *libelli* containing offices for Alban and Birinus, however, indicate that individual communities were also enhancing their festal observance in the period between the tenth-century reform and the Conquest, and warn against the temptation to assign a post-Conquest date to the less closely datable lection annotations found in pre-Conquest copies of the *Historia ecclesiastica*.[60] Such evidence, together with that for the provision of proper lections for saints who were not of special local significance, helps to place the more politically-motivated promotion of local saints' cults in the post-Conquest period within a wider religious context of liturgical development from the later tenth to the twelfth centuries, in which the festal liturgy came gradually to be embellished through additional readings, prayers and chants – a process that had its origins in developments on the Continent from the eighth century, and which received various stimuli in England from the tenth century onwards. Such activity could sometimes be of a modest and incremental nature: the initiative of a cantor responding in a more routine fashion to the duties of his office rather than necessarily to external stimulus.[61] Particular circumstances might focus special attention upon a saint of local importance but not to the exclusion of the introduction or embellishment of universal feasts, as has been shown in a recent study of the accretions to the Homiliary of Paul the Deacon, and in particular additions for the celebration of the feast of All Saints.[62]

Canterbury and the Norman Conquest, 53–85; J. Rubenstein, 'The life and writings of Osbern of Canterbury', in ibid. 27–40; idem, 'Liturgy against history', 279–309; P.A. Hayward, 'Translation-narratives in post-Conquest hagiography and English resistance to the Norman Conquest', *ANS* xxi (1999), 67–93; idem, 'Gregory the Great as "Apostle of the English" in post-Conquest Canterbury', *JEH* lv (2004), 19–57. See also the caution expressed by Christopher Brooke, with reference to determining Lanfranc's views, given the evident 'variety of opinion and attitude': *Monastic constitutions of Lanfranc*, ed. Knowles and Brooke, xxxvi–xxxviii.

[60] For new hagiographical production during this period, see M. Lapidge and R.C. Love, 'The Latin hagiography of England and Wales (600–1550)', in G. Philippart (ed.), *Hagiographies: international history of the Latin and vernacular hagiographical literature in the West from its origins to 1550*, iii, Turnhout 2001, 203–325, at 222–3; *Three Anglo-Latin saints' Lives*, ed. Love, xxxvii–xxxix.

[61] For the incremental 'properization' of the office chants, see, for example, R. Hankeln, '"Properization" and formal changes in high medieval saints' offices: the offices for Saints Henry and Kunigunde of Bamberg', *Plainsong and Medieval Music* x (2001), 3–22.

[62] T.N. Hall, 'The development of the common of saints in the early English versions of Paul the Deacon's Homiliary', in T.N. Hall and D. Scragg (eds), *Anglo-Saxon books and their readers: essays in celebration of Helmut Gneuss's* Handlist of Anglo-Saxon manuscripts, Kalamazoo, MI 2008, 31–67.

Non-liturgical Uses of the *Historia Ecclesiastica* as a Source of Hagiographical Readings and Reference

The office of matins was not the only occasion for readings from the *Historia ecclesiastica*. In several copies, both those that contain lection marks and those that do not, passages of hagiographical narrative not ostensibly divided into liturgical lections have been annotated or rubricated in ways that are suggestive of oral delivery.

For example, in late-Anglo-Saxon copies, such as Cambridge, Trinity College, MS R. 7. 5 and BL MS Royal 13. C. v, in which year-dates were originally written in roman numerals, verbal forms of the dates were supplied as interlinear glosses (in later copies, the dates were written as words from the outset). Several copies were also annotated with stress-marks (in the form of a hairline acute stroke) above the syllable that received the stressed accent in unfamiliar polysyllabic words or words that might otherwise be accented incorrectly.[63] Such marks need not necessarily be evidence of preparation for public reading but may have been intended to provide assistance in other contexts (such as the schoolroom) in the correct accentuation of the text. Nevertheless, the heavy incidence of stress-marks only in the account of the life of St Æthelthryth (*HE* iv. 19 (17)) in a late-eleventh- or early-twelfth century copy from St Neots, BL MS Add. 38130 (fos 73r–74r), would seem to indicate a more specific intent to prepare this particular passage for reading aloud. Although there are no liturgical lection marks in this copy of Bede, the manuscript also contains a copy of a *Vita S. Neoti* that is marked up as eight lections, together with other texts for the commemoration of St Neot (fos 1–9v).

Passages were also adapted to form discrete readings by the addition of alternative opening and/or closing formulae. In Winchester Cathedral, MS 1, for example, a new clause was supplied in a late-eleventh- or twelfth-century hand to provide a more precise chronological context than 'Eo tempore' at the start of the account of the martyrdoms of the two Hewalds (*HE* v. 9; fo. 91r) together with a conventional termination, 'Prestante domino nostro iesu cristo..' (fo. 92v).[64] A similar termination plus an explicit rubric to mark the end of the

---

[63] See, for example, S. Keynes, *Anglo-Saxon manuscripts and other items of related interest in the library of Trinity College, Cambridge* (Old English Newsletter, Subsidia xviii, 1992), pl. xviii, which shows the beginning of *HE* ii. 5 in Trinity R. 7. 5, with examples of accents over stressed syllables, and numerals written out in full, as well as corrections to the punctuation.

[64] Winchester Cathedral, MS 1 (fo. 91r): '\Anno dominicę incarnationis prope modum sescentesimo nonagesimo secundo. uenerabilis quidam cristi sacerdos de natione anglorum uocabulo egberhctus/... (fo. 92v) fluenti sui dona perfundat. \prestante domino nostro iesu cristo. qui cum patre et spiritu sancto uiuit et regnat per omnia secula seculorum amen.' These adaptations were noted by Charles Plummer, who also drew attention to similar

account of St Oswald at the start of book iii. 14 was added during the second half of the twelfth century to the copy from Christ Church, Canterbury (Bodl. Lib. MS Hatton 43, fo. 80r).[65] Incipit and explicit rubrics were likewise added in the margins to top-and-tail the narrative of the life and miracles of Oswald in Bodl. Lib., MS Laud Misc. 243 (fos 42v and 50r), as well as directions on fos 46r and 47r (in the form 'non' and 'hic') to omit book iii. 8 (where the narrative breaks off to deal with the kingdom of Kent) and, on fo. 50r, to incorporate the outlying miracle of Oswald recorded in *HE* iv. 14.[66] In the same manuscript similar rubrics were added to demarcate the *vitae* of Alban (*HE* i. 7; fo. 3v) and Augustine (*HE* i. 23–33, ii. 2–3; fos 11v and 27v), including directions to the reader to omit *HE* i. 24 – ii. 1.[67] A further notable feature of the presentation of the Augustine narrative in this copy is that the text of the processional antiphon 'Deprecamur te domine in omni misericordia dei' (*HE* i. 25; fo. 18r), which, according to Bede, was sung by Augustine and his companions as they approached Canterbury, is notated in neumes on a four-line stave, perhaps suggesting that the lector at this point would sing the melody rather than simply intone it.[68] Incipit rubrics for lives of Oswald and Hild were also added in the lower margins of the pages containing the start of respectively books iii. 1 and iv. 23 (21) in the copy from Selby abbey (Bodl. Lib. MS Fairfax 12).[69]

The only annotations that specify the precise context in which such passages were to be read are a set of thirteenth-century annotations supplied at the beginning and end of the narrative of the Augustinian mission (*HE* i. 23 – ii. 3), in Bodl. Lib. MS Digby 211, a twelfth-century copy from Waltham abbey. These indicate that the passage (omitting the digression at book ii. 1 concerning Pope

---

wording incorporated into the text itself at the opening of *HE* i. 7, the account of St Alban, in Bodl. Lib. MS Douce 368: *Venerabilis Baedae Historiam ecclesiasticam gentis Anglorum, Historiam abbatum, Epistolam ad Ecgberctum una cum Historia abbatum auctore anonymo*, ed. C. Plummer, Oxford 1896, i. pp. cxii and cxvi.

[65] 'Regnante domino nostro iesu cristo. qui cum patre et spiritu sancto uiuit et regnat per immortalia secula seculorum amen. Explicit passio sancti oswaldi regis et martiris.' The excision of a leaf between fos 66 and 67 has caused the loss of the start of the narrative at the beginning of book iii, and thus any opening rubric that may have been provided.

[66] 'Est in sequenti libro scriptum qualiter natalicius dies sancti oswaldi diuinitus est ostensus et celebrari preceptus est signo tali prescripto + suo quidem loco pro temporum accidentis ibidem scriptus sed hic ubi finis ac miracula eius contexta sunt recensendus.' The same direction is found in the original hand in the copy from Battle abbey, now Hereford P. v. 1, fo. 82r.

[67] fo. 22r: 'Hoc pretermisso ubi signum crucis inueneris in quarto folio lege'.

[68] For the chant, see K. Levy, 'A Gregorian processional antiphon', *Schweizer Jahrbuch für Musikwissenschaft / Annales suisses de musicologie* new ser. ii (1982), 91–102.

[69] fo. 52v: 'Hic incipit passio sancti oswaldi regis martiris', fol. 99v 'Hic incipit uita sancte hylde virginis et abbatisse'.

Gregory) should be read each year in the refectory (presumably on the feast of St Augustine).⁷⁰ A similarly worded thirteenth-century directive, referring explicitly to the feast but without the reference to the refectory, accompanies the same passage in BL MS Add. 14250 (fo. 18r), a mid-twelfth-century copy from the Augustinian priory of Plympton in Devon.⁷¹ Over the course of the eleventh and twelfth centuries annual cycles of refectory reading that incorporated hagiographical readings on feast days came to be adopted within all the different monastic traditions and those of the regular canons.⁷² The mid-twelfth-century *Liber ordinis*, the custumal of the Augustinian abbey of St Victor, Paris (to my knowledge, the earliest surviving full record of an annual cycle), for example, concludes the description of the cycle of biblical and exegetical reading with the general allowance that 'in festiuitatibus sanctorum legantur uitae uel passiones eorum'.⁷³ Unfortunately most of the detailed evidence for the content of the refectory reading post-dates the twelfth century, and surviving English records are not as full as those from the Continent; none provides so full a list of the hagiographical readings and various books used as is found in the early-thirteenth-century Fécamp ordinal.⁷⁴ The absence of any specific reference to the *Historia ecclesiastica* in the English evidence should not, therefore, preclude the refectory from being the most likely context outside the office for reading lections from this text.

Nevertheless, mealtimes in the refectory were not the only non-liturgical occasion for public reading within religious communities. Readings were also delivered during the morning chapter office, the evening collation and periods of manual labour. The norms that governed the choice of readings during the chapter office and collation (although not manual labour) can be established from surviving monastic custumals and booklists.⁷⁵ I have not yet encountered

---

⁷⁰ fo. 13v: 'Hic incipit ad legendum in refectorio de s. augustino anglorum apostolo; fo. 23r: 'va-' (the corresponding '-cat' is no longer visible at the end of the chapter); fo. 27v: 'usque huc legitur in refectorio de sancto augustino anglorum apostolo'.

⁷¹ 'Ab hoc loco debet legi in festiuitate sancti augustini anglorum apostoli usque ad capitulum quartum proximi libri quod sic incipit successit augustinus et cetera.'

⁷² G. Philippart, *Les Légendiers latins et autres manuscrits hagiographiques* (Typologie des sources du Moyen Âge occidental xxiv–xxv, 1977), 115–16; B. de Gaiffier, 'À propos des légendiers latins', *AB* xcvii (1979), 57–68, at 61.

⁷³ *Liber ordinis sancti Victoris Parisiensis*, ed. L. Jocqué and L. Milis (Corpus christianorum continuatio medievalis lxi, 1984), 211–15, at 214.

⁷⁴ *The ordinal of the abbey of the Holy Trinity Fécamp (Fécamp, Musée de la Bénédictine, MS 186)*, ed. D. Chadd (HBS cxi–cxii, 1999–2002), ii. 674–85; D.-B. Grémont, 'Lectiones ad prandium à l'abbaye de Fécamp au xiiie siècle', *Cahiers Léopold Delisle* xx (1971), 3–41.

⁷⁵ Although the custumals do not specify particular texts to be read during manual labour, the *Liber tramitis*, a mid-eleventh-century Cluniac custumal from the abbey of Farfa, states that the reading could come from the book from which the refectory reading had been

a reference to the *Historia ecclesiastica* in such lists; instead, by contrast with the lists of refectory books and reading, the hagiographical texts that are mentioned are of a particularly restricted kind: in the case of the chapter office, only the Martyrology, and, for collation, lives of the early Desert Fathers (in particular, the collection known as the *Vitas patrum* and Gregory's *Dialogi*).[76] It is possible that such evidence may not take account of occasional variations from the norm, and therefore it would be unwise to exclude the possibility that other *vitae*, including those embedded in the *Historia ecclesiastica*, might have been read on especially important feasts. The full extent of the use of the *Historia ecclesiastica* for public reading is unlikely to be recoverable.

Finally, several twelfth-century copies of the text contain forms of apparatus (running titles and marginal subject headings) that suggest consultation of hagiographical passages perhaps also for the purposes of personal devotion, edification or reference. BL MS Stowe 104, for example, was rubricated from the outset with running titles across the relevant openings in the form 'De sancto augustino', De sancto oswaldo', that refer to Alban, Augustine, Oswald, Aidan, Fursey, Cedd, Æthelthryth, Cuthbert, John of Beverley and Wilfrid. Similarly worded marginal subject headings added to BL MS Add 38817 (from the Augustinian priory of Kirkham) mark passages on Augustine and the northern saints Oswine, Chadd, Oswald, Hild and Cuthbert. A marginal heading, 'De sancto oswine', was also added both in the list of capitula to book iii, beside the capitulum for book iii. 14, and beside the relevant passage in ch. 14 (at 'Habuit autem') in Cambridge, Pembroke College, MS 82 (fo. 45v), a copy from Tynemouth priory (a cell of St Albans). Although Oswine was specially culted at the priory (which claimed to possess his relics, translating them to a shrine within the newly completed church in 1110), the marginal headings are unlikely to mark the passage for use as public reading on his feast. Instead, the liturgical lections, and probably those also for the refectory, were drawn from a recent and more extended *Vita, inventio et miracula* which was more explicit about Oswine's sanctity.[77]

---

taken: 'legatur ibi lectio de libro quo legitur in refectorio, si talis est qui ad aedificationem pertineat': *Liber tramitis aevi Odilonis abbatis*, ed. P. Dinter (Corpus consuetudinum monasticarum x, 1980), 201.

[76] For the readings in the chapter office, see Graham, 'Cambridge, Corpus Christi College 57', 34–7; for reading in the chapter office and at collation, see also T. Webber, 'Monastic space and the use of books in the Anglo-Norman period', *ANS* xxxvi (2014), 221–40, at 231–6.

[77] P.A. Hayward, 'Sanctity and lordship in twelfth-century England: St Albans, Durham, and the cult of Saint Oswine, king and martyr', *Viator* xxx (1999), 105–44; Hughes, 'British rhymed offices', 271–3. The now fragmentary compendium of texts for the liturgical and extra-liturgical commemoration of Oswine in Corpus Christi College, Oxford, MS 134,

Other evidence contributes to the impression that Bede's history came to be regarded during the twelfth century as a compendium of English saints' lives. Such a perception may have lain behind the inclusion in three textually related copies (BL MS Harley 3680, from Rochester; Dublin, Trinity College, MS E. 2. 23 (492), from Bury St Edmunds, and Bodl. Lib. MS e Museo 115, of unknown provenance) of an eleventh-century Latin translation of the Old English *List of saints' resting-places* – a list of the locations of the relics of (mostly) Anglo-Saxon saints.[78] Henry of Huntingdon's own compendium of English saints and their miracles (modelled on Jerome's *De uiris illustribus*), which forms book ix of his *Historia Anglorum*, drew heavily (and with due acknowledgement) from the *Historia ecclesiastica*: 'In fact, in this little book I have added none, or nearly none, to the miracles which that man of the Lord, the venerable Bede, whose authority is completely secure, has written in his *History*.'[79] Most striking is a list (in a late-twelfth-century hand) made to accompany a now-lost copy of the *Historia ecclesiastica*, which provides an index, book by book, to the lives to be found in each, headed with the qualification 'Plura sunt nomina et gesta sanctorum in hoc libro que non sunt hic intitulata'.[80]

Whether used for readings within or outside the liturgy or for other purposes, the accounts of the saints of the early English church in the *Historia ecclesiastica* had an authority that was unquestionable. For Henry of Huntingdon, Bede's authority was 'firmissima' – 'completely secure'. His perceived status from the Carolingian period onwards as one of the orthodox Fathers of the Church was manifested, for example, in the inclusion of his homilies alongside those of Augustine, Jerome, Gregory and other Catholic Fathers in the Homiliary of Paul

---

is described in R.M. Thomson, *A descriptive catalogue of the medieval manuscripts of Corpus Christi College, Oxford*, Cambridge 2011, 66–7.

[78] *Die Heiligen Englands: angelsächsisch und lateinisch*, ed. F. Liebermann, Hanover 1889.

[79] 'In hoc siquidem libello, exceptis miraculis que uir Domini Beda uenerabilis, cuius auctoritas firmissima est, in historia sua conscripsit, nulla uel fere nulla apposuimus.' Henry, archdeacon of Huntingdon, *Historia Anglorum: the history of the English people*, ed. D. Greenway, Oxford 1996, p. lxv and n. 45, ix (pp. 622–97), at ix. 1 (pp. 622–3).

[80] The list is written on a bifolium now mounted on a stub at the end of a fourteenth-century copy of Bede's *Ecclesiastical history* (CCCC, MS 264, fos xiir–xiiir). The handwriting is rather idiosyncratic but has parallels in some of the more formalised renditions of proto-cursive writing found in local charters of the late twelfth century. It is not clear whether the bifolium was first bound with this copy when the manuscript was put together for Simon Bozoun, prior of Norwich, in the mid-fourteenth century, or only when the volume came into the hands of Matthew Parker, who had the relevant chapter numbers written on to the stub to which it is fixed and a copy of the entire list added at the front of the eleventh-century copy of the *Ecclesiastical history* that is now Cambridge, Trinity College, MS R. 7. 5.

the Deacon.[81] Those whose lives he recounted were thereby exempt from the tests of authenticity required by sceptical Norman bishops and abbots for the relics of saints who lacked so authoritative an account. Bede may not have described every one of these men and women as 'sanctus' or 'beatus', but, to his eleventh- and twelfth-century readers, his authority meant that their sanctity was not in doubt. In this they, and the custodians of their relics, were fortunate indeed, for, as Henry of Huntingdon wrote, 'Although wonderful and magnificent men have lived in subsequent ages, yet their deeds lack either a known author or one so trustworthy as Bede, the servant of God.'[82]

---

[81] J. Hill, 'Bede and the Benedictine reform' (Jarrow Lecture, 1988), esp. 4–8, 10–11; R.W. Pfaff, 'Bede among the Fathers? The evidence from liturgical commemoration', *Studia patristica* xxvii (1993), 225–9.

[82] 'Quia quamuis succedentium temporum uiri mirabiles et magnifici fuerint, tamen eorum gesta uel auctore carent certo, uel quantum seruus Dei Beda probato.' HH ix. 1 (pp. 622–3).

Appendix: English-made Copies of the *Historia Ecclesiastica* Dating from the Late Tenth to the Late Twelfth Centuries

(Manuscripts that contain lection marks are given in bold; references to religious houses indicate medieval provenance not place of origin.)

Aberystwyth, National Library of Wales, MS Peniarth 381 (Hengwrt 102) s. xii[1]
   Colgrave and Mynors, lii.[83]

Cambridge, Pembroke College, MS 82, s. xii^{med} (Tynemouth, Benedictine priory)
   Colgrave and Mynors, xlix;), N.R. Ker, *Medieval libraries of Great Britain*, 2 edn, London 1964, 191 (hereafter *MLGB*); Thomson, *Manuscripts from St Albans abbey*, i. 38, 116–17; M. Gullick, 'The origin and importance of Cambridge, Trinity College, MS R. 5. 27', *Transactions of the Cambridge Bibliographical Society* xi (1998), 239–62, at 243.

Cambridge, Trinity College, MS R. 5. 27, s. xii$^{1/4}$
   Colgrave and Mynors, liii; perhaps produced at St Mary's, York: Gullick, 'Origin and importance', 239–62.

Cambridge, Trinity College, MS R. 7. 5, s. xii$^{in.}$ – s. xi[2] (perhaps written in two stages; some text re-written in the twelfth century)
   Colgrave and Mynors, xlvii–xlviii; Gneuss, *Handlist*, no. 181; Keynes, *Anglo-Saxon manuscripts*, no. 18, p. 30, pl. xviii; G. Henderson, '*Sortes biblicae* in twelfth-century England: the list of episcopal prognostics in Cambridge, Trinity College, MS R.7.5', in D. Williams (ed.), *England in the twelfth century: proceedings of the 1988 Harlaxton Symposium*, Woodbridge 1990, 113–35.

Dublin, Trinity College, MS E. 2. 23 (492), s. xii$^{med.}$
   Colgrave and Mynors, lviii; Ker, *Catalogue of manuscripts containing Anglo-Saxon*, no. 104; *MLGB*, 19; M.L. Colker, *Trinity College Library Dublin: descriptive catalogue of the mediaeval and renaissance Latin manuscripts*, Aldershot 1991, ii. 901–3; E. Parker, 'The scriptorium of Bury St Edmunds in the twelfth century', unpubl. Ph.D. diss. London 1984, 319–20. Probably the copy recorded in a later-twelfth-century booklist from Bury: *English Benedictine libraries: the shorter catalogues*, ed. R. Sharpe, J.P. Carley, R.M. Thomson and A.G. Watson (Corpus of British Medieval Library Catalogues iv, 1996), B13.211, p. 82 (hereafter CBMLC).

Durham, Dean and Chapter Library, MS B. II. 35 (fos 38–120), s. xi^{ex} (Durham, Benedictine cathedral priory)
   Colgrave and Mynors, xlix; R.A. B. Mynors, *Durham cathedral manuscripts to the end of the twelfth century*, Oxford 1939, no. 47; *MLGB*, 67; Gneuss, *Handlist*, no. 238; M. Gullick, 'The scribe of the Carilef Bible: a new look at some late-eleventh-century Durham cathedral manuscripts', in L.L. Brownrigg (ed.), *Medieval book production: assessing the evidence. Proceedings of the second conference of The Seminar of the History of the Book to 1500*, Los Altos Hills, CA 1990, 61–83, at 68; Gullick, 'Origin and importance', 243–4, n. 18.

---

[83] I am grateful to Dr Elizabeth New for examining this manuscript for me.

Hereford Cathedral, MS P. v. 1, pt ii (fos 29–152) + Oxford, Bodleian Library, MS e Museo 93 (*SC* 3632), *s.* xii¼ (Battle, Benedictine abbey; later at Brecon, a cell of Battle)
>Colgrave and Mynors, lvi; Ker, *Catalogue of manuscripts containing Anglo-Saxon*, no. 121; *MLGB*, 8 and n. 9; R.A.B. Mynors and R.M. Thomson, *Catalogue of the manuscripts of Hereford Cathedral Library*, Cambridge 1993, 95–6.

London, British Library, MS Add. 14250, *s.* xii^med. (1140?) (Plympton, Augustinian priory)
>Colgrave and Mynors, liii; Andrew G. Watson, *Catalogue of dated and datable manuscripts, c.700–1600 in the Department of Manuscripts, the British Library*, London 1979, no. 103, pl. 75; *MLGB*, 152.

London, British Library, MS Add. 25014, *s.* xii² (Newminster, Cistercian abbey)
>Colgrave and Mynors, xlix; *MLGB*, 134 (with a query); Gullick, 'Origin and importance', 243–4.

London, British Library, MS Add. 38130, *s.* xi/xii (St Neots, Benedictine priory)
>Colgrave and Mynors, xlviii; not in *MLGB*, but the addition of a mass set for St Neot, and the inclusion from the outset of his *vita* (the first part of which is marked up for eight lections), *translatio* and two sermons on his translation, suggests a St Neots origin and twelfth-century provenance: Gullick, 'Origin and importance', 244, n. 17.

London, British Library, MS Add. 38817, *s.* xii² (Kirkham, Augustinian priory)
>Colgrave and Mynors, liv; *MLGB*, 106; Gullick, 'Origin and importance', 239–40.

London, British Library, MS Cotton Vitellius E. i + E. vii, fos 1–2, *s.* xii^med.? (Guisborough, Augustinian priory)
>Heavily damaged during the Cottonian fire of 1731, and largely illegible. Colgrave and Mynors, lx; *MLGB*, 94 and n. 4.

London, British Library, MS Harley 3680, *s.* xii¼ (Rochester, Benedictine cathedral priory)
>Colgrave and Mynors, lviii: *MLGB*, 161. Katherine Mary Waller, 'The library, scriptorium and community of Rochester cathedral priory, *c*.1080–1150', unpubl. Ph.D. diss. Liverpool 1981, 269; CBMLC iv, B79.50. Although this manuscript was produced by scribes active at Rochester during the first quarter of the twelfth century, the copy recorded in the earlier twelfth-century Rochester catalogue (CBMLC iv, B77.65) is described as being in two volumes.

London, British Library, MS Harley 4124, *s.* xii² (Worksop, Augustinian priory)
>Colgrave and Mynors, xlix; *MLGB*, 215; Gullick, 'Origin and importance', 244.

London, British Library, MS Royal 13. C. v, *s.* x/xi or xi¹ (fos 1–2 are mid- or late-eleventh-century replacements) (Gloucester, Benedictine abbey, by *s.* xiii^in.)
>Colgrave and Mynors, li–lii; *MLGB*, 92; Thomson, 'Books and learning at Gloucester abbey', 3, 11, 19. An eleventh- or earlier-twelfth-century Gloucester provenance is unlikely given the presence of lection markings for feasts of twelve lessons for both Mellitus (24 April/18 September) and Æthelburh (7 July/11 October), both of whom are absent from the twelfth-century Gloucester liturgical kalendar (Oxford, Jesus College, MS 10, fos 1–6v: Wormald,

English Benedictine kalendars after a.d. 1100, ii. 39–55. T.A.M. Bishop identified one of the scribes as that of Cambridge, Corpus Christi College, MS 448, ii: Bishop, *English Caroline minuscule*, 20, n. 1. For the date, see Dumville, *English Caroline script*, 55–6, n. 245; the characteristics of the hands of the original manuscript more closely resemble those of the late tenth and earlier eleventh centuries than that of English Caroline minuscule of the second half of the eleventh century. The later dates assigned by Colgrave and Mynors, *MLGB* and Thomson may have been influenced by the handwriting of the replacement leaves at the start of the volume.

London, British Library, MS Stowe 104, *s.* xii[ex.]
    Colgrave and Mynors, liii.

London, College of Arms, *sine numero* s. xii[2] (Chichester, secular cathedral)
    Colgrave and Mynors, liii; *MLGB*, 51.

Oxford, Bodleian Library, MS Bodley 163 (*SC* 2016), *s.* xi[in.] (fos 1, 6, 7 *s.* xii[med.]; fos 136–7, s. xi/xii) (Peterborough, Benedictine abbey, by *s.* xii)
    Colgrave and Mynors, li; Ker, *Catalogue of Anglo-Saxon manuscripts*, no. 304; *MLGB*, 151; Gneuss, *Handlist*, no. 555. The identification of the main hand as that of Cambridge, Pembroke College, MS 301 (T.A.M. Bishop, 'Notes on Cambridge manuscripts, part i', *Transactions of the Cambridge Bibliographical Society* i (1953), 432–41, at 441) has been challenged: D.N. Dumville, 'On the dating of some late Anglo-Saxon liturgical manuscripts', *Transactions of the Cambridge Bibliographical Society* x (1991), 40–57, at 41–2; idem, *English Caroline script*, 139–40, n. 116, and Rebecca Jane Rushforth, 'The eleventh- and early twelfth-century manuscripts of Bury St Edmunds abbey', unpubl. Ph.D. diss. Cambridge 2002, 169–70.

Oxford, Bodleian Library, MS Digby 211 (*SC* 1812), *s.* xii[4/4] (Waltham, Augustinian abbey)
    Colgrave and Mynors, lvi; Ker, *Catalogue of Anglo-Saxon manuscripts*, no. 321; *MLGB*, 193; Otto Pächt and J.J.G. Alexander, *Illuminated manuscripts in the Bodleian Library Oxford, 3. British, Irish, and Icelandic schools*, Oxford 1973, no. 308.

Oxford, Bodleian Library, MS Douce 368 (*SC* 21943), *s.* xii[2/4] (Winchcombe, Benedictine abbey)
    Colgrave and Mynors, lii; *MLGB*, 199; Pächt and Alexander, no. 104, pl. x.

Oxford, Bodleian Library, MS e Museo 115 (*SC* 3537), *s.* xii[ex.]
    Colgrave and Mynors, lviii; Pächt and Alexander, no. 252, pl. xxiv.

Oxford, Bodleian Library, MS Fairfax 12 (*SC* 3892), *s.* xii[med.] (Selby, Benedictine abbey)
    Colgrave and Mynors, liii; *MLGB*, 177; Pächt and Alexander, no. 73, pl. viii; Gullick, 'Origin and importance', 239.

Oxford, Bodleian Library, MS Hatton 43 (*SC* 4106), *s.* xi[in] (Christ Church, Canterbury, Benedictine cathedral priory, by *s.* xii[in])
    Colgrave and Mynors, xlii–xliii, lvii; Ker, *Catalogue of manuscripts containing Anglo-Saxon*, no. 326; Gneuss, *Handlist*, 630.

Oxford, Bodleian Library, MS Laud Misc. 243, *s.* xii[1]
    Colgrave and Mynors, liii; Ker, *Catalogue of manuscripts containing Anglo-Saxon*, no. 341.

Oxford, Balliol College, MS 176, *s*. xii[2]
: Colgrave and Mynors, li; R.A.B. Mynors, *Catalogue of the manuscripts of Balliol College, Oxford,* Oxford 1963, 180; J.J.G. Alexander and E. Temple, *Illuminated manuscripts in Oxford college libraries, the University archives and the Taylor Institution*, Oxford 1985, no. 114.[84]

Oxford, Lincoln College, MS lat. 31, *s*. xii[med.]
: Colgrave and Mynors, liv; Ker, *Catalogue of manuscripts containing Anglo-Saxon*, no. 356.

Oxford, Magdalen College, MS lat. 105, *s*. xii[2]
: Colgrave and Mynors, lvi; Ker, *Catalogue of manuscripts containing Anglo-Saxon*, no. 357; Alexander and Temple, no. 60, pl. v. The combination of flex punctuation and single-colour initials suggests a Cistercian origin.

Oxford, New College, MS 308, *s*. xii[2]
: Colgrave and Mynors, lii; Alexander and Temple, no. 106, pl. vi, where Cistercian ownership is suggested: an added early-thirteenth-century list of popes (fos 2v–3v) describes Pope Eugenius III as 'nostri ordinis'.[85]

Oxford, Pembroke College, MS 3, *s*. xii/xiii
: Colgrave and Mynors, lii; N.R. Ker, *Medieval manuscripts in British libraries, III. Lampeter–Oxford*, Oxford 1983, 674; Alexander and Temple, no. 152.

Oxford, St John's College, MS 99, *s*. xii[2] (Jervaulx, Cistercian abbey)
: Colgrave and Mynors, liv; Alexander and Temple, no. 48; Gullick, 'Origin and importance', 239.

Winchester Cathedral, MS 1 + London, British Library, MS Cotton Tiberius D. iv, vol. 2, fos 158–66, *s*. x/xi (Winchester, Benedictine cathedral priory, by *s*. xiv)
: Colgrave and Mynors, l–li; N.R. Ker and A. Piper, *Medieval manuscripts in British libraries, IV. Paisley-York*, Oxford 1992, 578–9; Ker, *Catalogue of manuscripts containing Anglo-Saxon*, no. 396; *MLGB*, 201; Gneuss, *Handlist*, no. 759.

---

[84] It was not possible to examine this manuscript due to library renovations.
[85] I am grateful to Dr James Willoughby for examining this manuscript for me.

PART II
Anglo-Saxon England in the Narrative of Britain

Chapter 5
Danish Ferocity and Abandoned Monasteries: The Twelfth-century View

Julia Barrow

When, in the second half of the twelfth century, the author of the opening section of the *Liber Eliensis* got to the passage where he needed to explain how what had been a flourishing nunnery in the time of Bede had become a community of secular clerics by the middle of the tenth century, he invoked the Danes as agents of change, and accused them of having burned the monastery and slaughtered all the nuns.[1] He had access to a brief comment about the burning of the monastery of Ely and the killing of its inmates in the *Libellus Æthelwoldi* of the early twelfth century,[2] but this was insufficiently detailed for his purposes, and so, to set the scene, he described the arrival of the Danes in terms borrowed from John of Worcester, Abbo of Fleury and the prophet Jeremiah. The following may serve as an example:

---

[1] *LE* 53–6 (bk i. 39–41): 'Mactatur, ut victima innocua, sanctimonialium caterva ... sicque monasterio quod vera Dei christicola Ædeldreda construxerat cum virginibus et ornamentis et reliquiis sanctorum sanctaruque combusto ... inimici Domini redierunt ad propria'. For translation, see *Liber Eliensis: a history of the Isle of Ely from the seventh century to the twelfth*, tr. J. Fairweather, Woodbridge 2005, 71–6; on the dating, see ibid. pp. xiii and xxii–xxiii: the work was completed after 1169 but perhaps before 1177.

[2] *LE* Appendix A (p. 396): 'Qui locus multum erat famosus, reliquiis et miraculis celeberrimus. Sed pagani seva invasione olim irruentes eundem locum igni cremandum dederant et, sanctimonialium caterva quamplurium ibi crudeliter necata omnibusque bonis undeunde sublatis, locum cum reliquiis, quasi quoddam exterminium, reliquentes abierunt'. For translation, see *Liber Eliensis*, tr. Fairweather, 487. On the dating of the *Libellus Æthelwoldi*, see S. Keynes, 'Ely abbey 672–1109', in P. Meadows and N. Ramsay (eds), *A history of Ely cathedral*, Woodbridge 2003, 3–58, at 7–8, and A. Kennedy, 'Law and litigation in the *Libellus Æthelwoldi episcopi*', *ASE* xxiv (1995), 131–83, at 132–3. The *Libellus* (largely copied into *Liber Eliensis* as cc. 1–49 of Book II, but also surviving on its own) was written in Latin by a monk of Ely under Bishop Hervey 1109–31, but was based on an Old English text, either a set of memoranda about land transactions or a more fully worked-out narrative, of about 990; however, Kennedy suggests that the opening four chapters were the work of the early-twelfth-century author/translator himself. See also *LE* p. xxxiv and Dorothy Whitelock's foreword to that volume, pp. ix–xviii.

All these men were persecutors of Christians, so cruel in their inborn ferocity that they did not know how to become gentle in the face of the miseries of mankind but, without any pity, they fed on people's agonies and, in accordance with the oracular statement of prophecy that 'all evil comes from the North', this same wicked race came leaping forward as the North Wind blows.[3]

Most of this passage just quoted was taken from Abbo's *Passion of St Edmund*, including the term 'ferocity' in connection with the northern peoples.[4]

The author of this part of the *Liber Eliensis* was only one of several twelfth-century English authors who felt moved to write descriptions of Viking destruction of monasteries in the ninth century. We find such accounts in William of Malmesbury's *Gesta pontificum*; in one of the Peterborough interpolations in the E-version of the Anglo-Saxon Chronicle, and, also at Peterborough, in Hugh Candidus' chronicle; in the Abingdon Chronicle; in the Whitby cartulary and in Symeon of Durham's *Libellus de exordio*.[5] Orderic Vitalis makes a brief reference to the Danes burning the churches of monks and clerics in his account of how the English church declined between the days of Bede and 1066.[6] This is by no means a comprehensive list, but it includes a work that circulated widely and was influential (*Gesta pontificum*) as well as ones whose audiences were essentially local, so it is reasonably representative. Symeon's *Libellus* forms a special case in this list, for reasons that will become clear in due course. Several twelfth-century historical works, however, say relatively little about Viking violence towards monasteries. The only account of Viking violence against monasteries in William of Malmesbury's *Gesta regum* is a sequence of quotations from Alcuin's letters mentioning the destruction of

---

[3] *LE* 53–5 (bk i. 39–40), here esp. c. 39 on p. 53: 'Hi omnes persecutores christianorum erant adeo crudeles naturali ferocitate ut nesciant malis hominum mitescere. Absque ulla miseratione pascuntur hominum cruciatibus et, iuxta prophetie vaticinium, quod ab aquilone venit omne malum, flante borea … gens eadem iniqua prosilivit'; for translation, see *Liber Eliensis*, tr. Fairweather, 71. The author of Book I also took care to include in his account of the life of St Æthelthryth a description drawn from Bede on how the monastery of Coldingham burned down not long after Æthelthryth had left it: ibid. 31 (i. 14); for Bede's account of Coldingham, see *HE* iv. 25.

[4] *Three Lives of English Saints*, ed. M. Winterbottom, Toronto 1972, 72; older edition in *Memorials of St Edmund's abbey*, ed. T. Arnold (RS [xcvi], 1890–96), i. 9 (Abbo, *Passio Sancti Eadmundi*, c. 5).

[5] Malmesbury, *GP*; *The Anglo-Saxon Chronicle MS. E*, ed. S. Irvine, Cambridge 2004 (hereafter ASC E), 48; *The chronicle of Hugh Candidus, a monk of Peterborough*, ed. W.T. Mellows, London 1949; *Historia ecclesie Abbendonensis: the history of the church of Abingdon*, ed. and tr. J. Hudson, Oxford 2002–7; *Cartularium abbathiae de Whiteby*, ed. J C. Atkinson (SS lxix, 1879); Symeon, *LdE*.

[6] OV ii. 240.

holy places, the despoliation of the church of St Cuthbert and the shedding of blood there.[7] Henry of Huntingdon, following a version of the Anglo-Saxon Chronicle that was close to E, turns the latter's account of the 793 attack on Lindisfarne into a statement that the churches in the 'province' (presumably diocese) of Lindisfarne were destroyed:

> Then there arrived the pagan people from Norway and Denmark, who first brought the Northumbrians to miserable ruin, and then on the Ides of January, in the province of Lindisfarne, they put Christ's churches to fearful destruction together with the inhabitants.[8]

Shortly after this, and again following a close relative of the E version of ASC, he narrates the sacking of *Donemuthe*: 'The pagans pillaged Northumbria, and despoiled Ecgfrith's monastery at *Donemuthe*'.[9] However, both these statements are very brief, and in the long and vivid passage about Danish savagery with which he opens Book V of his *History* he concentrates on the effects of the Vikings on the population in general, omitting any mention of monasteries. Similarly, he does not mention any attack on a monastery in the narrative of ninth-century events that follows.[10] John of Worcester also makes almost no reference to Viking violence to churches: strikingly, and although he was using the DE versions of the Anglo-Saxon Chronicle and often puts in Northumbrian annal material, he omits the accounts of the attacks on Lindisfarne and Jarrow. His only account of ninth-century Viking violence to churches is a passage copied from William's *Gesta pontificum* describing the Danish destruction of Hexham; he added this when he was enlarging his entry for 828, so that he could describe the later history of Hexham.[11]

It is easy to dismiss twelfth-century accounts of Viking violence to monasteries as worthless; indeed, most of them are worthless. However, as examples of views from their time, or, better still, as examples of a concerted effort in the twelfth century to build accounts of Danish destruction into a history of the monastic order in medieval England, they have some significance. They are also

---

[7] Malmesbury, *GR* i. 104–5 (bk i. 70).

[8] HH 256–7 (bk iv. 26); Henry places the event in the tenth year of Brihtric, king of Wessex, i.e. 793, where, as Greenway points out, the Ides of January is an error for 8 June. See ibid. pp. xci–xcii for discussion of the version of the ASC that he used; this was a version related to E, but not E itself, lacking E's Peterborough insertions but with the E annals down to 1133. On ASC E's entries for 793–94, which quote Northumbrian annals of the late eighth and early ninth centuries, see n. 19 below.

[9] HH 258–9 (bk iv. 27), dated to Brihtric's eleventh year, i.e. 794.

[10] HH 272–5 (bk v. pref.), general account of Danish savagery; 274–98 (bk v. 1–13), narrative of events to Alfred's death.

[11] JW *Chronicle*, ii. 248, s.a. 828; Malmesbury, *GP* i. 388 (bk iii. 117).

important because they have made such a contribution, all the stronger for not having been sufficiently analysed, to general understanding of the Viking attacks in the ninth century. This contribution has not only influenced popular writing in the Christopher Dawson tradition[12] but several more serious works.[13] An early attempt to get beyond this uncritical approach, Peter Sawyer's *The age of the Vikings*, which paid attention to when narratives were written, only made matters worse by condemning the ninth-century chroniclers out of hand for 'an easily recognisable bias against the Scandinavians', because 'they were written by churchmen'.[14] More recently research has tended to argue for survival, if with change, at many monastic sites; furthermore it is often possible to see bishops, or sometimes kings, taking over eighth- and ninth-century monastic sites, with consequent changes to their function.[15]

While twelfth-century accounts of Viking violence towards monasteries are often highly coloured, eighth- and ninth-century accounts in England are terse and very sparse. Indeed, the principal source, the A version of the Anglo-Saxon Chronicle, contains no records of Scandinavian destruction of English churches in the eighth, ninth or tenth centuries. Churches get mentioned in A in the eighth and ninth centuries only rarely, in the ninth century only when burials are

---

[12] C. Dawson, *Religion and the rise of Western culture*, London 1950, 99–103; see also R.H. Hodgkin, *A history of the Anglo-Saxons*, 3 edn, Oxford 1952, ii. 517–25, 608–17 and M. Deanesly, *The pre-Conquest Church in England*, 2 edn, London 1963, 244–75.

[13] See, for example, D. Knowles and R.N. Hadcock, *Medieval religious houses: England and Wales*, London 1971, 10–11, 463–87; C.P. Wormald, 'Viking studies: whence and whither?' in R.T. Farrell (ed.), *The Vikings*, London and Chichester 1982, 128–53, at 137–9 and idem, 'The ninth century', in J. Campbell (ed.), *The Anglo-Saxons*, Oxford 1982, 132–59, at 147–9; R. Fleming, 'Monastic lands and England's defence in the Viking Age', *EHR* c (1985), 247–65, at 247–9. Sarah Foot dismisses the twelfth-century accounts but still argues for cataclysm in 'Remembering, forgetting and inventing: attitudes to the past in England at the end of the first Viking age', *TRHS* 6 ser. ix (1999), 185–200. See also D.N. Dumville, *The churches of North Britain in the first Viking age*, Fifth Whithorn Lecture, Whithorn 1997, esp. 8–14: contemporary Irish sources make more frequent reference to Viking destruction of monasteries than do their Anglo-Saxon counterparts.

[14] P. Sawyer, *The age of the Vikings*, 2 edn, London 1971, 31, justly criticised by N. Brooks, 'England in the ninth century: the crucible of defeat', *TRHS* 5 ser. xxix (1979), 1–20, at 2–7, and by Wormald, 'Viking studies', 129–31.

[15] J. Blair, *The Church in Anglo-Saxon society*, Oxford 2005, 291–329; D.M. Hadley, *The Vikings in England: settlement, society and culture*, Manchester 2006, 192–36; J. Barrow, 'Survival and mutation: ecclesiastical institutions in the Danelaw in the ninth and tenth centuries', in D.M. Hadley and J.D. Richards (eds), *Cultures in contact: Scandinavian settlement in England in the ninth and tenth centuries*, Turnhout 2000, 155–76; F. Tinti, *Sustaining belief: the church of Worcester from c.870 to c.1100*, Farnham 2010, 165–211.

being recorded, and not often even then.¹⁶ In some cases, further details about burials are supplied by Æthelweard, but his chronicle also makes no mention of Viking violence to churches.¹⁷ Alfred the Great in his preface to the translation of Gregory the Great's *Pastoral care* provides a fleeting reference to the churches of England being full of treasures and books 'before everything was ransacked and burned'.¹⁸ The set of Northumbrian annals running down to 806 preserved within the DE versions of the Anglo-Saxon Chronicle and also in the twelfth-century Durham *Historia regum* records the classic accounts of the Viking raids on Lindisfarne and *Donaemuthan* (probably a monastery known as 'Ecgfrith's

---

¹⁶ *The Anglo-Saxon Chronicle, a collaborative edition*, 3: *MS. A*, ed. J.M. Bately, Cambridge 1986 (hereafter ASC A), makes specific references to churches and monastic life in the eighth and ninth centuries as follows: s.a. 718 (p. 34) mention of Cuthburh as foundress of Wimborne minster; s.a. 738 (p. 35) mention of how later Eadberht son of Eata king of Northumbria and his brother Archbishop Egbert of York were buried in the same chapel in the city of York; s.a. 874 (p. 49): mention of how Burgred king of Mercia was eventually buried in the church of St Mary in the *scola Anglorum* at Rome. ASC A refers to several ninth-century burials without naming churches as such: s.a. 716 (p. 33): Ceolred of Mercia at Lichfield, Ethelred son of Penda at Bardney; s.a. 755, for 757, looking ahead to 786 (p. 37): Cynewulf at Winchester, Cyneheard at Axminster; s.a. 755 for 757 (p. 37): Æthelbald of Mercia at Repton; s.a. 855 for 858 (p. 45): Æthelwulf at Winchester; s.a 860 (p. 46): Æthelbald at Sherborne and, likewise, Æthelbert (in fact d. 865); s.a. 867 (p. 47): burial of Bishop Ealhstan in the cemetery (*on tune*) of Sherborne; s.a. 871 (p. 48): burial of Alfred's brother Æthelred at Wimborne; s.a. 888 (p. 54): burial of Alfred's sister Æthelswith at Pavia. There are also some references to bishoprics, usually in the context of episcopal succession.

¹⁷ *Chronicon Æthelweardi*, ed. and tr. A. Campbell, London and Edinburgh 1962, iv. 1 (p. 35, burial of Æthelbert at Sherborne minster), iv. 2 (p. 36, burials of Bishop Ealhstan at Sherborne and of Ealdorman Eanwulf *in cenobio quod Glastingabyrig nuncupatur*, and of Edmund of East Anglia at *Beadeoricesuuyrthe*, i.e. Bury St Edmunds), iv. 2 (pp. 36–7, burial of Archbishop Ceolnoth at Canterbury), iv. 2 (p. 38, burial of Bishop Heahmund at Keynsham), iv. 2 (p. 39, burial of Æthelred in Wimborne minster), iv. 3 (p. 41, burial of Burgred *in templo Christi genetricis sanctae, quae nunc Anglorum scholae usitant nomen*), iv. 3 (p. 51, Guthfrid, king of the Northumbrians, in York minster: *Euoraca ... in urbe in basilica summa*, and Alfred in the city of Winchester).

¹⁸ *King Alfred's West-Saxon version of Gregory's Pastoral care*, ed. H. Sweet (Early English Text Society, original ser. xlv and l, 1871–72), i. 4–5 ('ærþæmþe hit eall forheregod wære & forbærned'); for the translation, see *Alfred the Great: Asser's Life of King Alfred and other contemporary sources*, tr. S. Keynes and M. Lapidge, Harmondsworth 1983, 125. By contrast, Asser sees plenty of continuity in monastic buildings (presumably in Wessex), but no interest in the monastic rule, either because of the attacks by foreigners, or because there was too much wealth: 'plurima adhuc monasteria in illa regione constructa permaneant, nullo tamen regulam illius vitae ordinabiliter tenente, nescio quare, aut pro alienigenarum infestationibus, qui saepissime terra marique hostiliter irrumpunt, aut etiam pro nimia illius gentis in omni genere divitiarum abundantia': *Asser's Life of King Alfred*, ed. W.H. Stevenson, rev. edn, Oxford 1959, 81 (c. 93); *Alfred the Great*, tr. Keynes and Lapidge, 103.

minster', next door to Jarrow) in the 790s,[19] for the former of which we possess supporting evidence in letters from Alcuin.[20] The Northumbrian annals clearly were interested in churches and Viking attacks on them; not so A, however. It recounts, very briefly, a series of attacks on towns and other settlements, for example London and Canterbury in 851, but, although presumably ecclesiastical establishments in these places were affected along with everything else, the authors of A felt no need to pick them out for special attention.[21]

A's lack of interest in what the Vikings could do to churches is wholly different from ninth-century continental annals, and also from the Irish and Northumbrian annals. In terse and unemotional language, the *Annals of St Bertin* quite often mention attacks on monasteries and other churches, for example in the years 859 (Saint-Valéry-sur-Somme), 861 (Saint-Vincent and Saint-Germain in Paris), 863 (Saint-Hilaire, Poitiers) and 865 (Fleury and the churches in Orléans).[22] The *Annals of Fulda* mention destruction of churches less often, but this was merely because eastern Francia was less affected; when it was, as in 881, the annalist provided a list of the sites attacked.[23] The *Annals of St Vaast* make frequent reference to the destruction of monasteries in the valley of the Scheldt and its environs between 879 and 892; they are written in

---

[19] *The Anglo-Saxon Chronicle, a collaborative edition*, 6: *MS. D*, ed. G.P. Cubbin, Cambridge 1996 (hereafter ASC D), 17; ASC E, 42; *HR* ii. 55–6; see also Rollason, this volume. The identification of *Donemuthan* has been disputed: W. Richardson, 'The Venerable Bede and a lost Saxon monastery in Yorkshire', *Yorkshire Archaeological Journal* lvii (1985), 15–22, followed by Rollason in *Libellus de exordio*, 90n, and in idem, *Northumbria, 500–1100: creation and destruction of a kingdom*, Cambridge 2003, 211, argues that it must have been a site on the river Don in southern Yorkshire, but more recently Ian Wood has argued for a site on the south of the Tyne, next to Jarrow: *The origins of Jarrow: the monastery, the Slake and Ecgfrith's minster* (Bede's World Studies i), Jarrow 2008, 18–20, and see idem, 'Bede's Jarrow', in C.A. Lees and G.R. Overing (eds), *A place to believe in: locating medieval landscapes*, University Park, PA 2006, 67–84, at 71–3; idem, 'The foundation of Bede's Wearmouth-Jarrow', in S. DeGregorio (ed.), *The Cambridge companion to Bede*, Cambridge 2010, 84–96, at 91–2; idem, 'The gifts of Wearmouth and Jarrow', in W. Davies and P. Fouracre (eds), *The languages of gift in the early middle ages*, Cambridge 2010, 89–115.

[20] *Alcuini sive Albini epistolae*, in, *Epistolae Karolini aevi* ii, ed. E. Dümmler (MGH Epistolae iv, 1895), 42–60, nos. 16–22.

[21] ASC A, s.a. 851 (p. 44); similarly, ASC A, s.a. 839 (*recte* 842; p. 43, slaughter in London and Rochester); ASC A, s.a. 867 (p. 47, slaughter of many Northumbrians in York). The attack on Winchester in 860 (ibid. 46) is entered in an addition made by a later hand, perhaps 'as late as *c.* 1000' (ibid. p. xxv).

[22] *Annales Bertiniani*, ed. G. Waitz (MGH Scriptores rerum Germanicarum v, 1883), 52, 54, 66, 75; *The Annals of St-Bertin*, tr. J.L. Nelson, Manchester 1991, 90, 94, 111, 122.

[23] *Annales Fuldenses, sive annales regni Francorum orientalis*, ed. F. Kurze (MGH Scriptores rerum Germanicarum vii, 1891), 97; *The Annals of Fulda*, tr. T. Reuter, Manchester 1992, 90.

a markedly less dispassionate tone than the *Annals of St Bertin*, with fire and the sword mentioned in the very first entry on Viking attacks.[24]

Before moving on to the twelfth-century English accounts we need to consider also those written in the tenth and eleventh centuries which in turn contributed imagery and details for later authors. Again, for England, there are few of these and some of those that exist contribute nothing to our purpose. Æthelwold's narrative of the refoundation of monasteries under Edgar tantalisingly has a gap where (if he had mentioned them) the Viking attacks could have been included.[25] It is tempting to think that he built a story about them into his explanation of how former monastic glories had withered (contemporary Continental sources were doing just this, for example a narrative in a tenth-century charter of Saint-Maixent)[26] but this can only be speculation. We have already noted that Æthelweard's *Chronicle* does include some material not in A concerning churches, but only on burials.[27]

Much more scope for future development was provided by Abbo of Fleury in his *Passio Sancti Eadmundi*, a work which is essentially unhistorical.[28] When

---

[24] *Annales Vedastini*, ed. G.H. Pertz (MGH Scriptores ii, 1829), 196–209, above all 197–206 (s.a. 879–92).

[25] *Councils and synods, with other documents relating to the English Church*, I: *871–1204*, ed. D. Whitelock, M. Brett and C.N.L. Brooke, Oxford 1981, i. 142–54; there is a gap in the text (p. 145) between the description of Augustine of Canterbury and that of King Edgar.

[26] A.T. Jones, 'Pitying the desolation of such a place: rebuilding religious houses and constructing memory in Aquitaine in the wake of the Viking incursions', *Viator* xxxvii (2006), 85–102, at 95 (Ademar of Chabannes developed the theme further a few decades later in the early eleventh century); for some Flemish parallels, see B. Meijns, 'Communautés de chanoines dépendant d'abbayes bénédictines pendant le haut Moyen Âge. L'exemple du comté de Flandre', *Revue bénédictine* cxiii (2003), 90–123, esp. 95; S. Vanderputten and B. Meijns, 'Gérard de Brogne en Flandre. État de la question sur les réformes monastiques du Xe siècle', *Revue du Nord* xcii (2010), 271–95.

[27] See above, n. 17.

[28] For a discussion of the literary qualities of Abbo's *Passio* and works derived from it, see esp. P. Cavill, 'Analogy and genre in the Legend of St Edmund', *Nottingham Medieval Studies* xlvii (2003), 21–45. D. Whitelock, 'Fact and fiction in the legend of St Edmund', *Proceedings of the Suffolk Institute of Archaeology* xxxi (1967–9), 217–33, at 218–22, underlined several of the fictional elements, but nevertheless was prepared to see some factual basis, for example Abbo's statement that Dunstan had, when young, heard the story from an aged man who claimed to have been Edmund's armour-bearer. On Abbo's approach to his work, see also A. Gransden, 'The legends and traditions concerning the origins of the abbey of Bury St Edmunds', *EHR* c (1985), 1–24, at 4–8, with comment on some of Abbo's possible hagiographical models on 6–8; S.J. Ridyard, *The royal saints of Anglo-Saxon England: a study of West Saxon and East Anglian cults*, Cambridge 1988, 212–14 on Abbo's general approach and 218–20 on a likely East Anglian *villa regalis* occurring in his account; P. Cavill, *Vikings: fear and faith*, Grand Rapids, MI 2001, 174–8; C. Phelpstead, 'King, martyr and virgin:

he wrote this, Abbo had been invited to teach at Ramsey Abbey by its founder, Archbishop Oswald of York. His period in England, 985–7, gave him the opportunity to meet Archbishop Dunstan of Canterbury, from whom he heard accounts of Edmund's death;[29] the story of an English king killed by Vikings had added relevance in the 980s, since from 980 onwards England was once more threatened by Scandinavian raids. Growing up as an oblate at Fleury, Abbo would early on have become familiar with an exciting narrative about Scandinavian raids on churches in the Loire valley: chapters 33–34 of Book I of the *Miracles of St Benedict*, written in the 860s by a monk of Fleury called Adrevaldus.[30] Adrevaldus' account of Viking mayhem supplied Abbo with a ready-made set of images of heathen northerners and the language in which to write about them. In the *Passio* he says that the Devil, seeking to put Edmund of East Anglia to the test, sends Inguar to him. Inguar and his partner Hubba belonged to the northern races that were so cruel in their inborn ferocity that they did not know how to become gentle in the face of the miseries of mankind.[31] Some of them were cannibals. The Danes were the northern people most involved in piracy on Christian territories because they lived nearest to them. Inguar and Hubba attacked Northumbria and then East Anglia with a mighty fleet, falling on 'a certain city' and burning it up. They killed the men in the open streets, sparing neither boys nor the elderly, and raped the women, sparing neither virgins nor matrons. Dying husbands lay sprawled over thresholds with their wives, and babies were snatched from their mothers' breasts and killed. It is a lively picture,

---

Imitatio Christi in Ælfric's *Life of St Edmund'*, in A. Bale (ed.), *St Edmund, king and martyr: changing images of a medieval saint*, Woodbridge 2009, 27–44, at 30–33.

[29] M. Mostert, *The political theology of Abbo of Fleury*, Hilversum 1987, 40–45; E. Dachowski, *First amongst abbots: the career of Abbo of Fleury*, Washington, DC 2008, 74–5.

[30] *Les Miracles de Saint Benoît écrits par Adrevald, Aimoin, André, Raoul Tortaire et Hugues de Sainte Marie, moines de Fleury*, ed. E. de Certain, Paris 1858, 71–6. On the *De miraculis*, see A. Vidier, *L'Historiographie à Saint-Benoît-sur-Loire et les miracles de Saint-Benoît*, Paris 1965, esp. 151–64 on Adrevaldus' section (Book I), and also D.W. Rollason, 'The Miracles of St Benedict: a window on early medieval France', in H. Mayr-Harting and R.I. Moore (eds), *Studies in medieval history presented to R.H.C. Davis*, London 1985, 73–90, esp. 76–82 on Book I. The possible models for Abbo's *Passio* noted by Gransden, 'The legends and traditions', 6–8, include several Frankish saints' lives but not Adrevaldus' *De miraculis*.

[31] Abbo seems to have been the earliest author to mention Hubba, though Inguar (Ívarr 'the Boneless') is mentioned by Asser in 878: Asser, *Life of King Alfred*, ed. Stevenson, 43 (c. 54). Byrhtferth in his *Vita Oswaldi* (*c.*1000); the *Annals of St Neots* pair Inguar and Hubba together, presumably following Abbo. For comment on Inguar and Hubba (Ubbe), see *Alfred the Great*, Keynes and Lapidge, 238–9; C. Downham, *Viking kings of Britain and Ireland: the dynasty of Ívarr to A.D. 1014*, Edinburgh 2007, 64–8; Byrhtferth of Ramsey, *The Lives of St Oswald and St Ecgwine*, ed. and tr. M. Lapidge, Oxford 2009, 16–17, n. 52. See also Bartlett in this volume.

though admittedly all made up of *topoi*, largely drawn from Adrevaldus.[32] However, Abbo doesn't mention Viking destruction of monasteries in the *Passio*, presumably to avoid setting up a rival object of sympathy to his hero Edmund. Nevertheless his imagery was useful to twelfth-century authors wanting to write about what the Danes could do to religious houses, as we shall see.

The *Historia de sancto Cuthberto*, which, following Ted Johnson South, we can place somewhere in the middle of the eleventh century,[33] omits the Viking raid on Lindisfarne in 793 altogether.[34] Here it is the capture of York in 866, followed by the defeat of the Northumbrians in 867, which provides the starting point for the narrative of Viking violence; York was of interest to the community of St Cuthbert because it owned property in the city.[35] King Ælle of Northumbria stole four vills from St Cuthbert and was duly punished when Ubba, duke of the Frisians, captured York and killed him, bringing the Northumbrian line of kings to an end. 'The Scaldings slew nearly all the English in the southern and the northern part, demolished and despoiled the churches'.[36] Later (*Historia de sancto Cuthberto* puts the election of Guthfrith as king and Alfred's vision of Cuthbert in first), Bishop Eardwulf and Abbot Eadred carried the body of Cuthbert away from Lindisfarne and wandered for seven years,[37] but the community continued to acquire lands (partly from Guthfrith and his Danish army) until the time of Ragnald ('the pagan king'), who divided its estates between his followers Scula and Onlafball.[38]

We can now turn to the twelfth-century narratives. The Durham material, because it is preserved in an almost continuous sequence of texts over a long

---

[32] See c. 33 of Adrevaldus' *De miraculis Sancti Benedicti* (*Les Miracles*, ed. de Certain, 71–5). This section of Adrevaldus, recounting Viking raids in the Loire valley, was copied with a few tiny alterations by William of Jumièges: *The Gesta Normannorum ducum of William of Jumièges, Orderic Vitalis and Robert of Torigni*, ed. E. van Houts, Oxford 1992–95, i. 20–22, bk i. 6(7)–7(8).

[33] *Historia de sancto Cuthberto: a history of Saint Cuthbert and a record of his patrimony*, ed. and tr. T. Johnson South, Woodbridge 2002, 25–36.

[34] W.M. Aird, *St Cuthbert and the Normans: the church of Durham, 1071–1153*, Woodbridge 1998, 24, notes this omission and points out that the *Historia de sancto Cuthberto* describes a translation of Cuthbert's relics to Norham under Bishop Ecgred (830–45) without mentioning a reason for this (*HsC*, c. 9).

[35] *HsC*, c. 10. For the property in York, see ibid. c. 5, and Domesday Book i, fo. 298a; *Domesday Book*, 30: *Yorkshire*, ed. M.L. Faull and M. Stinson, Chichester 1986, C 2.

[36] *HsC*, cc. 10, 11.

[37] *HsC*, c. 20; for Guthfrith's election, see ibid. c. 13, and for Alfred's vision, immediately before his victory over the Danes at *Assandune*, in error for Edington in 878, ibid. c. 16. See also D.W. Rollason, 'The wanderings of St Cuthbert', in idem (ed.), *Cuthbert: saint and patron*, Durham 1987, 47–59.

[38] *HsC*, cc. 22–3. On Ragnald, king of York from a point before 919 until his death in 920/1, see Symeon, *LdE* p. 130, n. 91; see also Rollason, 'The wanderings of St Cuthbert', 55.

period, is distinctive, and makes a convenient starting point. In looking back to the dawn of the Viking age, Symeon in his *Libellus*, written between 1104 and 1115,[39] could use the Northumbrian annals of the eighth and early ninth centuries. His version of the attack on Lindisfarne is slightly more elaborate than theirs: he adds that the raiders overthrew Lindisfarne's altars, seized its treasures, took some monks prisoner, cast out others naked and drowned others. The *Historia regum* is close to Symeon here but adds a quotation from one of the verses in Boethius' *Consolation of philosophy*, including a passage about evildoers trampling underfoot holy necks. However, as Symeon adds, although the church of Lindisfarne had been laid waste, it survived with its see; a handful of monks who had escaped were able to return and remained there with the body of St Cuthbert for a long time yet to come.[40]

Symeon, describing the Viking capture of York (which he dates to 1 November 867), expands on earlier sources to add that 'the heathen army ... destroyed monasteries and churches far and wide with sword and fire, and when they departed they left nothing except roofless walls, to such an extent that the present generation can recognise hardly any sign – sometimes none at all – of the ancient nobility of these places'.[41] The churches are not named, but Symeon presumably meant ones in southern Northumbria, because he says that the invaders did not go north of the Tyne at this point. However, the account lacks corroborative detail; instead, it falls back on conventional remarks about the destruction of war, including, as we have seen, the reference to fire and the sword. When Halfdan did reach the Tyne a few years later, Bishop Eardwulf left Lindisfarne with the body of St Cuthbert.[42] While the community moved around northern England in flight there was a savage slaughter of the population of Northumbria. Halfdan and his army burned monasteries and churches everywhere and killed monks and nuns after subjecting them to mockeries.[43] By contrast, the *Historia regum*, in both its ninth-century sections, misses out these accounts of monastic destruction, though it does mention the slaughter of the Northumbrians and the departure of the community of St Cuthbert from Lindisfarne.[44]

Symeon's *Libellus* thus contains a mixture of historical account, oral tradition and twelfth-century verbal padding added for excitement. Our next author is rather more circumspect. William of Malmesbury was perhaps the only twelfth-century English historian to think seriously about which monasteries actually had been attacked by the Danes across the country as a whole; he did this in

---

[39] Symeon, *LdE* p. xlii.
[40] Ibid. 88–91 (bk ii. 5); *HR* ii. 54–6.
[41] Symeon, *LdE* 96–7 (bk ii. 6).
[42] Ibid. 100–101 (bk ii. 6).
[43] Ibid. 104–5 (bk ii. 6).
[44] *HR* ii. 82, 110, 105–6, 114–15.

Gesta pontificum, the first recension of which he completed in 1125.[45] William's own abbey had remained unscathed by Danish attacks, a piece of good fortune that he attributes to Aldhelm's sanctity.[46] Elsewhere in the *Gesta pontificum* he comments on the effects of the Vikings as follows. At Chertsey the Danes had 'destroyed the place like so much else, burning the church, abbot, monks and all'.[47] Barking, however, 'was never entirely destroyed' because of the prayers of its nuns.[48] The East Anglian see of Soham had been burned and razed to the ground.[49] At Abingdon the Danes had ranged around 'with barbaric petulance' and had razed the buildings to the ground'.[50] Glastonbury had survived until Alfred's reign; then the Danes had arrived and had left it desolate, lacking inmates for some years.[51] In the north of England, 'as for the monasteries that had shone like stars throughout the province, they had been destroyed long before this, in the time of the Danes. A few walls still stand in ruins, no pleasure to the eye, but a reminder of past sorrows'. William went on to mention Wearmouth and Whitby ('*Streneshalh* .. quod nunc Witebi dictum'), as examples, but added that many more of the northern houses were now unknown.[52] At Hexham, 'the Danish army, which had already been an object of fear in the days of Alcuin, finally arrived; they killed or drove out the inhabitants, set fire to their houses, and laid their secret places open to the sky'.[53] William uses this account as an explanation for why there were no bishops at Hexham after Tidferth. For what the Danes did at Lindisfarne William could quote Alcuin's letters.[54] At Gloucester (here

---

[45] Malmesbury, *GP* ii. pp. xix–xxv.

[46] Malmesbury, *GP* i. 610–13 (bk v. 256) recounts how the Danes came to Malmesbury in the reign of Æthelred and how one of them tried to loot precious stones from Aldhelm's shrine, but was repulsed by the saint: 'so it came about that, while all the neighbouring monasteries were robbed and plundered, this one alone never had too serious a calamity to bewail' (ibid. 613).

[47] Malmesbury, *GP* i. 228–9 (bk ii. 73).

[48] Ibid.

[49] Malmesbury, *GP* i. 242–3 (bk ii. 74). There is also a brief reference to Ely being burned and the nuns there being put to flight, though William has more to say on Ely later, on which see n. 56 below.

[50] Malmesbury, *GP* i. 300–301 (bk ii. 88).

[51] Ibid. i. 308–9 (bk ii. 91).

[52] Ibid. i. 386–7 (bk iii. 116). On the debate over the identification of *Streneshalh* (Bede's *Streanæshalch*) with Whitby, see T. Styles, 'Whitby revisited: Bede's explanation of *Streanæshalch*', *Nomina* xxi (1998), 133–48; P. Barnwell, L.A.S. Butler and C.J. Dunn, 'Streanaeshalch, Strensall and Whitby: locating a pivotal council', in M.O.H. Carver (ed.), *The cross goes north: processes of conversion in northern Europe, AD 300–1300*, Woodbridge 2003, 311–26; C. Hough, 'Strensall, *Streanæshalch* and Stronsay', *The English Place-name Society Journal* xxxv (2003), 17–24. Overall, Whitby is the most likely identification.

[53] Malmesbury, *GP* i. 388–9 (bk iii. 117).

[54] Ibid. i. 406–9 (bk iii. 127–8); see also Malmesbury, *GR* i. 104 (bk i. 70).

William conflated the old monastery of St Peter's with the new foundation of Æthelred and Æthelflæd) 'the house flourished till the time of the Danes … but the monks melted away in the face of the enemy'.[55] William found slightly more to say about Ely: the abbesses Æthelthryth, Seaxburh and Eormenhild

> had in the following period many to imitate their rule and their piety, right up to the time of the Danes, who forced their way into the Fens, put the women to flight, and destroyed their buildings. One, whose brutal heart inspired him with madness, snatched away the precious cloth that covered the tomb of the virgin Æthelthryth, and struck the marble with his axe. The surface of the stone broke apart under the blow, and the fragment, ricocheting off the ground, flew straight into the blasphemer's eye, so that he fell senseless to the floor.[56]

William includes rhetorical flourishes and – as in Ely – miracle stories, but he does not say that Danish destruction was global. It is noticeable, for example, that he says nothing about the history of *Medeshamstede* (Peterborough) before Æthelwold's foundation in the later tenth century.[57] He also tends to say that monks and nuns fled when the Danes arrived rather than that they were massacred.

In 1121 or just after, slightly earlier than William's *Gesta pontificum*, an anonymous historian at Peterborough was copying out the E version of the Anglo-Saxon Chronicle and inserting materials concerning his abbey. For the year 870, after the account of the Danes defeating and killing King Edmund of East Anglia, the E interpolator added 'and they destroyed all the monasteries they came to. In this same time they came to *Medeshamstede*, burned and destroyed it, killed the abbot and monks and all they found there, and brought it to pass that it became nought that had been very mighty'.[58] Some monasteries in the Fens found that they could use the martyrdom of King Edmund as a peg on which to hang stories about their own past; the stories they wanted to tell were ones of destruction that would explain why their monastery had had to be refounded in the reign of Edgar.

---

[55] Malmesbury, *GP* i. 446–7 (bk iv. 155). Æthelred and Æthelflæd's foundation was also dedicated to St Peter, hence perhaps the confusion; later the dedication was changed to St Oswald: see M. Hare, 'The documentary evidence', in C. Heighway and R. Bryant (eds), *The Golden Minster: the Anglo-Saxon minster and later medieval priory of St Oswald at Gloucester* (Council for British Archaeology Research Report cxvii, 1999), 33–45, at 35–7; Hare, 39, thinks William was attributing Danish destruction to the reign of Cnut, but that 'William was inclined to ascribe all manner of ills to the Danes and it is perhaps best to regard his invocation of "the time of the Danes" as a topos'.

[56] Malmesbury, *GP* i. 488–9 (bk iv. 183).
[57] Ibid. i. 480–83 (bk iv. 180).
[58] ASC E, s.a. 870 (p. 48).

Hugh Candidus, when writing his Peterborough Chronicle probably between 1155 and 1175,[59] based his account of what he thought had happened at Peterborough in the late ninth century on the *Passio Sancti Eadmundi*. Thus we find the killing of young and old and the dishonouring of matronly and virginal respectability and plenty of burning.[60] In addition, however, Hugh says monasteries with their male and female inmates were burned, first in Northumbria and then throughout all England. Then Inguar and Hubba reached East Anglia and martyred Edmund, and 'in that stormy time even that most renowned monastery of Medeshamstede with its monks was burned by fire just like the rest'.[61] Hugh at that point breaks off to criticise those who interpret adversities as punishment for sin. Rather, God allows the elect to undergo testing, as in the case of Job, and also in the case of St Benedict's own monastery.[62] After the servants of God had been martyred their monasteries remained deserted and in ruins for many years. Some of them were subsequently restored but many remained abandoned, with merely fragments of their walls showing how they had been laid out.[63]

Book I of *Liber Eliensis*, written at about the same time (it was completed just after 1169), is textually even closer to Abbo's *Passio*, with more verbatim borrowings, though with large slabs of John of Worcester's *Chronicle* as well. Here too we have Inguar and Hubba, the cruel people from the chilly north and the cannibalism. The admixture of John of Worcester allowed better chronology and more interest in events in Northumbria and Mercia. Neither Abbo nor John talked about the destruction of English monasteries in the later ninth century and so the author of the *Liber Eliensis* provided his own comment to the effect that resting-places of the saints and monasteries had been burned.[64] Then the Danes got to Ely, crossing to it easily by boat; they invaded the nunnery, stretched their swords over the milk-white necks of the nuns and sacrificed them (presumably by beheading) like innocent victims. The nunnery was burned with its virgins, its ornaments and its relics and the city was sacked and burned.[65] After this the author recounts how one of the Danes rashly tried to break into St Æthelthryth's tomb with his axe, but lost his eyes in the process.[66] The hint of decapitation in this story may reflect the beheading of St Edmund in Abbo's *Passio*, but headlessness was quite a common feature of Anglo-Saxon

---

[59] Ibid. p. xci.
[60] *Chronicle of Hugh Candidus*, 23.
[61] Ibid. 24.
[62] Ibid. 24–6.
[63] Ibid. 27.
[64] *LE* 53–4 (bk i. 39).
[65] Ibid. 54–5 (bk i. 40).
[66] Ibid. 55–6 (bk i. 41); see also n. 56 above.

saints' cults and there may be several possible sources here.[67] It is worth noting that at about this time, between 1163 and 1177, William de Vere, then a canon at the Augustinian priory of St Osyth's at Chich in Essex,[68] was writing a *Life* of the seventh-century St Osyth, supposedly a granddaughter of Penda, in which he made the 'pirates' Inguar and Hubba behead her for refusing to worship idols, and despoil her nunnery. Here, too, a variety of stock elements is visible.[69]

In the early 1160s the Abingdon Chronicle referred generally to the destruction of monasteries;[70] in a later version composed between the end of the twelfth and the mid-thirteenth centuries the chronicle describes the Danes moving 'from kingdom to kingdom and from people to people', finally reaching Wessex and the house of Abingdon:

---

[67] For Abbo, see *Three Lives of English saints*, ed. Winterbottom, 79 and 81; for Oswald of Northumbria, see A. Thacker, '*Membra disjecta*: the division of the body and the diffusion of the cult', in C. Stancliffe and E. Cambridge (eds), *Oswald: Northumbrian king to European saint*, Stamford 1995, 97–127; for Kenelm, see *Three eleventh-century Anglo-Latin saints' Lives*: Vita S. Birini, Vita et miracula S. Kenelmi *and* Vita S. Rumwoldi, ed. R.C. Love, Oxford 1996, 49–89, at 61; for Ethelbert of East Anglia, see M.R. James, 'Two Lives of St Ethelbert, king and martyr', *EHR* xxxii (1917), 214–44; for Osyth, see n. 69 below. See also Catherine Cubitt's comments on local and oral traditions in saints' cults in her article 'Universal and local saints in Anglo-Saxon England', in A. Thacker and R. Sharpe (eds), *Local saints and local churches in the early medieval West*, Oxford 2002, 423–53.

[68] For William's career, see J. Barrow, 'A twelfth-century bishop and literary patron: William de Vere', *Viator* xviii (1987), 175–89; *English episcopal acta*, vii: *Hereford 1079–1234*, ed. J. Barrow, Oxford 1993, pp. xliii–xlv and nos. 178–242; eadem, 'Vere, William de', in *ODNB*, http://www.oxforddnb.com/view/article/95042 (consulted 1 September 2011).

[69] William's *Life* is now lost, but notes of its contents were made by Leland: *Leland's Itineraries*, ed. L. Toulmin Smith, Oxford 1906–10, v. 167–72. Lessons for the feast of St Osyth are to be found in the Hereford Breviary: *Hereford Breviary*, ed. W.H. Frere and L.E.G. Brown, (HBS xxvi, xl, xlvi, 1904–15), ii. 361–4. On the cult of St Osyth, see C. Hohler, 'St Osyth and Aylesbury', *Records of Buckinghamshire* xviii (1966), 61–72. The Anglo-Norman *Life* of St Osyth has been edited twice: A.T. Baker, 'An Anglo-French Life of St Osith', *The Modern Language Review* vi (1911), 476–502; *La Vie seinte Osith, virge e martire*, ed. D.W. Russell, tr. Jane Dick Zatta, rev. and annotated by Jocelyn Wogan-Browne, *Papers on Language and Literature* xli (2005), 339–444, and see also, ibid. J. Wogan-Browne, 'The Life of St Osith: an introduction', 300–305, and J. Dick Zatta, 'The *Vie Seinte Osith*: hagiography and politics in Anglo-Norman England', 306–38. Curiously, Zatta and Wogan-Browne overlook the possibility that the Anglo-Norman *Life* was commissioned by Bishop William de Vere at Hereford, which is the likely explanation for the inclusion of the miracle of the crippled woman of Hereford; if so, it could have been largely based on William's own Latin *Life* (now lost, but probably written while William was a canon at Chich), but with a few additions. Hereford was an important centre for Anglo-Norman literature in the later twelfth century: Simon de Freine was a canon there and Hue de Rotelande lived near by at Credenhill.

[70] *Historia ecclesie Abbendonensis*, i. 28 (c. 14); for the dating, see ii. p. xvii.

> Finally, they entirely drove out the monks and destroyed with hostile hand, leonine ferocity, and detestable greed the sacrosanct and venerable house of Abingdon ... so that nothing is reported to have remained there besides the walls. However, it was divinely provided that the relics of saints with the charters of the house ... were secretly preserved.

The Danes (still pagan) occupied the monastery and one day, when they 'were sitting like monks in the refectory and were behaving themselves in all respects in a manner both scurrilous and disorderly' a miracle occurred; the figure of Christ on a crucifix, shocked by their gluttony, tore stones out of the wall and stoned them so that they fled.[71]

At Whitby, a short narrative of the post-Conquest refoundation was composed before 1180, and about six decades later it was copied into the abbey cartulary, whose earliest sections were written *c.*1240. This recounted how the 'very energetic' knight Reinfrid, when passing through Northumbria, came to *Streoneshalc*:

> When he learned that the holy place together with the province of Northumbria had been laid to waste, in a ferocious devastation (*depopulatio*) by the most cruel pirates Inguar and Ubba, leaders of the Alans and the Danes, and that thereafter the religious service of monks and nuns had ceased in that place for more than two hundred years, he was struck with compunction in his heart.[72]

It is now time to pull some threads together. Devastated monasteries and fleeing, or slaughtered, religious tend not to feature in historical works about kings, or written for kings. This may well be the reason why the A version of the Anglo-Saxon Chronicle omits all accounts of devastated monasteries in the late eighth and the ninth centuries;[73] it would also explain why such stories are largely omitted by William of Malmesbury from his *Gesta regum* and by Henry of Huntingdon from his *Historia Anglorum*. Presumably destroyed

---

[71] Ibid. i. 268–71; for dating of this recension (MS 'B', BL Cotton Claudius B. vi), see ibid. ii. p. xxxvii (s. xiii$^{2/4}$ or s. xiii^{med}).

[72] *Cartularium abbathiae de Whiteby*, 1; note also the description (ibid. 2) of walls and uncovered altars of almost forty oratories on the site. I have followed Atkinson (ibid. p. xxxii) on the dating of the narrative; for the dating of the cartulary, see G.R.C. Davis, *Medieval cartularies of Great Britain and Ireland*, rev. edn by C. Breay, J. Harrison and D.M. Smith, London 2010, 209.

[73] On Alfred's role in the commissioning and choice of material for the earliest version of the Anglo-Saxon Chronicle, see A. Scharer, 'The writing of history at King Alfred's court', *Early Medieval Europe* v (1996), 177–206, esp. 178–85; on probable royal involvement in several later sections of various versions of the chronicle, see N.P. Brooks, 'Why is the *Anglo-Saxon Chronicle* about kings?', *ASE* xxxix (2010), 43–70.

monasteries did not figure prominently in the list of suitable topics for royal audiences. Ecclesiastical audiences, however, wished to hear accounts of what the Vikings had done, or could be claimed to have done, to churches in general and their own community in particular. There were several reasons why claiming a violent break in ecclesiastical continuity in the ninth century was appealing: it might serve as an explanation for changes in monastic observance, or more especially for changes from monastic to clerical observance, and it could also show why monasteries had lost property, books and relics that they might now be trying to reclaim. Elsewhere in Europe, indeed, it was not uncommon for monastic historians of the tenth to the twelfth centuries to attribute the cessation of regular life in their houses, especially the replacement of monks or nuns by clergy, to damage caused by Vikings in the ninth century, or by the Hungarians at the turn of the ninth and tenth centuries;[74] in several instances, even though houses actually had been attacked, later accounts exaggerated the impact of the invaders, in particular their effect on the internal organisation of the communities they attacked.[75]

Twelfth-century English authors, too, often felt that Vikings could be used appropriately to mark a turning-point between what they saw as mid-Anglo-Saxon monastic fervour and early-tenth-century monastic decay, and in this line of thinking they may have received some of their inspiration from French historians. At least one Continental work containing a vivid account of Viking destruction, William of Jumièges' *Gesta Normannorum*, was widely circulated in England.[76] William of Malmesbury knew a large number of continental historical works.[77] However, unlike their French counterparts, who did often possess ninth-century accounts of Viking attacks on churches, English historians were faced with a shortage of material. Apart from Durham, whose monks could make use of early Northumbrian annals, their own community's summary accounts of property

---

[74] For examples of Viking attacks marking a caesura in the history of Norman abbeys in accounts by eleventh- and twelfth-century historians, see, for example, OV ii. 8–9, 14–17; *GND* i. 24–7.

[75] J. Nightingale, *Monasteries and patrons in the Gorze reform: Lotharingia, c.850–1000*, Oxford 2001, 66–7, 174–84; Jones, 'Pitying the desolation of such a place'. Vikings were also used by eleventh- and twelfth-century authors to explain the movement of relics in the ninth and tenth centuries: see F. Lifshitz, 'The migration of Neustrian relics in the Viking age: the myth of voluntary exodus, the reality of coercion and theft', *Early Medieval Europe* iv (1995), 175–92.

[76] William of Jumièges' copy of part of Adrevaldus was fairly well known in twelfth- and thirteenth-century England: *GND* i. pp. xcv–cxix on the surviving manuscripts, many of which are of English origin and provenance. Even so, twelfth-century monastic historians in eastern England seem to have preferred Abbo's *Passio Sancti Edmundi*, since it provided an East Anglian context for events.

[77] R.M. Thomson, *William of Malmesbury*, 2 edn, Woodbridge 2003, 67–9.

transactions and the eleventh-century *Historia de sancto Cuthberto*, English monastic communities were starved of sources about the ninth century. They could use the Anglo-Saxon Chronicle, or (more readily) works derived from it, such as John of Worcester's *Chronicle* and its dependent compilations, and they could draw on Abbo's *Passio Sancti Eadmundi* for colourful martyrdom imagery. Some had access to the accounts of the destruction of Lindisfarne preserved in the DE versions of the Anglo-Saxon Chronicle, more fully elaborated by William of Malmesbury and by the Durham historians. But all in all there was little to go on. Abbo's *Passio* was very widely used, as we see from the frequent occurrences of Inguar and Hubba in our stories. The 793 attack on Lindisfarne may have supplied the main mental image of destruction and of the slaughter of monks, but perhaps equally potent images were supplied by some Anglo-Saxon saints' *Lives*, or even by stories of early Christian martyrs. Bede's narrative of the late-seventh-century burning of the monastery of Coldingham in the *Historia ecclesiastica* seems to have had a particular appeal: the story of how Æthelthryth had taken the veil at Coldingham and how it had burned down shortly after she had left is retold with enthusiasm in the *Liber Eliensis*.[78] The burning of Coldingham may also have influenced the author of the *Libellus Æthelwoldi* and Hugh Candidus in their accounts of ninth-century destruction. Indeed, in the thirteenth century Roger of Wendover was to turn Bede's Coldingham story into a gripping account of a Viking attack on defenceless nuns, who managed to protect themselves from rape by cutting off their noses and lips, but who could not protect themselves from fire.[79] Overall, a very limited repertoire of narrative elements was reshuffled again and again to produce stories that answered what seems to have been a desire for excitement combined with a need for validation. Ecclesiastical communities, especially, but not only, Benedictine ones, may have felt that ninth-century fire and the sword, preferably inflicted by Inguar and Hubba, would help to justify their subsequent refoundation and thus their continuing existence.

---

[78] *LE* 31 (bk i. 14); *Liber Eliensis*, tr. Fairweather, 40–41.
[79] Matthew Paris, *Chronica majora*, ed. H.R. Luard (RS [lvii], 1872–83), i. 391–2.

Chapter 6

Symeon of Durham's *Historia de Regibus Anglorum et Dacorum* as a Product of Twelfth-century Historical Workshops*

David Rollason

This chapter is offered by way of some reflections on one aspect of the research agenda of this volume, but also by way of a report on a new edition and translation of Symeon of Durham, *Historia de regibus Anglorum et Dacorum*, which is being undertaken by Michael Lapidge and the present author, to be published by the Clarendon Press in the series Oxford Medieval Texts.[1] This text, which is currently available in full only in Thomas Arnold's now-antiquated and much criticised edition in the Rolls Series,[2] is a complex and composite one, as Peter Hunter Blair made abundantly clear,[3] and the new edition needs to reflect that, and to make it transparent to a reader what the various layers and attributions within it are. Michael Lapidge has demonstrated that the first part of the *Historia de regibus Anglorum et Dacorum* represents a compilation, containing some of his own work, of the early-eleventh-century English scholar Byrhtferth of Ramsey,[4] and the editors consequently intend to present it as such, within Symeon's more extended compilation. The title which Byrhtferth's compilation originally had is unknown. Lapidge favoured originally the neutral 'Historical compilation', although he has

---

* I am grateful to Pauline Stafford, Michael Lapidge and Lynda Rollason for commenting on earlier drafts of this paper.

[1] The title, *Historia de regibus Anglorum et Dacorum*, is taken from the contemporary rubric on fo. 51v of the only extant manuscript, CCCC, MS 139 (later twelfth century), and will be used in place of Arnold's long-accepted title, *Historia regum*, which was invented in the early-modern period.

[2] *Symeonis monachi opera omnia*, ed. T. Arnold (RS [lxxv], 1882–85), ii. 3–283.

[3] P.H. Blair, 'Some observations on the *Historia regum* attributed to Symeon of Durham', in N.K. Chadwick (ed.), *Celt and Saxon: studies in the early British border*, Cambridge 1963, 63–118, repr. in P.H. Blair, *Anglo-Saxon Northumbria*, ed. M. Lapidge and Pauline Hunter Blair, London 1984, no. ix.

[4] M. Lapidge, 'Byrhtferth of Ramsey and the early sections of the *Historia regum* attributed to Symeon of Durham', *ASE* x (1981), 97–122, repr. in M. Lapidge, *Anglo-Latin literature, 900–1066*, London and Rio Grande 1993, 317–42.

since wondered whether *Historia regum* might have been Byrhtferth's original title, and that is what will be used in the new edition.[5]

It is intended to include alongside the new edition and translation of Symeon's *Historia de regibus Anglorum et Dacorum* the work which was clearly regarded as the continuation to it, that is John of Hexham, *Historia .xxv. annorum*,[6] along with the anonymous *De obsessione Dunelmi et de probitate Uhtredi comitis, et de comitibus qui ei successerunt*, because it was associated with Symeon's work in the later twelfth century, and the only extant copy of it precedes the *Historia de regibus Anglorum et Dacorum* in CCCC, MS 139.[7] Also included will be Symeon's letter to Dean Hugh of York on the archbishops of York, which immediately precedes it in the manuscript.[8] It is also intended to include the *De primo Saxonum aduentu siue de eorundem regibus*, a text which is not found in CCCC, MS 139, but is closely linked to Symeon's work in its contents and therefore makes an appropriate complement to it.[9]

Research Agenda

On the understanding then that what follows are preliminary thoughts on a project which is still at an early stage, let me turn to the research agenda of this volume as it relates to Symeon of Durham's role in the *Historia de regibus Anglorum et Dacorum*, which is my principal concern, as distinct from the equally important role of Byrhtferth of Ramsey, which is Lapidge's principal concern.

As in so many topics to do with English history, inspirational ideas and questions have been provided by James Campbell, in this case in his Denis Bethell memorial lecture, 'Some twelfth-century views of the Anglo-Saxon past'.[10] There he reviewed the interpretations advanced by Richard Southern and others of why Anglo-Norman historical writing was so vigorous and varied. He argued that this activity was less the result of a Benedictine urge to celebrate pre-

---

[5] *Historia regum* is used for Byrhtferth's compilation in *Byrhtferth of Ramsey, the Lives of St Oswald and St Ecgwine*, ed. M. Lapidge, Oxford 2009, xxxix–xlii.
[6] *Symeonis opera*, ii. 284–332.
[7] Fos 50r–51v; see below, n. 22.
[8] Fos 48v–50r; see below, n. 17.
[9] Symeon of Durham, *Libellus de exordio atque procursu istius hoc est Dunhelmensis ecclesie*, ed. and tr. D.W. Rollason, Oxford 2000, lxxix–lxxx; D.W. Rollason and D. Gore, *Sources for York history before 1100*, Archaeology of York, York 1998, 26–7; for the text, *Symeonis opera*, ii. 365–84.
[10] J. Campbell, 'Some twelfth-century views of the Anglo-Saxon past', *Peritia* iii (1984), 131–50, repr. in J. Campbell, *Essays in Anglo-Saxon history*, London and Ronceverte 1986, 209–28.

Conquest monasticism, and more a response by writers, including non-monks such as Henry of Huntingdon, to the lack of historical writing produced in pre-Conquest England after the time of Bede, combined with a new intellectual and political imperative to take control of England and its past.

An especially striking aspect of his analysis was his emphasis on the modernity of twelfth-century historical writing, the emphasis that writers like Henry of Huntingdon and William of Malmesbury laid on comparison and reconciliation of sources, on the orderly arrangement of historical themes (as in Henry of Huntingdon's separation of secular and ecclesiastical history), and on the sorting-out of the confusing and complex sequences of the kings of the multifarious English kingdoms, as we see it for example in John of Worcester's tables and summaries relating to the various kingdoms, shires and bishoprics, with diagrams of family trees, in the sections of his *Chronicle* still awaiting a modern edition.[11] As Campbell commented, 'His is indeed a work of reference. His table and trees are not just materials for a *Handbook of British chronology*; they are its true ancestor'.[12] Moreover, twelfth-century historical writing provides, Campbell argued, one of those formative moments when our vision of the past is shaped, when the broad lines of pre-Conquest English history which we have all been taught ever since, were basically laid down, in Henry of Huntingdon's case in the form of the concept of the Heptarchy.[13] Campbell's view that twelfth-century historical writing marked a turning point derives from the fact that there were new and varied sorts of text, such as John of Worcester's tables and summaries, and that new historical methods were brought into play. The richness of post-Conquest Durham historical writing seems to offer the opportunity to investigate the extent to which this was the case.

Types of Historical Writing at Durham

First, the question of types of historical texts. Campbell drew a sharp line between writers such as William of Malmesbury and Henry of Huntingdon on the one hand, the scientific historians of whom his paper so approved, and the likes of Geoffrey of Monmouth and the hagiographers of saints like Edmund

---

[11] *Florentii Wigorniensis monachi Chronicon ex chronicis*, ed. B. Thorpe (English Historical Society, 1848–49), i. 231–80, although the editor gives a very inadequate impression of the ingenuity and creativity of these pages as they appear, for example, in OCCC, MS 157. They are currently being edited by David Woodman as part of the forthcoming first volume of *The chronicle of John of Worcester*, ed. R.R. Darlington, P. McGurk, J. Bray, and D.A. Woodman, Oxford 1995–.

[12] Campbell, 'Some twelfth-century views', 214.

[13] Ibid. 221.

and Osyth on the other, writers liberal in his view in the application of fantasy and destructive of the onward progress of history as an academic discipline.[14] Yet, in Anglo-Norman Durham, the sheer variety of historical writings, or at least quasi-historical writings at what David Dumville called 'a hotbed of historiographical activity',[15] should lead us to consider why such a range of historians' methods were used in the same period, the same place, and perhaps in some cases even by the same scholars and in the same works. The corpus of historical writings includes the following texts. First, there was Symeon's *Libellus de exordio*, written between 1104 and sometime between 1107 and 1115, and representing a blending of annalistic information, hagiographical source material, and apparently oral tradition, to produce a work which seems much more aimed at making a point about the history of the church of Durham and its alleged ancestry in the ancient foundation of Lindisfarne, perhaps (as W.M. Aird has suggested) in response to the pressure on Durham cathedral priory of the bishop, Ranulf Flambard (1099–1128).[16] Secondly Symeon's letter addressed to Dean Hugh of York, possibly composed after 1114, dealt with the history and succession of the archbishops of York.[17] Thirdly, the *Capitula miraculorum et translationum sancti Cuthberti* form an exaggerated blend of the hagiographical and the historical,[18] and have much in common with the *Historia de sancto Cuthberto*, which, although composed probably in the 1030s, was evidently being copied and used in Anglo-Norman Durham.[19] Fourthly, the *De iniusta uexacione Willelmi episcopi primi*, written

---

[14] Ibid. 226.

[15] D.N. Dumville, 'Textual archaeology and Northumbrian history subsequent to Bede', in D.M. Metcalf (ed.), *Coinage in ninth-century Northumbria: the tenth Oxford symposium on coinage and monetary history* (British Archaeological Reports, British Series clxxx, 1987), 43–55, repr. in D.N. Dumville, *Britons and Anglo-Saxons in the early Middle Ages*, Aldershot 1993, no. x, at 45.

[16] Symeon, *LdE* p. xlii, for the date; W.M. Aird, 'The political context of the *Libellus de exordio*', in D.W. Rollason (ed.), *Symeon of Durham: historian of Durham and the North*, Stamford 1998, 32–45.

[17] *Symeonis opera*, i. 222–8. For discussion, see R. Sharpe, 'Symeon as pamphleteer', in Rollason (ed.), *Symeon of Durham: historian*, 214–29 at 218–19.

[18] CCCC, 139, fos 48v–50r; printed *Symeonis opera*, i. 229–61, ii. 333–62; for comment, see B. Colgrave, 'The post-Bedan miracles and translations of St Cuthbert', in C. Fox and B. Dickins (eds), *The early cultures of north-west Europe (H.M. Chadwick Memorial Studies)*, Cambridge 1950, 305–32; and W.M. Aird, 'The making of a medieval miracle collection: the *Liber de translationibus et miraculis sancti Cuthberti*', *Northern History* xxviii (1992), 1–24.

[19] *Historia de sancto Cuthberto: a history of Saint Cuthbert and a record of his patrimony*, ed. and tr. T. Johnson South, Woodbridge 2002, for an edition, translation and discussion of the possible 1030s dating. But see also H.H.E. Craster, 'The patrimony of St Cuthbert', *EHR* lxix (1954), 177–99, and L. Simpson, 'The King Alfred/St Cuthbert episode in the *Historia*

probably shortly after 1081, constituted a record (or so it claimed) of the trial of Bishop William of Saint-Calais at Old Sarum before his exile.[20] Fifthly, the so-called *Annales Lindisfarnenses et Dunelmenses* were a set of annals entered in the ancient manner of earlier centuries in the margins of the Easter tables now preserved in the Hunterian Library in Glasgow.[21] Sixthly, there was the *Historia de regibus Anglorum et Dacorum* itself, to which we must turn in more detail in a moment. Finally, the *De obsessione Dunelmi et de probitate Uhtredi comitis* was a text composed in the late eleventh century or early twelfth century, almost certainly at Durham.[22]

This last text is in some ways the most interesting of all, not only because of its content, which the late Richard Fletcher explored so vividly in his last book,[23] but also because of its form. This is a work far removed from Campbell's scientific history. Its author was careless with dates, and much ink has been spilled over the very first chronological indication in the text, that for the siege of Durham by the Scots, which is clearly wrong.[24] But more importantly the author appears primarily concerned to draw on traditions about the successive wives of Earl Uhtred of Northumbria, about the feud which he became involved

---

de sancto Cuthberto: its significance for mid-tenth-century English history', in G. Bonner, D.W. Rollason and C. Stancliffe (eds), *St Cuthbert, his cult and his community to AD 1200*, Woodbridge 1989, 397–411.

[20] *De iniusta uexacione Willelmi episcopi primi per Willelmum regem filium Willelmi magni*, ed. H.S. Offler in *Camden miscellany* xxxiv (Camden 5 ser. x, 1997), 49–104; still worth consulting is H.S. Offler, 'The tractate *De iniusta uexacione Willelmi episcopi primi*', *EHR* lxvi (1951), 321–41. On the probable authenticity of the text, see esp. M. Philpott, 'The *De iniusta uexacione Willelmi episcopi primi* and canon law in Anglo-Norman Durham', in D.W. Rollason, M. Harvey and M. Prestwich (eds), *Anglo-Norman Durham, 1093–1193*, Woodbridge 1994, 125–37.

[21] W. Levison, 'Die "Annales Lindisfarnenses et Dunelmenses" kritisch untersucht und neu herausgegeben', *Deutsches Archiv für Erforschung des Mittelalters* xvii (1961), 447–506. For commentary on the script and content of these annals, see M. Gullick, 'The hand of Symeon of Durham: further observations on the Durham martyrology scribe' and J.E. Story, 'Symeon as annalist', in Rollason (ed.), *Symeon of Durham: historian*, 14–31, at 17–18; 202–13, at 207–8.

[22] *Symeonis opera*, i. 215–20. For a very capable translation and discussion, see C.J. Morris, *Marriage and murder in eleventh-century Northumbria: a study of 'De obsessione Dunelmi'* (Borthwick Paper no. 82), York 1992.

[23] R. Fletcher, *Bloodfeud: murder and revenge in Anglo-Saxon England*, Harmondsworth 2002; see also W.E. Kapelle, *The Norman conquest of the north: the region and its transformation*, London 1979, 3–85.

[24] See, for example, B. Meehan, 'The siege of Durham, the battle of Carham and the cession of Lothian', *Scottish Historical Review* lv (1976), 1–19; Morris, *Marriage and murder*, 10–12; and, more recently, A. Woolf, *From Pictland to Alba, 789–1070*, Edinburgh 2007, 233.

in as a result of his marriage to the daughter of Styr, son of Ulf, on condition that he should kill his enemy Thurbrand, about the devastating effect of that feud on subsequent generations, and about the fate of the estates which had come to Uhtred with his first wife, the bishop of Durham's daughter, and had not been returned to the church after the marriage's break-up. No one who has read the account of how two of Uhtred's descendants were reconciled, only for one to kill the other as they waited for a ship to go on pilgrimage together, can doubt that we are dealing here with an account closer to what we would normally regard as literature, or maybe oral tradition, than to scientific history.

Yet, there seems little doubt that the *De obsessione Dunelmi* was a Durham product, and that it was in the scriptorium around the time when the *Historia de regibus Anglorum et Dacorum* was being composed.[25] Certainly, it is likely to have come from the pen of one of of Symeon of Durham's colleagues in Durham cathedral priory, and its purpose was in part at least to keep alive the church's claim to the lost estates, some of which it actually did recover in due course.[26]

The 'modern' approach to history discussed by James Campbell is certainly in evidence, of course, in parts of the *Libellus de exordio*, and in the *Historia de regibus Anglorum et Dacorum*, but we should perhaps accept that, in Durham as elsewhere, history had a range of different forms and purposes which deserve our attention more than our condemnation.

Collaboration and Historical Workshops

As regards new methods of historical research, it seems possible to pursue in the context of the *Historia de regibus Anglorum et Dacorum* the importance of collaboration between contemporary historical writers. For it may be that part of the power of Anglo-Norman historical writing to shape a definitive image of the pre-Conquest past, and indeed the Anglo-Norman past, derived from the fact that scholars collaborated, developing a sense not only of a discipline of history, but of the existence of a specialism in historical writing. Nor need this have been limited to individuals. Since Martin Brett identified Worcester in the twelfth century as an 'historical workshop' with regard to the collaborative work taking place there between a group of scholars on the successive versions of John of Worcester's chronicle,[27] it seems worth asking whether such historical

---

[25] Symeon, *LdE* pp. lxxviii–lxxix; Morris, *Marriage and murder*, 9–10.
[26] Morris, *Marriage and murder*, 12–16.
[27] M. Brett, 'John of Worcester and his contemporaries', in R.H.C. Davis and J.M. Wallace-Hadrill (eds), *The writing of history in the middle ages: essays presented to Richard William Southern*, Oxford 1981, 101–26, at 124.

workshops, either in one institution or spread between two or more, were an important factor in the advances in twelfth-century historical writing.

Let us review the structure of the text of the *Historia de regibus Anglorum et Dacorum*. The only complete manuscript is Cambridge, Corpus Christi College, MS 139, which contains all the elements listed in the following numbered and sectionalised scheme, which will be used in the forthcoming edition:[28]

> A. Symeon of Durham (d. 1128/9), *Historia de regibus Anglorum et Dacorum*:
>   A.1: Rubric
>   A.2: Byrhtferth of Ramsey (*c*.970–*c*.1020), *Historia regum*
>   A.2.1 [ByrhtHR, pars i]: *Passio SS. Æthelberhti et Æthelredi*
>   A.2.2 [ByrhtHR, pars ii]: The early Northumbrian kings, including material derived mainly from Bede (d. 735), *Historia abbatum*; poems on the times and seasons; Bede, *Versus de die iudicii*; and extracts from Bede, *Historia ecclesiastica*
>   A.2.3 [ByrhtHR, pars iii]: The Northern annals: from 732 to 740; from 740 to 781; from 783 to 802
>   A.2.4 [ByrhtHR, pars iv]: A chronicle from 849 to 887, derived mainly from Asser, *Vita Ælfredi*
>   A.3: A chronicle from 888 to 957
>   A.4: Extracts from William of Malmesbury, *Gesta regum*
>   A.5: A chronicle from 848 to 1118 derived mainly from the *Chronicle* of John of Worcester
>   A.6: A chronicle from 1119 to 1129 drawing on John of Worcester and on Eadmer, *Historia nouorum*
>   A.7: Rubric
> [Interpolated into A.2.3, probably at Hexham in the early twelfth century:
>   A.2.3.1: Interpolated into the annal for 740: Burial, translation, and miracles of Bishop Acca of Hexham
>   A.2.3.2: Interpolated into the annal for 781: Translation of Bishop Ealhmund of Hexham]
> B. John of Hexham, *Historia .xxv. annorum*
>   B.1: Annals from 1130 to 1138
>   B.2: Annals from 1138 to 1152
> [C. Interpolated into B.2 in the annal for 1138
>   C.1: John of Worcester on the burning of London and natural phenomena in 1133
>   C.2: Serlo on the Battle of the Standard
>   C.3: William, *De morte Sumerledi*
>   C.4: Ailred of Rievaulx, *Tract on the Battle of the Standard*]

---

[28] For more detail on the sections, see Blair, 'Observations', 76–118.

The opening rubric (A.1) states that the text which follows is the 'history of Symeon of holy and sweet memory, monk and cantor of the church of St Cuthbert at Durham', and that this history extends 'from the death of the venerable priest Bede up to the death of King Henry I, son of William the Bastard who obtained England, that is 429 years and four months'.[29] The closing rubric (A.7) repeats the number of years and months which the history is said to cover. As Peter Hunter Blair noted, the statement that A extends to the death of Henry I – that is, 1135 – is incorrect because it ends in 1129; and the period of 429 years from the death of Bede in 735 would in any case mean that it extended to 1164 rather than to 1135. Blair's conclusion was that, in the light of other items in the manuscript, it was likely that the rubrics had been composed in 1164, and were thus in a confused way referring to the year of their composition rather than the terminal date of the *Historia de regibus Anglorum et Dacorum*.[30] This may also be the approximate date of the manuscript itself, as Lapidge assumed,[31] but in fact the manuscript, which is probably in any case to be regarded as a series of booklets of somewhat varying dates, may only have reached its present form as late as *c.*1180.[32]

Our starting point, then, and the only really solid point we have in our understanding of the development of the *Historia de regibus Anglorum et Dacorum*, is a compilation known from a single late-twelfth-century manuscript, consisting of A, to the end of which has been added B, which has in its turn been interpolated with C. Let us call this compilation Version O_4.

The rubrics had been used, after 1164 and before the date of the manuscript, to define A as a unified work and to attribute it to Symeon of Durham, who is now known with reasonable certainty to have died in 1128 or 1129,[33] and who is also known with reasonable certainty as in some sense the author of the *Libellus de exordio atque procursu istius hoc est Dunelmensis ecclesie*, written between 1104 and some time between 1107 and 1115.[34] Version O_4 represents, then, the development of the *Historia de regibus Anglorum et Dacorum* as it was in the period 1164×*c.*1180.

---

[29] CCCC, 139, fo. 51v: 'Historia sancte et suauis memorie Symeonis, monachi et precentoris ecclesie sancti Cuthberti Dunelmi, de regibus Anglorum et Dacorum, et creberrimis bellis, rapinis, et incendiis eorum, post obitum uenerabilis Bede presbyteri fere usque ad obitum regis primi Henrici, filii Willelmi Nothi qui Angliam adquisiuit, id est ccccxxix annorum et iv mensium'.

[30] Blair, 'Observations', 77–8.

[31] *Lives of St Oswald and St Ecgwine*, p. xxxix.

[32] B. Meehan, 'A reconsideration of the historical works associated with Symeon of Durham' (unpubl. Ph.D. diss., Edinburgh 1979), 105–9, discussing *inter alia* D. Baker, 'Scissors and paste: Corpus Christi, Cambridge, MS 139 again', *Studies in Church History* xi (1975), 83–123.

[33] Symeon, *LdE* pp. xlvii, l; Gullick, 'The hand of Symeon of Durham', 21–2.

[34] Symeon, *LdE* p. xlii.

Where was Version O₄ compiled? An *ex libris* visible under ultraviolet light leaves no doubt that the manuscript itself once belonged to the Cistercian abbey of Sawley in Lancashire near to the town of Clitheroe. It is not impossible that it was copied there, although the relative poverty of Sawley abbey makes this unlikely.[35] The fact that the manuscript contains material of specifically Cistercian interest, notably the account of the foundation of Fountains abbey, raises the possibility that it could nevertheless have been copied at a Cistercian monastery, possibly at Newminster,[36] the mother-house of Sawley, possibly at Fountains itself, the mother-house of Newminster. It might be supposed that the elements of C were interpolated into B in such a context, especially as C.4 is a work of Ailred of Rievaulx. It is also possible, however, that the manuscript (or at least that part of it which contains A, B, and C, for it is a manuscript composed of 'booklets') was copied at Durham, which had close relations with the Cistercian monasteries of Yorkshire, especially with Rievaulx abbey.[37]

But, aside from the copying of the manuscript, it is nearly certain that the rubrics A.1 and A.7 were inserted at Durham, since they are closely comparable to those in a contemporary copy of Symeon's *Libellus de exordio* in a manuscript now split between Cambridge University Library, MS Ff. 1 .27, and Cambridge, Corpus Christi College, MS 66, which Christopher Norton has shown with reasonable certainty to have been produced at Durham. Norton has argued that this manuscript, which includes, in addition to the *Libellus de exordio*, Gilbert of Limerick's *De statu ecclesie*, was assembled in the context of the tensions between Durham cathedral priory and Hugh of le Puiset, bishop of Durham (1153–95). Those tensions, in Norton's view, led to a renewed interest at Durham in history 'as one component of a moral and theological world-view', an interest which accounts for the content and illumination of the manuscript and for the copying of Symeon's *Libellus de exordio* into it. The close connections between CUL, MS Ff. 1. 27/ CCCC, MS 66 and CCCC, MS 139 suggest that the material which the latter contains may have been assembled at Durham in the same context of using history for politico-ecclesiastical purposes.[38]

The development of the *Historia de regibus Anglorum et Dacorum* at Durham shortly before the creation of Version O₄ can be illuminated with the aid of a chronicle contained in BnF, MS nouv. acq. lat. 692, a late-twelfth- or early-

---

[35] Blair, 'Observations', 118, first reported the discovery of the *ex libris*, but had already strongly supported the view that the manuscript had been copied at Sawley (72–6). He was supported in this by D.N. Dumville, 'Nennius and the *Historia Brittonum*', *Studia Celtica* x–xi (1975–6), 78–95, at 79. On the implausibility of its being written at Sawley, see Baker, 'Scissors and paste', 104.

[36] Baker, 'Scissors and paste', 95–9.

[37] F.M. Powicke, 'Maurice of Rievaulx', *EHR* xxvi (1921), 17–29.

[38] C. Norton, 'History, wisdom and illumination', in Rollason (ed.), *Symeon of Durham: historian*, 61–105.

thirteenth-century manuscript which contains a chronicle entitled *Liber de gestis Anglorum*, running from 793 to 1153. This chronicle, which has never been printed, is clearly a derivative of some version of the *Historia de regibus Anglorum et Dacorum*, sometimes copying complete annals from it, sometimes drastically abbreviated ones, sometimes omitting them altogether.[39]

Collation of BnF, MS nouv. acq. lat. 692 with CCCC, MS 139, where the former contains sections of the *Historia de regibus Anglorum et Dacorum* in full, suggests that it derives from a copy which is closer to the original text than the copy we have in CCCC, MS 139, in that it does not have elements which can be argued on other grounds to have been later additions to the original text, while at the same time sharing its overall shape. As Offler and Todd showed, it follows that both manuscripts must derive from a now lost copy of the *Historia de regibus Anglorum et Dacorum*, not far removed in time from that in CCCC, MS 139.[40] The version of the *Historia de regibus Anglorum et Dacorum* which it was using, however, seems to have differed from Version O_4. In it, A had already been joined to a full text of B, as it is found in CCCC, MS 139, but clumsily interpolated with C.1–4. In addition, the account of the earls of Northumbria which occurs in Version O_4 under the year 1072, which is inappropriate since it in fact runs to 952, is found in its proper place in BnF, nouv. acq. lat., MS 692. Finally, the lists of archbishops of York and abbots of Whitby which have been updated in Version O_4 had apparently not been updated in the version from which BnF, nouv. acq. lat., MS 692's abbreviation was made.[41] BnF, MS nouv. acq. lat. 692 is therefore evidence for the existence after 1153 of an earlier version, O_3, which was modified in various ways to produce Version O_4 as we have it in CCCC, MS 139.

It is possible that BnF, MS nouv. acq. lat. 692 was compiled from a manuscript of Version O_3 at Durham, where the rubrics naming Symeon as 'of saintly and sweet memory' may already have been added. But Offler presented a very strong case that what we are calling Version O_3 was compiled at Hexham in the time of John of Hexham, whose *Historia .xxv. annorum* (B) runs to 1153.[42] This would explain not only why A is continued by a Hexham writer, but also why A.2.3.1–2, which were of specifically Hexham interest, had been interpolated into A.2.3. Offler wondered in addition whether the tendency of the text as we know it in

---

[39] J.M. Todd and H.S. Offler, 'A medieval chronicle from Scotland', *Scottish Historical Review* xlvii (1968), 151–9, repr. in H.S. Offler, *North of the Tees: studies in medieval British history*, ed. A.J. Piper and A.I. Doyle (Collected Studies, Aldershot 1996), no. xi; and, more recently, Meehan, 'A reconsideration of the historical works', 121–4.

[40] Todd and Offler, 'A medieval chronicle from Scotland', 153–4.

[41] For the texts contained in these manuscripts collated with Version O_4, see the forthcoming *Symeon, Historia de regibus Anglorum et Dacorum*, ed. Lapidge and Rollason.

[42] H.S. Offler, 'Hexham and the *Historia regum*', *Transactions of the Architectural and Archaeological Society of Durham and Northumberland*, NS ii (1970), 51–62, repr. in Offler, *North of the Tees*, no. x.

CCCC, MS 139 'to soften statements in the southern sources ... which were hostile or injurious to York and its archbishop' might not be another indication of Hexham modifications incorporated into Version O_3, in view of Hexham's close affiliation with York in the twelfth century. That version must have been completed after 1153, when B ends, and probably after 1155, if A.2.3.1–2 were dependent (as Offler argued) on Ailred of Rievaulx's tract on the saints of Hexham, written after that year.[43]

It may be then that in CCCC, MS 139 we have a version, O_4, which represents a form of Version O_3 modified either at Durham or at whichever Cistercian abbey had received it. (It could be argued that the modifications are unlikely to have occurred at Hexham itself since they involved the spoiling through interpolation with C.1–4 of the coherence of John Hexham's work (B), although it may be that in the context of medieval historical compilations this would have been less unthinkable than in the present day.)

The compilation which the rubrics (A.1 and A.7) assigned to Symeon was clearly thought to have extended to 1129, so there was presumably an earlier version which ended then and was produced at Durham (Version O_2). Two further texts, both derived from the *Historia de regibus Anglorum et Dacorum*, offer us the possibility of tracing still further back the stages of the text's development. The first is the *Historia post Bedam*, which extends to 1148, but follows the *Historia de regibus Anglorum et Dacorum* only down to 1121, after which it draws on Henry of Huntingdon's *Historia Anglorum*.[44] It is possible that the compiler of the *Historia post Bedam* merely changed his source from the *Historia de regibus Anglorum et Dacorum* to Henry of Huntingdon after 1121. There is, however, no obvious reason why he should have done this had his copy of the *Historia de regibus Anglorum et Dacorum* extended beyond that year, although we must acknowledge the perhaps unlikely possibility that what he had was an incomplete copy of a work which did in fact extend further. If we discount that possibility, it seems possible that the *Historia post Bedam* as we have it (in three manuscripts of the mid-twelfth century and later)[45] is a second stage of development, and that the original version extended only to 1121 and was entirely derived from the *Historia de regibus Anglorum et Dacorum*. Where collation between the *Historia post Bedam* and the *Historia de regibus Anglorum*

---

[43] Offler, 'Hexham', 55.
[44] A. Gransden, *Historical writing in England c.550 to c.1307*, London 1974, 225–30; *Chronica magistri Rogeri de Houedene*, ed. W. Stubbs (RS [li], 1868–71) i. xxv–lxxi for discussion, i. 3–214 for the text.
[45] Oxford, St John's College, MS 97, BL, Royal 13. A. vi, and London, Inner Temple, Petyt MS 511.2 (the last not used by *Houedene*, ed. Stubbs); see Todd and Offler, 'Medieval chronicle', 21 n. 16, citing *The chronicle of Walter of Guisborough: previously edited as the chronicle of Walter of Hemingford or Hemingburgh*, ed. H. Rothwell (Camden 3rd ser. lxxxix, 1957), p. x.

et Dacorum is possible, it may therefore offer us a glimpse of what the latter text was like before it was extended from 1121 to 1129 (Version O_1).

Another such glimpse may be offered by a text preserved in Liège, Bibliothèque Universitaire, MS 369C, and in BL, MS Cotton Caligula A. viii. The latter can probably be dated *c.*1170; but the former, despite serious misdatings in the past, has been convincingly shown to belong to the years 1124 × 1128.[46] The text which these two manuscripts contain (they are very similar copies of it) consists of a version of the account of the Anglo-Saxon kingdoms called in other compilations *De primo Saxonum aduentu*, followed by annals from 1066 to 1119. Those annals are clearly derived from a version (O) of the *Historia de regibus Anglorum et Dacorum*, which presumably did not extend beyond 1119 (that is it did not yet include most at least of A.6). The revised dating of Liège, MS 369C tends to confirm the early date of this version.

If we were to assume, as we have in the foregoing, that historical writers ceased to use a chronicle or a set of annals at a particular date because that source had come to an end, and that the latest date in an historiographical text points to its date of composition, the development of the *Historia de regibus Anglorum et Dacorum* in the twelfth century could be envisaged as in the diagram opposite (Figure 6.1).

It should be recognised at once, however, that the sequence of development proposed above is open to a serious objection arising from Symeon's use in his annals through to 1118 of passages from Eadmer's *Historia nouorum* which came to him as part and parcel of John of Worcester's chronicle from which he was extracting.[47] Richard Southern argued that the *Historia nouorum* had been written in two parts.[48] The first, which consisted of books 1–4, and had been written soon after the death of Archbishop Anselm in 1109, probably before 1115, had the purpose of presenting Anselm's political career in the most favourable possible light. The second, which consisted of books 5–6, and finished with the death of Ralph, archbishop of Canterbury, in 1122, had in Southern's view been begun after Eadmer's return from self-imposed exile in Normandy in 1119, and finished after 1122. Its purpose was to vindicate both Anselm and Ralph, and it should therefore be regarded as a unitary composition down to 1122. The importance of this for understanding the development of the *Historia de regibus Anglorum et Dacorum* lies in its use by John of Worcester. The earliest surviving version of his chronicle, that in OCCC, MS 157, extracts from the second part of Eadmer's *Historia*, and some

---

[46] Meehan, 'A reconsideration of the historical works', 121–43, where the views of earlier commentators are discussed.

[47] JW *Chronicle* ii. pp. lxxiii–lxxiv. For what follows, I am very grateful for the comments and suggestions of Martin Brett.

[48] R.W. Southern, *St Anselm and his biographer*, Cambridge 1963, pp. 298–309; R.W. Southern, *Saint Anselm: a portrait in a landscape*, Cambridge 1990, pp. 414–17.

Symeon of Durham's Historia de Regibus Anglorum et Dacorum 107

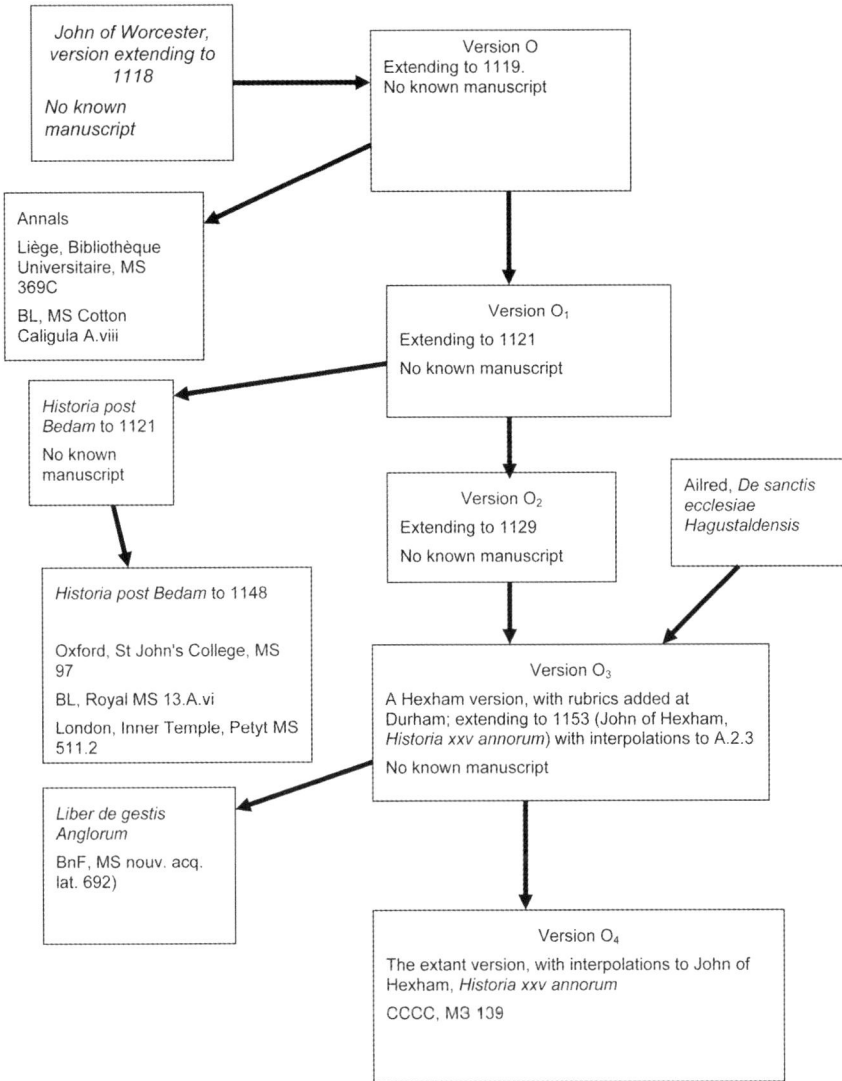

Figure 6.1 The development of the *Historia de regibus Anglorum et Danorum* (versions 0-0_4) and its relationship to other works.

of these extracts appear in the *Historia de regibus Anglorum et Dacorum* in the context of borrowings from John himself. If Southern's view of the dating and sequence of composition of Eadmer is correct, then there can have been no version of John of Worcester terminating in 1118, and the 1109–19 annals in the *Historia de regibus Anglorum et Dacorum* cannot have been composed before some date after the death of Archbishop Ralph in 1122.[49]

To resolve this issue, we might define two possible models for the development of the *Historia de regibus Anglorum et Dacorum*. The first would involve accepting that Southern's analysis and dating of Eadmer's *Historia nouorum* are correct. The dates and developmental sequence in the upper part of Figure 6.1 would then have to be revised, in particular to show that the *Historia de regibus Anglorum et Dacorum* could not have been written before 1122 and probably 1123. According to this model, we should have to assume that Symeon stopped using John of Worcester after 1119, possibly after 1120, even though he had a version which extended beyond that, and took the decision to create an independent set of annals. (The fact that Symeon began whole-heartedly to use Eadmer's *Historia nouorum* independently of John in his annal for 1119 and yet still seems to echo John's words in a sentence in his annal for 1120 might be seen as supporting this.)[50] We should also have to assume that the derivatives of his work in the Liège manuscript and in the putative early version of the *Historia post Bedam* finish when they do, in 1119 and 1121 respectively, because they were based on Symeon's early and incomplete drafts. The second model would involve accepting that the logic pursued to create the interpretation summarised in Figure 6.1 must stand, and that the dating and compositional sequence of Eadmer's *Historia nouorum*, and therefore of John of Worcester, is in need of reconsideration. In the case of the latter, it still remains a striking fact that the death-notice of Florence of Worcester, presented as if he were in some sense the author of the work occurs in the annal for 1118, and it might be thought that this strengthens the argument that the chronicle once existed in a form which finished in that year.[51] In the case of Eadmer's *Historia nouorum*, it might be time

---

[49] Brett, 'John of Worcester and his contemporaries', pp. 120–21.

[50] Ibid. p. 120. In John of Worcester, the sentence in question reads: 'Rex ... omnibus prospere et ad uelle peractis a Normannia in Angliam redit' (JW *Chronicle* iii. 146, s.a. 1120); in Symeon, it reads 'Itaque rex ... cunctis ... ad uotum prospere peractis ... in Angliam multo [nauigio] reuehitur' (*HR* ii. 258).

[51] R.R. Darlington (ed.), *William of Malmesbury, The Vita Wulfstani of William of Malmesbury* (Camden 3rd ser. lx, 1928), pp. xvi–xviii. The scholarship since then is added to and reinforced by Brett, 'John of Worcester and his contemporaries', p. 104 and n. 3. However, McGurk's note on this annal, which repeats earlier scholarship and reads, 'The death of Florence in 1118 is one of the arguments against his authorship of the chronicle' (JW *Chronicle iii*, p. 143, n. 5), might be seen as pointing to an element of circularity in need of reconsideration.

to reconsider the possibility that it was composed in a more complicated and long-drawn-out way, as its editor M.J. Rule proposed in an introductory essay which Southern's critique consigned to oblivion.[52] This second model would necessarily revolve around the idea that historical writing in the early twelfth century was much more akin to modern scholarship and that a series of drafts was circulating between historical writers, with constant revisions and updates taking place to existing texts, which would themselves have been preserved and worked on in 'scratch' copies. It would then not be unthinkable, for example, that a version of John of Worcester's chronicle had been written in 1118, used by Symeon for the earliest version of the *Historia de regibus Anglorum et Dacorum*, updated by John to make use of Eadmer's *Historia nouorum*, and then used again in this form by Symeon. There is at present no evidence for this, but we should at any rate recognise that the first model leaves us with the problem of why Symeon's use of John's text ceased in 1118, to which the second model might provide some sort at least of a solution.

The primary aim of the new edition of the *Historia de regibus Anglorum et Dacorum* is of course to make the text as usable as possible by modern scholars; but an important secondary aim is to explore that text and the versions of it in such a way as to illuminate the process of historical writing in its period. The validity or otherwise of the models sketched above is one of the challenges facing the editors, and no attempt is being made in this paper to offer a resolution at present. However, the fact that John of Worcester has now been edited, and in the case of the preliminary material is about to be edited, to the highest scholarly standards, offers unprecedented opportunities for examining the light that that chronicle can cast on the development of the *Historia de regibus Anglorum et Dacorum*. And, whatever the conclusions the new edition prompts, it seems likely that the picture ultimately to emerge will be one of modifications and rewritings which form an important part of the text's development, even if the early dates in Figure 6.1 need to be revised. It may be that the light it can cast on the process of historical writing is what is most important about the *Historia de regibus Anglorum et Dacorum*.

Envisaging the text as the product of a series of alterations and interpolations is to bring approaches to it into line with recent work on medieval historical writing. Dauvit Broun and Julian Harrison, for example, are preparing what they describe as a 'stratigraphic' edition of the Chronicle of Melrose, which seeks to reveal how a team of scribe-compilers added to and modified the annalistic record kept at Melrose Abbey.[53] Patrick McGurk has shown very clearly how study of the earliest

---

[52] *Eadmeri Historia Novorum in Anglia, et opuscula duo de vita Sancti Anselmi et quibusdam miraculis ejus*, ed. M. Rule (RS [lxxxi], 1884), pp. xlix–xl as concerns books 5–6, and Southern, *St Anselm and his biographer*, 298.

[53] *The chronicle of Melrose abbey: a stratigraphic edition: volume i: introduction and facsimile edition*, ed. D. Broun and J. Harrison (Scottish History Society, 6 ser. i), Woodbridge 2007.

manuscript of John of Worcester, OCCC, MS 157, can bring to light a similar process of ongoing revision and compilation, which is also evident in the other early manuscripts of the work and in John's own abbreviation of it.[54] On a smaller scale, it is clear that important elements in Symeon of Durham's *Libellus de exordio* were altered after its initial composition, perhaps at various stages in the twelfth century.[55] The process of historical research has emerged as every bit as interesting as the factual record which the historical writing purported to embody.

It is also necessary, however, to consider this in the context of, to borrow Brett's phrase, the historical workshops of the twelfth century. The Anglo-Norman shaping of an image of the past was a laborious process, involving change and development, and founded on the exchange of information between workshops and collaborative work of a high order. The process was clearly under way in the tenth century, for the similarities between the way in which Byrhtferth's *Historia regum* was assembled and edited,[56] and the way in which the Anglo-Norman compositions were produced, is striking. But it may be that the momentum in developing this process increased in the twelfth century. In his northern outpost on the river Wear, hemmed in by the threat of the aggression of the English kings no less than the Scottish, Symeon of Durham was evidently in touch with a range of centres of learning. The fact that he had Byrhtferth's *Historia regum* suggests that at once. How had he obtained it? Had it come north with the two Peterborough monks, Æthelric and Æthelwine, who became successively bishops of Durham from 1041 to 1071?[57] Or had it been unearthed by the busy researches in the Ramsey archives of Symeon or another member of his 'historical workshop'? Clearly, Symeon enjoyed close relations with Worcester, given his use of John of Worcester's work and the latter's use of the *Libellus de exordio*, possibly in the context of an exchange of work,[58] and with Canterbury, given his independent use of Eadmer's *Historia nouorum* from his annal for 1119. The subsequent history of Symeon's work suggests the same themes – ongoing modification in the light of new material, just as Symeon's *Libellus de exordio* was modified early in its life probably on the orders of

---

[54] JW *Chronicle* ii. pp. lxvii–lxxxi, acknowledging the importance of the 'fundamental article' by Brett, 'John of Worcester and his contemporaries'.

[55] D.W. Rollason, 'The making of the *Libellus de exordio*: the evidence of erasures and alterations in the two earliest manuscripts', in Rollason (ed.), *Symeon of Durham: historian*, 140–56.

[56] See, for example, Lapidge, 'Early sections'.

[57] B. Meehan, 'Insiders and property in Durham around 1100', *Studies in Church History* xii (1975), 45–58; for a discussion of the pre-Norman religious community at Durham, see D.W. Rollason, 'Symeon of Durham and the community of Durham in the eleventh century', in C. Hicks (ed.), *England in the eleventh century: proceedings of the 1990 Harlaxton Symposium*, Stamford 1992, 183–98.

[58] Brett, 'John of Worcester and his contemporaries', p. 121.

Symeon's superiors,[59] and modification, too, in other centres, Hexham certainly as Offler argued,[60] and perhaps in a Cistercian centre further south as well.

This collaboration, this movement of texts and materials, were clearly part of the strengths of the twelfth-century historical endeavour which was, as Campbell argued, so definitive. But how was such collaboration achieved? One clue may lie in the fact that Symeon was the cantor or precentor of Durham cathedral priory. As such he was responsible for the library of the monastery, for the scriptorium, and also for the remembrance of the dead.[61] That last activity involved remembrance in the church of Durham itself, but it involved also a massive network of contacts with other religious houses. Jean Dufour's edition of the mortuary rolls which were carried far and wide across England after the death of each abbot or prior shows fully the gargantuan scale of the traffic between religious houses,[62] and Lynda Rollason has shown the mobility and pattern of movement of the Durham *breuiatores* who carried these mortuary rolls.[63] Now, we know that other historical writers, notably William of Malmesbury and later Thomas of Walsingham, were also cantors of their churches,[64] although by no means all cantors of monasteries showed any interest in writing recent history as these cantors did, and Eadmer of Canterbury's work while he probably held the office of cantor was devoted much more to hagiographical than to historiographical writing. In some cases, nevertheless, it may be that a link between the role of cantor and the role of historian provides a clue to the vigorous collaborative historical culture of the twelfth century.[65]

---

[59] Symeon, *LdE* p. xliv.

[60] Offler, 'Hexham', passim.

[61] Symeon, *LdE* p. xliii; *The monastic constitutions of Lanfranc*, ed. and tr. D. Knowles and C.N.L. Brooke, 2 edn, Oxford 2002, 122–3.

[62] *Recueil des rouleaux des morts: (VIIIe siècle-vers 1536)*, ed. J. Dufour, Paris 2005–.

[63] L. Rollason, 'Medieval mortuary rolls: prayers for the dead and travel in medieval England', *Northern History* xlviii (2010), 187–223.

[64] R.M. Thomson, 'Malmesbury, William of (b. *c.*1090, d. in or after 1142)', in *ODNB*, Oxford 2004, s.n.; J. Taylor, 'Walsingham, Thomas (*c.*1340–*c.*1422)', in ibid., s.n.

[65] See L. Rollason, *Memorial books from the British Library*, London forthcoming, on which the preceding discussion is entirely dependent. See also the important discussion of M.E. Fassler, *The Virgin of Chartres: making history through liturgy and the arts*, New Haven 2010, 97–8, arguing that, at Chartres in particular but at other churches generally, 'the cantor was in control of the history-making enterprise'. Fassler particularly draws attention to Symeon of Durham's 'cantor's book', discussed by M. Gullick, 'The scribes of the Durham cantor's book (Durham, Dean and Chapter Library, MS B.IV.24) and the Durham martyrology scribe', in D.W. Rollason, M. Harvey and M. Prestwich (eds), *Anglo-Norman Durham*, 93–124; and A.J. Piper, 'The Durham cantor's book (Durham, Dean and Chapter Library, MS B.IV.24)', ibid. 79–92. On Eadmer as cantor, see Southern, *Saint Anselm: a portrait*, pp. 210–11.

Chapter 7
William of Malmesbury's Diatribe against the Normans

R.M. Thomson

> Norman saw on English oak,
> On English neck a Norman yoke;
> Norman spoon in English dish,
> And England ruled as Normans wish;
> Blithe world in England never will be more,
> Till England's rid of all the four.
>
> (Walter Scott, *Ivanhoe*, ch. 27.)

Sir Walter Scott put these words in the mouth of the brave jester, Wamba, as he confronted a group of unpleasant Norman barons. To us, the stark contrast drawn by Scott between oppressed English and overbearing Normans may seem anachronistic in its late-twelfth-century setting. But how long did this contrast, or at least the perception of it by the English, continue after 1066? One man at least was still tortured by it as late as the 1130s.

William, Benedictine monk of Malmesbury and historian of England (*c*.1095–?1143), thought hard about the Norman Conquest: What led to it? By what steps did it proceed? Why was it successful? What were its effects and significance? He thought hard about these things because he felt deeply about them. Michael Winterbottom has emphasised the 'enduring *feeling* of Englishness' that pervades William's historical works.[1] What mattered most to William about the Conquest was that it ended, or at least severely damaged, a great tradition. He felt himself to be an heir of that tradition, with a responsibility for recording if not preserving it. In some ways, his account of the Conquest is the centrepiece and lynchpin of the *Gesta regum Anglorum* – it does indeed occur about the halfway point of the work; probably it provides the overriding motive for its writing. And yet, William also said 'Vtriusque gentis sanguinem

---

[1] M. Winterbottom, 'The language of William of Malmesbury', in C.J. Mews, C.J. Nederman and R.M. Thomson (eds), *Rhetoric and renewal in the Latin West, 1100–1540: essays in honour of John O. Ward*, Turnhout 2003, 129–47, at 129.

traho';[2] this would impel him to try and write a balanced account of William the Conqueror and, we may infer, of the Conquest itself. And, indeed, from time to time during his narrative he identifies the differing English and Norman views: of the Conqueror himself, and of this or that turn of events, and either weighs them up and passes judgement even-handedly, or confesses his inability, for lack of information, to decide between them.

He begins his narrative at the end of book 2, which takes the story of England from the rise of the kingdom of Wessex to the end of Edward the Confessor's reign and Harold's succession: its last chapter, 228, recounts Edward the Confessor's disposition of the succession and death. Book 3 crosses the Channel and backtracks chronologically, beginning with the rise to power of William within Normandy and over neighbouring Maine, then comes to Hastings at cc. 238–44, with interpretation at 245–6.

At 228 Edward attempts to find a legitimate heir to the English throne, eventually fixing on William of Normandy. Harold then finds himself in Normandy, whether sent by Edward to convey his purpose or accidentally, driven by the wind, William of Malmesbury is unsure. Either way Harold promises to William Dover castle 'which was in his fief', and the kingdom after Edward's death; in return, he is betrothed to William's daughter, not yet of age. Edward dies and Harold, having 'exacted (*extorta*) an oath of loyalty from the chief nobles', seizes (*arripuit*) the crown. 'The English', says William, 'say that it was granted to him by the king', but William does not believe it, though he thinks that Harold was worthy of the position, had it come to him lawfully. There follow the invasion of Harald Hardrada and the battle at Stamford Bridge. Immediately after his victory, says William, Harold Godwinsson made a bad tactical error by refusing to distribute the booty among his followers, so that many of them left him in dudgeon, thus weakening the force available to him at Hastings. At this point come some significant, if obscure, interpretative comments:

> It was God's hidden and stupendous purpose that never again should Englishmen feel together and fight together in defence of their liberties, as though all the strength of England had fallen away with Harold, who could and should have paid the penalty for his perfidy, even through the agency of utter cowards. In so saying I make no reflections on the valour of the Normans; they have my loyalty, both for my own origins and for what I owe them.[3]

---

[2] Malmesbury, *GR* bk iii. prol. 1. We interpreted this as meaning that one of his parents was English, the other Norman. But William's assertion of Englishness, as outlined in this chapter, makes one wonder whether the Norman genetic infusion occurred further back in his ancestry: M. Winterbottom, 'William of Malmesbury and the Normans', *Journal of Medieval Latin* xx (2010), 70–77, at 74 n. 11.

[3] Malmesbury, *GR* i. 422–3 (bk ii. 228. 11–12).

The English were no cowards either, he continues, but fought bravely at Hastings though outnumbered.

At 238 William of Malmesbury explains how Harold broke his oath to Duke William and the arguments which he used to justify it to William's envoys – arguments 'that either had, or seemed to have, some force'. Harold makes another tactical error in not pleading his cause to the pope, who promptly legitimised William's attempt on the English throne.

At 239–40 Harold is characterised as rash, and thus it is unsurprising that when William sends him a counterclaim for the throne and a proposal for avoiding battle, he refuses. In 241 the English, too, are shown to be impetuous, spending the night before the battle, 'so I have heard', 'in song and wassail', while the Normans (242) piously confess their sins and take communion. Then we have a detailed account of the battle, in which both leaders and their sides fought bravely, the Normans winning because of superior tactics.

Cc. 245 and 246 are important chapters of interpretation. 'That was a day of destiny for England, a fatal disaster for our dear country as she exchanged old masters for new', William begins 245. He then goes on to praise England's achievement in learning and religion in the age of Bede. 'But zeal both for learning and for religion cooled as time went on, not many years before the coming of the Normans'. And he puts some interesting detail to this statement: 'The English of those days wore garments half way to the knee, which left them unimpeded; hair short, chin shaven, arms loaded with gold bracelets, skin tattooed with coloured patterns, eating till they were sick and drinking till they spewed'. Not everyone was like this, he admits, 'But as in tranquil times God's serene kindness often fosters bad and good men equally, so in the hour of captivity His stern judgement sometimes grips good as well as bad.' In 246 he turns to the Normans, drawing up a balanced list of their good and bad features and effects on England. Perhaps the most important of their positive effects is that 'the standard of religion, dead everywhere in England, has been raised by their arrival: you may see everywhere churches in villages, in towns and cities monasteries rising in a new style of architecture; and with new devotion our country flourishes, so that every rich man thinks a day wasted if he does not make it remarkable with some great stroke of generosity.'[4] On the basis of such passages, William can hardly be seen as anti-Norman, even if he obviously regretted the passing of Bedan England and the end of the house of Wessex.

This was all written by early 1126, mostly in the course of 1124 and 1125. A decade or so later he appears to be singing a starkly different tune. William wrote his *Commentary on Lamentations* c.1135, after a period of inactivity

---

[4] At Malmesbury, *GR* i. 458–9 (bk iii. 245. 6) William notes that the English had since the Conquest passed on their vices of gluttony and drunkenness to their conquerors. In ch. 14 of *Ivanhoe* Walter Scott seems to echo William's comparison of the races.

as a writer.[5] In its prologue, addressed to a (presumably local) monk ('frater amantissime'), he speaks slightingly of his youthful writings on history; now, he says, he intends to write works unambiguously in praise of God and for the spiritual edification of his readers. His fellow monk had asked him to summarise the *Commentary* by the Carolingian Paschasius Radbertus, and William obliges, though adding much learning and free-wheeling comment of his own: whether Lamentations attracted him for his own reasons we can only speculate. Certainly it includes a great deal of lamentation on William's contemporary environment.

One of these passages of lament is an impassioned outpouring of anguish for England's state as a result of the Norman invasion. The correct interpretation of this particular passage was first made by Michael Winterbottom, who has recently published it with elegant commentary.[6] My remarks in this chapter are supplementary to his, and reflect my approach as a historian and the theme of this volume. The context is William's discussion of the notion of God using a godless nation to punish His chosen people who have become errant. The verse of Lamentations being commented is 1. 14: 'The yoke of my iniquities hath watched: they are folded together in his hand, and put upon my neck: my strength is weakened within me: the Lord hath delivered me into a hand out of which I am not able to rise'.[7] In the translation below I have italicised the salient points.

> Behaviour like this makes God's people subject to pagan nations, under the yoke of miserable slavery. Behaviour like this weakens armed peoples and overthrows fortified cities.
>
> It made the Jews, once beloved of God, no match in war first for the Babylonians, then for the Macedonians, and finally for the Romans: clients in subservience, captives in defeat, tributaries in money. A just outcome! They had been ungrateful for God's clemency; now for their pride they were whisked away at the whim of their conquerors.
>
> Behaviour like this has often made Christian armies yield to Gentiles, so that more than 200 years ago the Turks and Saracens took control of the places that had known God's birth and passion.

---

[5] *Willelmi Meldunensis monachi liber super explanationem Lamentationum Ieremiae prophetae* (henceforward *CL*), ed. M. Winterbottom and R.M. Thomson (Corpus Christianorum, Continuatio Mediaevalis ccxliv, Turnhout 2011), I, lines 2194–212 (p. 84).

[6] Winterbottom, 'William of Malmesbury and the Normans', 70–74. My own original position was that the passage referred to the advance of Islam (R.M. Thomson, *William of Malmesbury*, 2 edn, Woodbridge 2003, 174–5). Winterbottom's interpretation had already been arrived at, independently, by S. Sønnesyn in '"Ad bonae uitae institutum": William of Malmesbury and the ethics of history', Ph.D. diss. Bergen 2007, now published: *William of Malmesbury and the ethics of history*, Woodbridge 2012, 143 n. 167.

[7] *CL* p. 82.

Look how few of us are left as the result of such behaviour – though once we were a race, if not large numerically, at least superior to many in learning and courtesy (eruditione et affabilitate). Surely in us is seen to be fulfilled what the Psalmist said in stigmatising the Jews: 'Scatter them by thy power; and destroy them, O Lord, my protector' (Ps. 58. 12). Thus some of us were brought down and lost their worldly glory, some were turned out and sigh for their sweet homeland, some have died and taken consciousness of their misery away with them. But as for those of us who remain, let us put up with evil fortune, until triumphant felicity puts an end to our troubles. Let us not therefore look at what we suffer, or at whose hands: rather at why. *It would certainly be a consolation in our distresses if we could see in our oppressors some distinction in learning, some holiness of character, some excellence of lineage superior to our own. Solace in calamity would be provided by the worth of those inflicting calamities. For we could tell ourselves that they are wiser than we, that they display right judgement when they reproach us for our mistakes. But in fact they are themselves of low birth, base in character, and quite without literary knowledge.* Who then would tolerate this? – though we should remember an incident in the life of the blessed David: when the son of Gera abused him, and Abisai, a tried and tested soldier, burned to avenge his lord, David stopped the furious man in his tracks with the reply: 'Let him alone and let him curse: for the Lord hath bid him curse' (2 Reg. 16. 10). In saying this, one who had surpassed the glory of all his predecessors surpassed himself also. Hence Solomon's dictum: 'Better is the patient man than the presumptuous: and he that ruleth his spirit, than he that taketh cities' (Prov. 16. 32). So this instance helps us to preserve patience, because the Lord's is all our life, the Lord's is all we suffer. Hence our most glorious athlete, when he entered upon the scene of his contest, said: 'The Lord gave, and the Lord hath taken away: as it hath pleased the Lord so is it done: blessed be the name of the Lord' (Job 1. 21).

But since we are concerned with the unworthiness of persecutors, let us remember that what we are suffering is not new. It is the way of the world and virtually a law of nature that the wicked ride roughshod over the wretched. If they were good, they would not act thus. But God, finding a good use for their badness, uses them to chastise those He loves, because a father generally throws into the fire the stick he beats his son with, once the boy has been corrected. Let us remember that the Babylonians were no better than the Jews, worse in fact, because while the Jews served one God, if only in a shadowy way, the Babylonians openly worshipped their absurd idols, and went so far as to claim for themselves the right to be God's agent in the punishment of the Jews. Yet they conquered them and led them away: even their liberty went into exile. God showed by this that He was concerned not to weigh the merits of those who inflicted punishment, but to punish the sinner. He showed too that He would rather have a few good worshippers than many bad ones. He also wished to rouse the rest to give up in this world the hopes they had entertained in vain, and allow God's grace to embrace them: grace easy to attain if you long for it, and not liable to slip from your hands if you hold fast to it. For often, indeed almost always, men in the straits of illness or punishment cry to God then in particular, though previously they had forgotten Him out of negligence or even blasphemed against Him out of arrogance. The world is full of relevant examples, so I will return from *personal grief* to my general exposition in relation to the Church.

A number of questions arise from this remarkable passage, of which I will consider just two: Why did William hold this view, that is, what ills did he think the Normans had inflicted on England? And, does this view mark a violent change from his earlier one, as outlined above, and, if so, why?

As to the first question: we can easily enough identify some explicit reasons for William's unhappiness. William thought the contemporary and near-contemporary secular clergy – most, if not all, Norman – corrupt and antagonistic to the monastic order. This is a theme running through the Commentary and a line run quite strongly in the earlier *Gesta pontificum*, which was arguably more oriented towards a monastic audience than the *Gesta regum*. For instance, in *Gesta pontificum* 68. 3 we find: 'For a horde of Norman abbots had flooded the land at that time, bringing to the English sermons they had practised and polished in their own country, and enjoying a leisurely life in successive places at the expense of others'. Even stronger is 73. 22 (later censored):

> For it is now openly said ... that he is unsuitable for a bishopric who is unwilling or unable to misemploy worldly power in the pursuits of the forest, the stimulation of the appetites, the elaboration of his dress, and the rowdiness of his retinue. Little or no account is taken of the winning of souls. And when it is objected that bishops were once looked to for piety and education, not ambition and money, people answer: 'Now we have another age, and other manners to suit the age', thus using a slick reply to palliate harsh reality.

Some of the Norman bishops and abbots described in the *Gesta pontificum* are said to be virtuous, others not. But none is a hero like Aldhelm, Wilfrid, Dunstan, Æthelwold or Wulfstan.[8] The same is true of the rulers. There is no Norman equivalent of Alfred, Æthelstan or Edgar: he did not think much of William Rufus (a wasteful and cynical oppressor) and was ambivalent about William

---

[8] Malmesbury, *GP* i. 500–579 (bk v. 188–231) (Aldhelm), i. 324–75 (bk iii. 99–110) (Wilfrid), i. 32–41 (bk i. 18–19) (Dunstan), i. 260–67 (bk ii. 75. 31–45) (Æthelwold), i. 423–43 (bk iv. 137–48) (Wulfstan).

I and Henry I.⁹ The great new buildings, then, were reason for praise, but the upper echelons of the Norman ecclesiastical hierarchy were not impressive.

Then there are some reasons that we can conjecture. One was that his monastery was without an abbot for most of his lifetime, and the *Gesta regum* at least was written in the (vain) hope of getting one.¹⁰ We can probably infer that the proportion of English monks compared with Norman was shrinking, as it was elsewhere. For this, our evidence is the hands of the more than fifty monks who helped William write his books.¹¹ A small number of these hands, among the books that can be dated earliest, still show the influence of Anglo-Caroline, the native script used for Latin texts in English manuscripts from the early eleventh century on. By far the majority, however, including the scribes most used by William, were either Continental themselves or wrote in hands showing Continental influence. Finally, the *Commentary on Lamentations* was bound to be oriented towards lamenting, and like the *Gesta pontificum* it was for the consumption of monks some at least of whom might be English, not the great Anglo-Norman laymen who might have read the *Gesta regum*, or had it read to them.

As to the second question: William's attitude was not altogether recent, for we find the bitterness anticipated in some passages of the *Gesta regum*. The most important of these occur earlier than the actual narrative of the Conquest. For instance, at c. 227: after the description of Edward the Confessor's deathbed prophecy of the green tree:

> The truth of this prophecy ... we now experience, now that England has become a dwelling-place of foreigners (*exterorum*) and a playground for lords of alien blood. No Englishman (*Anglus*) today is an earl, a bishop, or an abbot; new faces everywhere enjoy England's riches and gnaw her vitals, nor is there any hope of ending this miserable state of affairs. The time has come for my pen to attempt, as I promised long ago, a brief account of the cause of these disasters.

The promise here referred to was made at c. 207, which tells the story of the female Siamese twins on the border of Normandy and Brittany:

> Some people thought ... that these women signified England and Normandy, which, though geographically divided, are yet united under one rule. Whatever

---

⁹ Malmesbury, *GR* i. 180–95 (bk ii. 121–3 (Alfred), i. 206–29 (bk ii. 131–40) (Æthelstan), i. 238–63 (bk ii. 148–60), i. 460–77 (bk iii. 247–57), i. 492–513 (bk iii. 267–83) (William I), i. 542–77 (bk iii. 305–33) (William II), i. 708–63 (bk v. 390–419) (Henry I).

¹⁰ Malmesbury, *GR* i. 4–5 (ep. i. 7). A puzzle is why, in both his major works, William discusses the two Norman abbots of Malmesbury, Warin and Godfrey, but does not so much as mention the next abbot, the English Eadwulf (1106–18).

¹¹ Thomson, *William of Malmesbury*, ch. 4.

money these two engulf in their greedy jaws descends to a single maw, which may be either the greed of princes or the ferocity of neighbouring nations. Normandy, dead and nearly sucked dry, is supported by the financial strength of England, until maybe she herself is overwhelmed by the violence of her oppressors. O happy England, if the moment ever comes when she can breathe the air of that freedom whose empty shadow she has pursued so long! As it is, she bewails her lot, worn by calamity and wasted by taxation, with all the nobility of ancient days extinct.

Moving forward to around the time of the *Commentary*, another extreme statement occurs in William's *Life of Dunstan*.[12] Speaking of the reign of Æthelred II (the Unready), he says:

To prolong the harm he did so that it affected posterity, he contrived that his successors should lose all England, by marrying Emma, daughter of Richard duke of Normandy, the result being that in after years the Normans were able to claim England as of right and bring it under their control, something better seen today than put down in writing.

But the declaration that the Normans were actually inferior to the English *is* made for the first time in the *Commentary*, and is at first sight surprising. One thinks immediately of his evident admiration for Lanfranc and Anselm, as displayed in the lengthy treatment of their pontificates in both *GR* and *GP*: but he knew perfectly well – and emphasises the fact – that they were both Italian.[13] He also appears to have clearly separated, in his mind, the Normans from the French; the latter for him the exemplars of civilised ideals and behaviour.[14] In any case, I suppose that he is comparing the *pasts* of the two nations: the Normans had had no Age of Bede; they were the descendants of the barbarous Rollo and his Danes.[15] What we seem to have, at all times of his life, is a tension, never resolved, between William the Englishman, bitter and regretful about the Norman invasion, and William the historian, attempting objectivity according to his lights.

Finally, one wonders whether William's unhappiness was more widely spread; to this I have no answer.[16] Certainly his *Commentary* was not influential: it was known to Robert of Cricklade when he was canon of the Augustinian

---

[12] ii. 34. 3–4: William of Malmesbury, *Saints' Lives*, ed. and tr. M. Winterbottom and R.M. Thomson, Oxford 2002, 297.
[13] Malmesbury, *GP* i. 48–9 (bk i. 24. 1), i. 108–9 (bk i. 45. 2).
[14] Malmesbury, *GR* i. 152–3 (bk ii. 106. 2).
[15] Malmesbury, *GR* i. 200–203 (bk ii. 127).
[16] Martin Brett kindly reminds me of the attempted uprising in the Isle of Ely recorded in *Liber Eliensis* iii. 52, *c*.1137: *LE* 296–9; tr. J. Fairweather, *Liber Eliensis: a history of the Isle of Ely from the seventh century to the twelfth*, Woodbridge 2005, 364. It occurred *c*.1137; at a meeting in Stretham church 'abominable oaths were sworn ... in favour of the death

house at Cirencester, not long after 1137; Robert went on to become prior of St Frideswide's Oxford.[17] The two surviving copies, both from close to William's lifetime, are from Worcester and Eynsham respectively. At Worcester the monastic population and its culture remained strongly English for a long time.[18] Perhaps the presence of a copy at Eynsham, near Oxford, owed something to Robert's presence at St Frideswide's. However, the fact that in the *Gesta regum* William is able to say 'The English say that ...',[19] makes it clear that general English unhappiness with the Conquest persisted well into his lifetime.

---

of everyone of French birth'. However, none of the ringleaders of this conspiracy, above all Ranulf of Salisbury, had an English name and their motives are obscure.

[17] *CL*, pp. x, xxix.

[18] R.M. Thomson, 'The use of the vernacular in manuscripts from Worcester cathedral priory', *Transactions of the Worcester Archaeological Society* xx (2006), 113–19.

[19] Malmesbury, *GR* ii. 228. 7 (i. 418–21); cf. iii. pref. 1 (i. 424–5).

Chapter 8
Normandy's View of the Anglo-Saxon Past in the Twelfth Century

Elisabeth van Houts

'I firmly believe that the holy deeds of the Angles and Saxons of England could be no less edifying to northern Christians than the deeds of the Greeks and Egyptians which devoted scholars have fully recorded in lengthy narratives that are widely read and give much pleasure. Moreover, I believe little as these things are known amongst our countrymen, they must prove all the more pleasing and full of grace to men of ardent charity who lament their past sins from the bottom of their hearts.'[1]

So wrote Orderic Vitalis, the English monk at work in Normandy in the second decade of the twelfth century. There is a polemic hint in his comment justifying the reading about the Anglo-Saxon past compared with the Greek and Egyptian past. That he felt he had to insert this justification is not surprising as he was writing the history of his own monastery, Saint-Évroult in Normandy. At the stage where he inserted an abbreviation of Felix's *Life of St Guthlac* into his account of the Norman Conquest he had not touched upon the early history of England at all. Yet, Orderic's deliberate insertion of this Anglo-Saxon saint's *Life*, preceded by the quotation on the value of English saints, was the first step along the road to painting a far wider historical canvas that turned into his *Ecclesiastical history*. The polemic note was a reaction against generations of propagandistic Norman historical writing.

Before Orderic took up his pen, the history of Anglo-Saxon England, albeit in patches, was known to Norman historians. Judging by Dudo of Saint-Quentin's knowledge (see below) something was available around the first millennium, though it is fair to say that real interest did not start until at least half a century later when events leading up to the Norman Conquest of England forced the Normans to look westwards. Twelfth-century library catalogues mention Bede's *Historia ecclesiastica* at Saint-Évroult (in a copy written by Orderic), at Bec and at Jumièges, Gildas at Bec, Mont Saint-Michel and Lyre, and 'Nennius', *Historia*

---

[1] OV ii. 324–5. I am most grateful to Martin Brett and David Woodman for their editorial comments and corrections. Any remaining errors are mine.

Brittonum perhaps at Bec.[2] *Lives* of Anglo-Saxon saints are listed at Fécamp (St Edward), Bec (*Vita sancti Neoti*) and Jumièges (*Vita sancti Neoti* and *Vita sancti Swithuni*), but these library catalogue references considerably understate what was known.[3] Modern research in medieval chroniclers' use of sources, surviving manuscripts and other material objects, as we shall show below, reveals good knowledge of England's past.[4] However, as far as we can tell, this knowledge was employed by Norman chroniclers in a highly selective manner, in the first instance to stress England's debt to Norman leaders. More than a century before Orderic's time his predecessor Dudo of Saint Quentin had written a history of the dukes of Normandy from the semi-legendary Hastings to Duke Richard I (d. 996).[5] In the second book on Rollo, Richard I's grandfather, Dudo devoted several chapters to 'King Alstemus', almost certainly the late-ninth-century Viking leader Guthrum of East Anglia, who after baptism was known as Athelstan.[6] Great store is set by their mutual support. First Alstemus allows Rollo a stay in England as long as he promises that it is a temporary overwintering before he continues his journey to France. As a result of a mutual pact, Alstemus then sends support in the form of twelve ships laden with corn, wine and bacon to Rollo once he had landed in Walcheren (in the Netherlands, now the province of Zeeland). Their second encounter comes later after Rollo's withdrawal from the siege of Paris, when he rushed to England where Alstemus was under attack from his subjects. Another pact follows, with the king promising Rollo half his kingdom and half his moveables provided he becomes a Christian. Rollo consents as he wants to fulfil his dream of conquering France with Alstemus' agreement. The story of Rollo's encounters with Alstemus, set in the late ninth century, and thus about a hundred years before Dudo's time, are legendary but very interesting in that they reflect the view of the Norman ducal court in the late 990s.[7] Only a few years earlier, in 991, Richard I had agreed a reciprocal pact with King Æthelred, suggested by Pope John XV (985–96), and backed up by

---

[2] G. Nortier, *Les Bibliothèques médiévales des abbayes bénédictines de Normandie*, Paris 1971, unpaginated Appendix, listed by author's name.

[3] Nortier, *Les Bibliothèques*, Appendix, listed under *Vita* or saint's name.

[4] M. Chibnall, 'Les Normands et les saints anglo-saxons', in P. Bouet and F. Neveux (eds), *Les Saints dans la Normandie médiévale. Colloque Cerisy-la-Salle (26–29 Septembre 1996)*, Caen 2000, 259–68.

[5] *De moribus et actis primorum Normanniae ducum auctore Dudone sancti Quintini decano*, ed. J. Lair, Caen 1865; *Dudo of St Quentin, History of the Normans*, tr. E. Christiansen, Woodbridge 1998.

[6] *De moribus*, 149–51, 158–9 (bk ii. 9, 17–18); *Dudo*, tr. Christiansen, 32–3, 39–40.

[7] For the date of Dudo's history, completed by around *c*.1001, see M. Arnoux, 'Before the *Gesta Normannorum* and beyond *Dudo*: some evidence on early Norman historiography', *ANS* xxii (1999), 29–48.

guarantors from both the English and the Norman side.[8] Otherwise, in Book III Dudo inflated William Longsword's dealings with the historical King Æthelstan (924–39) by recording that it was Duke William (instead of Count Hugh of Vermandois and Hugh Capet) who had taken the initiative in the return to power of the Carolingian King Louis IV after his exile at the English royal court.[9]

The historiographical theme of Normans as saviours of the English increased in strength as time went on. It was picked up and continued by Dudo's successor, William of Jumièges, in his *Gesta Normannorum ducum (GND)*.[10] He drastically abbreviated Dudo's work on the first four Norman leaders before updating it with three books on Richard II (996–1027), Richard III (1027–8) and Robert the Magnificent (1028–35), and William the Conqueror (1028–87) until *c*.1070. In the process he cut out all history of Rollo before he was baptised, including the encounters with Alstemus, on the grounds that 'they are mere flattery and do not offer a model of what is honourable or edifying'.[11] His updated history, however, is important for the Norman view of England soon after the middle of the eleventh century, as it functioned as prelude to his account of the Norman Conquest of England. As in a much briefer account in the *Inuentio et miracula Sancti Vulfranni* (c. 18) written in the early 1050s at Saint-Wandrille, the point was to stress the legitimacy of Edward the Confessor's rule against that of Cnut and his sons, and the help he received from his Norman relatives.[12] Æthelred's marriage to the Norman Emma created the dynastic link that ultimately provided William the Conqueror with his argument to invade England. Books v, vi and vii of the *GND* provide a substantial account of Anglo-Norman relations based in intimate (if biased) knowledge of the end of Æthelred's reign due to the actions of the Danish kings Svein and Cnut, the exile of the aethelings

---

[8] *Papsturkunden 896–1046*, ed. H. Zimmermann (Denkschriften der Österreichischen Akademie der Wissenschaften, Phil.-hist. Klasse 174, 1984), i. 595–7, no. 307; F. Tinti, 'England and the papacy in the tenth century', in D. Rollason, C. Leyser and H. Williams (eds), *England and the Continent in the tenth century: studies in honour of Wilhelm Levison (1876–1947)* (Studies in the early Middle Ages xxxvii, 2010), 163–84. P. Bauduin, 'La papauté, les Vikings et les relations anglo-normandes: autour du traité de 991', in A. Gautier and C. Martin (eds), *Échanges, communications et réseaux dans le Haut Moyen Âge. Études offertes à Stéphane Lebecq*, Turnhout, Brepols (Collection Haut Moyen Age, 14), 2011, 197–210.

[9] *De moribus*, ed. Lair, 70; *Dudo*, tr. Christiansen, 193 and for historical commentary, 201 n. 259.

[10] *The Gesta Normannorum ducum of William of Jumièges, Orderic Vitalis and Robert of Torigni*, ed. and tr. E.M.C. van Houts, Oxford 1992–95.

[11] *GND* 'epistola' (i. 6–7): *animaduertens ea penitus adulatoria nec speciem honesti uel utilis pretendere*.

[12] *Inventio et miracula sancti Vulfranni*, ed. Dom J. Laporte (Société de l'histoire de Normandie, Mélanges 14 sér. 1938), 29–31; E.M.C. van Houts, 'Historiography and hagiography at Saint-Wandrille: the *Inventio et miracula sancti Vulfranni*', *ANS* xii (1990), 233–51.

in Normandy and their attempts to return to England.[13] Striking is William's knowledge of the St Brice's Day massacre in 1002 for which he is the earliest, and most critical, non-English source.[14] In contrast to Dudo's stories about 'Alstemus' and Orderic Vitalis's use of the *Life of Guthlac*, this was not ancient Anglo-Saxon history but relatively recent, almost contemporary history, history within living memory that highlighted important political links between the duchy and its far richer and more powerful neighbour across the Channel. In William's story the theme of the Normans as saviours of the English was needed in order to justify Duke William's own claim to the English throne which he argued had been unjustly taken by Edward's brother-in-law Harold. Upon Edward's death, Harold had committed perjury by not fulfilling his promise to Duke William given in 1064/65 to help the smooth handover to him. The Norman Conquest was the just punishment of the perjured leader Harold and a belated vengeance on Harold's father, Godwin, who was held responsible in some quarters for the death in 1036 of Edward's brother Alfred. The apologetic nature of Norman eleventh-century historiography reached its peak in William of Poitiers' biography of the Conqueror which worked out in far greater detail what William of Jumièges had already attempted. In the process he famously revealed some knowledge of Anglo-Saxon law. In a speech by Harold's messenger to William on the eve of the battle of Hastings, he claimed that both Harold and William were right in their respective claims to the English throne, but that Harold's took priority on the basis of King Edward's deathbed bequest which, according to Anglo-Saxon law, overrode any earlier promise: 'For ever since the time when St Augustine came to these parts, the common custom of this people has been that the gift that anyone made at the point of death shall be held as valid.'[15] Duke William's claim was based on an earlier promise by King Edward, valid according to Norman custom but not according to English. By the end of the eleventh century, then, Dudo's history, the *GND* and William of Poitiers' biography of the Conqueror were the standard reference works for Norman history. Their attention to Anglo-Saxon history was limited, highly selective and had no room for England's saints.

---

[13] *GND* ii. 10–15, 14–23 (bk v. 4, 6–9); ii. 76–9 (bk vi. 9 (10)–11 (12)); ii. 104–7 (bk vii. 5 (8)–6 (9)).

[14] S. Keynes, 'The massacre of St Brice's Day (13 November 1002)', in N. Lund (ed.), *Seksogtyvende tværfaglige vikingesymposium Københavns Universitet 2007*, Aarhus 2007, 32–67. For the most important English sources, see ASC E, s.a. 1002; and *English historical documents, c.500–1042*, ed. D. Whitelock, 2 edn London 1979, no. 127, translating S 909.

[15] *The Gesta Guillelmi of William of Poitiers*, ed. and tr. R.H.C. Davis and M. Chibnall, Oxford 1998, 118–19: *etenim ab eo tempore quo beatus Augustinus in hanc uenit regionem, commune gentis huius fuisse consuetudinem donationem quam in ultimo fine suo quis fecerit eam ratam haberi*. J. Beckermann, 'Succession in Normandy 1087 and in England 1066: the role of testamentary custom', *Speculum* xlvii (1972), 258–60.

At whom was Orderic's polemic pleading for the value of Anglo-Saxon saints in Normandy aimed? His inclusion of stories about Anglo-Saxon saints followed his own revisionist use of his predecessors' work as he downplayed the propagandistic and triumphant style of the two Williams' work by allowing occasionally the subjected English to be heard. He made it his life's task to be that voice, albeit subtly enough not to upset his Norman paymasters. First, around 1110, he revised the *GND* by adapting the Latin style to his own rhymed prose, by inserting information pertaining to Saint-Évroult and its benefactors and by explaining events for a younger audience. By far the most important aspect was his toning down of the triumphalist pro-Norman flavour of William of Jumièges' original account of the Norman Conquest. In the earlier sections of the *GND*, including those on eleventh-century England, Orderic did not change the original all that much. Secondly, he wrote his *Ecclesiastical history* with which I began this chapter. For the story of the Norman Conquest he mainly used William of Poitiers' work, for which he now is our prime witness, as the end of the original text is lost.[16] There, too, he wove into his narrative comments highly critical of the Conqueror, especially the criticisms aimed at the lack of control Odo of Bayeux and William FitzOsbern exercised over their troops on King William's behalf, and the devastation caused as a result of the 'Harrying of the North' in 1068/69.[17] It is in the Norman Conquest part of the narrative, too, that he came to insert the history of Crowland in the Fens where he spent five weeks at the invitation of his former colleague at Saint-Évroult, Abbot Geoffrey of Orléans (1109–24).[18] Crowland had become the last resting-place of Earl Waltheof, one of the three earls punished for their rebellion against William the Conqueror in 1075, but the only one to be executed in 1076. A minor cult had sprung up round his tomb and Orderic was asked to provide an epitaph for him.[19] It is in this context that we have to place Orderic's research on the early history of the abbey founded by St. Guthlac in the eighth century.[20] A summary of his life as written by Felix was inserted in the *Ecclesiastical history* with an update on its refoundation in *c*.971. While Orderic clearly had a copy of Felix's text in front of him, the more recent history of the abbey was based mostly on oral information from Abbot Geoffrey, sub-prior Ansgot and some

---

[16] For a reconstruction, see R.H.C. Davis, 'William of Poitiers and his *History of William the Conqueror*', in R.H.C. Davis, J.M. Wallace-Hadrill, R.J.A.I. Catto and M.H. Keen (eds), *The writing of history in the middle ages: essays presented to Richard William Southern*, Oxford 1981, 71–100, at 98–100.

[17] OV ii. 202–3, 232–3.

[18] OV ii. 324–5 and p. xxvi; at OV i. 32 the editor suggests that the visit may be dated to 1114–15.

[19] C. Watkins, 'The cult of Earl Waltheof at Crowland', *Hagiographica* iii (1996), 95–111.

[20] OV ii. 324–39.

senior monks as well as his own research into records.[21] Orderic's hand has been identified in the calendar of Thorney Abbey (Oxford, St John's College, MS 17, fo. 21v) where he added the name of St Évroult on 29 December, evidence that he visited the nearby abbey where he presumably made inquiries as well.[22] His information about the succession of English kings, which he uses to give chronological guidance to his readers in dating the stories he tells, derived from a chronicle of Worcester, another house he visited perhaps during the same journey. This was John of Worcester's work.[23] Apart from the Crowland story, he mentions the conversion of the Angles and Saxons by St Augustine (for which incidentally compare William of Poitiers' knowledge, above) and the reform movement of the tenth century.[24] For him they were the stories of the holy deeds of the Anglo-Saxons which he felt deserved a place in his work on the Normans. Alongside his revision of the *GND* and his *Ecclesiastical history*, Orderic copied manuscripts, including a complete copy of Bede's *Ecclesiastical history* now preserved in Rouen, BM MS 1343.[25] He also compiled hagiographical dossiers such as that for St Æthelwold, bishop of Winchester and associated saints, now Alençon, BM MS 14, probably based on manuscript material from Winchester's Old Minster.[26] Thus, there is no doubt that Orderic actively promoted the knowledge of some Anglo-Saxon saints at Saint-Évroult and incorporated their cults into his *Ecclesiastical history*.

Orderic's agenda for the inclusion of Anglo-Saxon ecclesiastical heritage in his work was probably a reaction to some of the outrageously violent attitudes

---

[21] OV ii. 338–9.

[22] OV i. Appendix 1, Manuscripts copied or annotated by Orderic, 200–203, at 203; M. Chibnall, *The world of Orderic Vitalis*, Oxford 1984, 36. For Orderic's use of his Thorney abbey research, see OV vi. 150–53.

[23] OV ii. 186, n. 1; JW *Chronicle* ii. pp. xvii–viii; M. Brett, 'John of Worcester and his contemporaries', in R.H.C. Davis and others (eds), *The writing of history in the Middle Ages*, 101–26.

[24] For kings' lists deriving from Bede and 'Nennius' (OV vi. 386 n. 3), see OV ii. 188–9, 240–41, 264–5, 338–9, iii. 62–3, iv. 42–3, v. 298–9, vi. 386–7; for the conversion of the Angles and Saxons, see OV ii. 240–41, iii. 62–3; for the reform movement and in particular Æthelwold, see OV ii. 240–43, vi. 150–53.

[25] OV i. Appendix 1, 203; *Bede's ecclesiastical history of the English people*, ed. B. Colgrave and R.A.B. Mynors, Oxford 1969, p. lxi (where Orderic's text is identified as a c-redaction). D. Escudier, 'Orderic Vital et le scriptorium de Saint-Évroult', in P. Bouet and M. Dosdat (eds), *Manuscrits et enluminures dans le monde normand (xe–xve siècles)*, Caen 1999, 17–28 who at 26–7 argues for more witnesses to Orderic's handwriting particularly in the form of musical annotation (see 26, figures 7 and 8). For Orderic's references to Bede, see OV iii. 66–9, vol. v. 288–9.

[26] Wulfstan of Winchester, *The Life of St Æthelwold*, ed. and tr. M. Lapidge and M. Winterbottom, Oxford 1991, pp. clvii–clviii; Chibnall, 'Les Normands et les saints anglo-saxons', 265. OV i. Appendix 1, 202. For Orderic's use of this material, see OV vi. 150–53.

of the Normans against the Anglo-Saxon past in the first generation after the Conquest. This had manifested itself in two main ways: through looting of Anglo-Saxon (religious) art and scepticism about Anglo-Saxon saints. Firstly, gold and silverware, richly embroidered vestments, decorated books and other treasures were taken from English monasteries to provide rewards for Norman and French supporters (ecclesiastical and lay).[27] This large-scale looting, though pretty standard by contemporary norms, had no regard for the local and national sentiments attached to the objects.[28] The conquerors had had their eye on England's riches (as the Danes and other invaders before them), which after the Conquest were legitimately, so they argued, theirs. Even if they admired the characteristic Anglo-Saxon craftsmanship of gold work and embroidery, what counted for them was the monetary and prestige value more than the 'Englishness' of the objects. Although Orderic does not spell this out, by including stories of English gifts dating from before the Conquest he bears witness to Norman awareness and appreciation of the quality of Anglo-Saxon artisanship. Queen Emma's gift of an illuminated Psalter (*magnum psalterium variis picturis decoratum*) to her brother Robert, archbishop of Rouen (989–1037), found its way to Saint-Évroult but is now lost. According to Orderic, Robert's son William 'carried it from his father's chamber, as sons do, and gave it to his beloved wife, whom he sought to please in all things'.[29] William and Hawisa's son Robert, abbot of Saint-Évroult, gave it in turn to his monastery. Other Anglo-Saxon liturgical books are the early-eleventh-century sacramentary in Latin and Old English, now Rouen BM MS 274, containing an English calendar and some masses for English saints, and the Latin pontifical, now Rouen BM MS 369; both are products of Winchester.[30] The former was given by Robert Champart (d. 1055), bishop of London (1044–51) and archbishop of Canterbury (1051–52) to his former abbey, Jumièges, where he had been monk and later abbot (1037–45),

---

[27] C.R. Dodwell, *Anglo-Saxon art: a new perspective*, Ithaca, NY 1982, ch. 8 'Anglo-Saxon art and the Norman conquest', 216–34; for stolen books, see D.N. Dumville, 'Anglo-Saxon books: treasure in Norman hands?' *ANS* xvi (1993), 84–99, Appendix at 98–9.

[28] T. Reuter, 'Plunder and tribute in the Carolingian empire', *TRHS* 5th ser. xxxv (1985), 75–94 and idem, '"You can't take it with you": testaments, hoards and moveable wealth in Europe, 600–1100', in E. Tyler (ed.), *Treasure in the medieval West*, York 2000, 11–24.

[29] OV ii. 42–3; E.M.C. van Houts, *Memory and gender in medieval Europe, 900–1200*, Basingstoke 1999, 114.

[30] *The missal of Robert of Jumièges*, ed. H.A. Wilson (HBS xi, 1896) (MS 274); J. Backhouse, D.H. Turner and L. Webster (eds), *The golden age of Anglo-Saxon art, 966–1066*, London 1984, nos 40 (colour pl. viii) [MS 274] and 50 (xiv) [MS 369]. It is less likely that the Robert who gave MS 274 was Archbishop Robert of Rouen.

and the latter probably came to Normandy through him as well.³¹ Secondly, the heavy-handedness of some of the Norman clergy in charge of English churches and monasteries after the Norman Conquest did not endear them to their new flock.³² Coming from a continental reform background characterised by increased regulation about what constitutes sainthood, the Normans demanded much more intense scrutiny before individuals could be declared saints. Faced with English saints in the calendars of the houses they colonised, occasionally abbots proposed a limited purge of calendars or liturgical music depriving the indigenous clergy of much loved saints. During the second generation after the Conquest it was Orderic in Normandy who set out to restore the place of Anglo-Saxon saints and their cults in a wide-ranging history that had started as a modest local chronicle of his own monastery. By stressing the capacity of saints, including Anglo-Saxon ones, to provide grace for penitent sinners (i.e. his readers) he justified their inclusion in his work. But times changed during Orderic's career. Whereas Normandy's interest in England was focused primarily on the demise of the Anglo-Saxon state (and events leading up to it) in 1066, by the 1130s the Normans turned their attention to its Anglo-Saxon beginnings. This in turn meant an evaluation of the demise of their precursors, the Britons, in whose accounts saints featured only sporadically.

Orderic included the prophecies of Merlin, written by Geoffrey of Monmouth probably in the 1120s, in his *Ecclesiastical history*; his younger colleague and historian Robert of Torigni at Bec showed Geoffrey's complete history of the Britons to Henry of Huntingdon in January 1139, Wace translated most of it (except the prophecies) in the early 1150s, and Stephen of Rouen used its contents for his *Draco Normannicus* in the late 1160s. It is truly astounding how the chroniclers of England's past – not only in England but across the sea – so dramatically switched their attention from the defeat of the Anglo-Saxons to the defeat of their predecessors. Orderic reinterpreted the prophecies of Merlin about the two dragons, one white and one red, symbolising the Saxons and British respectively, but reversed their colours.³³ He saw the red one as William Rufus and the white one as Robert Curthose, while one of the prophecies' other animals, the lion of justice, was interpreted as standing for Henry I.³⁴ Although the prophecies formed part of the history of the Britons, as Merlin was supposed to have told them to King Vortigern, Orderic does not seem to have known the full text of Geoffrey

---

³¹ V. Gazeau, *Normannia monastica*, ii, Prosopographie des abbés bénédictins (xie–xiie siècle), Caen 2007, 150–51.

³² S. Ridyard, '*Condigna veneratio*: post-Conquest attitudes to the saints of the Anglo-Saxons', *ANS* ix (1987), 179–206 and for a more nuanced interpretation P.A. Hayward, 'Translation-narratives in post-Conquest hagiography and English resistance to the Norman Conquest', *ANS* xxi (1999), 67–93.

³³ OV vi. 380–88 and p. xviii.

³⁴ G. Mon. 144–5 (bk vii. 112)); OV vi. 386–7.

of Monmouth's *History of the kings of Britain*. There is one potential paraphrase in the early part of his work when he has Guitmund (later bishop of Aversa) say to William the Conqueror that the Angles and Saxons who arrived 600 years before the Normans 'won dominion over the Britons now called the Welsh' (*Britonibus qui nunc Guali uocantur*).[35] The phrase is reminiscent of Geoffrey of Monmouth's at the very end of his *History* in Book xi, c. 207: *iam non uocabantur Britones sed Gualenses*.[36] However, the section is too short to use it categorically as evidence for Orderic's knowledge of Geoffrey's full text.

Yet, not Saint-Évroult but the monastery of Bec in Normandy is the place most intimately associated with interest in the British past of England. There Robert of Torigni, monk and prior, and from 1154 abbot of Mont Saint-Michel, took over Orderic's mantle as Normandy's historian.[37] He, too, had revised the *GND* by using Orderic's version of the text, reinstating much of Dudo's work on Rollo (including the stories about Rollo 'the pagan' and Alstemus) which William of Jumièges had omitted.[38] Robert also updated the text with Book VIII, which is in effect a biography of Henry I (1100–1135) containing at the same time invaluable prosopographical material on the main Anglo-Norman noble families. However, he left an update concerning Geoffrey of Anjou, who in the 1140s became duke by right of his wife Empress Matilda, to others better informed about Angevin history.[39] Like Orderic before him, Robert then moved on to writing history on a wider canvas by continuing Sigebert of Gembloux's world chronicle.[40] Robert's updating of the *GND* and Sigebert's chronicle as well as his sense of his own limitations as historian are important to bear in mind when we evaluate his stand on the history of the Britons.

---

[35] OV ii. 276–7.

[36] G. Mon. 280–81 (bk ix. 207). The sentence does not feature in 'Nennius'.

[37] For Robert of Torigni as historian of English history, see D. Bates, 'Robert of Torigni and the "Historia Anglorum",' in David Roffe (ed.), *The English and their Legacy, 900–1200. Essays in Honour of Ann Williams*, Woodbridge 2012, 175–84. I am most grateful to David Bates for allowing me to read his paper in advance of publication

[38] *GND* i. pp. lxxvii–xci.

[39] Robert of Torigni to Prior Gervase of Saint-Céneri, a priory of Saint-Évroult, asking him to write a continuation of the *GND* with a biography of Count Geoffrey (*Venerabilis Guiberti abbatis b. Mariae de Novigento opera omnia*, ed. L. d'Achery, Paris 1651, 715–16 and *Chronique de Robert de Torigni*, ed. L. Delisle, Rouen 1872–73 [RT], ii. 338–40; for a discussion, see E.M.C. van Houts, 'Latin and French as languages of the past in Normandy during the reign of Henry II: Robert of Torigni, Stephen of Rouen and Wace', in R. Kennedy and S. Meecham-Jones (eds), *Writers of the reign of Henry II: twelve essays*, Basingstoke 2006, 53–78, at 62–3.

[40] *Chronique de Robert*, ed. Delisle; see also *The chronicle of Robert of Torigni abbot of St. Michael-in-Peril-of-the-Sea*, in *Chronicles of the reigns of Stephen, Henry II and Richard I*, ed. R. Howlett (RS [lxxxii], 1884–89), iv.

By January 1139, when Robert had completed his revision of the *GND*, he had got hold of Geoffrey of Monmouth's full work, as in that month he showed it at Bec to his fellow historian Henry of Huntingdon.[41] The archdeacon had accompanied Theobald, archbishop of Canterbury (1138–64), until the previous year abbot at Bec, on his journey to Rome to receive his pallium. Henry was stunned as he had not seen it before. This is most surprising as both he and Geoffrey formed part of the same intellectual circle of secular clergy in England. Henry was archdeacon (of Huntingdon) in the diocese of Lincoln, as was Geoffrey's close friend Walter (of Oxford), who Geoffrey claimed had given him 'the book in British ... brought back from Brittany' (Book xi, c. 208).[42] Both Henry and Geoffrey dedicated versions of their work to Bishop Alexander of Lincoln.[43] As members of the highest secular clergy, Geoffrey of Monmouth and Walter of Oxford must have known Theobald, as clearly Henry did. And how do they link up with Robert of Torigni? Perhaps Robert was known in England as an historian of Normandy and may have been approached for information about the more obscure aspects of Normandy's (British, i.e. Celtic) past (see below). Perhaps Theobald, freshly arrived at Canterbury, spread knowledge of Robert's expertise and love of books in England. Or Geoffrey himself may have travelled via Bec, as Henry of Huntingdon did in 1139, en route to one of the French schools where he studied – as we know that he carried the title of *magister* which he must have earned there.[44]

Interestingly, too, Robert himself remains silent about Geoffrey and only reveals his knowledge about him through Henry of Huntingdon. As David Bates has recently emphasised, Robert was interested in English history because he used Henry of Huntingdon's chronicle both for the Anglo-Saxon past and for contemporary English (and Norman) history in his *World chronicle*.[45] But to say that Robert himself absorbed and digested Geoffrey's work would be wrong. He copied Henry's 'Letter to Warin the Breton' which formed part of Henry's *History of the English*, but not in the chronologically correct place, that is after the Romans and before the arrival of the Angles and Saxons. Instead, it was inserted after the account of Henry I's death where he lists some of the woes of his own time.[46] In the 'Letter to Warin' Henry explains how he had found the

---

[41] Henry of Huntingdon, *Historia Anglorum: the history of the English people*, ed. and tr. D. Greenway, Oxford 1996 [HH].

[42] G. Mon. 280–81. For Geoffrey and Walter as witnesses of the same charters, see H.E. Salter, 'Geoffrey of Monmouth and Oxford', *EHR* xxxiv (1919), 382–5.

[43] HH 4–7, Prologue ; G. Mon. 142–3 (bk vii. 109–10).

[44] Salter, 'Geoffrey of Monmouth', 383, no. 3 (January 1139 charter for Godstow styles Geoffrey as *magister*).

[45] Bates, 'Robert of Torigni'.

[46] HH 558–83, Letter to Warin.

full copy of Geoffrey's work at Bec and then presents him a summary of it.[47] In Robert's own autograph manuscript of the *World chronicle* (Avranches, BM MS 159) he interpolated Henry's 'Letter to Warin' with a short passage revealing himself as the person who showed Henry the book and describing himself as 'a man devoted to the investigation and collection of books upon subjects divine as well as secular'. He also added the name of Archbishop Theobald.[48] Robert, like Henry before him, therefore included Geoffrey's information in a drastically abbreviated form not at the chronologically correct place in his *World chronicle*, but around *c.*1100, the point where he declares himself to be the continuator of Sigebert's *Chronicle*. By doing so, he uses the same technique of inserting relevant information but of unknown authority as he had used in his revision of the *GND* when at the end he added the so-called *Additamenta* dealing with issues relating to the history of much earlier dukes than Henry I.[49] In this way Robert, like Henry, 'sat on the fence', by inserting the information yet refraining from explicitly voicing scepticism about his sources' dubious authenticity. With regard to Geoffrey's *History of the kings of the British* it is highly significant that Robert used it only through the filter of Henry of Huntingdon's authority so he could not be blamed for putting faith in what many must have suspected, if not known, to be a hoax.

England's British, rather than Anglo-Saxon, past remained a topic of fascination for Norman historians as it seems to have inspired a mini hoax at Bec during Robert's lifetime, but after he had left the monastery to take up the abbacy at Mont Saint-Michel. The copy of Geoffrey's *History*, Leiden, UB BPL 20 fos 60r–101v, dating from *c.*1160 may well have been made for (if not copied by) another Bec monk, Stephen of Rouen.[50] He was the author of the *Draco Normannicus*, a versified Latin history of the Normans (based on Robert of Torigni's *GND*) but with lengthy sections on other related topics, written at Bec shortly after September 1167 when Empress Matilda died.[51] Written to celebrate

---

[47] HH 558–9, Letter to Warin.

[48] *Chronique* ed. Delisle, i. 97–8 (ed. Howlett, 65–6); see also HH 558 n. g. Note that HH pp. cxxii–iii, omits the description of Robert of Torigni's autograph manuscript with the siglum Av as announced in the index of manuscripts cited on p. 847.

[49] *GND* 'Additamenta' (ii. 280–89). However, note that where he was sure of the authenticity of his sources he included them in the correct chronological place. See, for example, his inclusion of a potted history of his monastery of Bec based among others on Gilbert Crispin's *Life of Herluin*; compare *Chronique*, bk vi. c. (9) with *GND* ii. 60–77 (bk vi. 9).

[50] For the manuscript, see E.M.C. van Houts, *Gesta Normannorum ducum. Een studie over de handschriften, de tekst, het geschiedwerk en het genre*, Groningen 1982, 229–31 with an updated summary in *GND* i. pp. cix–cx and J.C. Crick, *The Historia regum Britannie of Geoffrey of Monmouth, iii: a summary catalogue of the manuscripts*, Woodbridge 1989, 124–6.

[51] *DN*, ii. 589–782. For the death of Matilda, see 596, 708 and 713.

Henry II and his mother, Empress Matilda, whom Stephen knew very well, it contains a curious amalgamation of information.[52] The title *Norman Dragon* is without any doubt inspired by Geoffrey's prophecies of Merlin, where, as we have already noted, the white dragon stood as symbol of a conquering people.[53] One of the most perplexing sections in the poem occurs in the contemporary part on Henry II in the form of an exchange of fictitious letters between him and Arthur and between Arthur, the main protagonist of Geoffrey's *History*, and Rolland of Dinan, the (real) leader of the Britons.[54] The historical context was Henry II's campaign to infiltrate and subject Brittany. Henry II's first move dated from within a year of his accession to the English throne, followed by his acquisition of the county of Nantes in 1158 and the marriage alliance of his son Geoffrey with the Breton heiress Constance in 1166, which led to marriage in 1181.[55] Clearly, the resurgence of Arthur as a 'live' ruler berating Henry II for his military expeditions into the duchy is a fiction. Nevertheless the fantasy reveals how by the late 1160s the history of the Britons had become synonymous with the case of Welsh and Breton resistance against the Angevin dynasty in Britain and on the Continent.[56] Stephen of Rouen used Arthur to voice the discontent amongst Henry II's subjects and to warn the king of potential dangers inherent in his imperial policies. For us, however, it becomes clear that Stephen is interested in Arthur not so much as pre-Anglo-Saxon ruler in England but as pre-Norman/Angevin 'ancestor' on the Continent. If this proposition can be accepted for Stephen, it raises the intriguing question whether the same held true for Robert of Torigni in the late 1130s. So let us retrace our steps and return to Robert's interest in Geoffrey's work, this time looking at the topic from a new angle.

---

[52] For Stephen of Rouen, see L. Shopkow, *History and community: Norman historical writing in the eleventh and twelfth centuries*, Washington, DC 1997, 50–51, 112–16, 170–72, 209–11, 239–41; van Houts, 'Latin and French', 55–6, 57–9. For Rolland's identification, see J.A. Everard, *Brittany and the Angevins: province and empire, 1158–1203*, Cambridge 2000, 44, 56–7.

[53] Shopkow, *History*, 141.

[54] *DN* 696 (Rolland to Arthur and Arthur to Rolland), 697–705 (Arthur to Henry II), 707 (Henry to Arthur). P. Johanek, 'König Arthur und die Plantagenets', *Frühmittelalterliche Studien* xxi (1987), 346–86, at 384–6, where it is suggested that Stephen of Rouen used an existing fictional correspondence (in prose). From 1157 dates a (fictional) letter from Arthur to Hugh, chaplain at Braine-sur-Avre, the home of Agnes de Baudemont and her second husband, Robert of Dreux, brother of King Louis VII. The text is printed in J.C. Crick, *The Historia regum Brittanie of Geoffrey of Monmouth iv: dissemination and reception in the later Middle Ages*, Woodbridge 1991, 92–3 but the identification of *Hugoni cappellano de Branno* is mine (van Houts, 'Latin and French', 58).

[55] Everard, *Brittany and the Angevins*, 34–45; van Houts, 'Latin and French', 58.

[56] Johanek, 'König Arthur'.

Arthur's exploits on the Continent, especially in France (Brittany, Anjou and Normandy) as recounted in the final three books of Geoffrey's *History* (Books IX–XI), may well have brought Geoffrey and Robert of Torigni together in the first place. Having just completed the *GND* Robert must have been fascinated to learn in detail about a Briton ruler Arthur who roamed through western Europe well before the Merovingians and Carolingians, and in particular about Arthur's dealings with Estrusia (Neustria, as Normandy used to be called), which he gave to his butler Bedverus (from Bayeux), and where his base camp was at Barfleur.[57] Bedverus together with Arthur's steward, Kaius (who had been given Anjou), were given a prominent role in the defeat of the giant of the Mont Saint-Michel who had murdered Hoel of Brittany's niece Helena, after whose grave on the smaller rock next to Mont Saint-Michel, Tombelaine (*Tumba Helena*) was called.[58] As I suggested above, both Robert's and Henry's insertion of the 'Letter of Warin' in their chronicles in their own time rather than in the supposedly correct chronological place is an indicator of their doubts about the authenticity of its information. Having said that, their scepticism does not preclude prior contact between Robert and Geoffrey, as it was common for historians across western Europe to seek one other out for knowledge about areas further away from home whose past was less well known to them. In *c*.980 Æthelweard famously asked Abbess Matilda of Essen for news of the whereabouts of King Æthelstan's sister 'who [was] married to a certain king near the Alps', and Robert himself confessed to not being well enough informed about Anjou to write a biography of Count Geoffrey (d. 1151).[59] Could Geoffrey have been in touch with Robert about the 'Neustrian' aspects of his fantastic story? There is no direct evidence for my question but the possibility ought to be raised.

The 1160s Bec copy of Geoffrey's *History* cited earlier contains a striking phrase on Bedverus' burial in Bayeux where the Neustrians carried him after his death: 'There the body was buried with honour in a cemetery in the southern

---

[57] G. Mon. 192–223 (bk ix), on Arthur's Continental campaign which occurs mostly in the Neustrian area. The most comprehensive discussion of this material remains J.S.P. Tatlock, *The legendary history of Britain: Geoffrey of Monmouth's Historia regum Britanniae and its early vernacular versions*, Los Angeles 1950, repr. New York 1974, 87–92, who on p. 89 stresses the fact that only two Norman toponyms are mentioned, Bayeux and Barfleur.

[58] Tatlock, *The legendary history*, 87–8; note that the occurrence of Arthur's butler and steward, but not their 'duchies', predates Geoffrey, as P. Sims-Williams has pointed out ('The early Welsh Arthurian poems', in R. Bromwich, A.O.H. Jarman and B.F. Roberts (eds), *The Arthur of the Welsh: the Arthurian legend in medieval Welsh literature*, Cardiff 1991, 33–71, at 39. For the geography of the two rocky promontories, see 'La baie du Mont Saint-Michel', in M. Baylé, P. Bouet, J.-P. Brighelli and others (eds), *Le Mont Saint-Michel. Histoire et imaginaire*, Paris 1998, 11–16.

[59] *The chronicle of Æthelweard*, ed. and tr. A. Campbell, London and Edinburgh 1962, 2.

part of the city next to its wall'.[60] While the specificity is indeed striking it is also puzzling, as the main Bayeux cemetery was at Saint-Vigor-le-Grand in the north, not south of the city.[61] One just wonders whether Geoffrey might have consulted a Norman historian for the information or, alternatively, was ticked off and persuaded to omit it. The hypothesis that Robert may have advised Geoffrey can in the absence of any other information simply not be verified.

Robert of Torigni's implicit doubt about the *History of the Britons* and Stephen of Rouen's playful use of Geoffrey's Arthur have to be set alongside the Arthurian knowledge of their contemporary Wace. In contrast to the two monks, Wace was a secular clerk who, having studied at Paris, settled at Caen and later became a canon of Bayeux.[62] He was the first major Norman author to adapt Latin prose to Anglo-Norman verse. Apart from saints' lives, his two major works are his verse adaptations: the *Roman de Brut*, based on Geoffrey's *History of the Britons* and written in the early 1150s, and the *Roman de Rou* based on the *GND* which he wrote in the 1160s and abandoned around 1174.[63] Like Robert and Stephen, Wace was conscious of the doubtful nature of much of Geoffrey's text, something he reiterated when he introduced the story of the attribute for which the Arthurian legend became most famous: the Round Table.[64] Other smaller revisions to the text of Geoffrey pertain to elaborations of descriptions of places, with some in the south-west corner of England, an area he probably visited.[65] He also consulted William of Malmesbury's two chronicles on the kings and bishops of England and had access to Goscelin of Saint-Bertin's miracles from St Augustine, Canterbury.[66] Whereas Geoffrey would refer to Neustrians and Neustria, Wace consistently used Normans and Normandy. If he was puzzled by Bedverus' link with Bayeux, he expressed it through another innovation by setting him over the Herepeis (the men from Hurepoix or La

---

[60] G. Mon. 248–9, lines 469–70 (bk x. 176) and p. xxiv; for a discussion, see Tatlock, *The legendary history*, 89–90, where he suggests that Bayeux's prominence may have been inspired by Geoffrey's patron Robert of Gloucester who held lands there by right of his wife.

[61] Tatlock, *The legendary history*, 90 and E. Deniaux, C. Lorren, P. Bauduin and T. Jarry (eds), *La Normandie avant les Normands. De la conquête romaine à l'arrivée des Vikings*, Rennes 2002, 234–6. For Wace's ignorance of the cemetery, see below.

[62] F.H.M. Le Saux (ed.), *A companion to Wace*, Woodbridge 2005; for his adaptation of the *Roman de Brut*, Tatlock, *The legendary history*, chapter 22, pp. 463–82 remains indispensible.

[63] *Wace's Roman de Brut: a history of the British*, ed. and tr. J. Weiss, Exeter 1999, rev. edn 2002; Wace, *The Roman de Rou*, tr. G.S. Burgess with the text of A.J. Holden and notes by G.S. Burgess and E.M.C. van Houts, Jersey 2002.

[64] Wace, *Brut*, lines 9787–98 (pp. 246–7).

[65] Tatlock, *The legendary history*, 464, 469; Wace, *Brut*, pp. xx–xxi.

[66] Tatlock, *The legendary history*, 468–9.

Hérupe, the ancient name for Neustria).⁶⁷ As for Bedverus' burial, Wace, like Geoffrey's 1160s Bec copy, locates it too in the south of the city of Bayeux.⁶⁸

Thus far we have seen that the early Norman chroniclers knew some Anglo-Saxon history which they manipulated to provide a narrative in which Normans are portrayed as knowing what is best for the English. Their successor Orderic chose a different tack and, at the same time as he toned down the propagandistic tone in Norman's historiography, he began to give voice to the victimised English by drawing attention to the good that could come from venerating their old saints. Orderic, in turn, was succeeded by Robert of Torigni, Stephen of Rouen and Wace who, like their English contemporaries, had to deal with a whole new dimension of England's history, namely that of its British past which incorporated Arthur's French campaigns. This new twist to English history, though no less Christian, did not allow for an hagiographical infusion along the lines Orderic had advocated. Anglo-Saxon saints were clearly venerated in Normandy, yet Anglo-Saxon cults never flourished widely in the duchy.⁶⁹

Before the Norman Conquest, Jumièges almost certainly acquired relics of St Aidan, bishop of Lindisfarne, St Oswald and perhaps also those of St Edmund through Robert Champart as bishop of London or archbishop of Canterbury. All three feature in a twelfth-century Jumièges calendar where they are joined by St Wilfrid.⁷⁰ The Anglo-Saxon manuscripts that came to Normandy contained information about Anglo-Saxon liturgical practices and one, as we have seen, had a calendar with indigenous saints in it. Many other Anglo-Saxon books formed part of the treasure distributed to Norman houses after 1066. Among the surviving ones three are known from Jumièges (an early-eleventh-century pontifical, a late-eleventh-century psalter, a customary from c.1000), two from Rouen (of which one is a late-tenth/mid-eleventh-century benedictional), Saint-Évroult (a benedictional, and a kalendar, both from the first half of the eleventh century), Mont Saint-Michel (an eighth-century gospel fragment and a homiliary c.1000), Saint-Wandrille (one is a missal of the second half of the eleventh century) and Fécamp (a late-eighth-century gospel book and a customary of c.1000) and one from Évreux (a pontifical of c.1000), Avranches (documents first half of eleventh century) and Cherbourg (tenth-century gospel book).⁷¹ These books would provide the Norman historians with

---

⁶⁷ Wace, *Brut* line 12170 (pp. 306–7; and 307 note 1).

⁶⁸ Wace, *Brut* lines 13003–6 (pp. 326–7): A Bayeues en Normendie/dunt il aveit la seignurie/ unt Beduer enseveli/ devers la porte, vers midi. 'Midi' surely stands for 'in australi' (G. Mon. 248–9, line 469 (bk x. 176), i.e. south [gate], not as in the translation here 'at noon'.

⁶⁹ Chibnall, 'Les Normands', 259–68, at 86 where she notes that the greatest popularity for an English saint was reserved for Thomas Becket (d. 1170, canonised 1173).

⁷⁰ Chibnall, 'Les Normands', 260, 267.

⁷¹ Dumville, 'Anglo-Saxon books', 98–9. Dumville's inventory also lists Anglo-Saxon books which ended up in non-Norman continental collections.

stories attached to them about their previous English owners, as in the case of Orderic's story about Queen Emma and the book she presented to her brother. Their contents would inform the Normans about English liturgical or other ecclesiastical practices, not all of which would be appreciated as we know from Norman scepticism. Yet, despite such explicit criticism in some quarters, Anglo-Saxon script and illumination exercised considerable influence on the writing and decorating of post-Conquest manuscripts by Normans in England and, to a lesser extent, in Normandy.[72] How conscious Norman and English scribes after 1066 were of the Anglo-Saxon legacy in manuscript culture is a difficult question to answer given the lack of explicit commentary. Among the looted treasure which according to William of Poitiers was distributed in Normandy were precious objects, many of which had saintly associations. Evidence form Waltham Abbey confirms that the despoliation went on after the Conqueror's death when William Rufus confiscated 6,666 pounds worth of treasure.[73] The late-twelfth-century Waltham chronicler explains that he found the evidence in a list compiled by Master Adelard, one of the canons established at Waltham by King Harold, that is, before 1066 but still clearly alive in Rufus' time.[74] According to the Waltham chronicler some of the loot went to St Stephen and Holy Trinity at Caen, the twin monasteries founded by Rufus' parents in the 1060s, where: 'even to this day they rejoice in the spoils thus acquired, and have inscriptions on the very reliquaries and gospel books of the names of the leading men who ... bestowed them on the church of Waltham.'[75] Significantly, these words prove that owner marks were on some of the relics and treasure, and these in turn served as potential sources of information for the Normans who

---

[72] For studies of manuscripts written in England in the first century after the Conquest, see N.R. Ker, *English manuscripts in the century after the Norman Conquest: the Lyell Lectures Oxford, 1952–3*, Oxford 1960, and R. Gameson, *The manuscripts of early Norman England (c.1066–1130)*, Oxford 1999.

[73] *The Waltham chronicle*, ed. and tr. L. Watkiss and M. Chibnall, Oxford 1994, 58–9. The thirteenth-century *Life of Harold* is more specific as it lists: 'seven shrines, of which three were gold and four silver-gilt, full of relics and precious jewels; four codices ornamented with gold silver and jewels; four large gold and silver censers ... four altars with relics, of which one was gold and the remainder silver gilt ... ten reliquaries one of which was made from two marks of gold and jewels, the remainder from gold and silver' (*Vita Haroldi. The romance of the life of Harold, king of England*, ed. and tr. W. de G. Birch, London 1885, 24–5. N. Rogers, 'The Waltham abbey relic-list', in C. Hicks (ed.), *England in the eleventh century* (Harlaxton Medieval Studies ii, 1992), 157–81, at 163 (translation)).

[74] *Waltham chronicle*, 58–9, c. 22; Adelard also wrote a list of Harold's relics into the Waltham chapter book (ibid. 36–7, c. 17).

[75] *Waltham chronicle*, 58–9, c. 22.

henceforth held them in their churches.[76] Archbishop Anselm of Canterbury (1089–1109) gave the *ossa* of St Neot to his old abbey of Bec as one of their English priories at Eynesbury was dedicated to this saint.[77] According to his letter to Bishop Robert of Lincoln (1094–1123) and others, it was the complete body 'except for the arm which it is said is already [at St. Neot's] in Cornwall and a small part which out of memory and veneration for the saint I have kept myself.'[78] He added that he himself had taken the key of the shrine in which the relics were kept to the abbey. Bec thus claimed to have relics of St Neot but as far as is known none for the Anglo-Saxon saints who were also listed in its liturgical calendar: St Dunstan, archbishop of Canterbury (959–88), St Edmund, king of East Anglia (855–69) and St Augustine, 'Apostle of the English'.[79]

Around the year 1000 a Norman reader interested in Anglo-Saxon history had only at his disposal the works of Bede and 'Nennius' plus the rather fantastic sections in Dudo's *History* which we have discussed. By *c.*1200, however, the choice of history books was larger but by no means generous. The most obvious start for our curious Norman would probably be Robert of Torigni's *World chronicle* for which he used Henry of Huntingdon's work, probably in the fourth version.[80] If he was ambitious, he could turn directly to Henry's own work known at Bec, Mont Saint-Michel and Jumièges.[81] No trace of the Anglo-Saxon Chronicle has ever been found in the duchy. William of Malmesbury's *Gesta regum Anglorum* and John of Worcester's *Chronicle* are known only indirectly, as we have seen through Wace and Orderic respectively, and both could have consulted them during visits to England. On the basis of what I have assembled here it would be difficult to argue that the twelfth-century Normans in Normandy were passionate in their quest for knowledge about the Anglo-Saxon past. This was left to their compatriots and descendants

---

[76] It should be noted that no trace of the Waltham treasure has been identified at Caen; see *Waltham chronicle*, 58–9, n. 4, c. 22.

[77] St Anselm, Letter 473 in *S. Anselmi Cantuariensis archiepiscopi opera omnia*, ed. F. Schmitt, London 1946–61, v. 421–2 – though a note in M. Brett and J. Gribbin (eds), *English episcopal acta xxviii: Canterbury, 1070–1136*, Oxford 2004, no. 31, discusses some serious difficulties with that text.

[78] Letter 473, p. 421.

[79] A. Porée, *Histoire de l'abbaye du Bec*, Évreux 1901, ii. Appendix v, pp. 579–91 Calendar of Bec: 583: St Dunstan, 19 May and St Augustine, 26 May; 585: St Neot, 31 July; 589: St Edmund, 20 November.

[80] Cf. note 42 above.

[81] HH pp. cxxii–iii, BnF MS lat. 6042 fos 3r–120v, a twelfth-century Norman copy possibly listed *c.*1163 in the catalogue of the library of Bec, but taken by Robert of Torigni to Mont Saint-Michel (siglum B); HH p. cxxxii, Cambridge, UL MS Gg. 2. 21 fos 3r–91r (siglum Gg); HH p. cxxxviii, Rouen BM MS 1177 fos 62r–166r, 276–78v (siglum R) around 1200 from Jumièges.

in England. It would be true to say that, of all Norman historians discussed here, it was only the Englishman Orderic Vitalis who campaigned for the Anglo-Saxon heritage to be taken seriously.

Chapter 9

Richard of Devizes and 'a rising tide of nonsense': How Cerdic Met King Arthur

John Gillingham

Richard of Devizes, a Benedictine belonging to Winchester cathedral priory (St Swithun's), is best known as the author of a contemporary chronicle of the early years of Richard I's reign.[1] This, it has been said, 'gives us a teasing entrance into an earthbound society' and reveals 'an entire absence of a Christian interpretation of history'.[2] It is also widely accepted that he wrote another, though little-known – and much more puzzling – historical work.[3] Parts of it were printed by H.R. Luard in the Rolls Series as the annals of Winchester.[4] Elsewhere it has been variously described as a 'chronicle of English history', as a 'Brut' chronicle,

---

[1] *The chronicle of Richard of Devizes*, ed. R. Howlett, in *Chronicles of the reigns of Stephen, Henry II and Richard I* (RS [lxxxii], 1886), iii. 379–454 and by J.T. Appleby, *The chronicle of Richard of Devizes*, London 1963.

[2] The quotations are taken from the chapter on Richard in N. Partner, *Serious entertainments: the writing of history in twelfth-century England*, Chicago 1977, 143–79, 151, 179.

[3] The case for his authorship was made by both Howlett and Appleby. Antonia Gransden was sceptical, however, partly on the grounds that annals being 'by their nature, merely brief chronological notes for each year' are difficult to compare with Richard's chronicle, *Historical writing in England, c.550 to c.1307*, London 1974, 252. But although this may be said of some entries, it is very far from being true of others, for example the entries for 828, 959, 979 and 1040. Indeed, Freeman described this last entry as 'a long romance'. E.A. Freeman, *The history of the Norman Conquest of England, its causes and its results*, Oxford 1873, ii, Note A.

[4] *Annales de Wintonia*, in *Ann. mon.* ii. 3 ff. Luard thought that Richard was the most likely author, but hedged his bets. Freeman's summary of the annalist's narrative of Earl Godwin's hand in the murder of Alfred illustrates the uncertainty over authorship created by Luard. 'Godwine wishes to open the succession to his son Harold. He entices Alfred over – Duke Robert, notwithstanding his death and burial in the East, keeps Edward back in Normandy – and causes one tenth of his companions to be beheaded, the rest to be tortured and crucified, and the Ætheling himself to be disembowelled. Godwine's instructions to his agents are given in two very graphic speeches. I trust that so pleasant a writer as Richard of Devizes is not answerable for this stuff.' Freeman, *Norman Conquest*, i, Note SSS.

and as a Winchester chronicle.⁵ No short title is entirely satisfactory, but for convenience sake I shall use the term 'annals'. In these annals we can see what Richard of Devizes made of Anglo-Saxon history and how he fitted it into what went before and came after. Given the fact that Richard's contemporary chronicle has long been celebrated as 'one of the most amusing products of the middle ages',⁶ we might have thought that his view of his country's more distant past would have attracted some interest. Nothing could be further from the truth. The account of the Anglo-Saxon period printed in the Winchester annals has been almost universally ignored – though not, inevitably, by Freeman in some of the wondrous notes in his Appendices. As for Richard's strikingly original reworking of Geoffrey of Monmouth's *De gestis Britonum*, including his depiction of the passage of dominion from British to Saxon rule, this remains unprinted and, so far as I can see, entirely unknown.⁷

That twentieth-century historians primarily interested in Anglo-Saxon England should have taken no notice of Richard's view of, and information on, the subject is hardly surprising. After all he was writing so much later, and was so clearly dependent on earlier sources, notably William of Malmesbury. But Richard has been all but ignored even by those interested in the historiography of Anglo-Saxon England. The one exception is Pauline Stafford's treatment of his tale of Queen Emma's ordeal. Under the year 1043, the longest of Richard's 'annals' tells how Queen Emma was accused of ill-treating Alfred and Edward and of taking the bishop of Winchester as a lover, and how she then in Winchester cathedral, thanks to St Swithun, came unharmed through the ordeal of walking barefoot over nine red-hot ploughshares.⁸ Stafford called Richard a 'chivalric chronicler' and his 'strange tale' of Emma 'a story which brings together eleventh-century facts and twelfth-century romanticisation with hagiographical traditions'.⁹ But I know of no one else who has shared her historiographical interest in Richard's

---

⁵ *Chronicle*, ed. Howlett, iii. p. lxviii; G.H. Martin, 'Devizes, Richard of (*c.*1150–*c.*1200)', in *ODNB*; BL online Manuscripts Catalogue, MS Cotton Domitian A. xiii. It is probably best described, as in the Corpus Christi College catalogue of manuscripts, as *Historia Angliae a Bruto ad primordia regni regis Stephani* with the note that according to Bale its author was Richard of Devizes.

⁶ *Chronicles*, ed. Howlett, iii. p. lxvii.

⁷ Most unluckily for him, it was certainly unknown when R.W. Leckie wrote *The passage of dominion: Geoffrey of Monmouth and the periodization of insular history in the twelfth century*, Toronto 1981.

⁸ *Ann. mon.* ii. 20–25.

⁹ P. Stafford, *Queen Emma and Queen Edith: queenship and women's power in eleventh-century England*, Oxford 1997, 19–21. It seemed to Freeman that the author whom he called the Winchester annalist displayed 'a remarkable acquaintance with the less decent parts of the satires of Juvenal', Freeman, *Norman Conquest*, ii, Note H.

reworking of the past – this despite him having much to say about Kings Cerdic, Ecgberht and Alfred.¹⁰

True, by contrast with the work of the writers of the second quarter of the twelfth century, above all William of Malmesbury and Henry of Huntingdon, the historians of the later twelfth century, Richard included, had little to contribute. As James Campbell put it, 'The greatest advances in the study and understanding of Anglo-Saxon history made before the 19th century were those of the twelfth. They were in large measure accomplished by historians working during the reigns of Henry I and Stephen'.¹¹ Rees Davies agreed: 'the twenty years from 1120 to 1140 were an explosively creative period in the shaping of the Matter of England'.¹² In James Campbell's view, 'Not the least interesting thing about the story of the recovery of knowledge of the distant past of England is that it is by no means one of continuous progress'. There was 'a rising tide of nonsense', much of it the responsibility of Geoffrey of Monmouth who 'poisoned most educated Englishmen's view of their own past'.¹³ In this chapter I wish to look a little closer at one who contributed more than most to that rising tide, and who in some ways out-geoffreyed Geoffrey, by daring to invent a decisive confrontation between King Arthur and Cerdic of Wessex.

Richard's annals survive in two manuscripts, CCCC MS 339, fos 1–24 (=A) and BL Cotton Domitian A. xiii, fos 3v–44r (=B).¹⁴ In both manuscripts they precede his chronicle. The copy of his chronicle in A is generally agreed to be Richard's autograph working text and, since annals and chronicle were written in the same hand, it seems hard to escape the conclusion that, as Bale long ago asserted, Richard composed both.¹⁵ Moreover, as Howlett and Appleby pointed out, both chronicle and annals contain the same turns of speech and the same classical quotations.¹⁶ In A the annals begin with Brutus arriving at an island

---

¹⁰ Richard does not, for example, figure in Simon Keynes's fine study of the cult of King Alfred, which in effect moves straight from William of Malmesbury to St Albans and Roger of Wendover, 'The cult of Alfred the Great', *ASE* xxviii (2000), 225–356, at 231.

¹¹ J. Campbell, 'Some twelfth-century views of the Anglo Saxon past', *Peritia* iii (1984), 131–50, repr. in idem, *Essays in Anglo-Saxon history*, London and Ronceverte 1986, 209–28, at 209.

¹² R.R. Davies, *The matter of Britain and the matter of England*, Oxford 1996, 12–17.

¹³ Campbell, 'Some twelfth-century views', 221.

¹⁴ For help and advice I am indebted to Suzanne Paul and Gill Cannell in Cambridge and to Julian Harrison in the British Library.

¹⁵ 'the Annals of Winchester … were copied by the same hand as the Chronicle', P.R. Robinson, *Catalogue of dated and datable manuscripts, c.737–1600, in Cambridge libraries*, Woodbridge 1988, i. 56; cf. R. Vaughan, cited in Appleby, *Chronicle*, pp. xviii–xix; M.B. Parkes, *Their hands before our eyes: a closer look at scribes*, Aldershot 2008, 18.

¹⁶ Howlett, *Chronicles*, iii. pp. lxxi–lxxii; *Chronicle*, ed. Appleby, pp. xxiv–xxv; J.T. Appleby, 'Richard of Devizes and the annals of Winchester', *Bulletin of the Institute of*

inhabited only by giants (an event dated 1,200 years after the Flood) and end in 1138 with Brian building Wallingford and Oxford as an illustration of a general point, made in the margin, that in England there was no one who mattered who did not raise or strengthen a fortress.[17] In B the text of the annals from AD 519 to 1065 is, like the chronicle of Richard's reign, clearly copied from A. But B's earlier and later annals are different. The earlier ones begin not with Brutus but with the birth of Jesus Christ and are written in a late-thirteenth-century hand; the annals for the period from 1066 to 1202 are written in the early-thirteenth-century hand which was also responsible for copying the annals for 519 to 1065.[18] Because the post-1065 annals in B are longer and apparently more informative than those in A, Luard chose to print A for 519 to 1065 and B for 1066 and after. In 1963 Appleby printed what he called 'the more interesting' of A's annals between 1066 and 1138, but he left out more than he printed.[19] Even more astonishing is the fact that both Luard in 1865 and Appleby in 1963 decided not to print the first nine folios of A, the early history of Britain as composed by one of the twelfth century's most remarkable authors.

Given that Appleby was keenly interested in proving that Richard was also the author of the Winchester annals, and that he, too, like Howlett before him, saw Richard's chronicle as 'one of the most interesting and amusing productions of the twelfth century',[20] it is surprising that he showed not the slightest interest in that part of his work in which Richard came to terms with another interesting and amusing production, the *Gesta Britonum* of Geoffrey of Monmouth. It is less surprising that Luard decided not to print a text which he referred to as 'a description of Britain, the early portion being chiefly taken from Geoffrey of Monmouth'. Nonetheless there is something distinctly odd about the fact that in making his edition of what he called 'the real Annals of Winchester',[21] he chose to begin with the year 519, for the contrast between the annals for 519 onwards and the earlier ones is nothing like as marked as he implied. The entries for 519, 534 and 552 all contain material taken from Geoffrey. While the last of these is no more than a five-word note of the succession of Constantine, son of Cador of Cornwall, as the king of the Britons, the entries for 519 and 534 are more substantial. In a remarkably original and inventive piece of history Richard explained, s.a. 519, the year of the accession of Cerdic as king of the West Saxons, that all the while Arthur was busy in Gaul the Saxons built those fortresses on the tops of hills the remains of which can still be seen today (*remanent usque hodie*). In the entry for 534 we are told that Cerdic was succeeded by his son

---

Historical Research xxxvi (1963), 70–77.

[17] A, fo. 24v. Extensive use of the margins is a well-known feature of Richard's chronicle.
[18] BL online catalogue, p. 2.
[19] Appleby, 'Richard of Devizes', 75–7.
[20] Appleby, 'Richard of Devizes', 70. Cf above, n. 6.
[21] *Ann. mon.* ii. p. ix.

Cynric, and that not until the seventh year of his reign (i.e. 541) did King Arthur, having heard of Modred's temerity, bring an army back from Gaul against his nephew. Modred was killed in battle while Arthur, wounded, was carried to the Isle of Avallon, and had stories told about him by future generations (*futuris de se fabulam fecit*).[22]

What makes Luard's decision to print a text beginning in 519 particularly odd is the fact that Cerdic of Wessex had appeared in several of the pre-519 entries. In a long entry accompanied by marginal dates of 491, 495, 499 and 504, Richard explained how King Arthur, having brought peace to Britain and then conquered most surrounding countries (Ireland, Orkney, Norway, Flanders, Gothia, Dacia and Gaul), was challenged by the arrival (seemingly in 495) of Cerdic with five ships. The two then fought long and hard (marginal date 499), but every time that Cerdic was driven out, he returned all the more fiercely, until finally Arthur, worn down by the unprofitable struggle, took an oath of fealty from Cerdic and granted him Hampshire and Somerset. Since his new territory was in west Britain, Cerdic named it Wessex and his fellow-warriors West Saxons. In 504 he made Winchester the capital of his duchy.[23] In 508 Arthur crossed over into Gaul. When Modred rebelled (no date given, but evidently before Cerdic's death in 534), his only fear was that Cerdic would remain loyal to Arthur, and so he granted him seven more *pagi*: Sussex, Surrey, Berkshire, Wiltshire, Dorset, Devonshire and Cornwall, together with all their fortresses. It was agreed that both of them should be crowned: Modred as king over the Britons, Cerdic as king over the West Saxons and those Britons in his territory who, if they wished to live peacefully, would not be expelled. Cerdic then brought over 800 shiploads of Saxons to whom he distributed estates in his new provinces. He was crowned heathen fashion at Winchester and Modred in Christian fashion at London.[24] In this astonishingly creative way Richard

---

[22] Ibid. 3.

[23] 'Et ecce quidam Cerdicius nomine de Germania Saxonia cum v ceolis venit Britanniam, aususque est Arturum provocare ad praelium. Diu et sepe decertatum est inter eos. Omni altero mense Cerdicius de insula expellebatur, omni altero mense acrior revertebatur. Ad postremum Arturus tedio victus, considerans quod dimicando cum illo cotidie nichil proficeret, in gratiam recepto et fidelitate iurata, dedit in possessionem Hamtesiram et Sumersetam. Qui aliquantum quod desiderabat adeptus, datam sibi provinciam quia in occidentali parte erat Britannie apellavit Westsexam et commilitones suos Westsaxones. Caput autem ducatus sui habuit Wintoniam.' A, fo. 9r-v.

[24] 'Modredus interea nepos Arturi cui regnum et reginam Arturus commiserat volebat usurpare coronam Britannie sed timebat solum Cerdicium ne sibi foret impedimento propter fidelitatem quam Arturo promiserat. Communicato demum illi secreto, praeter duos pagos quos ab Arturo perceperat, dedit illi alios vii, scilicet Suhsexam, Surream, Berchesiram, Wiltesiram, Dorsetam, Devenesiram et Cornubiam et omnia munita eorum tradidit. Tali inter eos conditione formata ut uterque eorum coronaretur in regem, unus super Britones

succeeded in uniting two traditions, bringing together in one story both the great British hero and the founding father of the West Saxon dynasty and hence of the kingdom of all England.

In some ways it might have seemed a natural step for an audacious reader of Henry of Huntingdon's history. Chapters 11, 13, 14, 16, 17 and 20 of Henry's *Historia Anglorum*, Book Two, *De adventu Anglorum*, are dominated by Cerdic and his son Cynric, and their battles against the Britons. Into this section Henry interpolated in chapter 18 the list of Arthur's twelve battles, drawn from the *Historia Brittonum*. 'None of these battle-sites can be identified now', Henry wrote, adding that meanwhile there were numerous battles everywhere and that, although first one side was victorious, then the other, the Saxons kept coming.[25] Despite this juxtaposition of Arthur and Cerdic in Book Two, Henry nowhere hinted that they fought against each other. That was left for Richard to invent. No other author had dared to do this, not even that other reader of Henry of Huntingdon's history, Geoffrey of Monmouth.[26]

Geoffrey of Monmouth's cast of characters included a Cherdic, a name very likely based, as Tatlock surmised, on Cerdic of Wessex. But Geoffrey placed this Cherdic in the time of Hengest and Vortigern, far too early to be a contemporary of King Arthur.[27] Richard's Cerdic has a closer affinity with Geoffrey's *Chelricus dux Saxonum*. Both of them ally with Modred and return from Germany with 800 ships of reinforcements.[28] This Chelric, it must be said, has to be distinguished from Geoffrey's other Chelric who early in Arthur's reign had brought 600 ships from Germany to Scotland, who fled from the battle of Mount Badon and was eventually hunted down and killed in Thanet

---

alter super Westsaxones et Britones qui in predictis pagis manebant si vivere vellent imbelles non expellerentur. Consensit Cerdicius et recepit oblata Modredi, missique in Germaniam nuncios, reduxit inde dccc naves plenas Saxonibus quibus distribuit in datis sibi provinciis possessiones. Cerdicius coram omni gente sua coronatus est in regem gentili more super Westsaxones apud Wintoniam et Modredus consecratus est in regem christiano more apud Londoniam.' A, fo. 9v.

[25] HH 100–101 (bk ii. 18).

[26] For Geoffrey as reader, teaser and subverter of other historians, see C. Brooke, 'Geoffrey of Monmouth as a historian', in C. Brooke and others (eds), *Church and government in the middle ages*, Cambridge 1976, 77–91; V. Flint, 'The *Historia Regum Britanniae* of Geoffrey of Monmouth: parody and its purpose: a suggestion', *Speculum* liv (1979), 447–68; J. Gillingham, 'The context and purposes of Geoffrey of Monmouth's *History of the kings of Britain*', *ANS* xiii (1991–92), 99–118, repr. in idem, *The English in the twelfth century: imperialism, national identity and political values*, Woodbridge 2000, 19–39.

[27] J.S.P. Tatlock, *The legendary history of Britain: Geoffrey of Monmouth's* Historia regum Britanniae an*d its early vernacular versions*, Los Angeles 1950, repr. New York 1974, 147.

[28] G. Mon. 248–51 (bk xi. 177).

by Duke Cador of Cornwall.[29] Indeed, this earlier Chelric also appeared in Richard's narrative of Arthur's pacification of Britain, as a *Cheldricus* done away with by Duke Cador of Cornwall.[30] Yet Richard's Cerdic was not simply Geoffrey's second Chelric under another name. According to Geoffrey, Modred offered Chelric not an embryonic Wessex, but a promise of the land from the Humber to Scotia as well as that which Hengest and Horsa had once held in Kent. Moreover, this Chelricus was killed together with Modred in the great battle explicitly dated (most unusually for Geoffrey who generally avoided year dates) to 542.[31] By contrast, Richard's Cerdic, having died in 534, was already dead by the time (in or after Cynric's seventh year) that Arthur and Modred came to blows. The implication of this was that Modred's grant to Cerdic must have taken place at least seven years before the final battle. It may have been this chronological awkwardness which led Richard to add the remarkable detail that Modred's usurpation would not have grieved Arthur overmuch, had he not, presumably some years later, also dared to invade the king's bedchamber.[32]

Richard of Devizes was not the first to turn Geoffrey of Monmouth's Chelricus into Cerdic. This step had already been taken in the later 1130s by Geffrei Gaimar in his *Estoire des Engleis*. In this, after an allusion to his (no longer extant) *Estoire des Bretuns*, Gaimar began by referring to the Cerdic to whom King Modred had granted the north of Britain.[33] Eight hundred lines of verse later he began to tell the story of the 'second Cerdic' who landed, as in the Anglo-Saxon Chronicle s.a. 495, at Cerdicshore, 'a hill that can still be seen today'.[34] Gaimar's Cerdic was given much greater prominence than Geoffrey of Monmouth had given Chelric. In Geoffrey's *Gesta Britonum* the Britons managed to maintain unified rule over their homeland for a long time after King Arthur's disappearance, but in Gaimar's *Estoire* the alliance of Cerdic – the first Cerdic – and Modred was followed by steady Saxon expansion. As Leckie pointed out, 'Gaimar established a direct causal link between Modred's treachery and English domination'.[35] It was at this point, the accession of Constantine after Arthur's death, that Gaimar stopped following Geoffrey of Monmouth and began his history of the English based mostly on the Anglo-Saxon Chronicle,

---

[29] G. Mon. 192–5 (bk ix. 143), 196–201 (bk ix. 147–8). In some manuscripts this figure is called Cheldricus.

[30] 'Et fugientem Cheldricum Cador oppressit'. A, fo. 9r.

[31] G. Mon. 250–53 (bk xi. 178).

[32] *Ann. mon.* ii. 3. Odd that in 1865 this was thought worth printing, but that not one of A's or indeed B's pre-519 entries was.

[33] Gaimar, *Estoire* lines 1–26. For discussion of the extent to which in his lost *Estoire des Bretuns* Gaimar had been following Geoffrey, see I. Short, 'What was Gaimar's *Estoire des Bretuns*?', *Cultura neolatina* lxxi (2011), 147–9.

[34] Gaimar, *Estoire* lines 822–72.

[35] Leckie, *Passage of dominion*, 81–2.

a chained copy of which was to be found, he said, in Winchester cathedral.³⁶ But by the time Gaimar got to write about the war between Cnut and Edmund Ironside, he seems to have forgotten that it was his first Cerdic who received Modred's donation. In a speech put into Cnut's mouth, the Dane told Edmund: 'It was Modred who granted Cerdic his fief .. and your family is descended from him'. If the Cerdic of the alliance with Modred was Edmund's ancestor then this has to have been Cerdic of Wessex, and in that case Modred's donation would not have consisted, as 4,000 lines earlier Gaimar had said it did, of 'all the land between the Humber and Caithness'.³⁷ On the other hand, in one respect Gaimar's treatment tended to conflate the two Cerdics by explicitly seeing both of them, as well as all the other Saxons, as descendants of Hengest.³⁸ Richard of Devizes followed Gaimar in stopping using Geoffrey of Monmouth at this same point. But whereas, initially at least, Gaimar had followed the Galfridian story by placing Modred's donation in the north, Richard broke new ground. By running with and developing Gaimar's later reference to Modred's donation to an ancestor of Edmund Ironside, he explicitly turned Modred's and Arthur's grants into the foundation of Wessex, and hence of England itself. There is much here which suggests that Richard read Gaimar, and then set about creating a drastic and dramatic clarification of the rather confused references to Cerdics which he had found in the *Estoire des Engleis*.

But Richard's version appears to have been all too much for one late-thirteenth-century reader of his history. After all, none of the acknowledged authorities, not the *Historia Brittonum* ('Nennius'), nor Geoffrey, nor the Anglo-Saxon Chronicle, nor William of Malmesbury nor Henry of Huntingdon had ever mentioned anything like this. It may have been this reader who was responsible for the fact that in B everything which Richard had written about the centuries before 519 has been jettisoned and replaced by six leaves (fos 3v–8v) containing the text of another annalistic chronicle.³⁹ This one, written in a late-thirteenth-century hand, begins at the birth of Christ and is more concerned with Frankish and monastic history than Richard's British chronicle had been. It did not, however, remove all trace of Geoffrey of Monmouth's history. Here, too (fo. 5v), King Lucius, having converted to Christianity, turned London, York and Caerleon into archiepiscopal sees. Here, too, we find (fo. 7v), under the year 468, a summary of the career of Arthur, king of the Britons, including his conquests in Gaul, and his final removal to Avallon. Indeed this chronicle continues on past the year 519, ending under the year 594 with Germund, the

---

³⁶ Gaimar, *Estoire* lines 2329–38.
³⁷ Ibid. lines 11 and 4319–22.
³⁸ Ibid. lines 9–16, 23–7, 827–54. This despite the fact that neither Hengest nor Horsa figure in the West Saxon genealogical tradition.
³⁹ Luard observed of these six leaves 'one would think that they were put in to replace others formerly there', *Ann. mon.* ii. p. x.

heathen African king, and Ysembert, apostate nephew of the king of the Franks, invading and ravaging Britain, forcing the archbishops of London and York to flee to Wales – all just as in Geoffrey's chapters 184–6. B's entry for 594 is placed at the top of fo. 8v and the rest of the page is left blank, so that fo. 9r begins with the entry for 519 written in the early-thirteenth-century hand which goes up as far as 1202. It seems that in Winchester *c.*1300 King Arthur and Germund were fine, but notions such as that Cerdic had been one of King Arthur's most redoubtable opponents and that Wessex owed its origins to donations by Arthur and Modred, were perceived as obvious mistakes, better destroyed and replaced.[40] In deciding to begin his edition of the Winchester annals with the year 519, Luard all too mechanically followed in the track of this unknown editor of *c.*1300.

Yet in fact Richard's pre- and post-519 annals present an interwoven history, the product of a single mind, to which the decision to print nothing from before 519 does an injustice. Consider the new genealogy which Richard provided for Ecgberht of Wessex, s.a. 828. In the traditional manner of West Saxon genealogies this went back from Cerdic to Woden and beyond. By making Woden the son of Fridewald, who was the son of Finn, the son of Godwin, son of Getius, he was staying roughly within the tradition represented by William of Malmesbury's genealogy of Æthelwulf and Ecgberht. But at this point Richard diverged, making Getius the son, not of Tetti, as in William of Malmesbury, but of Phillida, daughter of Assaracus, son of Ebraucus, son of Mempricius, son of Mandanus, son of Locrinus, son of Brutus.[41] Assaracus, Ebraucus, Mandanus and Locrinus were all taken from Geoffrey of Monmouth, but Phillida is a name which is entirely Richard's invention. It is she who as Getius's mother is represented as the crucial link in the chain linking the British and West Saxon kings. At about the time that Roger of Howden – whether inadvertently or not – changed King Arthur from *rex Britonum* to *rex Anglie*, Richard of Devizes claimed dynastic continuity between British and English kings.[42] Indeed, he took the trouble to invent an explanation of how it came about.

According to Geoffrey, Ebraucus, the sixth British king and founder of York, had twenty sons and thirty daughters. Of these only Brutus Greenshield stayed behind in Britain to inherit his father's throne. Ebraucus's daughters

---

[40] This was not, however, the view taken by the fifteenth-century chronicler Thomas Rudborne, also of St Swithun's Winchester, who in his *Historia major ecclesiae Wintoniensis* made use of Richard's version of the origins of Wessex, despite the problems he had in fitting Arthur's reign into his chronology, *Anglia sacra*, ed. H. Wharton, London 1691, i. 187–8. On Rudborne, see A.R. Rumble in ODNB and A. Gransden, *Historical writing in England, II: c.1307 to the early sixteenth century*, London 1982, 394–8.

[41] *Ann. mon.* ii. 8. Malmesbury, *GR* i. 176–7 (ii. 116).

[42] For the context in which Roger made this change, see Gillingham, 'Context and purposes', n. 23.

went to Italy where they married Trojan nobles. Ebraucus's other sons all sailed to Germany and there, led by Assaracus, and with the help of their sisters' husbands, they subdued the inhabitants and conquered the kingdom.[43] This was an episode in the legendary history which attracted little attention. Neither Henry of Huntingdon, nor Ralph Diceto nor Gervase of Canterbury nor Roger of Wendover, even so much as mentioned it in their summaries of Geoffrey of Monmouth.[44] But Richard of Devizes seized upon it and made it a key moment. In his version the children of Ebraucus took a large number of their fellow Britons with them to Germany. They settled there and as a consequence of the change of location they themselves changed in customs, name and language. Their descendants were those Angles and Saxons who in later times, led by Horsa and Hengist, by conquering Britain recovered the inheritance of their fathers.[45] This idea was significant enough for Richard to return to it for a second time. In describing the arrival of Hengist and Horsa with three ships full of armed men, all of them heathen, he explained again that they were descended from those Britons who had gone to Germany with the sons of Ebraucus, though distance and the passage of time meant that they had considerably degenerated from the language and manners of their brethren.[46] In other words, Richard presented the leading Angles and Saxons of the fifth century as men who possessed hereditary claims in Britain. In the case of Cerdic, by his manipulation of the genealogy of Ecgbert he made explicit that the claim went through a woman, Phillida, daughter of Assaracus. Why this invention? Perhaps as a polite gesture in the direction of the reigning king of England, whose claim to the throne was as son or grandson of a woman, the 'Empress' Matilda.[47]

---

[43] G. Mon. 34–7 (bk ii. 27).

[44] Though, not surprisingly in a work dedicated to Otto IV, Gervase of Tilbury's summary of Geoffrey does include their acquisition of Germany, Gervase of Tilbury, *Otia imperialia*, ed. and tr. S.E. Banks and J.W. Binns, Oxford 2002, 404.

[45] 'Unus qui et primogenitus filiorum nomine Brutus cum patre remansit, alii omnes maximam secum ducentes multitudinem Britonum adierunt Germaniam et subdiderunt eam sibi et mutauerunt cum loco mores Britonum et nomen et linguam; de quorum posteritate egressi sunt Angli et Saxones qui futuris temporibus Britanniam patrum suorum hereditatem conquiserunt super Britones fratres suos, quorum primi fuerunt Hors et Hengestus.' A, fos 1v–2r.

[46] 'Omnes erant gentiles. Isti fuerunt de genere Britonum qui cum xxx filiis Ebrauci regis qui condidit Eboracum in Germaniam detenderant. Sed vetustate temporum ex remotione a fratribus moribus et lingua multum a Britonibus degenerati.' A, fos 7v–8r.

[47] The theme of women as rulers or as carriers of claims to kingship is, of course, far more prominent in Geoffrey of Monmouth's British history, composed at a time when Matilda's claim was a live issue. For the evidence that Richard had his own day very much in mind when composing the annals see below n. 70. On the probable date of composition, see below 155.

In other ways, too, Richard signalled the high significance of Ecgberht's reign. According to him, Ecgberht was crowned king of all Britain at Winchester, on which occasion he decreed that the island should in future be called England, and that those who were called Jutes or Saxons should all bear the common name of English.[48] By the late twelfth century, as the writings of Ralph Diceto, Gervase of Canterbury and even the northerner Roger of Howden show, it had become common form to accord pivotal importance to Ecgberht's reign as the moment which saw, in William of Malmesbury's words, 'the union of the four kingdoms of Britain into one'.[49] Richard was particularly indebted to William of Malmesbury. For example, Richard's statement in the annal for 781 that Ecgberht, having been exiled to Gaul, made good use of his time *in schola disciplinae militaris* was clearly based on William's statement that Ecgberht learned new ways when in exile among people who led the western world in military skill and polished manners.[50] Only Richard, however, had Ecgberht crowned at Winchester and portrayed him, like Cerdic in 499/504, as a name-giving ruler.[51]

Yet King Alfred was, in Richard's eyes, an even more important figure than Ecgberht. Here, too, we see the portrait of a ruler whose achievements were both measured in the terms set by William of Malmesbury and prefigured in

---

[48] 'Veniunt Wintoniam clerus et populus, et assensu omnium partium coronatus est Egbirtus in regem totius Britanniae. Edixit illa die rex Egbirtus ut insula in posterum vocaretur Anglia, et qui Juti vel Saxones dicebantur, omnes communi nomine Angli vocarentur', *Ann. mon.* ii. 8. G.T. Beech relied upon this annal to argue that Egbert saw himself as the ruler of a unified English nation, i.e. that the idea of England existed very much earlier than was previously thought, 'Egbert's England', *History Today* lxiii, issue 2 (2013), 38–43. See also J. Gillingham, 'Questioning Egbert's Edict', *History Today* lxiii, issue 4 (2013), 4–5.

[49] Malmesbury, *GR* i. 152–3 (bk ii. 106). Cf. Gervase of Canterbury, 'sic Anglia in unam demum reducta monarchiam de uno et solo principe gaudeat, ne per plures divisa proprio scismate polluatur', in *The historical works of Gervase of Canterbury*, ed. W. Stubbs (RS [lxxiii], 1879–80), ii. 23; 'Nunc ergo quia Angliam nostram tam gravi scismate dissipatam ad unitatem unius reduximus regnum, restat ab hoc rege Egbrihto quasi novum aliquid incipiamus,' ibid. 41; *The historical works of Master Ralph de Diceto*, ed. W. Stubbs (RS [lxviii], 1876), ii. 233–4 (where he noted 'Qui vocati sunt huc usque reges West Saxonum, abhinc appellati sunt solummodo reges Anglorum sed nondum monarchiam optinuerunt'); *Chronica magistri Rogeri de Houedene*, ed. W. Stubbs, (RS [li], 1868–71), i. 29–30, adding after *rex* the word *magnus* to his predecessor's account of Ecgberht's reign. See below n. 67.

[50] *Ann. mon.* ii. 6; Malmesbury, *GR* i. 152–3 (bk ii. 106). On this theme, see J. Gillingham, 'Civilizing the English? The English histories of William of Malmesbury and David Hume', *Historical Research* lxxiv (2001), 17–43; idem, 'French culture, twelfth-century English historians and the civilising process', in C. Arrignon et al. (eds), *Cinquante années d'études médiévales. À la confluence de nos disciplines. Actes du colloque organisé à l'occasion du Cinquantenaire du CESCM, 2003*, Turnhout 2006, 729–40.

[51] On the importance of these name changes, see R.R. Davies, *The first English empire: power and identities in the British Isles, 1093–1343*, Oxford 2000, 48–9.

the pre-519 section of Richard's annals. William's special emphasis on Alfred the translator – 'no Englishman had a keener understanding or could translate with greater elegance' – included the earliest list of his translations.[52] No doubt this tempted Geoffrey of Monmouth into teasing William by inventing works not in that list: Alfred's translations of the Molmutine laws and of Marcia's new British laws.[53] This was not something that struck Henry of Huntingdon as being important. In his summary of Geoffrey he omitted both references, just as he had already, following the Anglo-Saxon Chronicle, said nothing about this aspect of the king's achievement in his account of the reign (Book Five, chapters 7–13). By contrast, Richard of Devizes accorded enormous importance to Alfred's translations. 'King Alfred translated the British laws into English, and they were then called the laws of King Alfred; and he translated many books in the same way'. He laid further emphasis on Alfred's laws by stating s.a. 1017 that Cnut ordered that English and Danes should be one people and all should hold the laws and rights of Alfred king of the English.[54] Richard saw a process by which, as a consequence of direct royal intervention, translation and command, different peoples could be brought to share a common law, first Britons and English, then Britons, English and Danes. Not surprising, then, that in his summary version of Geoffrey's British history he should twice have found room to mention Alfred's work of translation.[55] No one matched Richard's insistence on the importance of this achievement.[56]

Richard also adopted William of Malmesbury's statement that Alfred 'instituted the centuries which they call hundreds and the divisions into tenths called tithings, so that every law-abiding Englishman had his century and his tenth.'[57] He was far from being the only late-twelfth-century historian to quote

---

[52] Malmesbury, *GR* i. 192–3 (bk ii. 123); and see the relevant commentary of R.M. Thomson at ii. 102.

[53] G. Mon. 52–3, 60–61 (bk iii. 39, 47).

[54] *Ann. mon.* ii. 10, 15. The entry for 1017 was based on John of Worcester's entry for 1018, but changing Edgar's law to Alfred's law.

[55] A, fos 2v, 3r. Another of Richard's contributions to the cult of Alfred is to claim for him the authorship of proverbs, ibid. 10, noted by Keynes, 'Cult', 233.

[56] Gervase had Marcia and Alfred's Merchenelage in his abstract of Geoffrey, but not the Molmutine laws and Alfred: *Historical works of Gervase*, ii. 10. Roger of Wendover likewise, see Matthew Paris, *Chronica majora*, ed. H. R. Luard (RS [lvii], 1872–83), i. 60. Gervase of Tilbury also had Alfred translate British laws, in this case those established by Belinus and recorded by Gildas, *Otia imperialia*, 406–8.

[57] 'Centurias quas dicunt hundrez et decimas quas tithingas vocant instituit, ut omnis Anglus legaliter dumtaxat vivens haberet et centuriam et decimam.' Malmesbury, *GR* i. 188–9 (bk ii. 122). For discussion P. Wormald, *The making of English law: King Alfred to the twelfth century*, Oxford 1999, 137–42. On the importance of this attribution for the cult of Alfred, see Keynes, 'Cult', 352.

William on this. So also did Ralph Diceto, Gervase of Canterbury and then Roger of Wendover.[58] Indeed, the idea was taken up so enthusiastically by the London Collector, writing in John's reign, that he, as in other cases such as the pope's letter to the British King Lucius, thoughtfully supplied the 'missing' Alfredian laws which established the tithings and peace gilds.[59] William of Malmesbury's interest in the history of institutions evidently made good sense to readers later in the century, living at a time which witnessed the creation of a new kind of literature, the administrative manual, notably *The Dialogue of the Exchequer*, composed by an author, Richard FitzNigel, who was himself interested in the history of the institution.[60] But more than any other historian of the time Richard of Devizes bought into William of Malmesbury's notion that English history was a story of cultural and social improvement, and for him, even more than for William, Alfred's reign marked the pivotal point in the civilising process. 'This kingdom which before his time was uncultured and underdeveloped, he taught and entirely refashioned, bringing it up to a proper standard.'[61]

Modern historians have treated Richard of Devizes almost exclusively as a chronicler of contemporary events. Nancy Partner, for instance, while acknowledging that Richard wrote part of the Winchester Annals, focused exclusively on the annals for 1196–1202.[62] R. William Leckie mentioned him only in an end note in support of the general point that 'the leading historians in the third and fourth quarters of the century began their depictions with events which belong to the Anglo-Norman era'.[63] But this generalisation should be qualified. True, in the works for which they are famous, the 'leading historians'

[58] *Historical works of Ralph de Diceto*, ii. 234; *Historical works of Gervase*, ii. 44–5; Paris, *Chronica majora*, i. 428.

[59] F. Liebermann, *Über die* Leges Anglorum saeculo XIII ineunte Londoniis collectae, Halle 1894, 16–20. In Liebermann's eyes, the London Collector was a bare-faced liar and forger who also contributed to a rising tide of nonsense.

[60] J. Hudson, 'Administration, family and perceptions of the past in twelfth-century England: Richard FitzNigel and the Dialogue of the Exchequer', in P. Magdalino (ed.), *The perception of the past in twelfth-century Europe*, London 1992, 75–98. On the new administrative history, see J. Gillingham, 'Expectations of empire: some twelfth- and early thirteenth-century English views of what their kings could do', in S. Duffy and S. Foran (eds), *The English Isles: cultural transmission and political conflict in Britain and Ireland, 1100–1500*, Dublin 2013, 56–67.

[61] 'Iste regnum Anglorum ante dies suos rude et incompositum, totum erudivit et informavit ad regulam', *Ann. mon.* ii. 10. This was perhaps only to be expected from the reign of a king who had shown such patience and gentleness (*tantae fuit patientiae et mansuetudinis*) that he allowed his three brothers, none of them anointed kings, to wear the crown before him, ibid. 8–9.

[62] Partner, *Serious entertainments*, 143, 149, 171, 178.

[63] Leckie, *Passage of dominion*, 22, 126 n. 36.

writing in the later twelfth century did begin with the Anglo-Norman era. But, with the exception of William of Newburgh – though he, too, found ways in which to demonstrate his interest in the British and Anglo-Saxon past – they all also composed brief accounts of earlier ages. Much less interesting to those generations of modern historians who were looking for reliable facts, these 'lesser' works should not be entirely forgotten. Although sometimes little more than lists of names, they were composed in order to locate their own place and time within a larger temporal and geographical context.[64] In the late 1180s Ralph Diceto, best known for the *Imagines*, his history of modern times, composed the *Abbreviationes chronicorum*. In this he used works such as Sigebert of Gembloux's universal history in order to place annals derived from information supplied principally by Bede, William of Malmesbury, Henry of Huntingdon and Geoffrey of Monmouth within what J.F.A. Mason described as 'the most ambitious attempt at a world history made until then by an Englishman'.[65] He also wrote *De regibus Britonum, Saxonum et Anglorum, Danorum, Normannorum*, one of the short historical tracts (*opuscula*) which he pulled together in the mid 1190s and sent to William Longchamp.[66] In the 1190s Roger of Howden tacked a Durham history beginning with the year 732, and to which he made a few additions of his own, on to the beginning of a revised version of the contemporary chronicle he had been maintaining since the 1170s.[67] Gervase of Canterbury, after composing his chronicle of events from Stephen's reign to 1199, moved on to write what he called *Exceptiones brevissimae de numero et gestis regum Britanniae*, beginning with Brutus and ending with King John. It was chiefly based on Geoffrey of Monmouth and William of Malmesbury, and Gervase advised those who wanted to know more to read those two.[68]

In one sense this is the company in which Richard's annals belong. Indeed Richard seems to have had a copy of Dean Ralph's *Abbreviationes* before him. Although West Saxon events, particularly those said to have occurred in Winchester, are central to Richard's annals, at times – notably on the pages relating to sixth- and seventh-century history – they are located within a world

---

[64] 'At the close of the century ... concern for the broad sweeps of history is very much in evidence', ibid. 97.

[65] *Historical works of Ralph de Diceto*, i. 3–263; J.F.A. Mason, 'Diceto, Ralph de (d. 1199/1200)', in *ODNB*.

[66] *Historical works of Ralph de Diceto*, ii. 222–39. In so far as there is a pattern in Ralph's view of Anglo-Saxon history it is more readily discernible in this short tract than in the *Abbreviationes*. In the table of contents with which he prefaced the *opuscula*, he explained that he listed the kings of Britons in order to deal with the *alter orbis*, ibid. 183–4.

[67] Stubbs printed this Durham history in *Chronica magistri Rogeri de Houedene*, i, with Roger's additions in large print.

[68] *Historical works of Gervase*, ii. 3–106, 23. The earliest (British and Anglo-Saxon) sections of this seem to have circulated separately, ibid. pp. ix–x.

history context. The notes of papal, Frankish and Persian history which adorn the margins of his text seem to come from Diceto rather than directly from Sigebert.[69] This disposes of Luard's suggestion that the annals were written before 1173.[70] It seems likely that the earlier annals, those of interest here, were composed in the late 1180s or early 1190s, and possible that he had reached 1138 when the drama of Richard I's crusade made him put them aside and turn instead to the writing of his contemporary chronicle.[71] But in another sense Richard's annals were something entirely different. He used his imagination in order to create a new past. No one came up with a more theatrical reworking of the passage of dominion. Apart from Richard of Devizes himself, no author suffered more from Luard's editorial decision than Leckie, the historian of the passage of dominion.

In this chapter I have focused on Richard's reinterpretation of Anglo-Saxon history. But his reworking of the earlier parts of Geoffrey of Monmouth would also repay attention. It is noteworthy, for example, that his annalistic narrative of British history from the time of Lucius, the first Christian king, onwards is much more focused around the theme of religious difference and conflict than was Geoffrey's original. Presumably because Richard knew that second-century Rome was still a pagan empire, he described the wars between Severus and Fulgenius, between Bassianus and Geta, and between Allectus and Asclepiodotus, not in simply secular terms, whether as British resistance to Roman authority or as brother against brother, as in Geoffrey, but as a series of struggles between Christian and pagan.[72] By the time he reached the threshold of the landing of new pagans led by Hengist and Horsa, it seemed clear to him

---

[69] See *Ann. mon.* ii. 3–5, and A, fos 5v and 9r. The entry *Johannes papa* s.a. 564 suggests that Richard had the B text of the *Abbreviationes* in which the dean stated his intention of taking the work up to 1190, *Historical works of Ralph de Diceto*, i. 98 n. 5. Where Richard obtained the note *Mahumet apud Gentiles deificatus est* which he placed under 648, I do not know.

[70] Luard believed this on the basis of an allusion in the entry for 837 to a king of the present day who rejoiced as much in his sons as Ethelwulf had done in his, *Ann. mon.* ii. p. xiii. But this is to ignore the likelihood that, far from not knowing about the rebellion against Henry II in 1173–74, Richard was actually commenting ironically on it. In view of his allusion to scandal involving Louis VII's first wife, the beautiful (his word) Eleanor of Aquitaine (Appleby, *Chronicle*, 25–6), it is possible that he had had Louis in mind when referring, in his account of Edgar's reign, to a husband of modern times who had cause to regret his wife's beauty, *Ann. mon.* ii. 12.

[71] One hypothesis would then be that later in the 1190s he resumed composing his annals, first extensively revising what he had earlier written about the years between 1066 and 1138, and then continuing, possibly going up as far as 1202, the point at which the scribe (not Richard himself) responsible for fos 9r–44r in B, laid down his pen. BL online Manuscripts Catalogue, Cotton Domitian A. xiii.

[72] A, fo. 6r–6v

that there were no native pagans left in Britain. This he explained by turning the 101st British king, Constantine – in Geofffrey's book a king who did nothing except father three sons, Constans, Aurelius Ambrosius and Utherpendragon – into a forceful ruler who rid the kingdom of all unbelievers and enemies of his people.[73] This injection of religion into Geoffrey's secular narrative is to show an unexpected side to the author whose contemporary narrative of the Third Crusade has been judged to present it as a war 'dominated by ordinary earthly considerations'.[74] As for his Anglo-Saxon history, that ends, exactly as his British history ends, with a great battle and the disappearance of a king who might one day return: *Volunt tamen quidam Anglorum quod Haroldus vivus evaserit et adhuc vivat cum Arturo rege Britonum*.[75] On the other hand, these two endings do appear to support the view that Richard was 'a man with an ironic eye for the absurd'.[76] An author indeed whose ideas on King Arthur and Cerdic were too absurd and too clever for his most influential readers in both the later middle ages and in the nineteenth century to stomach.[77]

---

[73] 'Iste exterminavit omnes incredulos et hostes gentis sue', A, fo. 7v.

[74] Partner, *Serious entertainments*, 175.

[75] A, fo. 22r, printed by Luard, *Ann. mon.*, ii. p. xv, and by Appleby, 'Richard of Devizes', 75.

[76] Partner, *Serious entertainments*, 146.

[77] I would add the twentieth century, too, if I could be confident that Appleby did read the earliest annals.

PART III
Anglo-Saxon Law and Charter

Chapter 10
Historical Literacy in the Archive: Post-Conquest Imitative Copies of Pre-Conquest Charters and Some French Comparanda*

J. Crick

This chapter examines an aspect of historical activity whose association with the long twelfth century is well established but which has no acknowledged place within received models of the twelfth-century discovery of the past.[1] It was not

---

* The research for this chapter was conducted during the tenure of a Leverhulme Research Fellowship on Script and forgery in England to AD 1100 and I acknowledge with thanks the generosity of the Leverhulme Trust. For access to manuscript and microfilmed materials I thank the custodians of the William Salt Library and Staffordshire Record Office, Stafford, Winchester College, and in Paris the Archives nationales (CARAN) and the Bibliothèque nationale de France. Some of the material in the present chapter was discussed at the second workshop on 'Production and use of English manuscripts 1060 to 1220', organised by Dr Mary Swan (University of Leeds) and Professor Elaine Treharne (Florida State University), funded by the Arts and Humanities Research Council and held at the University of Leicester in April 2010. I thank the organisers of the Leicester and Cambridge meetings for their invitations and have learned from the comments and suggestions of the audiences on both occasions. Nicholas Brooks and Simon Keynes have been kind enough to discuss with me the palaeographical and textual details of S 602 and I have profited from Alice Rio's and Bruce O'Brien's comments on a draft text. I have been assisted in the preparation of this chapter by the images from the Single Sheet Database made available on the Kemble website http://www.kemble.asnc.cam.ac.uk/ and I acknowledge their use with thanks.

[1] For classic accounts of these models, see R.W. Southern, 'Aspects of the European tradition of historical writing: 4. The sense of the past', *TRHS* 5 ser. xxiii (1973), 243–63, repr. in R.J. Bartlett (ed.), *History and historians: selected papers of R.W. Southern*, Oxford 2004, 66–83; B. Guenée, *Histoire et culture historique dans l'Occident médiéval*, Paris 1980; R.H.C. Davis and J.M. Wallace-Hadrill (eds), *The writing of history in the middle ages: essays presented to Richard William Southern*, Oxford 1981; R.M. Thomson, 'England and the twelfth-century Renaissance', *Past and Present* ci (1983), 3–21, repr. in his *England and the twelfth-century Renaissance*, Aldershot 1998; P. Magdalino (ed.), *The perception of the past in twelfth-century Europe*, London 1992; R.L. Benson and G. Constable (eds), *Renaissance*

triggered by changes in education or exposure to the Latin classics. It cannot be claimed to be a novel activity because it belongs to a continuum, but it does attest important historical processes: archival control, the sorting and processing of information about the Anglo-Saxon past, and, in an unusually literal sense, how contemporaries viewed English antiquity. I refer to the production of imitative copies of Anglo-Saxon charters.[2]

The immense importance of the English past to twelfth-century devotion is attested in literary output so voluminous that much remains unedited, although the effort of writing and rewriting saints' lives has been well studied.[3] This work of renewal is an activity closely analogous to another, also well attested and well recognised: the need to maintain and, indeed, to stabilise the archives whose contents documented and protected the material resources which sustained cult sites.[4] The status and even survival of individual religious communities was jeopardised by the destruction of the assumptions which had sustained territorial and jurisdictional rights before the Norman Conquest. The death or exile of senior patrons left English institutions exposed to the threat of predation by newly appointed bishops attuned to the different expectations and standards of religious life in vogue on the Continent. Although the dangers posed to monastic communities were particularly acute in William's reign, the contested succession of subsequent monarchs, up to and including Henry II, will have destabilised some secular patronage networks on a lesser scale, as new men were preferred and dissenters deprived of landed property.[5] In the post-Conquest era communities had to keep rewriting their documents in order

---

and renewal in the twelfth century, Cambridge, MA 1982; J. Le Goff, 'What did the twelfth-century Renaissance *mean*?', in P. Linehan and J.L. Nelson (eds), *The medieval world*, London 2001, 635–47; C.S. Jaeger, 'Pessimism in the twelfth-century "Renaissance"', *Speculum* lxxviii (2003), 1151–83.

[2] The production of imitative charters in the long twelfth century has been established in a series of published studies: below, Table 10.1, nn. a–r.

[3] R. Bartlett, 'The hagiography of Angevin England', *Thirteenth-century England* v (1993), 37–52; *William of Malmesbury: Saints' Lives: Lives of SS. Wulfstan, Dunstan, Patrick, Benignus and Indract*, ed. and tr. M. Winterbottom and R.M. Thomson, Oxford 2002. On Wales and Ireland, see R. Bartlett, 'Rewriting saints' lives: the case of Gerald of Wales', *Speculum* lviii (1983), 598–613; J.W. Evans, J.M. Wooding (eds), *St David of Wales: cult, church and nation*, Woodbridge 2007; H. Birkett, *The Saints' Lives of Jocelin of Furness: hagiography, patronage and ecclesiastical politics*, Woodbridge 2010.

[4] Southern, 'Aspects', 246–56. M.T. Clanchy, *From memory to written record: England 1066–1307*, 3 edn Oxford 2012, chs 1 and 5. See also B. O'Brien, 'Forgery and the literacy of the early Common Law', *Albion* xxvii (1995), 1–18; N. Karn, 'Information and its retrieval', in J. Crick and E.M.C. van Houts (eds), *A social history of England, 900-1200*, Cambridge 2011, 373–80, esp. 377–8.

[5] For an example, see J. Sayers, '"Original", cartulary and chronicle: the case of the abbey of Evesham', *Fälschungen im Mittelalter* (MGH Schriften xxxiii, 1988), iv. 371–95, at

to fight obsolescence.⁶ As Frank Barlow showed more than sixty years ago, charters could not be expected to perform their work indefinitely, but needed to be adapted to changing circumstances.⁷ Fresh copies were required when draftsmen improved existing documents through interpolation or fashioned new texts outright from reclaimed textual material. Some of these creations survive in the form of imitative copies, although the possibility remains that unimproved texts, too, were preserved in replacement copies.

Sir Richard Southern in the last of his presidential addresses to the Royal Historical Society encouraged scrutiny of archival evidence as a process central to understanding the historical movement of the twelfth century:⁸

> **The mistake is often made of looking for evidence of a historical revival only in the histories which it produces; and this mistake has obscured the character of the work done by these monastic scholars.** Just as the finest work of the modern historical movement is to be found in editions of texts, catalogues of material and critical notes on sources, symbols, and social habits, **so in the twelfth century the historical revival is to be seen as a continuous process of collecting and arranging charters, transcribing documents**, and carrying out minute investigations into chronology and topography, studying monastic buildings and inscriptions, assembling the texts of ancient learning, writing estate-histories, chronicles, and biographies – **and only at the end of the day the histories which we all know**.

In other words, the familiar and celebrated historical edifices of the twelfth century were buttressed by an accumulation of mundane data whose acquisition, by collecting, auditing, surveying and ordering, attests significant historical awareness and skill. It is well known that monastic historians in the Middle Ages used charters to construct narratives of monastic houses and chronologies of office-holders.⁹ Some charters in themselves attest the ordering of the past,

---

371. On the broader context, see J. Blair, *The Church in Anglo-Saxon society*, Oxford 2005, 505–12.

⁶ For examples, see *Charters of Malmesbury abbey*, ed. S.E. Kelly, Oxford 2005, 51–64; *Charters of St Albans*, ed. J.C. Crick, Oxford 2007, 58–74. On the general principle, see Clanchy, *From memory to written record*, 148–9.

⁷ F. Barlow, *Durham jurisdictional peculiars*, London 1950, xvii, 12–13.

⁸ Southern, 'Aspects', 249, with my emphasis.

⁹ A. Giry, *Manuel de diplomatique*, Paris 1925 [1 edn Paris 1894], 51–3; M. Chibnall, 'Charter and chronicle: the use of archive sources by Norman historians', in C.N.L. Brooke (ed.), *Church and government in the Middle Ages: essays presented to C.R. Cheney on his seventieth birthday*, Cambridge 1976, 1–17; *Historia ecclesie Abbendonensis: the history of the church of Abingdon*, ed. and tr. J. Hudson, Oxford 2002–7, i. xxviii–xxxiii, lxxii–lxxiv, lxxvii–lxxxi; *Charters of St Augustine's abbey, Canterbury, and Minster-in-Thanet*, ed. S.E. Kelly, Oxford 1995, xcix–cv. Compare the reflections of P.J. Geary, 'Medieval archivists as

either in the shape of text fabricated by a process of archival research, or in their physical form in which scribes altered one or more of their usual repertoire of scripts in response to, or in imitation of, a pre-Conquest model. Either situation bears out Stenton's observation that 'any medieval text which claims to be a copy of an ancient charter represents in itself an elaborate framework of local circumstance'.[10] A doubly complex process, of palaeographical as well as textual bricolage, must be presupposed when, as sometimes was the case, forged charters were copied in archaising script.

Scribal archaism suggests both a consciousness of the past and a distance from it. Just like forgery, which is its textual equivalent, it required modification of the practitioner's usual habits. As a matter of routine any draftsman or scribe will have constructed his text using elements learned from past practice, whether in the form of vocabulary and textual tags, or in the shape of letter-forms, marks of abbreviation and so forth. The draftsman of a spurious charter, by contrast, adopted a consciously discontinuous relationship with the past, importing formulae alien to his normal repertoire, and so introducing the anachronistic elements upon which the detection of a forgery by modern critics depends. The archaising scribe likewise deliberately modified his script to mimic the letter-forms and sometimes the ligatures and even the aspect of one or more distant historical targets. The phenomenon occurs across Europe from the *copie figurée* recognised by French diplomatists,[11] to Carlrichard Brühl's observation that charters were frequently written in deliberately antique, often completely archaising script.[12] Archaising script occurs not uncommonly in books as well, and Michelle Brown has usefully defined the deliberate modification of script by 'imitation and forgery' as 'a conscious attempt on the part of an artist or scribe to alter the usual appearance of their work to resemble that of another, whether for purpose of homogeneity or for motives of expediency'.[13] The tension between the scribe's normal practice and the model being imitated can be so poorly resolved that the results can be baffling: it is very difficult to reconstruct the processes

---

authors: social memory and archival memory', in F.X. Blouin and W.G. Rosenberg (eds), *Archives, documentation and institutions of social memory: essays from the Sawyer seminar*, Ann Arbor, MI 2006, 106–13.

[10] F.M. Stenton, *The Latin charters of the Anglo-Saxon period*, Oxford 1955, 19.

[11] Giry, *Manuel*, 12, 863. See also below, n. 49.

[12] C. Brühl, 'Die Entwicklung der diplomatischen Methode im Zusammenhang mit dem Erkennen von Fälschungen', in *Fälschungen im Mittelalter* (MGH Schriften xxxiii 1988), iii. 11–27, at 25–6. For examples, see J. Vezin, 'Écritures imitées dans les livres et les documents du haut moyen Âge (viie–xie siècle)', *BEC* clxv (2007), 47–66 and J.C. Crick, 'Script and the sense of the past in Anglo-Saxon England', in J. Roberts and L. Webster (eds), *Anglo-Saxon traces*, Tempe, AZ 2011, 1–29.

[13] M.P. Brown, *The Book of Cerne: prayer, patronage and power in ninth-century England*, London 1996, 27.

which led to their formation. On the other hand, some scribes mimicked their exemplars so successfully that their work can barely be distinguished from antique (i.e. pre-Conquest) models.[14] Both types of imitation attest an engagement with older documents, the influence of exemplars one or more centuries old being easier for the critic to detect than that of documents closer in date to the imitator's own time of writing.

Such encounters between medieval scribes and potentially ancient exemplars allow the scholar to assess the acuity of the scribe's observation of historical difference and the skill with which he was able to alter his own writing habits to imitate those of the older scribe. Later medieval and Continental examples have been investigated in the last generation by Malcolm Parkes, Peter Lucas and, most recently, Jean Vezin.[15] Examples from pre-Conquest England have also been discussed in print.[16] This chapter represents a foray into the immediate post-Conquest era and beyond, and involves the study of scribes working on both sides of the English Channel. In almost all cases the examples of imitation discussed here have previously been identified in print, most commonly by editors. Some of these identifications have been widely accepted but others remain controversial.[17]

During the long twelfth century, defined for the purposes of this chapter as extending from the start of the reign of William I to the end of that of John, scholars working in numerous English monastic archives processed pre-

---

[14] For an example of the former, see J.C. Crick, 'St Albans, Westminster and some twelfth-century views of the Anglo-Saxon past', *ANS* xxv (2003 for 2002), 65–83, at 67–70 and pl. 1. For examples of more successful imitation, see below, 172–7.

[15] P.J. Lucas, 'Scribal imitation of earlier handwriting: "Bastard Saxon" and its impact', in M.-C. Hubert, E. Poulle and M.H. Smith (eds), *Le Statut du scripteur au moyen age. Actes du XIIe colloque scientifique du Comité international de paléographie latine (Cluny, 17–20 juillet 1998)*, Paris 2000, 151–60; M. Hunter, 'The facsimiles in Thomas Elmham's History of St. Augustine's, Canterbury', *The Library* 5 ser. xxviii (1973), 215–20; M.B. Parkes, 'Archaizing hands in English manuscripts', in J.P. Carley and C.G.C. Tite (eds), *Books and collectors, 1200–1700: essays presented to Andrew Watson*, London 1997, 101–41. See also H. Atsma and J. Vezin, 'Le dossier suspect des possessions de Saint-Denis en Angleterre revisité (VIIIe–IXe siècles)', *Fälschungen im Mittelalter*, iv. 211–36, at 225–9, and below n. 53.

[16] J.C. Crick, 'Insular history? Forgery and the English past in the tenth century', in D. Rollason, C. Leyser and H. Williams (eds), *England and the Continent in the tenth century: studies in honour of Wilhelm Levison (1876–1947)*, Turnhout 2011, 515–44; Crick, 'Script and the sense of the past'.

[17] For the English material discussed here, the palaeographical judgements are my own but I am largely dependent on others for assessments of textual authenticity. I have been reliant to a greater extent on published discussion of the French material, although I have inspected, either in manuscript or in microfilm, examples housed in Paris.

Conquest documents as entries in cartularies and monastic chronicles.[18] More than twenty monastic cartularies fit squarely into this period, with at least as many dating from the thirteenth century.[19] Religious houses of substance possessed such books – Abingdon, Bury St Edmund's, Christ Church and St Augustine's Canterbury, Ely, Evesham, Eynsham, Peterborough, Rochester, St Albans, Sherborne, Winchester, Worcester – and these volumes preserve many pre-Conquest texts for which no single-sheet copy survives. Alongside these efforts of compilation stands a response to the pre-Conquest archival record of a different sort altogether. More than thirty single-sheet copies of purportedly pre-Conquest documents survive from the same period. Doubts attach to a much higher proportion of the texts than is the case for cartulary copies: indeed, only a few single-sheet copies are regarded as authentic texts. About half of the documents were copied in what looks like the scribe's customary hand, unmodified to reflect the nature or age of the document being copied but that of the remainder has been identified as imitative by a series of authorities. This significant residue can be divided into three categories: first, blatant imitation of pre-Conquest script which clearly belongs neither to pre-Conquest nor post-Conquest scribal traditions; secondly, subtler modification which it may take longer to discern because it departs only in minor details from a recognisable scribal tradition of the post-Conquest era; finally, imitation so successful that scholars remain divided about whether certain charters should be classified as pre-Conquest originals or post-Conquest copies.

---

[18] For pre-Conquest charters preserved in the Abingdon Chronicle, see *Historia ecclesie Abbendonensis*, i. cxcv-ccviii and *Charters of Abingdon abbey*, ed. S.E. Kelly, Oxford 2000–2001, i. liii–lxiii; in the historical works of William of Malmesbury, *Charters of Malmesbury abbey*, ed. S.E. Kelly, Oxford, 2005, 42–5. For Ely traditions, see S. Keynes, 'Ely Abbey 672–1109', in P. Meadows and N. Ramsay (eds.), *A history of Ely cathedral*, Woodbridge 2003, 3–58, esp. 5–10.

[19] G.R.C. Davis, rev. C, Breay, J. Harrison, and D.M. Smith, *Medieval cartularies of Great Britain and Ireland*, London 2010, nos 3, 118, 163, 163A, 364, 365, 366, 367, 368, 381, 382, 399, 596, 754, 817, 892, 1042, 1061, 1068, 1069. See further N.R. Ker, *English manuscripts in the century after the Norman Conquest: the Lyell lectures, 1952–3*, Oxford 1960, 20–21.

Table 10.1 Preliminary list of single-sheet copies of pre-Conquest diplomas and charters copied in the long twelfth century.[20]

Reference	Face Date	Archive	Date of copy	Facsimile	Status	Imitative
S 602	956	Burton	s. x or xi²	*Facsimiles*, ed. Keynes, no. 4	Disputed[a]	x
S 768	968	Burton	s. x or xi²	*Facsimiles*, ed. Keynes, no. 7	Disputed[b]	x
S 623	956	Burton	s. xi	OSF iii, Anglesey 1	Authentic[c]	x
S 360	900	NMWi	s. xi¹ or ? xi²	OSF ii, Winchester College, 1	Spurious[d]	x
S 879	996	Burton	s. xi²	*Charters*, ed. Sawyer, pl. II.b	Spurious[e]	x
S 906	1004	Burton	s. xi²	OSF iii, Anglesey 3	Authentic	
S 1536	1002 x 1004	Burton	s. xi²	OSF iii, Anglesey 2	Authentic	
S 794	974	Ely	s. xi²	*Facsimiles*, ed. Keynes no. 25	Spurious[f]	x
S 959, MS 21	1023	CaCC	s. xi²	OSF i.19	Disputed	
S 980, MS 1	1022 x 1023	Bury St Edmunds	s. xi^ex.	*Facsimiles*, ed. Keynes no. 33	Spurious	
S 1026, MS 1	?1062x1065	Evesham	s. xi/xii	*Facsimiles*, ed. Keynes no. 35	Spurious[g]	x
S 779, MS 1	970	Ely	s. xi/xii	OSF iii.32	Disputed	

(*continued*)

[20] Omitted from this list are Exeter charters copied in the pontificate of Bishop Leofric (1050–72) or before, a number of which were written in modified or archaising script: S 386, S 387, S 388, S 389, S 405, S 433.1, S 433.3, S 669. Here the conventional abbreviations for pre-Conquest foundations will be employed: CaCC (Christ Church Canterbury), NMWi (New Minster Winchester), OMWi (Old Minster, Winchester).

Table 10.1 (*continued*)

Reference	Face Date	Archive	Date of copy	Facsimile	Status	Imitative
S 959 MS 2	1023	CaCC	s. xi/xii	OSF i.20	Disputed	
S 959 MS 4	1023	CaCC	s. xi/xii	*Facsimiles*, ed. Keynes no. 34	Disputed	
S 553	950	Wells (ex Glastonbury)	s. xi/xii	*Facsimiles*, ed. Keynes no. 32	Spurious	
S 68	664	Peterborough	s. xi/xii		Spurious[h]	
S 1029	1060	Peterborough	s. xi/xii		Spurious[i]	x
S 1043 MS 1	1066	Westminster	s. xii[1]	*Facsimiles*, ed. Keynes no. 39	Spurious[j]	x
S 959 MS 1	1023	CaCC	s. xii[1]	OSF i.21	Disputed	
S 959 MS 3	1023	CaCC	s. xii[1]	OSF iii.40	Disputed	
S 1011	1045	Westminster	s. xii[1]	BMF iv.30	Spurious[k]	x
S 1043 MS 2	1066	Westminster	s. xii[1]	*Facsimiles*, ed. Keynes no. 38	Spurious[l]	x
S 731, MS 1	964	Worcester	s. xii[1]	*Facsimiles*, ed. Keynes no. 40	Spurious[m]	x
S 124 MS 1	785	Westminster	s. xii[med.]	Heslop, 'Twelfth-century forgeries', 54(b)[n]	Spurious[o]	x
S 1293	959	Westminster	s. xii[med.]	Heslop, 'Twelfth-century forgeries', 53, 54(a)	Spurious[p]	x
S 1060	1055 x 1060	Peterborough	s. xii[med.]		Spurious[q]	x
S 774	969	Westminster	s. xii[med]	*Facsimiles*, ed. Keynes no. 37	Spurious[r]	x
S 645	957	Westminster	s. xii	OSF ii. Westminster 3	?Authentic	

Reference	Face Date	Archive	Date of copy	Facsimile	Status	Imitative
S 1041, MS 1	1065	Westminster	s. xii$^{med.}$	OSF iii.34	Spurious	
S 1450, MS. 2	951/972/ 978/986	Westminster	s. xii	*Facsimiles*, ed. Keynes no. 36	Disputed	x
S 1062	1042 x 1065	OMWi	s. xii	BMF iv. 37	Spurious	
S 995	1038 x 1039	Bury St Edmunds	s. xi [2]		Spurious	

Notes (Table 10.1)

[a]   Identified as imitative in *Charters of Burton abbey*, ed. P.H. Sawyer, Oxford 1979, no. 17, pp. xiii–xiv, 28–9; *Facsimiles*, no. 4; D.N. Dumville, 'English square minuscule script: the mid-century phases', *ASE* xxiii (1994), 133–64, at 146 n. 71: 'imitative', citing Keynes.

[b]   Identified as imitative in *Facsimiles*, p. 4.

[c]   Identified as imitative by Dumville, 'English square minuscule script', 146 n. 71, with no indication of date given. Sawyer described it as a 'very clumsy eleventh-century copy of an authentic charter': *Charters of Burton*, no. 14, p. 24. The palaeographical evidence for imitation (not discussed by Sawyer) resides in the highly variable formation of the letters, for example **a** and **g**, the irregular spacing, shape and size of the letters, and the repeated copying errors, including omitted words inserted interlineally using *signes de renvoie* in lines 7 and 8. There are no specifically anachronistic letters, which lends weight to Sawyer's suggestion that the scribe was copying an original of 956. The ascenders are tagged, a symptom of eleventh-century production: N.R. Ker, *Catalogue of manuscripts containing Anglo-Saxon*, Oxford 1957, rev. imp. 1990, xxxii.

[d]   *Charters of the New Minster, Winchester*, ed. S. Miller, Oxford 2001, no. 3. Nicholas Brooks dated this to the eleventh century 'though we cannot yet define the date more precisely': N.P. Brooks, 'The Micheldever forgery', *Anglo-Saxon myths: State and Church, 400–1066*, London 2000, 239–74, at 243 (reprinted from R.A. Custance (ed.), *Winchester College: sixth-century essays*, Oxford 1981, 189–228). Examination of the single sheet (in August 2010) suggests a distance from the Old English scribal tradition which might be consistent with a date later in that century: the scribe's inability to write a consistently square **a**, the poor formation of **e**-ligatures, the very variable size of **d** and forms of **f**, including a form in which the top rises above the succeeding letter, the unusual angling of the top of **g** at almost 45 degrees to the horizontal. The scribe wrote *sociętate*, suggesting confusion about **ae/e** spellings of the sort common in the early twelfth century, some descenders drag leftwards on the top few lines as they do in vernacular script of the eleventh century, the rustic capitals used for display are clumsily written with horizontal feet on the base line and at the tops of strokes, and the *ond* form, with a very extended top stroke, looks alien to tenth-century practice.

[e]   On the date, see *Charters of Burton*, no. 26, pp. 44–5. Sawyer described the script as 'impure Caroline minuscule for the Latin' and noted 'many similarities' with S 602 but he did not describe the script as imitative. The scribe employs monumental rotund insular minuscule for Latin, with round **a**, round-backed **d**, rounded **e**, long **r** and **s**, and occasional ligature of **et**, alongside Caroline **a**, **h**, tall **s**. Ligature of **e** with **a, i, n, p, r, x** is usually avoided, which indicates a post-tenth-century date, as does the degree of abbreviation. The execution of eth, **Q** and the **ra** ligature suggest that the scribe might be contemporary with that of the will of Wulfric Spot (S 906/1536), s. xi^{ex}.

[f]   *Facsimiles*, p. 8. *Cartularium Saxonicum*, ed. W. de G. Birch, London, 1885–93, no. 1305.

[g]   The authenticity was discussed in *Facsimiles*, p. 10. This version of the text remains unpublished until Dr Richard Mortimer completes his new edition of the Westminster charters. See meanwhile *Codex diplomaticus aevi Saxonici*, ed. J.M. Kemble, London, 1839–48, no. 801. On the script see below, 170–71.

^h The single-sheet copy was discovered by Professor Nicholas Vincent in Northamptonshire Record Office in October 2012 and I record its discovery here with Professor Vincent's kind permission. For the text, see *Charters of Peterborough abbey*, ed. S.E. Kelly, Oxford 2009, no. 1.

ⁱ *Charters of Peterborough*, ed. Kelly, no. 23, esp. pp. 304–5.

^j Below, 172. *Codex diplomaticus*, ed. Kemble, no. 824.

^k B.W. Scholz, 'Two forged charters from the abbey of Westminster and their relationship with St. Denis', *EHR* lxxvi (1961), 466–75, at 467. *Codex diplomaticus*, ed. Kemble, no. 779.

^l Below, 172. *Codex diplomaticus*, ed. Kemble, no. 824.

^m On authenticity, see *Facsimiles*, p. 11; on script, below, 172. *Cartularium*, ed. Birch, no. 1135.

ⁿ T. A. Heslop, 'Twelfth-century forgeries as evidence for earlier seals: the case of St Dunstan', in N. Ramsay, M. Sparks and T. Tatton-Brown (eds), *St Dunstan: his life, times and cult*, Woodbridge 1992, 299–310, pl. 54(b). *Cartularium*, ed. Birch, no. 245.

^o Heslop, 'Twelfth-century forgeries', 308, n. 36; Crick, 'St Albans', 68.

^p Heslop, 'Twelfth-century forgeries', 301. *Cartularium*, ed. Birch, no. 1050.

^q *Charters of Peterborough*, ed. Kelly, no. 22, esp. p. 300.

^r *The Crawford collection of early charters and documents now in the Bodleian Library*, ed. A. S. Napier and W. H. Stevenson, Oxford 1895, no. 6 and p. 89. Also Heslop, 'Twelfth-century forgeries', 301 and 308 n. 36. On authenticity, see *Facsimiles*, p. 11.

Table 10.2   Preliminary list of single-sheet copies of purportedly pre-Conquest writs copied in the long twelfth century.

Reference	Face Date	Archive	Date of copy	Facsimile	Status
S 1120	n. d.	Westminster	s. xii	OSF ii, Westminster 9	Spurious
S 1121	1044 x 1051	Westminster	s. xii	BMF iv.34	?Interpolated
S 1124	1047 x 1065	Westminster	s. xii	BMF iv.35	Spurious
S 1125	1049 x 1066	Westminster	s. xii	OSF ii, Westminster 17	?Authentic
S 1137	1058 x 1066	Westminster	s. xii	OSF ii, Westminster 15	Spurious
S 1138	1053 x 1066	Westminster	s. xii	OSF ii, Westminster 13	Disputed
S 1140, MS 2	1062 x 1066	Westminster	s. xii	OSF ii, Westminster 11	Forged copy
S 1141	1042 x 1066	Westminster	s. xii	BMF iv.36	Disputed
S 1142	1053 x 1066	Westminster	s. xii	OSF ii, Westminster 10	Authentic basis
S 1145	1042 x 1066	Westminster	s. xii	OSF ii, Westminster 14	?Interpolated

According to the working definition to be adopted in this chapter, a scribe writing imitative script deliberately suspends his normal practices and temporarily modifies and distorts his taught repertoire of scripts. Script-imitation requires distance from the original, therefore. Few script-types represent a real break with the past, Caroline minuscule being a conspicuous exception. Most adopt familiar elements such as letter-forms and ligatures and some even indulge in deliberate throw-backs to the past, such as the early phases of English square minuscule in the tenth century, examples of which are discussed below.[21] In such instances a scribe, or group of scribes, imported features from the past into a standard repertoire of graphic forms and so made them their own. Imitative script, on the other hand, is by definition the inverse of a settled scribal style – rather, it is a performance for an occasion, and so usually concocted as a response to a particular set of circumstances. Even when the same scribe has employed archaising script on two occasions, as in two different charters, often the modification will be subtly different.[22] This degree of variation can be attributed in part to the subtlety of an individual scribe's response to the models in front of him, but it also reflects the instability inherent in imitative script: the pretence cannot be maintained. Julian Brown wrote of faker's palsy, a physical tremor caused by the mental and physical effort of copying something unfamiliar.[23] Scribes rarely achieved consistency in their importation of alien script forms. Even an ambitious scribe who was able to execute ligatures or blocks of words brilliantly often failed to sustain the rhythm of his writing and so the aspect of the page. Moreover, imitative campaigns are often accompanied by elementary copying errors, as if the task of imitation occupied so much of the scribe's concentration that he was unable to focus on the primary task in hand.[24] In the process of imitation the scribe consciously

---

[21] For example, Dumville, 'English square minuscule script', 135–6, 141. Below, 172–7, on S 624 and 646. The script is exemplified by the use of graphic features familiar in eighth-century insular script: letter-forms borrowed from insular half-uncial, such as **oc a** and capital **N**, and capitals echoing the form of uncials and rustics in use in the eighth century.

[22] Crick, 'Script and the sense of the past', 14–19. Atsma and Vezin argued that a Saint-Denis scribe varied his imitative script in copying charters of different dates: 'Le dossier suspect', 227–8.

[23] [T.J. Brown], 'The detection of faked literary manuscripts', in J. Bately, M.P. Brown and J. Roberts (eds), *A palaeographer's view: the selected writings of Julian Brown*, London 1993, 253–62, at 259. See also below, n. 72.

[24] For example, the scribe copying the imitative Exeter charter S 389 MS. 1 (Exeter, Dean and Chapter, MS. 2517), purportedly of AD 670 wrote *domicę* for *dominicę* after 'Anno' in the opening line. Bischoff also identified scribal error as a symptom of forgery in charters: B. Bischoff, tr. D.Ó Cróinín and D. Ganz, *Latin palaeography: antiquity and the Middle Ages*, Cambridge 1990, 46.

interrupted his own habitual practices, observed those of the historic scribe(s) whose work he sought to imitate, and reproduced them to the best of his ability.

The charters listed in Table 10.1 include examples of all three categories of imitation just outlined. The first category, blatant imitation of pre-Conquest script which clearly belongs neither to pre-Conquest nor post-Conquest scribal traditions, embraces a great variety of possibilities. One is represented by S 1026, an Evesham charter purporting to be of AD 1055. The scribe copied the vernacular boundary clause in a form of insular minuscule employing features typical of the mid-eleventh century and later: descenders which drag to the left at their lowest extent, eth with a tall ascender looping over at the top, while the round **a**, hooked **e** and avoidance of **e**-ligatures are all consonant with an eleventh- or twelfth-century date.[25] The script of the Latin text and attestations is altogether more curious, not least because the scribe pursues the anachronistic goal of copying the Latin text of a diploma of Edward the Confessor in insular minuscule. Royal diplomas were routinely copied in Caroline minuscule from the 980s.[26] The form of insular minuscule employed is differentiated from that of the boundary clause by features borrowed from Caroline minuscule. Hence a ligature resembling ampersand is used instead of the **et**-nota, and the **ct**-ligature characteristic of Caroline minuscule is imperfectly reproduced by the addition of a semicircular stroke above those two letters. The ligature representing **et** is confirmed as an imitation by comparison with the larger version of the same compendium employed in the attestations, where it represents Æ in initial position. This failure to differentiate between **ae** and **et** is a marked anomaly in the script.[27] Long **s** is routinely positioned so that it has the tall form reminiscent of Caroline minuscule: the head is at approximately the same height as neighbouring ascenders (for example, **l** and **k**). Norman influence is apparent in the use of **W** in Old English and Norman names in the attestations. In the middle of the twelfth century another Evesham scribe imitated insular script in the production of a forged papal bull of 713.[28] On this occasion the scribe modified his normal bookhand by adding a flourished top to **t**, and by the use of round **a**, round **d**, long **f**, **r** and **s**, insular **g** and open-bowled **p**, all features suggesting imitation of an eighth- or ninth-century model. In other respects – the adoption of hook-backed

---

[25] Ker, *Catalogue*, xxxi–xxxiii.

[26] For the last square minuscule diplomas, see Dumville, 'English square minuscule script', 156 n. 125. The general rule that Latin was written in Caroline minuscule in the eleventh century was formulated by Ker, *Catalogue*, xxv–xxvi. Exceptions have been discussed by P.A. Stokes, 'English vernacular script, *ca* 990–*ca* 1035', unpubl. Ph.D. diss. Cambridge 2006.

[27] For another example, see *infra*, B.R. O'Brien, 'Pre-Conquest laws and legislators in the twelfth century', 255 and n. 89 (on Paris, BnF, lat. 4771).

[28] The second privilege of Pope Constantine for Evesham (713) (BL, Cotton Cleopatra E. i, fos 64–5): Sayers, '"Original", cartulary and chronicle', iv. 377 and pl. I.

e and the leftwards drag of the descenders – he shows awareness of eleventh-century models and in the inappropriate addition of hairline extensions to the foot of minim letters he was probably influenced not by an English model, but possibly by Continental practice.[29]

This first category of imitation also embraces examples which are much more extreme, as illustrated by a twelfth-century imitation whose scribe has departed so far from his training that at first sight the results are almost unintelligibly hybrid. This is Offa's grant of Aldenham, Herts, to Westminster, AD 785 (S 124), which belongs to a series of feigned originals produced at Westminster in the middle years of the twelfth century in connection with a dispute over the estate.[30] The twelfth-century scribe successfully imitated a number of letter-forms of set-cursive minuscule of his target period, the later eighth or early ninth century, letting **f**, **r**, and **s** fall below the baseline and reproducing with moderate success a pinched **a** and open-headed **q**, and the rising tops of **e** and **t**.[31] However, the script utterly fails to convince. It is characterised by irregularity, inconsistency and some telling anachronisms. An eighth-century scribe would have ligatured **e** with a following consonant, but our twelfth-century scribe shirks this. The e-ligature characterised insular script from half-uncial downwards until the middle of the tenth century, but thereafter even scribes trained to write insular minuscule reproduced the compendium rarely, and a post-Conquest scribe unfamiliar with insular script would have found it complex to execute and difficult to imitate. The scribe adopted a leftward turn at the foot of descenders, a feature common in the eleventh century but quite alien to his target period, the eighth or early ninth century, which influenced other features of his imitation, and this feature apparently reflects the influence of models of different date. Our twelfth-century scribe wrote with a degree of lateral compression, for example in the letters constructed from minim strokes, which is uncharacteristic of an English scribal performance before the Norman Conquest.

The second category comprises examples written in post-Conquest script which has been only lightly modified, perhaps to reflect the purported antiquity of the text being copied. Here, it is important to bear in mind Ker's observation that many scribes, even as late as 1160, copied charters in bookhand or in a

---

[29] On the form of **e** and the descenders, see Ker, *Catalogue*, xxix, xxxii. For an example of trailing minims, see the purported confirmation of exemption and immunity to the monastery of Ebermünster, dated 12 August 801, scraped and rewritten in the twelfth century: F. Lot and P. Lauer (avec la collaboration de G. Tessier), *Diplomata Karolinorum: recueil de reproductions en fac-similé des actes originaux des souverains carolingiens conservés dans les archives et bibliothèques de France*, 10 parts, Paris, 1936–, I, pl. xli (no. 24), Bibliothèque-Archives de Sélestat, Ebermünster B.

[30] Above, Table 10.1, n. n.

[31] See also Crick, 'St Albans', 68 and n. 23.

modification of it, with round-backed **d** and long **f**, **r** and **s**.³² One must also focus on the Latin text, as scribes throughout the twelfth century continued to use Old English letter-forms in the copying of Old English texts and name-forms.³³ Candidates for classification as mildly imitative charters include S 731, a forgery copied in bookhand of the first half of the twelfth century, which employs frequent round **d** and long **r**, and occasional insular **r** in Latin in the attestations (*archuntorum*; *dorouuernensis*); S 1043 MS 2, copied by a mid-twelfth-century scribe who perpetrated other imitations, as Heslop showed (in this instance **r** extends below the baseline and descenders trail to the left); and S 1043 MS 1, in which **f** and **s** also descend below the baseline.

So far this discussion has focused on relatively crude examples, but imitation can be remarkably sophisticated. The last purported pre-Conquest charter to be discussed here has attracted controversy and continues to do so. Most commentators have accepted the charter as an authentic tenth-century single sheet, but Peter Sawyer and Simon Keynes have suggested in print that it is an eleventh-century copy.³⁴ The following discussion will set out palaeographical evidence which supports their judgement.³⁵ The charter in question, S 602 from the archive of Burton abbey, purportedly dates from 956 and records King Eadwig's gift to his thegn, Æthelnoth, of land at Darlaston, Staffs (see Figure 10.1). On first inspection, the charter bears a remarkable resemblance to authentic originals of 956 and 957, whose production Chaplais assigned to the fifth of eight 'so-called royal scribes' whose work he associated with the Winchester scriptorium of the period 931–63.³⁶ They are S 624, King Eadwig's grant to Ealdorman Edmund of land at Annington, Sussex, from the Abingdon archive, and S 646, from Ely, which records King Eadwig's grant to Archbishop

---

[32] Ker, *English manuscripts*, 18–19. The phenomenon has been explored in an important paper by T. Webber, 'L'écriture des documents en Angleterre au xiie siècle', *BEC* cv (2007), 139–65.

[33] As Ker reported: *Catalogue*, xxvi–xxvii.

[34] Above, Table 10.1, n. a.

[35] The discussion here is based on purely palaeographical criteria. Any consideration of the authenticity of the text is a separate matter not entered into here. The identification of a single sheet as an imitative copy does not automatically condemn the text as fabricated, although it of course opens the possibility that it might be so: see below, 185. I am most grateful to Professors Nicholas Brooks and Simon Keynes for discussion of this matter.

[36] P. Chaplais, 'The origins and authenticity of the royal Anglo-Saxon diploma', *Journal of the Society of Archivists* iii (1966), 160–76, repr. in F. Ranger (ed.), *Prisca munimenta: studies in archival and administrative history presented to Dr A.E.J. Hollaender*, London 1973, 28–42, esp. 41. Keynes doubted, with good reason, that the two charters were written by the same scribe: *Facsimiles*, p. 4.

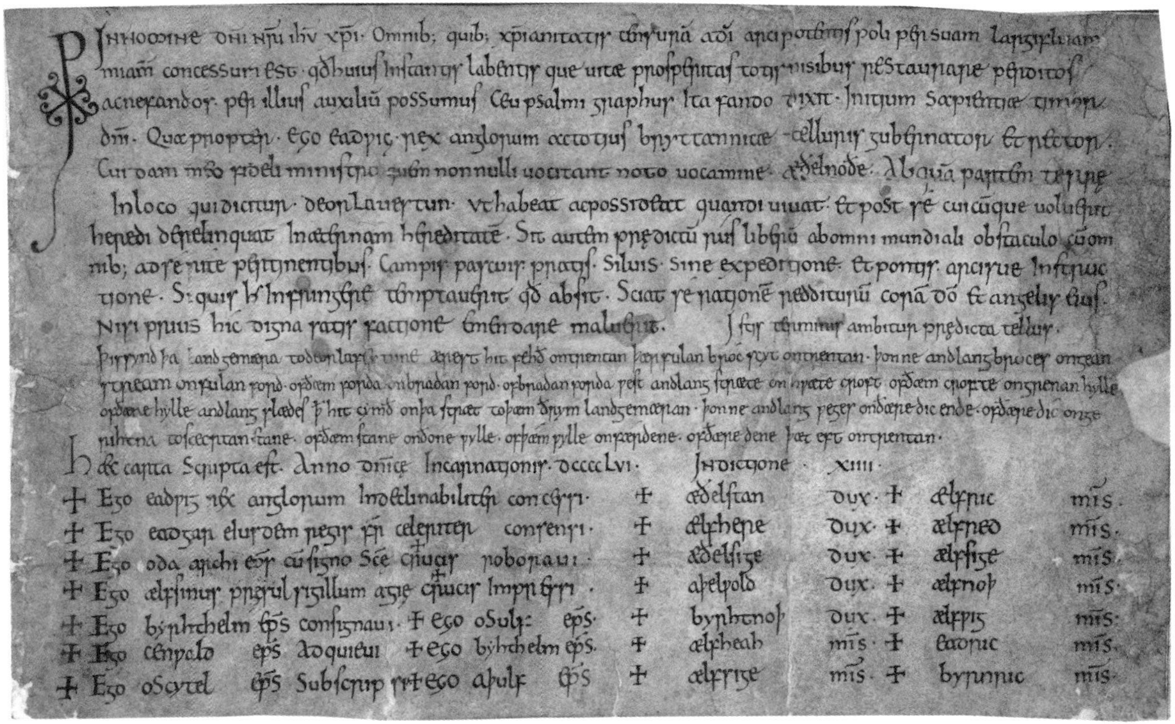

Figure 10.1 S 602. King Eadwig's grant to his thegn, Æthelnoth, of land at Darlaston, Staffs. Purported original of AD 956, from the archive of Burton. Stafford, William Salt Library, MS. 84/1/41 (230 × 360 mm), reproduced at a scale of 45% of the original size. Reproduced by permission of the Trustees of the William Salt Library, Stafford.

Oda of forty hides at Ely, Cambs. (AD 957) (see Figure 10.2).³⁷ Overlapping features link the three documents together, and these will be discussed below before any attempt is made to establish the chronological relationship between the Darlaston charter and its comparanda.

The three charters share a common format. All three open with a pictorial invocation in the form of a chi-rho monogram in the left-hand margin. The crosses which mark the attestations are aligned with the chi-rho, to the left of the text-block, and in the first column of attestations the word *Ego* begins with a square capital *E*. In all three charters the ministerial style is abbreviated *mis*, a common trait in charters of the mid-tenth century.³⁸ Also unremarkable is the writing of a small cross above the word *crucis* where it occurs in episcopal attestations (S 602 lines 18–19; S 624 line 17; S 646 lines 9, 12). All three employ the same mixed capitals for the verbal invocation, the donor's name, and in the dating clause, with uncial **d**, **e**, **g** and **m**, rustic capital **v** for **u** and **g**, but with frequent use of lower-grade letter forms, such as minuscule **e** and the characteristic half-uncial form of **a** in the shape of a conjoined **o** and **c**. The scribe of the Darlaston charter is noticeably more conservative than the scribes of the tenth-century originals, writing most of the dating clause in minuscule, and avoiding the lambda-shaped **A** imported from rustic capitals, which the other scribe(s) use in writing the king's name in capitals on the first line of their texts. These eclectic majuscules are typical of tenth-century scribal inventiveness, and the use of the form of **G** terminating in a left-wards trailing descender is particularly favoured in that period.³⁹ All three charters employ a variant form, with the tail of the **G** turning to the right (S 602 line 4 Eadwig; S 624 line 1 Eadwig; S 646 line 2 Eadwig).⁴⁰ Such revivals are characteristic of the so-called decorative style of square minuscule which David Dumville associated with the court of Eadwig, his successor Edgar, and his predecessors Edmund and Eadred.⁴¹ All three charters show the deployment of features imported from the higher grades of eighth- and ninth-century insular minuscule: the so-called **oc**-form of **a** characteristic of insular half-uncial of the eighth century and hybrid minuscule of the ninth, the **ti** ligature with pendant **I**. They also employ an outsized round **S** which rises above adjacent minims letters (e.g. S 602 line 2 *concessum*; S 624 line 5 *scilicet*; S 646 line 5 *constructione*).

---

³⁷ Keynes, 'Ely', 5 n. 13 and 17. Keynes identified S 646 as a comparandum: *Facsimiles*, p. 4.

³⁸ S.D. Thompson, *Anglo-Saxon royal diplomas: a palaeography*, Woodbridge 2006, 96–7.

³⁹ Besides these three charters the form is found, for example, in S 470 (AD 940), S 512 (AD 943), S 497 (AD 943), S 528 (AD 947).

⁴⁰ In S 602 and 624 the preceding 'ego' employed the variant form. In S 646 the parchment has been damaged and the word 'ego' lost so no comparison is possible.

⁴¹ Dumville, 'English square minuscule script', 144–51.

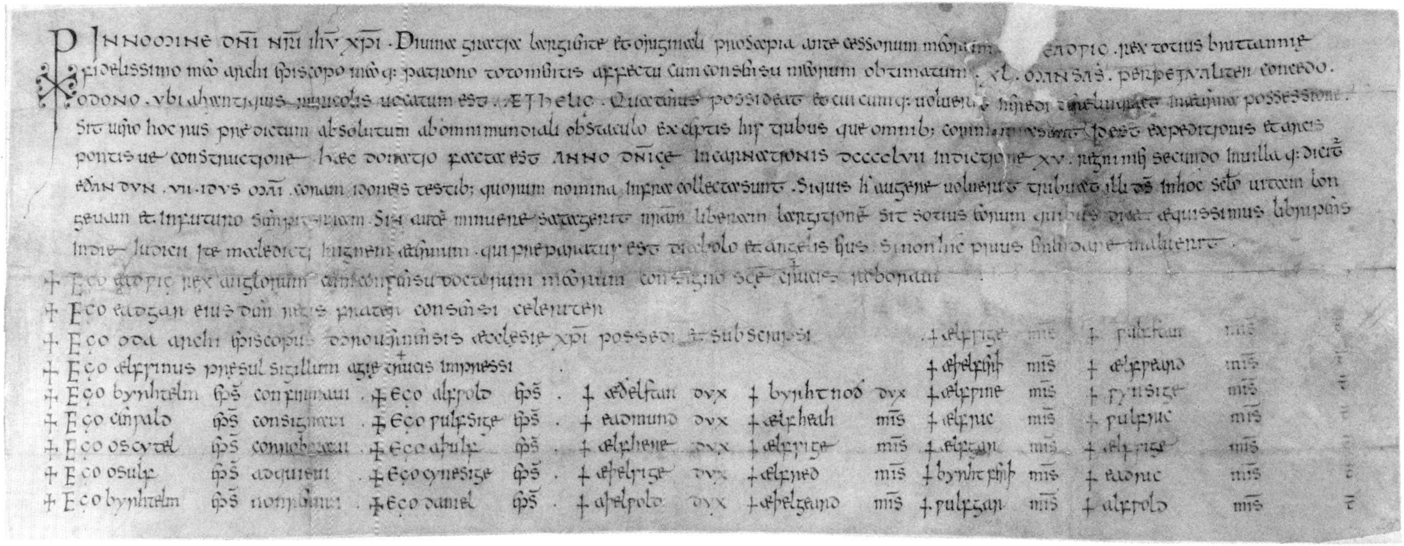

Figure 10.2 S 646. King Eadwig's grant to Archbishop Oda of forty hides at Ely, Cambs. Original of AD 957, from the archive of Ely. Oxford, Bod'eian Library, MS. Eng. Hist. a. 2, no. V (190 × 490 mm), reproduced at a scale of 35% of the original size. Reproduced by permission of the Bodleian Libraries, the University of Oxford.

Certain features link two of the three charters. The two unambiguously tenth-century productions employ capitals more boldly than does S 602, for the names not just of the king but of the beneficiary and estate, and for the bulk of the dating clause. Their scribes wrote a fully rounded uncial **e** (S 624 line 1 *Ego Eadwig*; S 646 lines 13–17 *Ego*), a feature shirked in S 602 in which the scribe reproduces the effect using an enlarged minuscule **e** with the top compartment joined at the right to the cross-stroke. Other features of their script will be discussed in due course. S 624 displays a generic resemblance to the Darlaston charter, notably in the inclusion of a vernacular boundary clause. The link between S 646 and the Darlaston charter is much closer and more striking, marked by three rare, or unique, features. One is a particularly elaborate form of pictorial invocation. Each of the arms of the cross of the *chi-rho* terminates in two tendril-like flourishes and the *rho* descends straight, like a capital P, until level with the midpoint of the fourth line of text, at which point it trails leftwards in a long flourish.[42] A second idiosyncrasy is the anachronistic use of the old insular compendium for *autem* (S 602 line 9; S 646, line 6) which occurs in only two other purportedly tenth-century charters, one also from Burton.[43] A third is that both charters bear two purportedly contemporary endorsements, a feature logged in only one other charter.[44]

There are a number of reasons for believing that these rare occurrences do not simply reflect contemporary practice but are explained by deliberate imitation, either of S 646 or of a lost charter very like it. First, the script of S 602 displays features far removed from the norms of the mid-tenth century. Even allowing for provincial production it is difficult to explain away the scribe's inability not only to write flat-topped square minuscule but also to exercise consistency in his script. So, he attempts to use a flat-topped **d**, as would be normal in the 950s (and is standard in S 624 and S 646), but he regularly employs a tall-backed **d** as a variant; **a** is almost never square, as one would expect before the later decades of the tenth century, but round, as is common in the eleventh. Our scribe occasionally executes *e*-ligatures but he often avoids high **e**, as comparison of the boundary clauses of S 624 and S 602 indicates (also S 602 line 7 *heredi derelinquat*), and he occasionally wrote a high **e** where there was no possibility of, or attempt at, a ligature (line 2 *restaurare*; line 4 *telluris*). In fact, the failure of the scribe to write convincingly insular script in the boundary clause suggests that he was not familiar with the insular tradition, at least in its pre-Conquest guise. There are two marked and unconscious anachronisms in S 602 which

---

[42] Thompson, *Anglo-Saxon royal diplomas*, 35: she records it also in S 649.
[43] S 768. Simon Keynes has suggested that S 768 might itself be an imitative copy: above, Table 10.1, n. b. The *autem* compendium occurs also in S 464: Thompson, *Anglo-Saxon royal diplomas*, 94.
[44] S 163: Thompson, *Anglo-Saxon royal diplomas*, 50.

place it beyond doubt as a later, probably eleventh-century product. The first is the form of the *autem* abbreviation. Insular scribes, among them that of S 646, constructed the compendium from a hooked **h**, the base letter-form being invariably insular, whether half-uncial or insular minuscule. The scribe of the Darlaston charter, on the other hand, constructed his compendium using a Caroline **h**, indicating a primary familiarity with that script, which must place him late, possibly after the Norman Conquest.[45] He abbreviated *misericordiam* using the contraction *miam*, which Bischoff recorded in his list of abbreviations for the twelfth to the fifteenth centuries, although he reported that it was an older creation.[46] Of forty-five occurrences of the word in Anglo-Saxon charters, only eight survive in pre-twelfth-century single sheets, usually unabbreviated. Apart from S 602 the only other occurrence of this abbreviation for *misericordia* occurs in another Burton charter, S 879, firmly established as a late imitative copy.[47] The Continental abbreviation *qd* for *quod* is reported relatively rarely in the last Anglo-Saxon century, almost always written with a straight-backed **d**.[48] In S 602 it is written with a round-backed **d** bisected by the abbreviation stroke, as is common after the Norman Conquest. A tenth- or eleventh-century scribe trained in the insular tradition is likely to have read this crossed round-backed **d** as the Old English letter eth (**ð**); indeed, it may be compared with the form of eth employed by this scribe (S 602 line 12 *of ðæm*). This muddying of the distinction between two different graphic forms suggests a scribe working after the Conquest. I conclude that the scribe of S 602 produced a remarkably faithful post-Conquest copy of an original diploma of Eadwig.

These eleventh- and twelfth-century examples represent only one segment of a longer and more widespread scribal tradition. Imitative charters are a phenomenon well recognised in France and identifiable in England from about the early tenth century onwards. The French tradition has been discussed in the writings of the great diplomatists of the École des chartes, notably in a series of case studies.[49] The

---

[45] J.C. Crick, 'English vernacular script', in R. Gameson (ed.), *The Cambridge history of the book in Britain, Volume 1: c.400–1100*, Cambridge 2012, 174–86, esp. 182–4.

[46] Bischoff, *Latin palaeography*, 153, 163. Lindsay associated it with Italy: W.M. Lindsay, *Notae Latinae: an account of abbreviation in Latin MSS. of the early minuscule period (c.700–850)*, Cambridge 1915, 126–9 and D. Bains, *A supplement to Notae Latinae (abbreviations in Latin MSS. of 850 to 1050 A.D.)*, Hildesheim 1963, 22–3.

[47] The other occurrences are S 111, S 168, S 470, S 956, S 1064, S 1203 (all unabbreviated) and S 319 (*miscda*). On S 879, see above, n. 25.

[48] Thompson reports six occurrences of this form of the abbreviation: Thompson, *Anglo-Saxon royal diplomas*, 96. To these may be added S 959 line 19. I have checked S 706 (line 10), S 892 (line 12), S 1003 (line 12), S 1027, listed by Thompson and all employ straight-backed **d**.

[49] J. Quicherat, 'Critique des deux plus anciennes chartes de l'abbaye de Saint-Germain des Prés', *BEC* xxvi (1865), 513–55; R. de Lasteyrie, 'La charte de donation du

twentieth-century editors of the royal diplomas of the Carolingian kings amplified these findings.[50] They listed numerous documents as pseudo-originals, that is, as single-sheet copies, describing some as *copies figurées*, indicating replica documents made for safe-keeping in imitation of the original, and identifying a small number of these as written in archaising or imitative script, often displaying the maladroitness, misinterpretation and poor spacing seen in imitative performances in England.[51] A separate category of replacement document, which Giry dubbed 'actes récrits', describes later fabrications, sometimes passable imitations of older documents.[52] More recently, Vezin and Atsma have undertaken a series of detailed studies of the replica documents forged at the abbey of Saint-Denis in the eleventh century, including a portfolio of royal and papal documents allegedly dating from the Merovingian and Carolingian eras, written in imitative script on papyrus obtained by pasting authentic Merovingian papyrus documents on to parchment and reclaiming the unwritten dorse.[53]

Findings collated from these various campaigns of study are tabulated below (Tables 10.3 and 10.4). Table 10.3 will necessarily reflect the reporting habits of certain editors. Tessier, for example, made it his practice to describe in detail the script of *copies figurées*, while his fellow editors sometimes provided no palaeographical information.

---

domaine de Sucy à l'Église de Paris (811)', *BEC* xliii (1882), 60–78, at 62, 77; L. Delisle, 'Imitation d'anciennes écritures par des scribes du Moyen Âge', *Revue archéologique* 3 ser. xvi (1890), 63–5; A. Giry, 'La donation de Rueil à l'abbaye de Saint-Denis: examen critique de trois diplômes de Charles le Chauve', *Mélanges Julien Havet (1853–1893)*, Paris 1895, 683–717; L. Levillain, 'Les diplômes originaux et le diplôme faux de Lothaire 1er pour l'abbaye de Saint-Denis', *BEC* xcv (1934), 225–58; G. Tessier, 'Originaux et pseudo-originaux carolingiens du chartrier de Saint-Denis', *BEC* cvi (1946), 35–69.

[50] *Recueil des actes de Charles II le Chauve, roi de France*, ed. G. Tessier, Paris 1943–55; *Recueil des actes de Louis II le Bègue, Louis III et Carloman II, rois de France (877–884)*, ed. F. Grat, J. de Font-Réaulx, G. Tessier, R.-H. Bautier, Paris 1978.

[51] For an example of an unstable imitative performance, see the description by Giry, 'La donation de Rueil', 693–4. Giry defined *copies figurées* as transcriptions whose scribes attempted to imitate the originals in all particulars, and which are sometimes virtually indistinguishable from originals: *Manuel*, 14. The identifications listed here were checked against published photographs, notably in Lot and Lauer, *Diplomata Karolinorum*, and those housed in Paris were checked against microfilm in the Archives nationales (CARAN), and, where permitted, against originals in the Bibliothèque nationale de France in May/June 2010.

[52] Giry, *Manuel*, 14–15, 867–70.

[53] H. Atsma and J. Vezin, 'Les faux sur papyrus de l'abbaye de Saint-Denis', in J. Kervhervé et A. Rigaudière (eds), *Finances, pouvoirs et mémoire. Hommages offerts à Jean Favier*, Paris 1999, 674–99 and pls I–IX. See also Atsma and Vezin, 'Le dossier suspect'; Vezin, 'Écritures imitées', 62–5.

Table 10.3 Indicative list of published identifications of single-sheet imitative copies of Merovingian and Carolingian diplomas from the eleventh and twelfth centuries.

Shelfmark	Face date	Archive	Date of copy	Facsimile	Identification	Comments[a]	Text
Archives de l'Aude H 11 (fonds de Lagrasse)	20 June 859	Attigny	s. x or s. xi	*Diplomata Karolinorum* V.xxv	Tessier[b]	Interpolated: script imitates extant original (same date)	Charles the Bald
Archives de l'église Saint-Pierre, Ghent, III D a 1	13 April 870	Ghent	s. x/xi		Tessier[c]	Imitative script	Charles the Bald
Paris, Archives nationales, K.1 no. 7[2]	29 July 631 or 632	Saint-Denis	1060–71	Atsma and Vezin[d]	Atsma and Vezin[e]	Imitative script on papyrus	Dagobert I
Paris, BnF, Collection Baluze 390, no. 481	n.d. [1 November 898]	Narbonne	s. xi		Lauer[f]	*Copie figurée*	Charles the Simple
Archives de Maine-et-Loire H 1836	5 June 881	Saint-Florent	s. xi		Grat *et al*.[g]	*Copie figurée*	Carloman
Archives départmentales de la Côte d'Or H.244	7 June 916	Molesme	s. xi		Lauer[h]	*Copie figurée*	Charles the Simple
Archives des Bouches-du-Rhône 1H 4, no. 7	2 February 884	Marseille	s. xi		Grat *et al*.[i]	*Copie en partie figurée*	Carloman
Archives du Gard H 114	3 December 815	Psalmody	s. xi	*Diplomata Karolinorum* II(2).L		Modified script	Louis the Pious to Psalmody

(*continued*)

Table 10.3 (*continued*)

Shelfmark	Face date	Archive	Date of copy	Facsimile	Identification	Comments[a]	Text
Paris, Archives nationales, K 12 no. 5b	25 April 860	Saint-Denis	s. xi	*Diplomata Karolinorum* V.xxvi	Levillain; Giry; Tessier[j]	Forgery; imitative script; traces of seal	Charles the Bald
Paris, Archives nationales, K 1 no. 3	December 558	Saint-Germain	s. xi [in.]		Quicherat[k]	On papyrus	Childebert
Rouen, Bibliothèque municipale, MS 3123	25 December 840–75	Nôtre-Dame, Soissons	s. xi [in.]		Tessier[l]	Forgery in imitative script	Charles the Bald
Paris, Archives nationales, K 14 no. 9B	9 October 873	Saint-Denis	s. xi [in.]	*Diplomata Karolinorum* V.xxix	Giry; Tessier[m]	Imitation of extant original of 27 March 875	Charles the Bald to St-Denis (Rueil)
Angers, Musée Saint-Jean	17 July 847 (or 808)	Angers, Saint-Aubin,	s. xi [in.]		Tessier[n]	Forgery; imitative script	Charles the Bald
Archives de Maine-et-Loire H 1835	8 June 848	Saint-Florent	Before *c.*1040–60		Tessier[o]	Forgery; imitative script	Charles the Bald
Paris, Archives nationales, K 11 no. 3	10 July 845	Saint-Germain	s. xi[2] or later		Tessier[p]	Forgery; anachronistic script	Charles the Bald

Shelfmark	Face date	Archive	Date of copy	Facsimile	Identification	Comments[a]	Text
Paris, Archives nationales, K 10 no. 8	18 April 840–54	Saint-Germain	s. xi[2] or later		Tessier[r]	Forgery; imitative script[1]	Charles the Bald

Notes (Table 10.3)

a Unless otherwise stated, the information in this column is derived from the published comments referenced in the preceding Identification column.
b *Recueil des actes de Charles II*, i. 333 n. 3 (no. 145), 527 (no. 208) and 528 n. 1.
c *Recueil des actes de Charles II*, ii. 244–5 (no. 337) and 244 n. 2.
d Atsma and Vezin, 'Les faux', pl. II.
e Ibid. 677, 687–8.
f *Recueil des actes de Charles III le Simple, roi de France* (893–923), ed. P. Lauer, Paris 1940, i. 24 (no. 14, MS B).
g *Recueil des actes de Louis II le Bègue, Louis III et Carloman II*, 140 (no. 55).
h *Recueil des actes de Charles III*, i. 192–3 (no. 86, MS B); imitation not described.
i *Recueil des actes de Louis II le Bègue, Louis III et Carloman II*, 185 (no. 72); also p. XVI, n. 1 and no. 55. No description.
j Levillain, 'Les diplômes originaux', 230 and n. 1; *Recueil des actes de Charles II*, ii. 593–4 (no. 479) and 594 n. 2.
k Quicherat, 'Critique des deux plus anciennes chartes', 535, 540.
l *Recueil des actes de Charles II*, ii. 655 (no. 499) and n. 1.
m Ibid ii. 648–9 and n. 1 (no. 456); Giry, 'La donation de Rueil'.
n *Recueil des actes de Charles II*, ii. 548 n. 1 (no. 467).
o Ibid. ii. 554–55 n. 1 (no. 470).
p Ibid. ii. 545 n. 1 (no. 466).
q Ibid. ii. 562–3 n. 1 (no. 472). Scribe identified in charters of Henry I (1058).
r The script may be compared with the aspect of Paris, Archives nationales, K 8 no. 6 (1), Lot and Lauer, *Diplomata Karolinorum*, ii, pl. xxvii, in the manner in which descending strokes are angled and the ascenders and descenders curve. **p** is pinched very acutely in both.

Table 10.4 Indicative list of published identifications of single-sheet imitative copies of non-royal documents from the eleventh and twelfth centuries.

Shelfmark	Face date	Archive	Date of copy	Facsimile	Identification	Comments[a]	Text
Paris, Archives nationales, K 7 no. 17[2]	811	Notre-Dame, Paris	s. xi		Lasteyrie[b]	Imitating s. ix	Forged charter of Count Stephen
Paris, Archives nationales, K 1, no. 5	862	Saint-Denis	1060–71	Atsma and Vezin, 'Les faux', pl. I	Atsma and Vezin[c]	On papyrus	Forged record of the synod of Soissons
Paris, Archives nationales, K 5, no. 4[2]	26 February 757	Saint-Denis	1060–71	Atsma and Vezin, 'Les faux', pl. III	Atsma and Vezin[d]	On papyrus	Forged bull of Pope Stephen II
Paris, Archives nationales, K 7 no. 16[2]	27 May 798	Saint-Denis	1060–71	Atsma and Vezin, 'Les faux', pl. IV	Atsma and Vezin[e]	On papyrus	Forged bull of Leo III
Paris, Archives nationales, K 13 no. 10[3]	28 April 863	Saint-Denis	1060–71	Atsma and Vezin, 'Les faux', pl. V	Atsma and Vezin[f]	On papyrus	Forged bull of Nicholas I
Paris, Archives nationales, K 3 no. 1[1]	1 July 654	Saint-Denis	1060–71	Atsma and Vezin, 'Les faux', pl. VI	Atsma and Vezin[g]	On papyrus	Forged charter of Bishop Landri of Paris

Shelfmark	Face date	Archive	Date of copy	Facsimile	Identification	Comments[a]	Text
Paris, Archives nationales, K 4 no. 1[2]	4 November 757	Saint-Denis	1060–71	Atsma and Vezin, 'Les faux', pl. VII	Atsma and Vezin[h]	On papyrus	Forged bull of Zacharias
Paris, Archives nationales, K 7 no. 8[2]	1 July 786	Saint-Denis	1060–71	Atsma and Vezin, 'Les faux', pl. VIII	Atsma and Vezin[i]	On papyrus	Forged bull of Adrian I
Paris, Archives nationales, L220 no. 3	28 April 863	Saint-Denis	1060–71	Atsma and Vezin, 'Les faux', pl. IX	Atsma and Vezin[j]	On papyrus	Forged bull of Nicholas I

Notes (Table 10.4)

[a] Unless otherwise stated, the information in this column is derived from the published comments referenced in the preceding Identification column.
[b] Lasteyrie, 'La charte de donation', 62.
[c] Atsma and Vezin, 'Les faux', 688.
[d] Ibid. 688.
[e] Ibid. 688.
[f] Ibid. 689.
[g] Ibid. 689.
[h] Ibid. 689.
[i] Ibid. 689.
[j] Ibid. 690.

Table 10.5 Documents in the names of English kings from the archives of Saint-Denis in script showing influence of English exemplars.

Shelfmark	Face date	Date	Facsimiles	Discussion	Reference	Text
Paris, Archives nationales, K 7 no. 10	790	s. xi^med.	Atsma and Vezin[a]	Atsma and Vezin[b]	S 133	Offa, grant of privileges
Paris, Archives nationales, K 17 no. 3	960	s. xi^med.	Atsma and Vezin[c]	Atsma and Vezin[d]	S 686	Edgar, restoration of property
Paris, Archives nationales, AE III.60 (K 19 no. 6)	1059	s. xi^med.	*Facsimiles*, ed. Keynes, no. 21a	Bishop, no. 20;[e] *Facsimiles*, ed. Keynes, 7–8	S 1028	Diploma of Edward the Confessor
Paris, Archives nationales, AE III.60 (K 19 no. 6)	1053 x 1057	s. xi^med.	*Facsimiles*, ed. Keynes, no. 20	*Facsimiles*, ed. Keynes, 7	S 1105	Writ of Edward the Confessor

Notes (Table 10.5)

[a] Atsma and Vezin, 'Le dossier suspect', pls I–III.
[b] Ibid. 215–16, 225–6. Vezin, 'Écritures', 64–5.
[c] Atsma and Vezin, 'Le dossier suspect', pls IV–VI.
[d] Ibid. 219–24, 226–30 and pls IV–VI. Vezin, 'Écritures', 64–5.
[e] 'The nerveless and presumably imitative work of a scribe who was unfamiliar with the O. E. minuscule, probably not an Englishman': *Facsimiles of English royal writs to A.D. 1100 presented to Vivian Hunter Galbraith*, ed. T.A. M. Bishop and P. Chaplais, Oxford 1957, pl. XVIII (no. 20).

This body of documents offers an instructive comparison with the English material in a variety of respects, not least because of the superior volume of surviving evidence, both in the number of extant examples and in the richness of their archival context. Some texts extant in imitative copies have been preserved in other single-sheet forms in addition, as non-imitative copies and as originals, permitting an assessment of the fidelity of copying of text and script. Such multiple versions are extremely rare in English material of comparable date. Although the archives of Christ Church Canterbury preserve duplicate copies of two charters, in each case both copies have been identified as imitative and so no single-sheet original survives as a fixed point for textual or palaeographical comparison.[54]

Such contrasts reflect the very different ways in which charters were made and preserved on either side of the Channel. Thus, according to Giry, *copies figurées* constitute local copies of chancery documents, and carry no expectation of fraud or even of production after the face date of the charter. Even *actes récrits* could be relatively innocent. Different commentators report that copies did not enhance rights and claims documented elsewhere but that they simply replaced deteriorating charters. Three eleventh-century copies of a grant made in 811 by Count Stephen to the (cathedral) church of Paris, are extant, one in imitative script, which Lasteyrie argued represented the reconstruction of a lost charter of donation using Carolingian charters.[55] Levillain noted that six original diplomas of Pippin I in favour of different religious houses were replaced by tenth- and eleventh-century imitative copies in their respective archives and, in a later study, he discussed ninth-century copies of charters of Chlothar I made to replace originals 'qui étaient sans doute trop détériorés pour pouvoir être même encore utilisés'.[56] The presence of imitative script does not necessarily connote fraud in the French scholarly tradition, but charters written in imitative script have been associated with a variety of archival practices. Early scholars established that imitative copying sometimes disguised manipulation of an early text. In a paper published in 1895 Giry discussed two copies of a charter of Charles the Bald to Saint-Denis giving valuable property on the Seine at Rueil (Paris, Archives nationales, Carton des rois, K.14.9).[57] The imitative copy is almost identical with the other, except that the text of the imitative version has been subtly improved, the issue date has been changed to the feast of Saint-Denis, and the claims significantly enhanced by the insertion of a sentence clarifying the abbey's rights to fisheries in the Seine.[58]

---

[54] S 175, of AD 814, and S 546, of AD 949; both survive as two non-contemporary single-sheet copies.

[55] Lasteyrie, 'La charte de donation', 77–8.

[56] Levillain, 'Les diplômes originaux', 229; *Recueil des actes de Pépin Ier et de Pépin II, rois d'Aquitaine*, ed. L. Levillain, Paris 1927, vii–viii.

[57] Giry, 'La donation de Rueil'.

[58] Giry, 'La donation de Rueil', 695–6.

The French charters make an interesting comparison with the English material as a wider group, then, because they indicate that imitative script was a technique available to scribes when the occasion dictated. The Abingdon chronicler recorded that he had copied into his work the text of a charter whose state of physical deterioration made it almost illegible (*in uetustissimis et pene consumptis litteris*). The text is accepted as 'entirely acceptable' and its copying might have been occasioned by a post-Conquest dispute over Kingston Bagpuize, the estate to which it gives title.[59] It is conceivable that the Darlaston charter was likewise created in order to preserve the text of a damaged original, but this time in the form of a replacement copy. Sawyer had reached much the same conclusion about S 623, another Burton charter of AD 956, whose apparently authentic text survives in a later imitative copy, as had Simon Keynes about S 768 and S 602.[60]

The distribution and date of manufacture of French imitative charters fall into more distinct patterns, and these, too, offer material for cross-Channel comparison. The sample collected in Table 10.3 clusters in the eleventh century rather than the twelfth, and this bears out observations by Dufour and Giry, who associated the production of forged Carolingian charters with the tenth or eleventh century.[61] Despite the association between forgery and the twelfth century upheld in the English historiographical tradition, the English evidence for imitative copying of charters likewise suggests a distribution earlier rather than later, with few instances dating from after the middle of the twelfth century.[62] Another preliminary observation concerns the date of authority claimed. The bulk of the evidence for imitative copying filtered from editions of Carolingian charters fastens on Charles the Bald (ob. 877), and not the Merovingian or earlier Carolingian kings who were often the subject of forged charters.[63] In the long twelfth century the creators of extant imitative charters in England,

---

[59] S 1216; *Charters of Abingdon abbey, part 2*, ed. S.E. Kelly, Oxford 2001, no. 115 and p. 450; *Historia ecclesie Abbendonensis*, i. 136 and 136–7 n. 289.

[60] Above, Table 10.1, n. c. *Facsimiles*, p. 4.

[61] As observed by Jean Dufour, 'État et comparaison des actes faux ou falsifiés intitulés au nom des Carolingiens français (840–987)', *Fälschungen im Mittelalter*, iv. 167–210, esp. 208–9. Giry assigned the bulk of the production of *actes récrits* to the tenth or eleventh centuries: *Manuel*, 15.

[62] On the association with the twelfth century, Clanchy, *From memory*, 318; N.P. Brooks, 'History and myth, forgery and truth', *Inaugural lecture delivered in the University of Birmingham, 23 January 1986*, repr. in his *Anglo-Saxon myths*, 1–19, at 13.

[63] This finding may be skewed in part by the fact that different editors devoted varying degrees of space to palaeographical evidence (see above, 178), but Dufour noted that medieval forgers fastened particularly on Charles the Bald: 'Actes faux', 208. On the chronological distribution of forgeries, see Dufour, 'Actes faux' and also Brooks, 'History and myth', 12–13.

too, avoided remote antiquity. Pre-Conquest imitative copies tend to reach back into the distant Bedan past.[64] Their equivalents made after the Norman Conquest focus on post-Alfredian kings – from Edward the Elder (possibly) but particularly from Eadwig (955–59) onwards.[65]

Discussion

Although much work remains to be done on the texts and archival context of charters written in imitative script, some preliminary conclusions can be drawn:

1. Imitation went on before and after the Conquest in England and on the Continent, but the introduction of Continental-trained clerics and scribes from the reign of Edward the Confessor onwards created particular situations in which imitation was necessary or appropriate.[66] It is entirely probable that established traditions of imitative copying in France renewed or changed the parallel English practice. Scribes trained outside the English tradition and encountering the archival remnants of the English tradition and needing to reproduce them for posterity had to imitate in order to reproduce graphic forms with whose formation or meaning they were unfamiliar. New incumbents viewing the ruined archives of old-established monastic houses might have sought to replace charters by the creation of imitation copies, as in the French tradition. Defence of ancient privileges occasioned the manufacture of suitable documentation in single-sheet form, some of it visibly antique, and native-trained scribes are likely to have been involved.
2. Sometimes the mimicry is of a very high order. Certain pre- and post-Conquest scribes, especially those with access to substantial resources of palaeographical material (charters and books), demonstrate careful observation and well-honed skills. So at Canterbury, Westminster and Saint-Denis, for example, scribes with plenty of models to hand could dip into the past and reproduce what they saw very accurately. Much less convincing imitative essays by scribes at Leofric's Exeter presumably

---

[64] Crick, 'Insular history?', 522–6, 534–44.
[65] Above, Table 10.1. Bruce O'Brien has pointed out in correspondence the marked absence of imitative copies in the names of Cnut and Edward the Confessor, the two most important pre-Conquest kings in later English legal precedent. I deduce from the distribution of donors that scribes worked largely within the parameters of their own local institutional histories.
[66] S. Keynes, 'Regenbald the Chancellor (*sic*)', *ANS* x (1988 for 1987), 185–222 on the personnel; *Facsimiles of English royal writs*, xvi–xix on the script.

reflect the poverty of appropriate archival material at their disposal.[67] The quality of the imitative work at Burton attests scribal skill and access to one or more single-sheet originals from the mid-950s.

3. Imitation, I suggest, tells us something about training. An imitative performance takes a scribe outside what he has been trained to do, puts him under pressure – leads him to make mistakes or to hesitate, hence the instability symptomatic of imitative script.

So, I have been looking at the Anglo-Saxons across a caesura. Post-Conquest scribes independently and on multiple occasions recognised that tenth-century script looked distinct from their own, just as tenth-century scribes had looked back on the eighth century and recognised it as different. I am now going to take a very big step and move from a relatively modest set of data to two very bold conclusions, both influenced by studies of the early-modern past.

According to one established historiographical model, the creation of historical replicas can be interpreted as a mark of scholarly sophistication. Anthony Grafton has discussed the 'new forgery' of the Renaissance, in which technical scholarship was harnessed in the creation of faked antiquity. Thus Renaissance antiquaries produced faked inscriptions and leading Renaissance scholars, including Erasmus, were involved in the work of forgery.[68] The work demanded skill and imagination because '[the forger] must give his text the appearance – the linguistic appearance as a text and the physical appearance as a document – of something from a period dramatically earlier than and different from his own'. This, Grafton noted, marked the rediscovery of ancient critical techniques traceable to the fifth century, although 'forgers had sought since antiquity itself to give their works the appearance of age'.[69] Grafton conceded that forgery continues throughout the Middle Ages but he associated 'new [Renaissance] forgery' with renewed sophistication and scholarly involvement. The care and skill with which the past was recreated constitutes a mark of historical sophistication.

More than forty years ago Peter Burke, in an influential study, commented on the 'historical innocence' of medieval attitudes to the past, noting that 'there was no "sense of history" even among the educated'.[70] Elizabeth Eisenstein, a decade later, argued that only after the advent of printing could the past be viewed from

---

[67] For examples, see Crick, 'Script and the sense of the past', 16–19. For a list of charters, see above, n. 20.
[68] A. Grafton, *Forgers and critics: creativity and duplicity in Western scholarship*, London 1990, 25–8, 44–5.
[69] Grafton, *Forgers*, 54.
[70] P. Burke, *The Renaissance sense of the past*, London 1969, 1.

a 'fixed distance'.[71] Printing created more uniformity about arranging historical materials but 'Before then, there was no fixed spatial-temporal reference frame which men of learning shared'.[72] More recently, another early modernist, Daniel Woolf, has consolidated earlier 'orthodoxy' about the pre-modern past, and explored the growing sense of distance from the present which scholars have discerned during the Renaissance.[73] It was Woolf's contention that 'English men and women in 1500 were only dimly conscious, if at all, of the fact that the people, scenes, buildings and material culture of previous centuries would have looked different from those to which they were accustomed'. He argued that a 'grasp of the visual dimension of the past' developed in the post-medieval era.[74]

Such contentions may have validity within the precise frame of reference within which their authors conceived them, but we should hesitate to deduce from them broader principles about a lack of temporal distance and sophistication in the Middle Ages.[75] Contrary evidence for the long twelfth century lies not just in historical narrative but in the manuscripts which carry them – the additions and comments of annotators marking important reigns and events, certainly, but, most especially, the quantities of lists: kings, bishops, other office holders, genealogies, synchronisms. The works of Henry of Huntingdon, John of Worcester and Ralph Diceto all attracted such historical satellites, but they are only among the more famous examples of a much larger phenomenon.[76] Much of this material is unedited and too diverse and scattered to be readily editable and so it is essentially lost to scholarship except as an indistinct impression. Another core around which chronological information collected was documentary. Collections of charters attracted parahistorical texts: lists of

---

[71] E.L. Eisenstein, *The printing press as an agent of change: communications and cultural transformations in early-modern Europe*, Cambridge 1979, i. 183–7.

[72] Eisenstein, *The printing press*, i. 187.

[73] D. Woolf, *The social circulation of the past: English historical culture, 1500–1730*, Oxford 2003, 20–21.

[74] Woolf, *The social circulation*, 220, see also 20, 182, 394.

[75] For evidence that these views are beginning to be challenged, see Alexander Nagel and Christopher S. Wood, *Anachronic Renaissance*, New York 2010, esp. 45–6.

[76] For Henry of Huntingdon, see D.N. Dumville, 'An early text of Geoffrey of Monmouth's *Historia regum Britanniae* and the circulation of some Latin histories in twelfth-century Normandy', *Arthurian Literature* iv (1985), 1–36, at 10–13. For Diceto, see the elaborate episcopal lists in BL, MS Add. 40007: A.J. Watson, *Catalogue of dated and datable manuscripts, c.700–1600, in the Department of Manuscripts in the British Library*, London 1979, i. 83, no. 401, and ii, pl. 112. For further examples, see Corpus Christi College, Oxford, MS 157 (John of Worcester's Chronicle), viewable online in the collection Early Manuscripts at Oxford University [http://image.ox.ac.uk/show?collection=corpus&manuscript=ms157]. On the use of columnar format to present historical information see Anthony Grafton and Megan Williams, *Christianity and the transformation of the book: Origen, Eusebius and the library of Caesarea*, Cambridge MA 2006, 135–42.

estates, benefactors, abbots; inventories.[77] All served to order the past, to set it to rights, to make it manageable.

One prevalent form of management of the past was, of course, forgery: the creation of surrogate texts to replace lost texts or to displace inadequate ones. These reconstructions were themselves often works of consummate scholarship. To be credible, a forger had to have a sense of chronology, to know what historical actors were alive when and where, what kinds of textual protocols were appropriate. The best forgeries employed historical scholarship: their draftsmen manufactured new texts out of original documents and scoured narrative sources for additional information.[78] Indeed, they constituted a form of historical narrative in their own right.[79] But the entire process bespeaks historical literacy: the ability to order the past. Likewise the scribes who had occasion to create replacement documents, whether the text were forged or not, had engaged in a process of archival research and observation, locating examples of script of equivalent date, more or less accurately depending on the available resources and the scribe's own skill. The process itself was well attested before the Norman Conquest, though the quality of the best reproductions in the twelfth century surpasses earlier efforts by some margin. The fabrication of imitative charters indicates that their creators perceived historical difference, even anachronism, and, most importantly, that they anticipated such perceptions on the part of the audience for whom replica charters were intended.

Frank Barlow wrote of the 'ornamental quality' of Durham forgeries:[80]

> They satisfied the craving for a long history and ancient titles; and they were convenient and suitably distinguished for exhibition when in the later Middle Ages episcopal visitations took on *quo warranto* characteristics, and claims to any special privilege had regularly to be proved.

Products of the long twelfth century would have served this ceremonial function admirably. At their best their makers had created near-perfect simulacra of tenth-century originals calculated to deceive contemporaries and destined to confuse future generations.

---

[77] For an early-thirteenth-century example, see BL, Cotton Nero A. i.
[78] As Giry described: *Manuel*, 867.
[79] 'For a history to be asserted and acknowledged, it must be textualized': A. Hiatt, 'Forgery at the University of Cambridge', *New Medieval Literatures* iii (1999), 95–118, at 103.
[80] Barlow, *Durham jurisdictional peculiars*, 150–51.

Chapter 11

The Use and Abuse of Anglo-Saxon Charters by the Kings of England, 1100–1300

Nicholas Vincent

For much of our knowledge of the Anglo-Saxon past we depend upon the recital in later royal confirmations of charters first granted by the Anglo-Saxon kings. Preserved today in the National Archives at Kew, these confirmations range in date from the reign of Henry III to that of James I, and extend across a large number of chancery Patent, Charter and Confirmation rolls. They are closely linked to a further series of copies of Anglo-Saxon royal charters, strictly speaking not official royal 'confirmations' but semi-official records of charters, enrolled in the so-called Cartae Antiquae Rolls, an Exchequer source beginning at an indeterminate date, *c.* 1200. Duly searched and listed, these confirmations, enrolments and copies occupy two and a half pages of the manuscripts index to Peter Sawyer's *Anglo-Saxon charters*: more space than is occupied by any other group of sources save for those in the Cotton collection of the British Library.[1] All told, they account for sixty-six of the entries in Sawyer: roughly five per cent of the corpus of just under 1,200 writs or charters recorded for the pre-Conquest English kings.[2] Yet, despite their significance, they have never been surveyed as a distinct category of evidence, nor has any attempt been made to assess their collective contribution to twelfth- or thirteenth-century understanding of pre-Conquest history. In what follows, and covering the two centuries from 1100 to

---

*   For their assistance with what follows, I am indebted to Ilya Afanasyev, Martin Brett, Julia Crick, David Crouch, Hugh Doherty, Simon Keynes, Tom Licence, Tessa Webber and Ann Williams.

1   S pp. 58–60, as opposed to pp. 50–54 for the Cotton manuscripts. For the *Cartae antiquae rolls*, see the two volumes thus far published (covering the first twenty of a series in fact running to at least forty-seven rolls, now PRO/TNA C 52): *The Cartae antiquae rolls*, ed. L. Landon and J.C. Davies (Pipe Roll Society xvii, xxxiii, 1939–57).

2   S 6, 66, 82, 119, 136, 138, 184, 300, 454, 501, 538, 731, 769, 779, 792, 798, 804, 835, 838, 867, 880, 904, 909, 954, 980, 990, 1000, 1002, 1016, 1021, 1030, 1033, 1036, 1038, 1041, 1043, 1045, 1048, 1051, 1054–5, 1063–4, 1067, 1069, 1075, 1084–5, 1088–9, 1091–2, 1094–6, 1104, 1109–10, 1152–3, 1155, 1157, 1217, 1226.

1300, I shall endeavour to tackle both of these questions. In the process, I shall also engage with a related issue: the use (and occasional abuse) of Anglo-Saxon evidence cited as evidence in law courts and inquests from the 1150s onwards. Here there is a richer tradition of scholarly enquiry, extending from J.H. Round to Paul Brand and Bruce O'Brien.[3] Nonetheless, here too there are new points to be considered and new discoveries to report.

To the first two generations of Anglo-Norman kings, before 1135, the Anglo-Saxon past was hardly something that could be forgotten, even had kings and their officials been inclined to forget. Domesday Book, deposited in the king's treasury at Winchester, was only one (albeit the greatest) among many other reminders that Anglo-Norman administration was founded upon the traditions of the Anglo-Saxon state. Whether or not they chose specifically to mention the fact, a large number of the routine charters and writs issued by kings of England from William I through to Henry I were merely the renewal, under the new king's seal, of grants first issued by earlier English rulers. On occasion, as with the writs of Bury St Edmunds, studied in detail by Richard Sharpe, it is possible to trace a direct copying of the language and formulae of writs issued by Cnut or Edward the Confessor in writs supposedly issued *de novo*, not just by the Conqueror and Henry I but as late as the reigns of Stephen and Henry II, from the 1020s through to at least the 1150s.[4] This is hardly surprising given that at least some of the chancery staff of Edward the Confessor survived into the service of King William I.[5]

It is one of the paradoxes of our enquiry that a more specific interest in the Anglo-Saxon past, viewed now as history or the source of legal testimony rather than as contemporary reportage, emerged in the 1140s and 50s, at more or less precisely the same time, one hundred years on, that the last survivors of the pre-Conquest population of England quit the scene. Various chroniclers might assert, as late as the 1180s, that Harold Godwinson was alive and well and living as a hermit outside Chester, but in reality (as those who have recently witnessed the extinction of the last human memories of 1914 will appreciate) by 1150 or so, there can have been hardly anyone still alive who had been a child, let alone

---

[3] J.H. Round, 'Tales of the Conquest', in idem, *Peerage and pedigree: studies in peerage law and family history*, London 1910, i. 284–323; P. Brand, '"Time out of mind": the knowledge and use of the eleventh- and twelfth-century past in thirteenth-century litigation', *ANS* xvi (1994), 38–54; B.R. O'Brien, 'Forgery and the literacy of the early common law', *Albion* xxvii (1995), 1–18, and see also N. Vincent, 'More tales of the Conquest', in D. Crouch and K. Thompson (eds), *Normandy and its neighbours, 900–1250: essays for David Bates*, Turnhout 2011, 271–301.

[4] R. Sharpe, 'The use of writs in the eleventh century', *ASE* xxxii (2003), 247–91.

[5] S. Keynes, 'Regenbald the chancellor (sic)', *ANS* x (1988), 185–222, and for Bernard a royal scribe as late as the 1120s, see A. Williams, *The English and the Norman Conquest*, Woodbridge 1995, 122–4.

a combatant in 1066.⁶ 'The time of the English kings', no less than their history, was becoming an increasingly distant point of reference, and Hastings itself something to be associated with a grandfather or great-grandfather rather than with still-living memory.⁷

As James Campbell, has noted, those twelfth-century historians who commemorated the Anglo-Saxon past did so not merely from defensive nostalgia but in order to categorise and make sense of what in hindsight had come to seem a distinct but now firmly closed period of history.⁸ Only in rare instances after 1150 do we find casual references to events of the pre-Conquest past cited as markers in time: in the late 1160s or early 1170s, for example, when an Oxfordshire landholder referred merely in passing to land given to the parish church of Lower Heyford 'in dedicatione Wlfwini episcopi de Dorcacestra', presumably recalling the church's dedication by Bishop Wulfwig (1053–67).⁹ Much more common was a tendency to view the period before 1066 as the remotest of vanished pasts. By 1158, when Henry of Blois came to raise the body of Cnut and other old Saxon kings to their mortuary chests above the high altar of Winchester cathedral, or by 1161 when King Henry II obtained the long-sought canonisation of Edward the Confessor, the remains of such kings could indeed be viewed as historic relics, just as far distant from events of the present day as Bede had been from the mission of St Augustine or as Edward the Confessor from memories of St Dunstan.¹⁰ Even so, boxed or enshrined, saints and kings lived on in memory if not in fact. They did so in part because of the peculiar insecurities of King Henry II.

---

⁶ A. Thacker, 'The cult of King Harold at Chester', in T. Scott and P. Starkey (eds), *The middle ages in the North-West*, Oxford 1995, 155–76, esp. 160–62.

⁷ Note here the recourse by Wace, writing in the 1150s or 60s, to the memory of his father, who either claimed to have seen or to have been told of the size of William the Conqueror's invasion fleet: Wace, *Rou*, pp. xvi–vii, 163. For 'the time of the English kings', see below nn.109 and 125.

⁸ J. Campbell, 'Some twelfth-century views of the Anglo-Saxon past', *Peritia* iii (1984), 131–50, repr. in J. Campbell, *Essays in Anglo-Saxon history*, London and Ronceverte 1986, 209–28.

⁹ *Eynsham Cartulary*, ed. H.E. Salter (Oxford Historical Society xlix, li, 1907–8), i. 109 no. 134.

¹⁰ For Henry of Blois's translation of 1158, J. Crook, '"A worthy antiquity": the movement of King Cnut's bones in Winchester Cathedral', in A.R. Rumble (ed.), *The reign of Cnut King of England, Denmark and Norway*, London 1994, 165–92. To judge from their collapse during the fire of 1174, similar relic chests were displayed at Canterbury, previously stored on the roof beams: *The historical works of Gervase of Canterbury*, ed. W. Stubbs (RS [lxxiii], 1879–80), i. 4. For the cult of the Confessor, the classic article remains that by B.W. Scholz, 'The canonization of Edward the Confessor', *Speculum* xxxvi (1961), 38–60.

As the founder of a new Plantagenet royal family, Henry's chief claim to dynastic legitimacy lay through his descent from Henry I and Matilda of Scotland, and thence from the bloodlines both of Rollo and of Cerdic. Hence the attempts by Ailred of Rievaulx to present Henry II as the green tree reflowering that had been prophesied by Edward the Confessor, reuniting the split trunks of England and Normandy.[11] Hence the commissions to Master Wace not only to rewrite the history of the Norman dukes (the *Roman de Rou*) but to turn Geoffrey of Monmouth's *Historia* into a French vernacular *Roman de Brut*.[12] It was presumably in a courtly as well as a monastic milieu that William of Malmesbury's *History of the kings of England* continued to circulate (at least fifteen surviving manuscripts dating before *c*.1200).[13] Walter Map recounted long stories at Henry II's court of the Anglo-Saxons, of Edward the Confessor's dealings with the Welsh, of the origins of Earl Godwin and of the battles between Cnut and Edmund Ironside.[14]

Nor was it only Henry II who encouraged nostalgia for the Anglo-Saxon past. In the days of Sir Walter Scott, it used to be supposed that the Plantagenet kings continued the age-old hatred of Normans for Saxons, being themselves Frenchmen opposed by the abiding spirit of an English nation defended by such English heros as Thomas Becket or Robin Hood.[15] Those days have long passed. Even so, Henry II's most embittered enemy, his former chancellor Thomas Becket (a man who in pursuit of social status had boasted not of English but of Norman knightly ancestry, and whose massive correspondence includes not a single indexed references to the Anglo-Saxons or to English saints) cried out at the moment of his murder in 1170 commending his soul to God and

---

[11] *The Life of King Edward who rests at Westminster*, ed. F. Barlow, 2 edn, Oxford 1992, 118–19, 131–2; Ailred, 'Vita Sancti Edwardi', in *PL* 195, cols. 773–4, and Ailred, 'Genealogia regum anglorum' in *PL* cxcv, cols. 711–38, for which see now E. Freeman, *Narratives of a new order: Cistercian historical writing in England, 1150–1220*, Turnhout 2002, esp. 55–87.

[12] Wace, *Rou*, commissioned by Henry II, and Wace, *Brut.*, ed. and tr. J. Weiss, at p. xii noting the later claim, by Layamon, that this was presented by Wace to Eleanor of Aquitaine *c*.1155.

[13] William of Malmesbury, *Gesta regum Anglorum*, ed. and tr. R.A.B. Mynors, R.M. Thomson and M. Winterbottom, Oxford 1998–9, esp. i, pp. xiii–xxi for the manuscripts.

[14] Walter Map, *De nugis curialium: courtiers' trifles*, ed. M.R. James, revised by C.N.L. Brooke and R.A.B. Mynors, Oxford 1983, 192–5, 410–37.

[15] For an excellent survey here, see C.A. Simmons, *Reversing the Conquest: history and myth in nineteenth-century British literature*, New Brunswick 1990, esp. 117–23, for the influence of Scott's *Ivanhoe* over Augustin Thierry who, in the 1820s, was driven to present even the quarrel between Henry II and Becket as one of race hatred between Frenchmen and Saxons.

to the martyrs, St Denis of France and St Aelfheah of Canterbury.[16] After his martyrdom, and until his translation in 1220, Thomas lay buried in the crypt of Canterbury cathedral between the tombs of Archbishops Eadsige (d. 1050) and Aethelred (d. 889), perhaps in a site that he himself had selected.[17] The miracles reported at his shrine, and the rebuilding of the tombs of its pre-Conquest archbishops after the great fire at Canterbury cathedral of 1174, served as a stimulus to other old English cults.[18] As a result, both in the 1170s and 80s and again after his translation to a new shrine in 1220, St Thomas achieved a greater revival of interest in the Anglo-Saxon saints than anything seen since the 1090s and the days of Goscelin of Saint-Bertin or Osbern of Canterbury. All of this was to some extent anticipated by Becket himself, as early as 1163, when he had presided over the translation of the relics of St Edward the Confessor at Westminster abbey, taking the opportunity to acquire as a souvenir of the occasion the stone that had previously covered St Edward's tomb and in which St Wulfstan had planted his staff.[19]

The translation of the relics of Anglo-Saxon saints, the rewriting of their lives (sometimes in the French vernacular), and the cataloguing of their deeds and miracles from the 1170s onwards became central concerns of the English Church. The enthusiasm here stretched from Kent to Cornwall and from Winchester to Northumbria.[20] So rejuvenated was the power of such saints that even Ranulf de Glanville, Henry II's justiciar, presiding at the Exchequer in the 1180s, preferred to allow the absurdly generous claims to food and entertainment made by the servants of the abbey of Abingdon rather than risk the vengeance of

---

[16] *Materials for the history of Thomas Becket archbishop of Canterbury*, ed. J.C. Robertson (RS [lxvii], 1875–85), iii. 141, iv. 77, and for Becket's premonition before his death that Canterbury was about to produce another St Aelfheah, see ibid. iii. 130. Cf. ibid. v. 336–50 no. 176 for Herbert of Bosham, as early as the mid-1160s, presenting Thomas as a second Aelfheah, a reference that I owe to Julie Barrau.

[17] W. Urry, *Thomas Becket: his last days*, Stroud 1999, 148–9, using, though not citing, *Gervase of Canterbury*, ed. Stubbs, i. 16.

[18] For the Canterbury fire and the reburial of the pre-Conquest archbishops, see *Gervase of Canterbury*, ed. Stubbs, i. 9–26. Note also the effect of the subsequent fire at Bury and the reburial of the body of St Edmund in 1198, described in detail in *The chronicle of Jocelin of Brakelond*, ed. H.E. Butler, London 1949, 112–16.

[19] *Gervase of Canterbury*, ed. Stubbs, ii. 285; F. Barlow, *Edward the Confessor*, 2 edn, London 1979, 284.

[20] For a brief introduction here, with particular emphasis upon the new vernacular French legends of St Edward, St Edmund, St Osyth and St Aethelthryth, see R. Koopmans, *Wonderful to relate: miracle stories and miracle collecting in high medieval England*, Philadelphia 2011, 134–7. For the aftermath of 1220, see N. Vincent, *Peter des Roches: an alien in English politics, 1205–1238*, Cambridge 1996, 243–7.

St Aethelwold, supposedly the institutor of these payments.[21] Another of Henry II's servants, William de Courcy, having falsely obtained royal letters granting him the lordship of a manor claimed by the monks of Bury St Edmunds, was stricken with madness by St Edmund, the monks' protector, before ever these letters could be implemented.[22]

In all of this, we should not forget that Henry II had been just as keen to cultivate the memory of his Norman as of his Anglo-Saxon forebears. As an Angevin, the son of a mere count of Anjou, he was neither English nor Norman by birth and emerged from a milieu some way below the exalted status of dukes or kings.[23] After Gaimar's *L'Estoire des Engleis*, written to a private commission in the 1130s, there was to be no detailed reworking of the Anglo-Saxon chronicle in Plantagenet England.[24] Indeed, the last surviving recension of the chronicle, composed at Peterborough, croaked itself to a standstill in 1154, at almost the precise moment that Henry II ascended the English throne.[25] By contrast, both Master Wace and Benoît de Saint-Maur were called upon to commemorate Henry's descent from Rollo, Normanising a king whose Angevin birth perhaps made it even more difficult for him to obtain acceptance in his Norman duchy than in his realm of England. In March 1162, a year after his agents had obtained the canonisation of Edward the Confessor by a pope now entirely dependent upon the support of Henry II and Louis VII of France, Henry joined the pope's legate in translating the bodies of the Norman dukes, Richard I and Richard II, to new tombs in the abbey church at Fécamp.[26] There they were placed in sarcophagi almost certainly paid for by Henry, intended to emphasise the

[21] *Historia ecclesie Abbendonensis: the history of the church of Abingdon*, ed. and tr. J. Hudson, Oxford 2002–7, ii. 370–71.

[22] *The letters and chaters of Henry II, 1154–1189*, ed. N. Vincent, Oxford forthcoming, no. 739, citing the account given in *Memorials of St Edmund's abbey*, ed. T. Arnold (RS [xcvi], 1890–6), i. 148–51.

[23] For reflections upon Henry II as outsider and parvenu, see N. Vincent, 'The Court', in C. Harper-Bill and N. Vincent (eds), *Henry II: new interpretations*, Woodbridge 2007, 333–4.

[24] For the circulation of Gaimar, apparently neither wide nor within the court milieu, see Gaimar, *Estoire* esp. pp. xvii–xxii. Slightly earlier, Henry of Huntingdon had made extensive use of ASC, principally from the E (Peterborough) version, but with forays into other recensions: Henry, archdeacon of Huntingdon, *Historia Anglorum: the history of the English people*, ed. and tr. D. Greenway, Oxford 1996, pp. xci–viii.

[25] *The Peterborough chronicle, 1070–1154*, ed. C. Clark, 2 edn, Oxford 1970.

[26] Robert of Torigni, 'Chronicle', in *Chronicles of the Reigns of Stephen, Henry II and Richard I*, ed. R. Howlett (RS [lxxii], 1884–9), i. 212–13; E.M.C. van Houts, *Gesta Normannorum ducum. Een studie over de handschriften, de tekst, het geschiedwerk en het genre*, Groningen 1982, 44–5, 280, 282. For an indulgence issued on this occasion by the legate Henry cardinal priest of SS Neri e Achille (3 March 1162), see Fécamp, Musée de la Bénédictine ms. charte 47 (formerly no. 11), printed from a later inspeximus in *Neustria pia*,

potential sanctity of these, Henry's Norman forefathers.[27] Wace, Henry's court poet, was present to record the event.[28] All three of Henry's elder sons – William, Henry and Richard – were named in honour of dukes of Normandy or Aquitaine. Only with Geoffrey, born in 1158, was there any acknowledgement of Henry's heritage from Anjou.[29] No wonder, perhaps, that the nun of Barking, writing her vernacular translation of Ailred's *Life* of Edward the Confessor, probably in the 1170s or 80s, referred to Henry II's descent not just from 'that king of ancient lineage, the good Edward, the friend of God', but from the dukes of Normandy, from 'count Robert, the good Richard, and William the honest (or French, "franz") bastard', men who, if they could not quite be accounted saints, had led good lives and had each experienced holy, perhaps even saintly deaths ('Mes tant di ke lur bone vie fu par sainte mort acomplie').[30]

It was not to an exclusively Anglo-Saxon past that Henry II looked back. Even so, and allowing for Henry II's anxieties over both his Norman and Angevin ancestry, far more was preserved in Henry II's charters or administration of the memory of the Anglo-Saxon kings than there was of the early dukes of Normandy or Aquitaine, or of Henry's ancestors the counts of Anjou.[31] We might begin here with Domesday. Writers in and around the Plantagenet court were certainly aware of the existence of Domesday Book. Richard fitz Nigel accords it prominent notice in his *Dialogue of the Exchequer*, rehearsing

---

ed. A. Du Monstier, Paris 1663, 254. For a charter issued by Henry II on the same occasion, granting the land of Hogues, see *Letters of Henry II*, ed. N. Vincent, no. 919.

[27] S.E. Jones, 'The twelfth-century reliefs from Fécamp: new evidence for their dating and original purpose', *Journal of the British Archaeological Association* cxxxviii (1985), 79–88.

[28] A surmise based upon Wace, *Rou*, 116 (vv. 2240–6).

[29] The births of all of these children are noted by Torigni; see *Chronicles*, ed. Howlett, i. 176 (alleging that the name William was chosen for its Aquitanian rather than its Norman significance), 183, 195, 197.

[30] *La Vie d'Édouard le Confesseur: poème anglo-normand du XIIe siècle*, ed. Ö. Södergård, Uppsala 1948, 112–13 (vv. 105–31): 'Iceo set uncore Engletere /Ki par les sens fine sa guerre /Par le glorius rei Henri /Ki de ceo saint lignage eissi ... Mes Deu, par ki ad la bunté, /Lui doint lunge vic et santé ... /Et a ses heirs doinst Deu vertu /Ke si terre puissent tenir /Ke il a Deu seit a pleisir. /Tel sens lur doint et tel valur /Cum orent lur bon anceisur /Li quens Robert, li bons Richarz /Et Gillame li franz bastarz. /De quel jeo savreie mut dire, /Kar noble est et bele la matire, /Mes tant di ke lur bone vie /Fu par sainte mort acomplie. /Lur sainte mort aoist lur los, /En Deu lur est vie et repos.', and for Henry II as heir to St Edward, 264 vv. 4988–98. For these references, I am indebted to Ilya Afanasyev.

[31] In the entire corpus of Henry II's more than 3000 charters, leaving aside references to his father, there are only three references to his named predecessors as counts of Anjou (Geoffrey II Martel and Fulk V) and three to his predecessors as dukes of Aquitaine (Geoffrey and William X): *Letters and charters of Henry II*, ed. Vincent, nos 55, 1055, 1696, 2221, 2306, 2353. In part, of course, this is a function of the far greater survival rate of charters from England than from other parts of Henry II's dominion.

an account of its making that he claims was supplied to him by that fellow amateur of the Anglo-Saxon past, Henry of Blois, bishop of Winchester.[32] Not all twelfth-century writers were as familiar with the appearance as opposed to the general idea of Domesday. Jocelin of Brakelond and Alan of Tewkesbury both refer to it as a roll rather than as a book, perhaps supposing (from its name 'Domesday') that it might correspond to the rolls and scrolls that the angels and evangelists are shown carrying in portrayals of the Apocalypse.[33] The only charter attributed to Henry II in which Domesday is mentioned – as the 'Liber reg(ius)', reputedly guaranteeing possession of the manor of Brightlingsea to the Colchester hospital of St Mary Magdalene – is a forgery, detectable not least because Domesday makes no such guarantee.[34] Nonetheless, that Domesday was regularly consulted by Henry II's Exchequer clerks can be established from the fact that the Exchequer chose to copy out its entries for the county of Hereford into a distinct 'Herefordshire Domesday', at some point in the 1150s or 60s, updated in the margins with the modern names of manors and those who now held them.[35] This was identified by its editor, V.H. Galbraith, as the private enterprise of the Exchequer official, Master Thomas Brown, but might just as plausibly be seen as a working document from the archive of the sheriff of Herefordshire. It was to be followed by numerous Domesday 'breviates', including

---

[32] Richard fitz Nigel, *Dialogus de scaccario*, ed. E. Amt, Oxford 2007, 20–21, 84–5, 94–9, esp. 96, referring to what we know as Domesday as the 'Liber iudiciarius', and, in general, see J. Hudson, 'Administration, family and perceptions of the past in late twelfth-century England: Richard FitzNigel and the Dialogue of the Exchequer', in P. Magdalino (ed.), *The perception of the past in twelfth-century Europe*, London 1992, 75–98.

[33] M.T. Clanchy, *From memory to written record: England, 1066–1307*, 2 edn, London 1993, 136–7, and cf. N. Vincent, 'Rouleaux ou registres? Le choix et l'utilisation des enregistrements à la chancellerie Plantagenêt (XIIe–XIIIe siècle)', in O. Guyotjeannin and others (eds), *L'Art du registre à la chancellerie du roi de France*, Paris forthcoming. An alternative suggestion, proposed by V.H. Galbraith, is that the confusion between book and roll resulted from the early circulation of the sort of abbreviations of Domesday, in essence reducing it to a list of hides, known from other later examples to have circulated on occasion as rolls rather than as books. For later testimony, once again referring to a roll rather than a book, see BL Harley 742 (Spalding cartulary) fo. 339v, headed 'Extracta de rotulo Winton' dicto Domisdai de feodis Spald', Pincebek et aliarum quarumdam villarum', continuing with abstracts from the 1086 returns for Ivo Taillebois and Crowland abbey, but ending with a statement that 'in hundred(o) de Nesse Robertus de Dribi tenet in Baston' et Carleby terciam partem duarum feod(orum) militis de G(ilberto) de Gant' et ipse de rege', this latter derived not from Domesday but from the returns of 1242–43 as elsewhere in *The Book of Fees commonly called Testa de Nevill*, ed. H.C. Maxwell-Lyte and others, London 1920–31, ii. 1052

[34] *Letters and charters of Henry II*, ed. Vincent, no. 672, from *Calendar of charter rolls 1327–41*, 356.

[35] *Herefordshire Domesday*, ed. V.H. Galbraith and J. Tait (Pipe Roll Society new ser. xxv, 1950).

one for Kent copied out in the late twelfth century as a roll rather than a book. Here, for the first time and a hundred years too late, reality was for the first time made to correspond to the imaginings of the antiquaries.[36] All of this suggest that, rather like the 'Notitia dignitatum' of Rome or the diplomatic archives of Byzantium, the older it became the more Domesday acquired significance in 'modern' administrative affairs. Its true apotheosis, indeed, still awaited it, from the 1270s onwards, when it began to be cited as the chief point of reference for claims to ancient demesne status, freeing peasants and the manorial population from charges and services not recorded in 1086.[37]

The date chosen for the translation of Henry II's new saint, Edward the Confessor, Sunday, 13 October 1163, was almost certainly chosen deliberately, not just as a convenient occasion when king and churchmen were gathered together in London, but to commemorate the anniversary of William the Conqueror's great victory at Hastings, fought on Saturday 14 October 1066.[38] Henceforth, 13 October, the feast day of Edward's translation, trumped Edward's other feast (5 January, the anniversary of his death). Neither date is specified in the pope's bull of canonisation, issued in February 1161, so that 13 October was presumably chosen only after consultation between Henry II and the Westminster monks.[39] In light of this, it is also worth speculating whether Henry II's great enquiry into knight service, the so-called *Cartae baronum*, a Domesday for barons and knights, was intended to perform a commemorative as well as a practical function. Although launched perhaps as early as Christmas 1165, and provoked by the particular circumstances of that year and the need to raise feudal aid for the marriage of the king's daughter to the duke of

---

[36] Ibid. pp. xxviii–ix, citing the Kent roll, now BL Cotton Vitellius C. viii, and, in general, see also E.M. Hallam, *Domesday Book through nine centuries*, London 1986, 38–49.

[37] Hallam, *Domesday Book*, 49–51, 74–113.

[38] Though it is worth noting that Roger of Howden managed to misdate the battle, correctly naming the feast of St Calixtus but placing it on 22 rather than 14 October: *Chronica magistri Rogeri de Houedene*, ed. W. Stubbs (RS [li], 1868–71), i. 113, apparently copying an error already to be found in *The chronicle of John of Worcester, vol. II: the annals from 450 to 1066*, ed. and tr. R.R. Darlington and P. McGurk, Oxford 1995, ii. 604–5. It is left undated by Torigni (in *Chronicles*, ed. Howlett, i. 36–7), and correctly dated to Saturday, 14 October by Ralph of Diss, in *The historical works of Master Ralph de Diceto*, ed. W. Stubbs (RS [lxviii], 1876), i. 196.

[39] For the canonisation bull, and the date of the translation, see F. Barlow, *Edward the Confessor*, 282–4, 323–7. Since Henry III had to petition the pope in 1228 for the inclusion of Edward in the Roman calendar of saints, and since it was not until 1236 that Pope Gregory IX recommended the observance of his feasts to the entire English Church, it is likely that before that, the cult was almost entirely restricted to Westminster: P. Binski, *Westminster Abbey and the Plantagenets: kingship and the representation of power, 1200–1400*, New Haven 1995, 52.

Saxony, the enquiry itself was generally associated with 1166, the centenary of Hastings and hence of an event that Henry II as much as J.H. Round might have acknowledged as marking 'The introduction of knight service into England'.[40] When in 1198, King Richard came to command a new nationwide survey of landholdings towards his tax on plough-teams, the arrangements were such that Bishop Stubbs was prepared to describe them as 'a new Domesday'.[41] King John's uncompleted yet massively ambitious national inquest of 1212 would have out-Domesdayed Domesday, as indeed would Edward I's great Hundred Rolls enquiry of 1279–80. Henry III's most substantial inquest into knights' fees was launched in 1242, exactly two hundred years after the accession of Edward the Confessor, a saint for whose cult (and chronology) Henry III displayed peculiar devotion.[42] Domesday and the idea both of its preservation and imitation were firmly embedded in the traditions of royal government.

The *Cartae baronum* of 1166 were provoked by the Saxon marriage of Henry II's daughter, an event that involved the transfer of large quantities of treasure to northern Germany including, almost certainly, the head relic of St Oswald now in Hildersheim cathedral, decorated with eight panels depicting old English kings including Edward, Alfred and Cnut.[43] In this way, a relic of the Anglo-Saxons was suitably honoured in the Saxon homeland of Oswald's *gens*: a homeland from which both Henry II's mother and eldest daughter obtained husbands. Oswald was by no means the only Anglo-Saxon saint to be commemorated at the Plantagenet court. By the 1190s, besides their coronation in the Confessor's church at Westminster, the Plantagenet kings had come to consider a visit to the shrines of both St Alban and St Edmund at Bury as obligatory at the start of

---

[40] For the survey, apparently intended to be finished by 13 March 1166 (the first Sunday in Lent) when knights who had not previously rendered liege homage to the king were to do so, see the less than precise remarks of *The chronicles of Ralph Niger*, ed. R. Anstruther, London 1851, 171, and the term for the homage referred to in the 'carta' of the archbishop of York: *The Red Book of the Exchequer*, ed. H. Hall (RS [xcix], 1896), i. 412–13.

[41] Howden, *Chronica*, iv. 46–7; *Book of Fees*, i. 1–13.

[42] For 1212 and 1242, see *Book of Fees*, i. 52–228, ii. 637ff. For the 1279 inquest, see S. Raban, *A second Domesday? The Hundred rolls of 1279–80*, Oxford 2004. For Henry's awareness of the significance not only of the Confessor's feast days but of the fact that 13 October 1269, the date chosen for translation of the remains of St Edward to their new shrine in Westminster Abbey, fell on the same day in a year whose Easter calendar corresponded to that of 1163, see D. Carpenter, 'Westminster Abbey in politics, 1258–1269', in *Thirteenth century England* viii (2001), 54–5.

[43] D. Ó Riain-Raedel, 'Edith, Judith, Matilda: the role of royal ladies in the propagation of the Continental cult', in C. Stancliffe and E. Cambridge (eds), *Oswald: Northumbrian king to European saint*, Stamford 1995, 210–29, at 223–5.

each new reign.⁴⁴ The shrine of St Frideswide at Oxford had attracted the notice of Henry II, whatever was later claimed about the fate of his successors, not least Henry III, whose defeat at Lewes in 1264 was blamed upon a failure to heed the saint's prohibition against English kings entering Oxford.⁴⁵ Meanwhile, Henry II's refoundation of both Amesbury and Waltham abbeys, and elsewhere such ventures as his interference at St Sexburgh's on Sheppey, involved him in reshaping the destiny of institutions established by Anglo-Saxon benefactors, endowed with pre-Conquest cults and governed by pre-Conquest charters that themselves were read and taken into consideration at Henry's court.⁴⁶ At the battle of Fornham fought against the Flemish and French mercenaries who entered East Anglia in 1173, the supporters of Henry II achieved victory fighting under the banner of St Edmund, just as on crusade in 1191 King Richard I dispatched the captured golden banner of the tyrant of Cyprus to be preserved at the shrine of St Edmund at Bury.⁴⁷ King John was buried at Worcester, flanked by images of the sainted bishops Wulfstan and Oswald.⁴⁸

---

⁴⁴ N. Vincent, 'The pilgrimages of the Angevin kings of England, 1154–1272', in C. Morris and P. Roberts (eds), *Pilgrimage: the English experience from Becket to Bunyan*, Cambridge 2002, 12–45, at 18.

⁴⁵ For Henry II's role in the 1180 translation of St Frideswide, see *ASS October*, viii. 539, 550, 568–9. For her supposed curse, see William Rishanger, *Chronica et annales*, ed. H.T. Riley (RS [xxviii], 1865), 20.

⁴⁶ Waltham Abbey undoubtedly possessed a charter of Edward the Confessor (S 1036), copied into the abbey's cartularies and also into the Exchequer *Cartae antiquae rolls* (ii, no. 356) after the refoundation by Henry II: *The early charters of the Augustinian canons of Waltham abbey, Essex, 1062–1230*, ed. R. Ransford, Woodbridge 1989, 3–4 no. 1. It formed the basis, c.1180, of the account of Harold's foundation supplied in *The Waltham chronicle*, ed. and tr. L. Watkiss and M. Chibnall, Oxford 1994, pp. xxxviii–xliii, 32–9. Nothing survives today of the pre-Conquest archive of Amesbury, but in 1423 the then prioress produced what was claimed to be a diploma of Aethelred II: PRO/TNA E 368/195 (Exchequer LTR Memoranda Roll 1 Henry VI) Recorda of the Trinity term m. 3, whence H.P.R. Finberg, *The early charters of Wessex*, Leicester 1964, 103–4 no. 331 (not in Sawyer's catalogue), with commentary by S. Keynes, *The diplomas of King Æthelred 'the Unready', 978–1016: a study in their use as historical evidence*, Cambridge 1980, 107 n. 66, 268 n. 72, and cf. *Victoria County History, Wiltshire*, ii. 242–3. For St Sexburgh's, where Henry II's interventions are documented in a late but local source, see *Thomae Sprotti chronica*, ed. T. Hearne, Oxford 1719, 162–4, also in the chronicle of William Thorne, whence R. Twysden, *Historiae Anglicanae Scriptores X*, London 1652, 1931.

⁴⁷ Howden, *Chronica*, ii. 55, iii. 108. The king's victory at Limassol took place on 6 May, the octave of the feast of the translation of St Edmund (29 April).

⁴⁸ For the circumstances here, see *The letters and charters of Cardinal Guala Bicchieri, papal legate in England, 1216–1218*, ed. N. Vincent (Canterbury and York Society lxxxiii, 1996), 99, no. 138.

James Campbell has suggested that hagiography was one of the few fields in which twelfth-century study of the Anglo-Saxon past merged into pseudo-history and invention.[49] Yet even the interest first evidenced by Henry II in the memory and posthumous 'cult' of that most mythological of kings, Arthur of Britain, takes on new interest when viewed as one of the king's Anglo-Saxon attitudes. As has long been acknowledged, by portraying himself as the modern embodiment of Arthur, Henry II may have sought to bask in the reputation of Arthur as a conqueror of Ireland and the dukedoms and counties of western France.[50] The account given in Wace's *Roman de Brut*, for example, of Arthur's embarkation from Southampton en route for Barfleur and the conquest of Normandy, and ultimately of the whole of France, supplies a deliberate mirror-image of Henry II's crossing from Barfleur to Southampton in 1154 at the beginning of a reign that was likewise to combine rule over England and western France.[51] Yet, as this clever inversion also suggests, Arthur was every bit as much the conqueror of the Anglo-Saxon princelings and tyrants as he was of the rulers of Brittany or the Welsh. By clothing themselves as Arthur (or as Arthur's vanquishers), Henry II and his successors, most notably Edward I, laid claim not just to British empire but to a status greater than that of any mere Anglo-Saxon king.

Besides the saints or Domesday, other aspects of the Anglo-Saxon past had come to form part of court culture. Both at Winchester and Westminster, the principal centres of English government, not least of the Exchequer, the physical relics of Anglo-Saxon kingship remained very plain to view. The Confessor's shrine at Westminster, which we now think of as a magnificent Gothic fantasia of the 1260s, was to its earliest sponsors, not least to Henry II, something far simpler, visited in a church that the Confessor himself had planned and would have recognised as his own through to its rebuilding from the 1230s onwards.[52] Henry III's devotion to the Anglo-Saxon saints was such that he not only rebuilt Westminster in honour of St Edward the Confessor, on a scale of luxury unmatched by any contemporary European king, but named his two eldest sons, Edward and Edmund, to honour the Anglo-Saxon past. Matthew Paris tells us that, visiting St Albans in the 1250s, Henry III was able to perform a number of feats of memory: reciting the names of the electors to the throne of Germany, 250 of the English baronies, and the names of 'all the royal saints of England', here specified as Aethelberht (d. 794), Edward martyr (d. 978), Cynehelm (*fl.* 810), Oswald (d. 642), Oswine (d. 651), 'Neithan' (presumably

---

[49] Campbell, 'Some twelfth-century views', 224–6.
[50] For a conspectus here, see M. Aurell, 'Henry II and Arthurian legend', in Harper-Bill and Vincent (eds), *Henry II*, 362–94.
[51] Wace, *Brut* 280–83.
[52] See here the essays by E. Fernie and W. Rodwell, in *Edward the Confessor: the man and the legend*, ed. R. Mortimer, Woodbridge 2009, 139–67, esp. 154–5.

St Nectan of Hartland, *fl.* 450), Wigstan (d. 849), 'Fromund' (presumably St Freomund,venerated at Dunstable and elsewhere as a martyred son of King Offa), 'Edwulf' (presumably St Eardwulf, d. 810), Edmund (d. 869) and Edward the Confessor (d. 1065).[53] It was also under Henry III that the royal chancery issued what must be considered the very earliest genuine surviving inspeximus, word by word, of an Anglo-Saxon charter, thereby confirming a diploma of Aethelred in favour of the nuns of Wherwell, first granted in 1002, reissued under the seal of Henry III in October 1260.[54]

Henry III may have been the first king of England to issue a full inspeximus of an Anglo-Saxon diploma but he was by no means the first post-Conquest king to make use of Anglo-Saxon charters or writs. Again to paraphrase James Campbell, so scrappy was the historical record of Anglo-Saxon England that, from the twelfth-century onwards, those studying it had little alternative but to engage with the charter evidence.[55] And not only to engage, but to imitate. We have already found William the Conqueror, Rufus and Henry I referring to and on occasion simply copying the terms of privileges or writs issued by their English predecessors.[56] It was on the basis of his charters from Edward the Confessor, according to Gervase of Canterbury, that Archbishop Lanfranc was able to prove the rights and liberties of his church.[57] By Henry I's reign it was unusual although by no means unknown for a king to refer specifically in his charters to the name of any Anglo-Saxon king whose acts were in the process of being confirmed.[58] By Stephen's reign it

---

[53] Matthew Paris, *Chronica majora*, ed. H.R. Luard (RS [lvii], 1872–83), v. 617, and for various of the more obscure figures here, see J. Blair, 'A handlist of Anglo-Saxon saints', in A. Thacker and R. Sharpe (eds), *Local saints and local churches in the early medieval West*, Oxford 2002, 495–565, esp. 531–2, 535, a list drawn to my attention by Tom Licence and revealing, incidentally, the very considerable gaps in knowledge displayed by Henry III and/or Matthew Paris.

[54] *Calendar of charter rolls 1257–1300*, 31 (S 904). Sawyer, *Anglo-Saxon charters*, 58, includes a rare misprint, citing the Charter Roll 5 Henry III for S 1000 and S 1226, which should actually be assigned to the Charter Roll 51 Henry III (PRO/TNA C 53/56), as in *Calendar of charter rolls 1257–1300*, 70. The original charter of inspeximus by Henry III was sold at Sotheby's in 2012 from the Schøyen Collection, for £60,000. It is now BL Additional Charter 77735.

[55] Campbell, 'Some twelfth-century views', 215–17.

[56] See Sharpe, above n. 4.

[57] *Gervase of Canterbury*, ed. Stubbs, ii. 369, 'secundum cartas regum quas eadem habet ecclesia, et principaliter sancti Edwardi et omnium successorum ipsius'. As pointed out to me by Martin Brett, this in fact tells us more about Gervase than the events of 1070–72. In Lanfranc's own account, and by the terms of the 1072 settlement, kings appear only as answering the judgement of the Church or receiving letters from the pope.

[58] For examples from the reign of Henry I, in which specific reference to charters of Edward the Confessor is extremely rare, but in which there are frequent references to gifts made by, or to the time of King Edward, see *Feudal documents from the abbey of Bury St*

was perhaps rarer still, almost always confined to a reference to 'the time' (rather than to any specific gifts or charters) of King Edward the Confessor.[59] Hence the significance that attaches to the seventeen occasions in the charters of Henry II that specific reference is made to the confirmation of grants or charters issued by the kings of England, before 1066.

We must be on our guard here. In England, as in France or Sicily, conquest served as a great spur to the reinvention of a pre-Conquest and hence of a pre-lapsarian past. In such a context, references in a later charter to the deeds or time of some ancient or prestigious ancestor are often hallmarks of forgery, as is the recital of ancient documents written in another language or according to different diplomatic traditions from those in customary use by the confirming authority.[60] Henry II's purported charter for Glastonbury, for example, supposedly issued in the aftermath of the great Glastonbury fire of 1184 and referring to a succession of privileges granted by English kings through Arthur, 'Bringwalthius', Cenwalh, Baldred, Centwine, Ine, Cuthred, Alfred, Edward the Elder, Edmund (d. 946)

Edmunds, ed. D.C. Douglas, London 1932, 63 no. 22, 65 no. 27, 71–2 no. 40 (suspicious but referring to a 'breve' of Edward the Confessor), 77 no. 52 (reference to a charter of Edward) (*RRAN* ii. nos 656, 658, 1079, 1597–8), and for vaguer references, see W. Dugdale, *Monasticon Anglicanum*, ed. J. Caley, H. Ellis and B. Bandinel, London 1817–30, i. 109 no. 32, 111 no. 39 (*RRAN* ii. nos 840, 1055), vi. 1180 no. 31 (*RRAN* ii. no. 1083); *Cartae antiquae rolls*, i. nos 50, 51 (*RRAN* ii. nos 1048–9); *Calendar of charter rolls 1327–41*, 434 no. 1 (*RRAN* ii. no. 1576); V.H. Galbraith, 'Royal charters to Winchester', *EHR* xxxv (1920), 389–90 nos 13–14, 18, 393–4 no. 31 (*RRAN* ii. nos 627, 745, 1380); *Cartae antiquae rolls*, i. nos 50, 52 (*RRAN* ii. nos 1048–9); *The cartulary of Worcester cathedral priory*, ed. R.R. Darlington (Pipe Roll Society new ser. xxxviii, 1968), 18 no. 22 (not in *RRAN* ii); *Liber Eliensis*, ed. E.O. Blake (Camden, 3 ser. xcii, 1962), 260–61 (*RRAN* ii. no. 930). *RRAN* ii. no. 1039 (Henry I's confirmation of a charter of Eadred to Crowland) is a gross forgery, and *RRAN* ii. no. 644 (*Feudal Documents*, ed. Douglas, 62–3 no. 21), citing and confirming charters of Cnut and Edward the Confessor, is almost certainly to be identified as a twelfth- or thirteenth-century invention.

[59] *RRAN* iii. nos 4 (mentioning a charter), 99 (referring to 'priuilegia'), 144, 169, 171, 246, 261, 270, 506, 717 (referring to 'priuilegia'), 729, 760 (referring to a charter), 929, 937, 955, 966, 975, the rest either spurious or referring to the 'tempus regis Edwardi' rather than to specific diplomas or writs. See also *Worcester cartulary*, 29 no. 47, for Roger earl of Hereford, 1143×54, confirming an unspecified charter granted by Edward the Confessor to Worcester cathedral priory.

[60] J. Dufour, 'Etat et comparaison des actes faux ou falsifiés intitulés au nom des Carolingiens français (840–987)', *Fälschungen im Mittelalter* (MGH Schriften xxxiii, 1988), iv. 167–210, esp. 209, and for Sicily, see the horrifying statistics for the forgery of Greek as opposed to Latin privileges attributed to the Norman kings, supplied by G.A. Loud, 'The chancery and charters of the kings of Sicily (1130–1212)', *EHR* cxxiv (2009), 779–810, esp. 801–10. See also M.T. Clanchy, 'Remembering the past and the good old law', *History* lv (1970), 165–76.

and 'St' Edgar father of King Edward (the martyr), is undoubtedly a forgery, first fully recorded as late as 1313 when it was confirmed by King Edward II, but apparently already in circulation in 1227 when it is referred to, and partially recited, in an entirely genuine privilege of Henry III.[61] It is surely no coincidence that it should have been at much this same time, in the second quarter of the thirteenth century, that the Glastonbury monks seem first to have appropriated to themselves connections both to King Arthur and to Joseph of Arimathaea, connections that are alluded to in the forged charter of Henry II.[62] The chaotic order in which the names of kings in Henry II's charter are supplied (St Edgar, St Edward, Edmund, Edward the Elder, Alfred, 'Bringwalthius', Centwine, Baldred, Ine, Arthur, Cuthred and Cenwalh) is perhaps some indication of the inability of the Glastonbury monks, for all their antiquarian interests, to make chronological sense of early West Saxon history.[63] Another charter of Henry II, equally spurious, claims to offer a full inspeximus and recital of a charter of Athelstan in favour of the monks of Milton Abbey in Dorset. Of this we have no record earlier than the sixteenth century.[64]

---

[61] *Letters and charters of Henry II*, ed. Vincent, no. 1131 (citing charters that may include S 227, 236–8, 246–7, 250–51, 257, 371, 499, 783), noting a lost 'original' still apparently in existence as late as the 1530s, and the principal chancery copies whence *Calendar of charter rolls 1226–57*, 43; *Calendar of charter rolls 1300–27*, 214, 225. The 1227 copy does not as yet include the controversial preamble, the clauses relating to immunity from episcopal authority, the clause near the end (clearly inspired by disputes with Bath from the 1190s onwards) forbidding the erection of a cathedral at Glastonbury, or the references to the Glastonbury myths of King Arthur and of an apostolic consecration of Glastonbury by Christ in person. These 'additional' clauses first appear in Glastonbury copies after *c.*1250, and seem not to have been confirmed by any English king until 1313.

[62] N. Vincent, *The holy blood: King Henry III and the Westminster blood relic*, Cambridge 2001, 91.

[63] Although, as Julia Crick points out to me, it is conceivable that this disorder was itself the product of the fire of the 1180s, which is said to have resulted in a complete confusion amongst the abbey's relics, ornaments and books: *The chronicle of Glastonbury abbey: an edition, translation and study of John of Glastonbury's* 'Cronica sive antiquitates Glastoniensis ecclesie', ed. J.P. Carley and D. Townsend, Woodbridge 1985, 172–5, dating the fire to St Urban's day in a year when the abbey was vacant, i.e. 25 May 1184. Cf. *Ann. mon.* ii. 62, 243.

[64] *Letters and charters of Henry II*, ed. Vincent, no. 1804, known from a sixteenth-century copy of a lost Milton cartulary, the cartulary copy printed in *Monasticon*, ii. 350–51 no. 7, itself reciting S 391. A fire is said to have destroyed the majority of Milton abbey's muniments on 2 September 1309: *Registrum Simonis de Gandavo, diocesis Saresbiriensis, A.D. 1297–1315*, ed. C.T. Flower and M.C.B. Dawes (Canterbury and York Society xl–xli, 1934), i. 272–3, 343–4. The hidations recorded in the spurious charter of Athelstan accord better with those confirmed to the abbey by Edward II in 1311 (*Calendar of patent rolls 1307–13*, 389–90) than they do with those of Domesday, suggesting that both the Athelstan

Twelfth- and thirteenth-century writers were not above the creation *ex nichilo* of letters attributed to pre-Conquest kings. Most notorious are the letters attributed by Stephen of Rouen to King Arthur, said to have been sent to Henry II as a challenge to Plantagenet authority.[65] To this same genre of pseudo-history we can almost certainly add the exchange of letters between Offa of Mercia and Charlemagne recorded in the *Vitae duorum Offarum*, texts that are still sometimes accepted as genuine relics of the eighth century, even though they leave no trace before the 1250s and even though they fit all too neatly into a twelfth- or thirteenth-century context of Anglo-French rivalry.[66] Whether or not we accept them as true records of agreements between English and foreign rulers, all four of our surviving texts of Anglo-Danish or Anglo-Norman 'treaties' from before 1066 survive only in post-Conquest versions, the most plausible of them in a copy of letters of Pope John XV (associated with William of Malmesbury's *Historia regum*), itself by no means above a suspicion of reworking or embellishment.[67]

---

charter and its supposed Henry II inspeximus may have been forged in the aftermath of the fire of 1309.

[65] Stephen of Rouen, 'Draco Normannicus', in *Chronicles*, ed. Howlett, ii. 697, 707, with commentary by S. Echard, *Arthurian narrative in the Latin tradition*, Cambridge 1998, 85–93; M. Aurell, *L'Empire des Platagenêt 1154–1224*, St-Amand-Montrond 2003, 170–72, and especially by J.S.P. Tatlock, 'Geoffrey and King Arthur in "Normannicus Draco"', *Modern Philology* xxxi (1933), 1–18, at 9–11, noting the dependence here upon other such fictitious correspondence between kings, in G. Mon. 214–15 (bk ix. 158), and most notably in the letters of Alexander the Great reported in the medieval Alexander romances, for which, see, for example, *Der Alexanderroman des Archipresbyters Leo*, ed. F. Pfister, Heidelberg 1913, 65–6, 86–7, 103–4, 124–5. For Arthur, see also John Gillingham's contribution to the present volume and above, 134.

[66] *The Lives of the two Offas*, ed. M. Swanton, Crediton 2010, 51–2 (kings of England to Carloman), 57–8 (Charlemagne to Offa), 63–4 (Offa to 'Meredith' king of the Welsh), 75–80 (exchange of letters between Offa and Charlemagne), two of these reprinted from the seventeenth-century edition of the 'Lives', via Mansi's *Concilia*, as genuine letters of Charlemagne in *PL* 98, cols 893 no. 1, 907 no. 7, 937 no. 2. These are to be distinguished from the letters from Charlemagne to Offa in *PL* 98, cols 910–11 no. 12, that derive from a far more plausible tradition, transmitted together with the letters of Alcuin, ed. E. Dümmler (MGH *Epistolae*, iv, 1895); cf. 131 no. 87, 144–6 no. 100, with extracts from the second of these letters also supplied by William of Malmesbury, presumably from a copy of Alcuin, *GR* i. 136–7 (i. c. 93). Swanton, *Lives of the two Offas*, pp. xxxii–iii, xc, xciii, admits that the letters in the *Vitae duorum Offarum* keep bad company yet seems to accept their *bona fides* as later transcripts derived from the St Albans archive that might have preserved such 'correspondence with foreign princes'. For one such letter from precisely this source, undoubtedly spurious, see below n. 95.

[67] P. Chaplais, *English diplomatic practice in the middle ages*, London 2003, 36–42, citing in particular the papal letters in William of Malmesbury, *GR* i. 276–9 (i. c. 166).

Nonetheless, there are other instances amongst the charters of Henry II where references to the Anglo-Saxon kings seem entirely genuine. If we resort to tabulation here, we shall find a number of features worth remarking:

Table 11.1 References to pre-Conquest kings in the charters of Henry II, 1154–1189.

No.	Beneficiary	Date	King(s)
16	Abingdon	1159	Edward the Confessor (S 1066), William I, Henry I
364	Bury St Edmunds	1155×58	Edward the Confessor (S 1070), Henry I
368	Bury St Edmunds	1155×58	Edward the Confessor (S 1070), Henry I
465	Canterbury	1155×58	Edward the Confessor (?S 1089), William I, Henry I, cites merely as gifts
577	Chertsey	1154×58	Edward the Confessor (?S 1035), William I, Henry I
580	Chertsey	?Spurious	Edward the Confessor (?S 1093–5), William I, Henry I
815	Wm of Durnford	?Spurious	Edward the Confessor (not in S), cites merely as a gift
910	Fécamp	?Spurious	Edward the Confessor (?S 1054), William I, Henry I
1117	St Peter's Ghent	1156×1162	Edward the Confessor (S 1002), William I, Henry
1131	Glastonbury	Spurious	Edgar, Edward martyr, Edmund, Edward the Elder, Alfred, 'Bringwalthius', Centwine, Baldred, Ine, Arthur, Cuthred and Cenwalh
1318	St Benet Holme	1154×64	Edward the Confessor (S 1055)
1804	Milton Abbey	Spurious	Athelstan (S 391)
2047	Peterborough	1177×89	Edward the Confessor (S 1029), cites as gift without mentioning charter
2240	Romsey Abbey	1155×58	Edward the Confessor (not in S)
2806	Westminster	1155×58	Edward the Confessor (S 1011 etc.), Henry I
2807	Westminster	?Spurious	Edward the Confessor (S 1011 etc.), William I, Henry I
2852	St S Winchester	1154×58	Edward the Confessor (S 1152), William I, Henry I, cited merely as gifts

Note: Possession of lands or liberties held 'tempore reg(is) Edwardi' are also cited in nos 440 (Canterbury, ?S 1089), 611 (Cirencester abbey, not in S), 706 (Coventry, S 1000, 1098), 708 (Coventry, S 1098), 750 (Darley Dale church, not in S), 1068–9 (forged, Fordwich, S 1092), 1341 (men of Hythe, cf. S 1047), 1506 (Lincoln/Kilsby, cf. S 1000), 1534 (Lincoln, cf. *Regesta*, i, no. 337), 1571 (men of Lincoln, not in S), 1632 (London knyghtengild, not in S), 2754–5 (forged, men of Wallingford and Berkhamsted, not in S), 2801 (Westminster S 1011 etc.), 2811 (Westminster S 1040, 1043). The 'die qua rex Edwardus fuit vivus et mortuus' is cited as a term in no. 839 (Ely).

The first point to be made is that, with the exception of the Glastonbury and Milton forgeries, the only Anglo-Saxon king to be referred to in the entire corpus of Henry II's charters is Edward the Confessor. This is significant. It indicates a more general fascination at the royal chancery with the memory of King Edward. Over the entire period from *c*.1200 to the seventeenth century, during which the chancery and Exchequer issued copies or inspeximuses of Anglo-Saxon charters, whereas only 26 (2.6 per cent) of the 997 royal charters issued before the reign of King Edward were inspected in chancery or by the Exchequer, no less than 36 (26 per cent) of the 164 charters or writs of Edward were granted this distinction. In other words, it was ten times more likely that the chancery would inspect charters of the Confessor than that it would recite those of all previous English kings.[68]

With specific reference to the chancery of Henry II, furthermore, this suggests that, as for the Domesday commissioners or to those who in the 1160s compiled the Hereford Domesday with its endless references to land held 'tempore regis Edwardi', the reign of Edward the Confessor was considered an unofficial yet nonetheless convenient milestone in legal memory. References in Henry II's charters to 'the time of King Edward', and on one occasion to 'the day when King Edward was alive and dead', not only echo the usages of Domesday but are intended to fix a *terminus a quo*, as we shall see in due course, similar to the more formal decision to establish a date of legal memory to determine the acceptance or rejection of historical testimony as evidence acceptable in court.[69] My impression is that, by the reign of Henry II's son King John, such recourse to the *tempus Edwardi regis* was in decline though not entirely abandoned. The surviving letters and charters of King John refer to only three charters of Edward the Confessor, for the monks of Bury, Chertsey and Westminster, all of them already referred to in charters of Henry II.[70] 'The time of King Edward' nonetheless continues to occur in King John's charters, after 1200, as a period from which the privileges of the monks of Bury, St Peter's Ghent and of the men of Dover and Hythe might be confirmed.[71]

This is not to suggest that 'the time of Edward the Confessor' enjoyed anything more than unofficial or symbolic significance to Henry II and his successors. A forger working at Westminster carried things a great deal further, assigning to Henry II an undertaking to confirm to the Westminster monks the gifts made to them by Edward the Confessor, 'the king of blessed memory, my kinsman, who

---

[68] Statistics based upon the figures from Sawyer, above n. 2.

[69] *Letters and charters of Henry II*, ed. Vincent, nos 440, 611, 706, 708, 750, 1341, 1506, 1534, 1571, 1632, 2801, 2811. The 'die qua rex Edwardus fuit vivus and mortuus' cited as a term in no. 839 for Ely is merely inherited by Henry II from the terms of earlier confirmations of Ely's privileges by Henry I and Stephen: *Cartae antiquae rolls*, i, no. 50 (*RRAN* ii, no. 1048); *RRAN* iii, no. 261.

[70] *Rotuli chartarum*, ed. T.D. Hardy, London 1837, 38b, 117, 139b.

[71] Ibid. 38, 83, 153, 153b, 184.

appointed my great-grandfather and his sons as adopted heirs in his realm'.[72] Here we come perilously close to the legal straitjacket, proffered by George Garnett, in which the kings of England after 1066 justified their conquest as an act of succession, identifying themselves as the legitimate successors to Edward the Confessor, their ultimate 'antecessor'.[73] With the exception of the Westminster forgery, however, this is not the sense in which the Confessor or the *tempus Edwardi regis* is used in Henry II's charters. Here they appear not so much as legal but as historical phenomena, the equivalent to phrases such as 'the time of the old English kings' or references to the time of Alfred, or Edgar or Cnut, that occur in subsequent business before the courts of thirteenth-century English kings.[74]

Such references are, nonetheless, not without interest. Not all of Henry II's nods to the Confessor can today be matched to known Anglo-Saxon charters. A charter of the Confessor granting the manor of Northwood (Hampshire) to the nuns of Romsey (not recorded in Sawyer or Finberg) is unknown beyond its appearance in a confirmation by Henry II.[75] So is a supposed grant of liberties and customs at Deerhurst said to have been made by the Confessor to the ancestors of William of Durnford, although this reference comes to us from a charter of Henry II itself of doubtful authenticity.[76] References by Henry II to his confirmation of the liberties and customs enjoyed in the time of King Edward by beneficiaries including the canons of Cirencester, the church of Darley Dale in Derbyshire, the men of Lincoln, and the London knyghtengild, are likewise unmatched by any surviving charters of the Confessor, although in no case here can we be sure that Henry II was definitely referring to charters as opposed to the general *tempus regis Edwardi*, synonymous since Domesday Book with the

---

[72] *Letters and charters of Henry II*, ed. Vincent, no. 2807: 'Sciatis communiter me pro redemptione anime mee et patris et matris mee necnon et aui mei gloriosi regis Henr(ici) et beate memorie regis Eadwardi cognati mei, qui proauum meum liberosque illius in regnum suum adoptiuos heredes instituerat, accepisse in manu mea et defensione totum honorem ecclesie sancti Petri Westmonasterii', supposedly in a charter issed at Dover 1155×58, in reality a forgery by a Westminster scribe, late twelfth century.

[73] G. Garnett, *Conquered England: kingship, succession and tenure, 1066–1166*, Oxford 2007, esp. ch.1.

[74] For examples, see below nn. 109 and 125 and, in general, see Vincent, 'Tales of the Conquest', 298.

[75] *Letters and charters of Henry II*, ed. Vincent, no. 2240, also printed in *Calendar of charter rolls 1257–1300*, 105 no.19, 'totum boscum suum de Nortwuda sicut rex Eadwardus ei dedit et carta sua confirmauit'.

[76] *Letters and charters of Henry II*, ed. Vincent, no. 815, 'Concedimus etiam predictis Willelmo et heredibus suis omnes libertates et liberas consuetudines quas gloriosus rex sanctus Edwardus eis contulit et concessit'. The use of the first-person plural here is itself a clear indication of forgery.

time before the Norman Conquest.[77] A sum of twenty-two pence in 'the alms (or almoner) of King Edward' offset against the king's profits from the county 'donum' of Surrey, recorded in the Pipe Rolls in 1158, may likewise bear witness to an otherwise lost act of almsgiving by a king for whom Henry II demanded particular veneration.[78]

As this should remind us, the citation of earlier charters in later confirmations can often serve as our only evidence that an Anglo-Saxon charter once existed, or at least was supposed to exist. This is a point to which we shall return. For the moment, we should also note a further aspect to the citation of Anglo-Saxon charters in the charters of the Plantagenet kings: their extreme scarcity. As Paul Brand has remarked, Anglo-Saxon charters, indeed charters not only of the Anglo-Saxon kings but of William I, William II and Henry I, were very seldom cited in litigation in the twelfth or thirteenth centuries.[79] Despite Brand's strictures, it seems not to have been widely noticed how rarely, before 1300, the royal chancery officially 'renewed' ancient evidences. Henry III's first full inspeximus of an Anglo-Saxon diploma, expedited in October 1260, was issued more than sixty years after the first introduction of the full-blown inspeximus form to the English royal chancery.[80] Thereafter, only seven Anglo-Saxon charters were accorded full inspeximuses in the Charter or Patent Rolls of the royal chancery from 1260 through to the death of Edward I in 1307. Of these seven, four were recited in combination with later, post-Conquest awards.[81] Even if we allow for copies recorded in the Exchequer Cartae Antiquae Rolls (themselves an innovation of the 1190s and never intended as more than a semi-official record of ancient evidences claimed by petitioners at the Exchequer), we find our seven charters set alongside a mere twenty others recited in full before either the Exchequer or the Chancery during the entire course of the twelfth and thirteenth centuries.[82] Half of the texts on the Charter and Patent Rolls, and sixteen of the twenty from the Cartae Antiquae Rolls, are writs or diplomas

---

[77] Ibid. nos 611, 750, 1571, 1632.

[78] *The great rolls of the pipe for the second, third and fourth years of the reign of King Henry the second*, ed. J. Hunter, London 1844, 162, 'et elemos' regis Aedwardi xxii. d(enarios)'.

[79] Brand, '"Time out of mind"', 37–9.

[80] For the introduction of the inspeximus form, already by the reign of Richard I allowing for the full recital of earlier royal charters, see N. Vincent, 'The charters of Henry II: the introduction of the royal "inspeximus" revisited', in M. Gervers (ed.), *Dating undated medieval charters*, Budapest and Woodbridge 2000, 97–120.

[81] *Calendar of charter rolls 1257–1300*, 31, 70, 324, 327; *Calendar of charter rolls 1300–26*, 17; *Calendar of patent rolls 1281–92*, 26 (covering S 136, 838, 904, 1000, 1055, 1157, 1226).

[82] *Cartae antiquae rolls*, i, nos 47–8, 106–8, 264, 269–70; ii, nos 356, 436, 443–6, 480, 581, 615, and PRO/TNA C 52/21 no. 16; C 52/27 no. 1 (covering S 4, 779, 990, 1002, 1036, 1038, 1041, 1043, 1045, 1051, 1054–5, 1075, 1084–5, 1091, 1094–6, 1217).

of Edward the Confessor. But this does not rule out the recital of charters of Aethelbert of Kent, Offa, Aethelred and Leofric of Mercia.[83] Most are written in Latin and are without English boundary clauses, although no less than ten vernacular writs or boundary clauses are preserved in one or other of these rolls before 1307.[84] Similar constraints apply to the recital or confirmation of early Norman as of Anglo-Saxon charters. During the same period from the invention of the inspeximus form in the 1190s through to the reign of Edward I, four charters of William I were granted full inspection by the royal chancery, and a further eighteen were recorded in the Cartae Antiquae Rolls. The earliest of these chancery inspeximuses dates from 1253.[85]

It is important to notice that very few of these charters, either Anglo-Saxon or Anglo-Norman, appear as isolated texts recited alone and without supporting evidence. In the vast majority of cases, charters of the Anglo-Saxons or of William I were only recited in full in combination with later Anglo-Norman charters. Of our twenty Anglo-Saxon charters recited on the Cartae Antiquae Rolls, for example, only one (S 1041, Edward the Confessor for Westminster) occurs in isolation, unaccompanied by later post-Conquest royal charters for the same beneficiary.[86] For an explanation here we can turn to perhaps our most enlightening and certainly our most detailed report of a twelfth-century king confirming charters of his pre-Conquest ancestors. According to the account of the great dispute of 1163 between the monks of St Albans and the bishop of Lincoln, recorded in the *Gesta abbatum* of St Albans (in its present form a thirteenth-century source, probably reworked by Matthew Paris, but drawing upon extensive histories from the twelfth century), heeding a warning from the bishop of Lincoln that, if these things were not settled in the king's court, they might be carried before papal judges, the king took certain of his closest courtiers apart from the great meeting of his court at Westminster, ordering the abbot of St Albans to come to him with two monks bearing their privileges so that both the old and the new might be inspected:[87]

---

[83] Cf. S 4, 136, 779, 838, 904, 990, 1217, 1226; *Cartae antiquae rolls*, i, nos 47, 269–70; PRO/TNA C 52/21 no. 16; *Calendar of charter rolls 1257 1300*, 31, 70; *Calendar of charter rolls 1300–26*, 17.

[84] *Calendar of patent rolls 1281–92*, 26 (S 1157); *Cartae antiquae rolls*, i, nos 106–8 (S 1094–6, also in *Monasticon*, i. 429–30 nos 6–8), 264 (S 1091), ii. no. 356 (S 1036, with English boundary clauses), 443–6 (S 1045, 1075, 1084–5).

[85] *Regesta regum Anglo-Normannorum: the acta of William I (1066–1087)*, ed. D. Bates, Oxford 1998, nos 2, 3, 19(i), 20(ii), 22, 23(ii), 31(i), 38, 80–81, 111, 115, 122, 141, 146, 160, 181, 185, 187–8, 194, 220, 227, 272.

[86] *Cartae antiquae rolls*, ii, no.615.

[87] *Gesta abbatum monasterii sancti Albani*, i. 150–51. Offa's surviving charters to St Albans include the spurious S 136 and S 138 but no full foundation charter. In general,

And when the writings of the English kings, namely of Offa and certain others, were inspected, from which no seals hung, contrary to modern custom, but at the beginning of which had been placed golden crosses drawn in the hands of the kings themselves, so that it seemed to certain men of ill will that these writings were of no account because unsealed; when they arrived at the charter of King Henry (I), the (present) king's grandfather, in which were confirmed those things, both in lands and liberties granted by the English kings to the blessed Alban, the king declared: 'What is all this that the people from Lincoln mutter, claiming that unsealed privileges are of no account? Look! The seal of my grandfather serves as seal of all the original charters confirmed in his charter'.

According to the author of the *Gesta*, this was a judgement that proved Henry II as wise as Solomon, since the monks had previously found no means of countering the argument that their charters were invalid because unsealed, not least because in various monasteries the claim that none of the old English kings used a seal was considered demonstrably false. 'For at Westminster', the author writes, 'can be found the seal of King Edward'.[88]

This is not our only twelfth-century source to refer to the peculiarities and pitfalls of Anglo-Saxon diplomatic. Gervase of Canterbury, for example, asserted that Edward the Confessor was the first of the English kings to seal his charters in wax, and that charters earlier than this amounted merely to 'scedulas' marked with signs manual and known as 'landbooks', an interesting indication this of the survival not just of the physical artefacts but of some sense of the context and terminology of Anglo-Saxon charters.[89] The *Gesta*'s reference to 'golden crosses' (presumably signs manual in golden letters, confused by the *Gesta* with

---

see J.C. Crick, 'Liberty and fraternity: creating and defending the liberty of St Albans', in A. Musson (ed.), *Expectations of the law in the middle ages*, Woodbridge 2001, 91–103.

[88] *Gesta abbatum*, i. 151, 'Quod enim dicebant regum Anglorum nulla esse sigilla deprehensum esse falsum in quibusdam monasteriis, nam apud Westmonasterium inueniebatur sigillum regis Edwardi'.

[89] *Gervase of Canterbury*, ed. Stubbs, ii. 59, 'Hic est primus regum Anglie qui in cartis suis ad testimonium veritatis ceram impressam appendit. Non enim habebant antiquitus de donationibus aut venditionibus terrarum nisi scedulas tantum de pactione qualibet inscriptas cum nominibus et signis personarum ibidem presentium. Has scedulas tunc temporis "landbokes", id est libros terrarum Angli vocabant, idemque robur habebant quod nunc vix optinent carte nostre cum qualibet impressione', although it is not clear whether Gervase, like Matthew Paris writing of the seal of Offa, had in fact been bamboozled by the forged seal of Edward the Confessor in use for the monks of Westminster. The use of the word 'landboc' here is interesting, and might explain the title 'Landboc' applied to the Winchcombe cartulary, composed in the reign of Henry III, opening with Anglo-Saxon materials from 798 onwards: *Landboc sive registrum monasterii beatae Mariae Virginis et Sancti Cenhelmi de Winchelcumba*, ed. D. Royce, Exeter 1892–1903, i. 17.

the opening *Chrismon*) is echoed in the allegation of the Waltham chronicler, writing *c*.1180, that Edward the Confessor's charter to Waltham was written in golden letters and signed with a golden cross.[90] As late as the 1330s, the lack of sealing in the case of Edgar's foundation charter for Peterborough was cited by at least one official of King Edward III as a reason why such charters could not be accepted as evidence in court.[91] In fiction, at least, it was generally supposed that seals had existed since the very beginnings of English history. Certainly, the seal of King Arthur was among the treasures displayed at Westminster Abbey as late as the sixteenth century.[92] Perhaps as early as the 1150s, the Westminster monks had already manufactured for themselves what they claimed to be a seal of St Dunstan, and quite possibly the seals of kings Offa and Edgar into the bargain.[93] So impressive was the (genuine) seal of St Edith of Wilton (d. 984), daughter of King Edgar, that it continued to be used as the conventual seal of Wilton Abbey into the thirteenth century and beyond. Indeed, as pointed out to me by Simon Keynes, in 1539 it was attached to the deed of surrender by which Wilton itself was suppressed.[94] To the author of the *Vitae duorum Offarum*, written at St Albans more likely in the thirteenth than the twelfth century, it was the seal of

---

[90] *The Waltham chronicle*, ed. Watkiss and Chibnall, 36–7 (S 1036), 'carta sua litteris aureis scripta confirmasset, et propria crucem auream manu in eadem exarasset', and cf. p. xxxviii for the charter's listing as late as 1204 in a Waltham inventory as being 'aureis litteris in pluribus locis scripta'. For further examples of Anglo-Saxon charters using golden lettering, see J.C. Crick, '"Pristina libertas": liberty and the Anglo-Saxons revisited', *TRHS* 6 ser. xiv (2004), 47–72, at 54, 64 n. 82, with surviving original examples that include S 880 (Aethelred to Ealdred bishop of Cornwall, now Exeter Cathedral MS 2070, drawn to my attention by Julia Crick) and S 745 (Edgar to New Minster Winchester, now BL Cotton Vespasian A. viii). See also T.A. Heslop, 'Twelfth-century forgeries as evidence for earlier seals: the case of St Dunstan', in N. Ramsay, M. Sparks and T. Tatton-Brown (eds), *St Dunstan: his life, times and cult*, Woodbridge 1992, 299–310, at 301, 308, 310n.

[91] *Placita de Quo warranto temporibus Edw. I, II, et III in curia receptae scaccarii Westm. asservata*, ed. W. Illingworth, London 1818, 553–6 (citing charters of Wulfhere, Aethelred and Edgar, S 68, 72, 787), at p. 556 attempting to repudiate the charter of Edgar on the grounds that 'cartam dicit esse predicti regis Edgari nullo sigillo consignatam cui per consequens nulla fides est adhibenda'. The abbot's reponse, mirroring that of Henry II in the St Albans case of 1163, was to point out that all the substantive terms of Edgar's charter had been renewed in privileges under the seals of Henry II and Richard I.

[92] Vincent, *Holy blood*, 174 n. 59; J.J. Scarisbrick, *Henry VIII*, London 1968, 272.

[93] Heslop, 'Twelfth-century forgeries', 299–310, as drawn to my attention by Julia Crick.

[94] Ibid. 303 n., at 303–4 noting a similar case, in the use of a (forged) seal of St Nectan by the post-Conquest canons of Hartland in Devon, and cf. T.A. Heslop, 'English seals from the mid ninth century to 1100', *Journal of the British Archaeological Association* cxxxiii (1980), 1–16, at 4 and pl. 1a. For the 1539 deed of surrender, see PRO/TNA E 322/264.

Offa I (*fl.* ?*c.*400), and attempts to forge it in Offa's own lifetime, that were key to a large part of his (entirely mythologised) biography.[95]

Even so, the St Alban's story of Henry II's treatment of the unsealed diploma of Offa II is of peculiar significance, making it quite clear why Anglo-Saxon charters, when they were confirmed after 1200, tended only to be accepted if they came already accompanied by a series of confirmations from earlier Anglo-Norman kings. The royal chancery remained wary in its approach to the Anglo-Saxon past, taking the view that there was safety in numbers, so that eleventh-century charters that initiated a series of later confirmations and reissues were more to be trusted than those that stood alone. This was not a foolproof test. Forgers merely learned to fashion their own series of inspeximuses and confirmations to supply their confections with context, nowhere more notoriously than at Rochester, as revealed through the detective work of Martin Brett. Here, forged charter was embedded within forged charter and in turn within a series of forged inspeximuses intended, through sheer weight of numbers, to overwhelm even the most sceptical of critics.[96] Nonetheless, the insistence that the royal chancery, after the 1190s, would for the most part only reissue Anglo-Saxon charters that appeared at the head of a sequence of later, post-Conquest confirmations, rendered forgery that much less likely to succeed.

There was perhaps a second reason for the long delay, after 1066, in the inspection and full recital of Anglo-Saxon charters by the English royal chancery. As Julia Crick has noticed, in an article of fundamental significance, such charters were often cited, and if necessary rewritten, by their beneficiaries as defences against the more predatory aspects of royal 'dominium'. Above all the insertion in such charters, either by their original grantors or in the course of post-Conquest forgery, of claims to 'liberties' or 'immunities' rendered them potentially hostile to the king's claims to sovereignty. 'Libertas' in this reading became the negation not only of slavery, in its Roman or post-Roman sense, but of whatever term, up to and including 'dominium', might be adopted by kings to designate their own particular brand of lordship. No wonder then that kings thought long and hard before issuing official confirmations or inspeximuses of such privileges. The fact that a very high proportion of the Anglo-Saxon charters for the seventy or more churches of England that continued to preserve them were subject to post-Conquest 'improvement' or rewriting was itself yet another reason why the royal chancery had to be so cautious in its approaches.[97]

---

[95] *Lives of the two Offas*, ed. Swanton, 27–31. Swanton's attempt to attribute this text to a twelfth-century author does not convince.

[96] M. Brett, 'Forgery at Rochester', *Fälschungen im Mittelalter* (MGH Schriften xxxiii, 1988), iv. 397–412.

[97] Crick, '"Pristina libertas"', 47–71, esp. 50–51, citing a figure of forty 'preservers' of such evidence. The figure seventy-five is suggested to me by Simon Keynes, citing the list under 'Archives' at the Kemble site, http://www.kemble.asnc.cam.ac.uk/node/113.

Not that such rewriting was necessarily apparent to subsequent generations. The courts of twelfth- and thirteenth-century kings could experience great difficulty in establishing the authenticity of older documents, on occasion accepting even the most outrageous forgeries as if they were genuine records of the eleventh-century past. Once again, a few examples must suffice. Take, for instance, the absurd rhyming charter, written in Middle English, recited before the King's forest justices in 1324, by which Edward the Confessor was reputed to have granted the hundreds of Chelmsford and Dengie with rights in the Essex forest to a man named Ranulf Peperking, or earlier, and only slightly more plausible, the charter of Edward the Confessor in favour of his servant, Alpheius, granting a messuage in Oakhanger (Hampshire), confirmed but not recited by Henry III in 1250, apparently as part of ongoing disputes over the rights of the then tenant, James of Oakhanger, to alienate his lands, defined as a royal serjeanty, to Selborne priory.[98] Given that, even in respect to documents less than a decade old, the King's officials were sometimes hard put to establish proofs of forgery, it is perhaps not surprising that their *Quellenkritik* was so crude when applied to the documentary evidences of a more distant past.[99] Things did not necessarily improve here between the twelfth and the seventeenth centuries. If anything, the further removed the king's chancery became from the practices of the Anglo-Saxon past, the easier it became to persuade the chancery's officials to accept absurd or anachronistic forgeries attributed to remote ages.

Note, for example, the atrocious forgery of Athelstan for the men of Malmesbury (S 454), first recorded in its recital by the chancery of Richard II in the 1380s.[100] Or of equal absurdity, but slightly later date, the sequence of charters

---

[98] For both the Peperking charter (PRO/TNA E 32/16, Essex Forest Eyre 1324) and that to Alpheius, presumably the TRE tenant of Oakhanger named in Domesday as Alfwy (*Calendar of charter rolls 1226–57*, 349, from PRO/TNA C 53/43 (Charter Roll 35 Henry III) m. 14: 'Sciatis quod donationem et concessionem quam rex Edwardus fecit Alpheo seruienti suo de quodam mesuagio cum pertin(entiis) in Akehangr' ratam habemus et gratam et eam pro nobis et heredibus nostris concedimus et confirmamus sicut carta predicti regis Edwardi quam eidem Alpheo super hoc fieri fecit rationabiliter testatur'), see Vincent, 'Tales of the Conquest', 288 n. 37.

[99] For examples here, see the disputes of the 1220s between Fawkes de Breauté and William Marshal the younger which turned upon allegations of forgery (*Curia regis rolls*, viii. 249–52), or the subsequent claims by the men of Carlisle, Ilchester and Kingston upon Thames to have possessed charters of Henry II conveniently destroyed by fire, apparently leaving no enrolments against which such claims could be checked: *Letters and charters of Henry II*, ed. Vincent, nos 509, 1343, 1412.

[100] S 454, first recorded in *Calendar of patent rolls 1381–5*, 54, still being renewed by the royal chancery as late as 1604, and cf. Crick, '"Pristina libertas"', 55. For the lingering though invented memory of Athelstan's charter, see also A. Wood, 'The loss of Athelstan's gift: the politics of popular memory in Malmesbury, 1607–1633', in J. Whittle (ed.), *Landlords and tenants in Britain, 1440–1660: Tawney's agrarian problem revisited*, Woodbridge 2013, 85–99.

from Henry I onwards, intended to support the genealogical pretensions of the Wellesley family, later dukes of Wellington, native to Wellesley in Wells. The existence of the Wellesley forgeries can be inferred as early as 1242, when the then head of the family claimed in court to have held 'the serjeanty of the county of Somerset from the east of the river Parrett as far as the county of Dorset' by confirmation of Kings Henry II, Richard I and John.[101] The charters themselves, all of them forged, of Henry I, Henry II and Henry III, are not recorded until 1331 when they were granted a full inspeximus by the chancery of Edward III.[102]

Yet even these examples of naivity or mendacity should not lure us into supposing a universal or ahistorical primitivism in later-medieval approaches to the Anglo-Saxon past. We have already seen that Domesday Book remained in use at the court of Henry II and his successors. Meanwhile, the script of Domesday enjoyed a posterity almost as significant as the Book itself. As Alexander Rumble has shown, the lettering of the first surviving Exchequer Pipe Roll (1130), and hence of the great series of pipe rolls that followed it, was consciously influenced by the Domesday script.[103] For proof that a knowledge of Old English, both of language and of letters, was still available at the court of Henry II we need merely cite the Exchequer officials who drew up the Cartae Antiquae Rolls, themselves capable of accurately copying old-English writs, or the work of the scribe who, between 1154 and 1159, wrote an original charter of Henry II for Bordesley Abbey, employing the old-English letter 'thorn'.[104] The royal chancery script, like that of the Exchequer, was itself highly self-conscious. To some extent it shared in a tradition that, as Julia Crick has shown, ensured, from long before the Conquest, that Anglo-Saxon scribes could deliberately mimic ancient scripts. Furthermore, as Crick notes, the very success and promiscuity of twelfth-century forgery of ancient charters is testimony not just to ingenuity but to the expertise shown by twelfth-century scribes in imitating the letter forms of the distant past. Such scribes were assiduous readers as well as reinventors of ancient documents. Nor was script-imitation necessarily nefarious: on occasion

---

[101] *Curia regis rolls*, xvi, no. 1900, and cf. *Book of Fees*, ii. 1383; *Letters and charters of Henry II*, ed. Vincent, no. 2796.

[102] *Calendar of charter rolls 1327–41*, 217–18, still being recited as late as 1449, *Calendar of patent rolls 1446–52*, 260.

[103] A.R. Rumble, 'A Domesday postscript and the earliest surviving Pipe Roll', in I. Wood and N. Lund (eds), *People and places in northern Europe, 500–1600: essays in honour of Peter Hayes Sawyer*, Woodbridge 1991, 123–30.

[104] For English charters copied on to the Cartae antiquae rolls, see above n. 82. For the Bordesley charter, whose scribe remains unidentified, see BL Cotton Nero C. iii fos 175–6, whence *Letters and charters*, ed. Vincent, no. 267; T.A.M. Bishop, *Scriptores regis: facsimiles to identify and illustrate the hands of royal scribes in original charters of Henry I, Stephen, and Henry II*, Oxford 1961, no. 363.

it testified to respect for the past or an aesthetic determination to return to past excellence or authority.[105]

Forged charters to townsmen or laymen excite one further reflection. In general, and despite the wholescale destruction of Anglo-Saxon charters after 1066 (deliberate and accidental), and the poor traditions of record-keeping by laymen as opposed to clerical beneficiaries, we have a surprisingly large number of pre-Conquest charters issued in favour of lay as opposed to ecclesiastical beneficiaries. Yet, of these, only a tiny few were ever granted inspeximus or official confirmation by any post-Conquest king. As I have argued elsewhere, this must surely reflect not only inadequate record-keeping by the laity but a conscious decision by the King's courts to exclude any claim to land brought by a laymen on the basis of pre-Conquest charters or possession.[106] The consequences otherwise, had the dispossessed Anglo-Saxon aristocracy been allowed to reclaim their lost lands on the basis of charters issued before 1066, would have been as alarming to kings of the twelfth century as they are obvious to historians writing today.

From this flows one other peculiar contingency. Perhaps precisely because they were deprived of their status as legal testimony, the vast majority of charters issued to laymen by the Anglo-Saxon (as indeed by the early Norman) kings must be assumed destroyed. Very few, so far as I can establish, were ever pleaded in a royal court.[107] If they survive at all, it is generally because they found refuge at an early stage of their existence in the archives of one or other of the great churches of England. This, as I have suggested elsewhere, has profound consequences for our understanding of the question of chancery as opposed to 'beneficiary production' in the charters of England's eleventh- and twelfth-century kings.

Our chief evidence that kings such as Henry II or Richard maintained professional chanceries for the production of their letters and charters comes from the fact that virtually every one of the many dozens of charters issued by these kings for lay beneficiaries is written in the hand of a recognised chancery scribe. Other beneficiaries, such as monasteries or bishops, continued to use their own scribes to write royal charters, adopting standard royal formulae, but then merely presenting such 'beneficiary-produced' documents for confirmation under the King's great seal. The charters issued to laymen, however, who maintained no such army of scribes and who instead had to rely upon the scribes of the king, supply our chief proof that the king's scribes and chancery were prolific in their manufacture of documents. In our dealings with Anglo-Saxon

---

[105] J.C. Crick, 'Script and the sense of the past in Anglo-Saxon England', in J. Roberts and L. Webster (eds), *Anglo-Saxon traces*, Tempe, AZ 2011, 1–29, esp. 21–2, 27.

[106] Vincent, 'Tales of the Conquest', 291–2, 297–9, following Brand, 'Time out of mind', 37.

[107] Exceptions would include the Pepperking and Oakhanger charters noted above, n. 98, recited in the course of actions before the forest eyre or the King's courts.

kings and with kings such as William I, the impression that we receive that the vast majority of royal charters continued to be manufactured for these kings by beneficiaries rather than from within a royal 'chancery' may itself be nothing save the consequence of archival accident.[108] If we possessed rather more original charters issued by kings either before or after 1066 to lay beneficiaries (we in fact have none for either the Confessor or the Conqueror), we might receive a very different understanding of the degree to which the charters of these kings were in general produced either by the king's own chancery or by local beneficiary scribes.

Let us turn now from charters to the law, and from the full recital of Anglo-Saxon privileges, to an alternative source of information, no less significant for our knowledge of the Anglo-Saxon past. On occasion, and without full rehearsal of earlier documents, we find, both in court records and in the responses to inquests, claims to land or privileges warranted on the basis of the Anglo-Saxon past, most often in the form of a claim that X held the land of Y 'ante Conquestum', or that A held the land of B by grant of such and such a (named) Anglo-Saxon king.[109] Claims of this sort are to be found from the very earliest surviving rolls of the King's courts, from the 1190s onwards.[110]

Such evidence can be used to argue a number of points. Firstly it brings into clear relief the fact that, by the twelfth century, the concepts of a Norman Conquest and of a 'Conqueror' were implanted both in popular consciousness and in English law. Modern legal historians may argue that the kings of England after 1066 viewed themselves as the rightful successors to Anglo-Saxon predecessors, anchoring tenure in the 'tempus regis Edwardi' by a tradition of legal memory that overcame the problems of violent dispossession or the loss of any unifying authority at the death of each successive Anglo-Norman king.[111] In reality, however, it was both universally agreed that a conquest divided the era of William and his successors from the 'time of the old English kings', and that the lands of 'the Conqueror' and his successors had been won by violence, 'per conquestum', and by the sword.[112] The idea of a Norman 'conquest' blends on occasion into that of a 'coming of the Normans', an 'adventus Normannorum' (in the estimation of William of Malmesbury and Henry of Huntingdon) every bit as traumatic as the

---

[108] Vincent, 'Tales of the Conquest', 292.

[109] See, for example, *Book of Fees*, i. 51 (by gift of King Edward), 90 (claiming tenure 'de antiquo tempore regum Anglorum ante conquestum Normannorum').

[110] *Rotuli curiae regis*, ed. F. Palgrave, London 1835, i. 68, 347–8, 413–14, ii. 6, 10–11; *CRR*, i, 93.

[111] Garnett, *Conquered England*.

[112] Vincent, 'Tales of the Conquest', 291–9, and for further examples of the concept of tenure 'a conquestu' in the earliest records of the royal courts, see *Rotuli curiae regis*, i. 93, 358, 427, ii. 129, 259. For a European-wide contextualisation, see R. Bartlett, *The making of Europe: conquest, colonization and cultural change, 950–1350*, London 1993, 93–6.

'adventus Saxonum' described by Bede and by implication every bit as much an act of divine vengeance lying beyond mere earthly law.[113] Yet, as Paul Brand has shown, whatever the reluctance of lawyers in theory to accept testimony from before the date of legal memory – a date fixed initially, after the 1150s, in the reign of Henry I, moving forwards thereafter so that by the 1270s it had come to be anchored definitively in 1189, at the accession of King Richard I – on occasion, such reluctance was ignored or overcome, allowing for the citation of charters and other evidence from a period long before 1100, let alone 1189.[114]

Under King John, we find the monks of Westminster and Bury St Edmund's producing charters of Edward the Confessor in the King's courts, cited as warranty for particular liberties.[115] Through to the 1240s, although the citation of such evidence remained relatively infrequent and confined to the greater ecclesiastical corporations (Bury, Westminster and so forth, at least whenever it came to specific Anglo-Saxon charters), we find at least one occasion in the 1220s when a beneficiary, the bishop of Ely, produced full transcripts of his royal charters, including diplomas of Edgar and Edward the Confessor, themselves copied on to a separate schedule attached to the record of the court.[116] On another occasion, again from the 1220s, we find the bishops of Ely and the monks of Ramsey both citing charters of Edward the Confessor, from which extensive quotations were given in the court transcripts, to defend rival positions in respect to their jurisdictions within the Norfolk hundred of Clackclose.[117] The dean and chapter of Rouen, in 1241 laying claim to their lands in Devon and Hampshire, declared that such lands had been held by them in unbroken succession 'a tempore regis Eadwardi', perhaps with some vague memory here of the way in which Domesday sought to establish ownership both 'tempore

---

[113] For the 'adventus Normannorum', see, for example, the passing references by William of Malmesbury (*Gesta regum* i. prologue, i.15.4, ii. prologue, ii. 216, iii. 245.3 (Malmesbury, *GR* i, 16, 36, 150, 398, 458); *Gesta pontificum*, ii. 91.3, v. 267.5 (Malmesbury, *GP* i, 308, 634)) to events 'ante' or 'post aduentum Normannorum'; the title to book 6 of Henry of Huntingdon's *Historia Anglorum*, 338 ('De adventu Normannorum'), and the list of Rochester's benefactors divided between those 'ante aduentum Normannorum' and 'post aduentum Normannorum': BL Cotton Vespasian A. xxii (Rochester annals etc., s.xiii¹), fos 81v–82r (whence J. Thorpe, *Registrum Roffense*, London 1769, 116), a link to the world of Bede to some extent confirmed at fos 120v, 122v which supply lists of the archbishops of Canterbury from St Augustine to Stephen Langton and of the 'reges Kentenses' from Hengist to Henry III via Harold ('sed iniuste').

[114] Brand, 'Time out of mind', 53–4.

[115] *Rotuli curiae regis*, i. 413–14, ii. 10–11; *Curia regis rolls*, iii. 291.

[116] *Curia regis rolls*, x. 167n, from PRO/TNA KB 26/79 m. 28, not cited by Sawyer as a source for these particular charters (S 779, 1051).

[117] *Curia regis rolls*, xii, no. 2019 (S 1030, 1051).

regis Edwardi' and now.[118] Without necessarily producing charters in court, other such claims involved the citation of gifts made by kings other than the Confessor. The monks of Pershore, for example, claimed liberties first granted by their founder, who they named as King Edgar, inferring, without specific citation, Edgar's foundation charter.[119]

By the time of the *Quo warranto* proceedings, from the 1270s onwards, such claims had become even more common, with Kings Egfrith, Wulfhere, Offa, Aethelred I, Alfred, Athelstan, Edgar, Cnut and Edward the Confessor all being cited as the source of privileges or lands, with or without reference to specific charters granted by these kings.[120] On occasion, such claims specifically refer to the fact that charters of Cnut or the Confessor survived in Old English.[121] Given the significance attached in recent scholarship to the eradication of Harold, as of King Stephen, from legal memory, it is worth noting that to those who drew up the 1212 inquests into serjeanties and knights' fees, there was no compulsion to exclude references to 'King' Harold.[122] Harold's kingship, indeed, viewed in something of a heroic rather than a sinister light, was commemorated in Henry II's reign not only by the legends of his survival at Dover or Chester, or in the pious memory of his foundation at Waltham, but in Gerald of Wales' claim that the Welsh Marches were still littered with stone monuments marking Harold's victories against the Welsh.[123]

Some of the references to Anglo-Saxon history in thirteenth-century charter or administrative sources are intriguing not least for the ignorance that they suggest prevailed as to the true nature of pre-Conquest England. Whom, for example, did the monks of Glastonbury assume the King's courts would

---

[118] *Curia regis rolls*, xvi, nos 1440, 1443, and cf. the recital by the monks of Fécamp of a charter of Edward the Confessor (S 1054) which survives only because it was copied into the Cartae Antiquae Roll, now PRO/TNA C 52/29 no. 1.

[119] *Curia regis rolls*, xi, no. 669, probably citing S 786.

[120] *Placita de quo warranto*, 186 (Athelstan), 187 (Egfrith), 197 (Athelstan), 275 (Edgar), 279b (Edgar), 288b (Offa), 302 (Edgar and Edward), 307 (Edgar), 341 (Cnut), 553–4 (Wulfhere and Aethelred), 560 (Cnut), 733 (Cnut), and for the Confessor, see pp. 65–6, 105, 256–7b, 288, 305b, 306, 318b–319, 341, 367, 409, 726, 727b, 729, 744b, 749.

[121] Ibid. 733 ('Anglice scriptum'), 318b–19 ('in Anglico'), and see p. 275 for a glossary of Saxon terms intended to expound the meaning of a charter of Edward the Confessor to Westminster.

[122] *Book of Fees*, i. 116, 'Wygodus de Walengheford tenuit honorem de Walingheford tempore regis Haraldi', and for what was otherwise Harold's exclusion from official memory, see Garnett, *Conquered England*, 18–19, 41–2, 299–300. For a later reference to Harold as king 'sed iniuste', see above n. 113.

[123] See above n. 6; *Vita Haroldi: the romance of the life of Harold, king of England*, ed. and tr. W. de G. Birch, London 1885; *The Waltham chronicle*, ed. Watkiss and Chibnall; Gerald, 'Itinerarium Kambriae' ii. c. 11, and 'Descriptio Kambriae' ii. c. 7 in *Giraldi Cambrensis opera,* ed. J.S. Brewer and J. Dimock (RS [xxi] 1861–91), vi. 140, 217.

comprehend from their forged charter of Henry II, manufactured by the 1240s, purporting to confirm the grants made by the Saxon king 'Bringwalthius', a figure so mythical as to be omitted even from the mythologising of Geoffrey of Monmouth?[124] Who was taken in by claims, to be found on several occasions in the 1220s and 30s, that individual knights' fees or military tenures had existed since before 1066, from 'before the Conquest', or from 'the time of the old English kings' (both of them, incidentally, significant terms, demonstrating that lawyers assumed a very real breach in the continuity of English history associated with the 'Conquest' of 1066, and that 1066 was itself assumed to have brought an end to the time of the 'English' kings)?[125] Claims by the abbots of Glastonbury or St Albans to the franchise of return of writs, argued on the basis of charters of the Anglo-Saxon kings, reveal monasteries using pre-Conquest charters to defend a legal privilege that was only brought into existence after the Conquest and that would have been meaningless to any Anglo-Saxon king.[126]

Charters of the Anglo-Norman as well as the Anglo-Saxon kings were occasionally rehearsed in full before thirteenth-century courts: a charter of William Rufus for the York hospital of St Leonard, recited before the Bench in 1223, for example; charters of the Conqueror and of Rufus to Battle abbey and for Archbishop Anselm recited in whole or in part before the special eyre of Hugh Bigod in 1258–59, or a charter of the Conqueror to the monks of Jumièges recited as part of a *Quo warranto* plea of 1280.[127] Much more often, litigants produced charters that were then merely abstracted in the court record. Even so, these abstracts are not without interest. Some lead us to 'new' charters of the Conqueror. For example, in the Trinity term of 1199, the abbess of Elstow in Bedfordshire produced a charter, duly abstracted in the court record, by which the Countess Judith (of Huntingdon), the Conqueror's niece, granted the nuns the vill of Hitchin and the chapel of Wymondley in Hertfordshire, 'in which charter is contained the grant and confirmation of King William the Conqueror

---

[124] Above n. 61.

[125] Vincent, 'Tales of the Conquest', 297, and cf. *Book of Fees*, i. 90 (with references to tenure 'de antiquo tempore regum Anglorum ante conquestum Normannorum' or 'de antiquo fefemento regum Anglorum'), 92 ('Abbas de Hyda Wintonie tenet Pidele Trentehydes in pura elemosina ad vestiendum monachos suos de dono regum Anglorum', referring to Piddletrenthide, listed in Domesday as a Hyde abbey manor from before 1066).

[126] As noted by Crick, '"Pristina libertas"', 53, and cf. p. 57.

[127] *CRR*, xi, no. 704 (*RRAN* i, no. 431 (lxxvi) from another source); *The 1258–9 Special eyre of Surrey and Kent*, ed. A.H. Hershey (Surrey Record Society xxxviii, 2004), nos 292, 351 (*RRAN* i, nos 62, 336, whence Bates, *Acta of William I*, no. 22, not noting this source); *Placita de quo warranto*, 702 (*RRAN* i, no. 194; Bates, *Acta of William I*, no. 160, not noting this source).

and the assent of William his son'.¹²⁸ Likewise, before the Bench in the Michaelmas term of 1232, the abbot of La Croix-St-Leuffroy (Eure, cant. Gaillon) produced a charter of King William granting the abbey seven hides and three virgates of land in the manor of Esher. Since this land appears in Domesday as the abbey's possession, the charter can be assumed to have been issued by William I rather than by William Rufus.¹²⁹ Neither of these charters, for Elstow or for La Croix-St-Leuffroy, appears in the standard modern edition of the Conqueror's acts.

In other instances, the court records abstract charters that are known and that are preserved elsewhere in much fuller form. Even here, however, our plea roll evidence is not without significance. It can on occasion provide us with a *terminus a quo*, offering us our earliest datable proof that a particular charter was in circulation. For example, there is today no surviving copy of William I's grant of Hayling Island to the monks of Jumièges earlier than the sixteenth century. Yet the charter itself was produced before the justices of King Henry III as early as 1242.¹³⁰ In other instances, the court record may supply information significant for the archival history of a particular charter. Thus, in 1204, the justices of King John were shown a charter of William I to the monks of Hyde

---

¹²⁸ *Rotuli curiae regis*, i. 391–2, from PRO/TNA KB 26/11 (Bench plea roll Trinity 1 John) m. 24 (22), briefly noted in *Placitorum in domo capitulari Westmonasteriensi asservatorum abbreviatio*, ed. W. Illingworth, London 1811, 8: 'Judith comitissa neptis reg(is) Will(elm)i conquestoris qui fundau(it) abbatiam de Aluestow' ded(it) ecclesie de Alnestow' villam de Hicch' cum ecclesia eiusdem ville et cum capella de Wim'dele que pertinet ad ecclesiam de Hich' per cartam suam quam protulit et que testatur quod ita ded(it) eam in liberam et perpetuam elemosinam, in qua etiam carta continetur concessio et confirmatio reg(is) Will(elm)i conquestoris in(de) et assensus Will(elm)i fil(ii) predicti reg(is)'. Duly noted in the account of the abbey given in *VCH Bedfordshire*, i. 353n., and cf. *VCH Hertfordshire*, iii. 7; *RRAN* ii, no. 1654; *Monasticon*, iii. 413–14; *Letters and charters of Henry II*, ed. Vincent, no. 820, where, *c*.1156, Henry II confirmed to the abbey 'ex dono regis Willelmi ecclesiam de Hiccha et totam terram presbiteri, scilicet duas hidas terre et i. virgatam cum omnibus decimis et consuetudinibus eidem ecclesie pertin(entibus) et nominatim ecclesiam suam de Westona' (i.e. Westoning, Bedfordshire, cf. *VCH Bedfordshire*, iii. 454).

¹²⁹ *Curia regis rolls*, xiv, no. 2013, from PRO/TNA KB 26/111 (Bench plea roll Michaelmas 16–17 Henry III) m.2d, also in KB 26/110 (Ibid.) m.4: 'abbas ... dicit quod non debet ei respondere quia tenet manerium de Esser' cum pertinentiis de dono regis Willelmi antecessoris domini reg(is) per cartam suam quam profert et que testatur quod idem dominus W(illelmus) dedit Deo et ecclesie sancti Leofridi de Cruce vii. hidas et tres virgat(as) terre in manerio de Esshour in perpetuam elemosinam. Profert etiam cartam reg(is) Henr(ici) proaui que testatur quod confirmat ei predictam terram in perpetuam elemosinam' (itself an addition to the charters of Henry I as recorded in *RRAN* ii) and, for the context, see *VCH Surrey*, iii. 448; *Book of Fees*, ii. 1363; *The 1235 Surrey eyre*, ed. C.A.F. Meekings and D. Crook (Surrey Record Society xxxi–xxxii, xxxvii, 1979–2002), ii. 418 nos 509, 552–3.

¹³⁰ *Curia regis rolls*, xvii, no. 1087, citing *RRAN* i, 21; Bates, *Acta of William I*, no. 159.

abbey in Winchester apparently from the same book, the *Liber vitae* of Hyde (now BL Stowe 944), from which it has been printed in modern times. In 1204 the accompanying sign of the cross was specifically advertised as the Conqueror's sign manual.[131] In the case of charters of both Edward the Confessor and William I for the monks of St Peter's at Ghent, the most recent edition of the William I charter being printed from an early-fourteenth-century copy, it is surely of significance, if only for the charters' documentary history, that both were cited in court in a *Quo warranto* plea of 1321 and that both were already known to the scribes who drafted Henry II's confirmation of the privileges of the monks of Ghent, as early as the 1150s.[132]

In such instances, the company kept by early charters, and the uses to which they were put in the King's courts, can be of assistance in establishing what are often their disputed claims to authenticity. This leads to a post-Conquest conundrum of no small significance. One of the most astonishing documentary discoveries made by the no less astonishing J.H. Round was the so-called 'Evesham writ': a letter of William I, commanding Abbot Aethelwig of Evesham to attend the king at Clarendon with the five knights his abbey owed in service. As trumpeted by Round, and assigned to 1072, the 'Evesham writ' was an essential building block in Round's history of the 'Introduction of knight service to England', and hence in his much broader assessment of the 'feudal' revolution effected after 1066.[133] The writ itself was found by Round in its sole surviving copy in an Evesham cartulary, itself written in a variety of late-twelfth- or early-thirteenth-century hands, now incomplete, with the original foliation and contents seriously disordered and disturbed.[134] Its authenticity has several times been questioned. Some have been puzzled by its nomination of Clarendon as a place of muster for a campaign directed against the Scots, others by the language of a writ that seems to correspond more with twelfth- than with eleventh-century expectations.[135]

---

[131] *Curia regis rolls*, iii. 118–19, citing and specifically noting the sign manual cross ('et profert quendam librum in quo carta predicti Willelmi notatur cum quodam singno crucis quod idem rex Willelmus, ut abbas dicit, propria manu scripsit') of *RRAN* i, no. 37; Bates, *Acta of William I*, no. 344.

[132] *Placita de quo Warranto*, 462–3, citing *RRAN* i, no. 141; Bates, *Acta of William I*, no. 150, and cf. *Letters and charters of Henry II*, ed. Vincent, no. 1117; *Rotuli chartarum*, 184.

[133] J.H. Round, 'The introduction of knight service into England', in Round, *Feudal England*, London 1909, 304.

[134] BL Cotton Vespasian B. xxiv, fo. 18r (15r), also including the so-called 'Evesham surveys', for which see *Domesday Book: Worcestershire*, Chichester 1982, appendix 4.

[135] Bates, *Acta of William I*, no. 131, rehearsing various of these objections, but opting for a delicate balancing act in which the authenticity of the writ is neither accepted nor denied. Other modern commentators, for whom the writ remains of supreme significance, allow even less room for doubt. For example, see Garnett, *Conquered England*, 58.

In the present context, it is surely crucial that we note Evesham's status as one of the most litigious and also the most mendacious Benedictine houses of northern Europe. Into the 1230s there is little doubt that the monks of Evesham were forging both royal and papal charters, including a writ of King William II incorporated into the same cartulary in which William I's 'Evesham writ' is preserved.[136] I would suggest that the William I writ can only be appreciated within a twelfth- or thirteenth-century context, manufactured as part of the ongoing dispute over Evesham's military obligations that led, after 1166, to a reduction in the abbey's 'servicium debitum' from the five knights' fees charged before that date to the four and a half knights' fees demanded thereafter. This in turn may have led to the forgery of letters of Henry I, first recorded in an inspeximus by Henry III issued in 1241 (at a time when the abbot of Evesham was serving in effect as royal chancellor), granting extensive liberties including exemption from scutage save for the abbey's service of four and a half knights' fees 'in expeditione me presente', itself an unparalleled restriction to body service to Henry I, with the explicit reference to scutage being likewise unparalleled so early in the twelfth century.[137] In 1241, it might be noted, Henry III was about to embark for a continental expedition, to Gascony, that might or might not be expected to involve his bodily leadership of all parts of the army but that certainly led to the imposition of a scutage and other extensive fiscal liabilities.[138] The Evesham cartulary, Cotton Vespasian B. xxiv, is itself testimony to the mastery acquired by Evesham's monks over their documentary past, written in a series of self-consciously archaised hands that

---

[136] J. Sayers, '"Original", cartulary and chronicle: the case of the abbey of Evesham', *Fälschungen im Mittelalter* (MGH Schriften xxxiii, 1988), iv. 371–95, esp. 379 for the William II writ, *RRAN* i, no. 429, printed in *Monasticon*, ii. 18 no. 9.

[137] *RRAN* ii, no. 831, first recorded in an inspeximus by Henry III, 3 March 1241: *Calendar of Charter Rolls 1226–57*, 257–8, with the original inspeximus of 1241 now surviving as London, College of Arms MS Charters 182. For confirmation that the charter is a forgery, as declared both by its language and its diplomatic, I am indebted to Richard Sharpe. For the abbot of Evesham's involvement in the affairs of the royal chancery in 1241–42, see T. F. Tout, *Chapters in the administrative history of mediaeval England*, Manchester 1920–33, vi. 4; *Liber memorandorum ecclesie de Bernewelle*, ed. J.W. Clark, Cambridge 1907, 78–9; *Calendar of patent rolls 1232–47*, 330; *Close rolls of the reign of Henry III 1237–42*, 519. A charter of Henry III issued at Portsmouth on 7 May 1242, addressed to the barons of the Exchequer and granting the abbot of Evesham and his successors the right to collect all monies elsewhere paid to sheriffs for aids, view of frankpledge and other levies, in effect freeing the abbey's lands from accounting via the sheriff, is described by its modern editors as a forgery when first reported in an inspeximus of 1329: *Calendar of charter rolls 1327–41*, p. xi and 151. In reality, it is almost certainly an authentic charter whose opening clauses appear at the now mutilated end of the Charter Roll 26 Henry III: *Calendar of charter rolls 1226–57*, 275.

[138] S.K. Mitchell, *Studies in taxation under John and Henry III*, New Haven 1914, 222–39, and in general for the extraordinary financial demands of these years, see R.C. Stacey, *Politics, policy and finance under Henry III, 1216–1245*, Oxford 1987.

might lead the unwary to suppose a much earlier date of composition than its true date somewhere in the period after 1200.

In this instance, as in many others, establishing the first date at which early evidences were in circulation and, above all, establishing the company that such documents keep, can be crucial in establishing their *bona fides* (or more often their lack of such). That the company kept by the Evesham writ is especially disreputable should perhaps not be surprising for an abbey whose treatment of historical evidence was elsewhere so cavalier. However dear to its discoverer, J.H. Round, the 'Evesham writ' is probably best regarded as a confection of the mid-to late twelfth century, related to the disputes over 'servicium debitum' aired in 1166, themselves perhaps associated with the extension of claims to scutage under Henry II, after 1159. As such, it may tell us less about the 'Introduction of knight service' than about that equally significant post-Conquest (though still little-understood) phenomenon, the 'Introduction of scutage'.[139]

Scutage and the charters of William the Conqueror carry us rather further from the Anglo-Saxon past than the remit of this chapter allows. Nonetheless, to the extent that they too demonstrate events of the eleventh century being transformed in the understanding of twelfth- and thirteenth-century royal officials from private memory into public 'history', they are none the less relevant to our pursuit of the processes by which the charters of Anglo-Saxon England were filtered into English law via the confirmations, inspeximuses and other public recitals issued from the 1150s onwards. I hope that I have cited sufficient evidence here to suggest that not only was the Norman Conquest widely accepted as a legally significant *caesura* in English history, but that from the 1150s through to the fourteenth century, litigants and kings trod warily in their acceptance or citation of pre-Conquest evidence in English courts of law. By the 1150s what had once been the ready adoption by Norman kings of Anglo-Saxon administrative processes yielded place to scepticism and a reluctance to accept untested testimony from a period now viewed as a historical rather than an immediate past. Henry II was the last English king to issue a bilingual charter, like William the Conqueror and others before him, confirming the privileges of the monks of Canterbury both in Latin and what had now become not so much Old as Middle English.[140] He was also the first English king, in his dealings with

---

[139] For various reflections here, pending a more detailed study, see N. Vincent, *A brief history of Britain, 1066–1485*, London 2011, 80–81.

[140] D.A.E. Pelteret, *Catalogue of English post-Conquest vernacular documents*, Woodbridge 1990, 77–8 no. 51, 80–81 no. 54; *Letters and charters of Henry II*, ed. Vincent, nos 440, 465. Pelteret, *Catalogue*, 79–80 nos 52–3, 81–2 no. 55, charters of Henry II for Rochester (*Letters and charters of Henry II*, ed. Vincent, nos 2225–6) are not truly bilingual charters, and contain only brief lists of liberties in English.

St Albans, known to have baulked at a request that he authenticate or accept the written evidence preserved in charters of the Old English kings.[141]

As a result of such sceptical reluctance, from the 1150s onwards, relatively few Anglo-Saxon charters were ever pleaded in the King's courts. Through to the fourteenth century, surprisingly few Anglo-Saxon charters were presented for confirmation or copying either in the royal chancery or at the Exchequer. This in turn raises significant questions about their preservation in monastic archives. Given that so few of these documents were ever cited before twelfth- or thirteenth-century law courts, as title deeds or as warranty, why should the twelfth century be regarded as the golden age for forgery of Anglo-Saxon charters? Why, given their slim chances of acceptance as legal evidence, did such charters continue to be preserved, 'improved' or copied, as they were so often copied, into monastic cartularies? Perhaps we need to tread with greater caution here and shun the lawyerly insistence that evidence either be acceptable or unacceptable, true or false. Not every child is entirely a little Liberal or else a little Conservative, just as in the twelfth century it was accepted that the best stories, even the best histories (witness Geoffrey of Monmouth), need not be absolutely true. Writing of King Arthur, Wace himself had declared that the stories of Arthur were not to be disregarded just because fact had become intermixed with fable: 'Not all lies, not all truth, neither total folly nor utter wisdom'.[142]

On occasion in the twelfth and thirteenth centuries the King's courts were prepared to grant a hearing to Anglo-Saxon charters, sometimes even to charters written in the Anglo-Saxon vernacular, albeit that such charters were generally considered to date from before the dawn of what was acceptable legal memory. In general and in theory, laymen were not allowed to plead possession from before 1066 as warranty for present possession, so that, from the 1150s onwards, only Anglo-Saxon charters for monasteries or churches obtained confirmation from English kings. Charters of Edward the Confessor were more frequently pleaded than charters of any earlier ruler. Even so, the occasional layman, James of Oakhanger in the 1230s or the men of Malmesbury a century later, could persuade the king to confirm their liberties based on grants by Edward the Confessor or other Anglo-Saxon kings, even on the basis of Anglo-Saxon charters that were very crudely forged. 'Liberty', although first used in Anglo-Saxon diplomas as a deliberate negation of the enhanced 'dominium' claimed by various Anglo-Saxon kings, was by no means entirely written out of the record of the Anglo-Saxon past. Thus Henry II might aspire to the 'dominium'

---

[141] Above n. 87.
[142] Wace, *Brut*, pp. xxi, 246–7 vv. 9791–4: 'Ne tut mençunge, ne tut veit, ne tut folie ne tut saveir'.

exercised by King Arthur yet recognise the 'libertates' claimed in charters of Offa or Edward the Confessor.

In these circumstances, it made perfect sense for archivists and cartulary-makers to preserve and where necessary to 'improve' their Anglo-Saxon writs and diplomas, not just as keepsakes or proofs of antiquity but as potential hostages against an uncertain future. Had they not done so, and were we instead reliant upon only those charters pleaded in the King's courts, nine-tenths of such charters would long ago have vanished without trace. The willingness of twelfth-century monks to 'improve' their ancient charters tells us a great deal of the need felt by ecclesiastical corporations to arm themselves with defences against an increasingly predatory and aggressive royal power.[143] In much this same way, it was by improving or inventing their earliest papal letters that communities such as St Augustine's or Christ Church Canterbury, St Albans and Evesham had successfully prosecuted their claims to immunity before ecclesiastical and in certain cases royal courts. Where a bull of Constantine I or Leo III could come in handy 500 years after its supposed date of issue, so potentially might a charter of Offa or a writ of Aethelred.[144] Had this not been the case, or had the post-Conquest kings of England rejected, as the legal historians are inclined to suggest that they most certainly should have rejected, all claims based on circumstances or evidence earlier than 1066, then we would be deprived of much of what we know of the Anglo-Saxon past. We would also have forfeited at least something of our understanding of the distinctly crooked timbers both of history and of humanity.

---

[143] Crick, "Pristina libertas", 52, 57, citing Patrick Wormald, 'Frederic William Maitland and the earliest English law', *Law and History Review* xvi (1998), 1–25, repr. in P. Wormald, *Legal culture in the early medieval West: law as text, image and experience*, London 1999, 45–69, at 51: 'The manufacture of so many fraudulently ancient liberties implies that something in the post-conquest climate was creating a new demand for them.'

[144] For examples of early papal letters preserved in monastic cartularies or employed in litigation, see Thomas of Marlborough, *History of the abbey of Evesham*, ed. J. Sayers and L. Watkiss, Oxford 2003, 314–21; *Papsturkunden in England*, ed. W. Holtzmann, Abhandlungen der Gesellschaft der Wissenschaften zu Göttingen, Philologisch-historische Klasse, neue Folge 25 (1930–31), 3. Folge 14–15 (1935–6) and 33 (1952), iii. 124–8 nos 1–3; E. John, 'The litigation of an exempt house, St Augustine's Canterbury, 1182–1237', *Bulletin of the John Rylands Library* xxxix (1957), 390–415; R.W. Southern, 'The Canterbury forgeries', *EHR* lxxiii (1958), 193–226.

Chapter 12

Pre-Conquest Laws and Legislators in the Twelfth Century*

Bruce O'Brien

The early twelfth century has received a good deal of attention from English legal historians because the texts and manuscript copies of Anglo-Saxon law codes produced before *c*.1125 can be used as evidence both for pre-Conquest law and for the impact of the Norman Conquest on English law. The late twelfth century is conversely a neglected period in the history of Anglo-Saxon law codes, despite the large number of Latin, Anglo-French and English texts created or copied between *c*.1150 and *c*.1200 which claim or were thought to represent the law in England before 1066. There are cogent reasons for this neglect. Scholars looking for records to show the consequences of the Conquest on law would say that they did not need to look beyond the evidence provided by the retrospective and present-minded creations of the post-Conquest period to c. 1150, and certainly not at the later copies of these same sources, except when these were needed to produce editions. Those interested in the developing law of the late twelfth century would aver that they were interested in texts that were statements of contemporary law, and especially texts of Henry II's assizes, the treatise known as *Glanvill*, charters, and fiscal and judicial rolls, which allowed them to study the stages of the careful crafting of the new system known to us as the common law. The later-twelfth-century copies of Anglo-Saxon laws satisfy neither interest. They appear to be late and derivative memorials of pre-Conquest law and self-evidently disengaged from contemporary legal developments. It is not an unreasonable conclusion that these late copies would not provide useful evidence of late-twelfth-century law.

Because such copies do fall outside the ambit of Anglo-Saxon legal historians, and are in fact for the most part merely derivative of texts created earlier in the twelfth century, their failure to find a place among the sources of those studying pre-Conquest law is understandable. The neglect from scholars of the early common law, however, arises from their anachronistic approach to law. Many legal historians of the common law have been all too ready to repeat *Glanvill*'s tendentious remark that, before his day, England's laws were unwritten.[1] With

---

* I would like to thank Julia Crick and the editors for their many comments on the whole piece; Michael Gullick and Tessa Webber for advice concerning the principal manuscript

such an authoritative judgement from the author of the first manual of the common law, as well as with the growing body of late-twelfth-century evidence for the actual application of this law, few have been willing to turn their gaze aside from these sources to look at the books of Anglo-Saxon law which were being produced and read in the 1170s, 1180s and 1190s.[2]

The mistake here is not that historians have concluded that these later copies of Anglo-Saxon law do not represent the realities of late-twelfth-century law, but rather that they assume that twelfth-century *thinking* about law can only be found in texts that appear to report the black-letter law of the day. These later Anglo-Saxon lawbooks, however, arose in *Glanvill*'s world. They were part of the thought, discussions and practices of those interested in the law, and were collected and read by some of the same individuals who collected and read *Glanvill* and the assizes. For that reason, scholars should be as interested in explaining the cultural products these Latin, Anglo-French and English lawbooks constitute as in understanding innovative English legal practices. It is worth asking, then, about more than any source's status as a contemporary legal authority, because memory of law's past was a significant dimension of late twelfth-century political debates about law, especially during and after the conflict between Thomas Becket and Henry II. The Anglo-Saxon lawbooks produced during this time are testaments to that memory of law, but testaments whose uneasy confluence with, and distance from, contemporary law as practised has suggested to scholars a treacherous memory at best. Nevertheless, these books attracted the attention of many patrons, compilers, writers, editors scribes, and readers in the second half of the twelfth century. Understanding why has the potential to help us describe in greater detail the actual culture out of which the common law came.

Another aspect of law's past and present on which they shed light is the languages of law, and, in particular, the role of English as a language of written law under the Angevin kings. We should take it as given, despite fairly modest

---

used for this study; Peter Stokes both for advice on its script and for copies of forthcoming work; John Blair for comments on burial rights; and Richard Sharpe for sharing with me his unpublished edition of the charters of Henry I. Abbreviations for all law codes are those used by the Early English Laws project and are listed online at www.earlyenglishlaws.ac.uk.

[1] *Treatise on the laws and customs of the realm of England commonly called Glanvill*, ed. G.D.G. Hall, with a guide to further reading by M.T. Clanchy, Oxford 1993, prologue, p. 2; for the falsity of Glanvill's remark, see B.R. O'Brien, 'The Becket conflict and the invention of the myth of lex non scripta', in J.A. Bush and A. Wijffels (eds), *Learning the law: teaching and the transmission of law in England, 1150–1900*, London 1999, 12–14.

[2] D.M. Stenton, *English justice between the Norman Conquest and the Great Charter*, Philadelphia 1964, 22–53; T.F.T. Plucknett, *Early English legal literature*, Cambridge 1958; J. Hudson, *The formation of the English common law: law and society in England from the Norman Conquest to Magna Carta*, London 1996, 151–5.

evidence, that written English was still a language used by a select group of people for some tasks – though none of these tasks was exclusive to English.[3] Homilies, liturgical books, translations of the Bible and glosses, for instance, all show the important place held by vernacular texts and collections alongside the growing volume of Latin and French texts. One class of evidence of written English not investigated yet are the English terms, phrases and sayings found embedded in many of the Latin law codes composed and copied after the Conquest.[4] Yet such a deployment of English has much to tell us about the authority of English as a language of the law. Further, in perhaps no genre of twelfth-century literature are all three major written languages – Latin, Anglo-French and English – as intertwined as they are in legal texts. Understanding, then, how twelfth-century writers and readers viewed Anglo-Saxon law and legislators has the ability to tell us about more than the evolving status of older written law. It can also help chart the changing and variable authority of law's written languages.[5] It adds a new dimension to current discussions of how English writings of any shape or size were valued and used at the very end of the century.

What then do the surviving manuscripts holding Anglo-Saxon law tell us about their late-twelfth-century writers, editors, and readers during the age of Angevin legal reforms? This chapter will identify evolving trends in the creation and copying of Anglo-Saxon laws throughout the twelfth century. It will then turn to the origins, shape, contents and languages of one particular lawbook, probably an exact contemporary of *Glanvill*, to see what it reveals about late-twelfth-century views of the Anglo-Saxon legal past, as well as what it can tell us about some widespread but curious ideas about law and its languages during a time when a good deal of careful thought was going into law's development. One clear conclusion is that the thinking about law behind *Glanvill* was a minority position in the late twelfth century, and that law's past then, regardless of its language, was still in some respects very much a part of law's present.

Let me begin by acknowledging that books of Anglo-Saxon laws in the late twelfth century, regardless of their language, are historical artefacts. These books are filled with texts of proscriptive law which are all or in part explicitly labelled as laws promulgated before or immediately after the Conquest. They were not intended to be principally records of law as practised or as experienced at the time of their copying, but instead are self-consciously constructed remembrances of the law. Both Latin and Anglo-French texts of this law are

---

[3] M. Faulkner, 'Rewriting English literary history, 1042–1215', *Literature Compass* ix (2012), 275–91.

[4] This class of English text is not covered by O. Da Rold, T. Kato, M. Swan and E. Treharne (eds), *The production and use of English manuscripts, 1060 to 1220*, University of Leicester 2010, available at http://www.le.ac.uk/ee/em1060to1220.

[5] B.R. O'Brien, *Reversing Babel: translation among the English during an age of conquest, c.800 to c.1200*, Newark, DE 2011, 211–21, with citations to earlier literature.

speckled with English words and phrases which evoke law's former vernacular, a language no longer being used as a vehicle for new legal compositions and whose older monuments were no longer even being copied. These legal texts are in one sense old, recording the desires and commands of kings long dead by 1100. But these texts were, for the most part, living artefacts rather than museum pieces dug fresh from the ground after a thousand-year slumber. They are monuments of the past whose every copying provided an opportunity to rewrite, reorder and recombine them – in a sense to revivify them.

The twelfth century as a whole has left more Anglo-Saxon lawbooks than all previous centuries combined. Excluding pontificals holding only ordeal manuals, excommunication formulas and coronation oaths, there are seventeen surviving twelfth-century manuscripts holding one or more texts that identified themselves as Anglo-Saxon law codes.[6] For the period before 1100, there are fifteen manuscripts of this pre-Conquest law which are either extant or well attested, even if now lost.[7] The number of manuscripts copied after 1100 is persuasive testimony to the long afterlife of interest in Anglo-Saxon law. Of course, the lesser number of earlier manuscripts may be a trick of survival. It does seem likely that there were more copies of laws around in *c.*950 or *c.*1025 than have in fact survived; how many more, however, can only be guessed.[8] But

---

[6] The extant MSS (hereinafter cited by sigla) are: BL Harley 55 (A); BL MS Add. 24066 (Ad); CCCC MS 383 (B); BnF, lat. 10185 (Ba); BnF, lat. 4771 (Cb); Bodl. Lib., MS Digby 13 (Di); BL Cotton Domitian viii (Dm); Medway Archives and Local Studies Centre, Strood, MS DRc/R1 (H); BL MS Add. 49366 (Hk); BL Royal 14. C. ii (Hv); Lambeth Palace Library, MS 118 (La), Lambeth Palace Library, MS 179 (Lb); The Law Society, London, MS 1 (Ls); John Rylands University Library, Manchester, MS Lat. 420 (M); BL Royal 11. B. ii (R); Bodl. Lib., MS Rawlinson C 641 (Rl); BL Cotton Titus A. xxvii (T). Images of the folios in these manuscripts holding legal texts are available online at http://www.earlyenglishlaws.ac.uk/laws/manuscripts/.

[7] The early manuscripts are listed in P. Wormald, *The making of English law: King Alfred to the twelfth century*, i. *Legislation and its limits*, Oxford 1999, 164–5. The total includes manuscripts (e.g., BL Cotton Otho A. x) which once existed, but are no longer extant and are of uncertain date.

[8] This is one of the implications of S. Keynes, 'Royal government and the written word in late Anglo-Saxon England', in R. McKitterick (ed.), *The uses of literacy in early medieval Europe*, Cambridge 1990, 232–44, D. Pratt, 'Written law and the communication of authority in tenth-century England', in D.W. Rollason and others (eds), *England and the Continent in the tenth century*, Turnhout 2010, 331–50, and S. Foot, *Æthelstan: the first king of England*, New Haven and London 2011, 138. A few of the manuscripts in Wormald's list survived by the slightest margin (for example, *Making of English law*, 256–62). How many did not? Some guessing could be done by studying the development of individual texts, and thus being at times in a position to justify the existence of hyparchetypes; this method, however, is not practised much these days by those who edit Old English texts. A welcome exception is Keynes, 'Royal government', 232.

even if earlier manuscripts suffered greater losses over time, the later ones at least demonstrate a strong and continuous desire throughout the twelfth century for records of the laws of pre-Conquest kings.

Interest in these records was not indiscriminately directed toward any pre-Conquest rulers, but was concentrated on the laws of two Anglo-Saxon kings, Cnut (1016–35) and Edward the Confessor (1042–66).[9] This narrower interest in the laws of these two kings rather than on the products of the entire roster of five centuries of Anglo-Saxon lawgivers was present, though not exclusive, at the beginning of the twelfth century, and this interest sharpened with each passing decade. Cnut's laws were the most important at the beginning of the twelfth century. Two of three legal encyclopedias composed in the early part of the century put Cnut's Winchester code at the head of their collections. *Quadripartitus*, whose first book, completed possibly before 1100, comes close to being a Latin translation of the laws of all pre-Conquest kings, begins not with its oldest code, Alfred's *Domboc*, but with Cnut's code.[10] *Textus Roffensis*, an equally comprehensive collection of Anglo-Saxon laws, mostly in their original languages, began with Cnut's, but in a Latin translation rather than the original Old English version.[11] This Latin version, known now as the *Instituta Cnuti*, was itself composed in the late eleventh or early twelfth centuries, and combines a number of legal sources, including Cnut's Winchester code, in a new text which travelled under Cnut's name. Like the *Instituta*, the *Consiliatio Cnuti*, created in the early decades of the twelfth century, holds a translation of the Winchester code to which have been joined several other pre-Conquest works, the whole of which is attributed to Cnut.[12] Instead of representing merely a soon-to-fade burst of interest in Cnut during the immediate post-Conquest period, these texts proved instead to be just the start of an upward trend in the copying of Cnut's laws. They provided the materials for an increasing multiplication of his laws which reached its crescendo in the final decades of the twelfth and the

---

[9] Laws attributed to Edward the Confessor are always recorded as if in a form confirmed by William I (1066–87).

[10] F. Liebermann, Quadripartitus: *ein englisches Rechtsbuch von 1114*, Halle 1892, 89–90 (hereinafter the law code will be cited as Quadr.); P. Wormald, 'Quadripartitus', in G. Garnett and J. Hudson (eds), *Law and government in medieval England and Normandy: essays in honour of Sir James Holt*, Cambridge 1994, 111–47. For the date of the translations, see R. Sharpe, 'The dating of *Quadripartitus* again', in S. Jurasinski, L. Oliver and A. Rabin (eds), *English law before Magna Carta: Felix Liebermann and 'Die Gesetze der Angelsachsen'*, Leiden 2010, 81–93, at 91. Alfred's *Domboc* follows immediately after I–II Cnut.

[11] *Textus Roffensis: Rochester cathedral library manuscript A. 3. 5*, ed. P. Sawyer, Copenhagen 1957, 11–12. A new edition of the *Instituta Cnuti* will appear in 2014 at www.earlyenglishlaws.ac.uk

[12] F. Liebermann, Consiliatio Cnuti*, eine Übertragung angelsächsischer Gesetze aus dem zwölften Jahrhundert*, Halle 1893, pp. v, 2–25.

beginning of the thirteenth centuries. By then, at least twenty-two copies of Cnut's laws in some Old English or Latin version had been created, of which sixteen are still extant.[13]

While references to the pre-Conquest laws in force under Edward the Confessor appear soon after the Conquest, interest in recording the actual contents of Edward the Confessor's laws began somewhat later than Cnut's, only appearing for the first time in the 1130s or 1140s with the composition of the *Leges Edwardi Confessoris* and *Leis Willelme*.[14] The *Leges Edwardi* claims to record the laws English nobles recited for William I at an assembly in 1070, but in reality represents an anonymous description of local customs dating probably from the late 1130s.[15] The *Leis Willelme* also pretends to be a record of the laws of Edward the Confessor as affirmed by the Conqueror, but is likewise a privately composed and unofficial collection of customs.[16] By 1200, however, these two works had been enriched and reworked by revisers, compilers and translators into eight distinguishable texts or versions of texts which continued to attribute the foundation of their laws to King Edward, with a ninth, the grandest of the lot, appearing in the first decade of the thirteenth century, imbedded within a chronological presentation of English royal laws from Ine on.[17] These nine versions themselves survive in twelve extant

---

[13] MSS A, B, Ba, Cb, Di, Dm, H, Hk, La, Lb, M, R, Rl and T. There are good reasons for including BL Cotton Nero A. i (MS G) in this list, as it is just as likely from after as before the Conquest: see Wormald, *Making of English law*, 224–8, and H. Gneuss, *Handlist of Anglo-Saxon manuscripts: a list of manuscripts and manuscript fragments written or owned in England up to 1100*, Tempe, AZ 2001, 64. I am also including John Rylands University Library, Manchester, MS Lat. 155 (MS Rs), which was copied in the first decade of the thirteenth century. The additional five copies of Cnut's laws represent the bare minimum count of no longer extant hyparchetypes, archetypes and autographs. For a stemma of the *Instituta Cnuti* (hereinafter cited as In Cn), see B.R. O'Brien, 'The *Instituta Cnuti* and the translation of English law', *ANS* xxv (2003), 177–97. For stemmata of the Old English text (hereinafter I–II Cn) and the *Consiliatio Cnuti* (hereinafter Cons Cn), see (with some reservation) *Die Gesetze der Angelsachsen*, ed. F. Liebermann, Halle 1903–16, iii. 193 and 333.

[14] The *Articuli Willelmi* (hereinafter Wl art.), which probably was composed or assembled in the late eleventh century, is attributed solely to William the Conqueror and appears to include an actual edict of that king. Although its contents are aimed at the immediate post-Conquest situation, it nevertheless does affirm the *lex Eadwardi*, for which see *Gesetze der Angelsachsen*, i. 488 (Wl art 7). In its early life this text appears as an appendix to the *Instituta Cnuti*, while in the second half of the twelfth century it also begins to accompany the *Leges Edwardi Confessoris*.

[15] B.R. O'Brien, *God's peace and king's peace: the laws of Edward the Confessor*, Philadelphia 1999, 31–48.

[16] Wormald, *Making of English law*, 407–9.

[17] The nine versions arising from the *Leges Edwardi Confessoris* (hereinafter ECf) and *Leis Willelme* (hereinafter Leis Wl) consist of four versions of ECf (ECf1, the 34-chapter text; ECf2, the 39-chapter text; ECf3, a revised version of ECf2 which Liebermann labelled

copies, and provide good evidence for an additional twelve copies consisting of autographs, archetypes or hyparchetypes.[18]

Only two post-Conquest writers saw a connection between the law-making of Cnut and of Edward, although each writer has a different explanation for this phenomenon. One, the author of *Quadripartitus*, tells us that the *laga Edwardi* often confirmed by Anglo-Norman kings meant, in practice, Cnut's laws. *Quadripartitus*' author begins the *Argumentum*, or preface, of his work with the statement that he is providing 'the laws that go by King Edward's name, derived from the institutes of Cnut in the first place, as we received them from our ancestors'.[19] More than that, the author tells us how Cnut came to issue his laws at an assembly of all the leading men of England and Denmark 'in order to suppress vices and increase virtues', and that these laws were what Edward later had to swear an oath to maintain before the thegns of England would make him their king.[20] That Edward was not legislating, but maintaining the laws of his predecessors is found not only in *Quadripartitus*, but also in William of Malmesbury's account of Cnut's laws. In the *Gesta regum Anglie*, William tells us that Cnut commanded that all the laws of ancient kings, especially those of Æthelred, should be observed. William links Cnut's command to a practice current in William's own time, when 'for the observance of these laws ... an oath is taken in the name of King Edward, not because he established them, but because he kept them'.[21] In William's *Gesta regum*, in fact, neither Cnut nor Edward is

---

the *Retractatio*; ECf4, a revision and enlargement of ECf3, appearing only in copies of the collection known as the London *Leges Anglorum*, the earliest of which, MS Rs, is from the first decade of the thirteenth century); ECf Hk, a hybrid text combining ECf2 and some of Cons Cn, called by me the Holkham *Leges Edwardi*; ECf3 Fr, an Anglo-French translation of ECf3 entitled *Le livre des leis de Engletere*; two Anglo-French versions of the *Leis Willelme* (a 28-chapter text and a 52-chapter text); and the *Leges Willelmi* (Leges Wl), a Latin translation of the long version of Leis Wl. For the stemma of ECf1, ECf2, with reference to that of ECf3, see O'Brien, *God's peace*, 109 and 138. For the stemma of Leis Wl, see *Gesetze der Angelsachsen*, iii. 284. Editions of ECf1 and ECf2 are available at www.earlyenglishlaws.ac.uk

[18] The extant manuscripts are: Ad, Ba, Cb, Hk, I Iv, La, Lb, Ls, Rl, Rs; BL Harley 746 (s.xiii ex./xiv in., for Leges Wl), and Cambridge, University Library, MS Ee. 1. 1 (1280–89, for ECf3 Fr).

[19] 'Leges quas dicunt Eadwardi regis ex Cnudi primum institutione diductas esse, sicut ab antiquis accepimus': Quadr, Argumentum 1, in Liebermann, *Quadripartitus*, 83; translation (as above) by R. Sharpe, 'The prefaces of *Quadripartitus*', in G. Garnett and J. Hudson (eds), *Law and government in medieval England and Normandy*, Cambridge 1994, 148–72, 162–3.

[20] Quadr, Argumentum 2–9, in Liebermann, *Quadripartitus*, 83–5. J. Maddicott, 'Edward the Confessor's return to England in 1041', *EHR* cxxii (2004), 650–66, argues that Quadr's account of Edward's affirmation of the law at his accession should be accepted.

[21] '... in quarum custodiam ... sub nomine regis Eduardi iuratur, non quod ille statuerit sed quod obseruarit': Malmesbury, *GR* i. 328–30 (bk ii. 183. 9).

much of a legislator.[22] Other twelfth-century narrative works, however, often give law-making credit to either Cnut or to Edward, and therefore allege no law-making or law-maintaining relationship between the two kings.[23] They merely parallel what is found in individual codes and lawbooks, where either Cnut's or Edward's laws are the basis for English law, the *laga Edwardi*, after 1066.

Affirmations by Norman kings of this *laga Edwardi* must in part be the explanation for the production of these texts in the seventy-five years after 1066. The well-known and probably official confirmation of the *laga Edwardi* by William I found in the brief collection entitled *Articuli decem* or *Decreta Willelmi* is matched by what he promised in some writs and charters.[24] These affirmations were followed in 1100 by Henry I's coronation edict's restoration of 'the law of King Edward along with changes by which my father improved it with the advice of his barons'.[25] In 1136 King Stephen offered similarly 'all liberties and good laws which my uncle Henry, king of the English, gave and conceded to his barons and men, and I concede to them all the good laws and good customs which held

---

[22] Even though William did include an act modern scholars treat as legislation, the letter Cnut sent in 1027 from Rome to the people of England, he did so because it was the letter of a royal pilgrim and showed both the king's 'reformed life' and his 'royal magnificence' ('... ad documentum emendatioris uitae et regalis magnificentiae'): Malmesbury, *GR* i. 324–5 (bk ii. 182).

[23] Gaimar, for example, gives all credit to Edward the Confessor: 'Puis tint la terre, asist ses lais; / unkes tels ne furent anceis. / Peis ama mult, dreit e justise, / pur ço les asist en tel guise / ke unc devant ço, ne puis son jur, / ne pout nul rei feire meillur' [Thereafter he ruled over the country and instituted laws the likes of which had never before been seen. He was sincerely committed to peace, the law and justice. So successfully did he lay down the law that neither before him nor after could any king have done better]: Gaimar, *Estoire*, ed. and tr. Short, 264–5 (lines 4861–6). I have slightly modified Short's translation. The Ramsey chronicler, on the other hand, records that Cnut 'coepit ... justas leges vel novas condere vel antiquitus conditas observare' [established just or new laws or observed laws established in the past]: *Chronicon abbatiæ Rameseiensis*, ed. W.D. Macray (RS [lxxxiii], 1886), pp. lxxx and 125.

[24] 'Hoc quoque precipio et uolo, ut omnes habeant et teneant legem Eadwardi regis in terris et in omnibus rebus, adauctis iis quae constitui ad utilitatem populi Anglorum': *Gesetze der Angelsachsen*, i. 488 (Wl art 7); William I's writ to London promises '... eallra þæra laga ƿeorðe þe gyt pæran on Eadƿerdes dæge kynges': *Regesta regum Anglo-Normannorum: the acta of William I (1066–1087)*, ed. D. Bates, Oxford 1998, no. 180, whose edition of this writ is also now available at www.earlyenglishlaws.ac.uk. I have restored the original's use of wyn.

[25] 'Lagam regis Eadwardi ... cum illis emendationibus quibus pater meus eam emendauit consilio baronum suorum': *Gesetze der Angelsachsen*, i. 522 (Hn cor 13); calendared at *RRAN* ii, no. 488. The text above is that of Richard Sharpe, whom I thank for sharing with me his forthcoming edition of the coronation charter of Henry I, which will appear in print, but is now available in part at www.earlyenglishlaws.ac.uk.

force in the time of King Edward'.²⁶ While William I has been dropped from the chain of legislators and amenders of law in Stephen's charter, the link to Edward the Confessor remained firm. These are only the most famous and broadest statements. Some charters issued to individuals or to ecclesiastical institutions by the Norman kings guaranteed to the recipients the customs and rights they had possessed in Edward's day, which, if not giving credit for promulgating good law to that king, at least directed the readers' gaze to Edward's reign as a legal benchmark.²⁷ And the link of his laws to Cnut's, clear in the minds of some contemporaries, especially in the fifty years after the Conquest, meant that this rising tide under the *laga Edwardi* floated both of these boats, but not others. The affirmations by the Norman kings were not generic promises to restore an unspecific *laga Anglorum*, *lex antiqua* or *lex terrae*, for instance, but were specific

---

²⁶ '... omnibus baronibus et hominibus meis de Anglia omnes libertates et bonas leges quas Henricus rex Anglorum avunculus meus eis dedit et concessit. Et omnes bonas leges et bonas consuetudines eis concedo quas habuerunt tempore regis Edwardi': *RRAN* iii, no. 270.

²⁷ There is in fact a variety of combinations in the charters of named kings and others whose reigns or specific grants defined the origins and authority of the rights and properties: Edward alone (*RRAN* ii. no. 1046 [1100×1116, prob. 1114]); Cnut and Edward (*RRAN* ii. no. 644 [1102×1103]); Edward and William I (*RRAN* ii. no. 487 [1087×1100]; *RRAN* ii. no. 579 [June 1102]); Edward, William I and William II (*RRAN* ii. no. 1072 [1115×1129, probably 1116]); Edward, William I and Archbishop Thomas (*RRAN* ii. no. 885 [27 May 1108]); William I and William II (*RRAN* ii. no. 1335 [1122]); William II (*RRAN* ii. no. 1969 [1100×1135]); William I and Henry I (*RRAN* iii. no. 1 [1149×54]); Henry I (*RRAN* iii. no. 10 [1139×54]); Henry I and other kings (*RRAN* iii. no. 2 [1136×54]); unnamed kings (*RRAN* iii. no. 100 [1138×54]). The later one goes in the twelfth century, the more likely a reference to Edward is due to the presentation of an older charter for confirmation which was issued by, or mentioned, King Edward: see, for example, *RRAN* iii. no. 4 (1140 or 1142x43), and *RRAN* iii. no. 99 (1136). A number of the above references fall into this category. It is only rarely, and under suspicious circumstances, that earlier kings are named – a particularly striking reluctance given the prestige of Cnut's laws after 1066 (and before): for example, the account of the York inquest of 1106, preserved in the Southwell White Book, credits the cathedral's special customs to King Æthelstan, but this is a reference to a grant by the king rather than to Æthelstan's reign in general or to his 'good laws' (*English lawsuits from William I to Richard I*, ed. R.C. van Caenegem, London 1990, i. no. 172). The York charter of Henry I, allegedly recording this inquest, refers to the customs of ancient kings and archbishops, especially King Edward and Archbishop Aldred (*RRAN* ii. no. 1083). The canons at York are to have the same customs as the king in his own lands and as the archbishop held them from King Edward, and so on for other customs. Stephen confirms this (*RRAN* iii. no. 975). In his forthcoming edition, Richard Sharpe presents convincing reasons for thinking that both of these York charters, Henry I's and Stephen's, were forged, possibly as late as the early thirteenth century.

references to the laws of the last acknowledged legitimate ruler of the English before 1066.[28] These were royal affirmations of royal law.

Whether or not writers were motivated by an affirmation by a Norman king, the path they took to create a text of the old law depended on whether they aimed to produce Cnut's or Edward's laws. The shape of Cnut in the twelfth century was controlled to a great extent by the existence of what was produced in the time of the actual king, the Old English text of his Winchester code, whose contents remained relatively intact into the twelfth century.[29] Latin translations either were based wholly on the Old English source, as was *Quadripartitus*' translation, or adopted it as the core source for a composite text, which was what the *Consiliatio Cnuti* and *Instituta Cnuti* did. Even a fabricated code, an imposture produced late in the twelfth century which claims to represent Cnut's regulations on use of royal forests, borrowed a good deal of language and some substance from the *Instituta Cnuti* – which resulted in a text that echoed here and there the phrasing of the most common version of Cnut's legislation in late twelfth-century legal collections.[30] Pseudo-Cnut (as the author is now called) did not borrow from any other Anglo-Saxon law codes. With this exception, the shape of Cnut in the twelfth century was determined largely by the shape of Cnut's laws in the early eleventh century.

Records of Edward's laws, however, are all new creations of the twelfth century, and not derived in any significant way from written sources. The *Leges Edwardi Confessoris* may borrow some language in its prologue and a story about Pippin's accession to the Frankish throne from existing narrative sources, but, except for one chapter on sanctuary, none of its actual laws is borrowed from any written law code.[31] Instead, the contents of the *Leges Edwardi* may have been derived in part from the contents of some ecclesiastical institution's writs and charters and in part from the experience of that institution's agents in courts.[32] The earliest form of the *Leis Willelme* also consists mostly of original material. At two points,

---

[28] Harold receives surprisingly high marks as a law-giver and just ruler, despite his condemnation by the Normans for perjury and rebellion: see JW *Chronicle* ii. 600–601, whose work was adopted wholesale by Symeon of Durham, *HR* ii. 179, and borrowed from Symeon by Roger of Howden, *Chronica*, ed. W. Stubbs (RS [li], 1868–71), i. 111. On the rejection and elimination of Harold as a legitimate ruler, which developed during the course of William I's reign, see G. Garnett, *Conquered England: kingship, succession, and tenure, 1066–1166*, Oxford 2007, 1–44.

[29] The copy of I–II Cnut in MS A, produced *c.*1150, shows fewer significant variants than the earlier copy in MS G.

[30] This text is the so-called *Constitutiones Canuti regis de foresta*, on which see *Gesetze der Angelsachsen*, i. 620–26; iii. 335–9, and F. Liebermann, *Über Pseudo-Cnuts* Constitutiones de Foresta, Halle 1894.

[31] O'Brien, *God's peace*, 32–4, 65, 69–70, 82–4.

[32] O'Brien, *God's peace*, 41–4.

however, it appears to follow the sequence of the amounts for heriots in Cnut's code and for fines for wounds to the face and hands in Alfred's *Domboc*, and shows some similarities with the structure of chapters or with certain phrases of a few additional chapters of these two codes.[33] Difference between the two codes' treatments of heriots make derivation of one from the other unlikely: the *Leis Willelme* mirrors neither II Cnut's order of the persons who owed heriot nor the contents and number of the actual items to be handed over according to the status of the deceased. The points of agreement between these two texts are probably a reflection of common knowledge.[34] Fines for wounds to the face and hands in Alfred are likely, however, to have been the source of what is found in the *Leis*; but even here, the differences between the two texts show that, if Alfred's *Domboc* was the source, it has been freely adjusted.[35] Other than these exceptions, the material in the two treatises claiming to record Edward the Confessor's laws is very probably original.

The implied corollary of our identification of this creative approach to producing the Confessor's laws in both the *Leges Edwardi* and *Leis Willelme* is that Edward produced no laws like Cnut's. Negative evidence is no evidence, but it would be odd for the author of *Quadripartitus* to have written that Cnut's laws were the *laga Edwardi* if a code of Edward's had in fact existed.[36] The authors of the *Leges Edwardi* and *Leis Willelme* were legal writers who did not know of any linkage between Cnut's laws and the *laga Edwardi*, or, at least, who did not share the belief in the link described by *Quadripartitus* and implied by the Latin translations of Cnut. So when a writer in 1135 came to ask 'What was the *laga*

---

[33] Leis Wl 10–11, 20; II Cn 71; Alfred's *Domboc* (hereinafter Af) 45, 56.1, 57, 59, 60, 66.

[34] While II Cn 71 lists the heriots of earls, king's thegns, ordinary thegns, king's thegns in the Danelaw, thegns close to the king, and men of inferior wealth, Leis Wl 20 covers reliefs owed by counts, barons, vavasours with or without equipment, and villeins. The amounts of the heriot/relief are similar in the two texts, but there are some significant differences: money payments included in II Cn are not part of relief in Leis Wl; while Leis Wl specifies the types of horses counts and barons must offer, II Cn does not. Given these differences, the agreement in the number of weapons and equipment in the three categories covering those of highest status may just as easily reflect well-known customary obligations as textual derivation.

[35] There is agreement on types of wounds covered and the amounts owed by the person who caused the wound (for example, in Af 45 wounds to the face, if hidden, are assessed at 1*s*., while visible ones are 2*s*.; in Leis Wl, the amounts are 4*d*. and 8*d*. respectively). This agreement demonstrates the derivation of Leis Wl from Af. It is also telling that the author of Leis Wl (ch. 11.1) has added a gloss to explain that an English shilling had four pence rather than the Norman twelve – this gloss would only have been necessary if the author took his amounts from an English source.

[36] Wormald, *Making of English law*, 128, admits the possibility that laws of Edward might have existed, but says that they also must have been lost before 'the "Law of Edward" acquired its talismanic force'.

Edwardi', there was little around to say that the post-Conquest generations had assumed it was Cnut's laws. The link between the *laga Edwardi* and Cnut had faded before the middle of the twelfth century; William of Malmesbury does not say whose laws Edward had maintained, except that they were issued by previous kings.[37] Knowledge of the Cnut-Edward connection was, in the most important sense for law, irrelevant. Versions of Cnut's and Edward's laws produced before *c*.1150 were not separate species of law codes, however different their origins and sources, but rather related sub-species, covering much the same territory of criminal and procedural law.[38]

These approaches to recording the *laga Edwardi* – translating Cnut's Winchester code or composing original descriptions of 'Edwardian' customs – though separate and distinguishable in their original early-twelfth-century versions, did not remain so. Although the Old English copies of I–II Cnut produced in the twelfth century remained stable, showing few differences from earlier witnesses, the Latin translations moved quickly away from being principally lexical equivalents of their Old English source.[39] Only in *Quadripartitus* is Cnut's law code derived almost entirely from an Old English source very similar but not identical to any of the three extant copies of the Old English text. The contemporary *Instituta Cnuti* and *Consiliatio Cnuti* grow Cnut's legislation by grafting on to his laws chapters selected from the corpus of pre-Conquest laws. The *Instituta* adds to I–II Cnut selections or complete copies of at least ten pre-Conquest codes, drawing particularly on Alfred's *Domboc* for its comprehensive list of compensations for bodily injuries.[40] The author has not simply added new codes to the end of II Cnut, to create a larger collection; rather, he has woven relevant sections from other codes into a core sequence of I–II Cnut in addition to tacking on at the end a long piece derived from Alfred's law code and a group of short tracts by Wulfstan. The original sequence of Cnut's laws has been broken in four places by the intrusion of borrowed passages from II Edgar, the Northumbrian Priests' Law and Alfred's *Domboc*.[41] In addition, the translator has reconfigured his sources. He has omitted and occasionally rearranged chapters throughout I–II Cnut and has reordered in his third book the long addition from Alfred-Ine: selections from Ine come first

---

[37] One exception is whoever was responsible for adding the *Instituta Cnuti* to the fifth version of Henry of Huntingdon's *Historia Anglorum*, on which, see below, 243–4.

[38] On the boundary between translation and original composition, see O'Brien, *Reversing Babel*, 45–52.

[39] On the existence of a post-Conquest 'vulgate' version of I–II Cnut, see Wormald, *Making of English law*, 351.

[40] F. Liebermann, 'On the *Instituta Cnuti aliorumque regum Anglie*', *TRHS* N.S vii (1893), 77–107, and *Gesetze der Angelsachsen*, iii. 330.

[41] The order of sources used in In Cn can most easily be seen at *Gesetze der Angelsachsen*, i. 612–13.

even though Ine's code always forms an appendix to Alfred's, and those parts of Ine are followed by chapters from Alfred that are out of their usual order.[42] The remaining section of the *Instituta*, which translates Wulfstan's short tracts, shows a similar rearrangement of its sources.[43] The combined and reordered laws all travel as Cnut's laws. The *Instituta* was a conscious attempt to craft a new version of Cnut's code. The same conclusion holds true, *mutatis mutandis*, for the *Consiliatio Cnuti*, which adds a new prologue and appends some or all of four other statements of the law. In the later part of the twelfth century, the only author who made an attempt to amend these two 'translations' of Cnut did so by combining them together, about which more in the second part of this chapter.

While Cnut's original code was being expanded and revised as it was being translated, some copies of the *Leges Edwardi* and *Leis Willelme* were also expanded by the addition of a translated portion of Cnut's laws. At some point between the composition of the *Leis Willelme* and the end of the twelfth century, someone (whether or not the author of the original version is hard to say) added a series of chapters on peasants, execution, inheritance, adultery, poisoning and shipwreck derived from Roman law and fourteen chapters translated from various parts of an Old English copy of II Cnut.[44] This long form of the *Leis*, which was the source of all later witnesses, was translated, according to Felix Liebermann, into Latin between c.1170 and c.1200.[45] The net result of the additions was to increase the treatise's length by 50 per cent and expand its treatment of both legal principles and judicial practices. Around 1175, at least one copy of the *Leges Edwardi* was similarly expanded, increasing in size by one-half.[46] Here the compiler added without break to the end of a copy of the second version of the *Leges Edwardi* thirty-seven chapters from the *Consiliatio Cnuti*

---

[42] The sequence is Ine 9, 13.1, 14, 15; Af 29–31.1, 44–77, 19–19.2, 23–23.2.

[43] For example, the short Wulfstanian code called *Grið* is reordered in In Cn with chapters 5 and 12 following chapters 6, 8, 7 and 11.

[44] Leis Wl 29–38 (from Roman law), and 39–52 (from II Cn); F. Liebermann, 'Über die *Leis Willelme*', *Archiv für das Studium der neueren Sprachen und Literatur* cvi (1901), 113–38; Wormald, *Making of English law*, 408–9. On the evidence showing that passages in Leis Wl are translated directly from an Old English source, see B.R. O'Brien, 'The *Instituta Cnuti*', 185–6.

[45] Liebermann, 'Über die *Leis Willelme*', 126, dates it to c.1200, but possibly from as wide a span as 1170–1300. In *Gesetze der Angelsachsen*, iii. 285–86, Liebermann shifts from c.1200 to 1170–1200, but still thought 1170–1300 was possible. The manuscript holding Leges Wl's only witness (BL Harley 746) was written between 1275 and the early fourteenth century: see O'Brien, *God's peace*, 144–5.

[46] Significantly enough for this text to be treated as a separate treatise: see my edition of the Holkham *Leges Edwardi* at http://www.earlyenglishlaws.ac.uk/laws/texts/ECf2-Hk/.

focused primarily on procedures, highly selective but in the sequence in which they appear in the source.[47]

For our purpose, there are three aspects to note about what has happened to these Edwardian texts. First, two compilers independently improved different versions of texts claiming to be the laws of Edward the Confessor by adding significant selections from Cnut's laws, and not those of any other king (assuming we can trust that they could tell whose laws they were borrowing). Second, in both cases, these additions consisted of more practical, procedural chapters from the secular half of the Winchester code (II Cnut), rather than from the ecclesiastical chapters of I Cnut or the homiletic chapters spread throughout. Last, neither the *Leis Willelme* nor *Leges Edwardi* identify their additions as Cnut's; the new chapters travel as part of the *laga Edwardi* attributed to King Edward and authorised by William I.

While created in different ways, the texts which recorded either the laws of Edward or the laws of Cnut were not mutually exclusive, and appear together in three legal collections of the latter half of the twelfth century as well as in one version of Henry of Huntingdon's *Historia Anglorum*. The first book, the Holkham lawbook, which includes the unique enlarged version of the *Leges Edwardi* and the only copy of the original version of the *Leis Willelme*, also holds a copy of *Quadripartitus* that starts with its translation of Cnut rather than with its prefatory matters.[48] The second, the Colbertine lawbook, holds the amalgamated version of the *Consiliatio Cnuti* and *Instituta Cnuti* which I call the Colbertine *Cnut* after its later home in the library of Jean-Baptiste Colbert de Torcy (1619–83).[49] The laws of Cnut are here joined to copies of the *Articuli* of William I, an early copy of the third version of the *Leges Edwardi*, and a royal genealogy.[50] The third lawbook, Oxford, Bodleian Library, Rawlinson C 641, is not wholly a legal collection.[51] Nevertheless, it holds among its legal

---

[47] See B.R. O'Brien, 'An English book of laws from the time of *Glanvill*', in S. Jenks, J. Rose and C. Whittick (eds), *Making the common law: institutions, lawyers, and texts: studies in medieval legal history in honour of Paul Brand*, Leiden 2012, 51–67.

[48] MS Hk, fo. 17r.

[49] MS Cb. The Colbert library, including this manuscript, was sold in 1732 to the Bibliothèque royale. How and when the book travelled from England to France before ending up in the Colbert library is unknown.

[50] An edition of Cnut's laws in this manuscript was published in *Legum regis Canuti magni*, ed. J.L.A. Kolderup-Rosenvinge, Copenhagen 1826. A new edition is in preparation for Early English Laws.

[51] In addition to contemporary copies of the Assize of Clarendon, a French verse version of the Constitutions of Clarendon, the *Instituta Cnuti*, *Articuli* of William I and *Leges Edwardi*, the manuscript also holds short treatises on original sin, the Incarnation, commands of Pythagoras, riddles of Aristotle, all in Latin, and a collection of proverbs in Latin and French.

materials a copy of *Textus Roffensis*' text of the *Instituta Cnuti* along with a copy of the *Leges Edwardi* related to the one appearing in the Holkham lawbook.[52] These two texts were not found by the compiler of the Rawlinson manuscript together in one book, but collected from different sources and joined in this book.[53] Although it is hard to say with absolute certainty, it appears that both the selections from the *Consiliatio Cnuti* and version 2 of the *Leges Edwardi* probably came from a common source. An early-fourteenth-century manuscript holding the only complete copy of the *Consiliatio Cnuti* and a copy of the second version of the *Leges Edwardi* related to, but not derived from, either the Holkham or Rawlinson copies, together with the combination of both texts in the Holkham lawbook, strongly suggests that these two texts were available at an early date in the same manuscript and this was used as the source for the construction of the Holkham *Leges Edwardi*.[54] This combination of texts was only one of many found in twelfth-century books. Given the mixing of short and long forms of the *Instituta* and *Quadripartitus*' translation of I–II Cnut with copies of the second and third versions of the *Leges Edwardi*, it is clear that all of these combinations of Cnut's and Edward's laws come not from a single common ancestor, but from several. These books are independent evidence of the desire of compilers in the later twelfth century, unlike their early twelfth-century predecessors, to have both Cnut's and Edward's laws together in the same book.[55]

The *Instituta Cnuti* and the third version of the *Leges Edwardi* were also added to a branch of the fifth version (5B) of Henry of Huntingdon's *Historia Anglorum*.[56] Who added them is unknown, though at least it was not Henry himself: the texts are not integrated fully into his narrative and neither code appears in his sixth and final version. While the *Instituta* has been inserted just

---

[52] P. Wormald, '*Laga Edwardi*: the *Textus Roffensis* and its context', *ANS* xvii (1994/95), 243–66, at 260–62, saw MS Rl as independent of MS H, and therefore both as witnesses to a now lost exemplar for *Textus Roffensis*. For the evidence that the copy in MS Rl is derived from MS H, see O'Brien, 'The *Instituta Cnuti*', 180, and n. 17; on the relation of the text of ECf2 in MS Rl to that in MS Hk, see O'Brien, *God's peace*, 149–50.

[53] In Cn in MS Rl came from MS H; however, the text of ECf2 does not appear in MS H, but elsewhere, and in any case was probably composed at least a decade after the copying of MS H.

[54] The fourteenth-century manuscript is BL Harley 1704 (Hr), which has ECf2 and Cons Cn: see O'Brien, *God's peace*, 142, for a description.

[55] Combinations of Cnut's and Edward's laws: the Rawlinson MS (Rl) combines a long form of the *Instituta* with the second version of the *Leges*; all other books (three early copies of version 5B of Henry of Huntingdon's *Historia*) combine the short form of the *Instituta* with the third version of the *Leges*. Although MS Hk subsumes Cons Cn in ECf2, the lawbook begins with a copy of Quadr's translation of Cnut, which is the only place these two texts (Quadr and ECf) appear together.

[56] HH, pp. lxviii–lxix, cxviii, 839–41.

before Cnut's obituary in book six of the *Historia*, the *Leges Edwardi*, along with the *Articuli decem* of William I and a genealogy of the Norman dukes (a commonly found combination of texts called by Liebermann the *Tripartita*), have been appended to the end of the *Historia*.[57] The insertion of the *Instituta* and appending of the *Tripartita* may have happened as late as *c*.1190, the earliest date of London, Lambeth Palace Library MS 118, the oldest extant witness to what Diana Greenway labels version 5B. This version along with version 5A (which holds only the *Instituta*) were relatively popular: three extant witnesses dating to the decades either side of *c*.1200 indicate that a further five hyparchetypes holding one or all three of these law codes had been created before then.[58]

Records of Anglo-Saxon laws did not shrink over time. Neither Cnut's nor Edward's laws, as they stood in the early twelfth century, diminish in length as the century proceeds. There is no evidence that they were ever abridged; selections taken from Cnut were not attributed to that king and were intended to increase the size of records of the *laga Edwardi* rather than reflect a shortened form of Cnut's laws. All versions of these laws either remained as they were created or grew. *Quadripartitus*' large collection continued to be copied. Other law codes began to congregate in what look like collections of not just laws, but of significant laws. In two cases – the Rawlinson lawbook and Roger of Howden's *Liber de legibus Anglie* – the older laws even appear alongside texts of Henry II's assizes, though one might argue that in Howden's *Liber*, the *laga Edwardi* texts served as a kind of Anglo-Saxon and Anglo-Norman Old Testament to Angevin legislation's New.[59] In another case, the first version of the *Leges Edwardi* always accompanies a text of *Glanvill*, probably intended to represent the varying laws of the counties whose recording *Glanvill* neatly sidesteps at the end of the treatise.[60] The growth of individual texts and the combination of old and new laws shows that interest in Anglo-Saxon laws grew throughout the century.

---

[57] Ibid. pp. cliv–clvi, 366 n. 89.

[58] Ibid. p. cxviii; the copies are MSS Ba, La and Lb.

[59] In addition to In Cn, ECf2 and Wl art, MS Rl holds a text of the Assize of Clarendon (fo. 19). The *Liber de legibus* Roger of Howden attached to his *Chronicle* holds Wl art (MS Hv, fos 214v–15r), ECf3 (215r–23v) and *Glanvill* (226r–74r) as well as the Assize of Northampton (156v–58r), articles of the eyre (274r–v), the Assize of Woodstock (274v–75r), Assize of Clarendon (275r–76v), Assize of Arms (Oxford, Bodleian Library, MS Laud misc. 582, fos 4r–5r), edictum regis (154r–v), Assize of Weights (166r), Pleas for itinerant justices (172r–v) and Assize de precepta de forestis (172v–73r). For discussion of these texts, see J.C. Holt, 'The assizes of Henry II: the texts', in D.A. Bullough and R.L. Storey (eds), *The study of medieval records: essays in honour of Kathleen Major*, Oxford 1971, 85–106; D. Corner, 'The texts of the assizes of Henry II', in A. Harding (ed.), *Law-making and law-makers in British history*, London 1980, 7–20. A useful chronological narrative covering the origins of most of these assizes is in Hudson, *Formation of the English common law*, 126–39.

[60] O'Brien, 'An English book of laws', 67.

One thing clear so far is that during this time the written evidence behind the image of the *laga Edwardi* was changing. All aspects of the laws were evolving: individual codes were being invented, the contents of many codes adjusted, the framework in which they were presented altered, and their language changed. This last aspect should be particularly noted, because the recent focus on the continuity of written English in the twelfth century, including Old English texts found in collections of laws, has minimised the shift. A search for Anglo-Saxon law undertaken in the first quarter of the century would as likely have led to large collections of Old English law texts as to similar Latin collections like *Quadripartitus*, or to an amalgamated text like the *Instituta Cnuti*. By mid-century, a greater variety of texts was available to those interested in Anglo-Saxon laws, texts in Old English, Latin and Anglo-French, but there was also an increasing probability that someone searching would find a Latin version of either Cnut's or Edward's laws first. During the second half of the century, yet more texts were in circulation, though almost all claimed to be Cnut's or Edward's laws, and Latin versions of both kings' laws would often be found together in the same books. So, for those in the twelfth century who wanted to know what Anglo-Saxon law was or had been, there was no single text to supply the need at any point in the century. By the end, while the variety of texts describing pre-Conquest law had increased, the kings to whom the laws were attributed had been reduced in all but one case to two, as had their languages, to Latin and Anglo-French. Based on what has survived, then, and despite worries about the representativeness of what has survived, it nevertheless appears that English as a language for legal collections or legal compositions faded away (if not disappeared) soon after *c.*1150.

By the last quarter of the twelfth century, then, judging from the number of texts and books produced, interest in Anglo-Saxon law – almost exclusively in those laws attributed to Cnut and Edward – was strong. Enough copies had been made for every episcopal household and many abbeys to have had one (though there is no evidence that they actually did).[61] These copies appeared in collections as grand as encyclopaedias or as modest as portable pamphlets.[62] They stood on their own, or alongside Roman law procedural manuals or canon law collections.[63] They were intruded into narrative histories, or, when they do

---

[61] Adding up extant manuscripts, hyparchetypes, archetypes and autographs gives us roughly 45 copies of Cnut's or Edward's laws by *c.*1200.

[62] For legal encyclopedias, see above, 233; the pamphlets are MSS A and Di.

[63] For Roman law texts alongside English law, see MS Hk, as described in O'Brien, 'An English book of laws', 57–9, 64–6; for canon law, see MS H (Textus Roffensis), where a short collection derived from the *Collectio Lanfranci* appears, described by M. Brett, 'The *Collectio Lanfranci* and its competitors', in L. Smith and B. Ward (eds), *Intellectual life in the middle ages: essays presented to Margaret Gibson*, London 1992, 157–74 at 162, and MS R, whose decretal collection is described and analysed in C. Duggan, *Twelfth-century*

not appear in the narrative itself, can be shown in at least one instance to have been used as a source by the author.[64] They were combined with genealogies, French poetry and even lapidaries. The motive behind this interest remains puzzling. Why were these texts and books created? What did they signify to contemporaries whose taste for them was specific, not random?

So far, what I have done is sweep through the collective evidence from different directions to find patterns in the treatment of individual texts and their extant copies. These patterns of preference and treatment, while real, I have described at some distance and this approach only hints at, but does not provide, answers to questions of purpose and significance. My focus on the patterns reduces, in fact, the individuality of each text and of each copy. A more persuasive explanation of the purpose of these texts can be provided only by studying the details of all of the texts and their copies. Since there is no typical artefact to represent the rest or even the majority of legal records, the only way forward is to examine them one by one. Some of these twelfth-century lawbooks – *Textus Roffesnsis*, Corpus Christi College 383 and the Holkham lawbook – have already been the subject of studies and have revealed both common drives, but also unique understandings of the law.[65] Another particular lawbook, produced during the late twelfth century, offers new evidence for how law and its languages were perceived at that time, evidence which differs from what these other books teach us. Its quirks may help clarify the terms by which some of the puzzling aspects of this interest in Anglo-Saxon law might be understood. This book is evidence for the usual late-twelfth-century combination of Cnut's and Edward's laws in one lawbook, but is also unusual, even unique, in how those responsible for the book treated their texts – from the reconstruction of the texts to the script used for individual words. This complex piece of evidence has not been studied before and yet has much to say about who was creating such books, what were their motives and goals, and perhaps what they expected of their readers.

The book, which I call the Colbertine lawbook, is a small, modestly produced English legal collection, written in the last decades of the twelfth century.[66] It

---

decretal collections and their importance in English history, London 1963, 69–70, 152–4, and M.G. Cheney, *Roger, bishop of Worcester, 1164–1179*, Oxford 1980, 200–202.

[64] Wace, *Rou*, 290–91 (bk iii vv 8997–9010) is based on his reading of ECf 34 in one of its first three versions.

[65] Wormald, '*Laga Edwardi*'; T. Gobbitt, 'Cambridge, Corpus Christi College, 383', in O. Da Rold, T. Kato and M. Swan (eds), *The production and use of English manuscripts 1060 to 1220*, University of Leicester 2010, available at http://www.le.ac.uk/english/em1060to1220/mss/EM.CCCC.383.htm; O'Brien, 'An English book of laws'.

[66] MS Cb (BnF lat. 4771). For previous descriptions, see *Legum regis Canuti magni*, pp. i–xii; Liebermann, Consiliatio Cnuti, pp. xv–xviii; F. Liebermann, *Über die* Leges Edwardi Confessoris, Halle 1896, 127; O'Brien, 'The Becket conflict', 5 n. 20. Descriptive terms used here are generally those of A. Derolez, *The palaeography of Gothic manuscript*

is made up of four quires, each consisting of four bifolia which have received continuous pagination in the modern period.[67] There are quire marks at the bottoms of the last pages of quires 2 (p. 32) and 3 (p. 48), and breaks between all quires are bridged by texts. The contents are in their original order, with no evidence that anything else which might have been part of the book has been detached. The pages are ruled sometimes in hard point, sometimes in pencil, with the margins of the writing area marked by double vertical lines. The writing itself is in long lines of twenty-six lines per page, an odd and old-fashioned format at a time when most texts were written with two columns per page. Chapters begin with large ink-drawn flourished initials in red, blue and green, with red or blue vine patterns within the empty spaces in the initials.[68] Brief chapters in one place begin with simple undecorated red, green and blue capitals, with each chapter beginning on the left margin with its own initial.[69] Only on two pages are black capitals beginning clauses within chapters given a red infill.[70]

At least three scribes collaborated to produce the book. One scribe (the main scribe) was responsible for almost all of the writing, including the rubrics. Another scribe (the illuminator) added the flourished initials and plain-coloured capitals.[71] The third scribe (the corrector) performed three tasks: he completed the last six lines of the final text, a genealogy, corrected the manuscript throughout, and added Old English terms and phrases in spaces left by the main scribe. Additional correctors probably did work on the book, though distinguishing their work from that of the principal corrector is not

---

books from the twelfth to the early sixteenth century, Cambridge 2003. The identification of the book as English I owe to Michael Gullick and Tessa Webber (pers. communication).

[67] The quires are as follows: $1^8\ 2^8\ 3^8\ 4^8$.

[68] The pattern of the initials is red, blue, red, green, red, blue and so on, with only occasional missteps (found on pp. 15–6, 29–30, 30–31, 32, 47–9, 51–2 and 53–7). Not all texts receive the same level of rubrication; the second text, the *Articuli Willelmi*, receives only one initial, the first letter of its first word (**S** written in error for **H**), and has no markings for chapter divisions other than black-ink capitals to begin each clause. Tessa Webber identifies (pers. comm.) this style of decoration as one found in English manuscripts from *c.*1175 to *c.*1225.

[69] Pp. 29–30.

[70] Pp. 1 and 17. For the first, they mark out the clauses of the preface. The second, however, is peculiar, as the red-filled capitals on this page distinguish not the clauses of a special chapter, but rather whatever sub-chapters from In Cn ii. 30.3 to 31.1a began on that page: these chapters cover the procedure for the triple ordeal forced on those who chose not to offer oath and the beginning of the description of a lord's suretyship over his *familia*.

[71] In a few places (for example, pp. 4, 5) the margins preserve the letter placed there to signal to the illuminator what letter to add; this suggests that the main scribe and illuminator were not the same person.

always possible.⁷² Someone (called here the reviser) was responsible for editing all of the texts before they were copied into the book, though whether this was done when and where the book was copied is unknown.

The book they created holds three law codes and a genealogy of the dukes of Normandy and their descendants, the kings of England. The first code is a unique text, which I call the Colbertine *Cnut*. It consists of a heavily edited version of the *Instituta Cnuti*, on to which have been grafted the prologue and first and last chapters of the *Consiliatio Cnuti* (pp. 1–35). The second text is the *Articuli decem* of William I (pp. 35–7).⁷³ The final code is a revised text of the *Leges Edwardi Confessoris* in its third version, created between *c.*1140 and the writing of the Colbertine lawbook (pp. 37–60). The untitled *Genealogy* follows directly after that; it begins with the reign of Rollo as duke (911–*c.*931) and ends with the coronation of Richard I in 1189 (pp. 60–63).⁷⁴ These last three texts travelled as a group in the twelfth century, forming, as was mentioned above, a popular collection labelled the *Tripartita* by Liebermann. The main scribe of the manuscript was responsible for all of the laws and for the *Genealogy* up to the coronation of Henry the Young King in 1170, where he stopped without supplying the full regnal years as was the pattern for the rest of the entries. The main scribe's hand is a competently drawn pregothic characteristic of the late twelfth and early thirteenth centuries.⁷⁵

Another scribe picked up directly from the coronation of the Young King and completed the *Genealogy* to the coronation of Richard I in 1189 (Figure 12.1). This change of script has been used to date the copying of the laws and most of the *Genealogy* by the main scribe to the period between those two coronations.⁷⁶

---

⁷² A number of corrections may not be by the principal corrector; some may even have been inserted by the main scribe. It is not always easy to tell because the cramped nature of the writing space between the lines reduces features that otherwise help identification.

⁷³ See above, n. 14.

⁷⁴ The edition of the *Genealogy* in Liebermann, *Über die* Leges Edwardi, 134–9 stops at the end of Stephen's reign despite being based on the copy in MS Cb; Liebermann argued that the author of the *Genealogy* might very well be responsible as well for creating ECf3, ibid. 119.

⁷⁵ Tessa Webber (pers. comm.) described the hand as 'well on the way towards a fully-developed *littera textualis*, with the treatment of the feet of minims that comes to characterise the variety of *textualis formata* known as *sine pedibus* or *prescissa*'. On this type of northern *textualis*, see Derolez, *Palaeography*, 76–7.

⁷⁶ Liebermann offered several dates for the copying of the texts other than the *Genealogy*, assigning the laws to *c.* 1150 in 1893 (*Consiliatio Cnuti*, pp. xv–xviii), and 'um 1160' in 1896 (Über die Leges Edwardi, 127), which remained his verdict in 1903 (*Gesetze der Angelsachsen*, i. pp. xx–xxi). According to Liebermann, the *Genealogy* was added later to MS Cb, though by the main scribe of the laws, who carried it up to 1170. This scribe's belief that the coronation of the Young King in 1170 signalled a change in rule suggested to Liebermann that this portion of the *Genealogy* must have been composed before 1173, when the rebellion made clear that Henry II, the father, was still ruling. In 1893 Liebermann noted

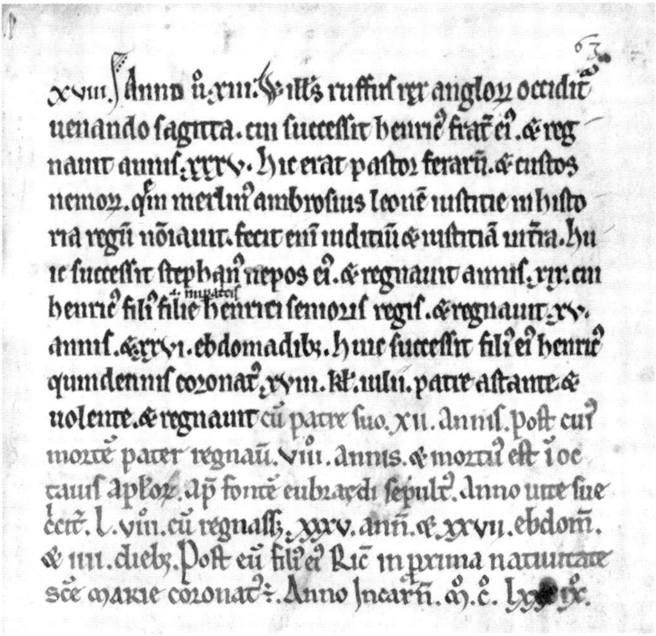

Figure 12.1   Paris, Bibliothèque nationale de France, lat. 4771, p. 63 (The End of the *Genealogy*).

The scribe who completed the genealogy, however, is very likely to have been the corrector of the manuscript, who was also responsible for adding Old English legal jargon throughout the text in spaces left by the main scribe. The evidence for this shared identity is the common letter forms and suspension marks used by both corrector and the scribe who completed the *Genealogy* (Figure 12.2 below). The scribe who did the latter employs a pregothic minuscule having a rounded, Caroline aspect, with feet curving up to the right; these characteristics are found in many corrections throughout the manuscript. Forms for **a**, **e**, **n** and **t** in some corrections, in the last lines of the *Genealogy*, and in some Old English words are very close if not identical to one another. The main scribe marks the vast majority of his suspensions with a crossbar with downward-angled tails, particularly thin and long on the right side; the corrections and *Genealogy* both exhibit a left-tilted **u** as a suspension mark for **m**, **n** and medial **s**, and the *Genealogy* shows the use of a crossbar for other

---

the change in ink between the main scribe's text and the continuation, but was uncertain whether it was a different hand as well (Consiliatio Cnuti, p. xvii n. 7); by 1896, he was more confident that it was a later hand (*Über die* Leges Edwardi, 139 n. 12).

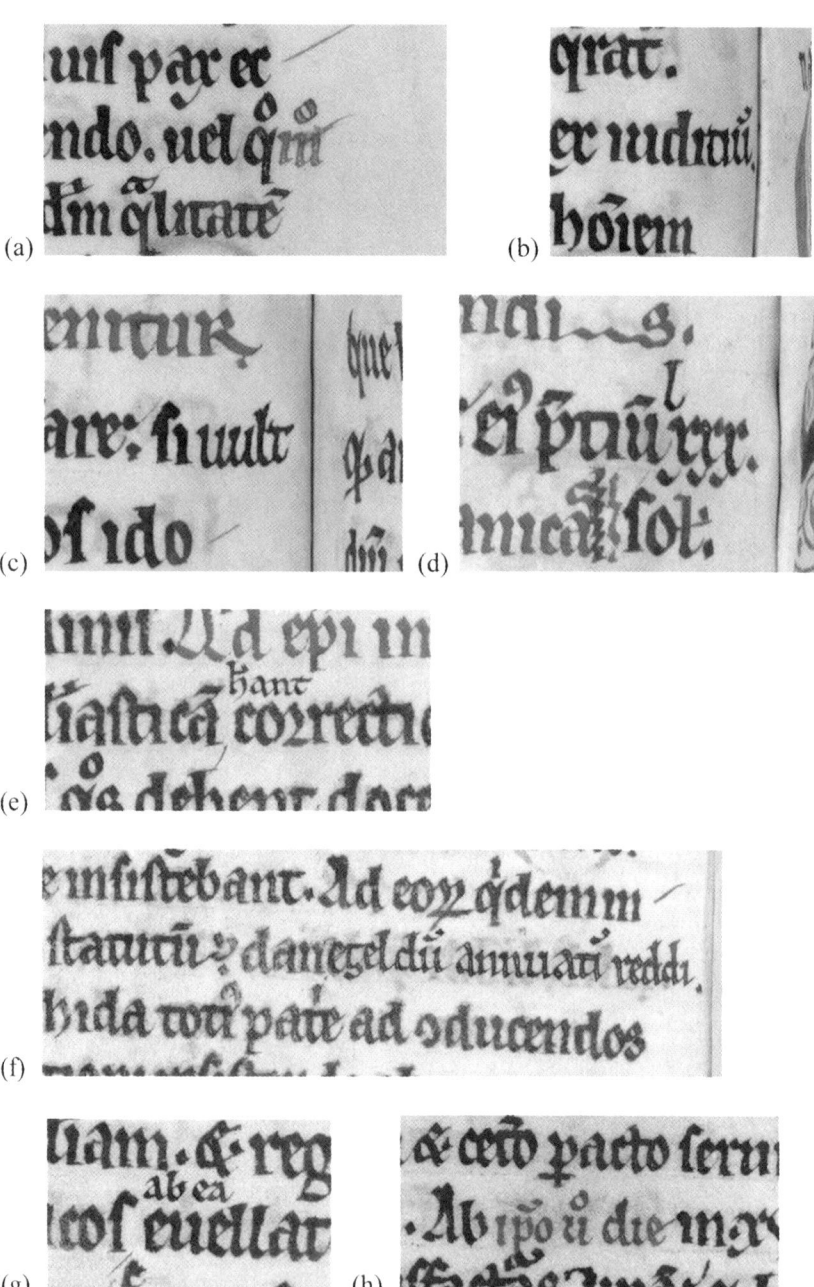

Figure 12.2 Paris, Bibliothèque nationale de France, lat. 4771, pp. 3, 14, 30, 34, 42, 46 and 58 (The Corrector's Hand).

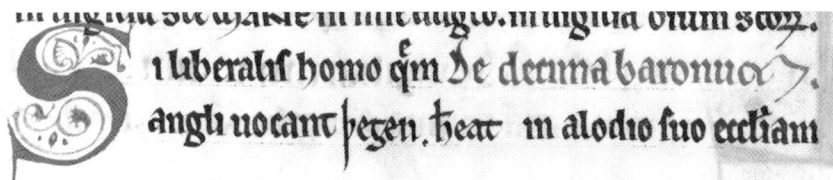

Figure 12.3   Paris, Bibliothèque nationale de France, lat. 4771, p. 7 (The Corrector's Insular and Pregothic Scripts).

suspended letters, such as **-ud**, **-it**, **-er**, **-os**, **-ardus** and **-ationis**; this crossbar often, but not always, has an angled tab up on the left side and down on the right.[77]

In one particularly telling example, the main scribe has, as usual, left space for the writing the Old English term *þegen*, which belonged in the text at that point (In Cn 1.11), but resumed writing with *in alodio*, accidentally skipping over the Latin word *habeat* which followed *þegen* in his source (Figure 12.3). It may be that the two words appeared to be one word in the source; the main scribe has left far more space than was needed for *þegen* alone and surely would have supplied the *habeat* if he had recognised his singular error. The corrector later filled in the Old English *þegen* and the missing Latin *habeat*, though switching from the insular letter-forms used for *þegen* to a round pregothic script for *habeat*. The hand of *habeat* looks identical to that of the end of the *Genealogy* and shares some letter forms (e.g. **a**) and ink colour with some examples of the corrector's hand elsewhere in the manuscript.[78] The letter-forms and ductus (and in part the ink colour) at the end of the *Genealogy* and in the English terms and phrases, compared with many of the Latin corrections spread throughout the book, lead to the conviction that some of the corrections and all of the insular script were written by the person who completed the *Genealogy*. This identification means that the manuscript cannot be older than 1189. A date at or near to that in fact is supported by the probable date of the script used by the main scribe.

The writing of embedded Old English terms by a separate scribe using vernacular letter-forms in a Latin text is peculiar. While the Latin text is written in a pregothic minuscule, many of the English terms were written in an insular script which is for the most part very much like some of those still used in the twelfth century for vernacular texts. Although there are a few imitative or archaising insular letter-forms, the hand as a whole does not appear to be

---

[77]   Pp. 14 (line 20), 58 (line 25). In the *Genealogy*, see suspension marks on p. 63 at line 10 (cu*m*), line 11 (morte*m*, regnau*er*it, i*n*), line 12 (ap*ud*, fonte*m*), line 13 (*circiter*, cu*m*, ann*is*, ebdom*adibus*), line 14 (eu*m*, Ric*ardus*) and line 15 (s*an*cte, Incarn*ationis*).

[78]   P. 7 (at In Cn i. 11) and corrections cited above, n. 77.

an imitative one.[79] Such a treatment of English in a Latin text of laws is to my knowledge unique.[80] Not all of the Old English terms in the texts were left for the corrector to insert (Figure 12.4).[81] In ninety-two places in the Colbertine lawbook, the corrector has filled spaces with words or phrases in his hand. In eighty-one other places where Old English terms appear, the main scribe left no blank spaces and instead simply wrote the terms in the pregothic script he uses for the Latin text. The key to the differing treatments lies in the presence or absence of certain vernacular letter-forms.[82] When an English word had the vernacular letter-forms þ, ð, ƿ or æ, the main scribe skipped the word, leaving space to be filled later by the corrector. When the English word had no vernacular letter-forms, it was almost always written in pregothic minuscule by the main scribe.[83] The same word appearing sometimes with and sometimes

---

[79] He used a form of **e** more often seen in English manuscripts of the tenth century than afterwards, forming it as a **c** with a long horizontal tongue centred and extending beyond the top and bottom limits of the horns of the **c** (i.e., ɛ). On distinguishing imitative from non-imitative script in the twelfth century, see M.B. Parkes, 'Archaizing hands in English manuscripts', in J.P. Carley and C.G.C. Tite (eds), *Books and collectors, 1200–1700: essays presented to Andrew Watson*, London 1997, 101–41; J.C. Crick, 'Script and the sense of the past in Anglo-Saxon England', in J. Roberts and L. Webster (eds), *Anglo-Saxon traces*, Tempe, AZ 2011, 1–29; eadem above in this volume, 159–90; and P.A. Stokes, 'The problem of grade in English vernacular minuscule, *c.*1060–1220', in E. Treharne, O. Da Rold and M. Swan (eds), *Producing and using English manuscripts in the post-Conquest period* (New Medieval Literatures xiii, 2011), 23–47.

[80] Liebermann noted in 1896 the use of 'Anglo-Saxon letters and runes' to write the English words in this manuscript: *Über die* Leges Edwardi, 127. Other lawbooks (Ad, Di, H, Hk, Hv, Hy, Ls, M, R, Rl, Rs and T) use on occasion a few vernacular letter-forms (þ, ð, æ, ƿ and, less often, **g**), but always integrated into the principal script of the Latin texts. The only analogue to Cb's practice is found in a near-contemporary copy of Adelard of Bath's translation of the astronomical tables of al-Khwārizmī, where a scribe uses a rubricated display script to represent transcribed Arabic technical terms retained in the Latin translation: C. Burnett, *The introduction of Arabic learning into England*, London 1997, 39–41, and pl. 3 (Bodl. Lib., MS Auct. F. 1. 9, fo. 99v), discussed in O'Brien, *Reversing Babel*, 102–4.

[81] Consider, for example, the following pattern of treatments seen in Figure 12.4 (p. 12 of the Colbertine lawbook), with the letters I (for insular) and P (for pregothic) identifying the scripts: 'fede oðe forðie' (line 1; I); 'gecydne utlage' (line 3; I); 'mertia' (line 3; P: both Wessex and East Anglia are done in insular script elsewhere); 'feohƿite' (line 5; I); 'ferdƿite' (line 6; I); 'Griðbrec\h/e' (line 6; I); 'hamsocne' (line 7; P); 'friðlesne man' (line 10; I); 'lashlit' [*sic*] (line 18; P); 'lashlit' (line 19; P); 'cherl man' (line 21; P); 'lashlit' (line 26; P).

[82] I am grateful to Peter Stokes for this observation.

[83] Consider the pattern of treatments in ECf3 12 on p. 43: 'kingeshandsealdegrið' (line 9; I); 'patling stret . Fosse . Ikenildestret . Ermingestret' (lines 12–13; I); 'hundreta' (line 20; P); 'dene-laga' (lines 20–21; P-I); 'were' (line 21; P); 'manbote' (line 22; P); 'Manbote' (line 23; P); 'de-nelage' (lines 23–4; P); 'manbote' (line 25; P). It would have been easy to have left blank spaces for many of the English words, given that a majority are prefaced by some

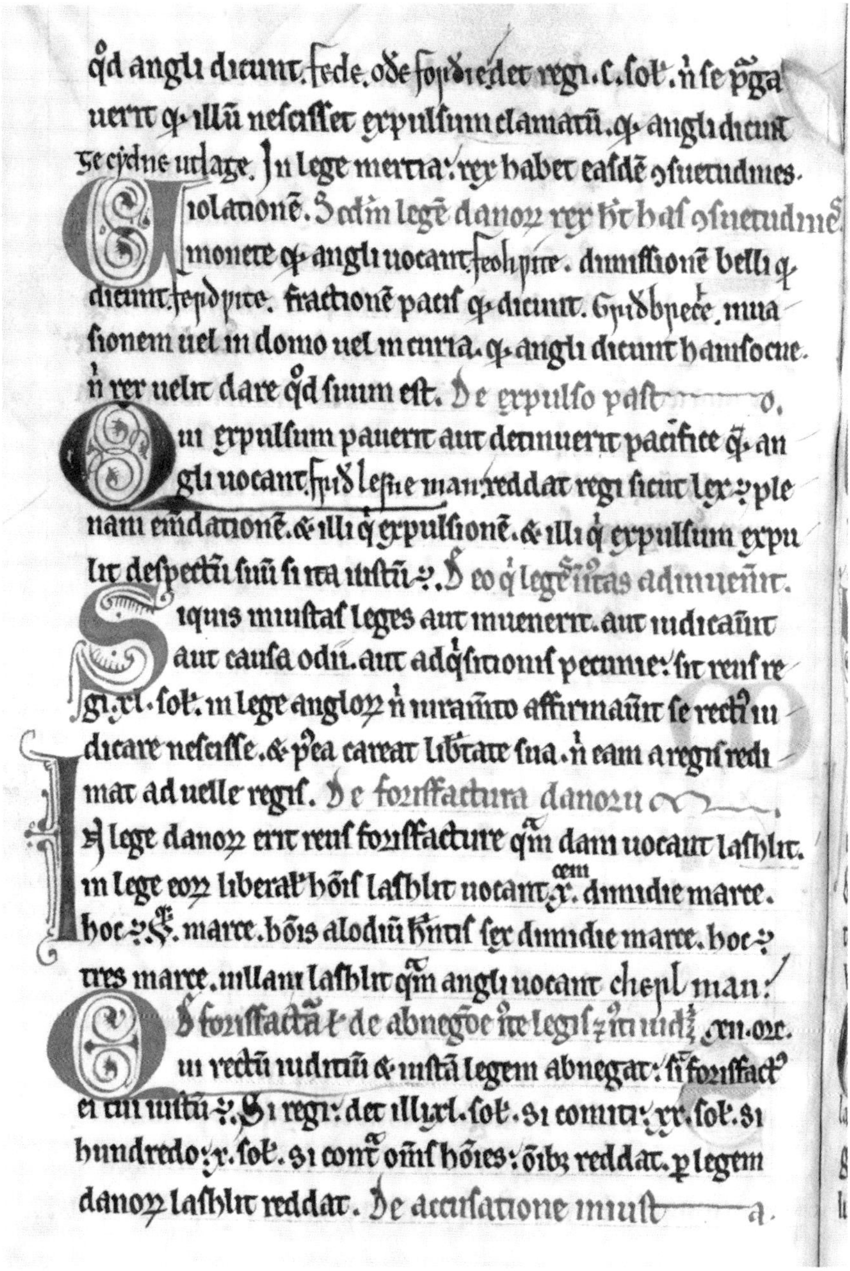

Figure 12.4 Bibliothèque nationale de France, lat. 4771, p. 12 (Insular and Pregothic treatments of pre-Conquest legal terms).

without special letter-forms received the expected treatments: 'æðeling' (In Cn 2.58) appears in the corrector's insular hand, while several occurrences of 'edeling'/'adeling' (ECf 35.1) appear in the main scribe's pregothic minuscule.[84] The exceptions to this rule suggest that more insular letter-forms (but not too much more) were better than less.[85] The main scribe could write at least one of these special letter-forms (þ), which raises the possibility that the decision to write these terms using different letter-forms and added by a different hand was not based on the main scribe's inability to write a few special letters, but rather on a desire by the person in control of the book to achieve greater distinctiveness or visibility for this special presentation of English words by assigning the task to a scribe with an obviously different hand.[86]

If the corrector had the best hand in the scriptorium for enhancing the Colbertine lawbook's vernacular visibility, his skill at writing the script, nevertheless, was not impressive, nor was his understanding of vernacular letters infallible. His insular hand resembles in some ways the novice hand responsible for writing the vernacular bounds of charters in *Codex Wintoniensis*. It may very well be that, as Alexander Rumble hypothesised about Scribe A of that cartulary, the corrector of the Colbertine lawbook 'had to learn [the vernacular's] special insular letter-forms during his transcription'.[87] In the case of **e**, the corrector appears to have adopted a letter-form current in the tenth century, but found

---

variation of 'quod Angli dicunt', and they all could exhibit some insular letter-forms (i.e., **f, g, r, s, t, ẏ**), albeit not ones representing letters used only in English words. The instructions to the main scribe could not have been to leave spaces for all English words, but only for those words having at least one of a select group of vernacular letter-forms.

[84]   The same is true of 'þere' / 'were': 'þere' at pp. 13 (ll. 4, 24), 17 (l. 24), 18 (l. 3), 21 (ll. 9, 16), 23 (l. 2), 24 (ll. 7, 16), 28 (ll. 6, 10, 12), 33 (l. 20) and 34 (l. 2) are all insular; it appears as pregothic 'were' at p. 43 (l. 21).

[85]   For example, 'saulescot' (In Cn 1.13); 'gecydne utlage' (In Cn 2.13.2); 'cherlman' (In Cn 2.15a and 3.42), are all in the corrector's hand though none has any of the four letter-forms exclusive to the vernacular.

[86]   The main scribe's three words that use þ are pregothic words in all other particulars except for this one letter-form. On p. 49, the main scribe has written 'infangeneþief' twice on the same line, once in the rubric and once at the beginning of the chapter. He also used a thorn for 'þrihinga' (ch. 31.1), and what appears to be a very tentative eth (ð) for **d** in 'leð' (p. 53, line 24; note that 'led' appears with a **d** five lines above on the same page). These three instances of þ written are noticeably inconsistent in form. As for who was in charge of the book project, it was probably the corrector, who would be expected to be a senior scribe.

[87]   A.R. Rumble, 'The structure and reliability of the *Codex Wintoniensis* (British Museum, Additional MS 15350); the cartulary of Winchester Cathedral Priory', unpubl. Ph.D. diss., London 1979, i. 57. For full analysis, see ibid. 56–60, 235–40. For similar observations about Ely and Bury St Edmunds, see Stokes, 'The problem of grade', 23–47.

rarely in twelfth-century insular minuscule.[88] He (and the main scribe) also at times misread the Old English letter ash (æ) as an ampersand (&), which both converted to 'et', garbling Old English words.[89] Overall, the compression and size of his letters are irregular. There is also a significant variety in some individual letter-forms. None of this suggests he had copied a great deal of English prior to his work on this lawbook. If he was the best available, then the Colbertine lawbook was probably created in a scriptorium with almost no experience copying English books.[90]

---

[88] See above, note 80. For examples of the corrector's fluctuating **e** letter-forms, see pp. 18 (l. 26, 'æþespyrðe'), 19 (l. 11, 'perelade'), 21 (l. 4, 'eðgelde', with initial and final **e** as ϵ and medial as the corrector's rounded pregothic **e**). Further examples can be found on pp. 5, 7, 12, 16 and 43. This same form of **e** is used as the standard minuscule **e** by a Westminster forger of the second quarter of the twelfth century for one of his creations: *Facsimiles of Anglo-Saxon charters*, ed. S. Keynes, Oxford 1991, 11 (no. 37).

[89] Both the corrector and the main scribe were confused by Old English ash. Resemblance between ash and ampersand in contemporary manuscripts can be close, a point also raised by Crick in this volume, 170: see MS R, fo. 146r, lines 19–20 (Quadripartitus). In MS Cb, on p. 17 (line 24) the corrector wrote 'petre' for what must have been 'pære' in the source (which itself is unusual), after which someone erased the **t**, leaving a gap. In three other places, the corrector has accurately copied ash (p. 7, l. 1; p. 17, l. 12 [this last on the same page as his 'petre']; p. 22, l. 14). In other places where we might expect to see the corrector writing **æ**, we find e and cannot say what was in the source (e.g., p. 13, l.6 ['hundr**e**d']; p. 14, l. 3 ['husf**e**st and folg**e**res']; p. 14, l. 3 ['b**e**rst']: all of these examples appear with **æ** in the oldest copy of In Cn [MS H]). The main scribe wrote 'metibote' for what must have been 'mæibote' in the source (p. 3, l. 10). At ECf 32 (p. 53), the main scribe wrote 'Gretue' (line 21) for what must have been 'Græue' (a mid-twelfth-century form of the Old English word 'gerefa' [reeve]) in the source, and four lines down again wrote 'gretue' (line 25); in both cases the **t** has been erased just as it had been in the insular script. On the bottom of the page (line 26), the word appears abbreviated as 'gue' with a suspension mark above the **g** used by the main scribe for **ra** and **ua**. On the next page (54), the word appears, without any erasure, as 'Gr&ue' (line 3), and this is clearly an ampersand rather than ash. On p. 53, at ECf 31, the word had appeared correctly in the compound 'trehingreue' (line 14). The error was spotted and the correction made to 'gretue' probably before the rubric was added by the main scribe, since he has spelled it as 'greue' in the rubric on the same line as his first 'gretue' (p. 53, l. 21).

[90] It is unlikely to have been produced at Christ Church, Canterbury, Rochester, or Worcester, all of which had a good deal of experience copying English-language books in the twelfth century. But does the corrector's inexperience mean that the book could not have been made at any of the other houses and cathedrals where we have some evidence for the production of English-language books, places like Abingdon, Barking, Bath, Bodmin, Bury St Edmunds, St Augustine's, Canterbury, Durham, Ely, Exeter, St Paul's London, Peterborough, Salisbury, Sherborne, Thorney, Winchester and York? The identification of sites of production is from O. Da Rold, 'EM in context', in O. Da Rold, T. Kato and M. Swan (eds), *The production and use of English manuscripts 1060 to 1220*, University of Leicester 2010, available at http://www.le.ac.uk/english/em1060to1220/culturalcontexts/2.htm.

Less noticeable to a twelfth-century reader than the treatment of the Old English terms is the level of revision that the texts have undergone. While I suspect that the particular deployment of insular script for English legal terms is probably original to this lawbook, it is far from clear whether the revisions are similarly original here, or had been done earlier in a different place by someone unconnected to the team of scribes who produced the lawbook. The problem of deciding the date when, and place where, the revisions were made is compounded by the fact that so many aspects of the lawbook are unique – the fundamental shape of one of its principal texts; the revised contents and wording of all of its law codes; and the use of insular script for many Old English terms in its two longest legal sources. We at least can say that the whole collection – Colbertine *Cnut, Articuli, Leges Edwardi,* and *Genealogy* – was assembled and revised probably at the same time, since the reviser's work appears on every page.

One scenario explaining the sequence of the book's creation might look like this: the *Genealogy*'s incompleteness – ending in mid-sentence – marks where the draft serving as the exemplar ended or where an initial extension of the *Genealogy* at the scriptorium reached. Once the main scribe had reached that point, the corrector added a newly composed final section of the *Genealogy*, corrected the texts, and filled in the spaces with Old English terms. Either after or more probably before the corrector did his work, the pen-drawn initials and capitals were added. It is in this scenario more likely that both the lawbook and its source, with its incomplete version of the *Genealogy*, were produced around the same time in the same place. The coordination between scribes, the complexity of their agenda, and the coherence of their product says as much. It is also much more likely that the blending of the *Instituta Cnuti* and *Consiliatio Cnuti*, as well as all of the other revisions, took place not in the Colbertine lawbook, but in its source.[91] The text in the lawbook is too cleanly written to be the actual object about which so many editorial decisions had to be made and successfully carried out; grammatically muddled revisions in any of the texts are exceedingly rare.[92] This seems to me to be the simplest hypothesis, though it is not testable, and other scenarios, while more complicated, might very well be closer to the truth.

That said, let us turn to the revisions. Someone has edited the book's contents to a degree not seen in any other twelfth-century lawbook. Most of these revisions are a matter of style preference, consciously or unconsciously enacted. The reviser, for instance, thought some words were interchangeable: he changed *dicunt* to *uocant* in some, but not all, 'quod Angli dicunt' phrases,

---

[91] By 'source' I mean the text copied into MS Cb. This source could be, and probably was, the reviser's draft.

[92] See In Cn 2.66 and 2.71.3.

and also switched *uocant* to *dicunt* elsewhere.[93] He replaced the *Instituta Cnuti*'s *insidiator* with *traditor*, a word which also appears in the *Leges Edwardi*.[94] Words that are redundant were sometimes removed: *et uolo* after *precipio*; *populi* from the phrase 'ad utilitatem populi Anglorum'; and many instances of *emendet* in the section of the *Instituta* that translates Alfred's personal injury penalties.[95] In the *Leges Edwardi*, changes of words, inversion of phrases, and rearrangement of syntax are frequent, but rarely do they amount to a substantive change in the law.[96] Some changes, like those in Colbertine *Cnut*, are simply different ways of writing the same thing: *in qua* for *ubi*; *regnum tenuit* for *regnauit*; and *malorum* for *uitiorum*.[97] Other instances suggest a reason behind the choice, though identifying that reason involves a guess: the reviser added *in Anglia* to the title perhaps to remind readers that the laws William I confirmed were for England and not for Normandy; he may have added *confirmate et* to enhance *corroborate* in describing William I's public endorsement of the laws and ancient customs of the English.[98] Longer omissions do not change the meanings of their chapters. For instance, he omits 'de suo proprio Anglorum lege' in the chapter on Peter's Pence, with no real change in the substance of the chapter.[99] Even if the reasons for some changes are opaque, it does seem as if the reviser was interested generally in making his texts clearer than their sources.[100]

For both the *Articuli* and the *Leges Edwardi*, no textual source for the revisions can be identified, and it is simplest to assume that changes are the product of the reviser's desire to tighten up their prose or to improve their idiom. For the Colbertine *Cnut*, stylistic changes are just as frequent, but many are derived from a known source. The reviser used, as Liebermann noted in 1893, a text of the *Consiliatio Cnuti* to supply words, phrases and clauses to replace

---

[93] For example, he changes 'dicunt' to 'uocant' at In Cn 2.20 (p. 13); 2.59d (p. 23); but not at In Cn 2.13.2 (p. 12) or Wl art 2 (p. 36). In Cn 3.5 (p. 28) shows the reviser moving in the opposite direction.

[94] In Cn 2.64 (p. 23); 'traditor' is what is used at ECf3 18.2 (p. 47).

[95] The first two examples are taken from Wl art 5 (p. 37); the omissions of 'emendare' are at In Cn 3.11, 3.13, 3.14, 3.15, 3.18, 3.19, 3.20 and so on (pp. 28–9). See also the omission of 'teneat et' from 'teneat et habeat' at Wl art 6 (p. 37), and 'uenire' at Wl art 7 (p. 37).

[96] Some changes are scribal error – eye skip at ECf3 12a (p. 43) caused the scribe to drop 'in natale domini dies octo, in pascha dies octo'.

[97] ECf3 10.3 (p. 42); 34.2 (p. 55); 37.1 (p. 59). See also 'redierit' for 'reditum fecerit' at 5.3a (p. 40). It may be that the reviser is trying to match the rhetorical *cursus* of his own day.

[98] ECf3 inscr. (p. 37) and 34.1a (p. 55).

[99] ECf3 10 (p. 42).

[100] His rubrics are often unique and more explicit than other witnesses' rubrics (e.g., ECf3 28 at p. 52). In the one place (ECf3 12.3, at p. 43) where an explanatory interlinear gloss has been added ('id est pacem regis', to explain an isolated *eam*), this may just as likely be the work of a corrector rather than the reviser.

those found in the section of the laws which come from the *Instituta Cnuti*.[101] Some emendations hide the seam between the two texts. For instance, the new prologue, borrowed from the *Consiliatio*, uses *decretum* to describe the 'common decision' of Cnut's council to fix the laws; the *Instituta*'s prologue has Cnut establish (*instituit*) his laws with the advice (*consilium*) of his chief counsellors.[102] The reviser retained the *Instituta*'s prologue, but changed *consilium* to *decretum*, which brings the two prologues into agreement and gives the counsellors a greater say in legislation.[103] Instances of more direct replacement are common.[104] The very order of the chapters in the *Instituta* has been rearranged in one place (I Cn 17–17.2) to match their order in the *Consiliatio*.

Felix Liebermann saw no logic behind these editorial moves because they did not enhance the substance of the laws. Logic or no, the identification of the source allows us to reconstruct the reviser's priorities and method more securely than we can with only the evidence of the revisions to the *Articuli* and *Leges Edwardi*. The reviser began with two Latin texts of Cnut which differed in major and minor ways. He chose the much longer *Instituta Cnuti* as his base text, perhaps not just because of its length and broader coverage of legal issues, but also because it, unlike the other text of Cnut, was filled with transcriptions of the technical vocabulary of Old English law. Although the second text, the *Consiliatio Cnuti*, is exceptional for having avoided virtually all transcription of Old English legal terms, nevertheless it had some unusual elements the reviser decided to borrow – most notably its prologue. He then read the *Instituta*'s text against the whole of the *Consiliatio* and borrowed language from the *Consiliatio*, it seems very likely, to improve the style and meaning of the composite text he was creating, even if his editorial judgements were mostly solipsistic. He directed more attention to religious matters than to anything else: his borrowings and emendations of all sorts are frequent in the ecclesiastical section of Cnut, and rare thereafter. This scenario still leaves two areas of revision to be explored:

---

[101] Liebermann, Consiliatio Cnuti, p. xviii. We have little or no knowledge of where copies of these texts could be found in the late twelfth century, but David Rollason's reminder to us of the movement of clerics in search of texts for Durham's historical works makes the question of where the reviser of Colbertine *Cnut* acquired his sources in an important sense moot: see Rollason in this volume, 110–12.

[102] Liebermann, Consiliatio Cnuti, 1; *Gesetze der Angelsachsen*, i. 279.

[103] Cb Cn prol., on p. 2 (line 9).

[104] See the apparatus to In Cn and text of Cons Cn in *Gesetze der Angelsachsen* i, at 1.2.1 ('propria'), 1.2.2 ('Christiani'), 1.2.3 ('concedat'), 1.3a ('dignitas'), 1.4.1 ('ad faciendum populo in necessitate'), 1.5.1a ('assumat sex secum et ipse sit septimus'), 1.5.2 ('uulgaris'), 1.5.2a ('audiutorium'), 1.6.2a ('uoluerit'), 1.7 ('commater'), 1.8.1 ('sicut carruca perarat' in In Cn, but omitted in Cons Cn and for that reason probably omitted from Cb Cn), 1.8.2 ('adeunt cum'), 1.8.2 ('illi dimittant'), 1.15 ('etiam'), 1.16 ('festum'), 1.16.1 ('natalis'), 1.17.1 ('festum'), 2.8.2 ('purgamine'), 2.22.3 ('condonetur'), 2.30.1 ('iuramentum') and 2.54.1 ('ei').

what was behind the substantive revisions made to some individual laws, and why was the prologue of the *Consiliatio Cnuti* adopted for this new amalgam?

The substance of the law has been changed in a handful of places in Cnut's laws, almost all of which are in the section dealing with ecclesiastical rights and protections (I Cnut). Though each change represents an editorial intervention in a text, the intention behind any one change is not always clear. Consider the following two examples. In one chapter, the Old English source (I Cnut 3.1–2) assigns different fines for breach of peace (*griðbrice*) to churches depending on their status, which it divides into four categories: chief minsters (*heofod mynstres*), middle-level minsters (*medemran mynstres*), lesser churches (*læssan [mynstres]*) and rural churches (*feld cyrice*) which have no graveyards.[105] The *Instituta Cnuti*, which provided the base text for this chapter in Colbertine *Cnut*, translates the four categories as principal churches 'such as bishoprics and abbeys', middle-level churches, minor churches and the smallest churches which have no cemeteries, and assigns each a *mund* amount that maintains for all but the smallest churches the numbers of the Old English source but changes the unit of account for middle-level and minor churches from West Saxon shillings to pounds, while converting the field churches' unit from shillings to pence.[106] The Colbertine *Cnut*, however, amended the *Instituta*'s identification of the churches which belonged in the top two categories: it changed the top category to archbishoprics and bishoprics while dropping abbeys down to the second category, where they joined middle-level churches.[107] It also restored some of the

---

[105] 'Ne synd ealle cyricean na gelicre mæðe wuruldlice weorðe, þeah hig godcundlice habban halgunge gelice· Heafod mynstres griðbrice is æt botwyrðum þyngum be cyninges munde, þæt is mid fif pundum on Engla lage· And medemran mynstres mid an hundred Ꞽ twentigum scyllingum – Ꞽ þæt is be cyninges wite· And þonne gyt læssan, þær litel þeowdom sy· Ꞽ legerstow þeah sy mid sixtigum scill'· And feld cyrice þær legerstow ne sy· mid ðrittigum scyll.': I Cn 3.1–2 (MS A, fos 5r–5v).

[106] 'Non enim sunt omnes ęcclesię unius eiusdemque honoris · quanuis habeant unam eandemque consecrationem· Principales autem ęcclesię sicut episcopatus & abbatię talem emendationem uiolatę pacis secundum legem anglorum habere debent: mundam regis · hoc est quinque libras· Secundum certe legem danorum · octo libras· Mediocris autem ęcclesię duas libras · hoc est secundum forisfacturam regis · & ad huc minoris ęcclesię hoc est ubi parum seruitii fit & tamen cimiterium habet: forisfactura est unius librę · minime uero ęcclesię quam angli feldcirice uocant · octoginta denariorum': In Cn 1.3.2 (MS H, fos 58v–59r).

[107] 'Non enim sunt omnes ecclesie dei unius eiusdemque honoris: quamuis unam habeant consecrationem· *De principalibus ecclesiis·* Principales uero ecclesie sicut archiepiscopatus & episcopatus: hanc emendationem uiolate pacis secundum legem anglorum debent habere: mundam regis · hoc est ·v· libras · secundum certe legem danorum: octo libras· *De mediocribus ecclesiis·* Mediocres autem ecclesie ut abatie & canonicatus · iuxta forisfacturam regis uidelicet ·xxc. solidos hoc est quatuor libras· *De minoribus ecclesiis·* Minores quidem ecclesie · hoc est ubi seruitium fit · & tamen cimiterium habent: xl [*recte* lx]· solidos · hoc est tres libras· *De minimis·* Minime uero ecclesie quam angli feldcherche dicunt: id est carentes cimiterio: xxx·

amounts of the fines and their unit of account to what is found in the original law code of Cnut. The source used for these restored amounts was not, however, the Old English text, but as for many stylistic changes the *Consiliatio*, which had kept the amounts as they appeared in its Old English source.[108]

These restored amounts raise the obvious question: why would the reviser care? In 1189 it is unlikely many readers would have known that these fines were originally calculated in West Saxon shillings of 4*d*., rather than the twelfth-century shillings of 12*d*.[109] The changes made to the Colbertine *Cnut*, then, gave all but the principal churches a hefty 300-per-cent increase over the *mund* amount in the *Instituta*, which merely converted pre-Conquest fines to the Norman 12*d*. shilling. The reviser here has also changed which churches the *Instituta* said belonged to the highest categories: in Colbertine *Cnut*, the top category is assigned to 'archbishoprics and bishoprics', while the second covers 'abbeys and houses of canons'. The reviser added 'archbishoprics' and 'houses of canons', which appeared in neither the *Instituta* nor in the *Consiliatio*, and demoted 'abbeys' from the first to the second category. One would like to see these changes to amounts and status as reasoned choices which provide clues to the purpose of the text and identity of the creators of the lawbook, and perhaps to developments in the law itself. However, it may not be wise to read these adjustments to *mund* literally; there is no independent evidence that churches in 1189 calculated their status based on *mund*, let alone were protected by fine amounts like these. The changes to this text might be more profitably read as statements of proportions and hierarchy, and the whole passage stands as a seasoned legal authority given retrospectively to the rising authority of archbishops and the status of canons regular in the ecclesiastical landscape. It is very much a bishop's book. The demotion of abbeys does suggest that, if the reviser was a monk, he was a humble one.

The second example appears to add new obligations to Cnut's chapter on soulscot, a payment owed at the burial of a corpse. I Cnut 13 states that, if a family wishes to bury the dead family member or friend in another parish, they were to pay soulscot first.[110] This was translated without change to the substance

---

solidos·': Cb Cn 1.3.2 (pp. 3–4). I have italicised the rubrics, kept the MS punctuation, but silently expanded abbreviations. All capitals at the start of chapters and some sub-chapters are two-line ink-drawn initials. The scribe has inverted the numbers for the fines of cxx and lx *solidi* – the pound amounts show that these inversions were scribal errors.

[108] For the amounts in Cons Cn 1.3.2, see Liebermann, Consiliatio Cnuti, 3.

[109] The author of the *Leis Willelme* over a half-century earlier had explained, as mentioned above (n. 35), that 'English' shillings contained only 4*d*. in order to avoid, no doubt, this very confusion.

[110] 'And saul sceat is rihtast þæt man symle geleste· æt openum græfe· Ænd gif man ænig lic of rihtscryftscire elles hwær legce gelæste man þone saþel sceat swa ðeah into þam mynstre þe hit to hyrde': I Cn 13–13.1, *Gesetze der Angelsachsen*, i. 294 (MS A, fo. 6v).

by the *Instituta*.[111] Colbertine *Cnut* took the *Instituta*'s text, but added that a person (grammatically the corpse) should 'honour his church from his own property according to what he himself is and thus he may be transferred to where he wishes with the licence of his own priest'.[112] This appears to describe a further mortuary which was based on a person's status and payable to the local church where the corpse should have been buried. This payment essentially purchases the licence of the local priest to bury the corpse somewhere other than the dead person's parish church's cemetery. Burial of corpses was an issue generally sorted out between older or mother churches and the newer parish churches and proprietary churches being built in their districts.[113] The right to the corpses of the elite was in particular defended fiercely by the older churches, since the dues such burials brought it, as well as the prestige of high-status corpses in the cemetery, were important to the viability and status of the church.[114] What had once been required became over time the default position, as it was expected in the next century that wealthy people in particular would choose their own burial sites.[115] Colbertine *Cnut* appears to be offering a scheme whereby the family and friends of a dead person could buy a licence to bury a corpse elsewhere, a step in the evolution of burial practices. That may well be what the text is doing, but caution about accepting that conclusion is warranted. Although the added clause may track the development of mortuaries, it may simply be a clumsy reiterative gloss on the meaning of soulscot; the poor quality of the grafting of new on old might justify reading this simply as a restatement of what it follows, rather than anything new.[116]

It is worth remembering that when amending particular laws in Colbertine *Cnut*, the reviser did not need to update everything. He needed only to update what he intended to draw attention to, or what seemed most useful to have the

---

[111] 'Si quis corpus parentis aut amici sui de propria parrochia alias portare ad sepeliendum uoluerit: faciat prius rectitudinem parrochię ad quam pertinet · scilicet redditus quod angli saulgescot uocant · quod recte persolui debet ad apertum sepulchrum': In Cn 1.13–13.1 (MS H, fo. 62r).

[112] '... & ctiam de substantia sua honoret ecclesiam suam secundum quod ipse est · & sic cum licentia proprii presbyteri transferatur quo uoluerit': Cb Cn 1.13–13.1 (MS Cb, p. 8).

[113] J. Blair, *The Church in Anglo-Saxon society*, Oxford 2005, 444 n. 76, 446–7, 451, 463–71. See the rich set of documents mentioning disputes or negotiations over burial rights in *English episcopal acta VII, Hereford 1079–1234*, ed. J. Barrow, Oxford 1993, nos 31, 56, 152, 153, 214 and 235. The earliest is 1131 x 1148; the latest *c.*1190 x 1198.

[114] *English episcopal acta VIII, Winchester 1070–1204*, ed. M.J. Franklin, Oxford 1993, no. 84 (1139 x 1143) and *English episcopal acta VII, Hereford*, nos 137 and 138 (1174 x 1186).

[115] *English episcopal acta VIII, Winchester*, no. 3 (1114).

[116] Though see *Episcopal acta VII, Hereford*, 104–5n, for no. 151 (1180 x 1186), on the separation of mortuaries and burials.

laws say. To ask for every chapter to be updated – especially when the code is an artefact of the old law – is to ask legal writers of the day to be something they are not – writers of legal textbooks. So the laws live simultaneously in the past and in the present according to what the writer needs or wants. For the Colbertine *Cnut*, then, the reviser wished to alter only a selection of chapters of the law, and these concern a cluster of issues which would have been of moment to some clerics of the day, rather than to the king's court or the secular elite.

A less ambiguous revision comes at the beginning of the Colbertine *Cnut*. The reviser has added a new prologue which recasts Cnut's legislation as an attempt to unify all of England's laws under the authority of its new conquering king (Figure 12.5).[117] This prologue was not composed for the Colbertine *Cnut*, but was borrowed with little change from the *Consiliatio Cnuti*. What the *Consiliatio*'s prologue, and hence the Colbertine *Cnut*'s prologue, says, however, is quite striking, and contrasts with the prologues of all other Old English and Latin versions of Cnut's laws. In the Colbertine *Cnut*, the conquering king learns that England had once been ruled by many kings and, as a consequence, had many different laws for its different and formerly independent regions. In response, King Cnut states that since England now had one king, it should also have one law ('... quatinus sicut uno rege: ita et una lege uniuersum Anglie regnum regeretur'). The anachronism of this imagined observation is beside the point. Cnut is here made to address the legal divisions which appear in the records of Anglo-Saxon law – the existence of the three major legal regions of West Saxon law, Mercian law and the Danelaw, and perhaps also local customs such as those of Kent or East Anglia, memory and textual evidence of which was still around in the twelfth century.[118]

The compiler of the Colbertine lawbook wanted a collection of texts of the *laga Edwardi*, and found a way to integrate these texts by borrowing the *Consiliatio*'s prologue and placing it at the head not only of the revised version of Cnut's laws, but of the lawbook itself. The whole lawbook gives voice to Cnut, Edward and William I, who together form a resounding chorus for the role kings and their barons (which included senior ecclesiastics) played in the creation and maintenance of law in a period of England's past which had already been singled out in the late eleventh and early twelfth centuries as the critical period for the kingdom's laws, the period when the *laga Edwardi* was in force as the good customs of the realm. That the Norman kings had endorsed this *laga* was known in the late twelfth century, even as current kings moved on to Henry I as

---

[117] See appendix to this article for an edition and translation of the prologue.

[118] The existence and identity of the legal regions of the kingdom appear in most of the codes and treatises: In Cn 2.14–15; Hn 9.10–10a; ECf 12.3–5, 30, 33; Leis Wl 2–3.3, 8, 21.3–4. Richard fitz Nigel also knows of them, though perhaps not independently: *Dialogus de scaccario*, ed. and tr. C. Johnson, F.E L. Carter and D.E. Greenway, Oxford 1983, 63.

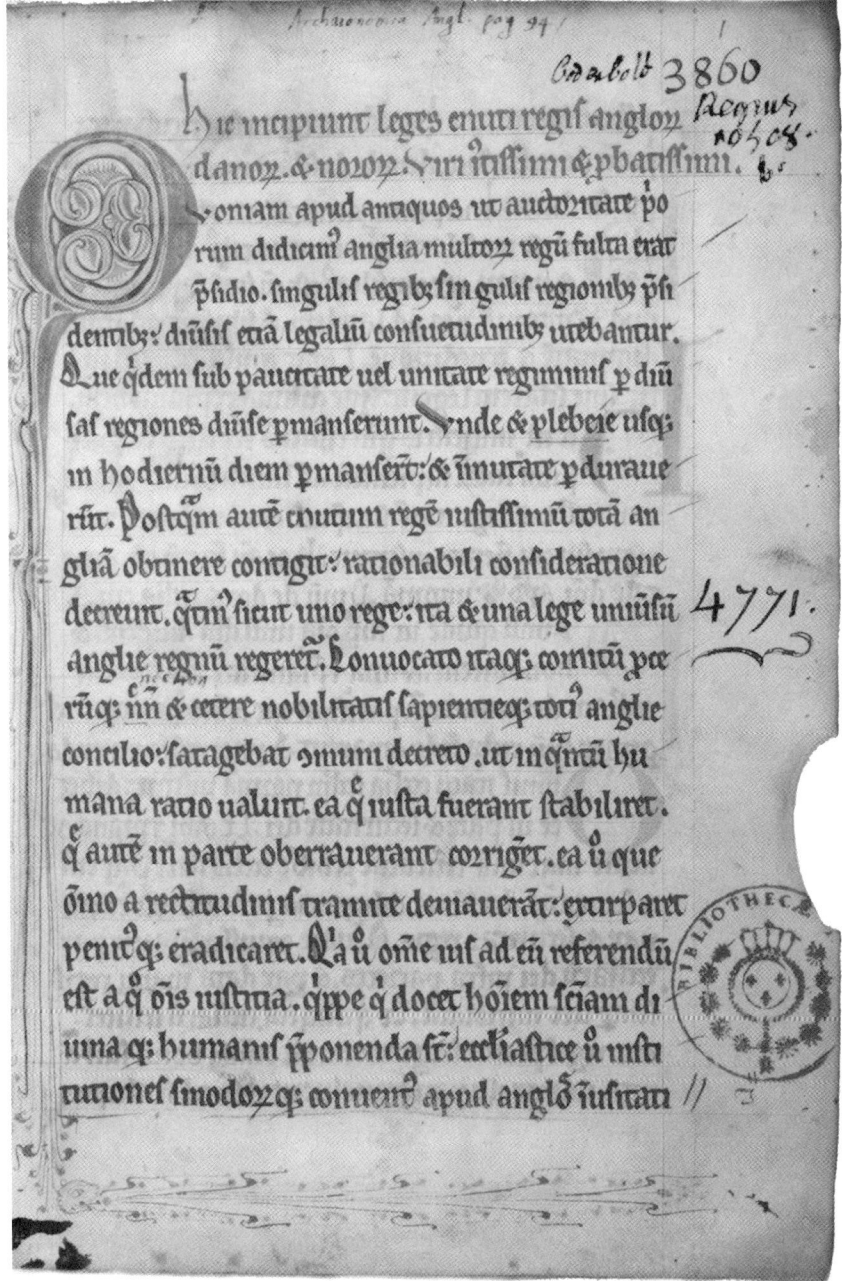

Figure 12.5   Paris, Bibliothèque nationale de France, lat. 4771, p. 1 (Colbertine *Cnut*'s Prologue).

their benchmark. In the 1160s or 1170s the Anglo-French writer Wace tells the story of William I's confirmation of the laws of Edward, a story he probably had learned from a copy of the *Leges Edwardi*.[119] That Henry I had confirmed the *laga Edwardi* was known by the rebels of 1215; their revision of his coronation charter, a document now known as the Unknown Charter, continued to affirm it. As late as 1215, it was possible, perhaps even usual, to trace back from Henry II's confirmation of the law of Henry I's day, to the reign of William I, and then to the *laga Edwardi* itself, the pre-Conquest law affirmed after the Conquest.[120] England's laws kept their genealogy even as the limits of legal memory and legal authority moved further away from 1066.

The borrowed prologue does serve the purpose of bringing into concord the messages of the laws of Cnut, of Edward the Confessor and of William I: all three legal texts now offer pictures of law's survival over a conquest, pictures which stress the power and authority of a new ruler to impose law, but who, regardless of that power, decided to work with law already in place (whether written or oral). The contents of the *Articuli* are 'what William, king of the English, and his magnates enacted after the conquest of England'; the individual chapters both impose new customs and affirm the *laga Edwardi*.[121] The *Leges Edwardi*'s lengthy two-part story of King William summoning his council of the English, hearing their customs, threatening to impose Norwegian law, and then acquiescing to the nobles' plea for the existing customs, offers a similar picture.[122] It acknowledges some introduction of foreign customs over time, but also royal support for the maintenance of the existing customary law of the kingdom. Such a willingness to both impose law and accept existing custom is missing, though, from the original prologue of the *Instituta Cnuti*. There, the author merely states that 'This is the ordinance which Cnut established with the advice of his wise princes for the praise of God, and for his own honour and the advancement

---

[119] 'Then he had all the barons summoned and all the English assembled, giving them the choice of which law they would uphold and which customs they wanted, either those of the Normans or of the English, of which lords and which kings. They said they should be those of King Edward; may the king uphold and protect his laws for them. The customs which they knew, which they used to hold at the time of Edward, those were the ones they wanted and those they asked for, those pleased them and those they adopted; this was their will and the king granted it to them' (Wace, *Rou*, 290–91, iii vv 8997–9010). Wace had earlier credited Edward the Confessor with establishing peace and good laws ('pais etabli e bones leis') (ibid. 204–5 [3.4739–40]).

[120] J.C. Holt, *Magna Carta*, 2 edn, Cambridge 1992, 113–14.

[121] '... quid Willelmus rex Anglorum cum principibus suis constituit post conquisitionem Anglie': *Gesetze der Angelsachsen*, i. 486 (Wl art inscr.).

[122] ECf prol., and 34, in O'Brien, *God's peace*, 158–9, 192–3.

of all the kingdom over which he presided'.[123] This Latin version discards what one of the two Old English witnesses has: Cnut's regnal titles to the kingdoms of England and Denmark.[124] Nothing in the *Instituta* reveals any hint of Cnut's rule of another kingdom. Reference to his rule of Denmark would have brought to mind the fact that he was a conqueror, and therefore had had the opportunity to impose new laws on his conquered kingdom. This was a lacuna which the borrowed prologue of the *Consiliatio* filled.

The Colbertine lawbook is not a revolutionary text, charting some new course taken by English legal writers during an age of legal reform. Nor, strictly speaking, can it seen as wholly reactionary, an antiquarian product whose gaze is fixed in the past. It is overly narrow to think of it as either one thing or the other. It would, like most if not all books, mean different things to different readers. To some, it might be read as a statement of the criminal law which the contemporary treatise known as *Glanvill* had dodged recording, much as were lawbooks such as the Holkham lawbook and contemporary combinations of *Glanvill* with the *Leges Edwardi*. To others, it could stand as a lightly retouched mirror of princes; only a few years later, a more ambitious writer or group of writers produced such a mirror in the *Leges Anglorum*, which in turn served as a first stage for putting in writing complaints about John's rule in the lead up to Magna Carta.[125] Others would see it as a historically valuable legal *summa*, illuminating the past much as did the inclusion, around the same time, of those same texts in one version of a popular English narrative history as well as in Howden's *Chronicle*. The Colbertine lawbook certainly had historical weight as a statement of the *laga Edwardi*, a term still in use in the late twelfth century, though principally of interest to political readers who raised a demand for it in the early thirteenth century.[126] Kings may have dropped references to the *laga Edwardi* from their charters – such was surely in their best interest – but kings and their councillors were not the only readers with a keen interest in law. Some readers might have seen in this collection a statement of how English kings ruled empires during times of political transition, an issue of some interest under the Angevins. Last, it could easily be seen as a rejoinder to Glanvill's dismissive comment that England was a land without

---

[123] 'Hęc est institutio quam cnud rex cum consilio principum suorum sapientium: ad laudem dei · & honorem sui ipsius · & profectum totius regni cui preerat · instituit': In Cn prol. (MS H, fo. 58r). The translator was working with something like the text in MS G as his source.

[124] *Gesetze der Angelsachsen*, i. 278 (MS A).

[125] Holt, *Magna Carta*, 93–5; B.R. O'Brien, 'Forgers of the law and their readers: the crafting of English political identities between the Norman Conquest and the Magna Carta', *PS: Political Science and Politics* xliii (2010), 467–73.

[126] Holt, *Magna Carta*, 113–16, 219–24, chronicles these demands.

written law.[127] For most if not all of the these readers, the lawbook would represent an attempted accommodation of the book's legal and political present to some part of the English legal and political past.

The reason there could be so many uses of this lawbook is simple – the viewers of the legal scene, and not just the objects they viewed, were changing. The prospect from which pre-Conquest law was surveyed was evolving. This evolution is shown by the evidence not only of this lawbook, but of all of the many legal works of the century. This period saw the composition and copying of the first Roman law procedural handbooks in England, as well as of the introduction of the teaching of Roman law.[128] In canon law, the writing of Gratian's *Decretum* in *c.*1140 did not end the study of older canon law collections, which continued to be copied, edited, and collated throughout the twelfth century.[129] Last, it was certainly a period of significant changes in some important areas of English law – namely the customs regarding land and inheritance as well as governing relations between lords and their vassals. Development of this nascent common law from the time of Henry II onwards, happening as it was in a period of accelerated changes in law and in the form and purpose of legal texts, would have shaped the kinds of questions contemporaries would ask of old law, and the questions they would have asked in *c.*1150 had certainly changed from what was asked in the immediate post-Conquest period, and by *c.*1200, the questions had changed from those of the mid-century. In

---

[127] In O'Brien, 'Becket conflict', 12–4, I argued that *Glanvill* could well have been a response to the multiplication of copies of these older royal laws after *c.*1164, a conclusion expanded here by considering the later texts as also, perhaps, responses to *Glanvill*.

[128] A. Gouron, 'Un traité écossais du douzième siècle: l'ordo "Ulpianus de edendo"', *Tijdschrift voor Rechtsgeschiedenis* lxxviii (2010), 1–13; P. Landau, 'The origins of legal science in England in the twelfth century: Lincoln, Oxford and the career of Vacarius', in M. Brett and K. Cushing (eds), *Readers, texts and compilers in the earlier middle ages: studies in medieval canon law in honour of Linda Fowler-Magerl*, Aldershot 2009, 165–82, whose case for Lincoln has been recently challenged by M. Brett, 'English law and centres of law studies in the later twelfth century', in T. Iversen (ed.), *Archbishop Eystein as legislator*, Trondheim 2011, 98–102. See further P. Landau, 'The origin of civil procedure: treatises in Durham during the twelfth century', in U.-R. Blumenthal, A. Winroth and P. Landau (eds), *Canon law, religion and politics. Liber amicorum Robert Somerville*, Washington, DC 2012, 136–44.

[129] Z.N. Brooke, *The English Church and the papacy from the Conquest to the reign of John*, Cambridge 1931, 84–105, 231–45, with corrections from M. Brett, 'Editions, manuscripts and readers in some pre-Gratian collections', in K.G. Cushing and R.F. Gyug (eds), *Ritual, text, and law: studies in medieval canon law and liturgy presented to Roger E. Reynolds*, Aldershot 2004, 205–19. R. Helmholz, *The Oxford history of the laws of England* I: *the canon law and ecclesiastical jurisdiction from 597 to the 1640s*, Oxford 2004, 67–105. For twelfth-century reworkings of pre-Gratianic collections in England, see Brett, 'The *Collectio Lanfranci*', 157–71 (esp. 161 n. 14); and M. Brett, 'Margin and afterthought: the *Clavis* in action', in Brett and Cushing (eds), *Readers, texts and compilers*, Aldershot 2009, 137–57, at 152–7.

England in particular, the Becket conflict and his murder in 1170 would have provoked talk of ancient customs which could not have been disengaged from discussion of writs, eyres and innovative assizes, let alone from evolving ideas of church reform and their implementation. Nevertheless, the function of the old law in this debate would have been changing. By the late twelfth century the laws of Cnut and Edward were no longer just a benchmark of criminal law, which they probably had been in the time of the Norman kings. Instead, the texts of these laws, while still a description of criminal law, supplementing contemporary practices in books like *Glanvill*, were also increasingly likely to be read as setting the historical and political context for a king's exercise of justice in the kingdom. The Colbertine lawbook probably would have been read as one such text.

The lawbook is also a complicated sign of the triumph of Latin as the language of law codes in the twelfth century. English-language lawbooks like Corpus Christi College MS 383 and Harley 55 merely highlight this preference. Law's Latinity was never in doubt throughout the century. This was not, however, the result of a rejection of English as one of the kingdom's languages of law. English did survive in law, but rather than being the principal vehicle for law as it had been before 1066, it became rather quickly a 'language of authenticity', not so much preserving a cultural memory of past status, but locking contemporary Latin into the semantic fields of the authoritative terminology of law.[130] It looks like the mid-century was the transitional period both for the end of English as a language for passing on the law, and for English's real as opposed to rhetorical value within Latin texts. Around that time, two pamphlets were produced – one an English copy of Cnut, the other a Latin copy of the *Instituta Cnuti* – showing the pragmatic place held by each language. It is noticeable, however, that this English pamphlet (BL Harley 55) was the last English lawbook to have survived. By the end of the century, the role of English in law codes was transformed. The Colbertine lawbook shows English to have become a thoughtfully chosen although inconsistently, even carelessly employed tag of authority and authenticity. This is not to say this is what happened to English in other genres.[131] It does suggest, however, that more immediate affairs rather than the Norman Conquest governed the status and function of all languages, and especially

---

[130] The phrase is borrowed from Faulkner, 'Rewriting English literary history', 279.

[131] See the particularly dynamic intermingling of languages analysed by M. Menzer, 'Multilingual glosses, bilingual text: English, Anglo-Norman and Latin in three manuscripts of Ælfric's Grammar', in J.T. Lionarons (ed.), *Old English literature in its manuscript context*, Morgantown, WV 2004, 95–119, and in B. Millett, 'The pastoral context of the Trinity and Lambeth homilies', in W. Scase (ed.), *Essays in manuscript geography: vernacular manuscripts of the English West Midlands from the Conquest to the sixteenth century*, Turnhout 2007, 43–64, at 52–60. The important collection that launched investigations of the post-Conquest production and use of English texts is M. Swan and E. Treharne (eds), *Rewriting Old English in the twelfth century*, Cambridge 2000.

English, in the late twelfth century.[132] Regardless of the occasional errors of orthography and infrequent appearance of English lemmata, contemporary readers of the Colbertine lawbook could not have avoided the conclusion that English held a special place among their written languages of law, a place in no way threatened by the increasing use of Anglo-French.

Much more work needs to be done before we can fully map the thought world of these readers – its debates and discussions about past and present law, the interaction between the written laws of kingdom, Church and Rome, the evolving reading tastes of courtiers and clerics, in or out of royal service – but we can at least see the possibility that a book like the Colbertine lawbook, with its positive picture of king-made law and of kings actually making law, of royal authority to lay down new laws, of the power of kings to rule not just kingdoms but empires, would not have been out of place in the royal court or with any of the king's justices, even if it was seen later to be out of the mainstream of England's legal development under the Angevins. *Glanvill*, the innovative work of a smart writer in the Angevin court, offered just one way of talking about law in the 1180s, one with a long future. Other ways were possible and in fact used. And lest these other ways of talking be dismissed as inconsequential to the law in its black-letter sense of forms of action or modes of proof, of descriptions of crimes, procedures, and penalties, let us not forget that the serious and hardened critics of King John did not ask for *Glanvill*'s law in 1215, but for Edward the Confessor's.[133] This thinking about the *laga Edwardi* was as important to the way that they conceived of law, understood it in its grandest sense, as were contemporary manuals of procedure and registers of writs and anything that happened in an actual court of justice.

---

[132] The contrary position is argued by E. Treharne, 'Periodization and categorization: the silence of (the) English in the twelfth century', *New medieval literatures* viii (2006), 247–73, and by the same scholar even more forcefully in her recent *Living through conquest: the politics of early English, 1020–1220*, Oxford 2012, chs 5–7. For analyses more sensitive to the historical, cultural and linguistic context, see M. Faulkner, 'Archaism, belatedness and modernisation: "Old" English in the twelfth century', *Review of English Studies* N.S. lxiii (2011), 179–203, and G.R. Younge, '"Those were good days": representations of the Anglo-Saxon past in the Old English homily on St. Neot', *Review of English Studies* N.S. lxiii (2012), 349–69. Both of these stimulating articles arise out of recently completed dissertations: M. Faulkner, 'The uses of Anglo-Saxon manuscripts c.1066–1200', unpubl. D.Phil. diss., Oxford 2008, and G.R. Younge, 'The Canterbury Anthology: an Old English manuscript in its Anglo-Norman context', unpubl. Ph.D. diss., Cambridge 2012.

[133] *Annales monasterii de Waverleia* for 1215, in *Ann. mon.* ii. 282.

Appendix: Prologue to the Colbertine *Cnut*

This is a transcription of the prologue of the Colbertine *Cnut* as found in its only witness, Paris, BnF lat. 4771, pp. 1–2 (MS Cb). The prologue derives from the *Consiliatio Cnuti*, but survives other than here in only one place: the sole witness to the complete text of the *Consiliatio*, the early-fourteenth-century London, BL Harley 1704, fo. 1 (MS Hr). The *Consiliatio* in MS Hr has been joined without break to a copy of version 2 of the *Leges Edwardi Confessoris*; both texts, which fill MS Hr's only quire, travel under a common title: 'Incipiunt leges que uocantur leges Edwardi quia cum diu essent dimisse ipsas fecit reparare et de legibus regis Willelmi'. Readings from MS Hr are provided in the notes. Figure 12.5 above shows the majority of the prologue. Images of all folios of MS Cb and MS Hr are available at www.earlyenglishlaws.ac.uk. The laws of Cnut in MS Cb were edited by J.A. Kolderup-Rosenvinge in his *Legum regis Canuti magni*, Copenhagen 1826. The prologue of the *Consiliatio Cnuti* was edited by Liebermann, *Consiliatio Cnuti*, 1–2, and in his *Gesetze der Angelsachsen*, i. 618; Liebermann used MS Cb in his reconstruction of the archetype of the *Consiliatio*. Wormald, *Making of English law*, 406, provides a partial translation. My edition of the Colbertine *Cnut* will appear at www.earlyenglishlaws.ac.uk

Text

Hic incipiunt leges cnuti regis anglorum danorum . et nororum . uiri iustissimi et probatissimi.[134]

Quoniam apud antiquos ut auctoritate priorum didicimus anglia multorum regum fulta erat presidio . singulis regibus[135] singulis regionibus presidentibus: diuersis etaim legalium consuetudinibus utebantur. Que quidem sub paucitate uel unitate regiminis per diuersas regiones diuerse permanserunt. Vnde et plebeie[136] usque in hodiernum diem permanserunt[137]: et immutate perdurauerunt. Postquam autem cnutum[138] regem iustissimum totam angliam obtinere[139] contigit: rationabili consideratione decreuit . quatinus sicut uno rege: ita et una lege uniuersum anglie regnum regeretur. Conuocato itaque comitum procerumque necnon et cetere nobilitatis sapeintieque totius anglie concilio: satagebat communi decreto . ut in quantum humana ratio ualuit . ea que iusta

---

[134] Incipiunt leges que uocantur leges edwardi quia cum diu essent dimisse ipsas fecit reparare et de legibus regis willelmi. *rubric in Hr*
[135] singulis regibus *om. Hr*
[136] consuetudines *add. Hr*
[137] indiscusse *Hr*
[138] *Originally* chutum *in Cb, but ascender of 'h' erased*; chuntum *Hr*
[139] optinere *Hr*

fuerant stabiliret . que autem in parte oberrauerant[140] corrigeret . ea uero que omnino a rectitudinis tramite deuiauerant: extirparet penitusque eradicaret. Quia uero omne ius ad eum referendum est a quo omnis iustitia . quippe qui docet hominem scientiam, diuinaque humanis[141] preponenda sunt: ecclesiastice uero institutiones[142] sinodorumque conuentus[143] apud anglos inusitati /p.2/ adhuc fuerant . ne quis ordo in regno suo[144] titubaret: primum de ecclesiastico . deinde de seculari iure tractare incepit sic dicens . Incipiunt decreta cnuti regis.[145]

Hec est consolatio[146] quam cnutus[147] totius anglie . danorum et nororum[148] rex consiliatus est cum suis sapientibus apud wintoniam deo ad laudem . et sibimet ad regiam dignitatem et expeditionem. Legat quilibet[149] utrum[150] malit . siue secularem legem: siue diuinam expeditionem.[151]

Hec est institutio[152] quam cnutus[153] rex decreto principum[154] suorum sapientum[155] ad laudem dei et honorem ecclesie . et dignitatem sui ipsius . et

---

[140] aber- *Hr*
[141] merito *add. Hr*
[142] institutiones uero *Hr*
[143] qui *add. Hr*
[144] in suo regno ordo *Hr*
[145] *No rubric in Hr*
[146] conciliacio *Hr*
[147] chuntus *Hr*
[148] norrorum *Hr*
[149] quelibet *Hr*
[150] utram *Hr*
[151] De iure ecclesiastico *rubric add. Hr*
[152] consiliacio *Hr*
[153] chuntus *Hr*
[154] decreto principum] meditacionem *Hr*
[155] sapientum *Hr*

ad utilitatem totius regni sui cui preerat: instituit.[156] Hoc autem factum est in natale[157] domini apud Wintoniam.

Translation

Here begin the laws of Cnut, king of the English, Danes and Norwegians, a most just and good man.

As we learn from the authority of those who came before, England in former times used to be secured by the protection of many kings, with separate kings governing in each region, and also with differing legal practices which continued in the different regions, whether they were under several governments or a single one. In this way the customs of the common people had continued up to the present day and endured unchanged. Afterwards, however, it happened that Cnut, the most just king, acquired all of England and he decided after reasonable consideration that in so far as the whole kingdom of England was ruled by one king, so also should it be ruled by one law. Having called a council, therefore, of the earls and chief men and also the rest of the great and the wise of all England, he endeavoured by a common decision, that, in so far as human reason was capable, he would make firm those customs which were just; he would correct, however, what was partly in error; and he would pull up and completely destroy those which deviated altogether from the path of righteousness. Since all law should refer to Him from whom all justice comes, and indeed, who teaches man knowledge, then divine matters ought to take precedence over human affairs. Before that time, ecclesiastical regulations and meetings of synods had been unusual among the English. Therefore, so that no order in his kingdom might falter, he began to draw together first from ecclesiastical law, and next from secular law, saying: Here begin the decrees of Cnut.

This is the alleviation which Cnut, king of all England, and of the Danes and Norwegians, deliberated with his councillors at Winchester for the praise

---

[156] ad laudem ... instituit] consiliatus est deo ad laudem et sibimet ad regiam dignitatem et expedicionem *Hr appears to have garbled its text at this point, repeating some, but not all of the preceding passage in a second short introductory chapter. The reviser in Cb has replaced most of this second introduction with language from the Instituta's translation of the source. It would be odd for the archetype or at least the autograph to have repeated itself intentionally. Might the explanation be that Hr reflects the Consiliatio as it appeared on the exemplar used by the scribe, but also that he has mistakenly included a version of the passage originally marked for deletion in the autograph, a passage which served as a first draft of the passage in the Old English source? It is impossible to say with any certainty. For reference, the passage in the earliest copy of the Instituta reads as follows:* 'Hęc est institutio quam cnud rex cum consilio principum suorum sapientium: ad laudem dei · & honorem sui ipsius · & profectum totius regni cui preerat · instituit.'

[157] natali *Hr*

of God and for his own dignity and advantage. Anyone whosoever can read whether he preferred either secular law or divine enterprise.

This is the ordinance which King Cnut established by the decision of his principal councillors to the praise of God and the honour of the church and his own dignity and for the utility of all his kingdom over which he ruled. This was done at Christmas in Winchester.

PART IV
Art History and the French Vernacular

Chapter 13
'History' in Anglo-Norman Romance: The Presentation of the Pre-Conquest Past

Judith Weiss

Many Anglo-Norman romances show a strong interest in 'history', in the sense that they use the past as 'a suitable locus for romance action', as Rosalind Field puts it, and create supposed histories of pre-Conquest English heroes to give their narratives plausibility.[1] Their poems also have close associations with history of the kind produced by twelfth-century chroniclers,[2] such as Gaimar, Wace and Geoffrey of Monmouth, and this is hardly accidental since the twelfth century is a highly productive period in England for both genres, romance and historiography. The historiographers provided the writers of romance with stories, supposedly from Britain's past, and it was of course a two-way process, since in turn the romance poets provided the chroniclers with stories.

But contemporary students of this body of romances are often careful to distance them from their historical context. For example, Field, the most perceptive commentator upon one of the romances I wish to discuss here, *Waldef*, remarks that it does not reflect 'the historical moment of the early thirteenth century'.[3] I'm not entirely happy with this observation. Of course I would not maintain that romances should be read entirely in terms of their relationship to

---

[1] R. Field, 'Romance as history, history as romance', in M. Mills, J. Fellows and C.M. Meale (eds), *Romance in medieval England*, Cambridge 1991, 164, 168. A notable example is *Boeve de Haumtone* (late twelfth century) where the fictitious pre-Conquest hero, by owning Southampton and building Arundel castle, can be seen as the Anglo-Saxon 'ancestor' and uninterrupted link to the Norman Albini family, who possessed the same land and probably were the patrons of the romance. See J. Weiss, 'The date of the Anglo-Norman *Boeve de Haumtone*', *Medium Aevum* lv (1986), 237–41 and I. Djordjevic, 'Mapping medieval translation: methodological problems and a case study', unpubl. Ph.D. diss. McGill 2003, 260–74.

[2] See L. Ashe, *Fiction and history in England, 1066–1200*, Cambridge 2007, 24.

[3] R. Field, '*Waldef* and the matter of/with England', in J. Weiss, J. Fellows and M. Dickson (eds), *Medieval insular romance: translation and innovation*, Cambridge 2000, 25–39, at 39.

the period in which they were written,[4] but I also share Laura Ashe's view that 'behind the changing meanings of the stories we tell ourselves lie the reasons for their being told',[5] and I believe some of those reasons may relate to contemporary issues and concerns.

The Anglo-Norman romances span almost a hundred years, from around 1170 to the 1260s, and they were written, so far as we can ascertain, for a close-knit group of baronial families – FitzGilberts, Albinis, FitzBaderons, Fitzwarins, perhaps also Clares and Bigods.[6] They 'show an awareness of contemporary developments in fiction and thus belong to a literary culture that is self-conscious, defensive and humorous'.[7] They are notable for their avoidance, or only oblique use of, Arthurian material, although they were obviously well acquainted with it, and this in itself suggests an agenda, or in Pearsall's terms, a reason for *not* telling a story.[8] In investigating how these romance narratives perceive and refashion the past, I propose to concentrate on just one question: when they present a picture of pre-Conquest peoples, are their views very similar to those of twelfth-century historians? Two of the romances will be discussed in some detail – the *Romance of Horn* and the *Romance of Waldef* – and aligned with a substantial body of recent scholarship, which explores what insular chroniclers felt about others who had occupied and ruled Britain before them, before the Normans arrived – and some peoples indeed who still lived there, in Celtic regions.[9] Are those historians'

---

[4] Field warns about 'explaining literature away' as propaganda: 'Romance as history', 166.

[5] Laura Ashe's introduction in L. Ashe, I. Djordjevic and J. Weiss (eds), *The exploitations of medieval romance*, Cambridge 2010, 1. Ashe is responding to an article by Derek Pearsall in 2004, on 'the dangers of reading literature solely in terms of its complicity with … cultural and political ideologies': Ashe, *Exploitations*, 1; D. Pearsall, 'Medieval literature and historical enquiry', *Modern Language Review* xcix (2004), xxxi–xlii.

[6] See J. Weiss, 'The power and the weakness of women in Anglo-Norman romance', in C.M. Meale (ed.), *Women and literature in Britain, 1150–1500*, Cambridge 1993, 7–19, at 17–19, I. Short, 'Patrons and polyglots: French literature in twelfth-century England', *ANS* xiv (1992), 229–49, and R. Field, '*Pur les francs homes amender*: clerical authors and the thirteenth-century context of historical romance', in R. Purdie and M. Cichon (eds), *Medieval romance, medieval contexts*, Woodbridge 2011, 175–88, at 178.

[7] Field, '*Pur les francs homes amender*', 180.

[8] Ibid. 181.

[9] See, for example, the articles by J. Gillingham: 'The context and purposes of Geoffrey of Monmouth's *History of the kings of Britain*', *ANS* xiii (1991–92), 99–118; 'The beginnings of English imperialism', *Journal of Historical Sociology* v. 4 (1992), 392–409; 'Conquering the barbarians: war and chivalry in twelfth-century Britain and Ireland', *Haskins Society Journal* iv (1993), 67–84 and 'Gaimar, the prose *Brut* and the making of English history', in Jean-Philippe Genet (ed.), *L'Histoire et les nouveaux publics dans l'Europe médiévale*, Paris 1997, 165–76. All of the articles cited above are reprinted in J. Gillingham, *The English in the twelfth century: imperialism, national identity and political values*, Woodbridge 2000. See

views on Anglo-Saxons and Celts reflected by the insular romances? The picture is interestingly mixed.

The developments and occasional contradictions of views found in twelfth-century historiography are fascinating. It seems the closer in time a writer from one people is to the preceding one, the more likely he is to depict it as barbarous, uncivilised, and punished for its moral turpitude, as shown by its defeat by his own people. Bede (much earlier, of course, than the twelfth century but a popular historical source for its historians)[10] provides a model here: he has no admiration for the Britons who preceded his own people, describing Cadwallon of Gwynedd as godless, savage, tyrannical and bent on exterminating the English race, sparing neither women nor children.[11] Henry of Huntingdon, on the other hand, sees the uncivilised Saxons, with their barbarous language and customs, as deservedly defeated by the Normans.[12] Geoffrey of Monmouth distorts and effaces Anglo-Saxon history of the seventh–tenth centuries, portraying the Anglo-Saxon arrivals as a treacherous collection of scoundrels while the British reach their glorious apogee with King Arthur (though Geoffrey, too, is keen on the idea of defeat arising from moral turpitude, which is evinced all too often by the British).[13]

But of course this picture is too simple. As Lesley Johnson puts it, 'twelfth-century writers tried to mediate between alternative images of the insular past, and to give it a shape'.[14] Some of these writers, like William of Malmesbury, were half-English and half-Norman, and envisaged English history in a slightly more benign light as a progress from barbarism to civilisation.[15] The Norman Gaimar in his *Estoire des Engleis* (first redaction 1137)[16] does not portray the

---

further, J. Gillingham, 'Henry of Huntingdon and the twelfth-century revival of the English nation', in S. Forde, L. Johnson and A.V. Murray (eds), *Concepts of national identity in the Middle Ages* (Leeds Texts and Monographs, N.S. XIV, 1995), 75–101. See also J.D. Niles, 'The wasteland of Loegria: Geoffrey of Monmouth's reinvention of the Anglo-Saxon past', in W.F. Gentrup (ed.), *Reinventing the middle ages and the Renaissance*, Turnhout 1998, 1–18; L. Johnson, 'The Anglo-Norman *Description of England*: an introduction', in I. Short (ed.), *Anglo-Norman anniversary essays*, London 1993, 11–30; F. Ingledew, 'The Book of Troy and the genealogical construction of history: the case of Geoffrey of Monmouth's *Historia Regum Britanniae*', *Speculum* lxix (1994), 665–704 and J. Campbell, 'Some twelfth-century views of the Anglo-Saxon past', *Peritia* iii (1984), 131–50; repr. in idem, *Essays in Anglo-Saxon history*, London and Ronceverte 1986, 209–28.

[10] See A. Gransden, *Historical writing in England, c.550 to c.1307*, London 1974, 16–17, 153, 169, 197–8.

[11] *HE* ii. 20 and iii. 1. Bede was rather kinder about the Irish Celts: see Gransden, *Historical writing*, 19.

[12] Gillingham, 'Henry of Huntingdon', 78.

[13] Niles, 'Wasteland of Loegria', 9–10.

[14] Johnson, 'Anglo-Norman *Description of England*', 24.

[15] Gillingham, 'Beginnings', 5, but see too Thomson in this volume.

[16] Gaimar, *Estoire*, ed. and tr. I. Short, p. xxv.

British king Arthur in an especially positive way (lines 409–18) (in his extant writing – his *Estoire des Bretuns* is lost) but pictures some Anglo-Saxon heroes sympathetically, at least those post-Alfred, like Edgar and Hereward (lines 3565–974 and 5468–700). Wace shows similar sympathy in his praise of the noble Oswald (lines 14435–8). The anonymous *Description of England* (1140s) depicts a continuous sequence of Saxon kings after Hengest instead of Geoffrey of Monmouth's depiction of the process of Saxon conquest as 'fitful and fractured'.[17] The powerful influence of Geoffrey's pro-British *Historia regum Britanniae* skews attitudes to the past for a while, and prompts other historians to revise their work;[18] but by the late twelfth century 'a developing sense of Englishness'[19] prevails, albeit in Normans whose first language was still French. By then, if not earlier, perhaps as early as 1138 with the address by Ralph, bishop of the Orkneys, at the Battle of the Standard, the Celts – Irish, Scots, Welsh – have replaced the Anglo-Saxons in the Norman view as barbarous, alien and uncivilised societies, living in rustic squalor, lazy and with deplorable sexual habits.[20]

Do Anglo-Norman romances perceive and refashion the past in alignment with these various views? In part. Most of the first generation of such romances, up to around 1200, have insular settings and insular heroes, but their sense of place varies from the occasionally precise to the (more often) vague, and that variation may partly be to do with their Anglo-Norman patrons. The Havelok story, as used in Gaimar's *Estoire* and the later *Lai d'Havelok* (c.1200) derived from it, comes from Lincolnshire (where Gaimar's patrons had land)[21] and dimly recalls a distant period of peaceful intermarriage between British in the kingdom of Lindsey and Angles in East Anglia.[22] Its topography is specific: Lincoln, Lindsey, Rutland, Colchester, Stamford, Grimsby. The heroine is half British, half English, the villains are British and Danish, and the hero Danish.[23] However, there is no sense that any one of these peoples is better (or worse) than the other. On the other hand, the hero of the *Romance of Horn* by Thomas

---

[17] Johnson, 'Anglo-Norman *Description of England*', 26.

[18] Campbell, 'Some twelfth-century views', 144–9.

[19] Gillingham, 'Henry of Huntingdon', 88.

[20] For Ralph's speech, see Henry, archdeacon of Huntingdon, *Historia Anglorum* in HH, x. 8 (pp. 714–5): 'There is among them [the Scots] no knowledge of military matters, experience in battle, or regard for discipline ... those who have violated the temples of God in this country have spilt blood on altars, have murdered priests, have spared neither children nor pregnant women ...' See also Gillingham, 'Beginnings', 7–11.

[21] Gaimar, *Estoire* pp. xi–xii, and I. Short, 'Gaimar et les débuts de l'historiographie en langue française', in D. Buschinger (ed.), *Chroniques nationales et chroniques universelles* (Göppinger Arbeiten zur Germanistik 508) Göppingen 1990, 155–63.

[22] See *The birth of romance in England*, tr. and intro. J. Weiss, Tempe, AZ 2009, 21–2.

[23] Gaimar puts the Havelok story at the start of his *Estoire* to support Cnut's later claim that Danes had sovereign rights in England long before Saxons.

appears to come from south-west England – 'Suddene' – and is keen to regain his heritage there, but spends long periods of time in two Celtic kingdoms, Brittany and Ireland, whose aristocratic cultures are depicted in detail and (in the case of the Irish) with great sympathy. But Suddene itself has no convincing literary existence as a place, and its culture is only alluded to in negative terms, one where people don't swear judicial oaths and don't interfere in chess games.[24] Horn's story has some close parallels with the fabulous parts of the story of Hereward (*Gesta Herewardi*, dated any time between 1109 and 1174), which likewise features close ties to the Celtic kingdoms of Cornwall and Ireland.[25] A strong Continental influence is, however, evident in the style of *Horn*, strongly influenced by the French *chanson de geste* with its crusading ethos and 'Saracen' enemies. This form of writing was probably popular with Norman patrons who imported it in the years after the Conquest. The same *chanson de geste* influence is felt in *Boeve de Haumtone* (1190s)[26] where the hero is English, son of Count Gui of Hampton and a Scottish mother. He is dispossessed by his wicked mother and exiled to the heathen regions of the Middle East. When he regains his lands, he is again dispossessed of them by an unjust English king, Edgar, and spends most of his life back in the Middle East. The poet's knowledge of English and foreign geography is alike imprecise and, although his story resembles those of Haveloc and Horn in their concentration on the importance of family and land, it seems not to matter how identifiable that land is. The story's 'Englishness' is also a shallowly rooted fiction. The poet's probable patrons were the francophone Albini family at the end of the twelfth century, now considering themselves 'English'.[27] Perhaps all that mattered to him was to provide them with a vague sense of connectedness to the pre-Conquest past.

So these early romances give a mixed picture in their portrayal of insular peoples in the past, perhaps because of the influence of Geoffrey's *Historia*: when the Celts appear (Irish, not Scots) in these narratives, they behave well, though that supreme Celtic figure, Arthur, never appears, while the English vary in their virtue, and no particular merit is attached to that people. Indeed in

---

[24] Thomas, *The Romance of Horn*, ed. M.K. Pope (Anglo-Norman Texts ix–x, xii–xiii, 1955–64), i. lines 939–40, 1979, 2754–5.

[25] See J. Weiss, 'Thomas and the earl: literary and historical contexts for the *Romance of Horn*', in R. Field (ed.), *Tradition and transformation in medieval romance*, Cambridge 1999, 1–13, at 9–13.

[26] See M. Ailes, 'The Anglo-Norman *Boeve de Haumtone* as a *chanson de geste*', in J. Fellows and I. Djordjevic (eds), *Sir Bevis of Hampton in literary tradition*, Cambridge 2008, 9–24.

[27] See above n. 1 and J. Weiss, '*Mestre* and son: the role of Sabaoth and Terri in *Boeve de Haumtone*', in *Sir Bevis of Hampton*, 25–36, at 34–6. On the Normans' perception of their identity in the period, see I. Short, '*Tam Angli quam Franci*: self-definition in Anglo-Norman England', *ANS* xviii (1995), 153–75.

Horn, while the hero is English, so is the principal villain (Wikele), and there is an incident suggesting a contemptuous view of the English as a people, to which I shall return. But first to consider the second generation of insular romances.

This is represented by *Waldef*, *Gui de Warewic* and *Fouke Fitz Warin*. Though the latter two will not be discussed at length here, it is interesting that *Gui* (which could be as late as the 1220s or, more likely, as early as 1204) is a romance strongly convinced of the virtues of England and England's king, Æthelstan.[28] So by the beginning of the thirteenth century the insular romance has become very positive about the English. I would like, however, to concentrate more upon the earlier *Waldef*, c.1200–1210, which presents a more mixed view of the English, far from uncritical. *Waldef* is indebted to Wace's version of Geoffrey's *Historia* and it has absorbed Wace's recurrent idea of history as conflict, violence and betrayal, often within a family. It has also absorbed the way Wace, like Gaimar, changes the *Historia*'s name for our island, from Bretaigne to Engleterre.[29] But *Waldef* goes one step further, by blotting out the British period from our history entirely. Its prologue depicts conquest, and the foundation of cities, by the civilising Romans, and proceeds directly from them to the aggressive East Anglians, whose incessant warfare with the neighbouring rulers recalls Gaimar's picture of Anglo-Saxon small kingdoms in the late eighth and early ninth centuries:

> En icel tens tel ert la lai:
> ki force aveit si feseit guere,
> a son veisin toleit sa terre …
> partut aveit itels seignurs:
> tresque alcuns pout un poi munter,
> si se fesait reis apeler.[30]

---

[28] For the revised dating of *Gui de Warewic*, initially placed in the 1220s by its editor (*Gui de Warewic: roman du XIIIe siècle*, ed. A. Ewert (Classiques français du Moyen Âge lxxiv-5, 1932–33), i. pp. v–vii), see E. Mason, 'Legends of the Beauchamps' ancestors: the use of baronial propaganda in medieval England', *Journal of Medieval History* x (1984), 25–40, Y. Liu, 'Romances of continuity in the English Rous Roll' (who corrects Mason's facts), in Purdie, *Medieval romance*, 149–59, at 151, and J. Weiss, 'The exploitation of ideas of pilgrimage and sainthood in *Gui de Warewic*', in *Exploitations of medieval romance*, 43–56, at 54–5. On Æthelstan, see I. Djordjevic, 'Saracens and other Saxons', in *Exploitations of medieval romance*, 28–42, at 41–2. Æthelstan was already admired by historians in the twelfth century: see Malmesbury, *GR* i. 210–11 (bk ii. 132–3).

[29] See Wace, *Brut*, p. xx. Wace may in turn have been influenced by Gaimar's *Estoire*, lines 29–34 (pp. 4–5).

[30] Gaimar, *Estoire* lines 2018–20 (pp. 110–11), 2286–8 (pp. 126–7): 'Such was the law at that time that whoever had the power to do so waged war and took his neighbour's land from him … There were sub-rulers all over the place, and as soon as an individual was able to

It is possible that, like the author of the *Gesta Herewardi*, the poet of *Waldef* wanted to correct the reputation of the English – found for example in Wace[31] – for being inexperienced in warfare, but he also puts their courage and skill in a context of constant vengeful violence, injustice and disorder, and is obviously concerned with *dreit* (law and justice) and its abuse by overwhelming force. The partiality of Waldef's own sons, Guiac and Gudlac, for foreign conquest puts the possessions and very life of their father at risk. As Rosalind Field has observed, it is precisely the absence of King Arthur in the romance, *except* as the dubious model whom Guiac and Gudlac cite and admire, which draws attention to the poet's 'suspicions of conquest and empire'.[32] The very long romance is unfinished but near its end Guiac imitates Arthur's defeat of the Roman emperor and arrogantly intends to surpass the British king by conquering Greece, the Holy Land and the Earthly Paradise. Like Arthur, too, the hubristic Guiac is stopped in his tracks by a messenger, and instead becomes a contrite pilgrim. It is an Englishman, not a Celt, who defeats the Emperor – a triumph of the imagined English past. But it is at great personal cost: in Guiac's absence his unsupported father has been murdered. The Celtic peoples are absent in person from this story but allusions to their most celebrated hero (and to other famous Britons like Belin, Brenne, Uther and Merlin too) suggest they provide bad examples that the English should on the whole avoid.[33]

Looking in detail at episodes in *Horn* and in *Waldef* reveals an insight into their poets' views that perhaps shows how far these twelfth- and early-thirteenth-century insular romances echo the attitudes of contemporary historians. In *Horn*, the hero has returned incognito from Ireland, where he has been treated with courtesy and kindness by an extremely cultured court, to Brittany to rescue his sweetheart, the princess Rigmel, from a forced marriage to King Modin. He meets Modin and Wikele, the English villain who has arranged this marriage, as they ride towards the bridal hall, and is angered by their talk of the princess, which spurs him into speech: 'Now he would say something, however cross it made them' (Ja lur dira un mot, ki qu'en seit coroçant):

'Seignurs,' fet il, 'bachelers, bien semblez gent bevant,
Ki a noces augez pur demener bobant,

rise to some sort of prominence, he had himself called king'. I am indebted to Gillingham, 'Gaimar', 121–2, for alerting me to this passage.

[31] See H.M. Thomas, 'The *Gesta Herwardi*, the English, and their conquerors', *ANS* xxi (1998), 213–32, at 220.

[32] R. Field, 'What's in a name? Arthurian name-dropping in the *Roman de Waldef*', in B. Wheeler (ed.), *Arthurian studies in honour of P.J.C. Field*, Cambridge 2004, 63–4.

[33] See J. Weiss, 'Emperors and Antichrists: reflections of empire in insular narrative, 1130–1250', in P. Hardman (ed.), *The matter of identity in medieval romance*, Cambridge 2002, 87–102.

> Bien jur(e)rez "Witegod"; quant avrez beü taunt
> Ke li vins vus eschaufe e seëz si jurant,
> Dorrai vus un sestier si gré m'estes savant,
> E si gré ne.m savez, n'en avrez taunt ne quant.'[34]

The villain, sure enough, *is* cross. Not only is 'bacheler' a jeer because it lowers the status of Modin and Wikele but also, in using the English oath 'witegod', or 'as God is my witness', Thomas (to quote his editor) 'appears to be having a fling at those Anglo-French barons who reveal in their cups the English origin they are usually at pains to conceal'.[35] It is impossible not to remember William of Malmesbury on the barbarous English:

> It is ingrained in this nation to dote on wassail rather than wealth ... Drinking in company was a universal practice, and in this passion they made no distinction between night and day ... [They ate] till they were sick and [drank] till they spewed.[36]

We recall too the introduction of the English words *wasseil* and *drincheil* by Geoffrey of Monmouth and (following him) Wace to Vortigern's banquet. Already in his cups (according to Wace), the British king is introduced to Hengist's daughter Ronwein and the Angles' custom of exchanging kisses while drinking more wine. The context, with Satan inflaming Vortigern with lust, gives the custom and the English words unsavoury connotations.[37] Then there are comments by Gaimar and Jordan Fantosme, Gaimar depicting King Edgar's passion for Ælfthryth as incited by heavy drinking:

> Baivres ourent a remüer,
> e la custome itele estait
> grant pris li ert ki bien beveit.
> Od cupes [d'or], od mazelins,
> od corns des bugles pleins de vins
> fu le wesheil e le drinchail ...[38]

---

[34] Thomas, *Romance of Horn*, lines 4011–16: 'My lords,' he said, 'young men, you seem like roisterers, going to a wedding to show off. You're sure to be swearing like a trooper, and, when you've drunk so much that you're inflamed with wine, and swearing in that way, I'll pour you a measure, if you thank me for it, and if not, you won't get anything at all'.

[35] *Romance of Horn*, ii. 164–5.

[36] Malmesbury, *GR* i. 458–9 (bk iii. 245–6).

[37] G. Mon. 128 (bk vi. 100); Wace, *Brut*, 174–7, lines 6945–98.

[38] Gaimar, *Estoire* 208–9, lines 3804–9: 'They had a wide variety of different drinks. The custom was that heavy drinking was highly prized. Wassailing there was, and toasts flew thick and fast, with golden goblets, mazers, and oxhorns brimming with different wines'.

And Fantosme (writing about 1173) puts a pejorative comment in the mouth of the Countess of Leicester:

> Li Engleis sunt bon vantus, ne savent ostëer;
> Mielz savent as gros hanaps beivre et gueisseillier.[39]

In introducing Horn's jeer, Thomas represents his hero as making fun of the very people he supposedly belongs to, the English.[40] In fact, in the hero's passion for combat evinced throughout the romance, he seems rather more like a Norman – the kind described by William of Malmesbury as 'hardly knowing how to live without fighting'[41] – and this may not be coincidental. There may have been an Irish context and inspiration for Thomas's romance, possibly composed and delivered at the Christmas feast of 1171–72 in the company of Henry II and the Norman Earl of Clare, Richard FitzGilbert, called Strongbow, perhaps as a compliment to the latter (part of whose Irish career resembles Horn's). The romance, probably elaborating a story already in circulation by 1170, has a number of touches suggesting first-hand knowledge of the Dublin area, and some knowledge of Irish culture, especially harping;[42] and whether Thomas was responsible for these elements or not, it is clear that, unlike contemporary historians, he is sympathetic to Celtic peoples.[43]

The poet of *Waldef* had first-hand knowledge of another region entirely, East Anglia, and his hero is from Norfolk. The writer portrays the area's towns – Thetford, Colchester, Taseburgh, Attleborough, Caister – as important and fought-over concentrations of power and wealth (even if he sometimes ascribes to them odd geographical features, for example being next to the sea rather than on rivers). Founded by the Romans, once these depart the towns fall into the hands of minor kings whose leader is the king of London. The poet's views on towns are mixed: on the one hand, they protect the coastline against invasion by *estranges gent* (foreigners, line 110); on the other hand, their burgesses may pragmatically desert their overlord for what they perceive to be the

---

[39] See Jordan Fantosme, *Chronicle*, ed. R.C. Johnston, Oxford 1981, lines 978–9: 'The English are great boasters, but poor fighters; they are better at quaffing great tankards and carousing'. (According to the *Anglo-Norman Dictionary*, 'gueisseillier' is related to 'wassailing'.)

[40] In *Boeve de Haumtone* there is perhaps a suggestion that English is regarded as the language of the nursery: the hero's wicked Scottish mother is reported as using it to address the child Boeve's *mestre*. See *Der Anglonormannische Boeve de Haumtone*, ed. A. Stimming, Halle 1899, line 331.

[41] Malmesbury, *GR* i. 460–61 (bk iii. 246). See also Thomas, 'The *Gesta Herwardi*', 220.

[42] Weiss, 'Thomas and the earl', 2–7.

[43] The portrait of the Breton court, which adopts Horn the foundling, is also detailed and sympathetic, even if its weak king does not treat the adult hero as he deserves.

winning side.[44] I want to focus on an episode where London's representative – the sheriff – thwarts the high-handed action of an unjust ruler and seems to appeal to ancient, pre-Conquest law. Okenard, a mercenary, once a supporter of Waldef's, has joined Waldef's enemy, King Fergus of London, but notwithstanding this switch of allegiance, he helps Waldef escape from Fergus's captivity and so incurs the king's anger and threats of execution. Okenard appeals to the 'judgement of your [Fergus's] court'. He is saved by the intervention of Edward, the sheriff, 'very wise in the laws and customs', who rebukes the king, saying that Okenard, as a mercenary, cannot be punished in the way a feudal vassal can; moreover, it is the business of the city of London's inhabitants, not the king's, to deliver judgement upon him:

> A itant estes vus Edward,
> Un halt hum iert de bone part,
> Vesquons estoit de la cité,
> Mult par estoit de grant eé
> E mult estoit sages des lois
> E d'establissement des rois ...
> 'Par vostre ire ne vus hastez
> De fere tant contre reisun,
> De treire hum a dampnaciun;
> N'est pas l'us de ceste cité ...
> Cest esguard n'avom pas veü,
> Ne vus apent rien d'esguard fere –
> Dire le vus voil e retreire –
> Mais vostre curt feire le doit,
> Iço apent a nostre droit.[45]

Edward decrees that Okenard may depart unharmed, owing Fergus neither loyalty nor pledge, and this judgement is praised by the king's allies. The London sheriff has upheld law and custom in the face of injustice and violence by the London king. It is no accident that the sheriff's name is Edward: this recalls

---

[44] For a detailed discussion of this and other episodes in *Waldef*, see J. Weiss, 'Anglo-Norman romance', in C. Saunders (ed.), *A companion to romance: from classical to contemporary*, Oxford 2004, 26–44, at 36–7.

[45] *Le Roman de Waldef*, ed. A.J. Holden (Texte, Bibliotheca Bodmeriana, v, 1984), lines 10701–6, 10712–35: 'Then here came Edward; he was a noble man of great authority. He was sheriff of the city and very old, and he was very learned in the laws and royal customs ... 'In your anger don't hurry to behave so unreasonably as to convict a man; it's not the custom of this city ... We have not made this judgement; it is in no way your prerogative to make a judgement – I wish to state this and tell you – but your court should do it. This belongs to our rights (*or*: our law)'.

the 'Laws of Edward', *Leges Edwardi Confessoris*, actually from the mid-twelfth century but claiming to document Saxon laws in Edward's reign, supposedly going back to Cnut and upheld via Edward the Confessor to William and his successors: the Coronation charters of Henry I and Stephen swore to maintain them.[46] The *Leges Edwardi* 'constituted the legal standard of the age'.[47] The romance has here invoked a positive aspect of a fictional English past, but in order to confront that past with a 'present' where those laws are threatened. Perhaps, in its picture of a London sheriff confronting a tyrannical king with a reminder of law and custom, the poem is making a veiled criticism of a contemporary monarch. Those opposing King John regarded Angevin rule as 'unlawful innovation standing in sharp contrast to the good and ancient custom of the Anglo-Norman kingdom, itself partly derived from pre-Conquest England'. John's opponents 'set out to ... bring government into line with ancient custom ... partly by glossing custom so that it was made relevant to the circumstances of their own day.'[48] There was a close association between the rebellious barons and Londoners (the mayor of London was one of the guarantors of Magna Carta), and it was in London *c.*1200 that the *Leges Anglorum* was compiled, a collection of laws and charters of English kings from Ine to Henry II.[49] The romance, if it belongs to the decade of 1200–1210, would seem to reflect the preoccupation of the baronage of the period with reform of the law, which leads up to Magna Carta, and with asserting the relevance of the Anglo-Saxon legal heritage.[50] *Waldef*'s editor has raised the possibility that the Bigod family were possible

---

[46] J.C. Holt, *Magna Carta and medieval government*, London and Ronceverte 1985, 21–2, 153–4; R. Sharpe, 'The prefaces of *Quadripartitus*', in G. Garnett and J. Hudson (eds), *Law and government in medieval England and Normandy*, Cambridge 1994, 148–72, at 162.

[47] Quoted from B.R. O'Brien, *God's peace and king's peace: the laws of Edward the Confessor*, Philadelphia 1999, 56, by J. Greenberg, '"St Edward's ghost": the cult of St Edward and his laws in English history', in S. Jurasinski, L. Oliver and A. Rabin (eds), *English law before Magna Carta*, Leiden and Boston 2010, 273–300, at 278.

[48] Holt, *Magna Carta and medieval government*, 153, 157.

[49] W. Ullmann, 'On the influence of Geoffrey of Monmouth in English history', in C. Bauer, L. Boehm and M. Müller (eds), *Speculum Historiale: Geschichte im Spiegel von Geschichtsschreibung und Geschichtsdeutung*, Freiburg and Munich 1965, 257–76; Holt, *Magna Carta and medieval government*, 165; and J. Catto, 'Andrew Horn: law and history in fourteenth-century England', in R.H.C. Davis and J.M. Wallace-Hadrill (eds), *The writing of history in the middle ages*, Oxford 1981, 367–91, at 376, 386. London actively opposed John in the 1190s; see J. Campbell, 'Power and authority, 600–1300', in D.M. Palliser (ed.), *The Cambridge urban history of Britain, volume I, 600–1540*, Cambridge 2000, 51–78, at 75.

[50] The long history of such assertions implies 'something widely and deeply felt': see P. Wormald, 'Quadripartitus', in G. Garnett and J. Hudson (eds), *Law and government in medieval England and Normandy: essays in honour of Sir James Holt*, Cambridge 1994, 111–47, at 145.

patrons for the romance;[51] both Roger II Bigod (d. 1221) and his son Hugh II (d. 1225) were among the twenty-five individuals charged with the enforcement of Magna Carta, and their ancestors had been sheriffs of Norfolk and Suffolk, so a poem where a sheriff stands up to a king could well have constituted acceptable light reading matter for them.[52]

But if this literary episode comes across as similar to baronial use of the Anglo-Saxon past as a warning about royal abuses of the law in the present, its presentation of Okenard the mercenary is somewhat surprising. He is portrayed sympathetically as a noble and honourable man, who will not desert Fergus even when he has helped Waldef escape: 'Jo ne voil pas ma foi mentir ... Kar a Fergus l'ai afié/ Servir le doie en lealté [I do not want to break my pledge of loyalty ... because I have promised it to Fergus, I should loyally serve him', lines 10467–70]. If the intervention by sheriff Edward reminds us of chapter thirty-nine of Magna Carta – no free man is to be imprisoned, dispossessed, outlawed, exiled or damaged without lawful judgement of his peers or by the law of the land[53] – chapter fifty-one of the same document is most unsympathetic to mercenaries. Such people were often highly trained professionals of considerable social standing, whose loyalty to their paymasters was respected, but by John's time the Angevin kings were heavily reliant on them.[54] There was resentment that John trusted them more than his vassals and rewarded their captains with offices the barons felt belonged to them.[55] At the very least the romance of *Waldef* has an ambivalent depiction of this particular mercenary that seems uncharacteristic of its period.

Our first romance, *Horn*, given its putative date of the 1170s, is surprisingly lukewarm about, even anti, English, and surprisingly pro-Irish – or should that be pro-Normanised Irish? To quote John Gillingham, if French speakers in

---

[51] Only to dismiss it: Holden, *Waldef*, 33–4.

[52] J.C. Holt, *Magna Carta*, 2 edn, Cambridge 1992, 478; J.A. Green, *The government of England under Henry I*, Cambridge 1986, 120.

[53] A.E.D. Howard, *Magna Carta: text and commentary*, Charlottesville and London 1998, 14; the same principle had been asserted in the Laws of Henry I.

[54] M. Chibnall, 'Mercenaries and the *familia regis* under Henry I', in M. Strickland (ed.), *Anglo-Norman warfare*, Woodbridge 1992, 84–92; J.O. Prestwich, 'The military household of the Norman kings', ibid. 93–127, and J.O. Prestwich, 'War and finance in the Anglo-Norman state', *TRHS*, 5 ser. iv (1954), 19–43. In 1102 the loyalty of mercenary knights to Robert de Bellême was respected by Henry I 'because they had served their master as was right', quoted from OV vi. 28–9. On the mercenary in *Waldef*, see S.D.B. Brown, 'Military service and monetary reward in the eleventh and twelfth centuries', *History* lxxiv (1989), 20–38.

[55] R.V. Turner, *King John*, London and New York 1994, 74, 184; W.L. Warren, *King John*, London 1961, 91 and G. Hindley, *The Book of Magna Carta*, London 1990, 29–30.

twelfth-century England could see the Anglo-Saxon past as *their* past,⁵⁶ then *Horn* (and his patrons?) show a rather critical view of that past. On the other hand, its pro-Irish slant may have much to do with the occasion and place of its delivery, if my hypothesis about these is correct. Our second romance, *Waldef*, is more predictably anti-British and, in the end, pro-English, but with many qualifications: if the English can stop fighting one other and stop following their imperial ambitions, and if they can observe law, they may struggle towards creating a civilised society. But the end of the poem is lost, and the supposed ending provided by a fifteenth-century Latin prose work does not help us, as it runs suspiciously counter to what the poet apparently envisaged earlier.⁵⁷ So we cannot be sure what his final word would be. What we *do* have fits the twelfth-century historians' view of England and the English before the Conquest: in a mess, in need of discipline and reform, but with the virtue of bravery and some respect for law. Some ten years later *Gui de Warewic* (which drew heavily upon *Waldef*) removed the mess and indiscipline from this picture and portrayed England and the English united under Æthelstan. At last there is a rosy portrayal, if rather far from historical actuality, of Anglo-Saxon England as far preferable to the lands in the Holy Roman Empire. And in this romance the nasty and treacherous foreigners are – German.⁵⁸

---

⁵⁶ Gillingham, 'Beginnings', 6.
⁵⁷ Johannes Bramis, *Historia regis Waldei*, drew on *Waldef* but also, he claims, on an English version (Holden, *Waldef*, 19–20). Field, '*Waldef* and the matter of/with England', 39 and Weiss, 'Anglo-Norman romance', 34 and n. 20, are not convinced by his ending of the narrative.
⁵⁸ On *Gui de Warewic*, the Germans and the Holy Roman Empire, see J. Weiss, '*Gui de Warewic* at home and abroad', in A. Wiggins and R. Field (eds), *Guy of Warwick: icon and ancestor*, Cambridge 2007, 1–11, at 2–3, 7; for *Gui* and the figure of Æthelstan, see I. Djordjevic, 'Saracens and other Saxons', 40–42.

Chapter 14

The Scribe Looks Back: Anglo-Saxon England and the Eadwine Psalter

C. Karkov

Any consideration of twelfth-century views of the Anglo-Saxon past should take account of the Eadwine Psalter: Cambridge, Trinity College, MS R. 17. 1, produced under the patronage of Prior Wibert at Christ Church Canterbury *c.*1155–60.[1] The Eadwine Psalter is the work of at least ten monastic scribes and six artists.[2] Eadwine, for whom the manuscript is named, may have been one of the scribes, possibly the main scribe; alternatively, he may have been in charge of designing the book or overseeing the project. Alternatively, some believe he may have been the manuscript's patron or possibly held a combination of these roles. Whatever his actual involvement in the production of the manuscript, however, the book itself presents him both verbally and visually as its scribe, and he will therefore be described as such in this chapter. In terms of its contents, the Eadwine Psalter is a scholarly collection of texts rather than a book designed for everyday use. It is a *psalterium triplex*, meaning that it brings together the three translations of the psalter text attributed to Jerome, the *Gallicanum* (the main text of Eadwine), the *Romanum* and the *Hebraicum* (both written in smaller script and narrower columns which run parallel down the sides of the page). The manuscript also contains an interlinear translation of the *Romanum* into Old English, and an interlinear translation of the *Hebraicum* (which is incomplete) into Anglo-Norman French, the *parva glosatura* or *glossa ordinaria* (a standard gloss or commentary on Psalms 1–150), a series of exegetical prologues, a calendar, *tituli* and collects, prognostics and, of course, the illuminations, which I have described elsewhere as providing both a comprehensive visual narrative and a gloss on the written text, that is, the psalms conveyed thorough a different form of language.[3] In addition to the drawings that accompany the psalter text, the book includes at its end the famous Eadwine portrait and drawings

---

[1] Portions of this chapter are based on C.E. Karkov, *The art of Anglo-Saxon England*, Woodbridge 2011, 175–8.

[2] See M. Gibson, T.A. Heslop and R.W. Pfaff (eds), *The Eadwine Psalter: text, image, and monastic culture in twelfth-century Canterbury*, London 1992.

[3] C.E. Karkov, 'Art and writing: voice, image, object', in C.A. Lees (ed.), *The Cambridge history of early medieval English literature*, Cambridge 2013, 73–98.

of the monastic precinct and waterworks of Christ Church, Canterbury. The manuscript now begins with the calendar, but it is most likely that it originally opened with a series of at least four leaves of painted narrative scenes consisting of Old and New Testament subjects from Exodus to the Acts of the Apostles (now separated from the manuscript and divided between London and New York),[4] in an expansion of the Anglo-Saxon tradition of typological psalter illustration. This development of Anglo-Saxon artistic practice is but one of the ways in which the manuscript is especially pertinent to the topic of this volume. It is, in part, a self-conscious look back at and appropriation of Anglo-Saxon traditions, some specific to Christ Church or to the larger Canterbury community, and an original translation of those traditions into a new visual language. Yet in some respects it also looks back beyond the Anglo-Saxons to some of the origins of their manuscript culture and their scribal and exegetical practices. The manuscript is a work of scholarship, indeed historical scholarship, but its heteroglossia can also be understood as symptomatic of the larger multilingual, postcolonial culture in which it was produced.

Some might still argue that the term 'postcolonial' is not appropriate to the culture of eleventh- and twelfth-century England; however, as numerous scholars have shown, that is far from the case. Postcolonial (as opposed to 'post-colonial') refers to a critical practice rather than to a linear history that assumes discrete colonising and colonised cultures, and thereby creates some sort of imaginary pre-colonial purity of culture.[5] I use the term here in reference to the ways in which the political and cultural encounter of an Anglo-Saxon past and an Anglo-Norman present is played out ideologically through the

---

[4] BL MS Add. 37472(1); London, Victoria and Albert Museum, MS 661; New York, Pierpont Morgan Library, MSS M. 521 and 724.

[5] On the term itself see C.E. Karkov, 'Postcolonial', in J. Stodnick and R. Trilling (eds), *A handbook of Anglo-Saxon studies*, Oxford 2012, ch. 10; K.E. Overbey, 'Postcolonial', *Studies in iconography* xxxiii (2012), 145–56. For its specific applicability to Anglo-Saxon and Anglo-Norman England, see, for example, K. Davis, 'National writing in the ninth century: a reminder for postcolonial thinking about the North', *Journal of Medieval and Early Modern Studies* xxviii.3 (1998), 61–37; N. Howe, 'Anglo-Saxon England and the postcolonial void', in A.J. Kabir and D. Williams (eds), *Postcolonial approaches to the European middle ages: translating cultures*, Cambridge 2001, 25–47; C.E. Karkov, 'The mother's tongue and the father's prose', *Parallax* xviii.3 (2012), 1–11; U. Mehan and D. Townsend, '"Nation" and the gaze of the other in eighth-century Northumbria', *Comparative Literature* liii.1 (2001), 1–26; K.E. Overbey, 'Taking place: reliquaries and territorial authority in the Bayeux embroidery', in M.K. Foys and K.E. Overbey (eds), *The Bayeux Tapestry: new approaches*, Woodbridge 2009, 36–50; M.R. Warren, *History on the edge: Excalibur and the borders of Britain, 1100–1300*, Minneapolis 2000; the essays collected in J.J. Cohen (ed.), *Cultural diversity in the British middle ages: archipelago, island, England*, New York 2008; E. Treharne, *Living through the Conquest: the politics of early English, 1020–1220*, Oxford 2012.

The Scribe Looks Back: Anglo-Saxon England and the Eadwine Psalter 291

Figure 14.1   Cambridge, Trinity College Library, MS R.17.1, fo. 5v. By permission of the Master and Fellows, Trinity College, Cambridge.

languages, images and contents of this one manuscript, the Eadwine Psalter. The manuscript is a space of encounter between cultures, but it does not establish a clear hierarchy of languages or 'cultural traditions', as suggested by some of the contributors to the 1992 volume on the psalter;[6] rather it puts those languages and traditions in an ongoing dialogue with one other.

In terms of its incorporation of the Latin, French and Old English languages, Eadwine is unusual, but far from unique – the *Production and use of English manuscripts 1060–1220* project has, for example, catalogued seventeen or eighteen manuscripts, which do the same, albeit not to the same extent or the same degree of complexity.[7] In terms of the way in which its texts and languages relate to each other, the Eadwine Psalter is distinctive, and its heteroglossia both more sustained and more ordered. The *Gallicanum*, the main text, was the version favoured on the Continent, as in the *c.*800 Utrecht Psalter, the ultimate model for Eadwine. The *Romanum* had been preferred by the Anglo-Saxons since at least the time of the tenth-century Benedictine Reform, but can be demonstrated to have been in particular favour at Canterbury from the earliest days of the Anglo-Saxon Church through to the period with which we are concerned.[8] It is the text used for the psalter in British Library, Harley 603, also thought to have been produced at Canterbury in the eleventh century, and also considered to have had an influence on the production of Eadwine, though perhaps not as direct as that of Utrecht. The *Romanum* was the official psalter in use in Rome, and might thus be considered an example of Anglo-Saxon *romanitas*, the Anglo-Saxons', and especially Canterbury's, own look back at their origins in the Church of Rome and Gregory. In any case, it is appropriate that in Eadwine this is the text accompanied by the Old English gloss. The *Hebraicum*, on the other hand, was a scholarly rather than a liturgical text. It was a central part of the history of biblical translation and, while known in Anglo-Saxon England, it can be associated more readily with the interest in Jewish texts and learning prevalent on the Continent, and in particular with the school of Theodulf (d. 821) at Fleury.[9] It is thus equally appropriate that it is accompanied by the Anglo-Norman French gloss. The arrangement does not in any way privilege the French over the English, as one might have expected of a manuscript produced

---

[6] Gibson, Heslop and Pfaff, *Eadwine Psalter*, 13, 136–7.

[7] O. Da Rold, T. Kato, M. Swan and E. Treharne (eds), *The production and use of English manuscripts 1060 to 1220*, University of Leicester 2010: http://www.le.ac.uk/ee/em1060to1220/.

[8] M. Gretsch, *The intellectual foundations of the English Benedictine reform*, Cambridge 1999, 289–90.

[9] S.L. Keefer and D.R. Burrows, 'Hebrew and the *Hebraicum* in late Anglo-Saxon England', *ASE* xix (1990), 67–80, at 67–8.

within a century of the Conquest.[10] Neither does it privilege the Old English;[11] rather it sets the two vernacular languages alongside and in dialogue with each other and puts them on an equal footing with respect to the dominant Latin of the Church. It might be possible to read a certain historicising of the texts on the page, as Jerome's *Hebraicum* was preceded by his *Romanum*, just as, perhaps, Anglo-Norman was preceded by Old English,[12] although there are places in the manuscript, such as the beginning of Psalm 1, where that order is reversed, with the Hebraicum and its Anglo-Norman gloss preceding the Romanum and its Old English gloss (Figure 14.2 below).

It is beyond doubt that the Eadwine Psalter looks back, but to what it looks back, and how and why it looks back, are not so easily pinned down. The close relationship between the words of the psalms and the miniatures that accompany them had already been established in the *c*.800 Utrecht Psalter (Utrecht, University Library, MS 32), one of the primary pictorial sources for Eadwine, although the *mise-en-page* of that manuscript, with its single text, is very different. In the Utrecht Psalter the drawings are all in a monochrome brown ink that visually unites them with the ink of the text, and helps not only to underscore the unity of image and text, but also to convey the fact that, for the most part, the images are a literal representation of the words of the text. Arguably the close visual correspondence between text and image established in Utrecht might be understood as compromised somewhat by the use of colour outline drawing for the images in British Library Harley 603, the earliest of the three 'copies' of Utrecht to be made at Christ Church after the manuscript arrived in England sometime shortly before the year 1000.[13] However, one could also argue that the coloured drawings in this manuscript serve to highlight the fact that text and image narrate the psalms through two different languages or narrative systems, and that while these are dependent on each other they are not the same. The dialogue between text and image established in Harley 603 might be seen as a move towards the heteroglossia of Eadwine. The interrelationship of text and image is established differently and possibly even strengthened in Eadwine by the extension of colourful images (the decorated, inhabited and historiated capitals) into the text, the addition of captions and words into some of the illustrations, and the general *mise-en-page* of the manuscript with its careful balancing of the images with the different versions of the psalms and commentaries on them. Eadwine might be seen then as performing a double look back to both Utrecht and Harley, although it cannot be said to be a literal

---

[10] E. Treharne, 'The architextual editing of Early English', in A.S.G. Edwards and T. Takako (eds), *Poetica* lxxi (2009), 1–13; eadem, *Living through the Conquest*, ch. 8.

[11] *Pace* Treharne, *Living through the Conquest*, ch. 8, in which the *Hebraicum* and its gloss are described as being marginalised to the gutter of the page.

[12] The *Romanum* was translated *c*.384, the *Gallicanum c*.392 and the *Hebraicum c*.400.

[13] Eadwine itself is the second copy. The third is BnF MS lat. 8846, produced *c*. 1180–90.

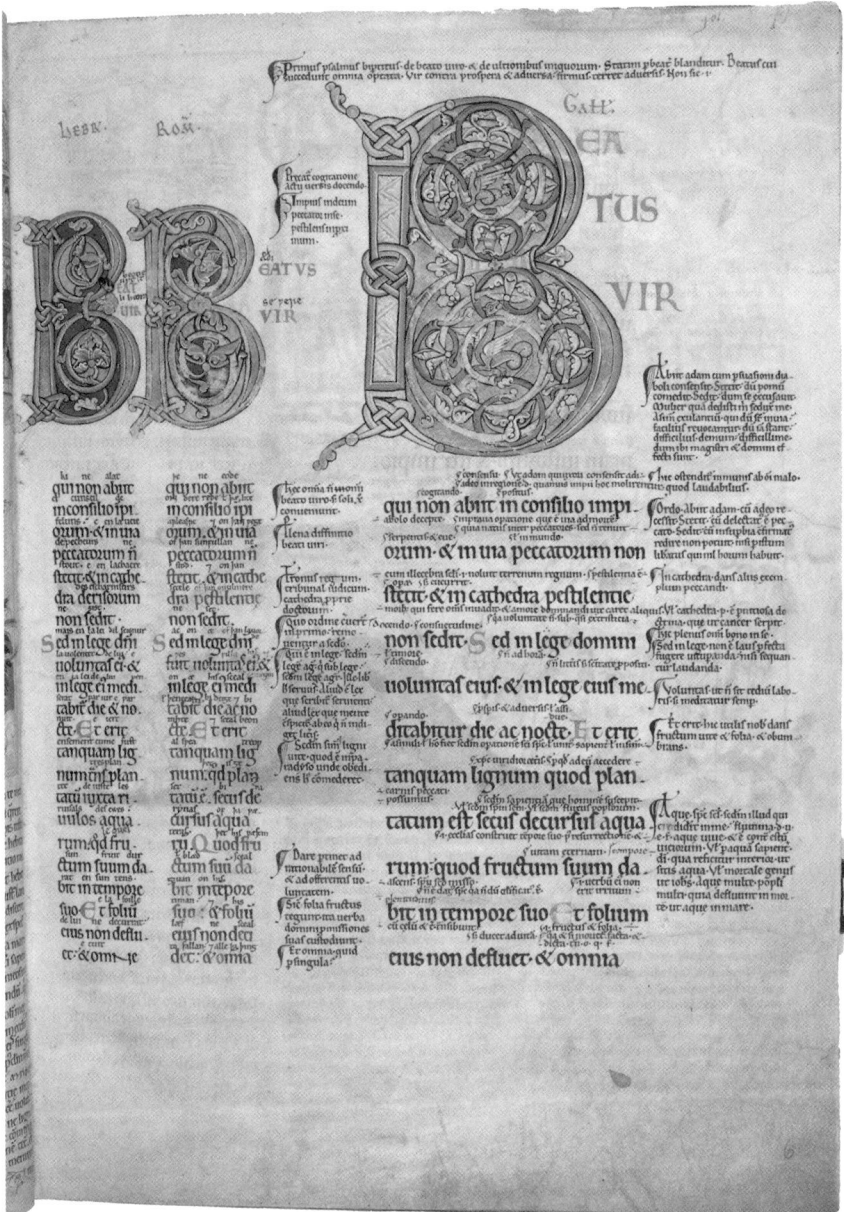

Figure 14.2: Cambridge, Trinity College Library, MS R.17.1, fo. 6r. By permission of the Master and Fellows, Trinity College, Cambridge.

copy of either. It mirrors them, but it does so in order to create something new and different. Indeed, a simultaneous process of doubling (or repetition) and division is very much a part of the way in which the Eadwine Psalter assembles its contents and conveys its meaning. The main Latin text is accompanied by the doubled Latin translations and the doubled vernacular glosses; the textual language of the psalms is doubled by the visual language of the illuminations. Yet equally, each language – the Latin, the Old English, the Anglo-Norman French, the imagery – is kept separate and distinct on the page, divided as well as doubled. I borrow the notion of doubling and division from postcolonial theory, in which it refers, in part, to the way in which the encounter between colonising and colonised cultures results in the repetition (or doubling) of the past in the present through the recreation or referencing of elements of the 'home' culture of the coloniser (which is always elsewhere and in the past) in the here and now of the culture that is colonised. The doubling, in other words, also creates difference, the same text written in, or story told in, two different languages, or in two different places, will never be the same text or story. Canterbury's Anglo-Saxon past revisited in its Anglo-Norman present, or the use of imported Norman stone and stone-cutting techniques in Archbishop Lanfranc's eleventh-century rebuilding of the Anglo-Saxon cathedral and cloister can, then, only ever be doublings that are always divided from that which they seek to double.[14]

Eadwine also creates, or has led later scholars to create, a similar doubling of the image of the scribe and scriptorium. Teresa Webber notes that 'there is much in the script of Eadwine which looks back to earlier English models, most notably the English Caroline minuscule perfected by ... Eadui Basan',[15] that most famous of pre-Conquest Canterbury scribes, though equally, there is much that does not. Richard Pfaff points out that Eadwine's calendar 'seems to be based' on a Canterbury calendar (or calendars) of the second third of the eleventh century.[16] And he also argues, albeit with due caution, that the portrait of Eadwine, and the status of 'prince of scribes' that the surrounding inscription gives him, are based on what was known of Eadui and his work at Canterbury just over a century after he flourished in the second and third decades of the eleventh century.[17] Eadui, as Pfaff points out, citing Nicholas Brooks, 'was involved in the securing of two key charters which safeguarded the possessions and liberties of the house

---

[14] On this process, see, for example, H.K. Bhabha, 'The world and the home', *Social Text* x. 31–2 (1992), 141–53; on the use of Norman stone and carving techniques at Canterbury, see R. Gem, 'Canterbury and the cushion capital: a commentary on passages from Goscelin's "De miraculis sancti Augustini"', in N. Stratford (ed.), *Romanesque and Gothic: essays for George Zarnecki*, Woodbridge 1987, 83–101, at 91.

[15] Gibson, Heslop and Pfaff, *Eadwine Psalter*, 24.

[16] Ibid. 77.

[17] R.W. Pfaff, 'Eadui Basan: Scriptorum princeps?', in C. Hicks (ed.), *England in the eleventh century: proceedings of the 1990 Harlaxton Symposium*, Stamford 1992, 267–83.

during the troubled times of the second decade or so of the [eleventh] century',[18] the implication being that Eadwine is also a guardian of Canterbury rights and traditions in a new time of trouble. Certainly, however, if Eadwine is concerned with the preservation of rights and possessions it is subtle to the point of silence in comparison with its near contemporary, *The Life and Miracles of Edmund king and martyr*, produced at Bury St Edmunds *c*.1130 (New York, Pierpont Morgan Library, MS M. 736), in which the manuscript's description and illustration of miracles performed by the saint in the Anglo-Scandinavian past are deployed as savage weapons against theft, corruption and unfair taxation in the Anglo-Norman present.[19] In particular, the images look back to the reigns of Swein and Cnut, so their focus is on the same period as the Eadui charters. It is certain that Eadwine looks back to the Anglo-Saxon Canterbury of the late tenth and eleventh centuries, but it also looks back to much broader Anglo-Saxon cultural phenomena such as the development of the typological psalter (a tradition arguably linked to Winchester), or the interest in the processes of writing, rewriting, copying and editing texts evidenced in such manuscripts as Oxford, Bodleian Library, MS Junius 11, or the Lindisfarne and Copenhagen Gospels (BL MS Cotton Nero D. iv and Copenhagen, Kongelige Bibliotek, MS Gl. Kgl. Sml 10, 2°). It is possible that Eadwine was indeed intended to reference Eadui and his manuscripts specifically, yet our lack of certainty and the ambiguity of the evidence have allowed Eadui to haunt the manuscript (and scholarship on it) in a way that is symptomatic of Eadwine's curious doubling and division, the way in which it allows us to read presence into what is in fact absence.

Eadui Basan is neither mentioned nor depicted in Eadwine, nor is his hand or image copied; nevertheless the placement of Eadui's image (if indeed it is Eadui) after Psalm 150 in the Eadui Psalter (BL Arundel 155) is believed to be mirrored in the placement of the prayer naming Eadwine after the same psalm in the Eadwine Psalter (fo. 262r). The prayer reads:

> Almighty and merciful God I humbly beseech your clemency that you allow me, your servant Eadwine, to serve you faithfully, and will deign to confer on me

---

[18] Gibson, Heslop and Pfaff, *Eadwine Psalter*, 85; N.P. Brooks and S.E. Kelly, *The Charters of Christ Church Canterbury*, Oxford 2013, i. 56–7, ii. 144, 145. The first is a forgery from Æthlered II, falsely dated 1006 and inserted into the Æthelstan Gospels (BL, Cotton Tiberius A. ii). The second is a charter of Cnut dated 1017–20, and copied into BL, Royal 1. D. ix, the 'main Christ Church gospel book' (ibid.). See also N. Brooks, *The early history of the church at Canterbury*, Leicester 1984, 257, 288.

[19] B. Abou-el-Haj, 'Bury St. Edmunds abbey between 1070 and 1124: a history of property, privilege and monastic art production', *Art History* vi (1983), 1–30; see also C. Hahn, 'Peregrinatio et natio: the illustrated Life of Edmund, king and martyr', *Gesta* xxx (1991), 119–39.

good perseverance and a happy end. And may this Psalter 'that I have sung in your sight' be perfected for the health and eternal salvation of my soul. Amen.[20]

Eadwine's words of humility do echo the pose of humility in which Eadui, if it is Eadui, is depicted but this is a standard topos of scribal humility. Similarly, Heslop states that the name Eadwine echoes that of his 'almost namesake',[21] but names beginning with 'Ead-' were extremely common in early-medieval England, so the comparison is not compelling. Moreover, Eadwine's prayer 'sung' in the Lord's sight picks up on the musical content of the psalm it follows in a way that Eadui's portrait does not. The psalm reads in part:

> 3. Praise ye him with the sound of trumpet: praise ye him with psaltery and harp.
> 4. Praise ye him with timbrel and choir: praise ye him with strings and organs. 5. Praise ye him on high sounding cymbals.[22]

The combination of psalm and prayer here convey not only the idea that Eadwine and the Psalmist sing the same song, but that Eadwine was aware of the ways in which his work both mirrored and continued that of the Psalmist.

Through a similar series of vague but persistent echoes, the portrait of the scribe Eadwine on fo. 283v at the end of the manuscript, has (by me, among others) been seen as mirroring Eadui's colophon at the end of St John's gospel in the Eadui Gospels (Hanover, Kestner Museum, WMXXIa 36), and also as referencing the writing-centred activities of the earlier manuscript's evangelist/scribal portraits.[23] However, Eadui's colophon asks simply for prayer and blessing for the scribe,[24] and is in no way comparable to the imposing figure of Eadwine presented in and by the psalter. The programme of evangelist portraits found

---

[20] Gibson, Heslop and Pfaff, *Eadwine Psalter*, 180 n. 10 (translation Heslop's): 'Omnipotens et misericors deus, clementiam tuam suppliciter deprecor, ut me famulum tuam Eadwinum tibi fideliter servire concedas, et perseverentiam bonam et felicem consummationem michi largiri digneris, et hoc psalterium quia in conspectu tuo cantavi ad salutem et ad remedium animae meae perficiat sempiternum. Amen.'

[21] Ibid. 181.

[22] '3. laudate eum in clangore bucinae laudate eum in psalterio et cithara
4. laudate eum in tympano et choro laudate eum in cordis et organo
5. laudate eum in cymbalis sonantibus laudate eum in cymbalis tinnientibus'.

[23] C.E. Karkov, 'Writing and having written: word and image in the Eadwig Gospels', in A.R. Rumble (ed.), *Writing and texts in Anglo-Saxon England*, Woodbridge 2006, 44–61.

[24] 'Pro scriptore precem ne temnas fundere pater. Librum istum monachus scripsit EADUUIUS BASAN. Sit illi longa salus. Vale seruus dei .N. et memor esto mei'. ('Father, do not refrain from pouring forth a prayer for the scribe. This book was written by the monk Eadwig Basan. May he have long-lasting health. Farewell servant of God, N, and remember me.')

Figure 14.3   Cambridge, Trinity College Library, MS R.17.1, fo. 5v (detail). By permission of the Master and Fellows, Trinity College, Cambridge.

in the Eadui Gospels, in which the evangelists are depicted as engaged in four sequential steps in the process of writing, thus clearly illustrating the process through which the manuscript was created, is not found in any earlier Anglo-Saxon manuscript (nor indeed in any earlier manuscript that I know of), but we cannot be certain that earlier manuscripts with similar types of portraits have not been lost. The Eadui Gospels programme was also copied by later Anglo-Saxon scribes/artists well before 1100, so any influence it might have had could well have been indirect.[25] There is no doubt that the Eadwine portrait (Figure 14.4 below) is based on the image of a writing evangelist, but there is nothing to suggest that it was modelled on one from a manuscript associated specifically with Eadui Basan, Christ Church or even Canterbury.

Among art historians, the Eadwine Psalter is best known for its 'portrait' of Eadwine, not only one of the most famous monuments of Anglo-Norman manuscript art, but also a poster child for the image of the medieval monastic scribe. Yet, while its place in the psalter is almost always acknowledged, art historians have most frequently studied it apart from, or as an addendum to, the manuscript in which it is contained. It has become emblematic of the new visibility of scribal status in the post-Conquest world, and of Canterbury tradition, but not much more. This may be due in part to its having been considered, largely on stylistic grounds, to be an addition to the manuscript, but this is in itself problematic. It takes no account of the length of time it may have taken to complete the original project, further assumes that all the psalter artists were working in a single style that did not change over time, and may also rest in part on the desire of some to read literally details of fashion, architecture and so forth, in the image. There is no reason to assume, for example, that the decorative foliate swirls that cover Eadwine's cloak reflect contemporary fashions, rather than being simply a formal device to help link the figure of the scribe with the border that surrounds him, and thus to create a carefully designed and balanced composition.[26] It also fails to take account of the distinctive work that this image is designed to do within the book as a whole. Moreover, medieval English works of art were often ongoing productions,[27] so when can something be said to be 'finished' so that it can be 'added to'? And how long a gap should

---

[25] C.E. Karkov, 'Evangelist portraits and book production in late Anglo-Saxon England', in S. Panayotova (ed.), *Cambridge illuminations. The conference papers*, London 2007, 55–63.

[26] See, for example, the comments of Heslop in Gibson, Heslop and Pfaff, *Eadwine Psalter*, 182.

[27] The Junius 11 *Genesis* might be described as a rewriting of two earlier poems, 'Genesis A' and 'Genesis B' (see C. E. Karkov, *Text and picture in Anglo-Saxon England: narrative strategies in the Junius 11 manuscript*, Cambridge 2001). The Nunburnholme Cross, for example, began life as a Roman architectural stone, was turned into a free-standing cross, and partially carved by a sculptor working in the Anglian tradition in the late ninth or tenth century, then recarved shortly thereafter by an Anglo-Scandinavian artist, and added to by an Anglo-Norman artist at some point after the Norman Conquest. On the cross, see C.E. Karkov, 'Postcolonial', in J. Stodnick and R. Trilling (eds), *A handbook of Anglo-Saxon studies*, Oxford 2012, 149–64. M.K. Foys, *Virtually Anglo-Saxon: old media, new media, and early medieval studies in the late Age of Print*, Gainesville, FL 2007, ch. 5.

Figure 14.4 Cambridge Trinity College Library, MS R.17.1, fo. 283v. By permission of the Master and Fellows, Trinity College, Cambridge.

there be between the moment at which we feel a manuscript is 'finished', and the moment at which we can describe it as having been 'added to' rather than simply 'continued'? However, even if we see it as a later addition, the portrait provides a fitting point of closure to the combined textual and pictorial programme of the psalter proper.[28] Adorned with the swirling arabesque patterns of the latest Anglo-Norman artistic style, Eadwine sits facing towards the past, his eyes glued to his book and his work. The page is carefully constructed and integral to the overall programme of the book.

In this manuscript, the arrangement of the miniatures which fill the whole width of the text block, after the prologue but before the psalm proper, means that the narrative images serve as a point of union for the multiple textual translations that follow, the images being equally applicable to each translation. The heteroglossia of the text, in other words both emerges from, and returns the eye to, the common language of the image. The process of reading sequentially through the psalter brings us finally to the portrait of Eadwine, from whose pen some portion of the text is likely to have flowed (or to whose design it is likely to have conformed). His image at the end serves as the ultimate sign of the inseparability of text and miniature that runs throughout the book. Eadwine in turn looks back over the book he has just 'written', for and by which he will be praised, his figure mirroring and balancing that of the blessed man of Psalm 1 with whose image and textual description the psalter Eadwine has sung began (Figures 14.1 and 14.3). Even the trilobed arch beneath which the writers sit, and the flanking towers that frame the arches, are doubled. And like that blessed man, Eadwine appears here with the book in which he can 'meditate day and night' on the law of the Lord (Ps. 1.2). Indeed, that is what he is depicted doing, as the copying of biblical texts was an acknowledged act of devotion from at least the days of Cassiodorus.[29] If Eadwine was indeed the scribe responsible for the beginning and end of the psalter, the closure the image gives to the book would be particularly fitting, and would provide a visual echo of the combined prayer and psalm that established Eadwine as a mirror of the Psalmist.

The portrait is also the culmination of the unity of text and image that characterises this manuscript, and in this respect it is both a closed, self-contained entity and open to a double past – the past of the book's production and the larger past of scribal activity that stretches back to the biblical authors

---

[28] The portrait is followed by large and small drawings of the Christ Church waterworks, but it would be hard to argue that those drawings are directly related to the writing and illumination of the psalms in the way that the portrait of the scribe clearly is. On the other hand, it is certainly possible to argue that, whatever other function the drawings are meant to fulfil, they do provide an image of the place in which the book would have been read, studied, performed or simply housed. See too below, 304–6.

[29] Cassiodorus, *Institutiones*, ed. R.A.B. Mynors, Oxford 1961, 75–6; *An introduction to divine and human readings by Cassiodorus Senator*, tr. L.W. Jones, New York 1966, 109.

themselves. The image is completely contained within the page, both by Eadwine's self-absorbed pose and by the inscribed border. It is surrounded by, and in dialogue with, its inscription in which the scribe speaks to his text (literally the letter) and the letter responds to his command, a closed dialogue that echoes the open visual dialogue between Eadwine and the blessed man of Psalm 1. The inscription reads:

> Scribe: I am the chief of scribes, and neither my praise nor fame shall die; shout out, oh my letter, who I may be. Letter: By its fame your script proclaims you, Eadwine, whom the painted figure represents, alive through the ages, whose genius the beauty of this book demonstrates. Receive, O God, the book and its donor as an acceptable gift.[30]

The inscription is arranged so that our eyes must cross the figure of the writing Eadwine as we read. It begins at the upper left, and runs across the top and then down the right-hand border, then goes back up to the top of the left-hand border, and runs down, and then across beneath Eadwine's feet – rather similar to the arrangement of the inscription on the Crucifixion page of the much earlier eighth-century Durham Gospels (Durham, Cathedral Library, MS A. II. 17). The meaning of the two images is very different; however, in both manuscripts, the arrangement and placing of the text is designed to demonstrate the intimate relationship between word and image, at the same time that it keeps our eyes very much aware of the image as we read: the image of Christ as Word and the image of Eadwine with his words. In Eadwine the last words written at the bottom of the right-hand border are *picta figura* (painted figure), and our eyes then have to cross the painted figure itself in order to read the remainder of the inscription (*Predicat Eadwinum ...*). It is possible that the arrangement was intended to suggest further that the conversation between the scribe and his text is taking place in the present, or in an eternal present of the book's creation and our reading – as the letter proclaims, Eadwine as scribe remains 'alive through the ages'. (Such a suggestion would certainly be in keeping with Cassiodorus' model of scribal genealogies and the power of writing, copying and reading scripture.)[31] Colour also seems to have been used to identify Eadwine as the

---

[30] Gibson, Heslop and Pfaff, *Eadwine Psalter*, 180 (Heslop's translation): 'Scriptor: s[c]riptorum princeps ego. Nec obitura deinceps laus mea nec fama. Quis sim mea littera clama.
Littera: Te tua s[c]riptura quem signat picta figura. Predicat Eadwinum fama per secula vivum. Ingenium cuius libri decus indicat huius. Quem tibi seque datum munus deus accipe gratum'.

[31] An excellent synopsis of Cassiodorus' ideas and their influence on the Anglo-Saxons is provided by J. O'Reilly, 'The library of scripture: views from the Vivarium and Wearmouth-Jarrow', in P. Binski and W.G. Noel (eds), *New offerings, ancient treasures: essays in medieval art for George Henderson*, Stroud 2001, 3–39.

author of the words that surround him, with green having been employed as the most prominent colour for the figure of the scribe himself, and used again for the words identifying and linking the speakers in the border dialogue, *scriptor* and *littera*, the latter word placed level with the book in which Eadwine writes. Eadwine sits copying the psalms (songs of praise), while the letter affirms the praise he will receive through his actions. Each becomes the product of the other.

But Eadwine's backward look and the relationship established between the painted figure and its inscription also open the book out to the past, a past that extends beyond the bounds of Christ Church Canterbury and the ghost of Eadui Basan, back to such early Anglo-Saxon speaking monuments as the eighth-century Ruthwell Cross on which imagery is contained within an inscription spoken in the first-person voice of the monument, or indeed the Durham Gospels Crucifixion image which demands a response from the reader by asking him or her to meditate on the two natures of Christ. The Eadwine Psalter is indeed a monument to the inherited textual and pictorial traditions of Christ Church Canterbury,[32] but it is more than that. It is not simply an 'edition' of Utrecht,[33] or of Harley 603, or simply a manuscript in the same tradition, though, as I have argued, it certainly engages in a double look back at both those earlier books, which served either directly or indirectly as two of its sources.[34] The expansion of the pictorial programme into the initials in Eadwine, and the emphasis on authorship and the relation between the book, its producers and its users is new – there is nothing like it in either Utrecht or Harley 603 – and these features should be understood as part of its scholarly agenda. Just as it brings together multiple texts and languages, it integrates an imported tradition (the basic visual content of the Utrecht derived miniatures), with Anglo-Saxon elements (for example the use of coloured-outline drawing, the relation between centre and margin), with a new style of illumination to create something that is simultaneously very traditional and highly innovative. The Eadwine portrait is key to this process. It is, as any number of art historians have emphasised, a new type of author portrait, which gives unusual prominence to the work and status of a contemporary named scribe. Eadwine is the chief or prince of scribes, not just a humble labourer for God like Eadui, and his book shouts out, not just reveals his identity and skills, or greets the reader, as does Aldred's famous tenth-century colophon in the Lindisfarne Gospels. Yet, as Aldred's colophon, and the

---

[32] P. Binski and S. Panayotova (eds), *The Cambridge illuminations: ten centuries of book production in the medieval West*, London 2005, cat. no. 25.

[33] Heslop in Gibson, Heslop and Pfaff, *Eadwine Psalter*, 48–9.

[34] On the relationship between the three manuscripts, see Heslop in Gibson, Heslop and Pfaff, *Eadwine Psalter*, 25–52; C.M. Kauffmann, *Romanesque manuscripts, 1066–1190*, London 1975, no. 68; W. Noel, 'The Utrecht Psalter in England: continuity and experiment', in K. van der Horst, W. Noel and W.C.M. Wüstefeld (eds), *The Utrecht Psalter in medieval art: picturing the psalms of David*, 't Goy, The Netherlands 1996, 120–65.

relationship between Eadui's colophon and the four evangelist portraits in the Eadui Gospels, constructed their authors verbally or visually as successors to the evangelist authors, Eadwine is represented in the guise of a writer of scripture.

The Eadwine Psalter is very narrowly about writing and texts, but it is also about collection and translation, and this gives it a certain lack of focus – as if the creators of this very carefully designed book wanted to include everything, all the world's knowledge – like the British Library. In its inclusion of Jerome's three translations, it is a collected edition of the Latin psalter. It is a compendium of glosses and commentaries on the psalter and also a comprehensive programme of illumination which is simultaneously literal and typological. It situates itself within a tradition of copying and editing that began with the Utrecht Psalter and a tradition of scribal production first articulated by Cassiodorus. In this it looks back beyond Anglo-Saxon England to the origins of what would eventually become themes in Anglo-Saxon art and manuscript production, doubling and dividing them in a way that provides both continuity with the past and a very new statement about what a book can be and what it can do with the past. As a collection it is all about Canterbury, but it is about the needs and desires of the Canterbury community in the twelfth century. It builds on, but it is not a memorial to, the ideals of the community in the Anglo-Saxon past.

Afterword

Peter Fergusson's *Canterbury cathedral priory in the age of Becket* (New Haven, 2011) appeared after this paper was originally written. In it Fergusson argues that the two drawings of the cathedral precinct with its new water system and its many new buildings (fos 284v–285 and 286) are integral to the manuscript and not later additions to it, as many scholars have believed.[35] He argues further that one of the purposes of the drawings is to represent and record the architectural innovations associated with Prior Wibert, the manuscript's patron. Fergusson's case is complex and convincing, but there is not room here to assess all the intricacies of his argument, especially as my focus is on the image of the scribe and not the patron. The precinct drawings are placed after the Eadwine portrait, and thus stand outside of the portion of the manuscript with which I am primarily concerned, as do the series of Old and New Testament narratives and calendar with which the manuscript began. However, whether contemporary with the rest of the manuscript or not, the precinct drawings are as carefully integrated into the overall design, content and function of the book as are all its other elements. Just as the portrait of Eadwine fits into a well-established

---

[35] See, for example, F. Woodman, 'The waterworks drawing of the Eadwine Psalter', in Gibson, Heslop and Pfaff, *Eadwine Psalter*, 168–85.

tradition of scribal portraiture that establishes a typological relationship between contemporary scribes and their biblical predecessors, so the precinct drawings can be understood in light of the maps or images of Jerusalem included in many earlier psalters. These maps were frequently paired with portraits of scribes or authors in manuscripts such as the eighth-century Anglo-Saxon Codex Amiatinus (Florence, Biblioteca Medicea, MS Amatiano 1), or twelfth-century Channel School psalters such as Brussels, Bibliothèque royale, MS 9823. In their pairing with author portraits (Ezra in the Codex Amiatinus, David in the later psalters), the images symbolised the coming together of the earthly and heavenly Jerusalem, and served as 'self-representations of the monastic community'.[36]

The precinct drawings of the Eadwine Psalter also make it clear to the reader in no uncertain terms that the book is above all a collection that is about Canterbury in the middle of the twelfth century. As Fergusson documents, in its original orientation the double-page drawing on fos 284v–285 gives a sense of being inside the monastic precinct, and experiencing its spaces as if part of the contemporary community.

A twelfth-century viewer would have read the image from left to right, replicating the way a monk or visitor would have experienced the space. Entering from the Green Court Gatehouse (originally on the verso at the left), he would have proceeded into the quasi-public Green Court, then entered the gated area of the strict enclosure, namely the Great Cloister and the Infirmary Cloister, and terminated at the cathedral (originally drawn on the outer side of the opposite recto).[37]

In contrast, the final drawing on fo. 286, originally the verso of a double-page spread, represents the precinct from the exterior, the point of view of someone leaving the enclosure.[38]

The precinct drawings can be understood in relation to the series of Old and New Testament images with which the manuscript originally began. That series established a relationship between two different eras, and the Eadwine Psalter, as I have argued above does the same. Further, the opening series of narrative images provided an entrance into the book as a whole, an abbreviated history leading up to the writing of the Psalms, and a typological tool for understanding the way in which they should be read. The precinct drawings provide an equally fitting exit from the book, simultaneously establishing a relationship between the earthly community and the heavenly Jerusalem, and suggesting with the final page that the reader is leaving the spiritual enclosure of the book just as he leaves

---

[36] M. Kupfer, Review of Gibson et al., *The Eadwine Psalter: text, image, and monastic culture in twelfth-century Canterbury*, *Speculum* lxix.4 (1994), 1168–71, at 1171; Fergusson, *Canterbury cathedral priory*, 44–6.

[37] Fergusson, *Canterbury cathedral priory*, 28–9.

[38] Ibid. 39.

the safety of the enclosed precinct. However, if the precinct drawings are indeed to be understood as paired with the Eadwine portrait, then it is also necessary to consider how they might relate to Psalm 1, that part of the book to which Eadwine most especially looks back in its mirroring of the words of the Psalmist and the image of the blessed man in the words and figure of Eadwine. Fergusson points out that the aedicule under which the blessed man of Psalm 1 sits differs from the classical tempietto of the corresponding image in Utrecht (and Harley 603), arguing that it is similar to the image of the Great Cloister's Fountain House in the precinct drawing on fo. 285, suggesting an 'exchange of ideas'.[39] The comparison between Fountain House and aedicule is not convincing, but one could also note that the numerous finials surmounting the aedicule in Eadwine are absent from the corresponding images in both Utrecht and Harley 603, and as twelfth-century Canterbury was known for its many such finials, perhaps the aedicule is intended to call to mind the monastery's architecture more generally. I have already suggested above that the aedicule's architecture was intended to mirror that of the Eadwine portrait. But the precinct drawings do evoke the imagery of Psalm 1 in a different way. The final image depicts the water flowing from its source through a field, a vineyard and an orchard before entering the precinct, and encourages the reader to reflect on this work – the drawing, book, abundant crops, water system, architecture – and on their maker, Prior Wibert. It is drawn, as noted, from the point of view of one looking in towards the monastery from the outside. Here, at the end of the book, the reader looks back over these works produced under Wibert's patronage, which again call to mind the words of the Psalm:

> 3. And he shall be like a tree which is planted near the running waters, which shall bring forth its fruit in due season.
> And his leaf shall not fall off: and all whatsoever he shall do shall prosper.

---

[39] Ibid. 37–8.

Chapter 15

The Anglo-Saxon Tradition in Post-Conquest Architecture and Sculpture[*]

Malcolm Thurlby

Introduction

The extent to which features associated with Anglo-Saxon architecture and sculpture continued after the Conquest, or were specifically revived in the later eleventh and twelfth centuries, is a much-debated topic.[1] For the most part,

---

[*] I am most grateful to the following for their help with aspects of this chapter: Richard Bryant, Eric Fernie, Chris Guy, Jackie Hall, Stuart Harrison, Barry Magrill, Guy Métraux, Roger Norris, Douglas Pocock, Michael Reed, Tom Russo and Roger Stalley. Martin Brett and David Woodman have been generous, informative and understanding editors. Research for this chapter was facilitated by generous grants from the Social Sciences and Humanities Research Council of Canada.

[1] The following abbreviations are used solely in this article:
– *Antiq. J.: Antiquaries Journal*
– *Archaeol. J.: Archaeological Journal*
– BAACT: *British Archaeological Association Conference Transactions*
– B/E: *The buildings of England*, Harmondsworth 1951–75; reprints and revised editions, New Haven and London
– Blair, *Minsters and parish churches*: J. Blair (ed.), *Minsters and parish churches: the local Church in transition, 950–1200*, Oxford 1988
– Butler and Morris, *The Anglo-Saxon Church*: L.A.S. Butler and R.K. Morris (eds), *The Anglo-Saxon Church. Papers on history, architecture and archaeology in honour of Dr H.M. Taylor*, CBA Research Report lx, London 1986
– CASSS: *Corpus of Anglo-Saxon stone sculpture*, Oxford 1977–2012
– Crook, *Winchester*: J. Crook (ed.), *Winchester cathedral: nine hundred years*, Chichester 1993
– JBAA: *Journal of the British Archaeological Association*
– JSAH: *Journal of the Society of Architectural Historians*
– RCHME: Royal Commission on Historical Monuments (England)
– Rollason and others, *Anglo-Norman Durham, 1093–1193*: D.W. Rollason, M. Harvey and M. Prestwich (eds), *Anglo-Norman Durham, 1093–1193*, Woodbridge 1994
– Temple, *Anglo-Saxon manuscripts, 900–1066*: E. Temple, *A survey of manuscripts illuminated in the British Isles, II, Anglo-Saxon manuscripts, 900–1066*, London 1976

architecture and sculpture have been studied separately, even though most post-Conquest sculpture is 'architectural'; in other words, the sculpture is an integral part of the building it adorns. In this chapter I endeavour to integrate the examination of architecture and architectural sculpture, and, in the case of Ely cathedral, incorporate investigation of the contemporary painted decoration. Formal analysis will provide the basis for determination of Norman versus Anglo-Saxon elements in the designs, and, for the latter, architectural representations in illuminated manuscripts are explored. In stone sculpture, examples which have been published as both Anglo-Saxon and Anglo-Norman are examined. Works are studied in association with the patronage and historical traditions connected with particular sites and monuments in an effort to understand reasons for the choices, although, as we shall see, clear separation of Anglo-Saxon versus Norman aspects will not always be absolute.

Historiography and the State of Research

In architecture, the great Anglo-Norman cathedral and monastic churches have generally been studied separately from smaller churches, and only recently has secular architecture been investigated in conjunction with contemporary ecclesiastical building.[2] The great churches are frequently grouped according to their starting date as either first or second generation after the Conquest. The austerity of first-generation buildings, such as St Albans abbey (from 1077) and Winchester cathedral (from 1079), is frequently contrasted with second-generation churches, like Durham cathedral (from 1093), with its rich arch mouldings, patterned columns, intersecting dado arcades, and variety of wall articulation. Quite apart from matters of detail, after 1066 we witness the total rebuilding of all major churches on a scale unprecedented before the Conquest to provide a monumental expression of the new Norman authority which was accompanied by a display of secular domination with the construction of castles across the landscape.[3]

Smaller churches are usually considered separately from the great churches except when they are seen to reflect developments in the latter. Minor churches have been grouped into period C3 (*c*.1050–1100) or under the banner of 'Saxo-Norman' or 'Overlap', and in the more recent scholarship the time line

---

– *TBGAS*: *Transactions of the Bristol and Gloucestershire Archaeological Society*; Most volumes are available on line at http://www.bgas.org.uk/publications/transactions.html.

[2] E. Fernie, *The architecture of Norman England*, Oxford 2000.

[3] E. Fernie, 'The effect of the Conquest on Norman architectural patronage', *ANS* ix (1986), 72–85; Eric Fernie, 'Architecture and the effects of the Norman Conquest', in D. Bates and A. Curry (eds), *England and Normandy in the middle ages*, London and Rio Grande 1994, 105–16.

has been extended as late as 1140.⁴ It is particularly in these smaller churches that continuity of a pre-Conquest tradition has been detected. But what of large Anglo-Saxon churches? The Anglo-Saxon cathedrals of Winchester and Canterbury have been excavated and a description of the use of Winchester has been investigated in conjunction with the form of the church.⁵ The cathedral of Sherborne has been partly excavated and its form analysed, as has the abbey (now cathedral) church of Peterborough, although fragments discovered there remain little explored.⁶ The pre-Conquest cathedrals of Canterbury and Winchester include many features found in great churches in Ottonian Germany. Archbishop Lanfranc's Canterbury cathedral (from 1070), which was based on the model of Saint-Étienne, Caen, was no larger than its Anglo-Saxon predecessor and thus the appearance of the new church proclaimed the new administration which accompanied the introduction of a new Norman liturgy, the Constitutions of Lanfranc, in place of the Anglo-Saxon *Regularis concordia*.⁷ On the other hand, the Norman cathedral at Winchester, commenced by the Norman Bishop Walkelin in 1079, greatly surpassed the scale of its pre-Conquest

---

⁴   G. Baldwin Brown, *The arts in early England, Anglo-Saxon architecture*, 2 edn, London 1925, 377–435; H.M. Taylor and J. Taylor, *Anglo-Saxon architecture*, Cambridge 1965; H.M. Taylor, *Anglo-Saxon architecture* iii, Cambridge 1977; E. Fernie, *The architecture of the Anglo-Saxons*, London 1983, 137–73; R. Gem, 'ABC: How should we periodize Anglo-Saxon architecture?', in Butler and Morris, *The Anglo-Saxon Church*, 83–105; R. Gem, 'The English parish church in the 11th and early 12th Centuries: a Great Rebuilding?', in Blair, *Minsters and parish churches*, 21–30; Fernie, *The architecture of Norman England*, 208–19; M. Thurlby, 'Anglo-Saxon architecture beyond the millennium: its continuity in Norman building', in N. Hiscock (ed.), *The white mantle of churches: architecture, liturgy and art around the millennium*, Turnhout 2003, 119–37; M. Thurlby, 'The Romanesque churches of St Mary Magdalen at Tixover and St Mary at Morcott', *Ecclesiology Today* xxxv (2005), 23–41 (http://www.ecclsoc.org/ET.35.pdf).

⁵   R.N. Quirk, 'Winchester Cathedral in the tenth century', *Archaeol. J.* cxiv (1957), 28–68; Fernie, *Architecture of the Anglo-Saxons*, 97–101; B. Kyølbye-Biddle, 'Old Minster, St Swithun's Day 1093', in Crook, *Winchester*, 13–20. On Anglo-Saxon Canterbury cathedral, see K. Blockley, M. Sparks and T. Tatton-Brown, *Canterbury cathedral nave: archaeology, history and architecture*, Canterbury 1997, 12–22, 95–110.

⁶   J.H.P. Gibb, 'The Anglo-Saxon cathedral at Sherborne, with an appendix on documentary evidence by R.D.H. Gem', *Archaeol. J.* cxxxii (1975), 71–110; Fernie, *The architecture of the Anglo-Saxons*, 121–4; J.T. Irvine, 'Account of the discovery of part of the Saxon abbey church of Peterborough', *JBAA* l (1894), 45–54, http://www.archive.org/stream/journalofbritish50brit#page/52/mode/2up; J.T. Irvine, 'Account of the pre-Norman remains discovered at Peterborough cathedral in 1884', *Associated Architectural Societies Reports and Papers* xvii (1883–4), 277–83, http://www.archive.org/stream/reportspapersofa17asso#page/n413/mode/2up; Fernie, *Architecture of the Anglo-Saxons*, 107–8, 121–4.

⁷   Fernie, *Architecture of Norman England*, 104–6.

predecessor.[8] The vast size referenced the great fourth-century imperial basilica of Old St Peter's, Rome, and thereby provided an association with the glory of early Christian Rome and, concomitantly, between the local St Swithun and St Peter. Doubtless size mattered to the most ambitious patrons of great post-Conquest churches, as the great scale of Winchester inspired analogous monumentality in the Benedictine abbey churches at Ely (begun 1081/82), Bury St Edmunds (1081), Old St Paul's cathedral in London (1087), Durham cathedral (1093), Norwich cathedral (1096) and the abbey at Peterborough (1117/18).

In order to understand Anglo-Saxon architecture beyond physical remains and documentary evidence, nineteenth-century architectural historians turned to representations of buildings in manuscripts illuminated in England before the Conquest. In 1844 Thomas Wright published 'Anglo-Saxon architecture, illustrated from illuminated manuscripts'.[9] The article had an immediate impact. In 1846, in the eighth edition of *The principles of Gothic architecture*, Matthew Holbeche Bloxam discussed and illustrated Anglo-Saxon architecture from Caedmon's paraphrase of Genesis (Bodl. Lib., MS Junius 11), and Paley's *Manual of Gothic architecture* refers to Wright's paper.[10] In 1848, in the fifth edition of his *Attempt to discriminate the styles of architecture in England*, Thomas Rickman included illustrations of architecture from Caedmon's MS and also recorded that long-and-short quoins are depicted in it.[11] Wright suggested that a significant number of architectural motifs used in pre-Conquest manuscripts accurately reflect those used in contemporary churches, including triangular arches, balusters, capitals with multiple horizontal mouldings. In 1890 J.P. Harrison published 'Anglo-Norman ornament compared with designs in Anglo-Saxon MSS', and this was followed in 1896 by a 'Note on English Romanesque architecture'.[12] He argued that many architectural motifs usually considered

---

[8] R. Gem, 'The Romanesque cathedral of Winchester: patron and design in the eleventh century', in T.A. Heslop and V. Sekules (eds), *Medieval art and architecture at Winchester cathedral, BAACT* vi (1983), 1–12; Fernie, *Architecture of Norman England*, 117–21.

[9] T. Wright, 'Anglo-Saxon architecture, illustrated from illuminated manuscripts', *Archaeol. J.* i (1844), 24–35.

[10] M.H. Bloxam, *The principles of Gothic architecture*, 8 edn, London 1846, 74–5; F.A. Paley, *Manual of Gothic architecture*, London 1846, 34–5.

[11] T. Rickman, *An attempt to discriminate the styles of architecture in England, from the Conquest to the Reformation, with a sketch of the Grecian and Roman orders; notices of numerous British edifices; and some remarks on the architecture of a part of France*, 5 edn, London 1848, xxx–xxxi.

[12] J.P. Harrison, 'Anglo-Norman ornament compared with designs in Anglo-Saxon MSS', *Archaeol. J.* xlvii (1890), 143–53; J.P. Harrison, 'Note on English Romanesque architecture', *JBAA* new ser. ii (1896), 268–72. See also J.P. Harrison, 'English architecture

post-Conquest already appeared in Anglo-Saxon manuscript illumination and therefore probably reflected lost Anglo-Saxon structures.

The Taylors included Wright's article in their bibliographies for Earls Barton (Northamptonshire) and Sompting (Sussex).[13] Dominic Tweddle characterised Wright's article as seminal, and referred to Wright's observation of turned balusters in late Anglo-Saxon manuscripts.[14] Tweddle further included details of baluster shafts, bases and foliage in Anglo-Saxon illuminations in his analysis of Anglo-Saxon sculpture.[15] Yet reference to manuscript illumination in relation to architectural detailing is relatively rare. The stripwork on the west tower of Earls Barton (Figure 15.1 below) has been paralleled with a chair in the Maeseyck Gospels,[16] and Eric Fernie has compared the bulbous capitals in various pre-Conquest manuscripts with those in Great Paxton (Huntingdonshire) (Figure 15.2 below), and indicated that intersecting arcading in canon tables of Anglo-Saxon manuscripts 'suggest that the motif was used in Anglo-Saxon buildings, though no examples survive'.[17] C.R. Dodwell read the tower of Babel in BL Cotton Claudius B. iv, fo. 19, as an Anglo-Saxon building.[18] Most recently, Katherine Karkov has related the imagery on the frontispiece of the *Regularis Concordia* in BL Cotton Tiberius A. iii, fo. 2v to late-tenth-century architectural developments at Winchester Old Minster.[19] I have yet to find a citation to Harrison's articles, perhaps because his pro-Anglo-Saxon interpretations were outweighed by the pro-Norman views of John Bilson and Baldwin Brown published at the turn of the century.[20] Be that as it may, Ella Armitage referred to Anglo-Saxon manuscript illuminations as representations of pre-Conquest burhs, and to the Bayeux Tapestry for a wooden tower inside a

---

before the Conquest', *Archaeologia Oxoniensis* 1892–95, 121–41: http://www.archive.org/stream/archaeologiaoxo00unkngoog#page/n163/mode/1up.

[13] Taylor and Taylor, *Anglo-Saxon architecture*, 47, 132, 179, 209, 226, 562.

[14] D. Tweddle and others *CASSS, IV, South-East England*, Oxford 1995, 65.

[15] Tweddle, *CASSS, IV, South-East England*, 64–71.

[16] M. Schapiro, 'A note on the wall strips of Saxon architecture', *JSAH* xvii (1959), 123–5, repr. in M. Schapiro, *Late Antique, early Christian and medieval art: selected papers*, New York 1979, 242–48. W. Rodwell, 'Anglo-Saxon church building: aspects of design and construction', in Butler and Morris, *The Anglo-Saxon Church*, 156–75, repr. in C.E. Karkov (ed.), *The Archaeology of Anglo-Saxon England: basic readings*, New York 1999, 195–231; M. Audouy, B. Dix and D. Parsons, 'The tower of All Saint's Church, Earl's Barton, Northamptonshire: its construction and context', *Archaeol. J.* clii (1995), 73–94.

[17] Fernie, *Architecture of the Anglo-Saxons*, 133–4, 273.

[18] C.R. Dodwell, *The pictorial arts of the West, 800–1200*, New Haven and London 1993, 119.

[19] C.E. Karkov, *The art of Anglo-Saxon England*, Woodbridge 2011, 109–13.

[20] J. Bilson, 'The beginnings of Gothic architecture in England', *Journal of the Royal Institute of British Architects* 3 ser. vi (1899), 259–69, 289–326; G. Baldwin Brown, *The arts in early England: Anglo-Saxon architecture*, London 1903.

Figure 15.1 Earls Barton, All Saints, W tower, exterior from SW.

Figure 15.2   Great Paxton, Holy Trinity, interior to W from chancel.

stockade on a motte.[21] Not all the manuscripts cited by Harrison were produced before the Conquest and therefore his observations have to be treated with caution. However, the principle of examining architectural representations in Anglo-Saxon illuminations is worthwhile and may be extended to depictions of architecture on ivory carving.

Richard Gem observed that the buildings depicted in the Bayeux Tapestry are 'strictly pictorial rather than documentary' but that they 'seem to have at least a general representational value'.[22] Both Gem and Eric Fernie used the image of Westminster abbey in the Bayeux Tapestry in connection with their reconstructions of Edward the Confessor's Westminster abbey.[23] Roger Stalley saw the depiction of King Harold's hall in the Bayeux Tapestry as an accurate representation of a stone-built hall, and Eric Fernie included it as evidence for Anglo-Saxon first-floor halls.[24] Accuracy in the Tapestry is indicated by the layers in the motte at Hastings, which

[21]   E.S. Armitage, *The early Norman castles of the British Isles*, London 1912, 19, 87, 158, 393.
[22]   R. Gem, 'The Romanesque rebuilding of Westminster abbey', *ANS* iii (1981), 33–60, at 36.
[23]   Gem, 'The Romanesque rebuilding' 36–7; Fernie, *Architecture of Norman England*, 96–8.
[24]   R. Stalley, *Early medieval architecture*, Oxford 1999, 88–9; Fernie, *Architecture of Norman England*, 82.

have been corroborated by excavation.[25] Jane Geddes referred to representations of ironwork on doors in Anglo-Saxon manuscripts as evidence for the form of hinges and scrollwork which presage ironwork on post-Conquest doors.[26] I shall now examine some of the motifs discussed by Wright and Harrison, and introduce some new observations in support of their thesis.

In the first place, the validity of architectural representations in manuscripts as accurate reproductions of the motifs used in buildings must be established. Cogent evidence for this may be found in the long-and-short quoins on the tower on the left of the scene of God in Majesty; Satan and his angels in Caedmon's paraphrase of Genesis etc. (Bodl. Lib., MS Junius 11, p. 17), *c*.1000. The west tower of Earls Barton is an excellent example of their use in pre-Conquest architecture (Figure 15.1).[27] In Aelfric's paraphrase of Pentateuch and Joshua, *c*.1025–50, fo. 9, middle register, Cain builds a city; there are round-headed and triangular arches and ashlar masonry.[28] Triangular arches are used in the windows of the second storey of the Earls Barton tower (Figure 15.1). Good examples are also found in the west wall of the nave of St Mary's, Deerhurst (Gloucestershire), and in the apse articulation at Wing (Buckinghamshire). Ashlar masonry is not normally associated with pre-Conquest churches but the early-eleventh-century St Laurence's, Bradford-on-Avon (Wiltshire), provides a fine example.[29] The tower of Babel in BL Cotton Claudius B. iv, fo. 19 is also shown with ashlar walls.[30] The red, yellow and blue painted ashlar may seem rather fanciful but blue and red masonry patterns are used in the main arcade arches of the south transept of Ely cathedral *c*.1082–93.[31] In the same miniature the arch above the door is set well below the capitals that carry the enclosing arch. An analogous differential of the springing points of arches is evident in the arcade and transverse arches of the upper storey of the bishop's chapel at Hereford constructed by Robert Losinga, bishop of Hereford 1079–95.[32] Even closer to the Hereford chapel is an architectural representation in Bodl. Lib., MS Junius 11, p. 77, Noah ploughing. In the scene of God closing the door of Noah's ark on p. 66 of the same manuscript, the top storey of the ark is articulated in

---

[25] Fernie, *Architecture of Norman England*, 52.
[26] J. Geddes, *Medieval decorative ironwork in England*, London 1999, 41, 51–7.
[27] Taylor, *Anglo-Saxon architecture*, iii. 944–6.
[28] *The Old English illustrated Hexateuch: British Museum Cotton Claudius B. IV*, ed. C.R. Dodwell and P. Clemoes (Early English manuscripts in facsimile xviii, 1974).
[29] Fernie, *Architecture of the Anglo-Saxons*, 145–51.
[30] *Old English illustrated Pentateuch*, ed. Dodwell and Clemoes.
[31] R. Baxter, 'Ely Cathedral, Ely Cambridgeshire', http://www.crsbi.ac.uk/search/location/ely%20cathedral/site/imagePopup/ed-ca-elyca/t18700.html.
[32] R. Gem, 'The bishop's chapel at Hereford: the roles of patron and craftsmen', in S. Macready and F.H. Thompson (eds), *Art and patronage in the English Romanesque*, London 1986, 87–96; Fernie, *Architecture of Norman England*, 233–6.

the same stepped tripartite manner as many Anglo-Norman clerestoreys.³³ The significance of this parallel is most evident when we contrast the clerestorey in the nave of Norwich cathedral with that in the nave of the abbey church of Saint-Vigor at Cerisy-la-Forêt (Manche) in which the side arches spring from the same point as the central arch.³⁴ While the Cerisy design also appears in England, the Norwich formula is not found in Normandy, which implies that the Norwich formula adheres to pre-Conquest precedent. In the representation of the Destruction of Sodom in BL, Cotton Claudius B. iv, usually dated to the second quarter of the eleventh century, the capitals bear a striking resemblance to volute capitals, a type always associated with Normandy, as in Saint-Étienne at Caen and Cerisy-la-Forêt. This raises the possibility that volute capitals were used by Anglo-Saxon architects.

In BL Cotton Claudius B. iv, fo. 58r, Potiphar's wife holding Joseph's garments, the bulbous capital to the left of Potiphar's right hand is remarkably similar to the nave arcade and north crossing arch capitals at Holy Trinity, Great Paxton (Figure 15.2). In the same miniature the capital adjacent to Potiphar's left hand has the appearance of a cushion capital, while in the canon tables of the Copenhagen Gospels (Kongelige Bibliotek, GL Kgl. Saml. 10, 2°) there are representations of cushion capitals carved with foliage.³⁵ It has been suggested that the cushion capital was introduced into England after the Conquest but the evidence of pre-Conquest manuscript illumination weighs against that case.³⁶ The birth of Abel in Bodl. Lib., MS Junius 11, p. 47 takes place before an arcade of plain, round-headed arches on bulbous capitals. Between the half-cylindrical responds there is another column and a column or pier framed by slim shafts. The difference in the form of the two free-standing supports is analogous to the nave arcade piers and crossing-arch responds at Great Paxton (Figure 15.2) and presages the greater variety in pier design in the nave of Rochester cathedral.³⁷ It

---

³³ L.R. Hoey, 'The design of Romanesque clerestories with wall passages in Normandy and England', *Gesta* xxviii (1989), 78–101.

³⁴ E. Fernie, *An architectural history of Norwich cathedral*, Oxford 1993; Hoey, 'The design of Romanesque clerestories with wall passages'.

³⁵ G. Zarnecki, 'The Romanesque capitals in the south transept of Worcester cathedral', in G. Popper (ed.), *Medieval art and architecture at Worcester cathedral: BAACT* i (1978), 38–42.

³⁶ R. Gem, 'Canterbury and the cushion capital: a commentary on passages from Goscelin's "*De Miraculis Sancti Augustini*"', in N. Stratford (ed.), *Romanesque and Gothic: essays for George Zarnecki*, Woodbridge 1987, 83–105; Fernie, *Architecture of Norman England*, 278–9. On the case for the use of cushion and scalloped capitals before the Conquest, see Thurlby, 'Anglo-Saxon architecture beyond the millennium', 131–4.

³⁷ For Great Paxton, see Taylor and Taylor, *Anglo-Saxon architecture*, 484–8; on the Rochester nave piers, see L.R. Hoey, 'Pier form and vertical wall articulation in English Romanesque architecture', *JSAH* lviii (1989), 258–83, at 279–81, fig. 26.

is also possible that the slim shafts were recessed in nooks in the manner of the respond of the arch to the south porticus at St Botolph's, Hadstock (Essex), or the chancel arch and west doorway at Kirkdale (Yorkshire), and in Romanesque compound piers, a point further discussed below. Moreover, the shafted support may have iconographic significance in focusing attention on the most important aspect of the scene, just as 'odd' supports articulate important spaces in Anglo-Norman churches and elsewhere in European Romanesque buildings.[38]

To the right of Abraham's feast in BL Cotton Claudius B. iv, fo. 35v is a portal with a trumeau (a central support in the doorway), plain tympanum and a round-headed arch with a moulding on the inner and outer edges. The latter relate to the north portal at Hadstock (Essex), which has been dated between 1050 and 1100.[39] A plain tympanum complete with framing arch cut on a single stone survives in a fragment of the pre-Conquest abbey at Peterborough, and in numerous doorways after the Conquest, as in the south portal at Brimpsfield (Gloucestershire).[40] The inclusion of a trumeau in the illumination is an intriguing detail in that there is no parallel for the motif in either Anglo-Saxon or Anglo-Norman architecture, yet it suggests that large portals with tympana may have existed before the Conquest.

The representation of Harold's hall at Bosham in the Bayeux Tapestry shows feasting taking place on the first floor, carried on a ground-floor arcade with compound piers on plinths with three steps and single lateral shafts and capitals carrying the arcade arches and a shaft between that rises to a capital at the bottom of the first floor. The design of the hall presages the *Aula nova* at Christ Church, Canterbury, complete with the articulation of the ground-floor arcade and the external stair to the first floor on the right of the hall. The form of the articulation has Norman associations, as in the compound piers of the nave arcades of the abbey churches of Jumièges and Mont Saint-Michel, and was introduced to England in Edward the Confessor's Westminster abbey. It seems unlikely that this type of articulation would have been used in Anglo-Saxon churches other than under the influence from Normandy, but the representation

---

[38] E. Fernie, 'The use of varied nave supports in Romanesque and early Gothic churches', *Gesta* xxiii (1984), 107–17; M. Thurlby, 'Articulation as an expression of function in Romanesque architecture', in J.A. Franklin, T.A. Heslop and C. Stevenson (eds), *Architecture and interpretation: a Festschrift for Eric Fernie*, Woodbridge 2012, 42–59.

[39] Fernie, *Architecture of Norman England*, 214, pl. 160. Hadstock belonged to Ely abbey and between the Conquest and 1086 it increased in value from £6 to £10, which may make the period *c*.1070–86 most likely for the construction of the church (*Domesday Book. Essex*, ii. fo. 19a, 10. 4).

[40] Irvine, 'Account of the discovery of part of the Saxon abbey church of Peterborough'; idem, 'Account of the pre-Norman remains discovered at Peterborough cathedral in 1884', 282–3, pl. III J.

in the Bayeux Tapestry at least suggests that it was used before the Conquest somewhere other than Westminster abbey.

The façade of Edward's palace at Winchester as shown in the Bayeux Tapestry includes many interesting details. The basic form is allied to the west façade of St Pantaleon, Cologne, and the west front of Jumièges abbey, although the main entrance to Edward's palace is approached by more steps. A secular analogue is also found in the main entrance tower at Ludlow castle.[41] The lozenge-patterned masonry on the façade presages that on the stair turret of the north transept at Christchurch (Twynham) priory and the north and south gables of the western block at Lincoln cathedral. At Twynham it is also significant that there is a multi-stepped plinth, as on the pre-Conquest crossing responds at Stow (Lincolnshire), surmounted by an intersecting blind arcade – a motif included in the canon tables of pre-Conquest gospel books – and the north-west corner of the transept is articulated with grouped shafts in the manner of the 'crossing' responds at Great Paxton (Figure 15.2). Finally, on the stair turrets of Edward's palace there are three designs for the windows each of which match left to right. The same variety is witnessed in the stair turret of the west tower at Hough-on-the-Hill (Lincolnshire) which is 'undoubtedly Anglo-Saxon' according to Stocker and Everson.[42]

It is clear that in matters of detail, many representations of architecture in Anglo-Saxon illuminated manuscripts are accurate depictions of real architectural motifs used in pre-Conquest buildings. Several features often associated with post-Conquest buildings in England can be shown to have been used there before 1066, and were probably part of a vocabulary of rich articulation used in the larger Anglo-Saxon churches.

Peterborough Abbey, Wittering and Kirkdale

The chancel arch of Wittering (Northamptonshire) is frequently discussed in the context of the 'Overlap' churches and the use of soffit-roll mouldings in Durham cathedral.[43] Wittering is not documented but is usually dated between

---

[41] M. Thurlby, *Romanesque architecture and sculpture in Wales*, Logaston 2006, 41–2, fig. 50.

[42] D. Stocker and P. Everson, *Summoning St Michael: early Romanesque towers in Lincolnshire*, Oxford 2006, 6, 13. It may be suggested that the representation of the palace at Winchester records the work of William the Conqueror's rebuilding of the pre-Conquest building. Even though I think this is unlikely, if it is early post-Conquest work that is shown then it records elaborate decoration on a building of that time.

[43] Fernie, *Architecture of Norman England*, 211–13; J. Bony, 'Durham et la traditionne saxonne', in S. McKnight Crosby, A. Chastel, A. Prache and A. Chatelet (eds), *Études d'art médiévale offertes à Louis Grodecki*, Paris 1981, 79–92, at 81.

1050 and 1100, which should perhaps be narrowed to *c*.1070–86.[44] In 1884 J.T. Irvine excavated a large voussoir and a corresponding jamb stone from the Norman sleeper wall under the south-west pier of the crossing of Peterborough cathedral.[45] He compared these stones with the chancel arch at Wittering and the comparison is a close one. In addition, he excavated another jamb stone with a slightly simpler profile (Irvine Pl. III B), 'part of an arch of a respond of an arcade' (Irvine Pl. III D), two 'capitals or pillars or responds' carved with different arrangements of horizontal steps and hollows (Irvine Pl. III e and F) of a less robust variety than on the tower arch at Barnack (Northamptonshire), various fragments of stripwork, and part of a plain tympanum (Irvine Pl. III J). Aside from passing mention in the Taylors' corpus, the Peterborough fragments have escaped notice in the literature.[46] Yet these stones are of great significance in our understanding of architectural articulation around the time of the Conquest. Irvine attributed the stones to the patronage of Leofric, abbot of Peterborough 1057–66.[47] The E version of the Anglo-Saxon Chronicle records that Leofric 'gilded the minster, so that it was called Gildenborough; and then waxed very much in land, and in gold, and in silver' (1051?), and that in 1059 'was consecrated the steeple at Peterborough, on the sixteenth before the calends of November (17 October)'. Leofric was succeeded as abbot by Brand, a monk of Peterborough, who died in 1069. He was followed by Thorold, a Norman, who was appointed by King William and remained in office until his death in 1098. There is no record of work on the abbey church by either Brand or Thorold, and the circumstances of Thorold's tenure make it unlikely that he made any modifications to the fabric of the church.[48] If Irvine's attribution of the Peterborough stones to Leofric is correct – and I believe it is – then we have evidence for the articulation of a major church immediately before the conquest complete with stripwork, richly moulded capitals and variety in elaborate responds and corresponding arches.

---

[44] Fernie, *Architecture of the Anglo-Saxons*, 164–8; Fernie, *Architecture of Norman England*, 211–13. In 1086 Wittering was held by Ansketil of the abbot of Peterborough and was worth £11. In the time of Edward the Confessor it was worth £3 (*DB Northamptonshire*, ed. F. and C. Thorn, Chichester 1979, fo. 221c, 6a, 4. The increase in value might be equated with construction of the church at some point in the twenty years after the Conquest.

[45] Irvine, 'Account of the discovery of part of the Saxon abbey church of Peterborough'; idem, 'Account of the pre-Norman remains discovered at Peterborough cathedral in 1884', 282–3, pl. III A and C.

[46] Taylor and Taylor, *Anglo-Saxon architecture*, 494.

[47] Irvine, 'Account of the pre-Norman remains discovered at Peterborough cathedral in 1884', 281; idem, 'Account of the discovery of part of the Saxon abbey church of Peterborough', 52.

[48] *VCH Northamptonshire and the Soke of Peterborough*, ii. 85–6.

Jeffrey West has dated a fragment of a decorated impost at Peterborough abbey carved with 'Winchester acanthus' to the late tenth or early eleventh century.[49] West's date may be correct but an attribution of Abbot Leofric should not be precluded. Either way, the fragment is a precious addition to our understanding of pre-Conquest architectural aesthetic.

Before turning to post-Conquest buildings, we must consider the church of Kirkdale (Yorkshire) in which there are nook shafts on the chancel arch and west doorway and three orders in the arch of the west doorway. Above the south doorway is an inscription which records that Orm Gamalsson rebuilt the minster 'in the days of Edward the king and the days of Tostig the earl', that is, between 1055 and 1065.[50] Baldwin Brown and Clapham associated the inscription with nave, chancel arch and west doorway.[51] More recently it has been suggested that the inscription has been reset and consequently the direct association between the inscription and the chancel arch and west doorway has been questioned; a date as late as the 1090s has been mooted for the extant fabric.[52] Yet Dominic Tweddle found no evidence to support the reuse of the inscription and added that 'the form of the bases to the angle shafts is not one encountered elsewhere in demonstrably post-Conquest Romanesque architecture'.[53] John Blair carefully considered the inscription and architectural details and concluded that 'the recognition of deliberate *Romanitas* in Orm's inscription might tend to strengthen the likelihood that the church which he built had its own pretensions to the up-to-date classical reference'.[54] Eric Fernie observed the use of nook shafts in the

---

[49] J. Backhouse, D.H. Turner and L. Webster (eds), *The golden age of Anglo-Saxon art, 966–1066*, London 1984, cat. 137.

[50] J. Blair, 'The Kirkdale dedication inscription and its Latin models: *Romanitas* in late Anglo-Saxon Yorkshire', in A. Hall and others (eds), *Interfaces between language and culture in medieval England: a Festschrift for Matti Kilpiö*, Leiden 2010, 139–45, at 140.

[51] Baldwin Brown, *Anglo-Saxon architecture*, 2 edn London 1925, 463; A. Clapham, *English Romanesque architecture before the Conquest*, Oxford 1930, 112–13. Fernie, *Architecture of the Anglo-Saxons*, 138, 159–60, follows Baldwin Brown and Clapham.

[52] S. Rigold, review of H. Taylor, *Anglo-Saxon architecture*, Cambridge 1977, in *JBAA* cxxxii (1979), 114; R.K. Morris and E. Cambridge, 'Beverley minster before the thirteenth century', in C. Wilson (ed.), *Medieval art and architecture in the East Riding of Yorkshire: BAACT* ix (1989), 9–32, at 19; R.K. Morris, 'Churches in York and its hinterland: building patterns and stone sources in the 11th and 12th centuries', in Blair, *Minsters and parish churches*, 191–9, at 196–7; J. Blair, 'The Kirkdale dedication inscription and its Latin models'; Fernie, *Architecture of Norman England*, 216–8, considers that a date as late as the 1090s is possible but does not rule out dating the fabric with the inscription.

[53] Tweddle, *CASSS, IV, South-East England*, 63–4.

[54] Blair, 'The Kirkdale dedication inscription', 143. Earlier, Blair observed that 'it seems on balance most probable, that the Romanesque details are contemporary with the sundial' (John Blair, *The Church in Anglo-Saxon society*, Oxford 2005, 358 n. 321), and cites L. Watts and others, 'Kirkdale – the inscriptions', *Medieval archaeology* xli (1997), 51–9, at 89 and n. 165.

windows of the lantern tower at Jumièges and that the nook shafts of the west doorway at Kirkdale may reflect Edward the Confessor's Westminster abbey.⁵⁵ Eric Cambridge took up Fernie's Westminster association and introduced the possibility that a link between Westminster and Kirkdale may have come via Beverley minster where building work is documented under Archbishop Kynesige (1051–60), and Archbishop Ealdred (1060–69), although later he was 'less confident' on the matter of the influence of Westminster.⁵⁶

I see little reason to doubt that the inscription refers to the present fabric of Kirkdale church. It is a small building and it is most unlikely that it would have been rebuilt less than half a century after Orm Gamalsson had constructed it. In addition to the nook shafts discussed above in connection with pre-Conquest manuscript illumination, painted fictive shafts are seen on the angles of the gallery piers in the first storey of the westwork at Corvey (873–85).⁵⁷ It is therefore possible that nook shafts are a three-dimensional expression of such painted articulation of piers. Nook shafts are not common in Roman architecture but there are examples in the Coenatio Jovis and the basilica of the Domus Flavia, Rome.⁵⁸ Subsequently, nook shafts are used in the central niche on the first storey of the façade of Theodoric's palace in Ravenna (493–526), in the ambulatory of S. Stefano, Verona, and the west window at Chapaize (Saône-et-Loire) and other First Romanesque churches in Burgundy. Nook shafts are used in the windows of the choir aisles and the arches to the choir-aisle apses at Bernay abbey, founded 1008–13, and in the west doorway at Kirk Hammerton (Yorkshire),⁵⁹ the south doorway of the west tower at Broughton (Lincolnshire),⁶⁰

---

⁵⁵   Fernie, *Architecture of the Anglo-Saxons*, 138, 159–60.

⁵⁶   Morris and Cambridge, 'Beverley minster before the thirteenth century', 13, 19; E. Cambridge, 'Early Romanesque architecture in North-East England: a style and its patrons', in Rollason, *Anglo-Norman Durham, 1093–1193*, 141–60, at 144 n.9.

⁵⁷   C.B. McClendon, *The origins of medieval architecture: building in Europe, A.D 600–900*, New Haven and London 2005, 189, ill. 194.

⁵⁸   W.L. Macdonald, *The architecture of the Roman empire: an introductory study*, rev. edn, New Haven and London 1982, pls 44 and 47. I am indebted to Guy Métraux for advice on this matter.

⁵⁹   R.K. Morris, 'Kirk Hammerton church: the tower and the fabric', *Archaeol. J.* cxxxiii (1976), 91–103.

⁶⁰   M. Shapland, 'St Mary's, Broughton, Lincolnshire: a thegnly tower-nave in the late Anglo-Saxon landscape', *Archaeol. J.* clxv (2008), 471–519. D. Stocker and P. Everson, *Summoning St Michael*, do not include a detailed discussion of Broughton tower but they note (47–8) the use of six-facetted capitals in the church and on the chancel arch at Honington and Wharram-le-Street (Yorkshire), dated to the first or second decade of the twelfth century by John Bilson and followed by Richard Gem. Gem has modified his views on the precise dating of Wharram-le-Street (48). Stocker and Everson (48) opt for a late eleventh-century date for this type of capital in Lincolnshire. Be that as it may, Kirkdale west doorway provides a dated example of this type of capital (1055–65).

Derby, St Alkmund, where Clapham dated two nook-shaft capitals recorded in the 1840s to the eleventh century;[61] and Bardsey, All Hallows (Yorkshire) which Elizabeth Coatsworth related to the west doorway at Kirk Hammerton, suggesting a date in the late tenth to eleventh century.[62] The Domesday survey records a church and priest at Kirk Hammerton, where the manor was valued at £4 in the time of Edward the Confessor but just 45 shillings in 1086.[63] This valuation tends to support a pre-Conquest date for the church. Nook shafts are also used in the west doorway at Hovingham (Yorkshire), along with a heavy roll moulding and a hollow moulding in the arch. In 1086 the whole manor, of which Hovingham was a part, was valued at 45 shillings, a significant drop from the £12 before the Conquest.[64] The Domesday survey also records a church and priest at Hovingham, and it seems entirely possible that the doorway and lower two storeys of the west tower are pre-Conquest. After the Conquest, the north portal of the west range at St Peter and St Paul, Jarrow, has nook shafts on bulbous bases and carrying cushion capitals, as well as a plain tympanum below an unornamented, two-order, round-headed arch. The extreme dates for the Jarrow cloister are 1074 and 1083, and Eric Cambridge makes a plausible case for 1076–80.[65] It is also worth noting that billet-ornamented imposts are used in the refectory doorway in the south walk of the cloister at Jarrow. Billet ornament is a favourite ornament in post-Conquest churches but it is also found on the north respond of the chancel arch at Great Paxton and on a stone excavated by Dimock from beneath the crossing at Southwell minster, examples which suggest that billet was part of a pre-Conquest architectural repertoire.[66]

It has been suggested that the three-order arches in the Romanesque fabric of St Albans abbey church may reflect Roman precedent, as in the Constantinian Baths at Trier, and the same may be true of the west doorway at Kirkdale.[67] In the essentially Norman design of St Albans abbey church Anglo-Saxon parallels have been cited for the rectangular crossing and accompanying rectangular crossing piers (in contrast to square plans for these elements in churches in Normandy), the arris between two half-shafts in the centre of the belfry openings and the triangular arches in the tympana above them in the crossing tower,[68] and the

[61] Clapham, *English Romanesque architecture before the Conquest*, 126–7, fig. 39; *Archaeol. J.* ii, 86–7.
[62] E. Coatsworth, *CASSS, VIII, Western Yorkshire*, Oxford 2008, 91–2.
[63] *Domesday Book. Yorkshire*, fo. 329c, 25W23.
[64] Ibid. fo. i. 327d, 23N23.
[65] Cambridge, 'Early Romanesque architecture in North-East England', 149.
[66] Thurlby, 'Anglo-Saxon architecture beyond the millennium', 132–4, figs 58 and 60.
[67] M. Thurlby, 'L'abbatiale romane de St. Albans', in M. Baylé (ed.), *L'Architecture normande au Moyen Âge*, Caen 1997, 79–90, at 87.
[68] Fernie, *Architecture of Norman England*, 114–15.

stepped bases and the variety of supports in the triforium of the crossing tower.[69] The baluster shafts in the transept triforia are generally regarded as reused Anglo-Saxon material.[70] Brooke sees 'very striking imitations of Anglo-Saxon arcading, which seem most probably to represent a deliberate emphasis on continuity with the past', and considers that Abbot Paul placed relics of earlier saints in the transept triforia, 'though presumably not St Alban himself'.[71] In a footnote Brooke adds: 'This is in contrast to the doubtful evidence of Matthew Paris that he showed contempt for the tombs of his predecessors'.[72] Brooke's interpretation of St Albans reflects Lanfranc's Canterbury where relics were removed to 'an upper room' which Brooke sees as 'evidently the triforium galleries'. Lanfranc's Canterbury had transept galleries but Abbot Paul's St Albans did not. The transepts at St Albans have triforia in the strict sense of that term: passages in the thickness of the wall in which there is no room for relics. The Biddles observe that the inclusion of mid-shaft rings on some of the balusters is a feature without parallel in Roman Britain, although it is possible that the material was reused because in the late eleventh century they were believed to be Roman or at least suggested Roman associations which would have been quite appropriate for Saint Alban.[73]

Great Churches of the First Generation after 1066

The articulation of the Peterborough and Wittering arches is in marked contrast to the early post-Conquest work in Abbot Paul of Caen's St Albans abbey and Bishop Walkelin's Winchester cathedral. Clear as this distinction may appear, the separation of first-generation churches from their richly articulated second-generation counterparts is not as straightforward as it first seems.[74] St Albans abbey church is faced with reused Roman brick, and therefore arch roll mouldings and

---

[69] Thurlby, 'L'abbatiale romane de St. Albans', 87.
[70] Tweddle and others, *CASSS, IV, South-East England*, 236–40. *The monastic constitutions of Lanfranc*, ed. and tr. D. Knowles, rev. C.N.L. Brooke, Oxford 2002, xxxvi.
[71] Ibid.
[72] Ibid. n. 33.
[73] Tweddle and others, *CASSS, IV, South-East England*, 236–40.
[74] On the division between the first generation of buildings up to *c.*1090, and the second generation post-1090, see, for example, P. Kidson and others, *A history of English architecture*, London 1965, 36–8; and Fernie, *Architecture of Norman England*, 19–41. Richard Gem prefers to divide the first 'generation' into two phases with phase 1 up to *c.*1080, and phase 2 in the 1080s: R. Gem, 'Bishop Wulfstan II and the Romanesque cathedral church of Worcester', in G. Popper (ed.), *Medieval art and architecture at Worcester cathedral: BAACT* i (1978), 15–37, esp. 32–3; R. Gem, 'The significance of the 11th-century rebuilding of Christ Church and St Augustine's Canterbury, in the development of Romanesque architecture', in N. Coldstream and P. Draper (eds), *Medieval art and architecture at Canterbury before 1220: BAACT* v

shafted responds were not an option.[75] If austerity was an overriding concern in the design of Abbot Paul's church then it would be hard to explain the consistent use of three orders to the main arcade and crossing arches and the corresponding steps in the responds. The three orders contrast with the two-order arches of Norman churches and the resulting seven steps to the nave aisle angles of the crossing piers at St Albans suggest a delight in aesthetic elaboration rather than simplicity. Whether one reads this as an Anglo-Saxon aesthetic adapted to brick construction, a specific attempt to recreate imperial Roman forms, or the next logical step from the complexity of the crossing piers at Saint-Étienne at Caen, is likely to remain a moot point. Unlike St Albans, which adopted the Norman liturgy of the Constitutions of Lanfranc, Winchester continued with Anglo-Saxon use and architecturally there are niches for altars in the east walls of the transept galleries.[76] Yet the architectural language at Winchester is essentially Norman and imperial.[77] Eric Fernie made the pertinent suggestion that the plainness of Winchester may be 'the result of a positive choice intended to make the building more like its imperial counterparts'.[78]

The windows of Lanfranc's dormitory at Christ Church, Canterbury, have a roll moulding in the arches and there is a single roll on the arch between the north nave gallery and the north-west tower of his cathedral church, and on the north-west tower itself. Such evidence suggests that similar mouldings featured in main arcade and gallery arches in Lanfranc's church. The relative scale of the moulding seems to be closer to the Irvine fragments at Peterborough than to anything at Saint-Étienne at Caen.[79] Lanfranc's tower differs from the western towers of Saint-

(1982), 1–19, esp. 17. On Lessay, see M. Thurlby, 'The Abbey Church of Lessay (Manche) and Romanesque Architecture in North-Eastern England', *Antiq. J.* xcvi (2014), 71–92

[75] On Romanesque St Albans, see Thurlby, 'L'abbatiale romane de St. Albans', 79–90.

[76] A.W. Klukas, '*Altaria superioria*: the function and significance of the tribune-chapel in Anglo-Norman Romanesque: a problem in the relationship of liturgical requirements and architectural form', Ph.D. diss. Pittsburgh 1978; idem, 'The architectural implications of the "*Decreta Lanfranci*"', *ANS* vi (1983), 136–71; idem, 'The continuity of Anglo-Saxon liturgical tradition in post-Conquest England as evident in the architecture of Winchester, Ely, and Canterbury cathedrals', in *Les Mutations socio-culturelles au tournant des XIe–XIIe siècles: études anselmiennes (IVe session)*, Paris 1984, 111–23.

[77] On Bishop Walkelin and Romanesque Winchester cathedral, see C. Brooke, 'Bishop Walkelin and his inheritance', in Crook, *Winchester*, 1–12, and Fernie, *Architecture of Norman England*, 117–21, with further bibliography.

[78] Fernie, *Architecture of Norman England*, 121.

[79] R. Gem, 'The significance of the 11th-century rebuilding of Christ Church and St Augustine's Canterbury', 14, suggested that the scale and deep recessing of Lanfranc's mouldings may 'perhaps be compared with Lessay'. Eudes de Capel was buried in the choir of the abbey church of Lessay in 1098 which suggests that at least the eastern arm of the building was completed by that date and, concomitantly, that construction commenced in the late 1080s or early 1090s.

Étienne at Caen or other Norman towers in that each storey is set back from the one below in the manner of the west tower at Earls Barton.[80] Moreover, column shafts carved with chevron and lozenge patterns are used in the passage to the dormitory. Could this be an aspect of Anglo-Saxon variety and adornment included at the insistence of the monks? More will be said on decorated shafts below.

Roll mouldings are also used on the windows of the north nave aisle at St Augustine's, Canterbury, commenced in 1073, which may have been used in the eastern arm as well. To differentiate between Anglo-Saxon and Norman parentage in the use of angle roll mouldings is a difficult, if not, impossible, task. Angle rolls are found at Anglo-Saxon Peterborough, and the transepts of the abbey church of Mont Saint-Michel (1048–58) and in the main arcade arches at Saint-Étienne at Caen.[81]

Chichester cathedral was richly articulated from the first. The see was moved to Chichester from Selsey in 1075. In 1108 Bishop Ralph Luffa (1091–1123) consecrated the new cathedral which, according to William of Malmesbury, he had built *a novo*. The *Victoria County History* suggested that an Anglo-Saxon minster church in the city served as the cathedral until construction of the present fabric was commenced early in the twelfth century.[82] Fernie pointed out that William of Malmesbury was 'describing the consequences of a fire in 1114 and so may have been referring to Ralph's repairs following the damage'. Gem suggested that the term *a fundamentis*, rather than *a novo*, would be expected if Luffa had founded the church.[83] Was there a delay of more than sixteen years between the transfer of the seat of the bishop of Chichester and the start of construction of the new cathedral? Tim Tatton-Brown proposed that work at Chichester commenced in the later 1070s and continued into the 1080s.[84] Earlier, Richard Gem had explored this idea but had reservations concerning such an early date for the use of three straight bays leading up to the apse and ambulatory, and for some of the capitals in the eastern arm, a point taken up by Eric Fernie who opined that the capitals may be easier to reconcile with the early twelfth century.[85] An apse-ambulatory plan with four straight bays was used from 1073 at St Augustine's, Canterbury, so there is no problem with three bays at Chichester in or soon after 1075. In the arches of the presbytery gallery, the second and third orders have simple roll mouldings which may derive from

---

[80] Fernie, *Architecture of Norman England*, 106.

[81] On the mouldings of the chancel at at Wittering in relation to the crossing arches at Saint-Étienne at Caen, see Fernie, *Architecture of the Anglo-Saxons*, 164–5.

[82] *VCH Sussex*, iii (1935), 105.

[83] R. Gem, 'Chichester cathedral: when was the Romanesque church begun?', *ANS* iii (1981), 61–4.

[84] T. Tatton-Brown, 'The medieval fabric', in M. Hobbs (ed.), *Chichester cathedral: an historical survey*, Chichester 1994, 25–46, at 25–9.

[85] Gem, 'Chichester cathedral', 61–4; Fernie, *Architecture of Norman England*, 130.

Lanfranc's Christ Church, Canterbury, or St Augustine's, Canterbury. Analogous mouldings appear on the main entrance at Colchester castle possibly as early as the 1070s and certainly before 1087. For roll-and-hollow mouldings on the aisle windows at Chichester there are close parallels in the external arcades of the apse of Saint-Nicolas at Caen, completed by 1083 and therefore in building *c.* 1075.[86] Similar mouldings are also used on the arches of the semicircular niches on the west front of Lincoln cathedral, probably begun between 1072 and 1075, when the seat of the bishop was moved from Dorchester to Lincoln, and largely finished by 1092. If construction moved from east to west then the west front may not have been reached until the mid-1080s but, given the fortified nature of the west block, it seems likely that building would have been undertaken at the east and west ends simultaneously. David Stocker has gone so far as to suggest that the eleventh-century western block of the cathedral was part of a free-standing fortified tower that pre-dates the work on the Norman cathedral.[87] Fragments of a variety of Norman arch mouldings from Archbishop Thomas of Bayeux's York minster may date from the early 1080s.[88] Such associations for the motifs in the Romanesque fabric of Chichester cathedral equate happily with the start of the work there in or soon after 1075.

The closest parallel for the Chichester mouldings is on the chapel doorway in the great tower at Corfe castle, a building normally attributed to Henry I prior to the imprisonment of Robert in the castle in 1106. Yet, the Domesday survey records that King William built a castle at Wareham and it is universally accepted that the reference is to work at Corfe.[89] In 1865 Bond suggested that the reference is to the Corfe great tower but this attribution has not received general approval.[90] More often the reference is associated with the herringbone masonry of the surviving south wall of a long rectangular structure by the south

---

[86] L. Musset, *Normandie romane, I, La Basse-Normandie*, 2 edn, La Pierre-qui-Vire 1975, 105.

[87] D. Stocker and A. Vince, 'The early Norman castle at Lincoln and a re-evaluation of the west front of Lincoln cathedral', *Medieval archaeology* xli (1997), 223–33, esp. 230–31.

[88] D. Phillips, *The cathedral of Archbishop Thomas of Bayeux: excavations at York Minster* ii, London 1985, 146, fig. 28. I am grateful to Stuart Harrison for sharing his views on the York minster mouldings prior to his publication on the eleventh- and twelfth-century work at York Minster.

[89] *Domesday Book, Dorset*, fo. 78d, 19.10.

[90] R. Willis, 'The architectural history of Winchester cathedral', *Proceedings of the Annual Meeting of the Archaeological Institute* (1846), 1–79, repr. in R. Willis, *Architectural history of some English cathedrals*, I, Chicheley 1972. T. Bond, 'Corfe castle', *Archaeol. J.* xxii (1865), 200–222, esp. 208–12, suggested that the great tower at Corfe may be the work of William the Conqueror but this attribution has not been generally accepted.

scarp of the west bailey.[91] Yet the rough tooling and broad joints in the ashlar masonry on the great tower at Corfe are more closely related to the post-1079 work than to the more smoothly finished and finely jointed stonework post-1107 work at Winchester cathedral which suggests that a date in the 1080s for the Corfe tower may be in order.[92]

Ely Cathedral

Anglo-Saxon liturgy continued after the Conquest in the Benedictine abbey church of Ely (cathedral after 1109), where construction of the Anglo-Norman church was commenced *c*.1081/82 for Abbot Simeon, brother of Walkelin, bishop of Winchester. The vast scale, aisled transepts and elevation of Simeon's church follow Winchester, along with terminal galleries in the transepts which were remodelled *c*.1110–20.[93] The unmoulded main arcade arches of the first phase of construction in the Ely transepts also follow Winchester.[94] The capitals of the eastern arcades of the south transept are based on Norman volute types, but the foliage has been convincingly compared to the pre-Conquest BL Cotton Claudius B. iv, fo. 37r.[95] Moreover, while there is no evidence for contemporary painted decoration in Walkelin's Winchester,[96] the painted designs on the arches of the east arcade of the south transept at Ely reflect Anglo-Saxon taste. In addition to the blue and red squares which we have compared with BL Cotton Claudius B. iv, fo. 19, the foliage scroll recalls this very motif on the pre-Conquest chancel arch of St Mary's, Deerhurst.[97] Sarah Ferguson has also related the roll moulding of the south window of the south-east chapel of the

---

[91] RCHME, 'Excavations in the west bailey at Corfe Castle', *Medieval Archaeology* iv (1960), 29–55; RCHME, *An inventory of historical monuments in the county of Dorset, II, South-East*, London 1970, 59.

[92] Willis, 'The architectural history of Winchester cathedral'.

[93] J.P. McAleer, 'A note about the transept cross aisles of Ely cathedral', *Proceedings of the Cambridge Antiquarian Society* lxxxi (1992), 51–70.

[94] S. Ferguson, 'The Romanesque cathedral of Ely: an archaeological evaluation of its construction', unpubl. Ph.D. diss. New York 1986; Fernie, *Architecture of Norman England*, 124–8; E. Fernie, 'The architecture and sculpture of Ely cathedral in the Norman period', in P. Meadows and N. Ramsay (eds), *A history of Ely cathedral*, Woodbridge 2003, 94–111. On the transept terminal aisles, see McAleer, 'A note about the transept cross aisles of Ely cathedral'.

[95] G. Zarnecki, *The early sculpture of Ely cathedral*, London 1958, 11–12, pl. 13.

[96] D. Park and P. Welford, 'The medieval polychromy of Winchester cathedral', in Crook, *Winchester*, 123–38, at 125.

[97] Baxter, 'Ely cathedral, Ely, Cambridgeshire', http://www.crsbi.ac.uk/search/location/ely%20cathedral/site/imagePopup/ed-ca-elyca/t18700.html; R. Gem, E. Howe, with R. Bryant, 'The ninth-century polychrome decoration at St Mary's church, Deerhurst', *Antiq. J.* lxxxviii (2008), 109–64.

south transept and the windows of the western aisle of the south transept to Anglo-Saxon precedent.[98] As with angle roll mouldings discussed above, it is difficult to be sure about the parentage of these Ely mouldings, but it is safe to say that they do not diverge from an Anglo-Saxon aesthetic. Eric Fernie has suggested that the form of the western transept is probably derived from the Empire, although this does not preclude Clapham's association of the design with the Anglo-Saxon church at Ely.[99]

The second phase of construction at Ely was commenced at gallery level on the east side of the north transept, and dates from either soon after Simeon's death in 1093 or after the appointment of Abbot Richard in 1100. Sarah Ferguson suggested that details of the second phase depend on Anglo-Saxon sources.[100] Specifically, she saw a 'two-surface wall' on the exterior of the gallery, the inner one plain and just pierced by a round-headed window; the outer plane with three arches supported on colonnettes. For Ferguson, '[s]uch a two-surface wall is unprecedented either in English large-scale buildings or in Normandy'.[101] She compared the articulation of the apse at Wing (Buckinghamshire), and blind arcading at Worth (Sussex), St Laurence's at Bradford-on-Avon, and Geddington (Northamptonshire).[102] Yet Norman precedent is surely more convincing, as in the exterior articulation of the nave clerestory at Saint-Étienne at Caen. Ferguson saw the articulation of the interior second phase in relation to Durham cathedral and suggested that 'the builders of Ely appear to be returning, almost consciously to an Anglo-Saxon heritage'.[103] Ferguson's analysis of Ely raises questions regarding Anglo-Saxon versus Norman sources concerning the articulation of wall surfaces and arches. The bold angle roll mouldings of the first-phase windows in the south transept are like those at Lanfranc's Christ Church, Canterbury, but at Ely they are accompanied by two quirks and a thin angle roll.[104] On the one hand, this multiplicity of mouldings may be seen against an Anglo-Saxon background, as at Seaham (Co. Durham), St Patrick's chapel at Heysham (Lancashire), Somerford Keynes (Gloucestershire) and Earls Barton. On the other hand, quirks between the roll mouldings suggest Norman

[98] Ferguson 'Romanesque cathedral of Ely', 88–9.
[99] Fernie, 'The architecture and sculpture of Ely cathedral in the Norman period', 110; Clapham, *English Romanesque architecture before the Conquest*, 90 and 94. The combination of central and western axial towers as in the pre-Conquest Canterbury cathedral, Durham cathedral, Ramsey abbey, Sherborne cathedral and Dover St Mary in Castro, also occurs after the Conquest at Petersfield (Hampshire), Kelso abbey and Lilleshall abbey.
[100] Ferguson 'Romanesque cathedral of Ely', 155–69.
[101] Ibid. 155.
[102] Ibid. 156.
[103] Ibid. 163–4.
[104] For illustrations of Ely, see Baxter, 'Ely cathedral, Ely, Cambridgeshire', http://www.crsbi.ac.uk/search/county/site/ed-ca-elyca.html.

analogues such as the crossing arches of Saint-Étienne at Caen, albeit with just single quirks. In the gallery arches of the north and south transepts at Ely, the soffit roll may be allied to Anglo-Saxon Peterborough and Wittering or the crossing arches of Saint-Étienne at Caen, while the quirked hollow roll on the outer order of the Ely gallery arches finds precedent in Caen but not in Anglo-Saxon England. The projecting heads at the top of the lower storey of the angle turrets of the Ely south transept recall Anglo-Saxon *prokrossoi*.[105] Analogous eclecticism is evident in the sculpture of the so-called monks' and prior's doorways, in which north Italian elements appear alongside pre-Conquest features. George Zarnecki related the Christ and angels on the tympanum of the prior's doorway with pre-Conquest illuminations of the 'Winchester' school for the 'dancing poses of the angels, their enormously long arms and large feet, and the floating draperies. The figures intrude from the tympanum onto the lintel like the figures in Anglo-Saxon manuscripts, which so often disregard the frames of the pages and are continued in the margins.'[106] He convincingly compared the aspects of the style and iconography of Christ with BL Cotton Tiberius C. vi; Cambridge, Corpus Christi College, MS 422, fo. 52v, and the prostrate figures of monks on the monks' doorway with BL Arundel 155.[107] The eclectic approach to design at Ely creates a richly articulated setting for its Anglo-Saxon saints. The significance of the continuity and promotion of St Etheldreda and her saintly relations, Sexburga, Eormenilda and Withburga, in post-Conquest Ely, so clearly presented by Susan Ridyard, is thus amply reflected in the articulation and decoration of the late-eleventh- and early-twelfth-century church.[108]

Worcester Cathedral, Great Malvern Priory and St Peter's Abbey, Gloucester

Bishop Wulfstan continued the use of the *Regularis concordia* at Worcester cathedral. Richard Gem's meticulous analysis of the Romanesque fabric of the cathedral church, commenced by Wulfstan in 1084 and consecrated in 1089, demonstrates that the major elements of the design conform to recent Anglo-Norman precedent at St Augustine's, Canterbury, Christ Church, Canterbury, St Albans abbey, Winchester cathedral and Bury St Edmund's abbey.[109] However, none of these great churches provides a model for Worcester's polygonal plan of the ambulatory and transept chapels. It is possible that such polygonal forms reflect Anglo-Saxon precedent at the cathedral where there were two churches,

---

[105] Taylor, *Anglo-Saxon architecture*, iii. 1057.
[106] Zarnecki, *The early sculpture of Ely cathedral*, 48.
[107] Zarnecki, *The early sculpture of Ely cathedral*, 31, 46, figs 27–29; Baxter, 'Ely cathedral, Ely, Cambridgeshire', http://www.crsbi.ac.uk/search/county/site/ed-ca-elyca.html.
[108] S.J. Ridyard, '*Condigna veneratio*: post-Conquest attitudes to the saints of the Anglo-Saxons', *ANS* ix (1987), 179–206, esp. 180–87.
[109] Gem, 'Bishop Wulfstan II and the Romanesque cathedral church of Worcester', 32–4.

St Mary and St Peter; the presbytery of St Peter's was rebuilt in the reign of Edward the Confessor and it is possible that it had a polygonal east end and/or chapels like St Mary's, Deerhurst.[110] Philip Barker suggested that Anglo-Saxon worked stones were reused in the Norman crypt and slype of Worcester cathedral including shafts, bases, and cushion and moulded capitals.[111] George Zarnecki has convincingly shown that the foliated cushion capitals of the west arch of the south transept chapel depend on Anglo-Saxon models, an idea with which Ute Engel concurs and expands to other elements of Wulfstan's cathedral.[112] Roll mouldings are used at Romanesque Worcester from the start, as evidenced in the west respond of the presbytery north gallery, the west arch of the south transept chapel, and the doorway to the dormitory from the west walk of the cloister. A closely related profile is in the arch from the north nave aisle to the north transept at Shrewsbury abbey and the chancel arch in the former collegiate church at Quatford (Shropshire), both founded by Roger, earl of Shropshire, in 1083 and 1086 respectively. An analogous roll moulding is used on the triumphal arch at Lastingham priory (1078–85) and the east crossing arch and arch from the north nave aisle to the north transept at Blyth priory founded 1088.

The Worcester chapterhouse has been dated *c*.1100–1115 by Neil Stratford in the most detailed analysis of its forms, and *c*.1100–1125 by Philip Barker (Figure 15.3 below).[113] Barker referred to excavation that revealed 'a substantial curving wall foundation concentric to the chapter house' which he read as 'the outer wall of a rotunda of Anglo-Saxon date'.[114] He believed that the pre-Conquest rotunda had 'an inner ambulatory arcade which was retained by Wulfstan and modified to form the outer wall of his chapter house'.[115] Stratford observed that

---

[110] Ibid. 16, 34. Polygonal apses are later found in the West Country school in the castle chapel at Ludlow, St Peter's abbey, Gloucester, and St Mary's, Dymock (Gloucestershire).

[111] P. Barker, *A short architectural history of Worcester cathedral*, Worcester 1994, 32–3, 40–41.

[112] G. Zarnecki, 'The Romanesque capitals in the south transept of Worcester cathedral', 38–42; U. Engel, *Worcester cathedral: an architectural history*, Chichester 2007, 78–82.

[113] N. Stratford, 'Notes on the Norman chapterhouse at Worcester', in Popper (ed.), *Medieval art and architecture at Worcester cathedral: BAACT* i (1978), 51–70. Stratford's dating is followed by Barker, *A short architectural history of Worcester cathedral*, 37; and P. Barker, 'Reconstructing Wulfstan's cathedral', in J.S. Barrow and N.P. Brooks, (eds), *St Wulfstan and his world*, Aldershot 2005, 167–88, at 167 and 175.

[114] Barker, 'Reconstructing Wulfstan's cathedral', 175. See also S. Crawford and C. Guy, 'As Normans tore down Saxon cathedrals', *British Archaeology* xxix (1997), 7 (http://www.britarch.ac.uk/ba/ba29/ba29feat.html).

[115] Barker, 'Reconstructing Wulfstan's cathedral', 175. See also, Fernie, *Architecture of Norman England*, 201–3. See also T.A. Heslop, 'Worcester cathedral chapterhouse and the harmony of the Testaments', in P. Binski and W. Noel (eds), *New offerings, ancient treasures, studies in medieval art for George Henderson*, Stroud 2001, 280–311, at 293 with reference to circular churches dedicated to St Mary.

Figure 15.3   Worcester cathedral, chapterhouse, interior.

the chapterhouse bases have a 'strongly archaic flavour', and compared them with bases in the crypt and generally with overlap buildings.[116] Similarly, he associated the roll moulding of the exterior window with the overlap and the east processional doorway in the south nave aisle at Great Malvern priory which he dated 'late eleventh century (?)'.[117] I do not know of a precise parallel for the Worcester chapterhouse window moulding in which a bold angle roll is framed by single thin rolls, but a family resemblance is found in the inner order of the east gallery arches in the north and south transepts of Ely cathedral in which the soffit roll is framed by a thin roll on the side of the transept for which the extreme dates are 1093–1106.[118]

The semicircular profile of the ribs of the chapterhouse vault is the same as the soffit roll of the south transept chapel arch. The intersecting blind arcade in the chapterhouse finds a parallel in the canon tables of Anglo-Saxon gospel books (BL Harley 76) and is used in the aisle dado arcade of Durham cathedral after

---

[116] Stratford, 'Notes on the Norman chapter house at Worcester', 61.
[117] Ibid. 62.
[118] For illustrations of the Ely cathedral arches, see: http://www.crsbi.ac.uk/search/location/ely%20cathedral/site/imagePopup/ed-ca-elyca/t18711.html; http://www.crsbi.ac.uk/search/location/ely%20cathedral/site/imagePopup/ed-ca-elyca/t18747.html.

1093.[119] The painted programme on the vault of the Worcester chapterhouse has been extensively studied by Sandy Heslop who considered that it shows a degree of continuity and development with the pre-Conquest monastic tradition at Worcester.[120] Heslop argued conclusively that the design of the chapterhouse and the painted programme were conceived together. Moreover, the chapterhouse would have been part of the original plan for the monastic buildings because the dormitory is located in the west range rather than the more usual location in the east range.[121] Heslop observed that there is 'little that is not explicable in terms of the major developments in elaboration of the mid-1090s associated with the work at the cathedrals of Durham and Norwich or St Anselm's choir at Canterbury'.[122] Yet, like others, he settled on a date in the first quarter of the twelfth century for the chapterhouse and its painted programme. This may be correct in terms of an absolute date seeing that chapterhouses were frequently constructed after the church was at least sufficiently advanced to be used for services. However, I see no compelling reason why the conception and indeed the building should not be placed in or soon after 1084 when construction on the cathedral was commenced. The vault shafts in the chapterhouse rest directly on the string course above the niched arcade. The absence of a base to the shafts is not paralleled in Norman architecture but is allied to the pre-Conquest north face of the east respond of the north crossing arch at Stow (Lincolnshire). Moreover, the setting of the shafts is analogous to that of the 'minor' high vault shafts above the main arcade in the presbytery of Durham cathedral, which Jean Bony has associated with the exterior articulation of the eastern arm of St Wystan's, Repton, and therefore an Anglo-Saxon trait rather than a feature to be associated with Norman or European Romanesque.[123] Sill-set shafts are used later in West Country Romanesque in the nave of St Peter's abbey, Gloucester, in the presbytery at Ewenny priory, the chapterhouse at Much Wenlock priory, the presbytery of Malmesbury abbey and the chapterhouse at St Augustine's, Bristol.

---

[119] A canon table of the Bury Gospel (BL Harley 76) is illustrated in colour in D.M. Wilson, *Anglo-Saxon art from the seventh century to the Norman Conquest*, London 1984, ill. 263.

[120] Heslop, 'Worcester cathedral chapterhouse', 297. See also T.A. Heslop, 'The English origin of the coronation of the Virgin', *Burlington Magazine* cxlvii (2005), 790–97.

[121] Fernie, *Architecture of Norman England*, 201–3; Heslop, 'Worcester cathedral chapterhouse', 296.

[122] Heslop, 'Worcester cathedral chapterhouse', 296.

[123] Bony, 'Durham et la tradition saxonne', 82. Reflections of the arrangement of sill-set vault shafts at Durham are in the nave of Lindisfarne Priory, the apse at Bamburgh castle chapel, the apse at Leuchars (Fife), the presbytery at Heddon-on-the-Wall and Warkworth (Northumberland).

St Oswald (d. 992) was venerated at Worcester and was strongly promoted by Bishop Wulfstan.[124] Anglo-Saxon associations in the design of Wulfstan's cathedral reflect this veneration of Oswald and the sense of continuity with the Anglo-Saxon past.

In addition to the Worcester cathedral and 'Overlap' associations for the east processional doorway at Great Malvern priory, the arch from south nave aisle to south transept incorporates one through stone. Through stones in arches are common in pre-Conquest buildings and also continue in use after the Conquest in the crypt and the ambulatory of the choir at St Peter's abbey, Gloucester. The west face of the arch at Great Malvern is adorned with chevron ornament which may also reflect Anglo-Saxon precedent, a point discussed further below.

Further Anglo-Saxon elements occur at St Peter's abbey, Gloucester. The single shafts on the exterior angles of the radiating chapels rest on the string course at the sill of the chapel windows in a manner allied to the ninth-century chancel of St Wystan, Repton. The arches of the Gloucester chapels have wedge-stone springers in an Anglo-Saxon tradition as in the arches of the nave porticus at Brixworth (Northamptonshire), rather than the traditional voussoirs of Norman construction. The alternation of continuous and non-continuous orders in the ambulatory wall arches and vault responds at Gloucester recalls the pre-Conquest tower east arch at St Mary-in-Castro, Dover (Kent). And, there is one particularly unusual trait in the rear arch of the north bay of the north transept gallery where the cushion capitals are not set horizontally at the top of the jamb but at an angle as the lowest stone in the arch.[125] The design probably derives from the setting of projecting blocks immediately above the impost of the jambs as in the south doorway of the west tower at Barnack, and the carved animals at the springing of the arch from the nave to the west tower at St Bene'ts, Cambridge. Such details are unlikely to have been specified by the Norman patron, Abbot Serlo, but indicate the practice of indigenous masons.

The Second Generation

Durham Cathedral and Lindisfarne Priory

Durham cathedral was commenced by Bishop William of Saint-Calais in 1093 to provide a magnificent architectural shrine for St Cuthbert (c.634–87). The

---

[124] E. Mason, 'St Oswald and St Wulfstan', in N.P. Brooks and C.R.E. Cubitt (eds), *St Oswald of Worcester: life and influence*, London 1996, 269–84; A. Gransden, 'Cultural transition at Worcester in the Anglo-Norman period', in Popper (ed.), *Medieval art and architecture at Worcester cathedral: BAACT* i (1978), 1–14.

[125] I am grateful to Richard Bryant for bringing this detail to my attention.

reference to Old St Peter's at Rome in the design of Winchester cathedral becomes more overt at Durham where, in addition to the overall length of the church, the 77-foot width of the choir and aisles repeats the width of Old St Peter's nave, and the spiral decoration of the columns and the ribs of the vaults at Durham are iconographically related to the St Peter's baldacchino.[126] Such associations establish a link between St Cuthbert and St Peter. A range of Anglo-Saxon motifs is also incorporated into the articulation of St Cuthbert's new home.[127] In addition to the intersecting arches of the aisle dado arcades, the paired shafts of the dado arcading are cut from monoliths in an Anglo-Saxon tradition, as in the grouped shafts at St Laurence's, Bradford-on-Avon. The Franks Casket, which is probably not far removed in date from the time of St Cuthbert, incorporates a number of motifs found in pre-Conquest buildings and in Durham cathedral.[128] The paired shafts of the canopy above the Virgin and Child in the Adoration of the Magi on the casket parallel those in the Durham dado arcade. The multiple roll mouldings in the central arch in the scene of the sack of Jerusalem by the Emperor Titus are reflected in the main arcade mouldings at Durham cathedral. The decorated columns in the scene of Egil defending his home may have inspired the Durham nave columns, albeit not with the same pattern. The incised zigzag on the arch in the same scene on the casket presages the chevron arches introduced in the nave at Durham. Similar *c.*700(?) incised chevron is also used on the interior face of the north nave window at Seaham (Co. Durham) and a more three-dimensional version is carved on pre-Conquest cross fragments at Jarrow and Northallerton (Yorkshire).[129]

The exterior articulation of the south transept east clerestorey at Durham speaks clearly of a regional, rather than a Norman, tradition. The string course that runs between the windows and continues as the hood of the windows is set one course above the abaci of the capitals of the window. This detail is paralleled in the north doorway of Laughton-en-le-Morthen (Yorkshire). Something

---

[126] M. Thurlby, 'The roles of the patron and the master mason in the first design of Durham cathedral', in Rollason and others (eds), *Anglo-Norman Durham, 1093–1193*, 161–84; Fernie, *Architecture of Norman England*, 131–40; E. Fernie, 'La seconda cattedrale di Durham', *Medioevo: l'Europa della cattedrali: Atti del Convegno internazionale di studi Parma, 19–23 settembre 2006*, Milan 2007, 132–40.

[127] Bony, 'Durham et la tradition saxonne', 79–92; Thurlby, 'The roles of the patron and the master mason in the first design of Durham cathedral', 161–84.

[128] For colour illustrations of the Franks' Casket, see Wilson, *Anglo-Saxon art*, ills 34–7.

[129] R. Cramp, *CASSS, I, County Durham and Northumberland*, Oxford 1977, 109, pl. 93 ills 497, 499, 500; J. Lang, *CASSS, VI, northern Yorkshire*, Oxford 2002, 180–81, 182–3, ills 662, 672–3. Incised chevron similar to that on the Franks' Casket is used on the soffit of the east window of the north nave wall at Seaham (Co. Durham). On the use of chevron in the pre-Conquest fabric of Southwell minster, see Thurlby, 'Anglo-Saxon architecture beyond the millennium', 132–3.

analogous also features in the belfry arches in the Saxo-Norman west towers in the North-East at Billingham, Bywell St Andrew, Monkwearmouth and Ovingham. The roll-and-hollow moulding at the angle of the Durham south transept east clerestorey windows is framed by a large expanse of plain archivolt on the front of the arch. This contrasts with Norman arches in which the moulded part of the arch forms its own order. Yet there is a pre-Conquest analogue for the expanse of stone between the angle moulding and the hood mould on the west doorway at Earls Barton (Northamptonshire). Moreover, if the restored archivolts of these Durham windows truly reflect the original masonry then the varied large size of the individual stones belongs to the tradition of Anglo-Saxon construction rather than Norman masoncraft with its smaller radiating voussoirs.

The Romanesque fabric of Lindisfarne priory church is a scaled-down version of Durham cathedral and as such serves as a perfect cenotaph for St Cuthbert. As at Durham, the main arcade of the Lindisfarne nave uses an alternating system of compound piers and columns with carved patterns. The first and third columns copy motifs from Durham, chevron and fluting, but the second column modifies the lozenge pattern at Durham by separating single rows of lozenges with incised rings. The latter recall the turned baluster shafts from the seventh-century abbey church at Jarrow. The delicate multiple mouldings of the interior of the Lindisfarne west doorway are even closer to the arch mouldings in the scene of the sack of Jerusalem in the Franks Casket.

Norwich Cathedral and the Patronage of Herbert Losinga

The great scale of Norwich cathedral, commenced by Bishop Herbert Losinga in 1096, follows Winchester cathedral and the great East Anglian Benedictine abbey churches of Bury St Edmunds and Ely. Like them, the elevation of Norwich follows the model of Saint-Étienne at Caen but certain aspects of its design echo Anglo-Saxon precedent. The use of three parallel shafts for the inner order of the major nave piers and the nave gallery piers is adapted from the grouped shafts of the 'crossing' at Great Paxton (Figure 15.2),[130] and the grouped shafts on the angles of the Norwich crossing tower also reflect that tradition. The motif is multiplied on the south-west tower of King's Lynn, St Margaret, also commenced by Herbert Losinga, where the exterior of the tower is adorned with a richly moulded stepped plinth in the manner of the crossing plinths at Stow and Hadstock.[131] Returning to Norwich, further pre-Conquest reference

---

[130] Kidson and others, *A history of English architecture*, 44.

[131] M. Thurlby, 'The influence of Norwich cathedral on Romanesque architecture in East Anglia', in I. Atherton, E. Fernie, C. Harper-Bill and H. Smith (eds), *Norwich cathedral: church, city and diocese, 1096–1996*, London and Rio Grande 1996, 136–57. It also seems likely that such Anglo-Saxon precedent lies behind the delicately moulded plinth of the great tower at Castle Hedingham (Essex).

is witnessed in the triangular blind arches and *prokrossoi* that enrich the interior of the terminal wall of the north transept, motifs that are also found in twelfth-century round towers in Norfolk as at Haddiscoe. The geometric patterning on the exterior walls of the crossing tower at Norwich reads like an ordered version of the stripwork on Earls Barton tower (Figure 15.1). A cloister capital from Norwich carved with a wingless dragon in interlace has long been linked with Urnes-style work especially with the Pitney brooch.[132] Other capitals from the Norwich cloister also reflect pre-Conquest exemplars. A damaged capital with the lower sections of three figures with fluttering edges to the draperies and the animated, cross-legged poses of the two side figures relates closely to Anglo-Saxon manuscripts.[133] Similarly, the round shoulders and almost horizontal protrusion of the neck and head of the man facing a figure carrying a situla on another Norwich cloister capital recall Anglo-Saxon precedent.[134]

While Anglo-Saxon motifs at Ely abbey and Worcester and Durham cathedrals may be associated with the presence of an Anglo-Saxon saint, the pre-Conquest reflections at Norwich Cathedral seem to be just a matter of aesthetic choice.

Hereford Cathedral Capitals

Anglo-Saxon antecedents for the figure style and aspects of the iconography of the historiated capitals from the east arch of the presbytery of Hereford cathedral (commenced 1107/15) have long been recognised.[135] Specifically, the flying angel with kicked-up legs and fluttering draperies evolves from the tradition of the pre-Conquest angels above the chancel arch at St Laurence's at Bradford-on-Avon, or in painted form in the dedication miniature in the Winchester New

---

[132] Zarnecki, *English Romanesque sculpture, 1066–1140*, 23, 38; G. Zarnecki, 'The sources of English Romanesque sculpture', *Actes du XVIIème Congrès internationale de l'histoire de l'art*, The Hague 1955, 171–8, at 176, pls 4 and 5; L. Stone, *Sculpture in Britain: the middle ages*, Harmondsworth 1955, 72; J. Franklin, *Medieval sculpture from Norwich cathedral*, Norwich 1980, cat. 3; J. Franklin, 'The Romanesque cloister sculpture at Norwich cathedral priory', in F.H. Thompson (ed.), *Studies in medieval sculpture*, London 1983, 56–70, at 57; Zarnecki and others, *English Romanesque art, 1066–1200*, cat. 126; O. Owen, 'The strange beast that is the English Urnes style', in J. Graham-Campbell and others (eds), *Vikings and the Danelaw: select papers from the proceedings of the Thirteenth Viking Congress, Nottingham and York, 21–30 August 1997*, Oxford 2001, 203–22, at 217–18.

[133] Stone, *Sculpture in Britain: the middle ages*, 73; Franklin, *Medieval sculpture from Norwich cathedral*, cat. 4.

[134] Franklin, *Medieval sculpture from Norwich cathedral*, cat. 2.

[135] For the starting date and the architectural history of Hereford cathedral, see M. Thurlby, 'Hereford cathedral: the Romanesque fabric', in D. Whitehead (ed.), *Medieval art, architecture and archaeology in Hereford: BAACT* xv (1995), 15–28.

Minster charter (BL Cotton Vespasian A. viii, fo. 2v) and above the chancel arch at Nether Wallop (Hampshire).[136] The iconography and style of the Harrowing of Hell capital belongs to the same tradition as the Tiberius Psalter (BL Cotton Tiberius C. iv, fo. 14r), and the carved slab in St Augustine's abbey (later cathedral), Bristol.[137] The pose of Milfrid(?) presenting a cross to Hereford cathedral is similar to that of Joachim in the annunciation to Joachim in the late pre-Conquest Hereford Troper (BL Cotton Caligula A. xiv, fo. 26).[138]

If the interpretation of Milfrid presenting a cross to Hereford cathedral is correct, reference to Anglo-Saxon sources for the Hereford capitals goes beyond fashion to recall a significant period in the history of the cathedral. About 830, Milfrid had erected a stone church at Hereford in honour of St Ethelbert which he enriched with silken vestments and admirable ornaments.[139]

Minor Churches

The chancel arch at Bosham and Stoughton (Sussex), the crossing arches at Stow and the tower arch at Corringham and Harmston (Lincolnshire) are all elaborately moulded and as such belong to the same family as Durham cathedral and the second campaign of construction at Ely.[140] Of these, the chancel arch at Bosham has been attributed to the patronage of Osbern, a royal clerk of Norman origin with rich landholdings in the area, who became bishop of Exeter in 1072.[141] Before the Conquest, Osbern was a chaplain of Edward the Confessor so it is difficult to determine whether the arch mouldings at Bosham reflect Norman or Anglo-Saxon taste.

---

[136] M. Thurlby, 'A note on the Romanesque sculpture at Hereford cathedral and the Herefordshire school of sculpture', *Burlington Magazine* cxxvi, no. 973 (1984), 233–4; M. Thurlby, *The Herefordshire school of Romanesque sculpture*, Logaston 1999; M. Thurlby, *The Herefordshire school of Romanesque sculpture (with a history of the anarchy in Herefordshire by Bruce Coplestone-Crow)*, Logaston 2013. The New Minster charter is illustrated in colour, in Wilson, *Anglo-Saxon art*, pl. 261. For Nether Wallop, see R. Gem and P. Tudor-Craig, 'A "Winchester school" wall painting at Nether Wallop, Hampshire', *ASE* ix (1981), 115–36.

[137] Zarnecki, *English Romanesque sculpture, 1066–1140*, 29; Stone, *Sculpture in Britain: the middle ages*, 49.

[138] S. Nichols and M. Thurlby, 'Notes on the Romanesque capitals from the east arch of the presbytery of Hereford cathedral', *The Friends of Hereford Cathedral Fifty-first Annual Report* (1985), 14–26, at 16; Temple, *Anglo-Saxon manuscripts, 900–1066*, cat. 97, fig. 294.

[139] G.M. Hills, 'The architectural history of Hereford cathedral', *JBAA* xxvii (1871), 46–84, at 52.

[140] T. Tatton-Brown (with B. Worssam), 'A new survey of the fabric of the church of the Holy Trinity, Bosham, West Sussex', *Sussex Archaeological Collections* cxliv (2006), 129–54.

[141] Ibid. 132.

The early fabric of St Mary at Bibury (Gloucestershire), including the carved capitals of the chancel arch, is traditionally dated before the Conquest.[142] In a recent article I argued that the work was created for Bishop Wulfstan of Worcester according to Anglo-Saxon design principles and techniques, probably around 1080–90.[143] Analogous continuity of the Anglo-Saxon tradition in architecture and sculpture after the Conquest is witnessed at Langford (Oxfordshire) probably under the patronage of the Englishman Aelfsige of Faringdon, and for Regenbald, former chancellor to Edward the Confessor, who continued in royal service under William I, Milborne Port (Somerset) where we witness a brilliant fusion of Anglo-Saxon and Norman motifs.[144] While the mouldings of the original crossing arches at Milborne Port are different in detail from those of the chancel arch at Bosham and the remains from Peterborough abbey, given the close association of Regenbald and Osbern with both Edward the Confessor and William I, one wonders whether the taste for elaborate articulation of the major arches of both churches may have been established in Edward's time.

Carved Tympana and Lintels

The depiction of a tympanum in BL MS Cotton Claudius B. iv, fo. 35v suggests that tympana were featured in the greater Anglo-Saxon churches. Whether or not there were carved tympana in English churches before the Conquest is quite another matter. George Zarnecki stated categorically that '[n]o carved tympana

---

[142] C.E. Keyser, 'Visit to the churches of Barnsley, Bibury, Aldsworth, Winson, Coln Rogers, and Coln St Denys', *TBGAS* xli (1918–19), 171–204, at 180; Baldwin Brown, *Anglo-Saxon architecture*, 2 edn, 444; W.H. Bird, *Old Gloucestershire churches: a concise guide, especially compiled for motoring folk and others interested in the architecture of our churches, and also their contents, screens, fonts, brasses, etc.*, London and Cheltenham 1928, 45–6; Clapham, *English Romanesque architecture before the Conquest*, 109n, 130, 135, 139; W.J. Croome, 'Gloucestershire churches', *TBGAS* lxxii (1953), 5–22, at 7; Taylor and Taylor, *Anglo-Saxon architecture*, 63–6; H.M. Taylor and J. Taylor, 'Architectural sculpture in pre-Norman England', *JBAA* 3 ser. xxix (1966), 3–51, at 8–9; C. Heighway, *Anglo-Saxon Gloucestershire*, Gloucester 1987, 113; D. Verey and A. Brooks, *B/E, Gloucestershire 1: The Cotswolds*, New Haven and London 2002, 167–8; R. Bryant, *CASSS, X, the Western Midlands*, Oxford 2012, 140–41.

[143] M. Thurlby, 'Aspects of the Anglo-Saxon tradition in architectural sculpture and decoration: the "overlap" and beyond', in M.F. Reed (ed.), *New voices on insular sculpture*, Oxford 2011, 57–69, at 57–8.

[144] J. Blair, *Anglo-Saxon Oxfordshire*, Stroud 1994, 175; Tweddle, *CASSS, IV, South-East England*, 62–6, 213–5; J. Blair, 'Secular minster churches in Domesday Book', in P. Sawyer (ed.), *Domesday Book: a reassessment*, London 1985, 104–42, at 134; Gem, 'The English parish church in the 11th and early 12th centuries: a great rebuilding?', 27; Fernie, *Architecture of Norman England*, 214; Thurlby, 'The Anglo-Saxon tradition in architectural sculpture and decoration', 94–9.

existed in pre-Conquest England'.[145] Yet several examples with clear Anglo-Saxon pedigree for various aspects of their style have been dated to before the Conquest, but in most cases they are not in pre-Conquest churches. Pamela Tudor-Craig listed examples at Strattenborough castle farm, Coleshill (Berkshire);[146] Lathbury (Buckinghamshire), Uppington (Shropshire), Byton (Herefordshire), Castor (Northamptonshire), Hoveringham (Nottinghamshire), Ipswich, St Nicholas (Suffolk), Little Tey (Essex), Little Braxted (Essex), Southwell minster, and the lintels at Bredwardine (Herefordshire) and St Bees (Cumbria) as possible pre-Conquest candidates.[147] To these may be added the confronted beasts with knotted tails carved in low relief on the tympanum reset in the interior south nave wall at St Leonard's, Ipstones (Staffordshire).[148] Many of these are *ex situ* and are often dated to the late eleventh or early twelfth century.[149] The small tympanum carved with the low-relief demi-figure of Christ reset in the gable of arch to the south porch at St Kyneburgha, Castor, has been attributed to the ninth century, but Ron Baxter rightly observed that the style of the figure is 'not incompatible with the figural capitals of the crossing, and may also be dated *c.*1100–1110'.[150] Zarnecki dated the St Bees lintel *c.*1120.[151]

Of the works *in situ*, the chip-carving on the Bredwardine lintels announces Norman parallels and groups the work with lintels in Welsh churches in the early twelfth century.[152] Similarly, the diapered lozenge pattern on the Little Tey tympanum is of Norman character as are the roll mouldings in the enclosing arch and the design of the single-cell apsidal plan of the church.

---

[145] Zarnecki and others, *English Romanesque art, 1066–1200*, 18.

[146] N. Pevsner, *B/E, Berkshire*, Harmondsworth 1966, 119, pl. 13.

[147] P. Tudor-Craig, 'Controversial sculptures: the Southwell tympanum, the Glastonbury respond, the Leigh Christ', *ANS* xii (1990), 211–31, at 219–24.

[148] Kendrick, *Late Saxon and Viking art*, 122, suggests that it is a twelfth-century rustic survival of the Urnes style; R. Baxter, 'St Leonard, Ipstones, Staffordshire', http://www.crsbi.ac.uk/search/county/site/ed-st-ipsto.html suggests a date in the first quarter of the twelfth century,

[149] Zarnecki, *English Romanesque sculpture, 1066–1140*, 27, ill. 15, dates Uppington late eleventh century; and 27, ill. 16, Byton to the early twelfth century. N. Pevsner and E. Williamson, *B/E, Buckinghamshire*, New Haven and London 2000, 424, suggest 1090–1100 for Lathbury.

[150] Clapham, *English Romanesque architecture before the Conquest*, 129, and Taylor, *Anglo-Saxon architecture*, 1059; R. Baxter, 'St Kyneburgha, Castor, Northamptonshire', http://www.crsbi.ac.uk/search/county/site/ed-nh-casto.html.

[151] Zarnecki and others, *English Romanesque art, 1066–1200*, cat. 124.

[152] Zarnecki, *English Romanesque sculpture, 1066–1140*, 29, ill. 23; Thurlby, *Romanesque architecture and sculpture in Wales*, 58–67.

The tympanum of the south doorway of St Margaret at Knook (Wiltshire) has been variously dated between 1000 and the early twelfth century.[153] Both Clapham and Zarnecki cite parallels for the tympanum in manuscript illumination which, although separated in date by about a hundred years, both appear visually convincing as parallels for the Knook tympanum. This is hardly surprising given the strong Anglo-Saxon influence on Norman illumination of the eleventh and early twelfth century.[154] The foliage on the tympanum belongs with the capitals of the south doorway and the chancel arch. The soffit roll of the south doorway may be related to both an Anglo-Saxon and a Norman tradition,[155] while the attic bases of the south doorway are most closely paralleled at Tewkesbury abbey, c.1090–1120.[156] Most significantly, distinct post-Conquest Norman associations are seen in the constructional detail of the chancel north window – the other chancel windows are from Butterfield's 1876 restoration – and the

---

[153] Clapham, *English Romanesque architecture before the Conquest*, 136, fig. 44, dated it to the mid-eleventh century and compared it with the Aldhelm, *De virginitate* in London, Lambeth Palace Library MS 200 (Part II) of the late tenth or early eleventh century (Temple, *Anglo-Saxon Manuscripts, 900–1066*, cat. 39). Subsequently, A. Clapham, 'Knook church', *Archaeol. J.* civ (1947), 163, revised the date to immediately before the Conquest which he 'determined by the character of the capitals of the side shafts of the doorway itself and the capitals of the chancel arch in the building'. Clapham's manuscript comparison was followed by Kendrick, *Late Saxon and Viking art*, 40–41, who dated the tympanum with the manuscript around 1000, as did Temple, *Anglo-Saxon manuscripts, 900–1066*, cat. 39. H.M. Taylor, 'Anglo-Saxon sculpture at Knook', *Wiltshire Archaeological and Natural History Magazine* lxiii (1968), 54–7, believed the tympanum to be Anglo-Saxon but in a Norman fabric. For Pevsner (*B/E Wiltshire*, Harmondsworth 1975, 17) the tympanum belongs to the 'so-called Saxo-Norman overlap, i.e. quite probably to after 1066'. He recognized that the tympanum scrolls bore a striking similarity to early-eleventh-century illumination but observed that it is on Norman shafts (Pevsner, *B/E Wiltshire*, 282). He considered that the tympanum, the capitals of the chancel arch and the single-splay chancel windows are Norman (Pevsner, *B/E Wiltshire*, 282–3). G. Zarnecki, 'Romanesque sculpture in Normandy and England in the eleventh century', *ANS* i (1978), 168–89, 233–5, at 183, argued against an Anglo-Saxon manuscript model for the tympanum and opted instead for a Norman source like an initial in a Jerome manuscript from Fécamp (Rouen, Bibl. municipale, MS 445, fo. 72 recto) dated to c.1100 by Jonathan Alexander. He stated that 'the tympanum is not Anglo-Saxon as it has been claimed by several writers, but must date to the first decade of the twelfth century'. R. Cramp, *CASSS, VII, South-West England*, Oxford 2006, 240, included the tympanum in the section on 'Stones wrongly associated with pre-Conquest period'.

[154] C.M. Kauffmann, *Romanesque manuscripts, 1066–1190*, London 1975, 19–20.

[155] Fernie, *Architecture of the Anglo-Saxons*, 151, fig. 89; Fernie, *Architecture of Norman England*, 274–6.

[156] S.E. Rigold, 'Romanesque bases, in and south-east of the limestone belt', in M.R. Apted, R. Gilyard-Beer and A.D. Saunders (eds), *Ancient monuments and their interpretation: essays presented to A.J. Taylor*, Chichester 1977, 99–137, at 114–16, fig. 4, nos 61–2.

form of the rear arch of the south doorway. In the latter there are approximately equal-sized radiating voussoirs, and there are neither through stones nor any large stones in the jambs.[157] In other words, construction was not according to an Anglo-Saxon tradition but followed the new technology introduced from Romanesque Normandy.[158] The evidence as a whole fits happily with attribution of Knook to Leofgeat around 1090. Her service as embroiderer to Edward the Confessor would account for the continuity of Anglo-Saxon motifs while her ongoing royal employment after the Conquest may explain the use of masons trained in the latest masonry techniques.

Elsewhere, Anglo-Saxon style was adopted by Norman patrons. The tympanum of the south doorway of Stratton (Gloucestershire) is carved with a Tree of Life flanked by animals and a serpent and is set beneath a plain enclosing arch. Brooks aptly called the animals 'almost Ringerike in style'.[159] The Domesday survey records that Roger de Lacy (c.1062–1106) held Stratton and that there was a priest.[160] A member of the de Lacy family married Ansfrid de Cormeilles and brought him the manor of Winstone.[161] This family link may explain the close parallel between the three rows of saltire crosses on the lintel of Stratton doorway and on the south doorway at Winstone, and makes a date in the late eleventh century before Roger de Lacy was banished from England in 1096 very likely. Chip-carved saltire crosses appear after the Conquest on the tympanum of the great tower at Chepstow castle under the patronage of William fitz Osbern before 1071.[162] There is no tradition of figured tympanum sculpture in Normandy; the earliest example seems to be the scene of Daniel in the lions' den on the west doorway at Bully (Calvados) which can be dated no more precisely than late eleventh century.[163] It is therefore no surprise that Norman patrons were happy to adopt English artistic forms when it came to the creation of impressive entrances to their churches.

At Barton-on-the-Heath (Warwickshire) the head of a lancet window on the north exterior wall of the chancel is cut from a tympanum with a ring knot

[157] Thurlby, 'Aspects of the Anglo-Saxon tradition in architectural sculpture and decoration: the "overlap" and beyond', 61–3, figs 10–12.
[158] Gem, 'The English parish church in the 11th and early 12th centuries: a great rebuilding?', 25.
[159] Verey and Brooks, *B/E Gloucestershire: the Cotswolds*, 645; C.E. Keyser, 'An essay on the Norman doorways in the county of Gloucester', in P.H. Ditchfield (ed.), *Memorials of old Gloucestershire*, London 1911, 122–71, 281–7 at 145–6.
[160] *Domesday Book. Gloucestershire*, fo. 168a, 39 17.
[161] R. Atkyns, *The ancient and present state of Gloucestershire*, London 1712, 698–9.
[162] Thurlby, *Romanesque architecture and sculpture in Wales*, 3–20.
[163] Baylé, *Les Origines et les premiers développements de la sculpture romane en Normandie*, 100, fig. 326.

Figure 15.4   Water Stratford, St Giles, tympanum of S doorway.

and a serpent.[164] Pevsner called it Anglo-Danish, of the early eleventh century.[165] A date in the late eleventh or early twelfth century seems to be more likely.

The tympanum of the south doorway at Water Stratford (Buckinghamshire), is carved with Christ in Majesty in a mandorla flanked by angels (Figure 15.4).[166] Kendrick related the subject to the prior's door at Ely cathedral, and attributed the Water Stratford tympanum to 'an English sculptor who was still inspired by the living tradition of his Saxon forefathers' Winchester art'.[167] Zarnecki supported the link with pre-Conquest models and emphasise sources in 'the miniatures of the Winchester School'.[168] He saw 'no connection with the Ely tympanum but it shows that similar subjects, derived from similar models, were current in English Romanesque sculpture'.[169] Lawrence Stone also saw Anglo-Saxon connections for

[164]   H. Sunley, 'St Lawrence, Barton-on-the-Heath, Warwickshire', http://www.crsbi.ac.uk/search/county/site/ed-wa-barto.html.
[165]   N. Pevsner, *B/E, Warwickshire*, Harmondsworth 1966, 86–7.
[166]   T.D. Kendrick, *Late Saxon and Viking art*, London 1949, 143; J.L. Myers, 'History and antiquities of Water Stratford', *Records of Buckinghamshire* vii (1897), 115.
[167]   Kendrick, *Late Saxon and Viking art*, 143–4. My thanks to Roger Stalley for drawing my attention to the stylistic similarity between the Water Stratford tympanum and the Benedictional of St Aethelwold.
[168]   Zarnecki, *The early sculpture of Ely cathedral*, 48.
[169]   Ibid. 48.

the tympanum and related the capitals to initials in Anglo-Saxon manuscripts except for the pelleting which he saw as 'a new Anglo-Norman device'.[170] There can be no doubt as to the Anglo-Saxon stylistic associations for the Water Stratford tympanum but it is difficult to equate this with any particular agenda that may be tied to the patronage of the work. At Domesday Water Stratford was held by Turstin of Robert d'Oilly.[171] On Robert's death in 1090 it passed to his brother Niel, and, on Niel's death in 1112, to his son Robert d'Oilly (d. c.1150).[172] Robert d'Oilly founded Osney priory in 1129 and gave two-thirds of the tithes of Water Stratford to his new foundation.[173] Perhaps the work at Water Stratford church may be associated with this gift. Be that as it may, the Anglo-Saxon seems to be a matter of taste, one that is parallel with the pre-Conquest appearance of the flyaway draperies in Henry I's third seal, and Stephen's third seal, missing on the seals of the Confessor and William I and II.[174]

The lively pose and calligraphic rendering of the draperies of St Michael killing the dragon on the tympanum reset in the south porch of Hallaton (Leicestershire), suggest Anglo-Saxon antecedents.[175] In 1086 Hallaton was held by Geoffrey Alselin of the king, and a Norman held of him.[176]

The angel on the tympanum of the north doorway at Halford (Warwickshire) has been convincingly related to Anglo-Saxon manuscript illumination.[177] It is also likely that the damaged figure in the niche to the right of the chancel arch is St John the Evangelist which was part of a rood with the Virgin in a niche to the left and the crucifix above the chancel arch in an Anglo-Saxon tradition. The architectural details of the Romanesque fabric, especially the heavy roll mouldings on the chancel arch and the adjacent niche to the right, suggest a late eleventh or early twelfth-century date. Halford is not recorded in the Domesday

---

[170] Stone, *Sculpture in Britain: the middle ages*, 51. D.M. Wilson, *Anglo-Saxon art from the seventh century to the Norman Conquest*, 211, detected Anglo-Saxon influence in the Water Stratford tympanum but saw the details as 'archaic and naïve'. He continued, 'There was an undoubted resistance to Romanesque sculpture in eleventh century England, a resistance which resulted in a style which inhibited the development of sculpture in the newly conquered land'. It is difficult to agree with this negative assessment.

[171] *Domesday Book. Buckinghamshire*, fo. 149c, 19.7.

[172] *VCH Buckinghamshire*, iv (1927), 260

[173] Ibid.

[174] F. Saxl, *English sculptures of the twelfth century*, London 1954, pls I a–d and IIa.

[175] G.C. Bellairs, 'Hallaton church and the recent discoveries there', *Transactions of the Leicester Architectural and Archaeological Society* (1890), 218–22, at 219, suggests that the tympanum is pre-Conquest.

[176] *Domesday Book, Leicestershire*, fo. 235c, 28.1.

[177] D. Kahn, 'The Romanesque sculpture of the church of St Mary at Halford, Warwickshire', *JBAA* cxxxiii (1980), 64–73.

survey, but in the time of Henry I it belonged to Henry of Newburgh, Earl of Warwick, who is a likely candidate as patron of the church.[178]

The lintel of the doorway to the vice in the north-west corner of the north transept at Southwell minster is carved with St Michael fighting the dragon and David rescuing his flock from the lion, and has been variously dated between the mid-tenth century and *c.* 1120.[179] The detailed study of the lintel by Philip Dixon, Olwyn Owen and David Stocker demonstrates conclusively that the carving on the underside of the lintel predates the work on the front of the stone, and that the stone may have originally served as an Anglo-Saxon grave cover. The St Michael and David composition probably dates from *c.* 1110 and is stylistically related to the tympanum reset above the north doorway at Hoveringham (Nottinghamshire), and the capitals of the east crossing arch at Southwell minster itself on which elements of style and iconography derive from Anglo-Saxon sources.[180]

Capitals, Arches and Label Stops

One side of a loose cushion capital at Campsall (Yorkshire) is carved with a lion in foliage in an Anglo-Scandinavian Ringerike manner.[181] In 1086 Campsall was held by Ilbert de Lacy and it is likely that he was the patron of the church.[182] As in the near-contemporary tympanum at Stratton, we find a Norman patron authorizing the use of pre-Conquest sculptural motifs in his church. Whether or not Ilbert de Lacy was aware of this as an illustration of continuity with the Anglo-Saxon past is difficult to decide for we must remember that in the 1040s

---

[178] W. Dugdale, *The antiquities of Warwickshire...*, London 1730, 616–7; W. Smith, *A new and compendious history of the county of Warwick*, Birmingham 1830, 84.

[179] Kendrick, *Late Saxon and Viking art*, 72, suggests that it is reused and therefore it is improbable that it is later than the mid-eleventh century. Stone, *Sculpture in Britain: the middle ages*, 48, pl. 29a, suggests mid- or late eleventh century. Zarnecki and others, *English Romanesque art, 1066–1200*, cat. 123, suggest that it was reset probably in the nineteenth century and date it *c.* 1120. P. Tudor-Craig, 'Controversial sculptures', 211–31, proposes that it comes from the church built by Archbishop Oskytel soon after 956. P. Dixon, O. Owen and D. Stocker, 'The Southwell lintel, its style and significance', in J. Graham Campbell and others (eds), *Vikings and the Danelaw: select papers from the proceedings of the Thirteenth Viking Congress, Nottingham and York, 21–30 August 1997*, Oxford 2001, 245–68 propose a date around 1110, and present detailed arguments for the use of the lintel before its setting above the door to the staircase in the north-west corner of the north transept.

[180] F. Kelly, 'The Romanesque crossing capitals of Southwell minster (together with a note on the lintel in the north transept and the tympanum at Hoveringham)', in J.S. Alexander (ed.), *Southwell and Nottinghamshire: medieval art, architecture, and industry: BAACT* xxi (1998), 13–23.

[181] Zarnecki and others, *English Romanesque art, 1066–1200*, cat. 103.

[182] *Domesday Book, Yorkshire*, fo. 315d, 9W36.

Figure 15.5   Bradbourne, All Saints, W tower, detail of S doorway.

at Jumièges abbey and later at Lion-sur-Mer (Calvados), Anglo-Saxon models had been used for motifs in carved capitals.[183]

Interlace designs on the right capitals of the south doorway at Kensworth (Bedfordshire, formerly Hertfordshire until 1897), suggest pre-Conquest origins.[184] The manor was held by Leofwine Cild of Edward the Confessor, and in 1086 it retained the same value under the canons of St Paul's, London.[185] In 1066 the manor was valued at 100 shillings but in 1086 it had fallen to 70 shillings. It is therefore likely that construction of the church took place some time after 1086.

The south doorway of the west tower at Bradbourne (Derbyshire) has a three-order arch with beakhead on the outer order while the two inner orders are adorned with two-plane carvings of animals with tails turning to interlace (Figure 15.5). For Arthur Gardner the animals 'can only be derived from Norse

---

[183]   M. Baylé, 'La sculpture du XIe siècle à Jumièges et sa place dans le décor architectural des abbayes normandes', in *Aspects du monachisme en Normandie (IV –VIII siècles), Actes du colloque scientifique de l'Annèe des abbayes normandes 1979*, Paris 1982, 75–96; M. Baylé, 'Interlace patterns in Norman Romanesque sculpture: regional groups and their historical backgrounds', *ANS* v (1983), 1–20, at 4–9.

[184]   H. Gardiner, 'St Mary, Kensworth, Bedfordshire', http://www.crsbi.ac.uk/search/county/site/ed-bd-kensw.html.

[185]   *Domesday Book, Hertfordshire*, fo. 136b, 13.1.

wood-work techniques'.[186] It seems likely that pre-Conquest references are more immediate. In 1086 the manor of Bradbourne was held by Henry de Ferrers and there was a church and priest. The inclusion of beakhead ornament on the tower doorway more-or-less precludes a date before 1130. Beakhead first appears in the 1120s at Sarum cathedral and Reading abbey,[187] the latter for King Henry I, the former for Bishop Roger (1102–39) who was second only in importance to the king. It is likely that ambitious patrons of architecture would wish to emulate such works without delay.

At St Mary's, Kirkburn (Yorkshire), two Urnes style capitals belong to the church which may be attributed to Robert de Brus II in the late 1120s after the gift of the church to Guisborough priory.[188] Maylis Baylé paralleled the Kirkburn capitals with a small group of sculptures at Sainte-Marie-du-Mont and Saint Côme-du-Mont (Manche).[189] She subsequently suggested a date around 1120–1130 for Sainte-Marie-du-Mont.[190] She also related the west capital in the second bay of the nave north wall at Kirkburn with the pre-Conquest tradition and related sculpture at Autheuil (Orne).[191] When seen in the context of Maylis Baylé's associations with similar sculpture in Normandy, it is clear that Anglo-Saxon motifs had been fully assimilated into Norman taste.

At Northampton, St Peter, some of the capitals of the nave arcade capitals have animals carved with 'fur' and two-strand interlace in the manner of pre-Conquest metalwork.[192] Henry Maguire also related the shaft rings on the arcade columns to pre-Conquest baluster shafts as in the belfry at Earls Barton.[193]

---

[186] A. Gardner, *English medieval sculpture*, Cambridge 1951, 53, fig. 82.

[187] F. Henry and G. Zarnecki, 'Romanesque arches decorated with human and animal heads', *JBAA* 3 ser. xx–xxi (1957–8), 1–35; Zarnecki and others, *English Romanesque art 1066–1200*, cat. 129–31; R. Baxter and S. Harrison, 'The decoration of the cloister at Reading abbey', in L. Keen and E. Scarff (eds), *Windsor: medieval archaeology, art and architecture of the Thames valley: BAACT* xxv (2002), 302–12. M. Thurlby, 'Sarum cathedral as rebuilt by Roger, bishop of Salisbury, 1102–39: the state of research and open questions', *Wiltshire Archaeological and Natural History Magazine* ci (2008), 130–40.

[188] *Cartularium prioratus de Gyseburne*, ed. W. Brown (SS lxxxvi, lxxxix, 1888–94), i. pp. vi–x, 3. For further discussion of the twelfth-century sculpture at Kirkburn, see Thurlby, 'The Anglo-Saxon tradition in architectural sculpture and decoration', 64–5.

[189] M. Baylé, *Les Origines et les premiers développements de la sculpture romane en Normandie*, Caen 1992, 98, 103.

[190] M. Baylé, 'Sainte-Marie-du-Mont: église Notre-Dame', in M. Baylé (ed.), *L'Architecture normande au Moyen Âge*, ii. 105.

[191] Baylé, *Les Origines et les premiers développements de la sculpture romane en Normandie*, 98, figs 310, 311 and 313.

[192] Gardner, *English medieval sculpture*, 62; H.P. Maguire, 'A twelfth-century workshop in Northampton', *Gesta* ix (1970), 11–35.

[193] Maguire, 'A twelfth-century workshop in Northampton', 20. See also R. Baxter, St Peter, Northampton, Northamptonshire, http://www.crsbi.ac.uk/search/location/northampton

The work is likely to date from the 1140s, possibly under the patronage of Simon de Senlis II, earl of Northampton.

Of all motifs of Anglo-Saxon origin that continued in use throughout the twelfth century, the most enduring is surely the beast-head label stop that first appeared on the chancel arch of St Mary's, Deerhurst, in the ninth century. The best known are in the nave arcades at Malmesbury abbey, where the vertical shafts above the nave arcade capitals are triplets in the manner of the north porticus gable articulation at St Laurence's, Bradford-on-Avon.[194] Also at Malmesbury, Kit Galbraith demonstrated the importance of Anglo-Saxon iconographic sources for the sculpture on the arch to the south porch.[195] The heads of the angels above apostles in the side lunettes of the south porch take on a distinctly Anglo-Saxon profile.[196] Such pre-Conquest references are particularly appropriate for the setting of the shrine of St Aldhelm.

Standing Crosses

Deidre O'Sullivan has amassed much evidence for the destruction of Anglo-Saxon church crosses and tombs in the north of England.[197] Be that as it may, as O'Sullivan has pointed out, several examples in Cumbria attest to retention of standing crosses after the Conquest, as at Bewcastle, Gosforth, Irton and elsewhere.[198] A number of post-Conquest standing crosses demonstrate at least

/site/ed-nh-nhstp.html.

[194] Allied beast-head label stops occur in Gloucestershire at Almondsbury – arch to N porch, Bibury – N nave arcade, Bishop's Cleeve – S and W doorways, Coln St Aldwyn – S doorway, Elkstone – W arch of former axial central tower, Forthampton – S doorway, Gloucester, St Oswald, Leonard Stanley – N and W doorways, Little Barrington – N and S doorways, Oddington – S doorway, South Cerney – S doorway, Tredington – N and S doorways, Withington – S doorway, and at Bolstone (Herefordshire) – N doorway, Ripple (Worcestershire) – W doorway, Ewenny priory (Glamorgan) – arch to N transept chapel, Llandaff cathedral – S presbytery window, Lincoln cathedral – W doorways, Freiston (Lincolnshire) – nave arcades, South Kyme (Lincolnshire) – S doorway, Sutterton (Lincolnshire) – N doorway, Southwell minster – north porch windows, Balderton (Nottinghamshire) – S doorway and N porch, South Collingham (Nottinghamshire), St John the Baptist – N nave arcade, Winkburn (Nottinghamshire) – S doorway, Cashel (Tipperary), Cormac's chapel – N doorway; Kilmalkedar (Kerry) – W doorway and E window of chancel, Roscrea, St Kronan – W front, Trondheim cathedral, N porch.

[195] K.J. Galbraith, 'The iconography of the biblical scenes at Malmesbury abbey', *JBAA* 3 ser. xxviii (1965), 39–56.

[196] Saxl, *English sculptures of the twelfth century*, pls liv, lv and lx.

[197] D. O'Sullivan, 'Normanising the north: the evidence of Anglo-Saxon and Anglo-Scandinavian sculpture', *Medieval Archaeology* lv (2011), 163–91.

[198] O'Sullivan, 'Normanising the north', 180.

some interest in prolonging or reviving the life of this traditional Anglo-Saxon monument. Various interlacing designs on St Leonard's Cross in the churchyard at Thrybergh (Yorkshire) reflect pre-Conquest sources but a standing figure beneath a pointed arch makes a date before the 1150s unlikely and it may be as late the thirteenth century.[199] Coatsworth attributed the cross shaft at Barnburgh, St Peter (Yorkshire) to the same sculptor and related both to the cross shaft at Rawmarsh, St Mary (Yorkshire).[200] Coatsworth also considered that the cross-shaft at St Peter's, East Marton (Yorkshire) 'seems to be an unequivocally Romanesque piece'.[201] Similar foliage and animal forms on the capitals of the chancel arch at Brayton (Yorkshire) and nave arcade capitals at Selby abbey suggest a date between 1130 and 1150 for the East Marton cross-shaft.[202]

The standing cross from the cemetery of the Dominican friary at King's Lynn, has been variously dated between the ninth and the thirteenth century.[203] The sculpture is very weathered and interpretation is therefore far from straightforward. The head of the cross has a crucifixion on one side and a figure of Christ on the other. On the shaft, St Michael killing the dragon is carved beneath the Crucifixion, and on the opposite side there is some relatively well-preserved foliage with a rectangular frame. The foliage is most closely related to the 'Byzantine blossoms' in the initials and borders of the Bury Bible. Such a comparison makes a date in the 1130s a possibility but similar foliage is still to be found in sculpture of the 1170s as on the frieze of the font at Great Kimble (Buckinghamshire).[204] The theme of the Crucifixion is also used on the tenth-century(?) cross-head at Kedington (Suffolk) while both the Crucifixion and Christ in Majesty appear in the head of the so-called Neasham cross brought from Low Middleton Hall to the chapel of the Nine Altars at Durham cathedral in 1938.[205] The proto-stiff-leaf foliage on the 'Neasham' cross arms is a dryer

---

[199] G. Baldwin Brown, *Anglo-Saxon sculpture: the arts in early England*, VI ii, London 1937, 142–6.

[200] Coatsworth, *CASSS, VIII, Western Yorkshire*, 286–9. N. Pevsner, *B/E, Yorkshire West Riding*, 2 edn revised by E. Radcliffe, Harmondsworth 1967, 517, asked 'Is it an Anglo-Saxon piece recarved in the C12?'

[201] Coatsworth, *CASSS, VIII, Western Yorkshire*, 288.

[202] For the Brayton and Selby capitals, see G. Zarnecki, *Later English Romanesque sculpture, 1140–1210*, London 1953, ill. 74.

[203] http://www.britishlistedbuildings.co.uk/en-384288-cross-beneath-greyfriars-tower-kings-lyn suggests ninth–tenth century; N. Pevsner, *B/E, North-West and South Norfolk*, Harmondsworth 1962, 228, dates the cross to the thirteenth century, but in the revised edition of the book, Nikolaus Pevsner and Bill Wilson, *B/E, Norfolk 2: North-West and South*, New Haven and London 2002, 471, a date in the eleventh century is proposed.

[204] Zarnecki, *Later English Romanesque sculpture, 1140–1210*, ill. 100.

[205] M.F. Reed, 'Sculpture and identity in late Saxon East Anglia', unpubl. Ph.D. diss. York 2008, 160, 164, 231–6, 361, fig. 19; N. Pevsner, *B/E, County Durham*, 2 edn rev. by

version of that on capitals from the late-twelfth-century chapterhouse at St Mary's abbey, York. Similarly, the figure style – especially the St John in the Crucifixion – relates to the figures from Archbishop Roger of Pont-l'Évêque's York minster and St Mary's abbey, York, and stained glass at York minster.[206] These parallels suggest a date in the late twelfth century for the 'Neasham' cross. Of similar date is the Kelloe (Co. Durham) cross carved with scenes from the invention of the True Cross. In the most detailed study of the Kelloe cross, Lang plays down Anglo-Saxon associations,[207] but Kendrick saw it as a 'distant descendant of the eighth-century panelled St Andrew Auckland cross, some ten miles away in the same county, and it is shouldered in a rather odd way that recalls the very late "full-length" crosses ...'[208] Kendrick rightly sees the figure style as Romanesque – Saxl parallels the death of Dives tympanum preserved in the Yorkshire Museum – but, as Kendrick indicates, the foliage grows from the frame as in Anglo-Saxon manuscript illumination.[209]

The wheel-head cross with collared shaft at Fletton (Huntingdonshire) with an inscription to William fitz Ralph has been dated 'not earlier than the twelfth century',[210] and late twelfth century.[211] The form of the cross is paralleled at Sproxton (Leicestershire), probably of the late tenth century, and Stanground, possibly twelfth century, but the animal-inhabited medallions joined with binding ties on the Fletton cross support a mid-twelfth-century date.

The cross in the churchyard of St Nicholas, Castle Hedingham (Essex), is carved with palmettes on the sides of the large square base and the shaft of the cross and a row of small bosses on the four chamfered angles of the

---

E. Williamson, Harmondsworth 1983, 200.

[206] J. Geddes, 'Twelfth-century metalwork at Durham cathedral', in N. Coldstream and P. Draper (eds), *Medieval art and architecture at Durham cathedral: BAACT* iii (1980), 140–48, at 144–5, suggested that the quatrefoil head of the cross may derive from objects like the Reliquary of Emperor Henry II.

[207] J. Lang, 'The St. Helena cross, Church Kelloe', *Archaeologia Aeliana* 5 ser. v (1977), 105–19. See also http://www.durham.anglican.org/userfiles/file/Durham%20Website/Diocese%20and%20Admin/Care%20of%20Churches/Archaeological%20Assessments/Kelloe.pdf

[208] Kendrick, *Late Saxon and Viking art*, 63.

[209] Kendrick, *Late Saxon and Viking art*, 146; Saxl, *English sculptures of the twelfth century*, 67–8. Saxl also sees Anglo-Saxon sources for the Doom slab in York minster. While the depiction of the Mouth of Hell reflects Anglo-Saxon precedent, I am not convinced by Saxl's suggestion of pre-Conquest sources for the figure style.

[210] A. Clapham, *English Romanesque architecture after the Conquest*, Oxford 1934, 159–60.

[211] *VCH Huntingdonshire*, iii (1936), 169–73. http://www.british-history.ac.uk/image.aspx?compid=66170&filename=fig125.gif&pubid=526 includes a drawing of all four sides of the cross from the Dryden Collection, Northampton Public Library.

shaft.²¹² The foliage is far removed from the tradition of Winchester acanthus and is most closely paralleled in the borders of full-page illuminations in the Bury Bible (Cambridge, Corpus Christi College MS 2, fo. 94) and the Bury Gospels (Cambridge, Pembroke College, MS 120, fo. 2v).²¹³ Both books were illuminated about 1130 at the abbey of Bury St Edmunds; a date between 1130 and 1150 may be suggested for the Castle Hedingham cross.

Built into the east wall of the nave to either side of the chancel arch of St Andrew, Minting (Lincolnshire), are two fragments of a cross framed vertically with nail-head ornament and foliage trails between.²¹⁴ To the north above the foliage is a Crucifixion with the Virgin and St John. The juxtaposition of the Crucifixion atop scrolls repeats that on the eleventh-century cross at Harmston (Lincolnshire).²¹⁵ The foliage has been compared with the Tree of Jesse panel from the west front of Lincoln cathedral which probably dates from the 1140s.²¹⁶ The individual trilobe leaves of the foliage trails find a closer parallel on a late-twelfth-century capital reused as a font base at All Saints, Winterton (Lincolnshire), on which nailhead adorns the impost.²¹⁷ A similar foliage trail appears on a fragmentary cross shaft at Revesby (Lincolnshire) where it is accompanied by dog-tooth ornament. The latter motif is used on the north doorway of the west front of Lincoln cathedral which has been dated as early as the 1140s, but the motif became more popular in the last quarter of the twelfth and in the thirteenth century. Christ's legs are crossed and his feet secured with one nail, which makes a date before the thirteenth century unlikely.²¹⁸

Fonts

George Zarnecki has convincingly compared figures of seated apostles of the Gloucestershire lead fonts with pre-Conquest manuscripts, BL, Arundel 155 and

---

[212] Brown, *Anglo-Saxon sculpture*, 148–9, pl. XL.
[213] R.M. Thomson, *The Bury Bible*, Woodbridge and Tokyo 2001, pls 5 and 52.
[214] P. Everson and D. Stocker, *CASSS, V, Lincolnshire*, Oxford 1999, 327–8, ills 460–61.
[215] For the Harmston crucifixion, see Everson and Stocker, *CASSS, V, Lincolnshire*, 176–7, ill. 195 and 199.
[216] Everson and Stocker, *CASSS, V, Lincolnshire*, 328. For the Lincoln Tree of Jesse fragment, see G. Zarnecki, *Romanesque Lincoln: the sculpture of the cathedral*, Lincoln 1988, fig. 93.
[217] T.E. Russo, 'All Saints, Winterton, Lincolnshire', http://www.crsbi.ac.uk/search/county/site/ed-li-winte.html.
[218] N. Pevsner and J. Harris, *B/E, Lincolnshire*, Harmondsworth 1964, 317; G. Schiller, *Iconography of Christian art, II. The passion of Christ*, London 1972, 146.

Cotton Caligula A. xiv.[219] On the allied stone font at Coleshill (Warwickshire), one figure with dancing cross-legged pose has been related to Anglo-Saxon manuscript illumination.[220] A standing angel with legs tapering pronouncedly to the feet on the lead font at Lower Halstow (Kent) has been associated with Anglo-Saxon manuscripts.[221] The association may well be correct but the drapery style also betrays knowledge of Byzantinising damp-fold style as on the St Anne portal on the west front of Notre-Dame, Paris, and the Christ in Majesty on the tympanum of the south portal at Barfreston (Kent).[222]

The interlace on the twelfth-century font at Toftrees (Norfolk) has been compared with the late-tenth-century Bosworth Psalter BL MS Add. 37517. Jane Geddes also associates interlace on the related fonts at Castle Rising, Inglethorpe, Sculthorpe and Shernborne with Anglo-Saxon sources.[223]

In all of these examples, there is nothing to indicate that the choice of Anglo-Saxon models is anything other than aesthetic preference.

Friezes

George Zarnecki cited iconographic and stylistic precedents in Anglo-Saxon art for aspects of the sculptured frieze on the west front of Lincoln cathedral.[224] The inclusion of a frieze on the Lincoln façade ultimately follows Roman precedent, but immediate inspiration for the sculpture may have been taken from the west front of Modena cathedral, possibly via the façade of Bury St Edmunds abbey, from which just one fragment of the frieze remains. There is also precedent for carved friezes in Anglo-Saxon England as early as the late seventh century at Monkwearmouth, Hexham and Jarrow, and later at Breedon-on-the-Hill (Leicestershire), Fletton and Winchester.[225] Other than Winchester, the scale of these pre-Conquest friezes is smaller than Lincoln, but fragments at Calverton (Nottinghamshire) and Barton-le-Street (North Yorkshire) and a lost panel

---

[219] G. Zarnecki, *English Romanesque lead sculpture*, London 1957, 11, 33, ills 31–4; Zarnecki and others, *English Romanesque art, 1066–1200*, cat. 243.

[220] Stone, *Sculpture in Britain: the middle ages*, 245 n. 26.

[221] Zarnecki, *English Romanesque lead sculpture*, 35, where he dates the font to the third quarter of the twelfth century; Zarnecki and others, *English Romanesque art, 1066–1200*, cat. 244, where he dates the font *c.*1130.

[222] M. Thurlby, 'A twelfth-century figure fragment from Lewes Priory', *Sussex Archaeological Collections* cxx (1982), 215–23.

[223] Stone, *Sculpture in Britain: the middle ages*, 241 n. 14; Geddes, *Medieval decorative ironwork*, 56.

[224] Zarnecki, *Romanesque Lincoln: the sculpture of the cathedral*.

[225] D. Kahn, 'Anglo-Saxon and early Romanesque frieze sculpture in England', in D. Kahn (ed.), *The Romanesque frieze and its spectator*, London 1992, 61–74.

from Chichester cathedral may follow a pre-Conquest tradition.[226] At Barton-le-Street (Yorkshire) the narrative panels, especially the agitated, dancing poses, recall Anglo-Saxon figure style.[227]

Disputed Examples

In the study of architectural sculpture, work *in situ* should be dated in connection with the building but, with *ex situ* carvings, there are 'disputed' examples, in other words, sculpture for which both Anglo-Saxon and Anglo-Norman dates have been suggested.

A number of works listed as pre-Conquest and dated *c.*1000 by Prior and Gardner, like the Barking rood, the ivory relief of the Deposition in the Victoria and Albert Museum and the Chichester reliefs, are now considered to be post-Conquest products.[228] The Barking rood is attributed to *c.*1150 by Zarnecki.[229] The Deposition ivory is grouped with the Herefordshire school of sculpture and dated *c.*1130–50.[230] Zarnecki convincingly reconstructed the Chichester reliefs on the former choir screen of the Romanesque cathedral, which he suggested was erected around 1120–30.[231]

The St Michael and the Dragon relief preserved loose in St Nicholas, Ipswich, was dated *c.*1000 by Prior and Gardner, but most recently to *c.*1120 by Zarnecki who convincingly suggests pre-Conquest influence.[232] Pre-Conquest associations are also evident on a tympanum carved with a boar, and three

---

[226] K.A. Morrison, 'Chichester Cathedral (Holy Trinity), Chichester, Sussex', http://www.crsbi.ac.uk/search/county/site/ed-sx-chica.html.

[227] Stone, *Sculpture in Britain: the middle ages*, 81.

[228] E.S. Prior and A. Gardner, *An account of medieval figure sculpture in England*, Cambridge 1912, fig. 114 (Barking Rood), 137, fig. 118 (Stepney rood), 137, fig. 117 (the ivory relief of the Deposition in the Victoria and Albert Museum, 139–40, figs 120–21 (Chichester reliefs).

[229] Zarnecki, *Later English Romanesque sculpture, 1140–1210*, 32, 58, ill. 65. See also Saxl, *English sculptures of the twelfth century*, 56, pls xxx–xxxi.

[230] Thurlby, *The Herefordshire school of Romanesque sculpture*, 153–6.

[231] G. Zarnecki, 'The Chichester reliefs', *Archaeol. J.* cx (1953), 106–19. A revised date for the reliefs around 1090–1100 may be proposed on the basis of a starting date for the cathedral around 1075.

[232] Prior and Gardner, *An account of medieval figure sculpture in England*, 130, fig. 109; K. Galbraith, 'Early sculpture at St Nicholas's church, Ipswich', *Proceedings of the Suffolk Institute of Archaeology*, xxxi, part 2 (1968), 172–84; Zarnecki and others, *English Romanesque art, 1066–1200*, cat. 122; S.J. Plunkett, 'Anglo-Saxon stone sculpture in Suffolk', in S. West (ed.), *A Corpus of Anglo-Saxon Material from Suffolk*, East Anglian Archaeology Report No. 84, Ipswich 1998, 323–57, at 352–4; R. Baxter, 'St Nicholas, Ipswich, Suffolk', http://www.crsbi.ac.uk/search/county/site/ed-sf-ipstn.html.

reliefs of standing apostles also preserved in St Nicholas's church, all of which are probably contemporary with the St Michael and the Dragon relief.[233] The apostles have been compared to tenth- to eleventh-century Irish metalwork, specifically the Soiscel Molaisse and the Breac Maedhog in the National Museum of Ireland.[234] While the ornamental bands on the draperies on the zoo-anthropomorphic evangelist symbols on the Soiscel Molaisse may be formally associated with one of the Ipswich apostles, one is left to ask how a sculptor in Ipswich in the twelfth century might have known such Irish metalwork. While Plunkett rejects Mercian parallels, it seems to me that the drapery abstractions in the Matthew miniature in the Book of Cerne (Cambridge, University Library, MS Ll. 1. 10, fo. 2v) are akin to those on the Ipswich apostles and may suggest that the sculptor made reference to English ninth-century sources.[235] Analogous reference to early medieval models is evident in the corbel carved with a male head in the Bedford Museum, which has been compared with insular manuscript illumination, especially the St Chad's Gospels in Lichfield cathedral.[236]

The Winchester narrative frieze fragment holds the rare distinction of having been included in both the *Golden age of Anglo-Saxon art* and *English Romanesque art, 1066–1200* exhibitions.[237] Zarnecki, Wilson, Alexander and Kahn opted for a date after the Conquest while for the Biddles it is a pre-Conquest work.[238] The archaeological evidence produced by the Biddles precludes a date after

---

[233] Plunkett, 'Anglo-Saxon stone sculpture in Suffolk', 352–7; R. Baxter, 'St Nicholas, Ipswich, Suffolk', http://www.crsbi.ac.uk/search/county/site/ed-sf-ipstn.html.

[234] Plunkett, 'Anglo-Saxon stone sculpture in Suffolk', 355. For illustrations of the Soiscel Molaisse and the Breac Maedhog, see P. Harbison, *L'Art médiévale en Irelande*, La Pierre-qui-Vire 1998, ills 141, 189–93.

[235] M.P. Brown, *The Book of Cerne: prayer, patronage and power in ninth-century England*, London 1996, pl. II(a).

[236] Zarnecki and others, *English Romanesque art, 1066–1200*, cat. 125. The Bedford head is unconvincingly compared with a corbel head reset inside the south nave doorway of St Mary, Luton (Bedfordshire) – F.W. Kuhlicke, 'A twelfth-century carved head from St Mary's church, Bedford', *Bedfordshire Archaeological Journal* vii (1972), 84–6. The suggestion of an Anglo-Saxon date in T.P. Smith, 'The Anglo-Saxon churches of Bedfordshire', *Bedfordshire Archaeological Journal* iii (1966), 7–14, is not convincing; cf. H. Gardiner, 'Bedford Museum, Bedfordshire', http://www.crsbi.ac.uk/search/county/site/ed-bd-bemus.html.

[237] J. Backhouse, D.H. Turner and L. Webster (eds), *The golden age of Anglo-Saxon art, 966–1066*, London 1984, 133–5, cat. 140; Zarnecki, *English Romanesque art, 1066–1200*, 150–51, cat. 97.

[238] Zarnecki and others, *English Romanesque art, 1066–1200*, 133–5; Wilson, *Anglo-Saxon art*, 198–200; Kahn, 'Anglo-Saxon and early Romanesque frieze sculpture in England', 71; M. Biddle and B. Kyølbye-Biddle in Tweddle and others, *CASSS, IV, South-East England*, 314–22 with full bibliography.

1093–94, and for the present writer, the probable date of 1017–35 suggested by the Biddles is quite acceptable.[239]

The standing figure of Christ triumphant with a cross at Leigh (Worcestershire) has been dated to the mid-eleventh century, 1050–1100, *c.*1100 and *c.*1220.[240] Pevsner thought that the sculpture was a coffin lid, but this was ruled out by Tudor-Craig given the subject matter, to which we should also add the shape of the stone. Tudor-Craig associated the long narrow nave at Leigh with a building dedicated to St Edburga, which she suggested was erected soon after the relics of St Edburga reached Pershore in the mid-eleventh century. She imagined the Christ in a gable above the west door or above the chancel arch. The account of the church in the *Victoria County History* dates the nave *c.*1100 and gives the dimensions as 58 feet 6 inches by 25 feet 6 inches.[241] Similar dimensions are found in Romanesque naves of Worcestershire churches as at Martley (61 ft 1 in. by 24 ft 10 in.), Eldersfield (58 ft 6 in. by 20 ft 9 in.), Rock (56 ft 6 in. by 27 ft 3 in.), and in Gloucestershire at Kempsford (58 ft 11 in. x 23 ft 6 in.), Temple Guiting: (58 ft 5 in. by 20 ft 7 in.), Stow-on-the-Wold (58 ft 6 in. by 28 ft) and Beckford (59 ft 8 in by 24 ft 10 in.). A *c.*1100 date would likely make the sculpture contemporary with the early Norman work in the church, which includes the cushion capitals of the chancel arch and a niche on the exterior north nave wall. Until 1970 the Christ was located in the niche above the north doorway.[242] In the absence of evidence to the contrary, should we not regard this as the original position of the sculpture? Large figures of Christ above doorways are found at Monkwearmouth (Co. Durham), Beverstone (Gloucestershire), Jevington (Sussex), Rous Lench (Worcestershire), North Newbald (Yorkshire), Lullington (Somerset) and at St Kronan at Roscrea (Tipperary). It is probable that both the Lullington and Roscrea figures reflect work undertaken for Bishop Roger on his cathedral at

---

[239] On the possibility of frieze sculpture on the tenth-century tower of Winchester New Minster, see R.N. Quirk, 'Winchester New Minster and its 10th-century tower', *JBAA* 3 ser. xxiv (1961), 16–54 esp. 34–5.

[240] Tudor-Craig, 'Controversial sculptures', 224–30, gives mid-eleventh century; J.H. Parker, *An introduction to the study of Gothic architecture*, Oxford 1849, 74, and *VCH Worcestershire*, iv (1924), 106 suggest *c.*1100; Prior and Gardner, *An account of medieval figure sculpture in England*, 177, 205, 728, discuss the sculpture in relation to others above doorways and in Romanesque arcades and give a twelfth-century date; N. Pevsner, *B/E, Worcestershire*, Harmondsworth 1968, 212, gives *c.*1220. In the revised *B/E Worcestershire*, rev. A. Brooks, New Haven and London 2007, 425, it is noted that Charles Avery of the Victoria and Albert Museum supported a *c.*1100 date, and Brooks added that '[i]t could be even earlier'. R. Bryant, *CASSS, X, the Western Midlands*, 374–5, gives 1050–1100 while noting that 'the date of *c.*1100 is perhaps more likely'.

[241] *VCH Worcestershire*, iv (1924), 106–7

[242] Illustrated in Parker, *An introduction to the study of Gothic architecture*, 74, and Pevsner, *B/E Worcestershire*, ill. 19.

Sarum – possibly a figure in a gable above the south transept south doorway.[243] At Balderton (Nottinghamshire) there is a standing figure of St Giles(?), and there is a similarly scaled figure of St Michael reset above the entrance to the north porch at Mere (Somerset). In terms of style, the fluttering edges of the drapery of the Leigh Christ and the Balderton St Giles relate to Anglo-Saxon exemplars. Similarly, the seated figure of Christ above the south doorway of Rous Lench has been compared to Christ in the tympanum of the prior's door at Ely cathedral.[244] The existence of the large figure of Christ above the entrance to the west porch at Monkwearmouth indicates that the location of the Rous Lench Christ follows a well established pre-Conquest precedent. The stylistic association with the Ely Christ is most likely to have come about through reference to similar Anglo-Saxon models rather by a direct borrowing.

The chancel arch at St James, Selham (Sussex) has been attributed to period C3 (1050–1100) but also dated as late as 1130–40, possibly reusing Saxon pieces.[245] Kathryn Morrison suggests the last quarter of the eleventh century.[246] The account in the *Victoria County History* dated the chancel and nave to the eleventh century and sees Byzantine influence in the capitals, 'that of Jerusalem rather than Constantinople'.[247] Dominic Tweddle assigns the chancel arch to the twelfth century yet he compares the interlace on the abacus of the north capital of the chancel arch with a fragment from Selsey (Sussex) for which he proposes a date of tenth to eleventh century.[248] The palmette on the abacus of the south capital fits typologically between the belfry capitals of the axial tower at Langford and the Chichester reliefs. The superimposed abaci and imposts of the chancel arch have more to do with the pre-Conquest layering of mouldings as on the imposts of the tower arch at Barnack. The north capital of the chancel arch is a debased Composite type with large volutes for which it is difficult to find Norman precedent. The angle roll moulding of the chancel arch is accompanied by two thinner rolls on the face of the arch; there is no hollow moulding. The narrow proportion and the relatively large size of the jamb stones and voussoirs of the north doorway have more in common with Anglo-Saxon building practice

---

[243] R.A. Stalley, 'A twelfth-century patron of architecture: a study of the buildings erected by Roger, bishop of Salisbury, 1102–1139', *Journal of the British Archaeological Association* xxxiv (1971), 62–83; M. Thurlby, 'Sarum cathedral as rebuilt by Roger, bishop of Salisbury, 1102–1139: the state of research and open questions', 130–40.

[244] Pevsner, *B/E Worcestershire*, 255. Pevsner dates the Rous Lench Christ *c*.1140–50, while *VCH Worcestershire*, iii (1913), 499 gives about 1130 for the south doorway.

[245] Taylor and Taylor, *Anglo-Saxon architecture*, 536–9, suggest period C3 (1050–1100); I. Nairn and N. Pevsner, *B/E Sussex*, Harmondsworth 1965, 358–9.

[246] K.A. Morrison, 'St James, Selham, Sussex', http://www.crsbi.ac.uk/search/location/selham/site/ed-sx-selha.html.

[247] *VCH Sussex*, iv. 81.

[248] Tweddle, *CASSS, IV, South-East England*, 94, 172.

than with a Norman tradition. Be that as it may, there are no through stones in either the chancel arch or the north doorway, and there are no long-and-short or side alternate quoins in the building. Much of the rubble masonry of the two-cell church is set in herringbone fashion which enjoyed great popularity in the late eleventh century but is not a sure guide to dating; herringbone is used in Roman villas at Barnsley and Chedworth (Gloucestershire), and in the ninth-century nave of St Mary's, Deerhurst (Gloucestershire).[249]

In 1086 the manor of Selham was held by Robert of Earl Roger. The value of the manor was £4 pounds in 1066, afterwards 30 shillings; now 64 shillings.[250] The fall in value of the manor after the Conquest makes church building unlikely but, if the financial improvement recorded in the Domesday survey continued, then construction of the church in the late eleventh or early twelfth century seems plausible.

The Stepney Rood is carved from Barnack stone and was located over the south door of the church by 1795.[251] It has been dated as early as the early eleventh century and as late as the late twelfth century. Sir Alfred Clapham grouped the Stepney rood with the Virgin and Child in the crypt of York minster and the Chichester reliefs as examples of early-eleventh-century sculpture, and noted the similarity between the foliage on the frame at Stepney and the Chichester relief.[252] Lawrence Stone observed that Christ's loincloth and the draperies of the Virgin and St John 'are obviously in the Winchester manner, and the feet of Saint John overstepping the frame is a typical trick of the Winchester school'.[253] On the other hand, the 'Maltese cross shape, the heavy acanthus border, and the angels in their medallions above the cross arms are all symptoms of imported work'. He considers that it was modelled on an ivory.[254] Dominic Tweddle assigned an eleventh-century date and related the varied moulded ends of the arms of the cross to the *c.*1000 Arenberg Gospels, although he recognised the parallel of the foliage borders with Chichester suggested by Clapham.[255] The comparison with Chichester is very much to the point in that the Stepney acanthus lacks the spikiness of the leaves on the Langford belfry openings, which

---

[249] J.H. Williams, 'Roman building materials', *TBGAS* xc (1971), 95–119.

[250] *Domesday Book, Sussex*, fo. 23c, 11.14.

[251] W.C. Pepys and E. Godman, *The church of St Dunstan, Stepney*, London 1905, 14 and 36, remark that it is generally assigned to the twelfth century – 'probably the latter portion'; B.F. Clarke, *Parish churches of London*, London 1966, 154 gives early eleventh century; cited in *VCH Middlesex*, xi (1998), 80.

[252] Clapham, *English Romanesque architecture before the Conquest*, 130 n. 2; 138–9, pl. 62.

[253] Stone, *Sculpture in Britain: the middle ages*, 240 n. 29.

[254] Stone cites O.M. Dalton, 'A relief representing the crucifixion in the parish church of St Dunstan's, Stepney', *Proceedings of the Society of Antiquaries of London* xxii (1907–8), 225–31.

[255] Tweddle, *CASSS, IV, South-East England*, 79, 229–30

suggests that the Stepney rood should be dated with the Chichester reliefs in the early twelfth century.

Richard Bryant has suggested that the panel carved with Christ in Majesty and the Harrowing of Hell above the Romanesque south doorway at All Hallows, South Cerney (Gloucestershire), as well as the beast-head label stops of the south doorway itself, are reused Anglo-Saxon work.[256] While the label stops derive from the pre-Conquest examples at Deerhurst, it has been shown that the type continues well into the twelfth century. Most importantly, contrary to Bryant's reading, the South Ceney label stops are closely related to the heads in the second order of the arch of the doorway, especially in the treatment of the eyes, ears and flared lips. Such a relationship surely indicates that the labels stops are contemporary with the doorway. And, seeing that there are beakheads in the arch, a date before the 1120s, when beakheads were introduced at Reading abbey and Sarum cathedral, is most unlikely. Bryant relates the Harrowing of Hell to the same subject on a slab at St Augustine's, Bristol, probably from the first half of the eleventh century. A closer comparison is found on the tympanum of the north doorway at Quenington (Gloucestershire), just nine miles from South Cerney, in which the scene is set beneath an arch just as at South Cerney, albeit as a mirror image. Bryant discusses the Quenington tympanum and dates it to the twelfth century on the basis of its setting in the richly carved Romanesque doorway.[257] It seems to me that the South Cerney panel is also twelfth century. Be that as it may, the fluttering edges to Christ's draperies at Quenington look more 'Anglo-Saxon' than at South Cerney, while the interlace adjacent to the capitals of the Quenington doorway, and carved on the very same stones, speaks clearly of a pre-Conquest tradition.

Late Twelfth and Thirteenth Century

References to Anglo-Saxon exemplars continued into the second half of the twelfth century and the early thirteenth century. At Kirkstall abbey, commenced in 1152, the Anglo-Saxon nature of the interlace on certain capitals, bases, a corbel, a piscina, has long been recognised.[258] The interlaced pattern of the tracery from the east rose window may be compared with the south belfry window of the west tower at Barnack.[259] In addition, the hood moulds of the nave west

---

[256] Bryant, *CASSS, X, The Western Midlands*, 247–9.
[257] Ibid. 271.
[258] J.T. Irvine, 'Notes on specimens of interlacing ornament at Kirkstall Abbey', *JBAA* xlviii (1892), 26–30; M. Thurlby, 'Some design aspects of Kirkstall Abbey', in L.R. Hoey (ed.), *Yorkshire monasticism: archaeology, art and architecture: BAACT* xvi (1995), 62–72, at 66.
[259] S. Harrison, 'Kirkstall abbey: the 12th-century window tracery and rose window', in Hoey (ed.), *Yorkshire monasticism*, 73–8. For Barnack, see Taylor and Taylor, *Anglo-Saxon*

windows terminate in heads of muzzled bears, like pre-Conquest hogback tombs as at Brompton-in-Allerton (Yorkshire).²⁶⁰ The design of the cluster piers of the nave arcades in which the foils are separated by angle fillets and rounded strips is most closely paralleled in the chancel arch responds, the responds of the arch to the north transept and the nave arcade piers at Great Paxton. In each case there is a delight in subtle variations in the use of all rounded strips or, at Kirkstall, an alternation of the two.²⁶¹

The iconography of the early gospel cycle on the north doorway of the Lady Chapel at Glastonbury abbey (1184–86/89) depends strongly on Anglo-Saxon iconographic sources and proclaims the proud pre-Conquest history of the site.²⁶² At Wells cathedral we witness precise Anglo-Saxon references in the retrospective effigies of bishops, and in the stiff-leaf capitals.²⁶³ For various aspects of the west front, such as quatrefoils and trefoil niches, Paul Binski cited Anglo-Saxon associations which extend to the Chorus of Virgins in the Benedictional of St Ethelwold (BL MS Add. 49598), and both may be associated with the sculpture recorded on the tenth-century tower of Winchester New Minster.²⁶⁴ To these parallels may be added the canopy over the Coronation of the Virgin with the sharply pointed gable integrated into the trefoil arch, which may be compared with the enclosing arches in the evangelist portraits in the mid-eleventh-century gospels in Monte Cassino (Archivio della Badia, MSS BB. 437, 439), in which there are also proto stiff-leaf capitals.²⁶⁵ Such pre-Conquest references at Wells recall its place as the historical seat of the see before it had been usurped by Bath.

---

architecture, fig. 22.

²⁶⁰ W.H. St John Hope and J. Bilson, 'Architectural description of Kirkstall abbey', *Publications of the Thoresby Society* xvi (1907), 1–140, at 22.

²⁶¹ Ibid. 124–5; Fernie, *The architecture of the Anglo-Saxons*, 129–34; Thurlby, 'Some design aspects of Kirkstall abbey'.

²⁶² M. Thurlby, 'The lady chapel of Glastonbury abbey', *Antiq. J.* lxv (1995), 107–70, at 138–40.

²⁶³ M.M. Reeve, 'The retrospective effigies of Anglo-Saxon bishops at Wells cathedral', *Somerset Archaeology and Natural History* cxlii (1998), 235–59; S. Gardner, *English Gothic foliage sculpture*, Cambridge 1927, 4, 22–6; P. Wynn-Reeves, 'English stiff-leaf sculpture', unpubl. Ph.D. diss., London 1952.

²⁶⁴ P. Binski, *Becket's crown: art and imagination in Gothic England, 1170–1300*, New Haven and London 2004, 109, 117–18; Quirk, 'Winchester New Minster and its 10th-century tower', 16–54.

²⁶⁵ Temple, *Anglo-Saxon manuscripts, 900–1066*, cat. 95, ills 287 and 288.

Conclusion

There is no clear-cut interpretation of Anglo-Saxon continuity or revival after the Conquest. In certain cases, it is difficult to decide whether a particular motif, such as the soffit roll, depended on Anglo-Saxon or Norman models. At least for the most ambitious patrons there seems to be a desire to have the best of both worlds. The vast scale of many Anglo-Norman great churches surpasses both Anglo-Saxon and Norman predecessors and, indeed, post-1066 churches in Normandy. The greater sense of monumentality in post-Conquest churches as a whole is a reflection of the Norman taste but in many cases this was accompanied by judicious borrowing from an Anglo-Saxon decorative vocabulary. The veneration of Anglo-Saxon saints at Ely, Worcester, Durham and Hereford is reflected in the inclusion of Anglo-Saxon motifs in the articulation of the fabric. Anglo-Saxon liturgy continued in Winchester, Ely and Worcester but at Durham Lanfranc's constitutions were adopted. Yet in architectural details Durham is the most consciously 'Anglo-Saxon' in its detailing. The Anglo-Saxon tradition in architectural sculpture and articulation of minor churches after the Conquest is exploited in a number of ways. At Bibury and Langford the continuity of Anglo-Saxon forms is witnessed virtually without change. At Milborne Port Anglo-Saxon aspects are juxtaposed with new elements, not least Norman masonry technique. The south doorway at Knook provides something similar. While these examples were produced for English patrons, works produced for Norman patrons frequently made use of pre-Conquest sources, not least in tympanum sculpture for which there was little in the way of an established tradition in Normandy, save geometric chip-carving. Moreover, given the influence of pre-Conquest exemplars on Norman manuscript illumination and sculpture before the Conquest, Norman patrons in England in the late eleventh and twelfth centuries had long been familiar with Anglo-Saxon aesthetics.[266]

---

[266] On Anglo-Saxon aspects of Norman illumination, see J.J.G. Alexander, *Norman illumination at Mont St.-Michel, 966–1100*, Oxford 1970; C.M. Kauffmann, *Romanesque manuscripts, 1066–1190*, 18–20; J.J.G. Alexander in Zarnecki and others, *English Romanesque art, 1066–1200*, 83–4.

Bibliography

Primary Sources

Abbo of Fleury, *Passio sancti Eadmundi*, in *Three Lives of English saints*, ed. M. Winterbottom, Toronto 1972
Acta of William I see *Regesta regum Anglo-Normannorum: the acta of William I*
Acta Sanctorum..., ed. J. Bollandus and others (Antwerp, Brussels and Paris 1643– , with partial reprint Paris 1863–70)
Ademarus Cabannensis, *Chronicon*, ed. P. Bourgain-Hemeryck, R. Landes and G. Pon (Corpus Christianorum, continuatio medievalis cxxix, 1999)
Ælfric's letter to the monks of Eynsham, ed. C.A. Jones, Cambridge 1998
Ælfric's Lives of saints: being a set of sermons on saints' days formerly observed by the English Church, ed. W.W. Skeat (Early English Text Society original ser. lxxvi, cxiv, 1881–1900)
Ailred of Rievaulx, *De sanctis ecclesiae Haugustaldensis*, in *The priory of Hexham*, ed. J. Raine (SS xliv, xlvi, 1864–65), i. 172–203
Alcuini sive Albini epistolae, in*, Epistolae Karolini aevi* ii, ed. E. Dümmler (MGH Epistolae iv, 1895), 1–493
Der Alexanderroman des Archipresbyters Leo, ed. F. Pfister, Heidelberg 1913
King Alfred's West-Saxon version of Gregory's Pastoral care, ed. H. Sweet (Early English Text Society, original ser. xlv and l, 1871–72)
Der Anglonormannische Boeve de Haumtone, ed. A. Stimming, Halle 1899
The Anglo-Saxon Chronicle, a collaborative edition, 3: *MS. A*, ed. J.M. Bately, Cambridge 1986
The Anglo-Saxon Chronicle, a collaborative edition, 6: *MS. D*, ed. G.P. Cubbin, Cambridge 1996
The Anglo-Saxon Chronicle, a collaborative edition, 7: *MS. F*, ed. S. Irvine, Cambridge 2004, and see *The Peterborough chronicle, 1070–1154*, ed. C. Clark, 2 edn, Oxford 1970
The Anglo-Saxon Chronicle, a collaborative edition, 1: *facsimile of MS. F, the Domitian bilingual*, ed. D.N. Dumville, Cambridge 1995 and see *Two of the Saxon chronicles parallel*
The Anglo-Saxon poetic records: a collective edition, ed. G.P. Krapp and E. van Kirk Dobbie, London 1931–42
Annales Bertiniani, ed. G. Waitz (MGH Scriptores rerum Germanicarum v, 1883), tr. as *The Annals of St-Bertin*, tr. J.L. Nelson, Manchester 1991

Annales Fuldenses, sive annales regni Francorum orientalis, ed. F. Kurze (MGH Scriptores rerum Germanicarum vii, 1891), tr. as *The Annals of Fulda*, tr. T. Reuter, Manchester 1992

Annales Lindisfarnenses et Dunelmenses, see Levison, W., 'Die "Annales Lindisfarnenses et Dunelmenses" kritisch untersucht' below

Annales monastici, ed. H.R. Luard (RS [xxxvi], 1864–69)

Annales Vedastini, ed. G.H. Pertz (MGH Scriptores ii, 1829)

Annales monasterii de Waverleia, in *Ann. mon.* ii. 129–414

Annales de Wintonia, in *Ann. mon.* ii. 1–125

S. Anselmi Cantuariensis archiepiscopi opera omnia, ed. F.S. Schmitt, London 1946–61

Asser's Life of King Alfred, ed. W.H. Stevenson, rev. edn Oxford 1959

Sancti Augustini sermones post Maurinos reperti, ed. G. Morin as *Miscellanea Agostiniana. Testi e studi publicati a cura dell'Ordine Eremitano di S. Agostino nel XV centenario dalla morte del santo dottore*, i, Rome 1930–31

Bede's ecclesiastical history of the English people, ed. and tr. B. Colgrave and R.A.B. Mynors, Oxford 1969; rev. edn 1991 and see *Venerabilis Baedae Historiam ecclesiasticam gentis Anglorum* below

Benedicti regula, editio altera emendata, ed. R. Hanslik (Corpus scriptorum ecclesiasticorum latinorum lxxv, 1977) and see *Rule of St Benedict* below

Boeve de Haumtone, see *Der Anglonormannische Boeve de Haumtone*

The Book of Fees commonly called Testa de Nevill, ed. H.C. Maxwell-Lyte and others, London 1920–31

Bovonis abbatis relatio de inventione et elevatione S. Bertini, ed. O. Holder-Egger (MGH Scriptores xv.1, 1887), 524–34

Breviarium Aberdonense, Edinburgh, 1510; facsimile reprint ed. W.J. Blew (Bannatyne Club xcix–c, 1854)

Byrhtferth of Ramsey, The Lives of St Oswald and St Ecgwine, ed. and tr. M. Lapidge, Oxford 2009

Calendar of the charter rolls preserved in the Public Record Office, London 1903–27 and see *Rotuli chartarum* below

Calendar of the patent rolls preserved in the Public Record Office, London 1891–

The Cartae antiquae rolls, ed. L. Landon and J.C. Davies (Pipe Roll Society xvii, xxxiii, 1939–57)

Cartularium abbathiae de Whiteby, ed. J.C. Atkinson (SS lxix, 1879)

Cartularium Saxonicum, ed. W. de G. Birch, London, 1885–93

The cartulary of Worcester cathedral priory ed. R.R. Darlington (Pipe Roll Society new ser. xxxviii, 1968)

Cassiodorus, *Institutiones*, ed. R.A.B. Mynors, Oxford 1961, tr. as *An introduction to divine and human readings by Cassiodorus Senator*, tr. L.W. Jones, New York 1966

Charters of Abingdon abbey, ed. S.E. Kelly, Oxford 2000–1

Charters of Burton abbey, ed. P.H. Sawyer, Oxford 1979
Charters of Malmesbury abbey, ed. S.E. Kelly, Oxford 2005
Charters of Peterborough abbey, ed. S.E. Kelly, Oxford 2009
Charters of St Albans, ed. J.C. Crick, Oxford 2007
Charters of St Augustine's abbey, Canterbury, and Minster-in-Thanet, ed. S.E. Kelly, Oxford 1995
Charters of the New Minster, Winchester, ed. S. Miller, Oxford 2001
Chronica magistri Rogeri de Houedene, ed. W. Stubbs (RS [li], 1868–71)
The chronicle of Hugh Candidus, a monk of Peterborough, ed. W.T. Mellows, London 1949
The chronicle of Jocelin of Brakelond, ed. and tr. H.E. Butler, London 1949
The chronicle of John of Worcester: ii, the annals from 450 to 1066, ed. R.R. Darlington and P. McGurk, tr. J. Bray and P. McGurk, Oxford 1995; iii, *the annals from 1067 to 1140*, ed. and tr. P. McGurk, Oxford 1998
The chronicle of Melrose Abbey: a stratigraphic edition: volume i: introduction and facsimile edition, ed. D. Broun and J. Harrison (Scottish History Society, 6 ser. i), Woodbridge 2007
The chronicle of Richard of Devizes, in *Chronicles of the reigns of Stephen, Henry II and Richard I*, ed. R. Howlett (RS [lxxxii], 1886), iii. 379–454
The chronicle of Richard of Devizes, ed. J.T. Appleby, London 1963
The chronicle of Robert of Torigni abbot of St. Michael-in-Peril-of-the-Sea, ed. R. Howlett (RS [lxxxii], 1886, iv. 61–315
The chronicle of Walter of Guisborough: previously edited as the chronicle of Walter of Hemingford or Hemingburgh, ed. H. Rothwell (Camden 3 ser. lxxxix, 1957)
Chronicon abbatiae Ramesiensis, ed. W.D. Macray (RS [lxxxiii], 1886)
Chronicon Æthelweardi, ed. and tr. A. Campbell, London and Edinburgh 1962
Chronique de Robert de Torigni, ed. L. Delisle, Rouen 1872–3
and see above, *Chronicle of Robert*
Close rolls of the reign of Henry III preserved in the Public Record Office, London 1902–38
Codex diplomaticus aevi Saxonici, ed. J.M. Kemble, London, 1839–48
Councils and synods, with other documents relating to the English Church, I: *871–1204*, ed. D. Whitelock, M. Brett and C.N.L. Brooke, Oxford 1981
The Crawford collection of early charters and documents now in the Bodleian Library, ed. A.S. Napier and W.H. Stevenson, Oxford 1895
Curia regis rolls ... preserved in the Public Record Office, London 1922– , and see *Rotuli curiae regis*
Das Decretum Gelasianum de libris recipiendis et non recipiendis, ed. E. von Dobschütz (Texte und Untersuchungen zur Geschichte der altchristlichen Literatur xxxviii/4, 1912)

De iniusta uexacione Willelmi episcopi primi per Willelmum regem filium Willelm magni, ed. H.S. Offler in *Camden miscellany xxxiv* (Camden 5 ser. x, 1997), 49–104

De moribus et actis primorum Normanniae ducum auctore Dudone sancti Quintini decano, ed. J. Lair, Caen 1865

Diplomata Karolinorum: recueil de reproductions en fac-similé des actes originaux des souverains carolingiens conservés dans les archives et bibliothèques de France, ed. F. Lot and P. Lauer with G. Tessier, Paris, 1936–52

Domesday Book, gen. ed. J. Morris (History from the sources, Chichester 1975–92)

The 'Draco Normannicus' of Étienne de Rouen in *Chronicles of the reigns of Stephen, Henry II and Richard I*, ed. R. Howlett (RS [lxxxii], 1884–89), ii. 589–782

Dudo of St Quentin, History of the Normans, tr. E. Christiansen, Woodbridge 1998 and see *De moribus et actis primorum Normanniae ducum*

Eadmer, *De reliquiis sancti Audoeni et quorundam aliorum sanctorum quae Cantuariae in aecclesia domini salvatoris habentur*, ed. A. Wilmart, in 'Eadmeri Cantuariensis cantoris nova opuscula de sanctorum veneratione et obsecratione', *Revue des sciences religieuses* xv (1935), 362–70

Eadmeri Historia novorum in Anglia, et opuscula duo de vita Sancti Anselmi et quibusdam miraculis ejus, ed. M. Rule (RS [lxxxi], 1884)

Eadmer, *Vita Bregwini*, ed. B.W. Scholz, 'Eadmer's Life of Bregwine, archbishop of Canterbury, 761–4', *Traditio* xxii (1966), 127–48

The early charters of the Augustinian canons of Waltham abbey, Essex, 1062–1230, ed. R. Ransford, Woodbridge 1989

The ecclesiastical history of Orderic Vitalis, ed. and tr. M. Chibnall, Oxford 1969–80

English episcopal acta:
    vii: *Hereford 1079–1234*, ed. J. Barrow, Oxford 1993
    viii: *Winchester 1070–1204*, ed. M.J. Franklin, Oxford 1993
    xxviii: *Canterbury, 1070–1136*, ed. M. Brett and J. Gribbin, Oxford 2004

English lawsuits from William I to Richard I, ed. R.C. van Caenegem (Selden Society cvi–vii, 1990–91)

Eynsham Cartulary, ed. H.E. Salter (Oxford Historical Society xlix, li, 1907–8)

Facsimiles of Anglo-Saxon charters, ed. S. Keynes, Oxford 1991

Facsimiles of Anglo-Saxon Manuscripts. photozincographed by command of Her Majesty Queen Victoria, tr. W. Basevi Sanders, Southampton 1878–84

Facsimiles of English royal writs to A.D. 1100 presented to Vivian Hunter Galbraith, ed. T. A.M. Bishop and P. Chaplais, Oxford 1957

Faricius, *Vita sancti Aldhelmi*, ed. M. Winterbottom, 'An edition of Faricius, *Vita S. Aldhelmi*', *Journal of Medieval Latin* xv (2005), 93–147

Felix's Life of St Guthlac, ed. and tr. B. Colgrave, Cambridge 1956

Feudal documents from the abbey of Bury St Edmunds, ed. D.C. Douglas (British Academy records of the social and economic history of England and Wales viii, 1932)

Florentii Wigorniensis monachi Chronicon ex chronicis, ed. B. Thorpe (English Historical Society, 1848–9)

Folcard, *Vita tertia Bertini*, in *ASS* Septembris ii. 604–13

Folcard, *Life of John of Beverley*, in *The historians of the church of York and its archbishops*, ed. J. Raine (RS [lxxi], 1879–94), i. 239–60

Geffrei Gaimar, *Estoire des Engleis (History of the English)*, ed. and tr. I. Short, Oxford 2009

Geoffrey of Burton, *Life and Miracles of St Modwenna*, ed. R. Bartlett, Oxford 2002

Geoffrey of Monmouth, *The history of the kings of Britain*, ed. M.D. Reeve, tr. N. Wright, Woodbridge 2007

Geoffrey of Wells, *De infantia sancti Edmundi*, in *Memorials of St Edmund's Abbey* (RS [xcvi], 1890), i. 93–103

Gervase of Tilbury, *Otia imperialia*, ed. and tr. S.E. Banks and J.W. Binns, Oxford 2002

Die Gesetze der Angelsachsen, ed. F. Liebermann, Halle 1903–16

Gesta abbatum monasterii sancti Albani, ed. H.T. Riley (RS [xxviii], 1867–69)

The Gesta Normannorum ducum of William of Jumièges, Orderic Vitalis and Robert of Torigni, ed. and tr. E.M.C. van Houts, Oxford 1992–95

Giraldi Cambrensis opera, ed. J.S. Brewer and others (RS [xxi] 1861–91)

Goscelin of Saint-Bertin, *Miracula sancte Ætheldrethe virginis*, in *The hagiography of the female saints of Ely*, ed. R.C. Love, Oxford 2004, 95–130

Vita beate Sexburge regine, ibid. 133–88

The great rolls of the pipe for the second, third and fourth years of the reign of King Henry the second, ed. J. Hunter, London 1844

Gui de Warewic: roman du XIIIe siècle, ed. A. Ewert (Classiques français du Moyen Âge lxxiv–5, 1932–33)

Die Heiligen Englands: Angelsächsisch und lateinisch, ed. F. Liebermann, Hanover 1889, and see Rollason, D.W., 'Lists of saints' resting-places' below

Henry, archdeacon of Huntingdon, *The history of the English people*, ed. and tr. D. Greenway, Oxford 1996

Hereford Breviary, ed. W.H. Frere and L.E.G. Brown (HBS xxvi, xl, xlvi, 1904–15)

Herefordshire Domesday, ed. V.H. Galbraith and J. Tait (Pipe Roll Society new ser. xxv, 1950)

Hermann the archdeacon, *Liber de miraculis sancti Edmundi*, in *Memorials of St Edmund's abbey*, ed. T. Arnold (RS [xcvi], 1890–96), i. 26–92

S. Hieronymi presbyteri opera, pars I, Opera exegetica vii: Commentariorum in Matheum libri IV, ed. D. Hurst and M. Adriaen (CCSL lxxvii, 1969)

Historia de sancto Cuthberto: a history of Saint Cuthbert and a record of his patrimony, ed. and tr. T. Johnson South, Woodbridge 2002
Historia ecclesie Abbendonensis: the history of the church of Abingdon, ed. and tr. J. Hudson, Oxford 2002–27
Historia post Bedam
See above, *Chronica magistri Rogeri de Houedene*, i. 3–210
Historia regum
See Symeon of Durham, below
The historical works of Gervase of Canterbury, ed. W. Stubbs (RS [lxxiii], 1879–80)
The historical works of Master Ralph de Diceto, ed. W. Stubbs (RS [lxviii], 1876)
Q. Horati Flacci opera, ed. E.C. Wickham, rev. H.W. Garrod, Oxford 1901
Inventio et miracula sancti Vulfranni, ed. Dom J. Laporte (Société de l'histoire de Normandie, Mélanges 14e sér., 1938)
The itinerary of John Leland in or about the years 1535–1543, ed. L. Toulmin Smith, Oxford 1906–10
Jean Bodel, *Le Jeu de Saint Nicolas*, ed. F.J. Warne, Oxford 1968
John of Tynemouth, *Sanctilogium*, see *Nova legenda Anglie*
John of Worcester, see *The chronicle of John of Worcester* and *Florentii Wigorniensis monachi Chronicon* above
Jordan Fantosme, *Chronicle*, ed. R.C. Johnston, Oxford 1981
Jocelin of Brakelond, see *The chronicle of Jocelin of Brakelond*
Landboc sive registrum monasterii beatae Mariae Virginis et Sancti Cenhelmi de Winchelcumba, ed. D. Royce, Exeter 1892–1903
Legum regis Canuti magni, ed. J.L.A. Kolderup-Rosenvinge, Copenhagen 1826
The letters and charters of Cardinal Guala Bicchieri, papal legate in England 1216–1218, ed. N. Vincent (Canterbury and York Society lxxxiii, 1996)
The letters and charters of Henry II, 1154–1189, ed. N. Vincent, Oxford forthcoming
Liber Eliensis, ed. E.O. Blake (Camden 3 ser. xcii, 1962), and Fairweather, J. (tr.), *Liber Eliensis: a history of the Isle of Ely from the seventh century to the twelfth*, Woodbridge 2005
Liber memorandorum ecclesie de Bernewelle, ed. J.W. Clark, Cambridge 1907
Liber monasterii de Hyda, ed. E. Edwards (RS [xlv], 1866)
Liber ordinis sancti Victoris Parisiensis, ed. L. Jocqué and L. Milis (Corpus christianorum continuatio medievalis lxi, 1984)
Liber tramitis aevi Odilonis abbatis, ed. P. Dinter (Corpus consuetudinum monasticarum x, 1980)
Liber vitae: register and martyrology of New Minster and Hyde Abbey, Winchester, ed. W. de Gray Birch (Hampshire Record Society, 1892)
The Life of King Edward who rests at Westminster, ed. F. Barlow, 2 edn, Oxford 1992
Lives of Saints Omer, Bertin and Winnoc see *Passiones vitaeque sanctorum*

The Lives of the two Offas, ed. M. Swanton, Crediton 2010

Le Livre des reliques de l'abbaye de Saint-Pierre-le-Vif de Sens, ed. G. Julliot and M. Prou, Sens 1887

Materials for the history of Thomas Becket archbishop of Canterbury, ed. J.C. Robertson and J.B. Sheppard (RS [lxvii], 1875–85)

Matthew Paris, *Chronica majora*, ed. H.R. Luard (RS [lvii], 1872–83)

Memorials of Bury St Edmunds, ed. T. Arnold (RS [xcvi], 1890–96), and see *Feudal documents*

Les Miracles de Saint Benoît écrits par Adrevald, Aimoin, André, Raoul Tortaire et Hugues de Sainte Marie, moines de Fleury, ed. E. de Certain, Paris 1858

The Miracles of St Æbbe of Coldingham and St Margaret of Scotland, ed. R. Bartlett, Oxford 2003

The missal of Robert of Jumièges, ed. H.A. Wilson (HBS xi, 1896)

The monastic constitutions of Lanfranc, ed. and tr. D. Knowles, rev. C.N.L. Brooke, Oxford 2002

Nova legenda Anglie, ed. C. Horstman, Oxford 1901

The Old English illustrated Hexateuch: British Museum Cotton Claudius B. IV, ed. C.R. Dodwell and P. Clemoes (Early English manuscripts in facsimile xviii, 1974)

Orderic Vitalis, see *The ecclesiastical history of Orderic Vitalis* and *Gesta Normannorum ducum*

Papsturkunden 896–1046, ed. H. Zimmermann (Denkschriften der Österreichischen Akademie der Wissenschaften, Phil-hist. Klasse clxxiv, clxxvii, cxcviii, 1984–89)

Papsturkunden in England, ed. W. Holtzmann, Abhandlungen der Gesellschaft der Wissenschaften zu Göttingen, Philologisch-historische Klasse, neue Folge 25 (1930–31), 3. Folge 14–15 (1935–6) and 33 (1952)

Passiones vitaeque sanctorum aevi Merovingici iii, ed. W. Levison (MGH Scriptores rerum Merovingicarum v, 1910), 729–75

Peterborough chronicle, see above, Anglo-Saxon Chronicle MS E

Placita de Quo warranto temporibus Edw. I, II, et III in curia receptae scaccarii Westm. asservata, ed. W. Illingworth, London 1818

Placitorum in domo capitulari Westmonasteriensi asservatorum abbreviatio, ed. W. Illingworth, London 1811

Ralph de Diceto, see *The historical works of Master Ralph*

Ralph Niger, see *The chronicles*

Recueil des actes de Charles II le Chauve, roi de France, ed. G. Tessier, Paris 1943–55

Recueil des actes de Charles III le Simple, roi de France (893–923), ed. P. Lauer, Paris 1940

Recueil des actes de Louis II le Bègue, Louis III et Carloman II, rois de France (877–884), ed. F. Grat, J. de Font-Réaulx, G. Tessier, R.-H. Bautier, Paris 1978

Recueil des actes de Pépin Ier et de Pépin II, rois d'Aquitaine, ed. L. Levillain, Paris 1927

Recueil des rouleaux des morts: (VIIIe siècle-vers 1536), ed. J. Dufour, Paris 2005–

The Red Book of the Exchequer, ed. H. Hall (RS [xcix], 1896)

Regesta regum Anglo-Normannorum, ii, 1100–1135, ed. C. Johnson and H.A. Cronne, Oxford 1956

Regesta regum Anglo-Normannorum, iii, 1135–1154, ed. R.H.C. Davis and H.A. Cronne, Oxford 1968

Regesta regum Anglo-Normannorum: the acta of William I (1066–1087), ed. D. Bates, Oxford 1998

Reginald of Durham, *Libellus de admirandis beati Cuthberti virtutibus*, ed. J. Raine (SS i, 1835)

The register of the priory of St Bees, ed. J. Wilson (SS cxxvi, 1915)

Registrum Simonis de Gandavo, diocesis Saresbiriensis, A.D. 1297–1315, ed. C.T. Flower and M.C.B. Dawes (Canterbury and York Society xl–xli, 1934)

Richard fitz Nigel, *Dialogus de scaccario*, ed. and tr. E. Amt, Oxford 2007 and *Dialogus de scaccario*, ed. and tr. C. Johnson, F.E.L. Carter and D.E. Greenway, Oxford 1983

Robert of Torigni, see *Chronique de Robert de Torigni*, ed. L. Delisle, *The chronicle of Robert of Torigni* ed. R. Howlett and *Gesta Normannorum ducum* above

Rodulfus Glaber, *Historiarum libri quinque*, ed. J. France, Oxford 1989

Le Roman de Waldef, ed. A.J. Holden (Texte, Bibliotheca Bodmeriana, v, 1984)

Rotuli chartarum in Turri Londoniensi asservati, ed. T.D. Hardy, London 1837

Rotuli curiae regis, ed. F. Palgrave, London 1835

The Rule of St Benedict in English, ed. T. Fry, Collegeville, MN 1982, and see *Benedicti regula* above

The saint of London: the Life and miracles of St. Erkenwald, ed. E.G. Whatley, Binghamton 1989

The 1258-9 special eyre of Surrey and Kent, ed. A.H. Hershey (Surrey Record Society xxxviii, 2004)

The 1235 Surrey eyre, ed. C.A.F. Meekings and D. Crook (Surrey Record Society xxxi–xxxii, xxxvii, 1979–2002)

Symeon of Durham, *Libellus de exordio atque procursu istius, hoc est Dunhelmensis ecclesie. Tract on the origins and progress of this the Church of Durham*, ed. and tr. D.W. Rollason, Oxford 2000

Symeon of Durham (attr.), *Historia regum* in *Symeonis monachi opera omnia*, ed. T. Arnold (RS [lxxv], 1885), ii, 3–283

Textus Roffensis: Rochester cathedral library manuscript A. 3. 5, ed. P.H. Sawyer (Early English manuscripts in facsimile vii, xi, 1957–62)

Thomas, *The Romance of Horn*, ed. M.K. Pope (Anglo-Norman Texts ix–x, xii–xiii, 1955–64)

Thomas of Marlborough, *History of the abbey of Evesham*, ed. and tr. J. Sayers and L. Watkiss, Oxford 2003

Thomas Rudborne, *Historia major ecclesiae Wintoniensis* in *Anglia sacra*, ed. H. Wharton, London 1691

Thomae Sprotti chronica, ed. T. Hearne, Oxford 1719

Three eleventh-century Anglo-Latin saints' lives: Vita S. Birini, Vita et miracula S. Kenelmi *and* Vita S. Rumwoldi, ed. R.C. Love, Oxford 1996

Treatise on the laws and customs of the realm of England commonly called Glanvill, ed. G.D.G. Hall, with a guide to further reading by M.T. Clanchy, Oxford 1993

Two of the Saxon chronicles parallel, ed. C. Plummer and J. Earle, Oxford 1892–99

Venerabilis Baedae Historiam ecclesiasticam gentis Anglorum, Historiam abbatum, Epistolam ad Ecgberctum una cum Historia abbatum auctore anonymo, ed. C. Plummer, Oxford 1896 and see *Bede's ecclesiastical history* above

Venerabilis Guiberti abbatis b. Mariae de Novigento opera omnia, ed. L. d'Achery, Paris 1651

La Vie d'Edouard le Confesseur: poème anglo-normand du XIIe siècle, ed. Ö. Södergård, Uppsala 1948

La Vie seinte Osith, virge e martire, ed. D.W. Russell, *Papers on language and literature* xli (2005), 339–445, and see A.T. Baker, 'An Anglo-French Life' below

Vie de S. Rumon, see Grosjean, 'Vie de S. Rumon; Vie, Invention et Miracles de S. Nectan'

Vita sanctissimi Ceolfridi abbatis, in *Venerabilis Baedae opera historica*, ed. C. Plummer, Oxford 1896, i. 388–404

Vita Haroldi. The romance of the life of Harold, king of England, ed. and tr. W. de G. Birch, London 1885

Vita Oswini regis Deirorum in *Miscellanea biographica*, ed. J. Raine (SS viii, 1838), 1–59

Vitae Audomari, Bertini, Winnoci ed. W. Levison (MGH, Scriptores rerum Merovingicarum v, 1910), 753–75

Wace's Roman de Brut. A history of the British, ed. and tr. J. Weiss, rev. edn, Exeter 1999

Wace, *The Roman de Rou*, tr. G.S. Burgess, with the text of A.J. Holden, and notes by G.S. Burgess and E.M.C. van Houts, Societé Jersiaise 2002.
The history of the Norman people. Wace's Roman de Rou, Woodbridge 2004 offers a revised translation, reprinting the essay by van Houts from the 2002 edition but omitting the Holden text.

Walter Map, *De nugis curialium: courtiers' trifles*, ed. M.R. James, rev. C.N.L. Brooke and R.A.B. Mynors, Oxford 1983

The Waltham chronicle, ed. and tr. L. Watkiss and M. Chibnall, Oxford 1994

William of Malmesbury

Gesta pontificum Anglorum. i. *Text and translation*, ed. and tr. M. Winterbottom, with R.M. Thomson, Oxford 2007; ii. *Introduction and commentary*, R.M. Thomson, Oxford 2007

Gesta regum Anglorum, [i] ed. and tr. R.A.B. Mynors, R.M. Thomson and M. Winterbottom, Oxford 1998, ii, *General introduction and commentary*, R.M. Thomson, Oxford 1999

Vita Dunstani, in William of Malmesbury, *Saints' Lives*. Lives of SS. Wulfstan, Dunstan, Patrick, Benignus and Indract, ed. and tr. M. Winterbottom and R.M. Thomson, Oxford 2002, 157–303

The Vita Wulfstani of William of Malmesbury, ed. R.R. Darlington (Camden 3 ser. lx, 1928) and William of Malmesbury, *Saints' Lives*, ed. Winterbottom and Thomson, 1–155

Willelmi Meldunensis monachi liber super explanationem Lamentationum Ieremiae prophetae, ed. M. Winterbottom and R.M. Thomson (Corpus Christianorum, Continuatio Mediaevalis ccxliv, Turnhout 2011)

The Gesta Guillelmi of William of Poitiers, ed. and tr. R.H.C. Davis and M. Chibnall, Oxford 1998

William fitz Stephen, *Vita sancti Thomae*, see *Materials for the history of Thomas Becket*, ed. J.C. Robertson (RS [lxvii], 1875–85), iii. 1–154

William Rishanger, *Chronica et annales*, ed. H.T. Riley (RS [xxviii], 1865)

William Thorne, *De rebus gestis abbatum sancti Augustini Cantuariae*, in *Historiae Anglicanae scriptores X*, ed. R. Twysden, London 1652, 1755–2202

Wulfstan of Winchester, *The Life of St. Æthelwold*, ed. and tr. M. Lapidge and M. Winterbottom, Oxford 1991

Secondary Sources

Abou-el-Haj, B., 'Bury St. Edmunds abbey between 1070 and 1124: a history of property, privilege and monastic art production', *Art History* vi (1983), 1–30

Ailes, M., 'The Anglo-Norman *Boeve de Haumtone* as a *chanson de geste*', in J. Fellows and I. Djordjevic (eds), *Sir Bevis of Hampton in literary tradition*, Cambridge 2008, 9–24

Aird, W.M., 'The making of a medieval miracle collection: The *Liber de translationibus et miraculis sancti Cuthberti*', *Northern History* xxviii (1992), 1–24

—, *St Cuthbert and the Normans: the church of Durham, 1071–1153*, Woodbridge 1998

—, 'The political context of the *Libellus de exordio*', in D.W. Rollason (ed.), *Symeon of Durham*, 32–45

Alexander, J.J.G., *Norman illumination at Mont St. Michel 966–1100*, Oxford 1970

Alexander, J.J.G., and Temple, E., *Illuminated manuscripts in Oxford college libraries, the University archives and the Taylor Institution*, Oxford 1985
Andrieu, M., *Les Ordines Romani du haut Moyen Âge* (Spicilegium sacrum Lovaniense. Etudes et documents xi, xxii–xxiii, xxviii–xxix, 1931–61)
Appleby, J.T., 'Richard of Devizes and the annals of Winchester', *Bulletin of the Institute of Historical Research* xxxvi (1963), 70–77
Armitage, E.S., *The early Norman castles of the British Isles*, London 1912
Arnoux, M., 'Before the *Gesta Normannorum* and beyond *Dudo*: some evidence on early Norman historiography', *ANS* xxii (1999), 29–48
Ashe, L., *Fiction and history in England, 1066–1200*, Cambridge 2007
Ashe, L., Djordjevic, I., and Weiss, J. (eds), *The exploitations of medieval romance*, Cambridge 2010
Atkyns, R., *The ancient and present state of Gloucestershire*, London 1712
Atsma, H., and Vezin, J., 'Le dossier suspect des possessions de Saint-Denis en Angleterre revisité (VIII^c–IXe siècles)', *Fälschungen im Mittelalter*, iv. 211–36
—, 'Les faux sur papyrus de l'abbaye de Saint-Denis', in J. Kerhervé et A. Rigaudière (eds), *Finances, pouvoirs et mémoire. Hommages offerts à Jean Favier*, Paris 1999, 674–99
Aurell, M., *L'Empire des Plantagenêt 1154–1224*, [Paris] 2003
Aurell, M., 'Henry II and Arthurian legend', in C. Harper-Bill and N. Vincent (eds), *Henry II: new interpretations*, Woodbridge 2007, 362–94
Backaert, B., 'L'évolution du calendrier cistercien', *Collectanea ordinis cisterciensium reformatorum* xii (1950), 81–94, 302–316; xiii (1951), 108–27
Backhouse, J., Turner, D.H., and Webster, L. (eds), *The golden age of Anglo-Saxon art, 966–1066*, London 1984
Bains, D., *A supplement to Notae Latinae (abbreviations in Latin MSS. of 850 to 1050 A.D.)*, Hildesheim 1963
Baker, A.T., 'An Anglo-French Life of St Osith', *The Modern Language Review* vi (1911), 476–502
Baker, D., 'Scissors and paste: Corpus Christi, Cambridge, MS 139 again', *Studies in Church History* xi (1975), 83–123
Baldwin Brown, G., *The arts in early England, Anglo-Saxon architecture*, 2 edn, London 1925
—, *The arts in early England*, vi (2), *Anglo-Saxon sculpture*, London 1937
Barker, P., *A short architectural history of Worcester cathedral*, Worcester 1994
—, 'Reconstructing Wulfstan's cathedral', in J.S. Barrow and N.P. Brooks (eds), *St Wulfstan and his world*, Aldershot 2005, 167–88
Barlow, F., *Durham jurisdictional peculiars*, London 1950
—, *Edward the Confessor*, 2 edn, London 1979
Barnwell, P., Butler, L.A.S., and Dunn, C.J., 'Streanaeshalch, Strensall and Whitby: locating a pivotal council', in M.O.H. Carver (ed.), *The cross goes

north: processes of conversion in northern Europe, AD 300–1300, Woodbridge 2003, 311–26

Barrow, J., 'A twelfth-century bishop and literary patron: William de Vere', *Viator* xviii (1987), 175–89

—, 'Survival and mutation: ecclesiastical institutions in the Danelaw in the ninth and tenth centuries', in D.M. Hadley and J.D. Richards (eds), *Cultures in contact: Scandinavian settlement in England in the ninth and tenth centuries*, Turnhout 2000, 155–76

—, 'Vere, William de', *ODNB* at: http://www.oxforddnb.com/view/article/95042

Bartlett, R., 'Rewriting saints' lives: the case of Gerald of Wales', *Speculum* lviii (1983), 598–613

—, 'The hagiography of Angevin England', *Thirteenth-century England* v (1993), 37–52

Bates, D., *Bishop Remigius of Lincoln, 1067–1092*, Lincoln 1992

—, *The making of Europe: conquest, colonization and cultural change, 950–1350*, London 1993

—, 'Robert of Torigni and the "Historia Anglorum"' (forthcoming)

Baxter, R., and Harrison, S., 'The decoration of the cloister at Reading abbey', in L. Keen and E. Scarff (eds), *Windsor: medieval archaeology, art and architecture of the Thames valley*, British Archaeological Association Conference Transactions xv (2002), 302–12

Baylé, M., 'La sculpture du XIe siècle à Jumièges et sa place dans le décor architectural des abbayes normandes', in *Aspects du monachisme en Normandie (IV –VIII siècles), Actes du colloque scientifique de l'Année des abbayes Normandes 1979*, Paris 1982, 75–96

—, 'Interlace patterns in Norman Romanesque sculpture: regional groups and their historical backgrounds', *ANS* v (1983), 1–20

—, *Les Origines et les premiers développements de la sculpture romane en Normandie*, Caen 1992

—, 'Sainte-Marie-du-Mont: église Notre-Dame', in M. Baylé (ed.), *L'Architecture normande au Moyen Âge*, Caen 1997, ii. 105

Baylé, M., Bouet, P., Brighelli, J.-P., and others (eds), *Le Mont Saint-Michel. Histoire et imaginaire*, Paris 1998

Beckermann, J., 'Succession in Normandy 1087 and in England 1066: the role of testamentary custom', *Speculum* xlvii (1972), 258–60

Beech, G.T., 'Egbert's England', *History Today* lxiii, issue 2 (2013), 38–43

Beeson, C.H., 'The manuscripts of Bede', *Classical Philology* xlii (1947), 73–87

Bellairs, G.C., 'Hallaton church and the recent discoveries there', *Transactions of the Leicester Architectural and Archaeological Society* viii (1890), 218–22

Benson, R.L., and Constable, G. (eds), *Renaissance and renewal in the twelfth century*, Cambridge, MA 1982

Bethell, D., 'The Lives of St Osyth of Essex and St Osyth of Aylesbury', *AB* lxxxviii (1970), 75–127

Bhabha, H.K., 'The world and the home', *Social Text* xxxi–xxxii (1992), 141–53

Bilson, J., 'The beginnings of Gothic architecture in England', *Journal of the Royal Institute of British Architects* 3 ser. vi (1899), 259–69, 289–326

Binski, P., *Westminster Abbey and the Plantagenets: kingship and the representation of power, 1200–1400*, New Haven 1995

—, *Becket's crown: art and imagination in Gothic England, 1170–1300*, New Haven and London 2004

Binski, P., and Panayotova, S. (eds), *The Cambridge illuminations: ten centuries of book production in the medieval West*, London 2005

Bird, W.H., *Old Gloucestershire churches: a concise guide, especially compiled for motoring folk and others interested in the architecture of our churches, and also their contents, screens, fonts, brasses, etc.*, London and Cheltenham 1928

Birkett, H., *The Saints' Lives of Jocelin of Furness: hagiography, patronage and ecclesiastical politics*, Woodbridge 2010

Bischoff, B., tr. D. Ó Cróinín and D. Ganz, *Latin palaeography: antiquity and the middle ages*, Cambridge 1990

Bishop, T.A.M., 'Notes on Cambridge manuscripts, part i', *Transactions of the Cambridge Bibliographical Society* i (1953), 432–41

—, *Scriptores regis: facsimiles to identify and illustrate the hands of royal scribes in original charters of Henry I, Stephen, and Henry II*, Oxford 1961

—, *English Caroline minuscule*, Oxford 1971

Bisson, T.N., *The crisis of the twelfth century: power, lordship and the origins of European government*, Princeton and Oxford 2009

Blair, J., 'Secular minster churches in Domesday Book', in P. Sawyer (ed.), *Domesday Book: a reassessment*, London 1985, 104–42

— (ed.), *Minsters and parish churches: the local Church in transition, 950–1200*, Oxford 1988

—, *Anglo-Saxon Oxfordshire*, Stroud 1994

—, 'A handlist of Anglo-Saxon saints', in A. Thacker and R. Sharpe (eds), *Local saints and local churches in the early medieval West*, Oxford 2002, 495–565

—, *The Church in Anglo-Saxon society*, Oxford 2005

—, 'The Kirkdale dedication inscription and its Latin models: *Romanitas* in late Anglo-Saxon Yorkshire', in A. Hall and others (eds), *Interfaces between language and culture in medieval England: a festschrift for Matti Kilpiö*, Leiden 2010, 139–45

Blair, P.H., 'Some observations on the *Historia regum* attributed to Symeon of Durham', in N.K. Chadwick (ed.), *Celt and Saxon: studies in the early British border*, Cambridge 1963, 63–118, repr. in P.H. Blair, *Anglo-Saxon Northumbria*, ed. M. Lapidge and Pauline Hunter Blair, London 1984, no. ix

Blockley, K., Sparks, M., and Tatton-Brown, T., *Canterbury cathedral nave: archaeology, history and architecture*, Canterbury 1997
Bloxam, M.H., *The principles of Gothic architecture*, 8 edn, London 1846
Bond, T., 'Corfe castle', *Archaeological Journal* xxii (1865), 200–222
Bony, J., 'Durham et la traditionne saxonne', in S. McKnight Crosby, A. Chastel, A. Prache and A. Chatelet (eds), *Études d'art mediévale offertes à Louis Grodecki*, Paris 1981, 79–92
Bosanquet, G., *Eadmer's history of recent events in England*, London 1964
Brand, P., '"Time out of mind": the knowledge and use of the eleventh- and twelfth-century past in thirteenth-century litigation', *ANS* xvi (1994), 38–54
Brett, M., 'John of Worcester and his contemporaries', in R.H.C. Davis and others (eds), *The writing of history in the middle ages*, 101–26
—, 'Forgery at Rochester', *Fälschungen im Mittelalter*, iv. 397–412
—, 'The *Collectio Lanfranci* and its competitors', in L. Smith and B. Ward (eds), *Intellectual life in the middle ages: essays presented to Margaret Gibson*, London 1992, 157–74
—, 'Editions, manuscripts and readers in some pre-Gratian collections', in K.G. Cushing and R.F. Gyug (eds), *Ritual, text, and law: studies in medieval canon law and liturgy presented to Roger E. Reynolds*, Aldershot 2004, 205–19
—, 'Margin and afterthought: the *Clavis* in action', in M. Brett and K.G. Cushing (eds), *Readers, texts and compilers in the early middle ages: studies in medieval canon law in honour of Linda Fowler-Magerl*, Aldershot 2009, 137–57
—, 'English law and centres of law studies in the later twelfth century', in T. Iversen (ed.), *Archbishop Eystein as legislator*, Trondheim 2011, 98–102
Brooke, C.N.L., 'Geoffrey of Monmouth as a historian', in C. Brooke and others (eds), *Church and government*, 77–91
—, 'Bishop Walkelin and his inheritance', in Crook (ed.), *Winchester*, 1–12
Brooke, C.N.L., Luscombe, D.E., Martin, G.H., and Owen, D. (eds), *Church and government in the middle ages: essays presented to C.R. Cheney on his seventieth birthday*, Cambridge 1976
Brooke, Z.N., *The English Church and the papacy from the Conquest to the reign of John*, Cambridge 1931
Brooks, N.P., 'England in the ninth century: the crucible of defeat', *TRHS* 5 ser. xxix (1979), 1–20
—, 'The Micheldever forgery', in R.A. Custance (ed.), *Winchester College: sixth-century essays*, Oxford 1981, 189–228)
—, *The early history of the church of Canterbury: Christ Church from 597 to 1066*, Leicester 1984
—, 'History and myth, forgery and truth', *Inaugural lecture delivered in the University of Birmingham, 23 January 1986*, repr. in his *Anglo-Saxon myths*, 1–19
—, *Anglo-Saxon myths: State and Church*, London 2000

—, 'Why is the *Anglo-Saxon Chronicle* about kings?', *ASE* xxxix (2010), 43–70
Brown, M., *The Book of Cerne: prayer, patronage and power in ninth-century England*, London 1996
Brown, S.D.B., 'Military service and monetary reward in the eleventh and twelfth centuries', *History* lxxiv (1989), 20–38
[Brown, T.J.], 'The detection of faked literary manuscripts', in J. Bately, M.P. Brown and J. Roberts (eds), *A palaeographer's view: the selected writings of Julian Brown*, London 1993
Brühl, C., 'Die Entwicklung der diplomatischen Methode im Zusammenhang mit dem Erkennen von Fälschungen', in *Fälschungen im Mittelalter*, iii. 11–27
Bryant, R., *Corpus of Anglo-Saxon stone sculpture, X, the Western Midlands*, Oxford 2012
Burke, P., *The Renaissance sense of the past*, London 1969
Burnett, C., *The introduction of Arabic learning into England*, London 1997
Butler, L.A.S., and Morris, R.K. (eds), *The Anglo-Saxon Church. Papers on history, architecture and archaeology in honour of Dr H.M. Taylor*, CBA Research Report lx, London 1986
Cambridge, E., 'Early Romanesque architecture in North-East England: a style and its patrons', in Rollason and others (eds), *Anglo-Norman Durham, 1093–1193*, 141–60
Campbell, J., 'Some twelfth-century views of the Anglo-Saxon past', *Peritia* iii (1984), 131–50, repr. in J. Campbell, *Essays in Anglo-Saxon history*, London and Ronceverte 1986, 209–28
—, 'Power and authority 600–1300', in D.M. Palliser (ed.), *The Cambridge urban history of Britain, volume I, 600–1540*, Cambridge 2000, 51–78
—, *The Anglo-Saxon state*, Hambledon and London 2000
Carley, J.P., and Townsend, D. (eds), *The chronicle of Glastonbury abbey: an edition, translation and study of John of Glastonbury's 'Cronica sive antiquitates Glastoniensis ecclesie'*, Woodbridge 1985
Carpenter, D., 'Westminster Abbey in politics, 1258–1269', in *Thirteenth-century England* viii (2001), 49–58
Catto, J., 'Andrew Horn: law and history in fourteenth-century England', in R.H.C. Davis and others (eds), *The writing of history in the middle ages*, 367–91
Cavill, P., *Vikings: fear and faith*, Grand Rapids, MI 2001
—, 'Analogy and genre in the Legend of St Edmund', *Nottingham Medieval Studies* xlvii (2003), 21–45
Chadd, D., 'Liturgy and liturgical music: the limits of uniformity', in C. Norton and D. Park (eds), *Cistercian art and architecture in the British Isles*, Cambridge 1986, 299–314
— (ed.), *The ordinal of the abbey of the Holy Trinity Fécamp (Fécamp, Musée de la Bénédictine, MS 186)* (HBS cxi–cxii, 1999–2002)

Chaplais, P., 'The origins and authenticity of the royal Anglo-Saxon diploma', *Journal of the Society of Archivists* iii (1966), 160–76, repr. in F. Ranger (ed.), *Prisca munimenta: studies in archival and administrative history presented to Dr A.E.J. Hollaender*, London 1973, 28–42
—, *English diplomatic practice in the middle ages*, London 2003
Cheney, M.G., *Roger, bishop of Worcester, 1164–1179*, Oxford 1980
Chibnall, M., 'Charter and chronicle: the use of archive sources by Norman historians', in C. N.L. Brooke and others (eds), *Church and government*, 1–17
—, *The world of Orderic Vitalis*, Oxford 1984
—, *Anglo-Norman England, 1066–1166*, Oxford 1986
—, 'Mercenaries and the *familia regis* under Henry I', in M. Strickland (ed.), *Anglo-Norman warfare*, Woodbridge 1992, 84–92
—, 'Les Normands et les saints anglo-saxons', in P. Bouet and F. Neveux (eds), *Les Saints dans la Normandie médiévale. Colloque Cerisy-la-Salle (26–29 Septembre 1996)*, Caen 2000, 259–68
Clanchy, M.T., 'Remembering the past and the good old law', *History* lv (1970), 165–76
—, *From memory to written record: England 1066–1307*, 2 edn, London 1993
Clapham, A., *English Romanesque architecture before the Conquest*, Oxford 1930
—, *English Romanesque architecture after the Conquest*, Oxford 1934
—, 'Knook church', *Archaeological Journal* civ (1947), 163
Clark, C., 'Notes on a *Life* of three Thorney saints, Thancred, Torhtred and Tova', *Proceedings of the Cambridge Antiquarian Society* lxix (1979), 45–52
Clarke, B.F., *Parish churches of London*, London 1966
Coatsworth, E., *Corpus of Anglo-Saxon stone sculpture, VIII, Western Yorkshire*, Oxford 2008
Cohen, J.J. (ed.), *Cultural diversity in the British middle ages: archipelago, island, England*, New York 2008
Colgrave, B., 'The post-Bedan miracles and translations of St Cuthbert', in C. Fox and B. Dickins (eds), *The early cultures of north-west Europe (H.M. Chadwick Memorial Studies)*, Cambridge 1950, 305–32
Colker, M.L., *Trinity College Library Dublin: descriptive catalogue of the mediaeval and renaissance Latin manuscripts*, Aldershot 1991
Conybeare, E., *Alfred in the chroniclers*, Cambridge 1900
Corner, D., 'The texts of the assizes of Henry II', in A. Harding (ed.), *Law-making and law-makers in British history*, London 1980, 7–20
Costambeys, M., 'Ívarr (d. 873)', *ODNB* xxix. 443–5
Coupland, S., 'The Vikings in Francia and Anglo-Saxon England to 911', in R. McKitterick (ed.), *The New Cambridge Medieval History*, Cambridge 1995, 190–201
Cramp, R., *Corpus of Anglo-Saxon stone sculpture, I, County Durham and Northumberland*, Oxford 1977; *VII, South-West England*, Oxford 2006

Craster, H.H.E., 'The patrimony of St Cuthbert', *EHR* lxix (1954), 177–99

Crawford, S., and Guy, C., 'As Normans tore down Saxon cathedrals', *British Archaeology* xxix (1997), 7

Crick, J.C., *The Historia regum Britannie of Geoffrey of Monmouth*, iii: *A summary catalogue of the manuscripts*; iv: *Dissemination and reception in the later middle Ages*, Woodbridge 1989–91

—, 'Liberty and fraternity: creating and defending the liberty of St Albans', in A. Musson (ed.), *Expectations of the law in the middle ages*, Woodbridge 2001, 91–103

—, 'St Albans, Westminster and some twelfth-century views of the Anglo-Saxon past', *ANS* xxv (2003 for 2002), 65–83

—, '"Pristina libertas": liberty and the Anglo-Saxons revisited', *TRHS* 6 ser. xiv (2004), 47–72

—, 'Script and the sense of the past in Anglo-Saxon England', in J. Roberts and L. Webster (eds), *Anglo-Saxon traces*, Tempe, AZ 2011, 1–29

—, 'Insular history? Forgery and the English past in the tenth century', in D. Rollason and others (eds), *England and the Continent in the tenth century*, 515–44

—, 'English vernacular script', in R. Gameson (ed.), *The Cambridge history of the book in Britain, Volume 1: c.400–1100*, Cambridge 2012, 174–86

Crook, J. (ed.), *Winchester cathedral: nine hundred years*, Chichester 1993

Crook, J., '"A worthy antiquity": the movement of King Cnut's bones in Winchester Cathedral', in A.R. Rumble (ed.), *The reign of Cnut King of England, Denmark and Norway*, London 1994, 165–92

Croome, W.J., 'Gloucestershire churches', *Transactions of the Bristol and Gloucestershire Archaeological Society* lxxii (1953), 5–22

Cubitt, C.R.E., 'Universal and local saints in Anglo-Saxon England', in A. Thacker and R. Sharpe (eds), *Local saints and local churches in the early medieval West*, Oxford 2002, 423–53

Dachowski, E., *First amongst abbots: the career of Abbo of Fleury*, Washington, DC 2008

Dalton, O.M., 'A relief representing the crucifixion in the parish church of St Dunstan's, Stepney', *Proceedings of the Society of Antiquaries of London* xxii (1907–8), 225–31

Da Rold, O., 'EM in context', in O. Da Rold and others (eds), *The production and use of English manuscripts, 1060 to 1220*

Da Rold, O., Kato, T., Swan, M., and Treharne, E. (eds), *The production and use of English manuscripts 1060 to 1220*, University of Leicester 2010, available at http://www.le.ac.uk/ee/em1060to1220

Davies, R.R., *The matter of Britain and the matter of England*, Oxford 1996

—, *The first English empire: power and identities in the British Isles, 1093–1343*, Oxford 2000

Davis, G.R.C., *Medieval cartularies of Great Britain and Ireland*, rev. edn by C. Breay, J. Harrison and D.M. Smith, London 2010

Davis, K., 'National writing in the ninth century: a reminder for postcolonial thinking about the North', *Journal of Medieval and Early Modern Studies* xxviii (1998), 61–37

Davis, R.H.C., 'William of Poitiers and his *History of William the Conqueror*', in R.H.C. Davis and others, *The writing of history in the middle ages*, 71–100

—, 'Bede after Bede', in C. Harper-Bill, C.J. Holdsworth and J.L. Nelson (eds), *Studies in medieval history presented to R. Allen Brown*, Woodbridge 1989, 103–16

Davis, R.H.C., Wallace-Hadrill, J.M., Catto, R.J.A.I., and Keen, M.H. (eds), *The writing of history in the middle ages: essays presented to Richard William Southern*, Oxford 1981

Davril, A., 'La longueur des leçons de l'office nocturne: étude comparative', in P. de Clerck and E. Palazzo (eds), *Rituels: mélanges offerts à Pierre-Marie Gy, O.P.*, Paris 1990, 183–97

Dawson, C., *Religion and the rise of Western culture*, London 1950

Deanesly, M., *The pre-Conquest Church in England*, 2 edn, London 1963

de Gaiffier, B., 'La lecture des actes des martyres dans la prière liturgique en Occident: à propos du passionaire hispanique', *AB* lxxii (1954), 134–66

—, 'La lecture des passions des martyrs à Rome avant le IXe siècle', *AB* lxxxvii (1969), 63–78

—, 'À propos des légendiers latins', *AB* xcvii (1979), 57–68

de Lasteyrie, R. 'La charte de donation du domaine de Sucy à l'Église de Paris (811)', *BEC* xliii (1882), 60–78

Delisle, L., 'Imitation d'anciennes écritures par des scribes du Moyen Âge', *Revue archéologique* 3 ser. xvi (1890), 63–5

Deniaux, E., Lorren, C., Bauduin, P., and Jarry, T. (eds), *La Normandie avant les Normands. De la conquête romaine à l'arrivée des Vikings*, Rennes 2002

Derolez, A., *The palaeography of Gothic manuscript books from the twelfth to the early sixteenth century*, Cambridge 2003

Dixon, P., Owen, O., and Stocker, D., 'The Southwell lintel, its style and significance', in J. Graham-Campbell and others (eds), *Vikings and the Danelaw: select papers from the proceedings of the thirteenth Viking congress, Nottingham and York, 21–30 August 1997*, Oxford 2001, 245–68

Djordjevic, I., 'Mapping medieval translation: methodological problems and a case study', unpubl. Ph.D. diss. McGill 2003

Djordjevic, I., 'Saracens and other Saxons', in L. Ashe, I. Djordjevic and J. Weiss (eds), *The exploitations of medieval romance*, Cambridge 2010, 28–42

Dodwell, C.R., *Anglo-Saxon art: a new perspective*, Ithaca, NY 1982

Dolbeau, F., 'Notes sur l'organisation interne des légendiers latins', in P. Riché (ed.), *Hagiographie, cultures et sociétés, ive–xiie siècles: actes du colloque organisé à Nanterre et à Paris (2–5 Mai 1979)*, Paris 1981, 11–31

Downham, C., *Viking kings of Britain and Ireland: the dynasty of Ívarr to A.D. 1014*, Edinburgh 2007

Dufour, J., 'État et comparaison des actes faux ou falsifiés intitulés au nom des Carolingiens français (840–987)', *Fälschungen im Mittelalter*, iv. 167–210

Dugdale, W., *The antiquities of Warwickshire illustrated...* rev. edn London 1730

—, *Monasticon Anglicanum*, ed. J. Caley, H. Ellis and B. Bandinel, London 1817–30

Duggan, C., *Twelfth-century decretal collections and their importance in English history*, London 1963

Du Monstier, A. (ed.), *Neustria pia*, Paris 1663

Dumville, D.N., 'Nennius and the *Historia Brittonum*', *Studia Celtica* x–xi (1975–6), 78–95

—, 'An early text of Geoffrey of Monmouth's *Historia regum Britanniae* and the circulation of some Latin histories in twelfth-century Normandy', *Arthurian Literature* iv (1985), 1–36

—, 'Textual archaeology and Northumbrian history subsequent to Bede', in D.M. Metcalf (ed.), *Coinage in ninth-century Northumbria: the tenth Oxford symposium on coinage and monetary history* (British Archaeological Reports, British Series clxxx, 1987), 43–55, repr. in D.N. Dumville, *Britons and Anglo-Saxons in the early middle ages*, Aldershot 1993, no. x

—, 'On the dating of some late Anglo-Saxon liturgical manuscripts', *Transactions of the Cambridge Bibliographical Society* x (1991), 40–57

—, *English Caroline script and monastic history: studies in Benedictinism, A. D. 950–1030*, Woodbridge 1993

—, 'Anglo-Saxon books: treasure in Norman hands?', *ANS* xvi (1993), 84–99

—, 'English square minuscule script: the mid-century phases', *ASE* xxiii (1994), 133–64

—, *The churches of North Britain in the first Viking age*, Fifth Whithorn Lecture, Whithorn 1997

Eales, R., and Sharpe, R. (eds), *Canterbury and the Norman Conquest: churches, saints and scholars, 1066–1109*, London 1995

Echard, S., *Arthurian narrative in the Latin tradition*, Cambridge 1998

Edwards, A.J.M., 'Odo of Ostia's history of the translation of St. Milburga and its connection with the early history of Wenlock Abbey', unpubl. Ph.D. diss. London 1960

Eisenstein, E.L., *The printing press as an agent of change: communications and cultural transformations in early-modern Europe*, Cambridge 1979

Engel, U., *Worcester cathedral: an architectural history*, Chichester 2007

Escudier, D., 'Orderic Vital et le scriptorium de Saint-Evroult', in P. Bouet and M. Dosdat (eds), *Manuscrits et enluminures dans le monde normand (xe–xve siècles)*, Caen 1999, 17–28

Evans, J.W., and Wooding, J.M. (eds), *St David of Wales: cult, church and nation*, Woodbridge 2007

Everard, J.A., *Brittany and the Angevins: province and empire, 1158–1203*, Cambridge 2000

Everson, P., and Stocker, D., *Corpus of Anglo-Saxon stone sculpture, V, Lincolnshire*, Oxford 1999

Excavations at St Ethernan's monastery, Isle of May, Fife, 1992–7 (Tayside and Fife Archaeological Commitee, Monograph 6, 2008)

Fassler, M.E., *The Virgin of Chartres: making history through liturgy and the arts*, New Haven 2010

Fälschungen im Mittelalter (MGH Schriften xxxiii, 1988–89)

Faulkner, M., 'The uses of Anglo-Saxon manuscripts c.1066–1200', unpubl. D.Phil. diss. Oxford 2008

—, 'Archaism, belatedness and modernisation: "Old" English in the twelfth century', *Review of English Studies* new ser. lxiii (2011), 179–203

—, 'Rewriting English literary history, 1042–1215', *Literature Compass* ix (2012), 275–91

Ferguson, S., 'The Romanesque cathedral of Ely: an archaeological evaluation of its construction', unpubl. Ph.D. diss. New York 1986

Fergusson, P., *Canterbury cathedral priory in the age of Becket*, New Haven 2011

Fernie, E., *The architecture of the Anglo-Saxons*, London 1983

—, 'The use of varied nave supports in Romanesque and early Gothic churches', *Gesta* xxiii (1984), 107–17

—, 'The effect of the Conquest on Norman architectural patronage', *ANS* ix (1986), 72–85

—, *An architectural history of Norwich cathedral*, Oxford 1993

—, 'Architecture and the effects of the Norman Conquest', in D. Bates and A. Curry (eds), *England and Normandy in the middle ages*, London and Rio Grande 1994, 105–16

—, *The architecture of Norman England*, Oxford 2000

—, 'The architecture and sculpture of Ely cathedral in the Norman period', in P. Meadows and N. Ramsay (eds), *A history of Ely cathedral*, Woodbridge 2003, 94–111

—, 'La seconda cattedrale di Durham', *Medioevo: l'Europa della cattedrali: Atti del Convegno internazionale di studi Parma, 19–23 settembre 2006*, Milan 2007, 132–40

—, 'Edward the Confessor's Westminster Abbey', in R. Mortimer (ed.), *Edward the Confessor: the man and the legend*, Woodbridge 2009, 139–50

Field, R., 'Romance as history, history as romance', in M. Mills, J. Fellows and C.M. Meale (eds), *Romance in medieval England*, Cambridge 1991, 163–73
—, '*Waldef* and the matter of/with England', in J. Weiss, J. Fellows and M. Dickson (eds), *Medieval insular romance: translation and innovation*, Cambridge 2000, 25–39
—, 'What's in a name? Arthurian name-dropping in the *Roman de Waldef*', in B. Wheeler (ed.), *Arthurian studies in honour of P.J.C. Field*, Cambridge 2004, 63–4
—, '*Pur les francs homes amender*: clerical authors and the thirteenth-century context of historical romance', in R. Purdie and M. Cichon (eds), *Medieval romance, medieval contexts*, Woodbridge 2011, 175–88
Finberg, H.P.R., *The early charters of the West Midlands*, 2 edn, Leicester 1961
—, *The early charters of Wessex*, Leicester 1964
Fleming, R., 'Monastic lands and England's defence in the Viking age', *EHR* c (1985), 247–65
Fletcher, R., *Bloodfeud: murder and revenge in Anglo-Saxon England*, Harmondsworth 2002
Flint, V., 'The *Historia Regum Britanniae* of Geoffrey of Monmouth: parody and its purpose. A suggestion', *Speculum* liv (1979), 447–68
Foot, S., 'Remembering, forgetting and inventing: attitudes to the past in England at the end of the first Viking age', *TRHS* 6 ser. ix (1999), 185–200
—, *Æthelstan: the first king of England*, New Haven and London 2011
Foys, M.K., *Virtually Anglo-Saxon: old media, new media, and early medieval studies in the late Age of Print*, Gainesville, FL 2007
Franklin, J., *Medieval sculpture from Norwich cathedral*, Norwich 1980
—, 'The Romanesque cloister sculpture at Norwich cathedral priory', in F.H. Thompson (ed.), *Studies in medieval sculpture*, London 1983, 56–70
Freeman, E.A., *The history of the Norman Conquest of England, its causes and its results*, Oxford 1867–79
Freeman, E., *Narratives of a new order: Cistercian historical writing in England, 1150–1220*, Turnhout 2002
Fritze, W., 'Zur Entstehungsgeschichte des Bistums Utrecht: Franken und Friesen, 690–734', *Rheinische Vierteljahrsblätter* xxxv (1971), 107–51
Galbraith, K.J., 'The iconography of the biblical scenes at Malmesbury abbey', *Journal of the British Archaeological Association* 3 ser. xxviii (1965), 39–56
—, 'Early sculpture at St Nicholas's church, Ipswich', *Proceedings of the Suffolk Institute of Archaeology*, xxxi, part 2 (1968), 172–84
Galbraith, V.H., 'Royal charters to Winchester', *EHR* xxxv (1920), 382–400
Galloway, A., 'Writing History in England', in D. Wallace (ed.), *Cambridge history of medieval English literature*, Cambridge 1999, 255–83
Gameson, R., *The manuscripts of early Norman England (c. 1066–1130)*, Oxford 1999

Gardner, A., *English medieval sculpture*, Cambridge 1951
Gardner, S., *English Gothic foliage sculpture*, Cambridge 1927
Garnett, G., *Conquered England: kingship, succession and tenure, 1066–1166*, Oxford 2007
Gatch, M. McC., 'The office in late Anglo-Saxon monasticism', in M. Lapidge and H. Gneuss (eds), *Learning and literature in Anglo-Saxon England: studies presented to Peter Clemoes on the occasion of his sixty-fifth birthday*, Cambridge 1985, 341–62
Gazeau, V., *Normannia monastica*, ii, Prosopographie des abbés bénédictins (xie–xiie siècle), Caen 2007
Geary, P.J., *Phantoms of remembrance: memory and oblivion at the end of the first millennium*, Princeton 1994
—, 'Medieval archivists as authors: social memory and archival memory', in F.X. Blouin and W.G. Rosenberg (eds), *Archives, documentation and institutions of social memory: essays from the Sawyer seminar*, Ann Arbor, MI 2006, 106–13
Geddes, J., 'Twelfth-century metalwork at Durham cathedral', in N. Coldstream and P. Draper (eds), *Medieval art and architecture at Durham cathedral*: British Archaeological Association Conference Transactions iii (1980), 140–48
—, *Medieval decorative ironwork in England*, London 1999
Gem, R., 'Bishop Wulfstan II and the Romanesque cathedral church of Worcester', in G. Popper (ed.), *Medieval art and architecture at Worcester cathedral*: British Archaeological Association Conference Transactions i (1978), 15–37
—, 'The Romanesque rebuilding of Westminster abbey', *ANS* iii (1981), 33–60
—, 'Chichester cathedral: when was the Romanesque church begun?', *ANS* iii (1981), 61–4
—, 'The significance of the 11th-century rebuilding of Christ Church and St Augustine's Canterbury, in the development of Romanesque architecture', in N. Coldstream and P. Draper (eds), *Medieval art and architecture at Canterbury before 1220*: British Archaeological Association Conference Transactions v (1982), 1–19
—, 'The Romanesque cathedral of Winchester: patron and design in the eleventh century', in T.A. Heslop and V. Sekules (eds), *Medieval art and architecture at Winchester cathedral*: British Archaeological Association Conference Transactions vi (1983), 1–12
—, 'ABC: How should we periodize Anglo-Saxon architecture?', in Butler and Morris (eds), *The Anglo-Saxon Church*, 83–105
—, 'The bishop's chapel at Hereford: the roles of patron and craftsmen', in S. Macready and F.H. Thompson (eds), *Art and patronage in the English Romanesque*, London 1986, 87–96

—, 'Canterbury and the cushion capital: a commentary on passages from Goscelin's "De miraculis sancti Augustini"', in N. Stratford (ed.), *Romanesque and Gothic: essays for George Zarnecki*, Woodbridge 1987, 83–101

—, 'The English parish church in the 11th and early 12th centuries: a Great Rebuilding?', in Blair (ed.), *Minsters and parish churches*, 21–30

Gem, R., Howe, E., and Bryant, R., 'The ninth-century polychrome decoration at St Mary's church, Deerhurst', *Antiquaries Journal* lxxxviii (2008), 109–64

Gem, R., and Tudor-Craig, P., 'A "Winchester school" wall painting at Nether Wallop, Hampshire', *ASE* ix (1981), 115–36

Gibb, J.H.P., 'The Anglo-Saxon cathedral at Sherborne, with an appendix on documentary evidence by R.D.H. Gem', *Archaeological Journal* cxxxii (1975), 71–110

Gibson, M., Heslop, T.A., and Pfaff, R.W. (eds), *The Eadwine Psalter: text, image, and monastic culture in twelfth-century Canterbury*, London 1992

Gillingham, J., 'The context and purposes of Geoffrey of Monmouth's *History of the kings of Britain*', *ANS* xiii (1991–92), 99–118, repr. in idem, *The English in the twelfth century*, 19–39

—, 'The beginnings of English imperialism', *Journal of Historical Sociology* v. 4 (1992), 392–409; repr. in idem, *The English in the twelfth century*, 3–18

—, 'Conquering the barbarians: war and chivalry in twelfth century Britain', *The Haskins Society Journal* iv (1993), 67–84, repr. in idem, *The English in the twelfth century*, 41–58

—, 'Henry of Huntingdon and the twelfth-century revival of the English nation', in S. Forde, L. Johnson and A.V. Murray (eds), *Concepts of national identity in the middle ages* (Leeds Texts and Monographs, new series xiv, 1995), 75–101

—, 'Gaimar, the prose *Brut* and the making of English history', in Jean-Philippe Genet (ed.), *L'Histoire et les nouveaux publics dans l'Europe médiévale*, Paris 1997, 165–76.

—, *The English in the twelfth century: imperialism, national identity and political values*, Woodbridge 2000

—, 'Civilizing the English? The English histories of William of Malmesbury and David Hume', *Historical Research* lxxiv (2001), 17–43

—, 'French culture, twelfth-century English historians and the civilising process', in C. Arrignon and others (eds), *Cinquante années d'études médiévales. À la confluence de nos disciplines. Actes du colloque organisé à l'occasion du Cinquantenaire du CESCM, 2003*, Turnhout 2006, 729–40

—, 'Questioning Egbert's Edict', *History Today* lxiii, issue 4 (2013), 4–5

—, 'Expectations of empire: some twelfth- and early thirteenth-century English views of what their kings could do', in S. Duffy and S. Foran (eds), *The English Isles: cultural transmission and political conflict in Britain and Ireland, 1100–1500*, Dublin 2013, 56–67

Giry, A., 'La donation de Rueil à l'abbaye de Saint-Denis: examen critique de trois diplômes de Charles le Chauve', *Mélanges Julien Havet (1853–1893)*, Paris 1895, 683–717
—, *Manuel de diplomatique*, Paris 1925
Gneuss, H., 'Liturgical books in Anglo-Saxon England and their Old English terminology', in M. Lapidge and H. Gneuss (eds), *Learning and literature in Anglo-Saxon England: studies presented to Peter Clemoes on the occasion of his sixty-fifth birthday*, Cambridge 1985, 91–141
—, *Handlist of Anglo-Saxon manuscripts: a list of manuscripts and manuscript fragments written or owned in England up to 1100*, Tempe, AZ 2001
Gobbitt, T., 'Cambridge, Corpus Christi College, 383', in O. Da Rold and others (eds), *The production and use of English manuscripts, 1060 to 1220*
Gouron, A., 'Un traité écossais du douzième siècle: l'ordo "Ulpianus de edendo"', *Tijdschrift voor Rechtsgeschiedenis* lxxviii (2010), 1–13
Grafton, A., *Forgers and critics: creativity and duplicity in Western scholarship*, London 1990
Graham, T., 'Cambridge, Corpus Christi College 57 and its Anglo-Saxon users', in P. Pusiano and E. Treharne (eds), *Anglo-Saxon manuscripts and their heritage*, Aldershot 1998, 21–69
Gransden, A., *Historical writing in England c.550 to c.1307*, London 1974
—, 'Cultural transition at Worcester in the Anglo-Norman period', in G. Popper (ed.), *Medieval art and architecture at Worcester cathedral: British Archaeological Association Conference Transactions* i (1978), 1–14
—, *Historical writing in England, II: c.1307 to the early sixteenth century*, London 1982
—, 'Bede's reputation as an historian in medieval England', *JEH* xxxii (1981), 397–425, repr. in eadem, *Legends, traditions and history in medieval England*, London 1992, 1–29
—, 'The legends and traditions concerning the origins of the abbey of Bury St Edmunds', *EHR* c (1985), 1–24
—, 'The composition and authorship of the *De miraculis Sancti Eadmundi* attributed to "Hermann the archdeacon"', *Journal of Medieval Latin* v (1995), 1–52
Green, J., *The government of England under Henry I*, Cambridge 1986
Greenberg, J., '"St Edward's ghost": the cult of St Edward and his laws in English history', in S. Jurasinski, L. Oliver and A. Rabin (eds), *English law before Magna Carta*, Leiden and Boston 2010, 273–300
Grégoire, R., 'L'homéliaire cistercien du manuscrit 114(82) de Dijon', *Cîteaux: Commentarii Cistercienses* xxviii (1977), 133–207
Grémont, D.-B., 'Lectiones ad prandium à l'abbaye de Fécamp au xiiie siècle', *Cahiers Léopold Delisle* xx (1971), 3–41

Gretsch, M., *The intellectual foundations of the English Benedictine reform*, Cambridge 1999

—, *Ælfric and the cult of saints in late Anglo-Saxon England*, Cambridge 2005

Grosjean, P., 'Vie de S. Rumon; Vie, Invention et Miracles de S. Nectan', *AB* lxxi (1953), 359–414

Guenée, B., *Histoire et culture historique dans l'Occident médiéval*, Paris 1980

Gullick, M., 'The scribe of the Carilef Bible: a new look at some late-eleventh-century Durham cathedral manuscripts', in L.L. Brownrigg (ed.), *Medieval book production: assessing the evidence. Proceedings of the second conference of The Seminar of the History of the Book to 1500*, Los Altos Hills, CA 1990, 61–83

—, 'The scribes of the Durham cantor's book (Durham, Dean and Chapter Library, MS B.IV.24) and the Durham martyrology scribe', in D.W. Rollason and others (eds), *Anglo-Norman Durham*, 93–124

—, 'The origin and importance of Cambridge, Trinity College, MS R. 5. 27', *Transactions of the Cambridge Bibliographical Society* xi (1998), 239–62

—, 'The hand of Symeon of Durham: further observations on the Durham martyrology scribe', in D.W. Rollason (ed.), *Symeon of Durham*, 14–31

Hadley, D.M., *The Vikings in England: settlement, society and culture*, Manchester 2006

Hahn, C., 'Peregrinatio et natio: the illustrated Life of Edmund, king and martyr', *Gesta* xxx (1991), 119–39

Hall, T.., 'The development of the common of saints in the early English versions of Paul the Deacon's Homiliary', in T.N. Hall and D. Scragg (eds), *Anglo-Saxon books and their readers: essays in celebration of Helmut Gneuss's Handlist of Anglo-Saxon manuscripts*, Kalamazoo, MI 2008, 31–67

Hallam, E.M., *Domesday Book through nine centuries*, London 1986

Hankeln, R., '"Properization" and formal changes in high medieval saints' offices: the offices for Saints Henry and Kunigunde of Bamberg', *Plainsong and Medieval Music* x (2001), 3–22

Harbison, P., *L'Art médiévale en Irelande*, La Pierre-qui-Vire 1998

Hardy, T.D., *Descriptive catalogue of materials relating to the history of Great Britain and Ireland* (RS [xxvi], 1862–71)

Hare, M., 'The documentary evidence', in C. Heighway and R. Bryant (eds), *The Golden Minster: the Anglo-Saxon minster and later medieval priory of St Oswald at Gloucester* (Council for British Archaeology Research Report cxvii, 1999), 33–45

Harper, J., *The forms and orders of Western liturgy from the tenth to the eighteenth century: a historical introduction and guide for students and musicians*, Oxford 1991

Harrison, J.P., 'Anglo-Norman ornament compared with designs in Anglo-Saxon MSS', *Archaeological Journal* xlvii (1890), 143–53

—, 'English architecture before the Conquest', *Archaeologia Oxoniensis* 1892–1895, 121–41

—, 'Note on English Romanesque architecture', *Journal of the British Archaeological Association* new ser. ii (1896), 268–72

Harrison, S., 'Kirkstall abbey: the 12th-century window tracery and rose window', in L.R. Hoey (ed.), *Yorkshire monasticism: archaeology, art and architecture*: British Archaeological Association Conference Transactions xvi (1995), 73–8

Hartzell, K.D., 'A St. Albans miscellany in New York', *Mittellateinisches Jahrbuch* x (1975), 20–61

—, *Catalogue of manuscripts written or owned in England up to 1200 containing music*, Woodbridge 2006

Hayward, P.A., 'The *Miracula inventionis beate Mylburge virginis* attributed to "the Lord Ato, cardinal bishop of Ostia"', *EHR* cxiv (1999), 543–73.

—, 'Sanctity and lordship in twelfth-century England: Saint Albans, Durham, and the cult of Saint Oswine, king and martyr', *Viator* xxx (1999), 105–44

—, 'Translation-narratives in post-Conquest hagiography and English resistance to the Norman Conquest', *ANS* xxi (1999), 67–93

—, 'Sanctity and lordship in twelfth-century England: St Albans, Durham, and the cult of Saint Oswine, king and martyr', *Viator* xxx (1999), 105–44

—, 'Gregory the Great as "Apostle of the English" in post-Conquest Canterbury', *JEH* lv (2004), 19–57

—, 'St Wilfrid of Ripon and the northern Church in Anglo-Norman historiography', *Northern History* xlix (2012), 11–35

Head, T., 'Saints, heretics, and fire: finding meaning through the ordeal', in S. Farmer and B. Rosenwein (eds), *Monks and nuns, saints and outcasts*, Ithaca, NY 2000, 220–38

—, 'The genesis of the ordeal of relics by fire in Ottonian Germany: an alternative form of "canonization"', in G. Klaniczay (ed.), *Procès de canonisation au Moyen Âge: aspects juridiques et religieux / Medieval canonization processes: legal and religious aspects*, Rome 2004, 19–37

Heighway, C., *Anglo-Saxon Gloucestershire*, Gloucester 1987

Helmholz, R., *The Oxford history of the laws of England I: the canon law and ecclesiastical jurisdiction from 597 to the 1640s*, Oxford 2004

Henderson, G., '*Sortes biblicae* in twelfth-century England: the list of episcopal prognostics in Cambridge, Trinity College, MS R.7.5', in D. Williams (ed.), *England in the twelfth century: proceedings of the 1988 Harlaxton Symposium*, Woodbridge 1990, 113–35

Henry, F., and Zarnecki, G., 'Romanesque arches decorated with human and animal heads', *Journal of the British Archaeological Association* 3 ser. xx–xxi (1957–8), 1–35

Heslop, T.A., 'English seals from the mid ninth century to 1100', *Journal of the British Archaeological Association* cxxxiii (1980), 1–16

—, 'Twelfth-century forgeries as evidence for earlier seals: the case of St Dunstan', in N. Ramsay, M. Sparks and T. Tatton-Brown (eds), *St Dunstan: his life, times and cult*, Woodbridge 1992, 299–310

—, 'The Canterbury calendars and the Norman Conquest', in R. Eales and R. Sharpe (eds), *Canterbury and the Norman Conquest*, 53–85

—, 'Worcester cathedral chapterhouse and the harmony of the Testaments', in P. Binski and W. Noel (eds), *New offerings, ancient treasures. Studies in medieval art for George Henderson*, Stroud 2001, 280–311

—, 'The English origin of the coronation of the Virgin', *Burlington magazine* cxlvii (2005), 790–7

Hiatt, A., 'Forgery at the University of Cambridge', *New Medieval Literatures* iii (1999), 95–118

Hiley, D., 'Chant composition at Canterbury after the Norman Conquest', in B. Hangartner and U. Fischer (eds), *Max Lütolf zum 60. Geburtstag. Festschrift*, Basel 1994, 31–46

—, 'The music of prose offices in honour of English saints', *Plainsong and Medieval Music* x (2001), 23–37

—, 'The office chants for St Oswald, king of Northumbria and martyr', in O. Kongsted, N. Krabbe, M. Kube and M. Michelsen (eds), *A Due: musical essays in honour of John D. Bergsagel & Heinrich W. Schwab: Musikalische Aufsätze zu Ehren von John D. Bergsagel & Heinrich W. Schabe*, Copenhagen 2008, 244–59

—, 'The saints venerated in medieval Peterborough as reflected in the Antiphoner Cambridge, Magdalene College, F.4.10', in E. Hornby and D. Maw (eds), *Essays on the history of English music in honour of John Caldwell: sources, style, performance, historiography*, Woodbridge 2010, 22–46

Hill, J., 'Bede and the Benedictine reform' (Jarrow Lecture, 1988)

Hills, G.M., 'The architectural history of Hereford cathedral', *Journal of the British Archaeological Association* xxvii (1871), 46–84

Hindley, G., *The Book of Magna Carta*, London 1990

Hodgkin, R.H., *A history of the Anglo-Saxons*, 3 edn, Oxford 1952

Hoey, L.R., 'The design of Romanesque clerestories with wall passages in Normandy and England', *Gesta* xxviii (1989), 78–101

—, 'Pier form and vertical wall articulation in English Romanesque architecture', *Journal of the Society of Architectural Historians* lviii (1989), 258–83

Hohler, C., 'St Osyth and Aylesbury', *Records of Buckinghamshire* xviii (1966), 61–72

Hohler, C., and Hughes, A., 'The Durham services in honour of St. Cuthbert', in C.F. Battiscombe (ed.), *The relics of St. Cuthbert*, Oxford 1956, 155–91

Holt, J.C., 'The assizes of Henry II: the texts', in D.A. Bullough and R.L. Storey (eds), *The study of medieval records: essays in honour of Kathleen Major*, Oxford 1971, 85–106

—, *Magna Carta and medieval government*, London and Ronceverte 1985

—, *Magna Carta*, 2 edn, Cambridge 1992

Hope, W.H. St John and Bilson, J., 'Architectural description of Kirkstall abbey', *Publications of the Thoresby Society* xvi (1907), 1–140

Hough, C., 'Strensall, *Streanæshalch* and Stronsay', *The English Place-Name Society Journal* xxxv (2003), 17–24

Howard, A.E.D., *Magna Carta: text and commentary*, Charlottesville and London 1998

Howe, N., 'Anglo-Saxon England and the postcolonial void', in A.J. Kabir and D. Williams (eds), *Postcolonial approaches to the European middle ages: translating cultures*, Cambridge 2001, 25–47

Hudson, J., 'Administration, family and perceptions of the past in twelfth-century England: Richard FitzNigel and the Dialogue of the Exchequer', in P. Magdalino (ed.), *The perception of the past*, 75–98

—, *The formation of the English common law: law and society in England from the Norman Conquest to Magna Carta*, London 1996

Hughes, A., 'British rhymed offices: a catalogue and commentary', in S. Rankin and D. Hiley (eds), *Music in the medieval English liturgy: Plainsong and Medieval Music Society centennial essays*, Oxford 1993, 239–84

Humphreys, K.W., and Ross, A.S.C., 'Further manuscripts of Bede's "Historia ecclesiastica", of the "Epistola Cuthberti de obitu Bedae", and further Anglo-Saxon texts of "Cædmon's hymn" and "Bede's death song"', *Notes and Queries* xxii (1975), 50–55

Hunter, M., 'The facsimiles in Thomas Elmham's History of St. Augustine's, Canterbury', *The Library* 5 ser. xxviii (1973), 215–220

Ingledew, F., 'The Book of Troy and the genealogical construction of history; the case of Geoffrey of Monmouth's *Historia Regum Britanniae*', *Speculum* lxix (1994), 665–704

Irvine, J.T., 'Account of the discovery of part of the Saxon abbey church of Peterborough', *Journal of the British Archaeological Association* l (1894), 45–54

—, 'Account of the pre-Norman remains discovered at Peterborough cathedral in 1884', *Associated Architectural Societies Reports and Papers* xvii (1883–4), 277–83

James, M.R., 'Two Lives of St Ethelbert, king and martyr', *EHR* xxxii (1917), 214–44

Jaeger, C.S., 'Pessimism in the twelfth-century "Renaissance"', *Speculum* lxxviii (2003), 1151–83

Johanek, P., 'König Arthur und die Plantagenets', *Frühmittelalterliche Studien* xxi (1987), 346–86

John, E., 'The litigation of an exempt house, St Augustine's Canterbury, 1182–1237', *Bulletin of the John Rylands Library* xxxix (1957), 390–415

Johnson, L., 'The Anglo-Norman *Description of England*: an introduction', in I. Short (ed.), *Anglo-Norman anniversary essays*, London 1993, 11–30

Jones, A.T., 'Pitying the desolation of such a place: rebuilding religious houses and constructing memory in Aquitaine in the wake of the Viking incursions', *Viator* xxxvii (2006), 85–102

Jones, L.W., *An introduction to divine and human readings by Cassiodorus Senator*, New York 1966

Jones, S.E., 'The twelfth-century reliefs from Fécamp: new evidence for their dating and original purpose', *Journal of the British Archaeological Association* cxxxviii (1985), 79–88

Kahn, D., 'The Romanesque sculpture of the church of St Mary at Halford, Warwickshire', *Journal of the British Archaeological Association* cxxxiii (1980), 64–73

—, 'Anglo-Saxon and early Romanesque frieze sculpture in England', in D. Kahn (ed.), *The Romanesque frieze and its spectator*, London 1992, 61–74

Kapelle, W.E., *The Norman Conquest of the north: the region and its transformation*, London 1979

Karkov, C.E., *Text and picture in Anglo-Saxon England: narrative strategies in the Junius 11 manuscript*, Cambridge 2001

—, 'Writing and having written: word and image in the Eadwig Gospels', in A.R. Rumble (ed.), *Writing and texts in Anglo-Saxon England*, Woodbridge 2006, 44–61

—, 'Evangelist portraits and book production in late Anglo-Saxon England', in S. Panayotova (ed.), *Cambridge illuminations. The conference papers*, London 2007, 55–63

—, *The art of Anglo-Saxon England*, Woodbridge 2011

—, 'Postcolonial', in J. Stodnick and R. Trilling (eds), *A handbook of Anglo-Saxon studies*, Oxford 2012, 149–64

—, 'The mother's tongue and the father's prose', *Parallax* xviii.3 (2012), 1–11

—, 'Art and writing: voice, image, object', in C.A. Lees (ed.), *The Cambridge history of early medieval English literature*, Cambridge 2013, 73–98

Karn, N., 'Information and its retrieval', in J. Crick and E.M.C. van Houts (eds), *A social history of England, 900–1200*, Cambridge 2011, 373–80

Kauffmann, C.M., *Romanesque manuscripts, 1066–1190* (A survey of manuscripts illuminated in the British Isles, III), London 1975

Keefer, S.L., and Burrows, D.R., 'Hebrew and the *Hebraicum* in late Anglo-Saxon England', *ASE* xix (1990), 67–80

Kelly, F., 'The Romanesque crossing capitals of Southwell minster (together with a note on the lintel in the north transept and the tympanum at Hoveringham)', in J.S. Alexander (ed.), *Southwell and Nottinghamshire: medieval art, architecture, and industry*: British Archaeological Association Conference Transactions xxi (1998), 13–23

Kendrick, T.D., *Late Saxon and Viking art*, London 1949

Kennedy, A., 'Law and litigation in the *Libellus Æthelwoldi episcopi*', ASE xxiv (1995), 131–83

Ker, N.R., *Catalogue of manuscripts containing Anglo-Saxon*, Oxford 1957

—, *English manuscripts in the century after the Norman Conquest. The Lyell Lectures Oxford 1952–3*, Oxford 1960

—, *Medieval libraries of Great Britain*, 2 edn, London 1964

Ker, N.R., and Piper, A., *Medieval manuscripts in British libraries*, Oxford 1969–92

Keynes, S., *The diplomas of King Æthelred 'the Unready', 978–1016: a study in their use as historical evidence*, Cambridge 1980

—, 'King Athelstan's books', in M. Lapidge and H. Gneuss (eds), *Learning and literature in Anglo-Saxon England*, 143–201

—, 'Regenbald the chancellor (*sic*)', ANS x (1988), 185–222

—, 'Royal government and the written word in late Anglo-Saxon England', in R. McKitterick (ed.), *The uses of literacy in early medieval Europe*, Cambridge 1990, 232–44

—, *Anglo-Saxon manuscripts and other items of related interest in the library of Trinity College, Cambridge* (Old English Newsletter, Subsidia xviii, 1992)

—, 'The cult of Alfred the Great', *ASE* xxviii (2000), 225–356

—, 'Ely abbey 672–1109', in P. Meadows and N. Ramsay (eds), *A history of Ely cathedral*, Woodbridge 2003, 3–58

—, 'The massacre of St Brice's Day (13 November 1002)', in N. Lund (ed.), *Seksogtyvende tværfaglige vikingesymposium Københavns Universitet 2007*, Aarhus 2007, 32–67

Keynes, S., and Lapidge, M., *Alfred the Great: Asser's Life of King Alfred and other contemporary sources*, Harmondsworth 1983

Keyser, C.E., 'An essay on the Norman doorways in the county of Gloucester', in P.H. Ditchfield (ed.), *Memorials of old Gloucestershire*, London 1911, 122–71, 281–7

—, 'Visit to the churches of Barnsley, Bibury, Aldsworth, Winson, Coln Rogers, and Coln St Denys', *Transactions of the Bristol and Gloucestershire Archaeological Society* xli (1918–19), 171–204

Kidson, P., and others, *A history of English architecture*, London 1965

Klukas, A.W., '*Altaria superioria*: the function and significance of the tribune-chapel in Anglo-Norman Romanesque: a problem in the relationship of liturgical requirements and architectural form', Ph.D. diss. Pittsburgh 1978

—, 'The architectural implications of the *Decreta Lanfranci*', *ANS* vi (1983), 136–71
—, 'The continuity of Anglo-Saxon liturgical tradition in post-Conquest England as evident in the architecture of Winchester, Ely, and Canterbury cathedrals', in R. Foreville (ed.), *Les Mutations socio-culturelles au tournant des XIe–XIIe siècles: études anselmiennes (IVe session)*, Paris 1984, 111–23
Knowles, D., *The monastic order in England*, 2 edn, Cambridge 1963
Knowles, D., and Hadcock, R.N., *Medieval religious houses: England and Wales*, 2 edn, London 1971
Koopmans, R., *Wonderful to relate: miracle stories and miracle collecting in high medieval England*, Philadelphia 2011
Kuhlicke, F.W., 'A twelfth-century carved head from St Mary's church, Bedford', *Bedfordshire Archaeological Journal* vii (1972), 84–6
Kupfer, M., Review of Gibson and others, *The Eadwine Psalter: text, image, and monastic culture in twelfth-century Canterbury*, *Speculum* lxix (1994), 1168–71
Laistner, M.L.W., with King, H.H., *A hand-list of Bede manuscripts*, Ithaca, NY 1943
Landau, P., 'The origins of legal science in England in the twelfth century: Lincoln, Oxford and the career of Vacarius', in M. Brett and K. Cushing (eds), *Readers, texts and compilers in the earlier middle ages: studies in medieval canon law in honour of Linda Fowler-Magerl*, Aldershot 2009, 165–82
—, 'The origin of civil procedure: treatises in Durham during the twelfth century', in U.-R. Blumenthal, A. Winroth and P. Landau (eds), *Canon law, religion and politics. Liber amicorum Robert Somerville*, Washington, DC 2012, 136–44
Lang, J., 'The St. Helena cross, Church Kelloe', *Archaeologia Aeliana* 5 ser. v (1977), 105–19
—, *Corpus of Anglo-Saxon stone sculpture, VI, northern Yorkshire*, Oxford 2002
Lapidge, M., 'Byhrtferth of Ramsey and the early sections of the *Historia regum* attributed to Symeon of Durham', *ASE* x (1981), 97–122, repr. in M. Lapidge, *Anglo-Latin literature 900–1066*, London and Rio Grande 1993, 317–42
—, *The cult of St Swithun*, Oxford 2003
— (ed.), *Byrhtferth of Ramsey, the Lives of St Oswald and St Ecgwine*, Oxford 2009
Lapidge, M., and Gneuss, H. (eds), *Learning and literature in Anglo-Saxon England: studies presented to Peter Clemoes on the occasion of his sixty-fifth birthday*, Cambridge 1985
Lapidge, M., and Love, R.C., 'The Latin hagiography of England and Wales (600–1550)', in G. Philippart (ed.), *Hagiographies: international history of the Latin and vernacular hagiographical literature in the West from its origins to 1550*, iii, Turnhout 2001, 203–325

Le Goff, J., 'What did the twelfth-century Renaissance *mean*?', in P. Linehan and J.L. Nelson (eds), *The medieval world*, London 2001, 635–47

Le Saux, F.H.M. (ed.), *A companion to Wace*, Woodbridge 2005

Leckie, R.W., *The passage of dominion: Geoffrey of Monmouth and the periodization of insular history in the twelfth century*, Toronto 1981

Levison, W., 'Die "Annales Lindisfarnenses et Dunelmenses" kritisch untersucht und neu herausgegeben', *Deutsches Archiv für Erforschung des Mittelalters* xvii (1961), 447–506

Levy, K., 'A Gregorian processional antiphon', *Schweizer Jahrbuch für Musikwissenschaft / Annales suisses de musicologie*, new ser. ii (1982), 91–102

Licence, T., 'History and hagiography in the late eleventh century: the life and work of Herman the archdeacon, monk of Bury St Edmunds', *EHR* cxxiv (2009), 516–44

—, *Hermits and recluses in English society, 950–1200*, Oxford 2011

Liebermann, F., Quadripartitus: *ein englisches Rechtsbuch von 1114*, Halle 1892

—, Consiliatio Cnuti, *eine Übertragung angelsächsischer Gesetze aus dem zwölften Jahrhundert*, Halle 1893

—, 'On the *Instituta Cnuti aliorumque regum Anglie*', *TRHS* new ser. vii (1893), 77–107

—, *Über die* Leges Anglorum saeculo XIII ineunte Londoniis collectae, Halle 1894

—, *Über Pseudo-Cnuts* Constitutiones de Foresta, Halle 1894

—, *Über die* Leges Edwardi Confessoris, Halle 1896

—, 'Über die *Leis Willelme*', *Archiv für das Studium der neueren Sprachen und Literatur* cvi (1901), 113–38

Lifshitz, F., 'The migration of Neustrian relics in the Viking age: the myth of voluntary exodus, the reality of coercion and theft', *Early Medieval Europe* iv (1995), 175–92

Lindsay, W.M., *Notae Latinae: an account of abbreviation in Latin MSS. of the early minuscule period (c.700–850)*, Cambridge 1915 (and see Bains)

Liu, Y., 'Romances of continuity in the English Rous Roll', in R. Purdie and M. Cichon (eds), *Medieval romance, medieval contexts*, Woodbridge 2011, 149–59

Loud, G.A., 'The chancery and charters of the kings of Sicily (1130–1212)', *EHR* cxxiv (2009), 779–810

Love, R.C. (ed.), *The hagiography of the female saints of Ely*, Oxford 2004

—, '"Torture me, rend me, burn me, kill me!" Goscelin of Saint-Bertin and the depiction of female sanctity', in P. Szarmach (ed.), *Writing women saints in Anglo-Saxon England*, Toronto 2013, 274–306

—, 'The Anglo-Saxon saints of Thorney Abbey and their hagiographer', in L. Lazzari and P. Lendinara (eds), *Hagiography in Anglo-Saxon England:*

adopting and adapting saints' Lives into Old English prose (c.950–1150), Porto, forthcoming

Lucas, P.J., 'Scribal imitation of earlier handwriting: "Bastard Saxon" and its impact', in M.-C. Hubert, E. Poulle and M.H. Smith (eds), *Le Statut du scripteur au Moyen Âge. Actes du XII*ᵉ *colloque scientifique du Comité international de paléographie latine (Cluny, 17–20 juillet 1998)*, Paris 2000, 151–60

Macdonald, W.L., *The architecture of the Roman Empire: an introductory study*, rev. edn, New Haven and London 1982

Maddicott, J., 'Edward the Confessor's return to England in 1041', *EHR* cxxii (2004), 650–66

—, 'Responses to the threat of invasion, 1085', *EHR* cxxii (2007), 986–97

Maddicott, J.R., and Palliser, D.M. (eds), *The medieval state: essays presented to James Campbell*, Cambridge 2000

P. Magdalino, P. (ed.), *The perception of the past in twelfth-century Europe*, London 1992

Martimort, A.G., 'La lecture patristique dans la liturgie des heures', in Giustino Farnedi (ed.), Traditio et progressio: *studi liturgici in onore del Prof. Adrien Nocent, OSB* (Analecta liturgica xii, 1988), 311–31

—, *Les Lectures liturgiques et leurs livres* (Typologie des sources du Moyen Âge occidental lxiv, 1992)

Martin, G.H., 'Devizes, Richard of (*c.*1150–*c.*1200)', in *ODNB* xv. 981–2

Mason, E., 'Legends of the Beauchamps' ancestors: the use of baronial propaganda in medieval England', *Journal of Medieval History* x (1984), 25–40

Mason, J.F.A., 'Diceto, Ralph de (*d.* 1199/1200)', in *ODNB* xvi. 40–42

McAleer, J.P., 'A note about the transept cross aisles of Ely cathedral', *Proceedings of the Cambridge Antiquarian Society* lxxxi (1992), 51–70

McClendon, C.B., *The origins of medieval architecture: building in Europe, A.D. 600–900*, New Haven and London 2005

Maguire, H.P., 'A twelfth-century workshop in Northampton', *Gesta* ix (1970), 11–35

Meehan, B., 'Insiders and property in Durham around 1100', *Studies in Church History* xii (1975), 45–58

—, 'The siege of Durham, the battle of Carham and the cession of Lothian', *Scottish Historical Review* lv (1976), 1–19

—, 'A reconsideration of the historical works associated with Symeon of Durham', unpubl. Ph.D. diss. Edinburgh 1979

Mehan, U., and Townsend, D., '"Nation" and the gaze of the other in eighth-century Northumbria', *Comparative literature* liii.1 (2001), 1–26

Meijns, B., 'Communautés de chanoines dépendant d'abbayes bénédictines pendant le haut Moyen Âge. L'exemple du comté de Flandre', *Revue bénédictine* cxiii (2003), 90–123

Menzer, M., 'Multilingual glosses, bilingual text: English, Anglo-Norman and Latin in three manuscripts of Ælfric's Grammar', in J.T. Lionarons (ed.), *Old English literature in its manuscript context*, Morgantown, West Virginia 2004, 95–119

Millett, B., 'The pastoral context of the Trinity and Lambeth homilies', in W. Scase (ed.), *Essays in manuscript geography: vernacular manuscripts of the English West Midlands from the Conquest to the sixteenth century*, Turnhout 2007, 43–64

Mitchell, S.K., *Studies in taxation under John and Henry III*, New Haven 1914

Morris, C.J., *Marriage and murder in eleventh-century Northumbria: a study of 'De obsessione Dunelmi'* (Borthwick Paper no. 82), York 1992

Morris, R.K., 'Kirk Hammerton church: the tower and the fabric', *Archaeological Journal* cxxxiii (1976), 91–103

Morris, R.K., 'Churches in York and its hinterland: building patterns and stone sources in the 11th and 12th centuries', in Blair, *Minsters and parish churches*, 191–9

Morris, R.K., and Cambridge, E., 'Beverley minster before the thirteenth century', in C. Wilson (ed.), *Medieval art and architecture in the East Riding of Yorkshire*: *British Archaeological Association Conference Transactions* ix (1989), 9–32

Mostert, M., *The political theology of Abbo of Fleury*, Hilversum 1987

Musset, L., *Normandie romane, I, La Basse-Normandie*, 2 edn, La Pierre-qui-Vire, 1975

Myers, J.L., 'History and antiquities of Water Stratford', *Records of Buckinghamshire* vii (1897), 115

Mynors, R.A.B., *Durham cathedral manuscripts to the end of the twelfth century*, Oxford 1939

—, *Catalogue of the manuscripts of Balliol College, Oxford*, Oxford 1963

Mynors, R.A.B., and Thomson, R.M., *Catalogue of the manuscripts of Hereford Cathedral Library*, Cambridge 1993

Nairn, I., and Pevsner, N., *The buildings of England, Sussex*, Harmondsworth 1965

Nelson, J.L., 'Presidential address: England and the Continent in the ninth century: II. The Vikings and others', *TRHS* 6 ser. xviii (2003), 1–28

Nichols, S., and Thurlby, M., 'Notes on the Romanesque capitals from the east arch of the presbytery of Hereford cathedral', *The Friends of Hereford Cathedral Fifty First Annual Report* (1985), 14–26

Nightingale, J., *Monasteries and patrons in the Gorze reform: Lotharingia, c.850–1000*, Oxford 2001

Niles, J.D., 'The wasteland of Loegria: Geoffrey of Monmouth's reinvention of the Anglo-Saxon past', in W.F. Gentrup (ed.), *Reinventing the middle ages and the Renaissance*, Arizona 1998, 1–18

Noble, T.F.X., and van Engen, J. (eds), *European transformations: the long twelfth century*, Notre Dame 2012

Noel, W., 'The Utrecht Psalter in England: continuity and experiment', in K. van der Horst, W. Noel and W.C.M. Wüstefeld (eds), *The Utrecht Psalter in medieval art: picturing the psalms of David*, 't Goy, the Netherlands 1996, 120–65

Nortier, G., *Les Bibliothèques médiévales des abbayes bénédictines de Normandie*, Paris 1971

Norton, C., 'History, wisdom and illumination', in D.W. Rollason (ed.), *Symeon of Durham*, 61–105

O'Brien, B.R., 'Forgery and the literacy of the early common law', *Albion* xvii (1995), 1–18

—, 'The Becket conflict and the invention of the myth of *lex non scripta*', in J.A. Bush and A. Wijffels (eds), *Learning the law: teaching and the transmission of law in England, 1150–1900*, London 1999, 1–16

—, *God's peace and king's peace: the laws of Edward the Confessor*, Philadelphia 1999

—, 'The *Instituta Cnuti* and the translation of English law', *ANS* xxv (2003), 177–97

—, 'Forgers of the law and their readers: the crafting of English political identities between the Norman Conquest and the Magna Carta', *PS: Political Science and Politics* xliii (2010), 467–73

—, *Reversing Babel: translation among the English during an age of conquest, c 800 to c.1200*, Newark, Delaware 2011

—, 'An English book of laws from the time of Glanvill', in S. Jenks, J. Rose and C. Whittick (eds), *Making the common law – institutions, lawyers, and texts: studies in medieval legal history in honour of Paul Brand*, Leiden 2012, 51–67

Offler, H.S., 'The tractate *De iniusta uexacione Willelmi episcopi primi*', *EHR* lxvi (1951), 321–41

—, *Medieval historians of Durham*, Durham 1958, repr. in idem, *North of the Tees: studies in medieval British history*, ed. A.J. Piper and A.I. Doyle (Collected Studies, Aldershot 1996), no. i

—, 'Hexham and the Historia regum', *Transactions of the Architectural and Archaeological Society of Durham and Northumberland* new ser. ii (1970), 51–62, repr. in H.S. Offler, *North of the Tees: studies in medieval British history*, ed. A.J. Piper and A.I. Doyle (Collected Studies, Aldershot 1996), no. x

O'Reilly, J., 'The library of scripture: views from the Vivarium and Wearmouth-Jarrow', in P. Binski and W.G. Noel (eds), *New offerings, ancient treasures: essays in medieval art for George Henderson*, Stroud 2001, 3–39

Ó Riain-Raedel, D., 'Edith, Judith, Matilda: the role of royal ladies in the propagation of the continental cult', in C. Stancliffe and E. Cambridge (eds), *Oswald: Northumbrian king to European saint*, Stamford 1995, 210–29

O'Sullivan, D., 'Normanising the north: the evidence of Anglo-Saxon and Anglo-Scandinavian sculpture', *Medieval Archaeology* lv (2011), 163–91

Overbey, K.E., 'Taking place: reliquaries and territorial authority in the Bayeux embroidery', in M.K. Foys and K.E. Overbey (eds), *The Bayeux Tapestry: new approaches*, Woodbridge 2009, 36–50

—, 'Postcolonial', *Studies in Iconography* xxxiii (2012), 145–56

Owen, O., 'The strange beast that is the English Urnes style', in J. Graham-Campbell and others (eds), *Vikings and the Danelaw: select papers from the proceedings of the Thirteenth Viking Congress, Nottingham and York, 21–30 August 1997*, Oxford 2001, 203–22

Oxford dictionary of national biography, Oxford 2004, with subsequent online additions at http://www.oxforddnb.com/ [citations are only given from the online version where there is no corresponding entry in the printed form]

Pächt, O., and Alexander, J.J.G., *Illuminated manuscripts in the Bodleian Library Oxford, 3. British, Irish, and Icelandic schools*, Oxford 1973

Palazzo, E., *A history of liturgical books from the beginning to the thirteenth century*, tr. M. Beaumont, Collegeville, MN 1998

Park, D., and Welford, P., 'The medieval polychromy of Winchester cathedral', in Crook (ed.), *Winchester*, 123–38

Parker, E., 'The scriptorium of Bury St Edmunds in the twelfth century', unpubl. Ph.D. diss. London 1984

Parker, J.H., *An introduction to the study of Gothic architecture*, Oxford 1849

Parkes, M.B., 'Archaizing hands in English manuscripts', in J.P. Carley and C.G.C. Tite (eds), *Books and collectors, 1200–1700: essays presented to Andrew Watson*, London 1997, 101–41

—, *Their hands before our eyes: a closer look at scribes*, Aldershot 2008

Partner, N., *Serious entertainments: the writing of history in twelfth-century England*, Chicago 1977

Pearsall, D., 'Medieval literature and historical enquiry', *Modern Language Review* xcix (2004), xxxi–xlii

Pelteret, D.A.E., *Catalogue of English post-Conquest vernacular documents*, Woodbridge 1990

Pepys, W.C., and Godman, E., *The church of St Dunstan, Stepney*, London 1905

Pevsner, N., *The buildings of England, North-West and South Norfolk*, Harmondsworth 1962

—, *The buildings of England, Berkshire*, Harmondsworth 1966

—, *The buildings of England, County Durham*, 2 edn rev. by E. Williamson, Harmondsworth 1983

—, *The buildings of England, Warwickshire*, Harmondsworth 1966

—, *The buildings of England, Wiltshire*, Harmondsworth 1975

—, *The buildings of England, Worcestershire*, Harmondsworth 1968

—, *The buildings of England, Yorkshire, West Riding*, 2 edn rev. by E. Radcliffe, Harmondsworth 1967
Pevsner, N., and Harris, J., *The buildings of England, Lincolnshire*, Harmondsworth 1964
Pevsner, N., and Williamson, E., *The buildings of England, Buckinghamshire*, New Haven and London 2000
Pevsner, N., and Wilson, B., *The buildings of England, Norfolk 2: North-West and South*, New Haven and London 2002
Pfaff, R.W., 'Lanfranc's supposed purge of the Anglo-Saxon calendar', in T. Reuter (ed.), *Warriors and churchmen in the high middle ages: essays presented to Karl Leyser*, London 1992, 95–108
—, 'Eadui Basan: Scriptorum princeps?', in C. Hicks (ed.), *England in the eleventh century: proceedings of the 1990 Harlaxton Symposium*, Stamford 1992, 267–83
—, 'Bede among the Fathers? The evidence from liturgical commemoration', *Studia patristica* xxvii (1993), 225–9
—, *The liturgy in medieval England: a history*, Cambridge 2009
Phelpstead, C., 'King, martyr and virgin: *Imitatio Christi* in Ælfric's Life of St Edmund', in A. Bale (ed.), *St Edmund, king and martyr: changing images of a medieval saint*, Woodbridge 2009, 27–44
Philippart, G., *Les Légendiers latins et autres manuscrits hagiographiques* (Typologie des sources du Moyen Âge occidental xxiv–xxv, 1977)
Phillips, D., *Excavations at York Minster, ii: the cathedral of Archbishop Thomas of Bayeux*, Royal Commission on the Historical Monuments of England, 1985
Philpott, M., 'The *De iniusta uexacione Willelmi episcopi primi* and canon law in Anglo-Norman Durham', in D.W. Rollason and others (eds), *Anglo-Norman Durham*, 125–37
Piper, A.J., 'The Durham cantor's book (Durham, Dean and Chapter Library, MS B.IV.24', in D.W. Rollason and others (eds), *Anglo-Norman Durham*, 79–92
Plucknett, F.T., *Early English legal literature*, Cambridge 1958
Plunkett, S.J., 'Anglo-Saxon stone sculpture in Suffolk', in S. West (ed.), *A corpus of Anglo-Saxon material from Suffolk, East Anglian Archaeology Report No. 84*, Ipswich 1998, 323–57
Porée, [A.], *Histoire de l'abbaye du Bec*, Evreux 1901
Powicke, M., 'Maurice of Rievaulx', *EHR* xxvi (1921), 17–29
Pratt, D., 'Written law and the communication of authority in tenth-century England', in D.W. Rollason and others (eds), *England and the Continent in the tenth century*, 331–50
Prestwich, J.O., 'War and finance in the Anglo-Norman state', *TRHS* 5 ser. iv (1954), 19–43
—, 'The military household of the Norman kings', in M. Strickland (ed.), *Anglo-Norman warfare*, Woodbridge 1992, 93–127

Prior, E.S., and Gardner, A., *An account of medieval figure sculpture in England*, Cambridge 1912

Quicherat, J., 'Critique des deux plus anciennes chartes de l'abbaye de Saint-Germain des Prés', *BEC* xxvi (1865), 513–55

Quirk, R.N., 'Winchester cathedral in the tenth century', *Archaeological Journal* cxiv (1957), 28–68

—, 'Winchester New Minster and its 10th-century tower', *Journal of the British Archaeological Association* 3 ser. xxiv (1961), 16–54

Raban, S., *A second Domesday? The Hundred Rolls of 1279–80*, Oxford 2004

RCHME, 'Excavations in the west bailey at Corfe Castle', *Medieval archaeology* iv (1960), 29–55

RCHME, *An inventory of historical monuments in the county of Dorset, II, South-East*, London 1970

Reed, M.F., 'Sculpture and identity in late Saxon East Anglia', unpubl. Ph.D. diss. York 2008

Reeve, M.M., 'The retrospective effigies of Anglo-Saxon bishops at Wells cathedral', *Somerset Archaeology and Natural History* cxlii (1998), 235–59

Reuter, T., 'Plunder and tribute in the Carolingian empire', *TRHS* 5 ser. xxxv (1985), 75–94

—, '"You can't take it with you": testaments, hoards and moveable wealth in Europe, 600–1100', in E. Tyler (ed.), *Treasure in the medieval West*, York 2000, 11–24

Richardson, W., 'The Venerable Bede and a lost Saxon monastery in Yorkshire', *Yorkshire Archaeological Journal* lvii (1985), 15–22

Rickman, T., *An attempt to discriminate the styles of architecture in England, from the Conquest to the Reformation, with a sketch of the Grecian and Roman orders; notices of numerous British edifices; and some remarks on the architecture of a part of France*, 5 edn, London 1848

Ridyard, S.J., '*Condigna veneratio*: post-Conquest attitudes to the saints of the Anglo-Saxons', *ANS* ix (1987), 179–206

—, *The royal saints of Anglo-Saxon England: a study of West Saxon and East Anglian cults*, Cambridge 1988

Rigg, A.G., *A history of Anglo-Latin literature, 1066–1422*, Cambridge 1992

Rigold, S.E., 'Romanesque bases, in and south-east of the limestone belt', in M.R. Apted, R. Gilyard-Beer and A.D. Saunders (eds), *Ancient monuments and their interpretation: essays presented to A.J. Taylor*, Chichester 1977, 99–137

—, Review of H. Taylor, *Anglo-Saxon architecture*, Cambridge 1977, *Journal of the British Archaeological Association* cxxxii (1979), 113–15

Robinson, P.R., *Catalogue of dated and datable manuscripts, c.737–1600, in Cambridge libraries*, Woodbridge 1988

Rodwell, W., 'Anglo-Saxon church building: aspects of design and construction', in Butler and Morris, *The Anglo-Saxon Church*, 156–75, repr. in C.E. Karkov (ed.), *The archaeology of Anglo-Saxon England: basic readings*, New York 1999, 195–231

—, 'New glimpses of Edward the Confessor's abbey at Westminster', in R. Mortimer (ed.), *Edward the Confessor: the man and the legend*, Woodbridge 2009, 151–67

Rogers, N., 'The Waltham abbey relic-list', in C. Hicks (ed.), *England in the eleventh century* (Harlaxton Medieval Studies ii, 1992), 157–81

Rollason, D.W., 'Lists of saints' resting-places in Anglo-Saxon England', *ASE* vii (1978), 61–93

—, 'The Miracles of St Benedict: a window on early medieval France', in H. Mayr-Harting and R.I. Moore (eds), *Studies in medieval history presented to R.H.C. Davis*, London 1985, 73–90

—, 'Relic-cults as an instrument of royal policy c.900–c.1050', *ASE* xv (1986), 91–103

—, 'The wanderings of St Cuthbert', in idem (ed.), *Cuthbert: saint and patron*, Durham 1987, 47–59

—, 'Symeon of Durham and the community of Durham in the eleventh century', in C. Hicks (ed.), *England in the eleventh century: proceedings of the 1990 Harlaxton Symposium*, Stamford 1992, 183–98

—, 'St Oswald in post-Conquest England', in C. Stancliffe and E. Cambridge (eds), *Oswald: Northumbrian king to European saint*, Stamford 1995, 164–77

—, *Northumbria, 500–1100: creation and destruction of a kingdom*, Cambridge 2003

—, 'The making of the *Libellus de exordio*: the evidence of erasures and alterations in the two earliest manuscripts', in D.W. Rollason (ed.), *Symeon of Durham*, 140–56

—, (ed.), *Symeon of Durham: historian of Durham and the North*, Stamford 1998

Rollason, D.W., M. Harvey and M. Prestwich (eds), *Anglo-Norman Durham, 1093–1193*, Woodbridge 1994

Rollason, D.W., and Gore, D., *Sources for York history before 1100*, Archaeology of York, York 1998

Rollason, D.W., Leyser, C., and Williams, H. (eds), *England and the Continent in the tenth century; studies in honour of Wilhelm Levison (1876–1947)* (Studies in the early Middle Ages xxxvii, 2010)

Rollason, L., 'Medieval mortuary rolls: prayers for the dead and travel in medieval England', *Northern History* xlviii (2010), 187–223

—, *Memorial books from the British Library*, London forthcoming

Round, J.H., *Feudal England*, London 1909

—, *Peerage and pedigree: studies in peerage law and family history*, London 1910

Rubenstein, J., 'The life and writings of Osbern of Canterbury', in R. Eales and R. Sharpe (eds), *Canterbury and the Norman Conquest*, 27–40

—, 'Liturgy against history: the competing visions of Lanfranc and Eadmer of Canterbury', *Speculum* lxxiv (1999), 279–309

Rumble, A.R., 'The structure and reliability of the *Codex Wintoniensis* (British Museum, Additional MS 15350); the cartulary of Winchester Cathedral Priory', unpubl. Ph.D. diss. London 1979

—, 'A Domesday postscript and the earliest surviving pipe roll', in I. Wood and N. Lund (eds), *People and places in northern Europe, 500–1600: essays in honour of Peter Hayes Sawyer*, Woodbridge 1991, 123–30

—, 'Rudborne, Thomas (*fl.* 1447–1454)', in *ODNB* xlviii. 74

Rushforth, R., 'The eleventh- and early twelfth-century manuscripts of Bury St Edmunds Abbey', unpubl. Ph.D. diss. Cambridge 2002

—, *Saints in English kalendars before A.D. 1100* (HBS cxvii, 2008)

Salter, H.E., 'Geoffrey of Monmouth and Oxford', *EHR* xxxiv (1919), 382–5

Sawyer, P.H., *Anglo-Saxon charters: an annotated list and bibliography*, London 1968

—, *The age of the Vikings*, 2 edn, London 1971

Saxl, F., *English sculptures of the twelfth century*, London 1954

Sayers, J., '"Original", cartulary and chronicle: the case of the abbey of Evesham', *Fälschungen im Mittelalter*, iv. 371–95

Scarfe, N., *Suffolk in the middle ages*, Woodbridge 1986

Scarisbrick, J.J., *Henry VIII*, London 1968

Schapiro, M., 'A note on the wall strips of Saxon architecture', *Journal of the Society of Architectural Historians* xvii (1959), 123–25, repr. in M. Schapiro, *Late Antique, early Christian and medieval art: selected papers*, New York 1979, 242–48

Scharer, A., 'The writing of history at King Alfred's court', *Early medieval Europe* v (1996), 177–206

Schiller, G., *Iconography of Christian art, ii. The passion of Christ*, tr. J. Seligman, London 1972

Scholz, B.W., 'The canonization of Edward the Confessor', *Speculum* xxxvi (1961), 38–60

—, 'Two forged charters from the abbey of Westminster and their relationship with St. Denis', *EHR* lxxvi (1961), 466–75

Schulenburg, J.T., *Forgetful of their sex: female sanctity and society, 500–1100*, Chicago 1998

Shapland, M., 'St Mary's, Broughton, Lincolnshire: a thegnly tower-nave in the late Anglo-Saxon landscape', *Archaeological Journal* clxv (2008), 471–519

Sharpe, R., 'Goscelin's St Augustine and St Mildreth: hagiography and liturgy in context', *Journal of Theological Studies* xli (1990), 502–16

—, 'Eadmer's letter to the monks of Glastonbury concerning St Dunstan's disputed remains', in L. Abrams and J.P. Carley (eds), *The archaeology and history of Glastonbury abbey*, Woodbridge 1991, 205–15

—, 'The prefaces of *Quadripartitus*', in G. Garnett and J. Hudson (eds), *Law and government in medieval England and Normandy*, Cambridge 1994, 148–72

—, 'The setting of St Augustine's translation, 1091', in R. Eales and R. Sharpe (eds), *Canterbury and the Norman Conquest*, 1–13

—, *A handlist of the Latin writers of Great Britain and Ireland before 1540*, Turnhout 1997

—, 'Symeon as pamphleteer', in D.W. Rollason (ed.), *Symeon of Durham*, 214–29

—, 'The use of writs in the eleventh century', *ASE* xxxii (2003), 247–91

—, 'The dating of *Quadripartitus* again', in S. Jurasinski, L. Oliver and A. Rabin (eds), *English law before Magna Carta: Felix Liebermann and 'Die Gesetze der Angelsachsen'*, Leiden 2010, 81–93

Sharpe, R., Carley, J.P., Thomson, R.M., and Watson, A.G. (eds), *English Benedictine libraries: the shorter catalogues* (Corpus of British medieval library catalogues iv, 1996)

Shopkow, L., *History and community: Norman historical writing in the eleventh and twelfth centuries*, Washington, DC 1997

Short, I., 'Gaimar et les débuts de l'historiographie en langue française', in D. Buschinger (ed.), *Chroniques nationales et chroniques universelles* (Göppinger Arbeiten zur Germanistik dviii), Göppingen 1990, 155–63

—, 'Patrons and polyglots: French literature in twelfth-century England', *ANS* xiv (1992), 229–49

—, '*Tam Angli quam Franci*: self-definition in Anglo-Norman England', *ANS* xviii (1995), 153–75

—, 'What was Gaimar's *Estoire des Bretuns*?', *Cultura neolatina* lxxi (2011), 147–9

Silvestre, H., 'Le hand-list de Laistner-King et les mss bruxellois de Bède', *Scriptorium* vi (1952), 287–93

—, Simmons, C.A., *Reversing the Conquest: history and myth in nineteenth-century British literature*, New Brunswick 1990

Simpson, L., 'The King Alfred/St Cuthbert episode in the *Historia de sancto Cuthberto*: its significance for mid-tenth-century English history', in G. Bonner, D.W. Rollason and C. Stancliffe (eds), *St Cuthbert, his cult and his community to AD 1200*, Woodbridge 1989, 397–411

Sims-Williams, P., 'The early Welsh Arthurian poems', in R. Bromwich, A.O.H. Jarman and B.F. Roberts (eds), *The Arthur of the Welsh: the Arthurian legend in medieval Welsh literature*, Cardiff 1991, 33–71

Smalley, B., *Historians in the middle ages*, London 1974

Smith, T.P., 'The Anglo-Saxon churches of Bedfordshire', *Bedfordshire Archaeological Journal* iii (1966), 7–14

Smith, W., *A new and compendious history of the county of Warwick*, Birmingham 1830
Smyth, A., 'The effect of Scandinavian raiders on the English and Irish Churches: a preliminary reassessment', in B. Smith (ed.), *Britain and Ireland 900–1300: insular responses to medieval European change*, Cambridge 1999, 1–38
Sole, L.M., 'Some Anglo-Saxon Cuthbert *liturgica*: the manuscript evidence', *Revue bénédictine* cviii (1998), 104–44
Sønnesyn, S., *William of Malmesbury and the ethics of history*, Woodbridge 2012
Southern, R.W., 'The Canterbury forgeries', *EHR* lxxiii (1958), 193–226
—, *Saint Anselm and his biographer*, Cambridge 1963
—, 'Aspects of the European tradition of historical writing: 4. The sense of the past', *TRHS* 5 ser. xxiii (1973), 243–63, repr. in R.J. Bartlett (ed.), *History and historians: selected papers of R.W. Southern*, Oxford 2004, 66–83
—, *Saint Anselm: a portrait in a landscape*, Cambridge 1990
Stacey, R.C., *Politics, policy and finance under Henry III 1216–1245*, Oxford 1987
Stafford, P., *Queen Emma and Queen Edith: queenship and women's power in eleventh-century England*, Oxford 1997
Stalley, R.A., 'A twelfth-century patron of architecture: a study of the buildings erected by Roger, bishop of Salisbury, 1102–1139', *Journal of the British Archaeological Association* xxxiv (1971), 62–83
—, *Early medieval architecture*, Oxford 1999
Stenton, D.M., *English justice between the Norman Conquest and the Great Charter*, Philadelphia 1964
Stenton, F.M., *The Latin charters of the Anglo-Saxon period*, Oxford 1955
Stocker, D., and Everson, P., *Summoning St Michael: early Romanesque towers in Lincolnshire*, Oxford 2006
Stocker, D., and Vince, A., 'The early Norman castle at Lincoln and a re-evaluation of the west front of Lincoln cathedral', *Medieval Archaeology* xli (1997), 223–33
Stokes, P.A., 'English vernacular script, *ca* 990–*ca* 1035', unpubl. Ph.D. diss. Cambridge 2006
—, 'The problem of grade in English vernacular minuscule, *c*.1060–1220', in E. Treharne, O. Da Rold, and M. Swan (eds), *Producing and using English manuscripts in the post-Conquest period* (New Medieval Literatures xiii, 2011), 23–47
Stone, L., *Sculpture in Britain: the middle ages*, Harmondsworth 1955
Story, J.E., 'Symeon as annalist', in D.W. Rollason (ed.), *Symeon of Durham*, 202–13
Stratford, N., 'Notes on the Norman chapter house at Worcester', in G. Popper (ed.), *Medieval art and architecture at Worcester cathedral: British Archaeological Association Conference Transactions* i (1978), 51–70
Styles, T., 'Whitby revisited: Bede's explanation of *Streanæshalch*', *Nomina* xxi (1998), 133–48

Swan, M., and Treharne, E. (eds), *Rewriting Old English in the twelfth century*, Cambridge 2000

Tatlock, J.S.P., 'Geoffrey and King Arthur in "Normannicus Draco"', *Modern philology* xxxi (1933), 1–18

—, *The legendary history of Britain. Geoffrey of Monmouth's* Historia regum Britanniae *and its early vernacular versions*, Los Angeles 1950, repr. New York 1974

Tatton-Brown, T., 'The medieval fabric', in M. Hobbs (ed.), *Chichester cathedral: an historical survey*, Chichester 1994, 25–46

Tatton-Brown, T. (with Worssam, B.), 'A new survey of the fabric of the church of the Holy Trinity, Bosham, West Sussex', *Sussex Archaeological Collections* cxliv (2006), 129–54

Taylor, H.M., 'Anglo-Saxon sculpture at Knook', *Wiltshire Archaeological and Natural History Magazine* lxiii (1968), 54–7

—, 'The Anglo-Saxon cathedral church at Canterbury', *Archaeological Journal* cxxvi (1969), 101–29

Taylor, H.M., and Taylor, J., *Anglo-Saxon architecture*, Cambridge 1965–77

Taylor, H.M., and Taylor, J., 'Architectural sculpture in pre-Norman England', *Journal of the British Archaeological Association* 3 ser. xxix (1966), 3–51

Taylor, J., 'Walsingham, Thomas (*c*.1340–*c*.1422), in *ODNB* lvii. 152–4

G. Tessier, 'Originaux et pseudo-originaux carolingiens du chartrier de Saint-Denis', *BEC* cvi (1946), 35–69

Thacker, A., '*Membra disiecta*: the division of the body and the diffusion of the cult', in C. Stancliffe and E. Cambridge (eds), *Oswald: Northumbrian king to European saint*, Stamford 1995, 97–127

—, 'The cult of King Harold at Chester', in T. Scott and P. Starkey (eds), *The middle ages in the North-West*, Oxford 1995, 155–76

Thomas, H.M., 'The *Gesta Herwardi*, the English, and their conquerors', *ANS* xxi (1998), 213–32

Thomas, I.G., 'The cult of saints' relics in medieval England', unpubl. Ph.D. diss. London 1974

Thompson, S.D., *Anglo-Saxon royal diplomas: a palaeography*, Woodbridge 2006

Thomson, R.M., *Manuscripts from St Albans abbey, 1066–1235*, Woodbridge 1982

—, 'England and the twelfth-century Renaissance', *Past and Present* ci (1983), 3–21, repr. in his *England and the twelfth-century Renaissance*, Aldershot 1998

—, 'Books and learning at Gloucester abbey in the twelfth and thirteenth centuries', in J.P. Carley and C.G.C. Tite (eds), *Books and collectors, 1200–1700: essays presented to Andrew Watson*, London 1997, 3–26

—, *The Bury bible*, Woodbridge and Tokyo 2001

—, *William of Malmesbury*, 2 edn, Woodbridge 2003

—, 'Malmesbury, William of (b. *c*.1090, d. in or after 1142)', in *ODNB* xxxvi. 348–51
—, 'The use of the vernacular in manuscripts from Worcester cathedral priory', *Transactions of the Worcester Archaeological Society* xx (2006), 113–19
—, *A descriptive catalogue of the medieval manuscripts of Corpus Christi College, Oxford*, Cambridge 2011
Thorpe, J., *Registrum Roffense*, London 1769
Thurlby, M., 'A twelfth-century figure fragment from Lewes Priory', *Sussex Archaeological Collections* cxx (1982), 215–23
—, 'A note on the Romanesque sculpture at Hereford cathedral and the Herefordshire school of sculpture', *Burlington Magazine* cxxvi, no. 973 (1984), 233–4
—, 'The roles of the patron and the master mason in the first design of Durham cathedral', in D.W. Rollason and others (eds), *Anglo-Norman Durham, 1093–1193*, 161–84
—, 'The lady chapel of Glastonbury abbey', *Antiquaries Journal* lxv (1995), 107–70
—, 'Hereford cathedral: the Romanesque fabric', in D. Whitehead (ed.), *Medieval art, architecture and archaeology in Hereford*: British Archaeological Association Conference Transactions xv (1995), 15–28
—, 'Some design aspects of Kirkstall Abbey', in L.R. Hoey (ed.), *Yorkshire Monasticism: Archaeology, Art and Architecture*: British Archaeological Association Conference Transactions xvi (1995), 62–72
—, 'The influence of Norwich cathedral on Romanesque architecture in East Anglia', in I. Atherton, E. Fernie, C. Harper-Bill and H. Smith (eds), *Norwich cathedral: church, city and diocese, 1096–1996*, London and Rio Grande 1996, 136–57
—, 'L'abbatiale romane de St. Albans', in M. Baylé (ed.), *L'Architecture normande au Moyen Âge*, Caen 1997, 79–90
—, *The Herefordshire school of Romanesque sculpture*, Logaston 1999
—, 'Anglo-Saxon architecture beyond the millennium: its continuity in Norman building', in N. Hiscock (ed.), *The white mantle of churches: architecture, liturgy and art around the millennium*, Turnhout 2003, 119–37
—, 'The Romanesque churches of St Mary Magdalen at Tixover and St Mary at Morcott', *Ecclesiology Today* xxxv (2005), 23–41
—, *Romanesque architecture and sculpture in Wales*, Logaston 2006
—, 'Sarum cathedral as rebuilt by Roger, bishop of Salisbury, 1102–1139: the state of research and open questions', *Wiltshire Archaeological and Natural History Magazine* ci (2008), 130–40
—, 'Aspects of the Anglo-Saxon tradition in architectural sculpture and decoration: the "overlap" and beyond', in M.F. Reed (ed.), *New voices on insular sculpture*, Oxford 2011, 57–69

—, 'Articulation as an expression of function in Romanesque architecture', in J.A. Franklin, T.A. Heslop and C. Stevenson (eds), *Architecture and interpretation: a Festschrift for Eric Fernie*, Woodbridge 2012, 42–59

—, *The Herefordshire school of Romanesque sculpture (with a history of the anarchy in Herefordshire by Bruce Coplestone-Crow)*, Logaston 2013

Tinti, F., *Sustaining belief: the Church of Worcester from c.870 to c.1100*, Farnham 2010

—, 'England and the papacy in the tenth century', in D. Rollason and others, *England and the Continent in the tenth century*, 163–84

Todd, J.M., and Offler, H.S., 'A medieval chronicle from Scotland', *Scottish Historical Review* xlvii (1968), 151–9, repr. in H.S. Offler, *North of the Tees: studies in medieval British history*, ed. A.J. Piper and A.I. Doyle (Collected Studies, Aldershot 1996), no. xi

Tolhurst, J.B.L. (ed.), *The monastic breviary of Hyde Abbey, Winchester, volume vi. Introduction to the English monastic breviaries* (HBS lxxx, 1942)

Tout, T.F., *Chapters in the administrative history of mediaeval England*, Manchester 1920–33

Toy, J., 'St Botulph: an English saint in Scandinavia', in M. Carver (ed.), *The cross goes north: processes of conversion in northern Europe, AD 300–1300*, York 2003, 565–70

—, *English saints in the medieval liturgies of the Scandinavian churches* (HBS, Subsidia vi, 2009)

Treharne, E., 'Periodization and categorization: the silence of (the) English in the twelfth century', *New Medieval Literatures* viii (2006), 247–73

—, 'The architextual editing of Early English', in A.S.G. Edwards and T. Takako (eds), *Poetica* lxxi (2009), 1–13

—, *Living through the Conquest: the politics of early English, 1020–1220*, Oxford 2012

Tudor-Craig, P., 'Controversial sculptures: the Southwell tympanum, the Glastonbury respond, the Leigh Christ', *ANS* xii (1990), 211–31

Tweddle, D., and others, *Corpus of Anglo-Saxon stone sculpture, IV, South-East England*, Oxford 1995

Turner, R.V., *King John*, London and New York 1994

Ugé, K., *Creating the monastic past in medieval Flanders*, Woodbridge 2005

Ullmann, W., 'On the influence of Geoffrey of Monmouth in English history', in C. Bauer, L. Boehm and M. Müller (eds), *Speculum Historiale: Geschichte im Spiegel von Geschichtsschreibung und Geschichtsdeutung*, Freiburg and Munich 1965, 257–76

Urry, W., *Thomas Becket: his last days*, ed. P. Rowe, Thrupp and Stroud 1999

Vanderputten, S., and Meijns, B., 'Gérard de Brogne en Flandre. État de la question sur les réformes monastiques du Xe siècle', *Revue du Nord* xcii (2010), 271–95

van Houts, E.M.C., *Gesta Normannorum ducum. Een studie over de handschriften, de tekst, het geschiedwerk en het genre*, Groningen 1982
—, 'Historiography and hagiography at Saint-Wandrille: the *Inventio et miracula sancti Vulfranni*', *ANS* xii (1990), 233–51
—, *Memory and gender in medieval Europe, 900–1200*, Basingstoke 1999
—, 'Latin and French as languages of the past in Normandy during the reign of Henry II: Robert of Torigni, Stephen of Rouen and Wace', in R. Kennedy and S. Meecham-Jones (eds), *Writers of the reign of Henry II. Twelve essays*, Basingstoke 2006, 53–78
van Uytfanghe, M., 'La controverse biblique et patristique autour du miracle, et ses répercussions sur l'hagiographie dans l'Antiquité tardive et le haut Moyen Âge latin', in *Hagiographie, cultures et sociétés, IVe–XIIe siècles, Actes du colloque organisé à Nanterre et à Paris 2–5 mai 1979*, Paris 1981, 205–33
Verey, D., and Brooks, A., *The buildings of England, Gloucestershire 1: the Cotswolds*, New Haven and London 2002
Vezin, J., 'Écritures imitées dans les livres et les documents du haut Moyen Âge (viie–xie siècle)', *BEC* clxv (2007), 47–66
Victoria history of the counties of England, ed. W. Page and others, London 1900–
Vidier, A., *L'Historiographie à Saint-Benoît-sur-Loire et les miracles de Saint-Benoît*, Paris 1965
Vincent, N., *Peter des Roches: an alien in English politics, 1205–1238*, Cambridge 1996
—, 'The charters of Henry II: the introduction of the royal "inspeximus" revisited', in M. Gervers (ed.), *Dating undated medieval charters*, Budapest and Woodbridge 2000, 97–120
—, *The holy blood: King Henry III and the Westminster blood relic*, Cambridge 2001
—, 'The pilgrimages of the Angevin kings of England 1154–1272', in C. Morris and P. Roberts (eds), *Pilgrimage: the English experience from Becket to Bunyan*, Cambridge 2002, 12–45
—, 'The Court', in C. Harper-Bill and N. Vincent (eds), *Henry II: new interpretations*, Woodbridge 2007, 333–4
—, 'More tales of the Conquest', in D. Crouch and K. Thompson (eds), *Normandy and its neighbours, 900–1250: essays for David Bates*, Turnhout 2011, 271–301
—, *A brief history of Britain 1066–1485*, London 2011
—, 'Rouleaux ou registres? Le choix et l'utilisation des enregistrements à la chancellerie Plantagenêt (XIIe–XIIIe siècle)', in O. Guyotjeannin and others (eds), *L'Art du registre à la chancellerie du roi de France*, Paris forthcoming
Waddell, C. (ed.), *Narrative and legislative texts from early Cîteaux* (Cîteaux: Commentarii cistercienses, Studia et documenta ix, 1999)
— (ed.), *Twelfth-century statutes from the Cistercian General Chapter* (Cîteaux: Commentarii cistercienses, Studia et documenta xii, 2002)

Wallace-Hadrill, J.M., *Early medieval history*, Oxford 1975
Waller, K.M., 'The library, scriptorium and community of Rochester cathedral priory, c.1080–1150', unpubl. Ph.D. diss. Liverpool 1981
Warren, M.R., *History on the edge: Excalibur and the borders of Britain, 1100–1300*, Minneapolis 2000
Warren, W.L., *King John*, London 1961
Watkins, C., 'The cult of Earl Waltheof at Crowland', *Hagiographica* iii (1996), 95–111
Watson, A.G., *Catalogue of dated and datable manuscripts c.700–1600 in the Department of Manuscripts, the British Library*, London 1979
Watts, L., and others, 'Kirkdale – the inscriptions', *Medieval Archaeology* xli (1997), 51–99
Webber, T., 'L'écriture des documents en Angleterre au xiie siècle', *BEC* cv (2007), 139–65
Weiss, J., 'The date of the Anglo-Norman *Boeve de Haumtone*', *Medium aevum* lv (1986), 237–41
—, 'The power and the weakness of women in Anglo-Norman romance', in C.M. Meale (ed.), *Women and literature in Britain, 1150–1500*, Cambridge 1993, 7–19
—, 'Thomas and the earl: literary and historical contexts for the *Romance of Horn*', in R. Field (ed.), *Tradition and transformation in medieval romance*, Cambridge 1999, 1–13
—, 'Emperors and Antichrists: reflections of empire in insular narrative, 1130–1250', in P. Hardman (ed.), *The matter of identity in medieval romance*, Cambridge 2002, 87–102
—, 'Anglo-Norman romance', in C. Saunders (ed.), *A companion to romance: from classical to contemporary*, Oxford 2004, 26–44
—, '*Gui de Warewic* at home and abroad', in A. Wiggins and R. Field (eds), *Guy of Warwick: icon and ancestor*, Cambridge 2007, 1–11
—, '*Mestre* and son: the role of Sabaoth and Terri in *Boeve de Haumtone*', in J. Fellows and I. Djordjevic (eds), *Sir Bevis of Hampton in literary tradition*, Cambridge 2008, 25–36
—, *The birth of romance in England*, Tempe, AZ 2009
—, 'The exploitation of ideas of pilgrimage and sainthood in *Gui de Warewic*', in L. Ashe, I. Djordjevic and J. Weiss (eds), *The exploitations of medieval romance*, Cambridge 2010, 43–56
Westgard, J.A., 'Dissemination and reception of Bede's *Historia ecclesiastica gentis Anglorum* in Germany c.731–1500: the manuscript evidence', unpubl. Ph.D. diss. Chapel Hill 2005
Whitelock, D., 'Fact and fiction in the legend of St Edmund', *Proceedings of the Suffolk Institute of Archaeology* xxxi (1967–9), 217–33
—, 'The pre-Viking age church in East Anglia', *ASE* i (1972), 1–22

—, (ed.), *English historical documents, c. 500–1042* (English Historical Documents i), 2 edn, London 1979

Williams, A., *The English and the Norman Conquest*, Woodbridge 1995

Williams, J.H., 'Roman building materials', *Transactions of the Bristol and Gloucestershire Archaeological Society* xc (1971), 95–119

Willis, R., 'The architectural history of Winchester cathedral', *Proceedings of the Annual Meeting of the Archaeological Institute* (1846), 1–79, repr. in R. Willis, *Architectural history of some English cathedrals*, I, Chicheley 1972

Wilson, D.M., *Anglo-Saxon art from the seventh century to the Norman Conquest*, London 1984

Winterbottom, M., 'The language of William of Malmesbury', in C.J. Mews, C.J. Nederman and R.M. Thomson (eds), *Rhetoric and renewal in the Latin West, 1100–1540: essays in honour of John O. Ward*, Turnhout 2003, 129–47

—, 'William of Malmesbury and the Normans', *Journal of Medieval Latin* xx (2010), 70–77

Wogan-Browne, J., 'The Life of St Osith: an introduction', in *Papers on language and literature* xli (2005), 300–305

Wood, A., 'The loss of Athelstan's gift: the politics of popular memory in Malmesbury, 1607–1633', in J. Whittle (ed.), *Landlords and tenants in Britain, 1440–1660: Tawney's agrarian problem revisited*, Woodbridge 2013, 85–99

Wood, I.N., 'Bede's Jarrow', in C.A. Lees and G.R. Overing (eds), *A place to believe in: locating medieval landscapes*, University Park, PA 2006, 67–84

—, *The origins of Jarrow: the monastery, the Slake and Ecgfrith's minster* (Bede's World Studies i), Jarrow 2008

—, 'The foundation of Bede's Wearmouth-Jarrow', in S. DeGregorio (ed.), *The Cambridge companion to Bede*, Cambridge 2010, 84–96

—, 'The gifts of Wearmouth and Jarrow', in W. Davies and P. Fouracre (eds), *The languages of gift in the early middle ages*, Cambridge 2010, 89–115

Woodman, F., 'The waterworks drawing of the Eadwine Psalter', in M. Gibson, T.A. Heslop and R.W. Pfaff (eds), *The Eadwine Psalter: text, image, and monastic culture in twelfth-century Canterbury*, London 1992, 168–85

Woolf, A., *From Pictland to Alba, 789–1070*, Edinburgh 2007

Woolf, D., *The social circulation of the past: English historical culture 1500–1730*, Oxford 2003

Wormald, P., 'Viking studies: whence and whither?', in R.T. Farrell (ed.), *The Vikings*, London and Chichester 1982, 128–53

—, 'The ninth century', in J. Campbell (ed.), *The Anglo-Saxons*, Oxford 1982, 132–59

—, 'Quadripartitus', in G. Garnett and J. Hudson (eds), *Law and government in medieval England and Normandy: essays in honour of Sir James Holt*, Cambridge 1994, 111–47, repr. in his *Legal culture*, 81–114

—, '*Laga Edwardi*: the *Textus Roffensis* and its context', *ANS* xvii (1994/95), 243–66, repr. in his *Legal culture*, 115–38

—, 'Frederick William Maitland and the earliest English law', *Law and History Review* xvi (1998), 1–25, repr. in his *Legal culture*, 45–69

—, *Legal culture in the early medieval West: law as text, image and experience*, London 1999

—, *The making of English law: King Alfred to the twelfth century*, i. *Legislation and its limits*, Oxford 1999

Wormald, F., *English kalendars before A.D. 1100* (HBS lxxii, 1934)

—, *English Benedictine kalendars after A.D. 1100* (HBS lxxvii, lxxxi, 1939–1946)

Wright, T., 'Anglo-Saxon architecture, illustrated from illuminated manuscripts', *Archaeological Journal* i (1844), 24–35

Wynn-Reeves, P., 'English stiff-leaf sculpture', unpubl. Ph.D. diss. London 1952

Younge, G.R., 'The Canterbury Anthology: an Old English manuscript in its Anglo-Norman context', unpubl. Ph.D. diss. Cambridge 2012

—, '"Those were good days": representations of the Anglo-Saxon past in the Old English homily on St. Neot', *Review of English Studies* new ser. lxiii (2012), 349–69

Zatta, J. Dick, 'The *Vie Seinte Osith*: hagiography and politics in Anglo-Norman England', *Papers on Language and Literature* xli (2005), 306–38

Zarnecki, G., *Later English Romanesque sculpture, 1140–1210*, London 1953

—, 'The Chichester reliefs', *Archaeological Journal* cx (1953), 106–19

—, 'The sources of English Romanesque sculpture', *Actes du XVIIème congrès internationale de l'histoire de l'art*, The Hague 1955, 171–8

—, *English Romanesque lead sculpture*, London 1957

—, *The early sculpture of Ely cathedral*, London 1958

—, 'The Romanesque capitals in the south transept of Worcester cathedral', in G. Popper (ed.), *Medieval art and architecture at Worcester cathedral*: *British Archaeological Association Conference Transactions* i (1978, 38–42

—, 'Romanesque sculpture in Normandy and England in the eleventh century', *ANS* i (1978), 168–89

—, *Romanesque Lincoln: the sculpture of the cathedral*, Lincoln 1988

General Index

Abbo of Fleury 17, 77–8, 83–4, 89, 92n, 93
abbots, character of Norman in England 118–19, 130
Abingdon, abbey 53, 87, 164, 172, 195
    abbot, *see* Faricius
    chronicle 78, 90–91, 186
acanthus-leaf 319, 349, 355
Adrevaldus, m. of Fleury 84–5, 92n
Adulfus, see Æthwulf
Ælfheah (Alphege), archbp of Canterbury and st 195
Ælfric of Eynsham 51–2, 314
Æthelberht II, kg and st 202, 211
Æthelburh st, 54–5, 58, 72
Æthelmund, ? kg of the South Saxons 41–2
Æthelnoth, thegn 172–3
Æthelred II, kg of England 120, 124–5, 201n, 203, 235
Æthelstan, kg of England 50, 135, 205, 215, 220, 280, 287
    and see Guthrum
Æthelthryth, abbess of Ely and st 54–6, 63, 65, 68, 78n, 88–9, 93
Æthelweard, chronicler 17, 81, 83, 135
Æthelwig, abbot of Evesham 223
Æthelwine, bp of Durham 22, 110
Æthelwold, abbot, bp and st 30–31, 36–8, 40, 45, 83, 88, 118, 128, 196
    and see Libellus
Æthwulf (*Adulfus,* Æthelwulf), bp? and st 30, 41
Aidan, bp of Lindisfarne and st 68, 137
Ailred of Rievaulx 15, 103, 194, 197
    on Battle of the Standard 101
    on saints of Hexham 105, 107
Alban, st 53–4, 63–4, 66, 68, 200
Alcuin 78, 82, 87, 87–8

Aldhelm, ab. and st 87, 118
    Life of 19
    shrine of 346
Alfred, kg of the Anglo-Saxons 81, 85, 118, 143, 151–3, 200, 204–5, 209, 220, 239, 241, 257
    and see Domboc
Alfred, the atheling 126, 141n, 142
Alphege, archbp of Canterbury and st, *see* Ælfheah
'Alstemus', kg 124
Amesbury, abbey 201
Ancarig, see Thorney
Anglo-Saxon Chronicle 4, 18–19, 79n, 81–2, 88, 91, 93, 139, 147–8
Anna, kg of East Angles 27, 41
annals, *see* St Neots, Winchester
Anselm, archbp of Canterbury and st 61, 80–81, 106, 120, 139, 221, 331
arcade, blind 317, 327, 330, 335
arches, triangular 310, 314, 321, 335
Arcoid, canon of St Pauls 20
Arthur, kg 134–7, 143–9, 155, 202, 204–6, 213, 226–7, 277–9, 281
Articuli decem 236, 244, 248, 256–8
Articuli Willelmi 234n, 242
Arundel, castle 275n
Ashdown, (*Assandune*) battle 18, 85n
Asser, bp 81n, 101
assizes of Henry II 229–30, 242n, 244, 267
Augustine, archbp of Canterbury and st 54, 56, 58, 62, 66–8, 128, 139, 193
Autheuil 345

Balderton 354
Baldred, kg in Wessex 204–5
baluster shafts 310–11, 322, 334, 345

Bardsey 321
Barfleur 135, 202
Barfreston 350
Barking, abbey 58, 87
Barnack 318, 354–6
Barnburgh 347
Barnsley, Roman villa at 355
Barton-le-Street 350–51
Barton-on-the-Heath 340
Bath 357
Battle, abbey 72, 221
Bayeux 135–6
    and see Odo, Wace
beakhead ornament 344–6
beast-head label stops 346, 356
Bec, abbey 123–4, 130–33, 139
    and see Robert, Stephen of Rouen
Bede 3, 23, 40, 44, 47–74, 93, 102, 123, 128, 193, 277
Bedverus 135–7
Benedict, st, *Rule* 48–9
Bernay, abbey 320
Bertin, st, *Life* of 34–6, 40, 42–4
Beverley, minster 320
Beverstone 353
Bewcastle, cross 346
Bibury, church of St Mary 337, 358
Billingham 334
Birinus, bp of Dorchester and st 53–4, 64
Blyth, priory 329
Boeve de Haumtone 275n, 279, 283
Bosham, church 336–7
    Harold's hall at 316
Botwulf (Botolph), st 27–45
Bovo, ab. 34–5
Bradbourne, church of All Saints 344–5
Bradford-on-Avon, church of St Laurence 314, 327, 333, 335, 346
Brand, ab. of Peterborough 318
Brayton 347
Breac Maedhog 352
Bredwardine 338
Breedon-on-the-Hill 350
Bregwin, archbp of Canterbury and st 20–21
Brimpsfield 316

Britons, assessment of character of 277–8
Brittany 23, 132, 134–5, 202, 279, 281
    and see Constance, Geoffrey
Brixworth 332
Brompton-in-Allerton, hogback tombs at 357
Broughton 320
Brutus 143–4, 153
Bully 340
burial, recorded in chronicles 80–81, 83, 101
    rights of churches to 261
Burton 23, 165, 172–3, 176–7, 186, 188
Bury St Edmunds, abbey 69, 71, 81n, 164–5, 192, 195n, 196, 200–201, 207–8, 219, 296, 310, 328, 334, 349–50
Byrhtferth of Ramsey 84n, 95–6, 101, 110
Byton 338
Bywell St Andrew 334

Cador, duke of Cornwall 144, 147
Caedmon 310, 314
Caen 136
    abbeys of 138, 309, 315, 323–5, 327–8, 334
calendar 56, 58, 61, 63, 72n, 129, 137, 199n, 289–90, 295
Calverton 350
Cambridge 332
Campsall 343
canonisation 193, 196, 199
canons, Augustinian (regular) 8, 48, 56
    secular, replacing monks or nuns 19, 77, 92
Canterbury 19, 81n, 82, 187, 195, 207, 225, 292, 295–6, 299, 304–6, 309, 322, 331
    archbishops, *see* Aelfhere, Ælfheah, Anselm, Bregwin, Dunstan, Oda, Ralph, Robert, Theobald, Thomas
    Christ Church (cathedral priory) 14, 51, 57–8, 60–61, 63, 66, 73, 164–6, 185, 185, 227, 289–90, 293, 299, 301n, 303, 316, 323, 325, 327–8
    and see Eadmer, Gervase

St Augustine's, abbey 8, 51, 58, 62, 164, 227, 324–5, 328
cantor, *see* precentor
capitals,
    bulbous 311, 315, 321
    cushion 315, 321, 329, 343, 353
    volute 315, 326, 354
Cartae antiquae rolls 191, 210, 216
Cartae baronum 199
Castle Hedingham, church of St Nicholas 348–9
Castle Rising 350
Castor 338
Celtic peoples, characterisation of 278–81, 286–7
Centwine, kg of Wessex 204–5
Cenwalh, kg of Wessex 204–5
Cerdic, kg of Wessex 143–56, 194
Cerisy-la-Forêt, church of Saint-Vigor 315
Chancery, treatment of pre-Conquest acts 208–11, 214
Charles [II] the Bald, kg, emperor 179–80, 185–6
charters
    Anglo-Saxon, in later confirmations 191–226, 237n
        cited in post-Conquest courts 192, 210–22, 226
        for laymen 217–18, 226–7
        models for later acts 192, 203–4
    copies figurées 162, 178–9, 185
    forgery, motives 6, 161–2, 171, 204, 214–15, 224, 227
        comparative chronology 185–6, 188–9
    fraudulently secured 196
    imitative 160–90
    Inspeximus form 203, 210–11, 214
    Merovingian and Carolingian 176–87
    sources for saints' lives 36–8, 83
    written in gold 212–13
Chedworth, Roman villa at 355
Chelric 146–7
Chertsey, abbey 87, 207–8
chevron pattern 324, 332–4

Chichester, bishops, *see* Ralph
    cathedral 324–5, 351
    reliefs 351, 354–6
Cistercians 47, 56–7, 74, 103, 111
Cnut, kg of England 125, 148, 187n, 192–4, 200, 209, 220, 233–46, 258, 260, 262, 264–5, 267, 285, 296
Coelfrith, ab. 27, 40
'Colbertine Cnut' 7–8, 242, 252–71
Colchester 278, 283
    castle 325
    hospital of St Mary Magdalene 198
Coldingham, monastery 22, 78n, 93
Coleshill 338, 350
Cologne 317
colophon 297, 303–4
Consiliatio Cnuti 233, 238, 240–43, 248, 256–9, 262, 265, 269
Constance of Brittany 134
Constantine, kg 144, 147, 156
Constitutiones Canuti regis de foresta 238n
Corfe, castle 325–6
coronation, 200, 248
    pledges given by kings at 232, 236–7, 252, 285
Corringham, church 336
Corvey 320
cross, free-standing 299n, 303, 346–9, 353
Crowland, abbey 40, 43, 127–8, 198n
Cuthbert, bishop of Lindisfarne and st 4, 18, 21, 23n, 85–6, 332–3
    community of 85
    liturgy for 50, 54–6, 63, 68
    and see Durham
    Lives of 50 -51

Darlaston 172–4, 176–7, 186
De obsessione Dunelmi 96, 98–100
De primo Saxonum adventu 106
decapitation, as topos 89–90
Decreta Willelmi 236
Deerhurst,
    church 314, 326, 329, 346, 355–6
Dombóc of Alfred 233, 239–40

Donemuthe, Donaemuthan 79, 81–2
Dorchester, bishops, *see* Birinus, Wulfwig
Dover 208, 220
   castle 114
   St Mary-in-Castro 332
Draco Normannicus, see Stephen of Rouen
Dudo of Saint-Quentin 123–6, 131, 139
Dunstan, bp, archbp of Canterbury and st 19, 83n, 84, 118, 139, 193, 213
Durham, Anglo-Saxon saints at 358
   bishops, *see* Æthelric, Æthelwine, Hugh of le Puiset, Ranulf, William of Saint-Calais
   cathedral priory 71, 98, 308, 310, 317, 327, 330–31, 332–6, 347
   chronicles 81–5, 92–3, 95–111
   and see Symeon
   Gospels 302–3

Eadmer, m. of Canterbury 3, 20–21, 58, 60–61, 111
   Historia nouorum 101, 106, 108–9
Eadred, kg of England 61, 174
Eadui Basan 295–7, 299, 303–4
Eadwig, kg of England 19, 172–5, 177, 187
Eadwine, psalter 7–8
   scribe 289, 296–7, 299, 301–4, 306
Ealdred, archbp of York 32, 320
Eardwulf, bp of Lindisfarne 85–6
Earls Barton 311, 314, 324, 327, 334–5, 345
East Marton 347
Ebraucus, kg 149–51
Ecgberht, kg of Wessex 143, 149–51
Ecgwine, st 19–20
Edgar, kg of England 36, 83, 174, 184, 205, 209, 213, 219–20, 278, 282
Edmund, kg of East Anglia, st and martyr 14–15, 17–18, 21, 38, 83–5, 88–9, 137, 139, 196, 200–201, 203
Edmund, kg of Wessex 174, 204
Edward I, kg of England 200, 202, 210–11
Edward II, kg 205

Edward III, kg 213, 216
Edward (the Confessor), kg of England and st 114, 119, 125, 194, 196, 204, 210, 317, 336–7, 340
   and Westminster, 195, 202, 208, 313, 316, 320
   charters, 6, 170, 184, 192–3, 199–200, 201n, 203, 207–8, 211–13, 215, 219–20, 223, 226–7,
   laws of, 233–40, 242–6, 262, 264, 267–8, 285
      and see laga Edwardi, *Leges Edwardi regis*
   Life of 34, 197
Edward the Elder, kg of the Anglo-Saxons 187, 204–5
Edward the Martyr, kg of England 202, 205
Edward, sheriff of London 7, 284–5
Ely, abbey, bishopric 18, 32, 40, 87n, 88–9, 120n, 164–5, 172, 174–5, 219
   church 308, 310, 314, 326–8, 330, 334–6, 341, 354, 358
   abbess, *see* Æthelthryth, Eormenhild, Seaxburh
   abbots, *see* Richard, Simeon
Emma, queen 125, 129, 138, 142
English church treasure, in Normandy 129, 137–8
   language, in twelfth century 14, 230–31, 245, 267–8, 289, 292–3, 295
   people, characterised 115, 277–83, 286–7
Erkenwald, bp of London and st 14, 20
evangelists, portraits of 198, 297–9, 304, 357
Evesham 23n, 164–5, 170, 227
   writ 223–5
Exeter, bishops, *see* Leofric, Osbern
Eynsham, abbey 121, 164
   and see Ælfric

facade, design 317, 320, 350
Faricius, ab. of Abingdon 19
Fécamp, abbey 52n, 67, 124, 137, 196–7, 220n, 339n

Felix, *see* Guthlac
Fergus, kg of London 7, 284, 286
fires, destruction of records by 13–16, 81, 204, 215n
Fletton 348, 350
Fleury, abbey of 82, 84
Florence of Worcester 108–9
Folcard of Saint-Bertin, m. of Saint-Bertin, ab. of Thorney 27–45
font 347, 349–50
Fouke Fitz Warin 280
Fountains, abbey 103
Franks' Casket 333–4
frieze 350–52, 353n
Fursey, ab. and st 54–5, 58, 60–61, 68

Gaimar 18, 196, 275
 Estoire des Engleis 147–8, 277–8, 280, 282
Geddington 327
Gelasius I, pope, supposed *Decretum* 50
genealogies 149–50, 189, 244, 246–8, 256
Geoffrey V, count of Anjou 131, 135
Geoffrey, duke of Brittany 134
Geoffrey Alselin 342
Geoffrey of Monmouth 5, 97, 130–37, 141–56, 194, 221, 226, 275, 277–80, 282
Gervase of Canterbury 151, 153, 203, 212
Gesta Herewardi 279, 281
Ghent 179, 207–8, 223
Glanvill 7, 229, 231, 244, 265, 266n, 268
Glastonbury, abbey 19, 81n, 87, 204–5, 207–8, 220–21, 357
glosses 65, 231, 239n, 257n, 261, 289, 293, 295, 304
Gloucester, abbey 58, 72, 88, 328–32
Godwin, earl 126, 141n, 194
Goscelin of Saint-Bertin 28, 40, 44n, 62, 136, 195
Gosforth 346
Gratian, *Decretum* 266
Great Charter 7, 265, 285–6
Great Kimble 347
Great Malvern, priory 328–32

Great Paxton 311, 315, 317, 321, 334, 357
Gregory I, pope and st 54–5, 66–8, 81
Gui de Warewic 280, 287
Guisborough, priory 72, 345
Guthlac of Crowland, st 40, 43–4
 Life by Felix 123, 127–8
Guthrum, kg 124

Haddiscoe 335
Hadstock 316, 334
Halford 342
Hallaton 342
Harmston 336, 349
Harold, kg of England 114–15, 126, 138, 141n, 156, 192, 220, 238n, 313, 316
Hastings, battle 114–15, 193, 199–200
 duke of the Normans 124
 motte at 313
Hengest, 147–8, 150, 278
Henry I, kg of England 119, 130–31, 134, 192, 194, 203, 210, 212, 216, 219, 224, 236, 262, 264, 285, 325, 342–3, 345
Henry II, kg 134, 160, 192–201, 204–10, 212, 214, 216–17, 220–21, 223, 225–6, 229–30, 264, 266, 283, 285
Henry III, kg 191, 199n, 200–203, 205, 210, 215–16, 222, 224
Henry of Blois, bp of Winchester 193, 198
Henry de Ferrers 345
Henry of Huntingdon 4, 18, 69–70, 79, 91, 97, 105, 130, 132–3, 139, 146, 189, 196n, 218, 242–3, 277
Henry of Newburgh, earl of Warwick 343
 the Young King 197, 248
Hereford 314, 335–6
 Anglo-Saxon saints at 358
Hereward 59, 278–9
Hermann the archdeacon 13–14
hermits 30–31, 36, 38–9, 43–5
herring-bone masonry 325, 355
Hexham 15–16, 79, 87, 101, 104–5, 111, 350
 bishop, *see* John of Beverley

and see Ailred, John
Heysham 327
Hild, abbess of Whitby and st 66, 68
Hingvar, *see* Ingvar
Historia de sancto Cuthberto 85, 93, 98
Historia de regibus Anglorum et Dacorum of Durham 4, 95–111
Historia post Bedam 105, 107
Hoel of Brittany 135
homilies, homiliary 30, 49–52, 64, 69, 137, 231
Horn, Romance of 276, 278–81, 283, 286–7
Hough-on-the-Hill 317
Hoveringham 338, 343
Hovingham 321
Hubba *see* Ubba
Hugh,
Hugh Bigod 221
Hugh Candidus 78, 89, 93
Hugh, dean of York 96, 98
Hugh of le Puiset, bp of Durham 103
Hyde, abbey 18, 222–4
    Book of 18
    'chronicle' 5n
    Liber vitae 223
    and see Winchester, New Minster

Iken (*Icanho, Icheanog*), monastery 27–8, 40–42
Ilbert de Lacy 343
Ine, kg of Wessex 204–5, 240–41, 285
Inglethorpe 350
Ingvarr (Hingvar, Imarr, Inguar, Ivarr) 17–18, 22, 84, 89, 93
inspeximus, *see* charters
Instituta Cnuti 233, 238, 240–44, 248, 256–8, 264
Ipstones 338
Ipswich 338, 351–2
Irton 346
Ivarr, *see* Ingvarr

James of Oakhanger 215, 226
Jarrow 27, 79, 321, 333–4, 350

and see Coelfrith, *Donaemuthan*
Jervaulx, abbey 56n, 74
Jevington 353
John, kg of England 7, 153, 163, 200–201, 208, 216, 219, 222, 265, 268, 285–6
John of Beverley, bp of Hexham, York and st 68
    lections for 54, 56,
    Life of 32, 34–6, 40, 44
John of Hexham, *Historia* 96, 101, 107
John of Worcester 3, 18, 79, 89, 93, 97, 100–101, 106–11, 128, 139, 189
Jordan Fantosme 282–3
Jumièges, abbey 123–4, 129, 137, 139, 221–2, 316–17, 320, 344

kalendar, *see* calendar
Kedington 347
Kensworth 344
King's Lynn 334, 347
Kirk Hammerton 320–21
Kirkburn, church of St Mary's 345
Kirkdale 316, 317–22
Kirkham, priory 56, 68, 72
Kirkstall, abbey 356–7
knight service 223–5
Knook 339–40, 358

laga Edwardi 235–40, 242, 244, 262–5, 268
Lai de Havelóc 278–9
Lanfranc, archbp of Canterbury 3, 120, 203, 295, 309, 322–3, 325, 327, 358
Langford 337, 354, 358
Lastingham, priory 329
Lathbury 338
law, Anglo-Saxon 126, 152, 218, 229–71
    Roman 7, 241, 245, 266
lectionary 3, 29, 48–74
Leges Anglorum (Londinienses), of *c.* 1200 7, 153, 235n, 265, 285
Leges Edwardi regis 234, 238–9, 241–4, 248, 256–7, 264–5, 269, 285
Leis Willelme 234, 238–9, 241–2
Leo III, pope 182, 227

Leofgeat 340
Leofric, ab. of Peterborough 318–19
   bp of Exeter 165n, 187
Leofwine Cild 344
Libellus Æthelwoldi 77, 93
Libellus de exordio 98, 100, 102, 110–11
   and see Symeon
Liber de gestis Anglorum 104, 106
Liber Eliensis 18, 33n, 77–8, 89, 93, 120n
Lichfield 81n, 352
   bishops, *see* Chad
Lincoln 209, 211–12, 278, 317, 325, 349–50
   bishop, *see* Remigius
Lindisfarne 18, 21, 79, 81, 85–7, 93, 98
   bishops, *see* Aidan, Cuthbert, Eardwulf
   Gospels 296, 303
   priory 331n, 332–4
lintel 338, 343
List of saints' resting places 39, 69
Little Braxted 338
Little Tey 338
liturgy 47–70
   influence on architecture 309–10, 323, 326, 358
   and see calendar, lectionary, pontifical, psalter
London 14, 82, 145, 148, 199, 283–5, 344
   archbp of 149
   bishops, *see* Cedd, Erkenwald, Mellitus, Richard FitzNigel, Robert Champart
   knyghtengild 209
   St Paul's cathedral 14, 310
      and see Arcoid, Ralph de Diceto
Louis I, the Pious, kg and emperor 179
Louis IV, kg of the Franks 125
Louis VII, kg of France 155n, 196
Low Middleton Hall 347
Lower Halstow 350
lozenge pattern 317, 324, 334, 338
Lucius, kg 148, 153, 155
Ludlow, castle 317
Lullington 353
Lyre, abbey 123

Magna carta, see Great Charter
Malmesbury, abbey 87, 119, 331, 346
   and see Aldhelm
   forgery of Æthelstan for 215
martyrdom 21–2, 37, 65, 88–9, 93, 195
Matilda, empress 131, 133–4, 150
Matthew Paris 22, 202, 211, 322
Medeshamstede, see Peterborough
Mellitus, bp of London and st 54–5, 58, 72
Melrose, chronicle 109–10
mercenaries 284–6
Merlin, prophecies of 130, 134
Milborne Port 337, 358
Milburga (Mildburh), st 14, 28
Milfrid 336
Minting 349
miracles, *see* saints
Modena, cathedral 350
Modred 145–9
monasteries, composition of community in 119, 121
monastic order, hostility to 118
   reform (tenth-century) 128, 292
Monkwearmouth 27, 87, 334, 353–4
   friezes at 350
Mont Saint-Michel 135
   abbey 123, 137, 316, 324
   and see Robert of Torigni
mortuary fees 261
   rolls 111
Much Wenlock, priory 14, 28

Nectan, st 202–3
'Nennius' 123–4, 139
Neot, st 72, 124, 139
Nether Wallop 336
Newminster, abbey 72, 103
Nicholas I, pope 182–3
nook shafts 316, 319–21
Norman Conquest
   architectural consequences 8, 308–58
   as historical pre-occupation 1–3, 113–16, 119–20, 125–6, 127, 218–19
   as legal *caesura* 6, 18–21, 225, 227
   consequences for Church 113

Normandy
  architectural influence of England in 343–5, 358
  chroniclers in 5, 123–40
  dukes of, *see* Hastings, Rollo, Richard, Robert, William
  influence of Anglo-Saxon books in 138, 339, 358
  treasure from England in 129, 137–8
Northallerton 333
Northampton 345
North Newbald 353
Norwich, cathedral 310, 315, 331, 334–5
nunneries 17, 22, 42, 77, 87, 89, 90–91, 93

oath, judicial 279
  and see coronation
Oda, archbp of Canterbury 172, 175
Offa, kg of Mercia 171, 184, 203, 206, 211–14, 220, 227
offices, monastic 48–74
Okenard 284, 286
Omer, st 34, 42, 44
ordeal 142
  manuals for 232
  and see relics
Orderic Vitalis 5, 15, 78, 123–4, 127–31, 137–40
Orm Gamalsson 319–20
Osbern, bp of Exeter 336
Osney, priory 342
Oswald, bp, archbp of York and st 84, 201, 332
Oswald, kg of Northumbria and st 54–5, 57, 59–60, 63, 66, 68, 90n, 200, 202
Oswin, kg of Deira and st 20, 22–3, 68, 202
Osyth, st 22, 90
Ovingham 334

Paris 185
  abbey of St Denis 169, 178–80, 182–5, 187
  abbey of Saint-Germain, 82, 180–81
  cathedral of Nôtre-Dame 182, 350

  and see Matthew
Paul, abbot of St Albans 322–3
Paul the Deacon, *Homiliary* 49n, 64, 69–70
Paulinus, bp, archbp of York and st 54–6
peace gilds, *see* tithings
Pershore 220, 353
Peterborough, abbey 39–40, 56, 59–60, 73, 78, 88–9, 164, 166, 196, 213, 309–10, 316, 317–24, 328, 337
  abbot, *see* Turold
  monks of, *see* Hugh Candidus
Phillida 149–50
Pippin I, kg of the Franks 185, 238
Plympton, priory 56, 67, 72
pontifical 129, 137, 232
popes, *see* Gelasius, Gregory, Nicholas
post-colonial theory 290–92, 295
precentor (cantor), as custodian of community's past 64, 111
prokrossoi 328, 335
psalter 129, 137, 289–306

Quadripartitus 233, 235, 238–44
Quatford 329
Quenington 356
Quo Warranto 220–23
quoins, long-and-short 310, 314, 355

Ragnald, kg in York 85
Ralph [of Sées], archbp of Canterbury 106, 108
Ralph Diceto (of Diss), dean of St Pauls 3, 151, 154–5, 189, 199n
Ralph Luffa, bp of Chichester 324
Ramsey, abbey 59, 84, 110, 219
Ranulf Flambard, bp of Durham 98
  de Glanville, justiciar 195
Ravenna 320
Rawmarsh 347
Reading 345, 356
Regenbald, chancellor 337
Regularis concordia 51, 309, 328
relics, reliquaries, *see* saints
Remigius, bp of Lincoln 30, 32
Repton, St Wystan's 331–2

Revesby 349
Richard, I, duke of Normandy 124–5, 196
Richard I, kg of England 155, 197, 200–201, 216–17, 219, 248
Richard II, duke of Normandy 125, 196
Richard III, duke of Normandy 125
Richard, abbot of Ely 327
Richard FitzNigel, treasurer, bp of London 153, 197, 262n
Richard of Devizes, m. of Winchester 5–6, 141–56
Rievaulx, abbey 103
Ringerike style 340, 343
Robert I (the magnificent), duke of Normandy 125, 141n
Robert II (Curthose), duke of Normandy 130
Robert de Brus II 345
Robert Champart, bp of London, archbp of Canterbury 129–30, 137
Robert of Cricklade 120–21
Robert d'Oilly 342
Robert of Torigny, m. of Bec, ab. of Mont Saint-Michel 5, 130, 131–9, 199n
Rochester 82n, 214
　cathedral priory 63, 69, 72, 164 , 315
Roger,
　(of Pont-l'Évêque), archbp of York 348
　bp of Salisbury 345, 353
　earl of Shropshire 329
　of Howden 149, 151, 153, 199n, 244, 265
　de Lacy 340
　of Wendover 22, 93, 153
Rolland of Dinan 134
Rollo, duke of the Normans 120, 124–5, 131, 194, 196, 248
romances, Anglo-Norman
　patronage 276, 279, 286
Rome 199, 268, 292, 310, 320, 333
Roscrea 353
Rouen 137, 219
Round Table 136
Rous Lench 353–4
Rumon, st 16

Life of 23

St Albans abbey 53, 68, 164, 202, 211, 213–14, 221, 226–7, 308, 321–3, 328
　abbots, *see* Paul
St Bees, priory 15, 338
Saint-Bertin, abbey 31–2, 34
　and see Bertin, Bovo, Folcard
St Brice's Day, massacre 126
Saint Côme-du-Mont 345
Saint-Évroult, abbey 15, 123, 127, 131, 137
Sainte-Marie-du-Mont 345
St Neots, priory 65, 72, 139
Saint-Omer, abbey 30, 42–3
Saint-Wandrille, abbey 125, 137
saints
　cult of 2–3, 48–70
　　authorisation for 63
　lives of, read in refectory and chapter 67–8
　miracles of 15–6, 20–21, 44, 51, 54, 69, 88–9, 195, 296
　relics of 13, 22, 24, 28, 38, 44, 58–61, 69–70, 91, 92, 137, 139, 353
　　tested by fire 22–3
　translated 15, 19, 21, 30, 34, 40–41, 53, 60–62, 68, 85–6, 101, 193, 195, 199
　and see Fécamp, Winchester
　scepticism towards English 70, 129–30
　shrines of 13–14, 16, 19–20, 59, 87n, 88, 138–9
　　archives attached to 160
Salisbury, bishop, *see* Roger
Sarum 345, 354, 356
Sawley, abbey 103
Scott, Sir Walter 112, 115n, 194
Sculthorpe 350
scutage 224–5
Seaham 327, 333
seal, use of before 1066 212–14
Seaxburh, abbess of Ely 88
Selby, abbey 66, 73, 347
Selham 354–5

Selsey 324, 354
Serlo, ab. of Gloucester 332
    of Wilton 101
sermons 36, 39, 51, 118
    and see homilies
Sexburga, abbess, queen and st 18
Sherborne, abbey 81n, 164, 309
Shernborne 350
shrines, *see* saints
Sigebert of Gembloux 131, 133, 154
Simeon, ab. of Ely 32, 326–7
Simon de Senlis II, earl of Northampton 346
soffit-roll moulding 317, 328, 330, 339, 358
Soham, church 87
Soiscel Molaisse 352
Somerford Keynes 327
Sompting 311
soulscot 260–61
Southampton 202, 275n
South Cerney 356
Southwell 321, 338, 343
    White Book of 237n
Sproxton 348
Stanground 348
Stephen, count 182, 185
Stephen kg of England 192, 203, 220, 236–7, 285, 342
Stephen of Rouen, m. of Bec 130, 133–4, 136–7, 206
Stepney 355–6
Stoughton 336
Stow 317, 331, 334, 336
Stratton 340, 343
Stretham church, 120n
stripwork 311, 318, 335
Symeon of Durham 78, 86, 95–111

Tavistock, abbey 16
Tewkesbury 339
Textus Roffensis 233, 243, 245n, 246
Thancred, st 30, 36–40, 45
Theobald, archbp of Canterbury 132–3
Thomas,
    of Bayeux, archbp of York 325
    Becket, chancellor, archbp of Canterbury 194–5, 230, 267
Thorney, abbey 27–45, 128
    abbot, *see* Folcard
Thorold, ab. of Peterborough 318
Thrybergh 347
tithings 153
Toftrees 350
Torhtred, st 30, 36–40, 45
Tostig, earl 22, 319
Tova, st 30–31, 36–40, 45
translation, *see* saints
Trier 321
trumeau 316
Turold, ab. of Peterborough 59
Turstin 342
Twynham 317
tympanum 316, 318, 321, 328, 337–43, 348, 350–51, 354, 356, 358
Tynemouth, priory 68, 71

Ubba (Hubba) 17–18, 22, 84–5, 89, 93
Uhtred, earl 99–100
'Unknown Charter' 264
Uppington 338
Urnes style 335, 338n, 345
Utrecht, bishop of, *see* Æthwulf
    Psalter 292, 302–4, 306

Verona 320
Vortigern, kg 130, 282

Wace 130, 136–7, 193n, 194, 196–7, 202, 226, 264, 275, 278, 280–82
Walchelin (Walkelin), bp of Winchester 30, 32, 40, 309, 322, 326
Waldef, Romance of 7, 276–87
Walter of Oxford 132
Waltham, abbey, church 66, 73, 138, 201, 213, 220
Waltheof, earl 127
Wareham 325
Water Stratford 341–2
Wearmouth, *see* Monkwearmouth
Wells 166, 216, 357

Westminster abbey, charters 166–8, 171, 187, 208–9, 211–13, 219
    church 195, 199–200, 202, 313, 316–17, 320
Whitby, abbey 15, 78, 87, 91
    abbess, *see* Hild
    abbots 104
Wibert, prior of Christ Church Canterbury 289, 304, 306
Wigstan, st 23n, 203
Wilfrid, archbp of York and st 54, 56, 58, 60–61, 68, 118, 137
William I, the Conqueror, duke and kg 114–5, 118–19, 125–6, 199, 317n, 318, 325
    charters of, 192, 203, 210–11, 218, 221–5,
    laws attributed to, 234, 236–7, 242, 244, 248, 257, 262, 264
William II, Rufus, kg 118, 130, 138, 203, 210, 221–2, 224
William IX, Count of Poitiers 197
William (Longsword), duke of Normandy 125
William fitz Osbern 127, 340
William fitz Ralph 348
William of Jumièges 92, 125–7, 131
William of Malmesbury 3, 5, 16, 19, 86–7, 92–3, 97, 111, 113, 136, 142, 151–3, 218, 240, 277, 282–3, 324
    Commentary on Lamentations 115–21
    Gesta pontificum 78–9, 118–20, 219n
    Gesta regum 78–9, 91, 101, 113–14, 118–21, 139, 194, 206, 219n, 235
    Life of Dunstan 120
William of Newburgh 154
William of Poitiers 126–7

William of Saint-Calais, bp of Durham 99, 332
Winchcombe, abbey 63, 73
Winchester 81n, 82n, 145, 151, 164, 172, 192–3, 202, 271, 296, 308–10, 317, 319, 322–3, 326, 328, 333–4, 341, 349–50, 352, 355, 358
    annals of 141–6, 151–5
    bishops, 142
        and see Aethelwold, Henry of Blois, Walchelin
    cathedral and priory (Old Minster) 52n, 53, 74, 128, 148, 167, 311
        and see Richard of Devizes
    New Minster 56n, 165, 335–6, 357
        and see Hyde
Wing 314, 327
Winnoc, st 34, 44
Winstone 340
Winterton 349
Wittering 317–22, 324n, 328
Worcester 164, 166, 201, 328–32, 335, 358
    bishops, *see* Wulfstan
    cathedral priory 58, 121
Worth 327
Wulfstan, bp of London, of Worcester and archbp of York 240–41
William II, bp of Worcester and st 118, 201, 328–9, 332, 337

York, 81n, 82n, 85–6
    archbishops 104, 149
        and see Ealdred, Oswald, Paulinus, Thomas, Wilfrid, Wulfstan
    bishop, *see* John of Beverley
    minster 81n, 348, 355
        and see Hugh, dean
    St Mary's abbey, church 44, 71, 348

Index of Manuscripts

[Note: single-sheet charters discussed in the contribution by Crick are not listed in this index.]

Abersytwyth, National Library of Wales,
    MS Peniarth 381 (Hengwrt 102): 71
Alençon, Bibl. municipale, MS 14: 128
Avranches, Bibl. municipale, MS 159: 133

Brussels, Bibliothèque royale, MS 9823: 305

Cambridge, Corpus Christi College,
—MS 2: 349
—MS 9: 58
—MS 57: 68n
—MS 66: 103
—MS 139: 95n, 96, 98n, 101, 102n, 103–5
—MS 183: 50
—MS 264: 69n
—MS 267: 58n
—MS 270: 48n, 62n
—MS 312: 312
—MS 339: 143, 144n, 145n, 150n, 152n, 155n, 156n
—MS 383: 232n, 234n, 246, 267
—MS 422: 328
—MS 448: 58n, 73
Cambridge, Magdalene College, MS F. 4. 10: 60
Cambridge, Pembroke College,
—MS 82: 68, 71
—MS 120: 349
—MS 301: 73
Cambridge, St John's College,
—MS 164 (F. 27): 62
—MS 209 (H. 6): 31n
Cambridge, Trinity College,
—MS O. 3. 55: 60
—MS R. 5. 27: 55, 63n, 71
—MS R. 7. 5: 65, 69n
—MS R. 17. 1: 289
Cambridge, University Library,
—MS Add. 4079: 57
—MS Ee. 1. 1: 235n
—MS Ff. 1. 27: 103
—MS Gg. 2. 21: 139n
—MS Ll. 1. 10: 352
Copenhagen, Kongelige Bibliotek, MS Gl. Kgl. Sml 10, 2°: 296, 315

Dublin, Trinity College, MS 492 (E. 2. 23): 69, 71
Durham,
    Cathedral Library,
—MS A. II. 17: 302
—MS B. II. 35: 55–6, 71
—MS B. IV. 24: 111n

Exeter, Cathedral Library, MS 2070: 213n

Florence, Biblioteca Medicea Laurenziana, MS Amatiano 1: 305

Hanover, Kestner Museum, WMXXIa 36: 297
Hereford, Cathedral Library, MS P. v. 1: 66n, 72

Leiden, Universiteitsbibliotheek, MS BPL 20: 133
Liège, Bibliothèque Universitaire, MS 369C: 106–8

London, BL,
—MS Add. 14250: 55–6, 67, 72
—MS Add. 15350: 254n
—MS Add. 17275: 15n
—MS Add. 24066: 232n, 235n, 252n
—MS Add. 25014: 56n, 72
—MS Add. 34633: 28n
—MS Add. 37472(1): 290n
—MS Add. 37517: 350
—MS Add. 38130: 65, 72
—MS Add. 38817: 56, 68, 72
—MS Add. 40007: 189n
—MS Add. 49366: 232n, 234n, 235n, 242n, 243n, 245n, 252n
—MS Add. 49598: 357
—MS Arundel 155: 61, 296, 328, 349
—MS Burney 335: 57
—MS Cotton Tiberius A. ii: 296n
—MS Cotton Tiberius A. iii: 311
—MS Cotton Tiberius C. iv: 336
—MS Cotton Tiberius C. vi: 328
—MS Cotton Tiberius D. iv: 51, 74
—MS Cotton Caligula A. viii: 106
—MS Cotton Caligula A. xiv: 336, 350
—MS Cotton Claudius B. iv: 311, 314–16, 326, 337
—MS Cotton Claudius B. vi: 91n
—MS Cotton Nero A. i: 190n, 234n, 238n, 265n
—MS Cotton Nero C. iii: 216n
—MS Cotton Nero D. iv: 296
—MS Cotton Otho A. x: 232n
—MS Cotton Vitellius A. xix: 51, 52n
—MS Cotton Vitellius C. viii: 199n
—MS Cotton Vitellius E. i: 72
—MS Cotton Vespasian A. viii: 213n, 336
—MS Cotton Vespasian A. xxii: 219n
—MS Cotton Vespasian B. xxiv: 223n, 224
—MS Cotton Vespasian D. vi: 62n
—MS Cotton Titus A. xxvii: 232n, 234n, 252n
—MS Cotton Domitian [A.] viii: 232n, 234n
—MS Cotton Domitian [A.] xiii: 142n, 143, 148–9, 155n
—MS Cotton Cleopatra E. i: 170, n. 28
—MS Egerton 874: 62n
—MS Egerton 3278: 48n
—MS Harley 55: 232n, 234n, 238n, 245n, 259n, 260n, 265n, 267
—MS Harley 76: 330
—MS Harley 603: 292–3, 303, 306
—MS Harley 742: 198n
—MS Harley 746: 235n, 241n
—MS Harley 1117: 51
—MS Harley 1229: 57
—MS Harley 1704: 243n, 269
—MS Harley 3097: 31n
—MS Harley 3680: 54–5, 63n, 69, 72
—MS Harley 4124: 72
—MS Royal 1. D. ix: 296n
—MS Royal 11. B. ii: 232n, 234n, 245n, 252n, 255n
—MS Royal 13. A. vi: 105n, 107
—MS Royal 13. C. v: 51, 54–5, 58, 63, 65, 72
—MS Royal 14. C. ii: 232n, 235n, 244n, 252n
—MS Stowe 104: 68, 73
—MS Stowe 944: 223
—Additional Charter 77735: 203n
London, College of Arms,
—MS Charters 182: 224n
—*sine numero*: 73
London, Inner Temple, Petyt MS 511.2: 105n, 107
London, Lambeth Palace Library,
—MS 118: 232n, 234n, 235n, 244
—MS 179: 232n, 234n, 235n, 244n
London, The Law Society, MS 1: 232n, 235n, 252n
London, PRO/TNA,
—C 52/21: 210n
—C 52/27: 210n
—C 52/29: 220n
—C 53/43: 215n
—C 53/56: 203n
—E 32/16: 215n

—E 322/264: 213n
—E 368/195: 201n
—KB 26/11: 222n
—KB 26/79: 219n
—KB 26/110: 222n
—KB 26/111: 222n
London, Victoria and Albert Museum, MS 661: 290n

Manchester, John Rylands University Library,
—MS Lat. 155: 234n, 235n, 252n
—MS Lat. 420: 232n, 234n, 252n
Medway Archives and Local Studies Centre, Strood, MS DRc/R1 (*formerly* Rochester, Cathedral Library, MS A. 3. 5): 232n, 234n, 243n, 245n, 252n, 255n, 259n, 261n, 265n
Monte Cassino, Archivio della Badia, MS BB. 437, 439: 357

New York, Morgan Library and Museum (Pierpont Morgan Library),
—MS M. 521: 290n
—MS M. 724: 290n
—MS M. 736: 296
—MS M. 926: 53–4

Oxford, Balliol College, MS 176: 74
Oxford, Bodl. Lib.,
—MS Add. C. 260: 61
—MS Auct. F. 1. 9: 252n
—MS Bodley 163: 51, 55, 57, 73
—MS Digby 13: 232n, 234n, 245n, 252n
—MS Digby 39: 53–4
—MS Digby 211: 66, 73
—MS Douce 368: 55–6, 63n, 66n, 73
—MS e Museo 93: 72
—MS e Museo 115: 69, 73
—MS Fairfax 12: 66, 73
—MS Hatton 43: 51, 54–7, 60–61, 63n, 66, 73
—MS Junius 11: 296, 299n, 310, 314–15

—MS Laud misc. 243: 57, 66, 73
—MS Laud misc. 582: 244n
—MS Rawlinson C 641: 232n, 234n, 235n, 242, 243n, 244n, 252n
Oxford, Corpus Christi College,
—MS 134: 68n
—MS 157: 189n, 97n, 106, 110
Oxford, Jesus College, MS 10: 58, 72
Oxford, Lincoln College, MS lat. 31: 74
Oxford, Magdalen College, MS lat. 105: 74
Oxford, New College, MS 308: 56n, 74
Oxford, Pembroke College, MS 3: 73
Oxford, St John's College,
—MS 17: 128
—MS 97: 105n, 107
—MS 99: 56n, 74

Paris, BnF,
—MS lat. 4771: 170n, 232n, 234n, 235n, 242n, 246-56, 259n, 261n, 269
—MS lat. 5362: 52n
—MS lat. 6042: 139n
—MS lat. 8846: 293n
—MS lat. 10185: 232n, 234n, 235n, 244n
—MS lat. 13092: 40n
—MS nouv. acq. lat. 311: 13n
—MS nouv. acq. lat. 692: 103–4, 107

Rochester, Cathedral Library, *see* Medway Archives and Local Studies Centre
Rouen, Bibl. municipale,
—MS 274: 129
—MS 369: 129
—MS 445: 339n
—MS 1177: 139n
—MS 1343: 128

Utrecht, University Library, MS 32: 293

Winchester, Cathedral Library, MS 1: 51, 55, 65, 74